Teachers, Schools, and Society

Teachers, Schools, and Society

TENTH EDITION

DAVID MILLER SADKER

University of Arizona and Professor Emeritus, American University

KAREN R. ZITTLEMAN

Ph.D., American University

Mc Graw Hill

Connect
Learn
Succeed™

The McGraw-Hill Companies

Connect
Learn
Succeed™

TEACHERS, SCHOOLS, AND SOCIETY, TENTH EDITION

Published by McGraw-Hill, a business unit of The McGraw-Hill Companies, Inc., 1221 Avenue of the Americas, New York, NY, 10020. Copyright © 2013 by The McGraw-Hill Companies, Inc. All rights reserved. Printed in the United States of America. Previous edition © 2010. No part of this publication may be reproduced or distributed in any form or by any means, or stored in a database or retrieval system, without the prior written consent of The McGraw-Hill Companies, Inc., including, but not limited to, in any network or other electronic storage or transmission, or broadcast for distance learning.

Some ancillaries, including electronic and print components, may not be available to customers outside the United States.

This book is printed on acid-free paper.

1 2 3 4 5 6 7 8 9 0 DOW/DOW 1 0 9 8 7 6 5 4 3 2

ISBN: 978-0-07-802445-0
MHID: 0-07-802445-5
AIE ISBN: 978-0-07-741110-7
AIE MHID: 0-07-741110-2

Senior Vice President, Products & Markets: *Kurt L. Strand*
Vice President, General Manager: Michael Ryan
Vice President, Content Production & Technology Services: *Kimberly Meriwether David*
Managing Director/Director: *Mike Sugarman*
Brand Manager: *Allison McNamara*
Director of Development: *Dawn Groundwater*
Development Manager: *Barbara A. Heinssen*
Content Development Editor: *Maureen Spada*
Editorial Coordinator: *Sarah Kiefer*
Director, Content Production: *Chris Gimlin*
Marketing Manager: *Ann Helgerson*
Project Manager/Content Project Manager: *Melissa Leick*
Buyer: *Sandy Ludovissy*
Design Coordinator: *Tara McDermott*
Interior/Cover Designer: *Greg Nettles/Squarecrow Creative*
Cover Images: © *Frank Rohde (background);* © *Shutterstock/Gualtiero Boffi (teacher);*
© *Photoeuphoria (dancing girl);* © *Konstantin32 (boy);* © *Photodisc (girl on left, basketball player, and graduate)*
Media Project Manager: *Sridevi Palani*
Typeface: *9/12 Utopia*
Compositor: *Laserwords Private Limited*
Printer: *R. R. Donnelley*

All credits appearing on page or at the end of the book are considered to be an extension of the copyright page.

Library of Congress Cataloging-in-Publication Data

Sadker, David Miller, 1942-
    Teachers, schools, and society / David Miller Sadker, Karen R. Zittleman.—10th ed., annotated instructor's ed.
      p. cm.
    ISBN 978-0-07-802445-0 (alk. paper)
    1. Teaching. 2. Education—Study and teaching—United States. 3. Teachers—Training of—United States. I. Zittleman, Karen R. II. Title.
    LB1775.2.S23 2013
    371.102—dc23

                                             2012028902

www.mhhe.com

About the Authors

David Sadker

Dr. Sadker is professor emeritus at American University (Washington, DC) and now teaches and writes in Tucson, Arizona. Along with his late wife Myra Sadker, he gained a national reputation for work in confronting gender bias and sexual harassment. The Sadkers' book, *Failing at Fairness: How Our Schools Cheat Girls,* was published by Charles Scribner in 1994 and, with Karen Zittleman, was updated in 2009, retitled *Still Failing at Fairness: How Gender Bias Cheats Girls and Boys and What We Can Do About It.* David Sadker co-edited *Gender in the Classroom: Foundations, Skills, Methods and Strategies Across the Curriculum* (Lawrence Erlbaum, 2007), as well as this introductory textbook.

David Sadker is a Courage & Renewal facilitator who works with healers, educators, social workers, lawyers, political and business leaders, as well as spiritual communities. David employs poetry, storytelling, music, art, reflection, and mindfulness to create a circle of trust, a place where individuals can explore their inner landscape. (Learn more at www.sadker.org/DavidSadker.html)

He has directed more than a dozen federal education grants and has written seven books and more than seventy-five articles in journals such as *Phi Delta Kappan, Harvard Educational Review,* and *Psychology Today.* The Sadkers' work has been reported in hundreds of newspapers and magazines, including, *BusinessWeek, The Washington Post, The London Times, The New York Times, Time,* and *Newsweek.* The Sadkers appeared on *The Today Show, Good Morning America, The Oprah Winfrey Show,* Phil Donahue's *The Human Animal,* National Public Radio's *All Things Considered,* and *Dateline: NBC* with Jane Pauley. The American Educational Research Association (AERA) honored the Sadkers for the best review of research published in the United States in 1991, for their professional service in 1995, and for "scholarship, activism, and community building on behalf of women and education" in 2004. The American Association of University Women awarded the Sadkers their Eleanor Roosevelt Award in 1995, and the American Association of Colleges of Teacher Education recognized their work with the Gender Architect Award in 2001. David Sadker has received two honorary doctorates and was selected as a Torchbearer by the U.S. Olympic Committee in 2002.

Karen R. Zittleman

Dr. Zittleman attended the University of Wisconsin for her bachelor's degree and American University for her master's degree and doctorate. Karen loves teaching and has taught in elementary and middle schools, at the collegiate level, and as an online virtual teacher for professional development courses. Her articles about gender, Title IX, and teacher education appear in the *Journal of Teacher Education, Educational Leadership, Phi Delta Kappan, Principal,* and other professional journals. Dr. Zittleman is the co-author of *Still Failing at Fairness,* which documents gender bias against girls and boys in school. She also wrote *Making Public Schools Great for Every Girl and Boy,* a guide for promoting equity in math and science instruction for the National Educational Association and educational film guides for *A Hero for Daisy* and *Apple Pie: Raising Champions.* She is Foundation Manager for the Myra Sadker Foundation. Her academic interests focused on educational equity, teacher preparation, and contemplative practices in education. Dr. Zittleman teaches and writes in Tucson, Arizona. You are invited to visit her website at www.sadker.org/zittleman.html.

Dedication

To Those Who Help & Inspire

Brief Contents

Preface xv

PART I: TEACHERS AND STUDENTS

Chapter 1: Becoming a Teacher 2
Chapter 2: Different Ways of Learning 25
Chapter 3: Teaching Your Diverse Students 51
INTASC   REFLECTIVE ACTIVITIES AND YOUR PORTFOLIO—INTRODUCTION 87
INTASC   REFLECTIVE ACTIVITIES AND YOUR PORTFOLIO—PART I 90

PART II: SCHOOLS AND CURRICULUM

Chapter 4: Student Life in School and at Home 100
Chapter 5: Purposes of America's Schools and the Current Reform Movement 133
Chapter 6: Curriculum, Standards, and Testing 166
INTASC   REFLECTIVE ACTIVITIES AND YOUR PORTFOLIO—PART II 201

PART III: FOUNDATIONS

Chapter 7: The History of American Education 210
Chapter 8: Philosophy of Education 245
Chapter 9: Financing and Governing America's Schools 273
Chapter 10: School Law and Ethics 302
INTASC   REFLECTIVE ACTIVITIES AND YOUR PORTFOLIO—PART III 332

PART IV: YOUR CLASSROOM

Chapter 11: Teacher Effectiveness 340
Chapter 12: Your First Classroom 373
Chapter 13: Q and A Guide to Entering the Teaching Profession 400
INTASC   REFLECTIVE ACTIVITIES AND YOUR PORTFOLIO—PART IV 418

TEXT APPENDICES

www.mhhe.com/sadker10e

1   Teacher Competency Exams *A-1*

2   State Offices for Teacher Certification and Licensure *A-2*

3   INTASC Standards: Concepts and Content in *Teachers, Schools, and Society*, Tenth Edition *A-5*

ONLINE APPENDICES

A   Classroom Observation Guidelines

B   State Offices for Teacher Certification and Licensure

Glossary G-1
Notes N-1
Credits C-1
Index I-1

Contents

Preface xv

PART I
TEACHERS AND STUDENTS

Chapter 1
Becoming a Teacher 2

A Teaching Career—Is It Right for You? 3

Professionalism at the Crossroads 8

From Normal Schools to Board-Certified Teachers 10

How Teachers Are Prepared Today 13
Urban Legends about Teaching 15

American Schools: Better Than We Think? 17

We Like Questions 19

Online Video Album to Accompany Teachers,
Schools, and Society, 10e 23
The Teachers, Schools, and Society Reader with
Classroom Observation Video Clips 23
Key Terms and People 24
Discussion Questions and Activities 24

Chapter 2
Different Ways of Learning 25

Multiple Intelligences 26

Instructional Technology 27
Assessment 28
The Five Minds 28

Emotional Intelligence 29

Learning Styles 31

Do Boys and Girls Learn Differently? 33

Brain Differences 34

Exceptional Learners 36

The Gifted and Talented 36
Special Education 39
Assistive Technology 46

Online Video Album to Accompany Teachers,
Schools, and Society, 10e 48

The Teachers, Schools, and Society Reader with
Classroom Observation Video Clips 48
Key Terms and People 49
Discussion Questions and Activities 50

Chapter 3
Teaching Your Diverse Students 51

Student Diversity 52

Failing at Fairness 52
Lesbian, Gay, Bisexual, and Transgender Students (LGBT) 54
Putting a Price on Racism 56
Theories of Why Some Groups Succeed and Others
Do Not 57
From the Melting Pot to Cultural Pluralism 58

Bilingual Education 60

Bilingual Education Models 63
The Bilingual Controversy 64
Research on Bilingual Education 65

Multicultural Education 66

The Multiculturalism Debate 67
Approaches to Multicultural Education 67

Culturally Responsive Teaching 69

Stereotypes 72
Stereotype Threat 72
Generalizations 73

Today's Classroom 74

Meet Your Seventh-Grade Class 74
Diversity Assets 81
Teaching Skills 82
We Are One 83

Online Video Album to Accompany Teachers,
Schools, and Society, 10e 84
The Teachers, Schools, and Society Reader with
Classroom Observation Video Clips 84
Key Terms and People 85
Discussion Questions and Activities 86

INTASC   REFLECTIVE ACTIVITIES AND
YOUR PORTFOLIO: INTRODUCTION 87

INTASC   REFLECTIVE ACTIVITIES AND
YOUR PORTFOLIO: PART I 90

PART II
SCHOOLS AND CURRICULUM

Chapter 4
Student Life in School and at Home 100

Rules, Rituals, and Routines 101

"Come Right Up and Get Your New Books": A Teacher's
Perspective 101
"Come Right Up and Get Your New Books": A Student's
Perspective 102

Watching the Clock 102

The Teacher as Gatekeeper 104

The Other Side of the Tracks 105

The Gendered World of Elementary and Middle Schools 109

GUEST COLUMN: Haunted by Racist Attitudes 110

High School: Lessons in Social Status 113

Social Challenges Come to School 116

Family Patterns 116
Wage Earners and Parenting 117
Latchkey Kids 118
Divorce 118
Poverty 118
Hidden America: Homeless Families 121

Children: At Promise or at Risk? 121

Dropping Out 122
Sexuality and Teenage Pregnancy 123
Substance Abuse 123
Obesity and Eating Disorders 125
Youth Suicide 127
Bullying 127

Online Video Album to Accompany Teachers,
Schools, and Society, 10e 129
The Teachers, Schools, and Society Reader with
Classroom Observation Video Clips 130
Key Terms and People 131
Discussion Questions and Activities 131

Chapter 5
Purposes of America's Schools and the Current Reform Movement 133

What Is the Purpose of School? 134

Purpose 1: To Transmit Society's Knowledge and Values
(Passing the Cultural Baton) 134

Purpose 2: Reconstructing Society (Schools
as Tools for Change) 135
Public Demands for Schools 137

Where Do You Stand? 138

What Makes a School Effective? 141

Factor 1: Strong Leadership 141
Factor 2: A Clear School Mission 141
Factor 3: A Safe and Orderly Climate 142
Factor 4: Monitoring Student Progress 143
Factor 5: High Expectations 144
Beyond the Five Factors 145

Educational Reform and School Choice 146

Charter Schools 147
Full Service Schools for the Whole Child 150
Vouchers 151
Magnet Schools 152
Open Enrollment 153
Schools.com 153
Schools for Profit 155
Home Schools 155
Green Schools 157

Teachers, Students, and Reform 158

The Importance of Trust 160
Students and School Reform 160
Rethinking Reform 162

Online Video Album to Accompany Teachers,
Schools, and Society, 10e 164
The Teachers, Schools, and Society Reader with
Classroom Observation Video Clips 164
Key Terms and People 165
Discussion Questions and Activities 165

Chapter 6
Curriculum, Standards, and Testing 166

The Saber-Tooth Curriculum 167

The Visible Curriculum 168

The Invisible Curriculum 168

The Extracurriculum 169

Who and What Shape the Curriculum? 170

Teachers 170
Parental and Community Groups 171
Students 171
Administrators 171
State Government 171
Local Government 171
Colleges and Universities 171

Contents

Standardized Tests *172*
Education Commissions and Committees *172*
Professional Organizations *172*
Special Interest Groups *172*
Publishers *172*
Federal Government *173*

The Reign of the Textbook *173*

The Testing Legacy of No Child Left
    Behind *176*

Common Core State Standards *177*

The Problem with Standardized Tests *179*

Evaluating Teachers by Student Test Scores *186*

Alternatives to High-Stakes Testing *187*

Tension Points *188*

Intelligent Design versus Evolution *188*
Censorship and the Curriculum *190*
Cultural Literacy or Cultural Imperialism? *192*

The Technology Revolution *193*

Ways Technology Is Used in the Classroom *194*
The Digital Divide *195*

Suggestions for Tomorrow's Curriculum *196*

Online Video Album to Accompany Teachers,
Schools, and Society, 10e *198*
The Teachers, Schools, and Society Reader with
Classroom Observation Video Clips *198*
Key Terms and People *199*
Discussion Questions and Activities *199*

INTASC   REFLECTIVE ACTIVITIES AND
        YOUR PORTFOLIO: PART II *201*

Native American Tribes: The History of
    Miseducation *216*

Spinsters, Bachelors, and Gender Barriers
    in Teaching *218*

The Secondary School Movement *219*

A Brief History of Educational Reform *221*

John Dewey and Progressive Education *222*

The Federal Government *223*

Black Americans: The Struggle for a Chance
    to Learn *225*

Hispanics: Growing School Impact *227*

Mexican Americans *227*
Puerto Ricans *228*
Cuban Americans *229*

Asian Americans and Pacific Islanders:
    The Magnitude of Diversity *229*

Chinese Americans *229*
Filipino Americans *230*
Asian Indian Americans *230*
Japanese Americans *231*
Southeast Asian Americans *231*

Arab Americans: Moving beyond
    the Stereotype *232*

Women and Education: A History of Sexism *234*

Hall of Fame: Profiles in Education *236*

Online Video Album to Accompany Teachers,
Schools, and Society, 10e *242*
The Teachers, Schools, and Society Reader with
Classroom Observation Video Clips *243*
Key Terms and People *243*
Discussion Questions and Activities *244*

PART III
FOUNDATIONS

Chapter 7
The History of American Education *210*

Christopher Lamb's Colonial Classroom *211*

Colonial New England Education: God's
    Classrooms *211*

A New Nation Shapes Education *214*

The Common School Movement *215*

Chapter 8
Philosophy of Education *245*

Finding Your Philosophy of Education *246*

Inventory of Philosophies of Education *247*

Interpreting Your Responses *249*

Five Philosophies of Education *250*

Teacher-Centered Philosophies *250*

Essentialism *250*
Perennialism *252*

Student-Centered Philosophies *254*

> *Progressivism 254*
> *Social Reconstructionism 255*
> *Existentialism 257*

Can Teachers Blend These Five
Philosophies? *261*

Psychological Influences on Education *261*

> *Constructivism 261*
> *Behaviorism 264*

Cultural Influences on Education *264*

The Three Legendary Figures of Classical Western
Philosophy *265*

Basic Philosophical Issues and Concepts *267*

> *Metaphysics and Epistemology 267*
> *Logic 269*
> *Ethics, Political Philosophy, and Aesthetics 269*

Your Turn *270*

> *Online Video Album to Accompany* Teachers,
> Schools, and Society, 10e *271*
> *The* Teachers, Schools, and Society *Reader with*
> *Classroom Observation Video Clips 271*
> *Key Terms and People 272*
> *Discussion Questions and Activities 272*

Chapter 9
Financing and Governing America's Schools *273*

Follow the Money: Financing America's
Schools *274*

> *Why Should Teachers Care Where the Money*
> *Comes From? 274*
> *The Property Tax: The Road to Unequal*
> *Schools 274*
> *Reforming Education Finance 275*
> *From Robin Hood to Adequacy 277*
> *Adequate Education in Difficult Times 278*
> *Does Money Matter? 280*
> *States Finding the Money 282*
> *The Federal Government's Role in Financing*
> *Education 283*

Schools, Children, and Commercialism *284*

> *Commercializing Childhood 284*
> *Brand Name Education: Should Schools Be*
> *Open for Business? 285*

What the Future May Hold for School Finance *287*

> *Accountability 287*
> *Choice Programs and the Neighborhood School 287*
> *Longer School Day and School Year 287*
> *The Economy's Impact on School Budgets 287*
> *The Rich–Poor School Divide Is Likely to Grow 287*
> *Decaying Infrastructure 288*
> *Commercializing Children and Schools 288*

Governing America's Schools *288*

> *School Governance Quiz 288*
> *The Legal Control of Schools 290*
> *State Influence Grows as School Boards Come*
> *under Fire 292*
> *The School Superintendent and Principal 293*
> *Covert Power in Schools 296*
> *Business and Schools 297*
> *Making Schools More Responsive 297*

Education in Finland *298*

> *Online Video Album to Accompany* Teachers,
> Schools, and Society, 10e *300*
> *The* Teachers, Schools, and Society *Reader with*
> *Classroom Observation Video Clips 300*
> *Key Terms and People 301*
> *Discussion Questions and Activities 301*

Chapter 10
School Law and Ethics *302*

Classroom Law *303*

What Is Your Rights Quotient? *303*

> *I. Teachers' Rights and Responsibilities 304*
> *II. Students' Rights and Responsibilities 312*

Teaching and Ethics *322*

> *Cheating: The Dishonor Role 322*
> *Social Networking Comes to School 323*
> *Protecting Your Students 324*
> *Moral Education: Programs That Develop Ethics and*
> *Values 326*
> *Classrooms That Explore Ethical Issues 328*
>
> *Online Video Album to Accompany* Teachers,
> Schools, and Society, 10e *330*
> *The* Teachers, Schools, and Society *Reader with*
> *Classroom Observation Video Clips 330*
> *Key Terms and People 331*
> *Discussion Questions and Activities 331*

INTASC REFLECTIVE ACTIVITIES AND
YOUR PORTFOLIO: PART III *332*

PART IV
YOUR CLASSROOM

Chapter 11
Teacher Effectiveness *340*

Are Teachers Born, or Made? *341*

Learning Time *342*

Classroom Management *343*

 Management Models 346
 Preventing Problems 346

The Pedagogical Cycle *349*

 Clarity and Academic Structure 349
 Questioning 351
 Student Response 354
 Reaction or Productive Feedback 356

Variety in Process and Content *359*

Technology as a Tool for Effective Teaching *360*

Models for Effective Instruction *362*

 Direct Teaching 362
 Cooperative Learning 363
 Mastery Learning 365
 Problem-Based Learning 366
 Differentiated Instruction 368

A Few More Thoughts on Effective Teaching *369*

 Online Video Album to Accompany Teachers, Schools, and Society, 10e *371*
 The *Teachers, Schools, and Society Reader with Classroom Observation Video Clips 371*
 Key Terms and People 372
 Discussion Questions and Activities 372

Chapter 12
Your First Classroom *373*

Stages of Teacher Development *374*

Your First Year: Induction into the Profession *374*

 Mentors 376
 Observation 376
 Your First Day: Creating a Productive Classroom Climate 380
 Professional Development Programs 382
 Personalizing Schools 384

The Intangible (But Very Real) Rewards of Teaching *386*

Educational Associations *389*

 The NEA and the AFT 390
 Professional Associations and Resources 391

Tomorrow's Classroom? *393*

 Online Video Album to Accompany Teachers, Schools, and Society, 10e *397*
 The *Teachers, Schools, and Society Reader with Classroom Observation Video Clips 397*
 Key Terms and People 398
 Discussion Questions and Activities 399

Chapter 13
Q and A Guide to Entering the Teaching Profession *400*

What Are My Chances of Finding a Teaching Position? *401*

Who Are My Teaching Colleagues? What Are the Demographics of Today's Teachers? *402*

What Are My Chances for Earning a Decent Salary? *403*

Do Private Schools Pay Less Than Public Schools? *403*

How Do I Apply for a Teaching Job? Do I Need a Résumé or a Portfolio? *403*

How Do I Prepare for a Successful Interview? *405*

What Do I Need in Order to Teach—a License or Certification? By the Way, What's the Difference? *407*

If I Want to Teach in Another State, Do I Need Another Teacher's License? *408*

What Is an Endorsement? *408*

What Are "Alternative" Or Nontraditional Routes to Getting a Teacher's License? *408*

What Are Teacher Competency Tests? *409*

How Do Teaching Contracts Work? *411*

What Are Some Advantages of Tenure? *411*

What Are Some Disadvantages of Tenure? *412*

Are Untenured Teachers Protected? *412*

What Teaching Positions Exist in Unique School Settings? *412*

What Kinds of Educational Careers Are Available Beyond Classroom Teaching? *413*

 Key Terms 417

INTASC   **REFLECTIVE ACTIVITIES AND YOUR PORTFOLIO: PART IV** *418*

APPENDICES

TEXT APPENDICES

1   Teacher Competency Exams *A-1*

2   State Offices for Teacher Certification
          and Licensure *A-2*

3   INTASC Standards: Concepts and Content
          in *Teachers, Schools, and Society,* Tenth Edition *A-5*

www.mhhe.com/sadker10e

ONLINE APPENDICES

A   Classroom Observation Guidelines

B   State Offices for Teacher Certification and Licensure

Glossary G-1

Notes N-1

Credits C-1

Index I-1

Preface

If you think that *Teachers, Schools, and Society* was written to introduce you to the world of teaching, you are only half right. This book also reflects our excitement about a life in the classroom and is intended to spark your own fascination about working with children. We wrote this book to share with you the joys and the challenges we feel about teaching, as well as the importance of fairness and justice in school and society. With this tenth edition, our goals are unchanged: to provide you with information that is both current and concise, and especially to create an engaging book—one that will give you a sense of the wonderful possibilities found in a career in the classroom.

The primary intent of introductory courses in education is to provide a broad yet detailed exposure to the realities of teaching and the role of education in our society. This text will help you answer important questions such as: Do I want to become a teacher? What do I need to become the best teacher possible? What should a professional in the field of education know? To help you answer those questions, we offer a panoramic and (we hope) stimulating view of education.

Hallmarks of *Teachers, Schools, and Society*

Several themes and resources have become the hallmarks of *Teachers, Schools, and Society* over the years.

Focus on Equity

Issues of social justice and equity are at the core of our book. In your reading, you'll examine the racial, economic, social, and gender issues that erect barriers to equal opportunity. Although discussions of equity are integrated throughout the book, several chapters specifically focus on diversity. Chapter 2, *Different Ways of Learning*, explores theories of learning styles, emotional and multiple intelligences as well as recent brain research, all intended to help us understand the different ways students learn. We also describe how teachers can work with learning disabled students as well as with the gifted. Chapter 3, *Teaching Your Diverse Students*, This chapter requires the reader to apply knowledge and concepts to a simulated classroom of students from different religious, racial, ethnic, and sexuality

backgrounds. In Chapter 4, *Student Life in School and at Home* we explore how current social forces affect families, children, and schools.

Student diversity, a critical issue facing our schools today and in the decades ahead, is a powerful theme integrated throughout the book. The text provides explanations of group differences in academic performance, as well as practical strategies for nonracist, nonsexist teaching. We believe that only through recognizing and appreciating diversity can teaching be both effective and joyful.

A Closer Look — Myths about Culturally Responsive Teaching

Myth 1—Culturally responsive teaching is a new approach intended to meet the needs of poor, urban students of color. Teaching has always been culturally responsive, but primarily responsive to the values of white, Euro-American, middle-class students. That is why schools historically have emphasized individual success more than group success, strict adherence to time schedules, knowledge valued through analytical reasoning, self-sufficiency, and even dress codes. More inclusive culturally responsive teaching embraces the values and experiences of other cultures as well.

Myth 2—Only teachers of color can actually be culturally responsive to students of color. Race is not an obstacle to culturally responsive teaching; ignorance is. Through teacher training, teachers of any cultural background can gain the knowledge, skills, and attitudes needed to teach children from diverse cultures. In turn, because most teachers are white, they can share important lessons about the dominant culture.

Myth 3—Culturally responsive teaching is little more than a collection of teaching ideas and practices to motivate students of color. Culturally responsive teaching offers a new way of looking at the roles of teachers and students. Culturally relevant teachers are committed to valuing the experiences of their students and working toward a more just

society, far more profound goals than simply a collection of teaching ideas.

Myth 4—Culturally relevant teachers must master all the critical details of many cultures. It is unrealistic to expect teachers to master the intricacies of many cultures. But over time, thoughtful teachers will abandon simplistic, stereotypic thinking as they gain insights into cultural differences that influence behavior and learning.

Myth 5—Culturally relevant teaching categorizes children, which feeds stereotypic thinking. Actually, culturally relevant teaching reduces stereotypic thinking by asking teachers to be reflective. They must consider student experiences and backgrounds, create teaching opportunities that respond to student learning styles, hold high expectations for all students, and help students experience academic success.

SOURCE: Adapted from Jacqueline Jordan and Beverley Jeanne Armento, *Culturally Responsive Teaching* (Boston: McGraw-Hill, 2001).

REFLECTION: Why do you think these myths are so prevalent? What additional myths about culturally relevant teaching can you add? How has your understanding of culturally relevant teaching expanded by reading this chapter?

Annotated Instructor's Edition

The Annotated Instructor's Edition provides a wealth of resources for both new and experienced instructors. It offers easily implemented suggestions for how and when to use our supplements.

GLOBAL VIEW
Describe the varied cultural, religious, or ethnic intelligences of your classmates.

Online Video Album to Accompany
Teachers, Schools, and Society 10e

New in the Tenth Edition is an Online Video Album to accompany *Teachers, Schools and Society* that highlights topics and issues in the text. This collection is another way that the authors keep the text relevant and fresh. Find the links in our Online Learning Center (OLC) and check back for updates. We hope you find this a useful addition to the text, and we welcome your feedback, ideas, and suggestions for future video links.

ONLINE VIDEO ALBUM TO ACCOMPANY *TEACHERS, SCHOOLS, AND SOCIETY, 10E*

Visit the Online Learning Center for a range of contemporary videos with content related to this chapter.

www.mhhe.com/sadker10e

Teaching Tip

Also new in the Tenth Edition are *Teaching Tip* boxes. At the suggestion of our readers, we added practical advice from practicing teachers, the kind of "Tip" that brings theory down to earth. For example, a first-year teacher shares the lessons she learned from dealing with "helicopter" parents.

Teaching Tip

HOW TO WORK WITH "HELICOPTER PARENTS"

It was the day before my first year of teaching, my room was all set up, and I felt ready. But I hadn't much thought about one thing: the other adults involved with my students—their parents! I learned *very* quickly to focus on parent relationships. My first semester teaching, I learned these lessons.

BE PREPARED FOR ANYTHING
"Meet the Teacher Day" brought students with their parents, and I was taken by surprise. I had a parent yell at me for having an "inappropriate book series" in my classroom (even though this is a well-loved children's series that had been approved by our school board). I had a parent inform me that they had searched me on the Internet and knew where I'd gone to school, my past jobs, that I'd recently gotten married, my age, etc. Thankfully, there wasn't any negative information for her to find.

STAND YOUR GROUND
About two months after our first class science experiment, I had a parent e-mail me saying she was very unhappy with the grade her child received and wanted an explanation. The parent made it very apparent that she wanted me to change the grade and also threatened to pull the child from the school. This was demoralizing. However, I knew in my gut it wouldn't be fair to change the grade and it wouldn't help the student in the long run. Following an in-person meeting, the grade stayed, and so did the child. I learned that some parents just want to test their power.

COMMUNICATE REGULARLY
Each week I send home a brief newsletter with announcements, updates from the classroom, and a list of what we learned in each subject that week. Parents are e-mailed unless they request otherwise at Parent Night. It takes me about 15 minutes to put it together. Several parents have thanked me, as they didn't feel they had ever been so informed of their children's daily work. They also like feeling part of a team.

COMMUNICATE POSITIVELY
I wanted students to realize how much I value effort in class, so I came up with an "Honor Roll." All students have to do to earn a place on the Honor Roll is turn in all of their homework; they don't have to perform perfectly. When I posted my first honor roll, students were so excited and proud. What I think they valued even more was the note I sent home to their parents. I had many tell me that their son or daughter had never been recognized for any sort of effort or achievement, or that a positive note had never been sent home.

By Amie Kemberling, an elementary school teacher in Tucson, Arizona

REFLECTION: Which of Amie's strategies resonate with you? Did any surprise you? Do you have a strategy to add?

Global View

This annotation provides an international perspective to the issues discussed, including relevant facts, and Web links.

NEW TO THIS EDITION

Previous users of *Teachers, Schools, and Society* will find the student-friendly writing style, the engaging features, and many of the chapters and topics familiar. But when we revise a textbook, we want those revisions to be meaningful and current. In this edition, we are pleased to provide a revised *Reader*. Published on a CD-ROM, *The Reader* offers greater depth on topics, different points of view, case studies, and video clips that allow you to apply your skills and insights to specific situations. *The Reader* includes fifty-two readings (more than twenty-nine are new in the tenth edition), twenty-three case studies, and seventeen classroom observation videos.

We are excited to announce our *Online Video Album to Accompany Teachers, Schools, and Society,* new *Teaching Tips* boxes, a contemporary design, and much more. To emphasize the growing awareness of education as a global enterprise, we've included our *Global View* annotations throughout the book, describing education issues and developments from around the globe. In Chapter 9, we also added a close-up view of education in Finland, a country receiving a great deal of attention for its educational reform done on a path quite different from the United States. All of the portfolio and reflective activities were reorganized to reflect the revised INTASC: Core Teaching Standards, and Appendix 3 details where INTASC Standards concept and content can be found in the text. Of course, throughout the book, we have updated the research, statistics, and figures. Here is a brief, chapter-by-chapter description of the revisions in the tenth edition:

Chapter 1. *Becoming a Teacher* More in-depth comparison of alternative versus traditional paths to teacher certification. Additional coverage of parental views of teaching. Analysis of the most effective aspects of a teacher education program. More in-depth discussion of the power of intrinsic rewards and the derivation and meaning of "vocation." This chapter offers a more personal and positive view of teaching, but also a realistic one.

Chapter 2. *Different Ways of Learning* Research on the concept of intelligence has been updated to include Carol Dweck's work on entity and incremental theories. Also included is a new discussion on learning styles, as well as recent research exploring male–female brain differences and whether girls and boys do, in fact, learn differently. The discussion on gifted and talented students has also been revised.

Chapter 3. *Teaching Your Diverse Students* An in-depth discussion of deficit theory is now included in this chapter, which continues to feature opportunities for the reader to apply multicultural concepts to a diverse student body.

Chapter 4. *Student Life in School and at Home* This chapter now includes revised sections on tracking, dropouts, bullying, poverty and homelessness, families, and obesity/eating disorders.

Chapter 5. *Purposes of America's Schools and the Current Reform Movement* This new chapter title better reflects the chapter progression from the purposes of schools, to research on effective schools, to today's school choice and reform movement. Revised descriptions are provided of educational reform, privatization, green schools (now including green ribbon schools), charter and virtual schools, vouchers, home schooling, and full-service schools (including Geoffrey Canada of Harlem Children's Zone). The pros and cons of "value added" are discussed at some length. A new section, "Rethinking Reform," explores some of the fundamental assumptions of the current reform movement. There is additional coverage on parent–teacher relationships.

Chapter 6. *Curriculum, Standards, and Testing* The expanded section on Common Core State Standards now investigates not only these standards, but forecasts some of the potential problems of implementing these standards. There is also a new section analyzing how standardized student test scores are being used to evaluate teachers and the inherent problems with this approach (including Campbell's law). The technology section has been updated, as well as an analysis of the continuing testing influence of No Child Left Behind, even as it fades from a national implementation. There is a also a new look at tomorrow's curricular trends.

Chapter 7. *The History of American Education* A new *Teaching Tip* discusses the use of primary sources, and there is now a section on the history of educational reform in this chapter. Updated research on Hispanics in the United States, and two new Educational Hall of Famers—Booker T. Washington and W. E. B. Du Bois—have been added.

Chapter 8. *Philosophy of Education* A new *Teaching Tip: Writing Your Philosophy of Education* is now included.

Chapter 9. *Financing and Governing America's Schools* The new section discussing education in Finland offers a view of a very different (and successful) approach to reforming education. Also discussed is the impact of the recession on the poor and how the concept of *adequate education* has been compromised. Additional insights on the pressures on and central role of principals in school improvement have been added.

Chapter 10. *School Law and Ethics* This chapter has updated research on religion in schools, sexual harassment, copyright laws (including digital materials), and discipline and zero-tolerance policies, especially relating to minority students, An expanded discussion on ethics includes cheating, social networking, and child abuse.

Chapter 11. *Teacher Effectiveness* Readers have asked for more information related to classroom management, and that is now included. Technology's role in effective instruction is also updated. Also new are discussions on the effective use of praise, using the revised Bloom's taxonomy to improve classroom interactions, and the role of reflective teaching to improve instruction.

Chapter 12. *Your First Classroom* The discussions on induction programs and mentoring have been revised, and examples of how first-year teachers could approach observations of their teaching have been included. The intrinsic drives of twenty-first-century workers are explored and contrasted with merit pay plans currently being used by a number of school districts.

Chapter 13. *Q and A Guide to Entering the Teaching Profession* Updated and expanded discussions on the education job market, teacher certification and licensure, nontraditional routes to teaching, teacher competency exams (including the newly proposed Teacher Performance Assessment), teacher tenure, and education-related job opportunities outside the classroom have been included. We added a new box, *Teaching Tip: That First Mistake.*

Acknowledgments

We are grateful for the contributions and insights of our colleagues. Professor John White of the University of North Florida reviewed and offered useful suggestions concerning the treatment of class and poverty in this edition. Professor Ian Macgillivray of James Madison University provided materials and insights for the discussion of gay, lesbian, bisexual, and transgendered students. We extend a special thanks to Dr. Carl Grant, University of Wisconsin, and Louise Wilkinson. Their insightful critiques and recommendations made Chapter 3, *Teaching Your Diverse Students,* a stronger, more relevant chapter.

Joe Kelly did a great job summarizing the many new readings in *The Reader,* as well as creating new questions. Ray Rose is the technolgy educator who never fails to promote the potential of technology on student learning, and we thank him for his updates. Classroom teachers like Eric Baylin, Diane Pettway, and Amie Kemberling added practical insights to our *Teaching Tips.* Sean Miller keeps our green school section ripe with updates, and Dan Otter used his years of practical school experience to develop the INTASC Reflective Activities and Your Portfolio (*RAP*) sections. Scott Grubbs, from Valdosta State College, worked on the supplements package. Kathy Bradley, from East Carolina University, and Annmarie Masi, from Miami Dade

College, acted as curators on our new Online Video Album, and every instructor using the text is in their debt. Of course, last and far from least is a force of nature, S. J. Miller, who added depth, clarity, and the spark of life to our writing.

Teachers, Schools, and Society was originally inspired by a wonderful woman and bright academic star—Myra Pollack Sadker. David's late wife co-wrote the text through several editions over a fifteen-year period. She was always the major force behind providing a student-friendly introduction to teaching. In March 1995, Myra died undergoing treatment for breast cancer. Yet her insights and passion for teaching still guide our efforts. Even when her name is no longer on the cover, her heart and mind shine through the book. We know that she will always be the primary author of this book. To learn more about Myra and her work, visit the Myra Sadker Foundation at www.sadker.org.

Our editor, Maureen Spada, has done an amazing job of taking on this challenging assignment. Maureen is a skilled, hardworking, and sensitive editor, and we are lucky to have her services. Cara Labell was our collaborator and wonderful editor before Maureen arrived, and she guided us through many editions of this text. Her thoughtful insights are still very much a part of this tenth edition. Senior Sponsoring Editor Allison McNamara has been the editorial godmother of this text. Her integrity and caring kept our spirits high, and we hold her support close to our hearts. She works with us to sort out changes in content and the features, and we owe her a great debt of gratitude. And overseeing all of this, Mike Sugarman generously shared his wealth of experience and publishing insights to bring this text to fruition. Denise Wright at Southern Editorial was responsible for assembling the many supplements that accompany the book, and we appreciate her efforts, as well as the contributions of Barbara Heinssen and Dawn Groundwater, in directing development. Sarah Keifer and Zachary Norton are editorial assistants on this project, and they both have worked on coordinating manuscript and information as it passes from one set of hands to another. Ann Helgerson worked on the marketing and sales of this edition. Melissa Leick is the production editor of this book, and the design is under the direction of Tara McDermott. The McGraw-Hill team continually makes us feel that this text could not have better publishing allies and friends, and we are proud to have them as our publishers.

We also thank the following reviewers of *Teachers, Schools, and Society* for generously sharing with us their experiences in teaching the book:

Kelley Bailey, Florida A&M University

Tom Bean, University of Nevada Las Vegas

Ben Berry, Cochise College

Kathy Bradley, East Carolina University

Barrie Brancato, Clarion University of Pennsylvania

Shakira Cain, Jackson State University

Tamara Calhoun, Schenectady Community College

Steven Fry, College of DuPage

Teri Gordon, Athens State University

Mark Guillette, Valencia Community College

Shannon Hart, University of North Carolina at Pembroke

Monique Henderson, Lone Star College

Glenda Hernandez, Montgomery College

Brenda Hurbanis, Anne Arundel Community College

Wanda Hutchinson, Athens State University

Krystall Kessee, Miami Dade College

Annmarie Masi, Miami Dade College

Mary Mattson, Georgia Perimeter College

Lottie McMillan, Miami Dade College

Nancy Moreau, Northampton Community College

Laurie Owen, Grace College

John Pisano, Luzerne County Community College

Phillip Russell, University of Arkansas

Candice Scott, Mercy College

Laura Daniels-Simmonds, Central Texas College

Richard Simmons, College of DuPage

Zeporia Smith, Montgomery College

Lois A. Stanciak, College of DuPage

Thomas Starmack, Bloomsburg University of Pennsylvania

Barbara Slater Stern, James Madison University

Deb Sutor, Minnesota State Community & Technical College

Long Tran, University of Cincinnati

Paul Wagner, University of Houston

Lucinda Waldron, Santa Fe College

Susan Woron, Delaware County Community College

Elaine Zweig, Collin College

Finally, we thank our students for keeping us honest, on track, and motivated. They are our inspiration.

David M. Sadker
Karen R. Zittleman
Tucson, Arizona

The student supplements package is designed to allow students to extend their learning.

The Teachers, Schools and Society Reader

The Reader has been revised for the Tenth Edition and includes fifty-two contemporary, thought-provoking readings as well as historically significant excerpts, each related to specific chapter content. Each reading includes a brief summary and analysis questions. In addition, twenty-three case studies based on actual school events help students confront significant and relevant educational questions and dilemmas. Finally, the *Reader* includes seventeen Classroom Observation Video Clips designed to allow students to see in action the issues they are reading about. For a listing of the readings, cases, studies, and classroom observations, see the inside front cover of book.

Online Learning Center—Study Guide and Interactive Resources

The Student Online Learning Center contains an online student *Study Guide* (including multiple-choice and true/false quizzes and study tools), *Interactive Activities, You Be the Judge* questions, *Reel to Real Teaching,* Classroom Observation Videos, and additional resources such as Web Links, the online appendices, and *RAP* forms.

NEW in 10e—Online Video Album to Accompany Teachers, Schools, and Society. The Online Album brings to the readers contemporary video resources tied to topics in the text. The video album will be updated from time to time to keep it relevant and fresh. You'll find the links in our Online Learning Center under the Course-Wide Content tab. We hope you'll find these a useful addition to your course and we welcome your feedback, ideas, and suggestions for future video links.

Resources to Prepare for the Praxis™ Exam

An overview of the Praxis™ Exam is presented in the book's appendix. For further study, *McGraw-Hill's Praxis I & II Exam* can be packaged with the text at a reduced price. Contact your sales representative for more information.

Teachers, Schools, and Societ

Teachers and Students

Chapter 1

Becoming a Teacher *2*

Chapter 2

Different Ways of Learning *25*

Chapter 3

Teaching Your Diverse Students *51*

Becoming a Teacher

FOCUS QUESTIONS

1. What are the advantages and the disadvantages of being a teacher?
2. What are the satisfactions—and the complaints—of today's teachers?
3. Is teaching a "good fit" for you?
4. Can we consider teaching to be a profession?
5. How has teacher preparation changed over the years?
6. Are America's schools a secret success story?
7. What steps can you take now on the road to becoming a teacher?

Do not ask yourself what the world needs. Ask yourself what makes you come alive, and then go do that. Because what the world needs is people who have come alive.

HOWARD THURMAN

For inspirational stories about people who have had a powerful impact on the lives of others, go to the Online Learning Center and read the "Class Acts."

www.mhhe.com/sadker10e

WHAT DO YOU THINK? Why do you want to be a teacher? Rate the factors influencing your decision whether to become a teacher, and see how other students have rated these factors.

CHAPTER PREVIEW

This chapter looks at classroom life through the teacher's eyes. You may be thinking: I have spent years in a classroom, watching teachers and what they do. If there is one thing I know, it is teachers and teaching! But during your years in the classroom, you have looked at teaching through "student-colored glasses," a unique but somewhat distorted view, like looking through a telescope from the lens that makes everything tiny instead of large. In this chapter, we will view the classroom from the teacher's side of the desk, a very different way of looking at school.

Some of you are taking this course because you want to learn more about schools and teaching. This text will answer many of your questions and offer useful information. We know that many of you taking this course are considering a major decision: Do I want to be a teacher? This first chapter is especially designed to help you answer that question.

The chapter is also about "us." Yes, us. We are now a team, this textbook, the authors, and you. When your authors were students, we did not much like our textbooks. They were far from exciting to read. By extension, we feared that we might not like teaching. In the end, we loved teaching—but still hated our textbooks. We want this textbook to be different—to be not only informative but also enjoyable. This first chapter offers us the opportunity to introduce the textbook and, in a sense, to introduce ourselves.

Welcome to our classroom.

A Teaching Career—Is It Right for You?

In this text, we will try mightily to include relevant information, witty insights, useful studies, and engaging chapters about teaching, school law, student diversity, and educational history—all kinds of topics that offer you a balanced view of teaching. We want you to understand the fundamentals of teaching and schooling in the United States, and we will present the information in as exciting a way as we can. To do this, we have created several features that encourage you to reflect and focus on key points. You will learn about both the positive and the negative aspects of many educational issues as you consider a possible career in teaching.

At some point, you will need to figure out if teaching is right for you. (And here's the hard part: Only you can do that.) Consider your friends' and relatives' advice, but realize that in the final analysis, it is your life, not theirs. You undoubtedly have met people who are doing work they love, and they are joyful and fulfilled. You have also met people who have made an unhappy choice, perhaps followed someone's advice that sounded good at the time—but wasn't. For them, every day is "a grind." Your goal is to find the career that puts you in that first group, a career that brings you joy and meaning. Where do you find such a vocation?

People think "vocation" is all about choosing and preparing for a career: learn about different careers, consider the external rewards and downsides of each career, weigh the pros and cons, and finally choose the one that makes the most sense. But if you haven't discovered this yet, life often defies such logic and planning. The clue about choosing the right vocation is hidden in plain sight, in the word itself. *Vocation* comes from the Latin root for *voice*; your voice. What career is your inner voice telling you to pursue? What, you don't hear an inner voice? Not surprising. In our society, schools teach us early on to be quiet and listen to others, to take notes on what others say, to study hard, and to do well on the test. But finding the vocation that is right for you is not about knowing what others believe; it is about learning about yourself. Theologian and Pulitzer Prize winner Frederick Buechner put it nicely when he said that finding your vocation in life is discovering the place ". . . where your deep gladness and the world's deep hunger meet." [1] We hope you find reflective, quiet times in this course so you can listen to your heart and discover where your deep gladness leads you.

As you read through this text, stop every now and then and ask yourself: "Does this speak to my heart? Am I enjoying what I am reading? Does teaching feel right for me?" We know, this heart talk is not what you typically read about in textbooks, but this is not a typical textbook.

In a *Peanuts* cartoon, Linus comments that "no problem is so big or complicated that it can't be run away from." Charles Schulz succinctly highlighted a human frailty shared by most of us—the tendency to put aside our problems or critical questions in favor of day-to-day routine. In fact, it is amazing how little care and consideration many of us give to choosing a career. It is always easier to catch a movie, surf the net, or even study for the next exam than it is to reflect on and plan for the future. That may be one reason why questions such as "What are you going to be when you grow up?" and "What's your next career move?" make so many of us uneasy. The big question facing many of you: Is teaching right for me? Some of you are in college or university programs and will be teaching in the next few years. Others of you may already be in a classroom, teaching as you work toward your license in one of several alternative teacher certification programs. For some of you, teaching may become a decades-long career filled with joy and satisfaction. For others, teaching may be limited to only a few years spent in the classroom, one of several careers you explore during your working years. And still

Like this perspective? In this chapter, you will look at classrooms from the teacher's side of the desk.

FOCUS QUESTION 1

What are the advantages and the disadvantages of being a teacher?

others may reach an equally useful and important realization: Teaching is not the ideal match for your interests or skills. We'd like to help you decide whether you and teaching are a good fit.

Throughout this text, we pose a variety of questions for you to consider. We have devised a feature called *You Be the Judge,* which presents several sides of an issue and encourages you to sort out where you stand. When the authors have a strong opinion about these or any of the issues in the text, we will not hide it from you. But our opinion is just our opinion, and we want you to form your own ideas. To that end, we will work hard to be fair, to present more than one side of the issue, and to help you form an independent point of view. *You Be the Judge* is one way that we hope to spark your interest and thinking on critical issues.

In the first *You Be the Judge,* where we highlight the joys and the concerns of a career in the classroom (see pp. 6–7), we include comments by teachers themselves that reveal their perceptions and feelings about their work. A more structured attempt to assess teachers' views on their careers was carried out by the National Education Association (NEA). Teachers from around the nation were asked why they decided to become teachers, and why they choose to stay in teaching.[2] Teachers elect a career in the classroom for the intrinsic rewards that make teaching unique, including a desire to work with young people, the significance of education generally, and even the love of a particular subject—not a bad bunch to have as colleagues. (See Figures 1.1 and 1.2).

Metropolitan Life has been surveying American teachers for a quarter of a century and reports that many teachers are more positive than they have been in decades. Their 2008

FIGURE 1.1

Why teach?

SOURCE: National Education Association, *Status of the American Public School Teacher,* 2006.

REFLECTION: Which of these reasons for teaching speak to you? Can you suggest others?

Reasons Teachers Teach	Teachers Agreeing
Desire to work with young people	71%
Value or significance of education to society	42%
Interest in subject-matter field	39%
Influence of teacher in elementary or secondary school	31%
Influence of family	19%

FIGURE 1.2

Where teachers teach?

SOURCE: C. Emily Feistritzer, *Profile of Teachers in the U.S.,* National Center for Education Information, 2011, www.ncei.com/Profile_Teachers_US_2011.pdf, chart 6, p. 16.

REFLECTION: Which of these geographic regions speak to you? Why?

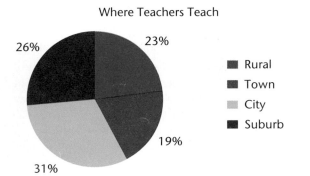

Where Teachers Teach

- Rural 23%
- Town 19%
- City 31%
- Suburb 26%

survey indicated that two-thirds of teachers feel that they are well prepared for their profession and better prepared for classroom challenges such as poverty, limited English proficiency, and lack of parental support. Nine out of ten teachers believe that their school curriculum is excellent or good. And while salaries remain a problem for many teachers, especially during times of tight budgets, about two out of three teachers felt they were paid a decent salary. The 2012 MetLife Survey was less optimistic. The impact of a struggling national economy led to the loss of many teaching positions, and as teachers' job security fell, little surprise that job satisfaction fell as well. But the survey also revealed that when teachers were treated as professionals, their job satisfaction increased. What exactly does being treated as a professional mean? Glad you asked, because we will revisit the concept of professionalism a bit later in this chapter.

But while most teachers feel better about their jobs than they did in the past, not all do. A Public Agenda survey (2009) described four in ten teachers as "disheartened" and almost the same ratio as "content." One reason for this mixed picture is the economic downturn that began in 2008 and affected many school budgets. Another has been the direction of the education reform movement. As people work to improve schools, some have decided that ineffective teachers are the problem with American education. Teachers in too many communities feel pressured by shrinking school budgets and public criticism. But even under these pressures, it is helpful to remember that almost one in four reported feeling great satisfaction in their work. They were described as "idealists,"[3] whose dedication makes a difference in people's lives; perhaps this is one reason Americans respect teachers more than they do scientists, judges, or television newscasters. Only doctors are more respected. And that is quite a compliment. (See Figure 1.3.)

Many believe that the path to improving education is monetarily rewarding good teachers and removing weak ones, so it is not surprising that pay-for-performance has gained popularity. **Pay-for-performance,** sometimes called **merit pay,** attempts to make teaching more accountable by linking teacher and student performance to teacher salary. Simply put: Better teachers earn more money. While this sounds like a pretty good idea, it has its problems. Although many of us feel we know a good teacher when we see one, being objective can be difficult. For example, several approaches use student test scores to decide which teachers are most effective. But does a test score measure teaching, or student attendance, or the family situation? Perhaps teachers who teach challenging subjects like physics or math should earn more money than first-grade teachers? (Or do we have that backward?) Perhaps teachers who

FOCUS QUESTION 2
What are the satisfactions—and the complaints—of today's teachers?

FOCUS QUESTION 3
Is teaching a "good fit" for you?

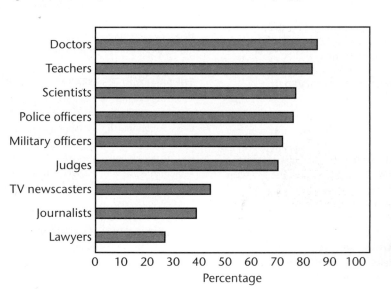

FIGURE 1.3
Public trust in various professions. "Would you generally trust each of the following types of people to tell the truth, or not?"

SOURCE: Statistics from *The Harris Poll* #61, August 8, 2006.

REFLECTION: Why do you think doctors and teachers garner so much trust? Why is there a significant drop in trust for TV newscasters, journalists, and lawyers?

You Be The Judge
A TEACHING CAREER

The Good News . . .

YOU ARE NOT WORKING ALONE, STARING AT A COMPUTER SCREEN OR SHUFFLING PAPERS

If you enjoy being in contact with others, particularly young people, teaching could be the right job for you. Young people are so often funny, fresh and spontaneous. As America's students become increasingly diverse, you will find yourself learning about different cultures and different life experiences. The children will make you laugh and make you cry. "I still can't get used to how much my heart soars with every student's success, and how a piece of my heart is plucked away when any student slips away."[1]

THE SMELL OF THE CHALKBOARD, THE ROAR OF THE CROWD

You carefully plan your social protest lesson. You bring your favorite CDs and DVDs of social protest songs, and prepare an excellent PowerPoint presentation to highlight key historical figures and issues. Thoughtful discussion follows, and students are spellbound. They make plans for researching current social protest. Wow, what a lesson!

When you have taught well, your students will let you know it. On special occasions, they will come up to you after class or at the end of the year to tell you "This class is awesome." At younger grade levels, they may write you notes (often anonymous), thanking you for a good class or a good year.

I'M PROUD TO BE A TEACHER

When you become a teacher, many people will accord you respect, because they admire teachers. You will be someone whose specialized training and skills are used to benefit others. Mark Twain once wrote, "To be good is noble, but to teach others how to be good is nobler." Which would have summed up this point perfectly, except, being Mark Twain, he added: "—and less trouble."

AS A TEACHER, YOU ARE CONSTANTLY INVOLVED IN INTELLECTUAL MATTERS

You may have become very interested in a particular subject. Perhaps you love a foreign language or mathematics, or maybe you are intrigued by contemporary social issues. If you decide you want to share that excitement and stimulation with others, teaching offers a natural channel for doing so. As one teacher put it: "I want them to be exposed to what I love and what I teach. I want them to know somebody, even if they think I'm crazy, who's genuinely excited about history."[3]

PORTRAIT OF THE TEACHER AS AN ARTIST

Some people draw clear parallels between teachers and artists and highlight the creativity that is essential to both:

. . . The Bad News

STOP THE CROWD—I WANT TO GET AWAY

Right in the middle of a language arts lesson, when fifteen kids have their hands in the air, you may feel like saying, "Stop, everybody. I feel like being alone for the next fifteen minutes. I'm going to Starbucks." For the major part of each day, your job demands that you be involved with children in a fast-paced and intense way, which could affect behavior beyond school. One kindergarten teacher warned her 40-year-old brother "to be sure and put on his galoshes. Wow! Did he give me a strange look."[2]

IS ANYBODY THERE?

After teaching your fantastic lesson on social protest literature, you want to share your elation with your colleagues, but it is hard to capture the magic of what went on in the classroom. It is rare to have another adult spend even ten minutes observing you at work in your classroom. Once you have obtained tenure, classroom observation becomes incredibly infrequent. The word may leak out—through students, parents, or even the custodian—if you are doing a really fine job; however, on the whole, when you call out, "Hello, I'm here, I'm a teacher. How am I doing?" there will be little cheering from anyone outside your classroom.

I DON'T GET NO RESPECT

Although many appreciate teachers, others do not. One reason is sexism. Occupations with large numbers of women, like teaching, generally face prestige problems (a situation we hope one day changes). Others are quick to blame schools for any and all of society's problems. Also, in our materialistic society, people's work is frequently measured by the size of the paycheck—and most teachers' wallets are only modestly endowed.

THE SAME MATTERS YEAR AFTER YEAR AFTER YEAR

Teaching, like most other jobs, entails a lot of repetition. You may tire of teaching the same subject matter to a new crop of students every September. If this happens, boredom and a feeling that you are getting intellectually stale may replace excitement. Because you are just embarking on your teaching career, you may find it difficult to imagine yourself becoming bored with the world of education. However, as you teach class after class on the same subject, interest can wane.

THE BOG OF MINDLESS ROUTINE

Although there is opportunity for ingenuity and inventiveness, most of the day is spent in the three Rs of ritual, repetition, and routine. As one disgruntled sixth-grade teacher in Los Angeles said,

The Good News . . .

I love to teach as a painter loves to paint, as a musician loves to play, as a singer loves to sing, as a strong man rejoices to run a race. Teaching is an art—an art so great and so difficult to master that a man [or woman] can spend a long life at it without realizing much more than his [or her] limitations and mistakes, and his [or her] distance from the ideal. But the main aim of my happy days has been to become a good teacher. Just as every architect wishes to be a good architect and every professional poet strives toward perfection.[4]

TO TOUCH A LIFE, TO MAKE A DIFFERENCE

Teaching is more than helping a child master a subject; each classroom is a composite of the anguish and the joy of all its students. You can feel the pain of the child in the fourth seat who is too shy to speak or the student who struggles to focus on any one task or project. You can be the one who makes a difference in their lives:

I am happy that I found a profession that combines my belief in social justice with my zeal for intellectual excellence. My career choice has meant much anxiety, anger, and disappointment. But it has also produced profound joy. I have spent my work life committed to a just cause: the education of Boston high school students. Welcome to our noble teaching profession and our enduring cause.[6]

BETTER SALARIES, LONGER VACATIONS

Salaries vary enormously from one community to another. Additional salary can be earned by working in the summer or accepting extra faculty responsibilities. Occupational benefits, such as health and retirement, are generally excellent, and you will enjoy long vacations. All these considerations make for a more relaxed and varied lifestyle, one that gives you time for yourself as well as your family. Whether you use your "free time" to be with your family, to travel, or to make extra money, time flexibility is a definite plus.[7]

. . .The Bad News

Paper work, paper work. The nurse wants the health cards, so you have to stop and get them. Another teacher wants one of your report cards. The principal wants to know how many social science books you have. Somebody else wants to know if you can come to a meeting on such and such a day. Forms to fill out, those crazy forms: Would you please give a breakdown of boys and girls in the class; would you please say how many children you have in reading grade such and such. Forms, messengers—all day long.[5]

THE TARNISHED IDEALIST

We all hope to be that special teacher, the one students remember and talk about long after they graduate. But too often, idealistic goals give way to survival—simply making it through from one day to the next. New teachers find themselves judged on their ability to maintain a quiet, orderly room. Idealistic young teachers find the worship of control incompatible with their humanistic goals. Likewise, they feel betrayed if a student naively mistakes their offer of friendship as a sign of weakness or vulnerability. As a result, many learn the trade secret—"don't smile until Christmas" (or Chanukah, Kwanzaa, or Ramadan, depending on your community)—and adopt it quickly. Even veteran teachers often throw up their hands in despair. Trying to make a difference may result in more frustration than satisfaction.

BUT SALARIES STILL HAVE A LONG WAY TO GO

Although teachers' salaries have improved, they still lag behind what most people would call a good income. Teachers would need a 30 percent pay increase to become competitive with other college-educated careers. Compared with teachers in other countries, U.S. teachers work longer hours for less pay. A history teacher says, "It's really difficult to maintain a family . . . I'm not sure I could have done it then except for a wife who's not demanding or pushy. She's completely comfortable with the things we have, and we don't have a great deal."[8]

www.mhhe.com/sadker10e

YOU DECIDE . . .

Which of these arguments and issues are most influential in determining if teaching is a good fit for you? Is there a particular point that is most persuasive, pro or con? What does that tell you about yourself?

On a scale from 1 to 10, where 10 is "really committed" to teaching, and 1 is "I want no part of that job," what number are you? Remember that number as you read the text and go through this course—and see if you change that rating in the pages and weeks ahead.

work at under-resourced schools in high-poverty areas should be paid more. (Does that mean we pay less to those who teach the gifted?) It is not unusual for school politics and personality issues to influence people's judgment about who is a terrific teacher. And schools can be very political places. Sometimes a plan that sounds fairly easy, like paying strong teachers more, is actually pretty difficult. Pay-for-performance has its challenges, but it is popular among many, and it is part of the current reform movement that we will talk more about later.[4]

In addition to identifying and rewarding superior teachers, the recent reform effort focuses on identifying and removing weak teachers, even those with tenure. What is tenure? After

GLOBAL VIEW

If there are international students in your class (or students who have been schooled abroad), perhaps they will be willing to discuss their experiences with teacher satisfaction in other cultures. Visit the Institute for International Education (www.iie.org) for information on teacher experiences in different countries. The site also describes opportunities to teach abroad, including the Fulbright scholarship program.

GLOBAL VIEW

Research teacher wages internationally. How might salary affect status and lifestyle issues abroad?

FOCUS QUESTION 4

Can we consider teaching to be a profession?

teaching satisfactorily during a probationary period (usually two to four years), teachers typically receive **tenure,** an expectancy of continued employment. Tenure is not an iron-clad guarantee of job security. It does not protect teachers who break the law, are debilitated by alcoholism, or theoretically have become terrible teachers. Tenure is intended to protect teachers from arbitrary and unfair dismissal. Unfortunately, in too many school districts, it has had the unintended effect of insulating some weak teachers from dismissal. (Did you ever have an awful teacher protected by tenure? Not much fun.) But many teachers worry that without tenure, it may not be just the weak teachers who are removed. Teachers may be fired because of personality conflicts, disputes with administrators, or other reasons unrelated to teaching skills. So although tenure protections are still in place in most school districts, much consideration is being given to the best ways to identify and remove incompetent teachers—and to possibly eliminating tenure entirely.[5] How do you feel about these possible tenure changes and the introduction of pay-for-performance? Both these modifications may well influence your life in the classroom.

Professionalism at the Crossroads

What noble employment is more valuable to the state than that of the man who instructs the rising generation?

(Cicero)

Education makes a people easy to lead, but difficult to drive; easy to govern but impossible to enslave.

(Lord Brougham)

I shou'd think it as glorius [sic] employment to instruct poor children as to teach the children of the greatest monarch.

(Elizabeth Elstob)

We must view young people not as empty bottles to be filled, but as candles to be lit.

(Robert Schaffer)

I touch the future; I teach.

(Christa McAuliffe)

Literature, philosophy, and history are replete with such flowery tributes to teaching. In many minds, in some of our greatest minds, teaching is considered the noblest of professions. But the realities of the job do not always mesh with such admirable appraisals, resulting in a painful clash between noble ideals and practical realities.

Many teachers feel that the satisfaction they realize inside the classroom is too often jeopardized by forces beyond the classroom: politicians mandating numerous standardized tests demanding parents offering little support, and textbook publishers or state officials deciding what should be taught and what topics are off-limits to teachers. Teachers desire more autonomy and control over their careers and, like all of us, want to be treated with more respect. Teachers increasingly see themselves as reflective decision makers, selecting objectives and teaching procedures to meet the needs of different learners.[6] They must know their subject matter, learning theory, research on various teaching methodologies, and techniques for curriculum development.[7] Some believe that the problems confronting teachers stem from the more pervasive issue of professional status and competence. Are teachers professionals? Are they treated like professionals? What does it take to be a professional, anyway? *Educating a Profession,* a publication of the American Association of Colleges for Teacher Education (AACTE), lists twelve criteria for a *profession.*

We have shortened these criteria here, and ask you to consider each one and decide if you believe that teaching meets these criteria. After marking your reactions in the appropriate column, compare your reactions with those of your classmates.

Criteria for a Profession	True for Teaching	Not True for Teaching	Don't Know
1. Professions provide essential services to the individual and society.	_____	_____	_____
2. Each profession is concerned with an identified area of need or function (e.g., maintenance of physical and emotional health).	_____	_____	_____
3. The profession possesses a unique body of knowledge and skills (professional culture).	_____	_____	_____
4. Professional decisions are made in accordance with valid knowledge, principles, and theories.	_____	_____	_____
5. The profession is based on undergirding disciplines from which it builds its own applied knowledge and skills.	_____	_____	_____
6. Professional associations control the actual work and conditions of the profession (e.g., admissions, standards, licensing).	_____	_____	_____
7. There are performance standards for admission to and continuance in the profession.	_____	_____	_____
8. Preparation for and induction into the profession require a protracted preparation program, usually in a college or university professional school.	_____	_____	_____
9. There is a high level of public trust and confidence in the profession and in the skills and competence of its members.	_____	_____	_____
10. Individual practitioners are characterized by a strong service motivation and lifetime commitment to competence.	_____	_____	_____
11. The profession itself determines individual competence.	_____	_____	_____
12. There is relative freedom from direct or public job supervision of the individual practitioner. The professional accepts this responsibility and is accountable through his or her profession to the society.[8]	_____	_____	_____

Do not be surprised if you find some criteria that do not apply to teaching. In fact, even the occupations that spring to mind when you hear the word *professional*—doctor, lawyer, clergy, college professor—do not completely measure up to all these criteria.

Where do you place teaching? If you had a tough time deciding, you are not alone. Many people feel that teaching falls somewhere between professional and semiprofessional in status. Perhaps we should think of it as an "emerging" profession. Or perhaps teaching is, and will remain, a "submerged" profession. Either way, teachers find themselves in a career with both potential and frustration.

Collectively, teachers struggle to empower their profession; individually, they struggle to empower their students.

Why does all this "profession talk" matter? You may be more concerned with *real* questions: Will I be good at teaching? Do I want to work with children? What age level is best for me? Will the salary be enough to give me the quality of life that I want for myself and my family? You may be thinking: Why should I split hairs over whether I belong to a profession? Who cares? The issue of professionalism may not matter to you now or even during your first year or two of teaching, when classroom survival has top priority. But if you stay in teaching, this idea of professionalism will grow in significance, perhaps becoming one of the most important issues you face. Even now, as a student, you can become more reflective in your views of teaching and learning; you can begin to refine your own professional behaviors and outlooks.

But let's keep all this in some perspective. Americans like to call themselves "professionals" because the term brings some status. But there are issues far more important than status. For example, no one would argue that a lawyer is a professional, but whereas some lawyers work to ensure that the environment is protected, others work to overturn environmental laws. Some lawyers work to protect the rights of the disenfranchised, while others serve the interests of the powerful. All these lawyers are professionals, but some of them make us proud, while the work of others saddens us. There is no reservation about the value of teachers' work. Teachers move the world forward—a meaningful way to spend one's life and more relevant than the word *professional,* and perhaps even more relevant than salary.

The unspoken dimension of this professional talk is salary. While doctors and lawyers might also fall short of professional status, many of them earn significantly higher salaries than teachers, so that must make their lives if not easier, than at least happier. Not necessarily. Psychologists and economists have found that after an economic threshold is met, the correlation between income and happiness is weak. At the University of Rochester, for example, researchers compared students who expressed extrinsic *profit* goals (wanting wealth and fame) with students who held intrinsic *purpose* goals (wanting to help others, improve their lives, grow and learn). A year or two later, the students with purpose goals in college reported being happier and more satisfied than they were in college. They had very low levels of anxiety or depression because they were finding fulfillment. But this was not the case for the graduates who had profit goals. Even though they were successfully accumulating money and status, they reported they were no happier than they were in college. Moreover, they were experiencing increased depression, anxiety, and other negative indicators. Attaining profit goals actually led to negative consequences. "People who have very high extrinsic goals for wealth are more likely to attain wealth, but they are still unhappy."[9] While all workers deserve to have an adequate salary, earning a large income is no guarantee of happiness. Living a purposeful life may well offer a happier future.

From Normal Schools to Board-Certified Teachers

As you read this brief history of teacher preparation, think about whether teachers are prepared in a way commensurate with belonging to a profession.

From colonial America into the twentieth century, teacher education scarcely existed. More often than not, teachers in colonial America received no formal preparation at all. Most elementary teachers never even attended a secondary school. Some learned their craft by serving as apprentices to master teachers, a continuation of the medieval guild system. Others were indentured servants paying for their passage to America by teaching for a fixed number of years. Many belonged to the "sink-or-swim" school of teaching, and the education of an untold number of students undoubtedly sank with them.

The smaller number of teachers working at the secondary level—in academies or Latin grammar schools and as private tutors—had usually received some college education, more often in Europe than in America. Some knowledge of the subject matter was considered desirable, but no particular aptitude for teaching or knowledge of teaching skills was considered necessary. Teaching was viewed not as a career but as temporary employment. Many of those who entered teaching, especially at the elementary level, were teenagers who taught for only a year or two. Others were of dubious character, and early records reveal a number of teachers fired for drinking or stealing.

From this humble beginning there slowly emerged a more professional program for teacher education. In 1823, the **Reverend Samuel Hall** established a **normal school** (derived from the French *école normale,* a school that establishes model standards) in Concord, Vermont. This private school provided elementary school graduates with formal training in teaching skills. Reverend Hall's modest normal school marked the beginning of teacher education in America. Sixteen years later, in 1839, **Horace Mann** was instrumental in establishing the first state-supported normal school in Lexington, Massachusetts. Normal schools typically provided a two-year teacher training program, consisting of academic subjects as well as teaching methodology. Some students came directly from elementary school; others had completed a secondary education. Into the 1900s, the normal school was the backbone of teacher education. The lack of rigorous professional training contributed to the less-than-professional treatment afforded teachers. The following is a teacher contract from the 1920s, a contract that offers a poignant insight into how teachers were seen . . . and treated.

MICHIGAN STATE NORMAL SCHOOL.

Many of today's noted universities began as normal schools a century ago and were established to prepare teachers.

FOCUS QUESTION 5

How has teacher preparation changed over the years?

Teaching Contract

Miss _____ agrees:

1. Not to get married. This contract becomes null and void immediately if the teacher marries.

2. Not to keep company with men.

3. To be home between the hours of 8 P.M. and 6 A.M. unless in attendance at a school function.

4. Not to loiter downtown in ice-cream parlors.

5. Not to smoke cigarettes. This contract becomes null and void immediately if the teacher is found smoking.

6. Not to drink beer, wine, or whiskey. This contract becomes null and void immediately if the teacher is found drinking beer, wine, or whiskey.

7. To keep the schoolroom clean:

    a. To sweep the classroom floor at least once daily.

    b. To scrub the classroom floor at least once weekly with soap and hot water.

    c. To clean the blackboard at least once daily.

    d. To start the fire at 7 A.M. so that the room will be warm by 8 A.M. when the children arrive.

8. Not to wear face powder, mascara, or to paint the lips.

(Reprinted courtesy of the *Chicago Tribune,* September 28, 1895, Section 1.)

As the contract indicates, by the 1900s, teaching was becoming a female occupation. Both female workers and teaching being held in low regard, the reward for the austere dedication detailed in this contract was an unimpressive $75 a month. But as the twentieth century progressed, professional teacher training gained wider acceptance. Enrollments in elementary schools climbed and secondary education gained in popularity, and so did the demand for more and better-trained teachers. Many private colleges and universities initiated teacher education programs, and normal schools expanded to three- and four-year programs, gradually evolving into state teachers' colleges. Interestingly, as attendance grew, these teachers' colleges expanded their programs and began offering courses and career preparation in fields other than teaching. By the 1950s, many of the state teachers' colleges had evolved into state colleges. In fact, some of today's leading universities were originally chartered as normal schools.

The 1980s marked the beginning of the modern effort to reshape education. A number of education reform reports fanned the flames of controversy regarding professionalism and teacher preparation, including one written by a group of prominent education deans. The Holmes Group, named for former Harvard Education Dean Henry H. Holm debated the teacher preparation issue for several years before releasing its report, titl *Tomorrow's Teachers* (1986).[10] The same year, the Carnegie Forum also issued a highly publicized report, *A Nation Prepared.*[11] Both reports called for higher standards and increased professionalism for the nation's teachers. The Carnegie report also called for an end to the undergraduate teaching major, to be replaced by master's-level degrees in teaching. While some universities followed this recommendation and created fifth-year teacher education programs (bachelor's and master's degrees required for teacher education candidates), other colleges continued their undergraduate education programs. Teacher education remains a hodgepodge of approaches. Some critics place much of the blame on universities themselves, for failing to adequately fund and support schools of education.[12]

But not all of the attention has been on initial teacher education. In the 1990s, the Carnegie Forum was influential in creating the **National Board for Professional Teaching Standards (NBPTS).** The goal of the NBPTS is to award *board certification* to extraordinary teachers whose skills and knowledge indicate their high level of achievement. Imagine yourself as a newly appointed NBPTS board member responsible for determining what skills and behaviors identify truly excellent teachers, teachers who will be known as board certified. How would you begin? The board identified five criteria: mastery of subject area, commitment to students, ability to effectively manage a classroom, continuous analysis of teaching performance, and a commitment to learning and self-improvement. (See *A CLOSER LOOK:* What Teachers Should Know and Be Able to Do).[13]

To demonstrate expertise to the NBPTS, teachers must complete a series of performance-based assessments, including written exercises that reflect mastery of their subject and understanding of the most effective teaching methods. Board candidates must also submit student work samples and videotapes of their teaching and participate in simulations and interviews held at special assessment centers. As you might imagine, the board assessment is not inexpensive, with a price tag of several thousand dollars. Fewer than half the states and a handful of school districts now pay for their teachers to prepare for board certification.

As the NBPTS evolves, the teaching profession faces new questions. What does board certification mean? Clearly, being recognized as exceptional is psychologically rewarding. Considering that there are literally millions of teachers in the United States, to be among a selected few is a major boost. To date, about 3 percent of teachers are board certified.[14] Many teachers

A Closer Look
What Teachers Should Know and Be Able to Do

The National Board for Professional Teaching Standards has described effective teachers with five core propositions.

1. TEACHERS ARE COMMITTED TO STUDENTS AND THEIR LEARNING

Accomplished teachers are dedicated to making knowledge accessible to all students. They act on the belief that all students can learn. They treat students equitably, recognizing the individual differences that distinguish one student from another and take account of these differences in their practice. They adjust their practice on the basis of observation and knowledge of their students interests, abilities, skills, knowledge, family circumstances, and peer relationships. Equally important, they foster students' self-esteem, motivation, character, and civic responsibility, and their respect for individual, cultural, religious, and racial differences.

2. TEACHERS KNOW THE SUBJECTS THEY TEACH AND HOW TO TEACH THOSE SUBJECTS TO STUDENTS

Accomplished teachers have a rich understanding of the subject(s) they teach and appreciate how knowledge in their subject is created, organized, linked to other disciplines, and applied to real-world settings. Their instructional repertoire allows them to create multiple paths to the subjects they teach, and they are adept at teaching students how to pose and solve their own problems.

3. TEACHERS ARE RESPONSIBLE FOR MANAGING AND MONITORING STUDENT LEARNING

Accomplished teachers create, enrich, maintain, and alter instructional settings to capture and sustain the interest of their students and to make the most effective use of time. They are as aware of ineffectual or damaging practice as they are devoted to elegant practice. They know how to engage groups of students to ensure a disciplined learning environment, and how to organize instruction to allow the schools' goals for students to be met. They are adept at setting norms for social interaction among students and between students and teachers. Accomplished teachers can assess the progress of individual students as well as that of the class as a whole.

4. TEACHERS THINK SYSTEMATICALLY ABOUT THEIR PRACTICE AND LEARN FROM EXPERIENCE

Accomplished teachers are models of educated people, exemplifying the virtues they seek to inspire in students—curiosity, tolerance, honesty, fairness, respect for diversity, and appreciation of cultural differences. They draw on their knowledge of human development, subject matter, and instruction, and their understanding of their students to make principled judgments about sound practice. Their decisions are grounded not only in the literature but also in their experience.

5. TEACHERS ARE MEMBERS OF LEARNING COMMUNITIES

Accomplished teachers contribute to the effectiveness of the school by working collaboratively with other professionals on instructional policy, curriculum development, and staff development. They can evaluate school progress and the allocation of school resources in light of their understanding of state and local educational objectives. Accomplished teachers find ways to work collaboratively and creatively with parents, engaging them productively in the work of the school.

SOURCE: www.nbpts.org. Adapted from © 2009, National Board for Professional Teaching Standards.

REFLECTION: Can you demonstrate your understanding of each proposition with a classroom example from your past? If your schooling offers little to brag about (or your memories are faded), let your imagination give credence to the task. Envision an example from the five areas to confirm you comprehend each concept.

who become board certified receive stipends or are placed on a higher salary scale. Others are given released time to work with new teachers. However, such recognition is not universal. When funds are in short supply or a school district's organizational structure is inflexible, board-certified teachers may receive few tangible rewards or new responsibilities, despite their excellence. As you enter the teaching profession, you will want to stay abreast of the activities concerning the national board and determine if you want to work toward board certification.[15] (For a current update of NBPTS activities, visit www.nbpts.org.)

How Teachers Are Prepared Today

Even as educators strive toward professional status, there is no consensus on how best to prepare teachers, and today we have many different paths to becoming a teacher. These different approaches have been categorized as traditional (undergraduate preparation at a college) or alternative (post-graduate preparation at a college or school district). The traditional teacher education path is found in hundreds of colleges where undergraduates study education and subject matter, then do student teaching en route to becoming a teacher. Alternative teacher preparation typically focuses on a structured apprenticeship, a sort of on-the-job training. For example, a candidate might learn the fundamentals of teaching in a summer program, then start teaching in the fall and continue to take university-level education courses in the evening, on weekends, or in the summer. At the end of a year, or perhaps two years, the individual is licensed to teach.

The growth of these alternative programs has led to a more mature and diverse teaching force. The vast majority of these new teachers are over 30 (almost half over 40 years of age), and about a third are male or nonwhites, quite a difference from traditional undergraduate teacher education populations. Alternative teacher preparation may graduate teachers better able to relate to today's more diverse students—little wonder that almost every state offers some form of alternative teacher training.[16] (Visit www.teach-now.org for details.)

Perhaps the best known of these alternative programs is Teach for America (TFA). TFA recruits, called corps members, agree to teach for two years in under-resourced urban and rural schools. Although relatively small in size, TFA has captured the imagination of many. Its founder, Wendy Kopp, conceptualized this program back in 1990 in her undergraduate thesis at Princeton. (That could be a motivator for you to view your class paper less as a task and more as an opportunity!) Why has TFA, a relatively small program, attracted so much attention? This program taps into the energy of recent college graduates who want to make a positive difference in the world. TFA is very selective, in 2010, for example, 4,500 were chosen from a candidate pool of almost 50,000. TFA identifies candidates with demonstrated leadership and organizational ability, evidence of critical thinking skills, respect for diversity, superior interpersonal skills, and a desire to work hard. Not surprisingly, these candidates often become strong teachers.[17]

But TFA alone is not an educational panacea. First, it is a relatively small program, just a few thousand teachers a year joining America's more than 3 million teachers. Second, although a majority of TFA corps members stay in teaching beyond their two-year commitment, the vast majority transfer out of their challenging schools to ones that offer better working conditions, or they transfer to non-teaching positions. Such transfers defeats at least part of the purpose of TFA.[18] Recommendations to strengthen TFA include more pre-teaching training, more support while in the classroom, and incentives to encourage corps members to stay in teaching.[19] What TFA has shown America is that teaching can and should attract the very best college graduates. And that's what the public wants as well. (See Figure 1.4.)

Let's mention one other exciting alternative program currently funded by the federal government: a *teaching residency program*. In this approach, talented teacher candidates commit to teaching for five years and are paid to spend the entire first year observing a master teacher while taking coursework. It is not until the second and third years that they teach under the supervision of a master teacher. Now doesn't that sound like a thoughtful approach![20]

But traditional undergraduate programs are not standing still either. Arizona State

Alternative teacher education programs attract more males and minorities into teaching than traditional programs.

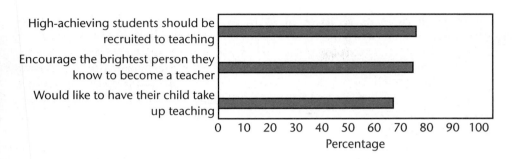

FIGURE 1.4

The public's view on who should become a teacher.

SOURCE: *Phi Delta Kappan*/Gallup poll in *Phi Delta Kappan*, September 2011.

REFLECTION: Why is there such a large gap between what the public wants, and the difficulty of recruiting top students to teaching?

University (ASU) now requires a yearlong student-teaching apprenticeship in local schools, and candidates are carefully evaluated for mastery of specific teaching skills. In fact, the National Education Association is promoting this approach for all teacher preparation programs. At ASU, this apprenticeship is an intense and focused experience, and ASU is the largest undergraduate education program in the country.[21]

Which is a better way to go, one of these alternative teacher preparation programs or the traditional undergraduate model? Trick question: strong and weak programs exist in both approaches.[22] Perhaps the better questions to ask of any teacher education program: Do the candidates have a strong background in their subject matter? Have they received effective pedagogical training? Has there been a carefully planned and implemented clinical experience?[23] As you begin your own teacher education program, whatever type it is, you may want to reflect on these questions and think about what subject matter content and teaching skills you would find most useful. (See TEACHING TIP: First, you get their attention.)

As you begin your own teacher education program, you may want to consider what goals education professors hold for tomorrow's teachers.[24] (Although there is no guarantee that your instructor in this course agrees with his or her colleagues, it may be fun to ask and find out.) Education professors want to prepare:

- Teachers who are themselves lifelong learners and are constantly updating their skills.
- Teachers committed to teaching children to be active learners.
- Teachers who have high expectations of all their students.
- Teachers who are deeply knowledgeable about the content of the specific subjects they will be teaching.

What are some effective strategies for you to consider as you begin teaching? Here's a hint: first year teachers report that they gain a great deal from discussions with fellow teachers, actual teaching experiences, and the help of mentors in the classroom.[25] It's not too surprising to learn that teachers who feel well prepared plan to stay in teaching longer than those who do not.[26] Strong teacher preparation has never been more important because of today's less experienced teacher workforce. The largest single group of teachers in today's schools has only one year of experience, compared with 15 years just two decades ago ago.[27]

Urban Legends about Teaching

Although sensible people take different routes to becoming a teacher, there are some pretty bizarre ideas out there about what it takes to be a teacher. You may have heard some of them

Teaching Tip

FIRST, YOU GET THEIR ATTENTION

I entered teaching through the back door and did not have the advantage of an effective classroom management mentor. What I would have loved in retrospect was to have someone say to me: One of the first things you need to establish is a simple and effective method of getting your students' attention. For example, in working with elementary-age children, I experimented with holding up an object. "Hey, look at this magic marker," I would say. All eyes would automatically look up because I had given them a task to perform. And with a note of wonder in my voice perhaps there was a good reason to look up. "Hey, look at this remarkable paper clip I just found and look what I can do with it."

This method was less effective as I started to work with middle schoolers. Some colleagues used the counting down method with this age group. "By the time I get to one, starting from five everyone should be quiet." It didn't work as well for me. Then I was attending an adult workshop one weekend and the facilitator said right at the start, "When you hear me say 'Focus up!' please repeat it and stop what you are doing." Well, it worked for a roomful of two hundred adults and it worked wonders with middle schoolers as well. To repeat the words required that they interrupt what they were doing, whether it was deep engagement with their work or more likely chatting with a neighbor. Sometimes I would have to repeat it again, but rarely did it take three times to quiet them down.

Most recently, I learned from a colleague who teaches kindergarten that a few simple rhythmic claps that in turn needed to be repeated by the class would achieve the same effect—simpler and easier on the voice, and a little less militaristic than the abrupt "focus up."

It is the nature of children's minds to wander, and it is the task of the teacher to gather and hold their attention when necessary instructions or other words are being spoken. What I gleaned from these experiments over the years was that the response that I needed from them was best achieved by having them perform a simple concrete action.

Eric Baylin, an art teacher for more than 40 years, currently teaches high school art at Packer Collegiate Institute in Brooklyn, NY.

REFLECTION: Do any of Eric Baylin's techniques appeal to you? Are there other techniques that you are considering to encourage your students to focus and stay on task?

---

yourself: "Teachers are born, not made," or "To be a good teacher, all you really need to know is the subject you are teaching." Like the urban legend of alligators cavorting in the New York City sewer system, these teaching myths have taken on a life of their own. Let's take a moment and clear the air about a few of these.

Teachers are born, not made: It is certainly true that some students enter a teacher education program with impressive instructional skills, yet training and practice is what is needed to transform a strong teacher into a gifted one. Teaching is far from unique in this. When a group of Olympians and their coaches were asked what it takes to become a champion, none of the answers suggested that they were "born" champions. On the contrary, the athletes credited well-designed practices and good coaching. Accomplished musicians attribute their performance to hours of focused practice, as do master chess players. So too, superior teachers are not born; they work at it.

All you really need to know is the subject you are teaching: Though it is true that subject mastery is critical in effective teaching, research reveals that teachers skilled in **pedagogy,** the art and science of teaching, especially teaching methods and strategies, outperform teachers with superior subject area knowledge. Clearly, the most successful teachers do not view this as an either/or proposition. Effective teaching requires both knowledge of the subject and instructional skills.[28]

Teacher education students are less talented than other college majors: (We never liked this one, either!) It is true that education majors are less likely to score in the top 25 percent on the SATs and too many who go into teaching are not strong academically. That is disappointing but true. On the other hand, adult literacy surveys show that teachers attain scores similar to those of physicians, writers, engineers, and social workers, which is much more encouraging.[29] It saddens us that no one seems to compare those becoming teachers with others in areas such as creativity, social consciousness, and honesty, for example. Why are such important human qualities overlooked? And why are teachers so often discounted in the public square and kept far from policy-making circles? When Andy Baumgartner, National Teacher of the Year in 2000, criticized the lack of significant teacher representation on a commission to reform education in his home state of Georgia, he quickly became *persona non grata*. The governor would not have his photo taken with him, and several politicians roundly criticized him for his audacity.[30]

Teachers' voices are silenced in the public square, but in the classroom, it is the teacher's voice that can make all the difference. It is discouraging for teachers to invest their talent and energy only to be told by politicians, journalists, and even the general public that they and our schools are doing poorly. Although a common complaint, that is only one side of the story. We would like to offer another side, a perspective we rarely hear.

American Schools: Better Than We Think?

Critics decry the low performance by U.S. students on international tests, but such criticisms may be way off the mark. In fact, today's schools may be doing as well as they ever have—perhaps even better than they ever have. Low test scores may simply reflect timing differences. Consider that Japanese middle school students score significantly higher than U.S. students on algebra tests, but most Japanese students take algebra a year or two earlier than U.S. students do. Moreover, most Japanese children attend private academies, called *Juku* schools, after school and on weekends. By 16 years of age, the typical Japanese student has attended at least two more years of classes than has a U.S. student. Yet, because of the greater comparative effectiveness of U.S. colleges in relation to Japanese colleges, many of these differences evaporate on later tests. [Perhaps there are two lessons here: (1) U.S. students should spend more time in school, and (2) the Japanese need to improve the quality of their colleges.]

Cultural differences in selecting which students take these exams also affect test scores. In other countries, students who do not speak the dominant language are routinely excluded from international exams. In some nations, only a small percentage of the most talented students are selected or encouraged to continue their education and go on to high school. As one might imagine, a highly selective population does quite well on international tests. In the United States, the full range of students is tested: strong and weak, English-speaking and non-English-speaking students. A larger number of American test takers are likely to be poor. Comparing all of America's students with another nation's best is unfair.

Americans value a comprehensive education, one in which students are involved in a wide array of activities, from theater to sports to community service. The U.S. public typically values spontaneity, social responsibility, and independence in their children, values that are not assessed in international tests. Consider the way a South Korean teacher identifies the students selected for the International Assessment of Education Progress (IAEP):

> The math teacher . . . calls the names of the 13-year-olds in the room who have been selected as part of the IAEP sample. As each name is called, the student stands at attention at his or her desk until the list is complete. Then, to the supportive and encouraging applause of their colleagues, the chosen ones leave to [take the assessment test].[31]

www.mhhe.com/sadker10e

INTERACTIVE ACTIVITY

What Should Teachers Learn? Create your own teacher education curriculum based on what you think teachers need to know.

FOCUS QUESTION 6

Are America's schools a secret success story?

GLOBAL VIEW

Juku schools have been called cram schools. Do you see Juku-type schools taking root in the United States?

U.S. students taking international exams do not engender cheers from their classmates and do not view such tests as a matter of national honor, as do the South Korean students. Too often, our culture belittles intellectuals and mocks gifted students.

Despite these obstacles, on several key tests our nation's students are doing quite well. By the late 2000s, the proportion of students scoring above 500 on the SAT reading and mathematics tests had reached an all-time high. The number of students taking Advanced Placement (AP) tests soared, a sign that far more students are in the race for advanced college standing. Improvements have been documented on the California Achievement Test, the Iowa Test of Basic Skills, and the Metropolitan Achievement Test—tests used across the nation to measure student learning. One of the most encouraging signs has been the performance of students of color, whose scores have risen dramatically. Among African American students, average reading scores on the National Assessment of Educational Progress NAEP tests rose dramatically.[32] Decades ago, many of these students probably would not have even been in school, much less taking tests. U.S. schools are teaching more students, students are staying in school longer, and children are studying more challenging courses than ever before. According to the 2006 Lemelson-MIT Invention Index, teenagers reported that they are pleased with the problem-solving and leadership skills, teamwork, and creativity they learned in school.[33] (See Figure 1.5.)

Then why is there a national upheaval about education—why all the furor about our failing schools and why the demands for radical school reform? Educators have advanced a number of possible explanations:[34]

- Adults tend to romanticize what schools were like when they attended as children, for they always studied harder and learned more than their children do. (And when they went to school, they had to walk through four feet of snow, uphill, in both directions!)

- Americans hold unrealistic expectations. They want schools to conquer all sorts of social and academic ills, from illiteracy to teenage pregnancy, and to accomplish everything from teaching advanced math to preventing AIDS.

- Schools today work with tremendous numbers of poor students, non-English-speaking children, and special education students who just a few years ago would not have been attending school as long or, in some cases, would not have been attending school at all.

- In *The Manufactured Crisis,* David Berliner and Bruce Biddle put much of the blame on the press, which has been all too willing to publish negative stories about schools— stories based on questionable sources. Sloppy, biased reporting has damaged the public's perception of schools.

FIGURE 1.5
Critical Skills.

SOURCE: The Lemelson-MIT Invention Index 2006, http://web.mit.edu/newsoffice/2006/lemelson-teens.html.

REFLECTION: Why do so few reports about U.S. schooling examine topics like these?

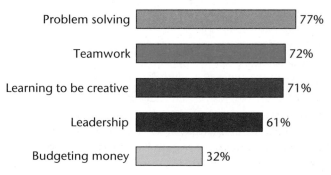

Percentage of Teens Who Feel They Have Learned Critical Skills While in High School

Problem solving	77%
Teamwork	72%
Learning to be creative	71%
Leadership	61%
Budgeting money	32%

It is helpful to remember two points. First, criticism can be fruitful. If additional attention and even criticism help shape stronger schools, then the current furor will have at least some positive impact. Second, there are countless students in all parts of the country who work diligently every day and perform with excellence. The United States continues to produce leaders in fields as diverse as medicine and sports, business and entertainment. To a great extent, these success stories are also the stories of talented and dedicated teachers. Although their quiet daily contributions rarely reach the headlines, teachers do make a difference. You represent the next generation of teachers who will, no doubt, weather difficult times and sometimes adverse circumstances to touch the lives of students and to shape a better America.

We Like Questions

Education is a dynamic field, rife with controversies, misperceptions, surprises, and constant change. Throughout this book, we will work hard to immerse you in that excitement, and to tweak your interest. (Okay, so it's not a Stephen King *Fright Night at the School Prom* novel for that rainy day at the beach. But we do want this text to be more exciting and interesting than most, to mirror the enthusiasm that we feel about education.) Issues discussed in this text may well spark questions. A sage once said that the only dumb question is the one not asked. (Although that particular sage might have been overrated, we concur with the premise.) This text is all about answering questions. In fact, at the end of the text, we list a number of questions that students typically ask: How do I get a teacher's license? Where are salaries and working conditions the best? What's a teacher competency exam like? We not only ask those questions, but also try our best to answer them. What if *your* question is not listed? Responding to your questions is one of the purposes of the website that accompanies this book. (Have you visited the Online Learning Center at www.mhhe.com/sadker10e yet?) In addition to attracting and answering student questions, the website is filled with useful web links, study hints, sample test questions covering each of the chapters in this text, and suggested student activities. We invite you to submit your questions through the text website, and we will try to answer them. In fact, we like questions so much that we will start the questioning ourselves. The following question is a good one to ask first, because if you are interested in becoming a teacher, there is no time like the present to begin.

What steps can I take between now and graduation to make myself an attractive teaching candidate?

Become informed about the job market.
Begin gathering current information about the job market and search out those particular content areas and skills that will increase your marketability. This information will help you select appropriate courses and extracurricular activities. Geography plays a role, because some local communities face critical teacher shortages and others have a teacher surplus. Special education and bilingual skills are often in demand, and demographics plays a big role as well. The nation's growing population of students of color is not matched by an adequate number of teachers of color, so there is a great need to attract African Americans, Hispanics, and Asian Americans into the teaching ranks. There are also too few male candidates for elementary teaching positions, and too few female teachers in physics and technology programs, so gender is yet another consideration. To find out more about the teaching job market, you can check educational associations and state departments of education, many of which are listed in the appendix of this text or found on our website. The National Teacher Recruitment Clearinghouse—www.recruitingteachers.org—is also a terrific resource for prospective teachers seeking jobs—and for school districts and states seeking qualified teachers. A central feature of the Clearinghouse is the unique gateway to job banks nationwide.

FOCUS QUESTION 7
What steps can you take now on the road to becoming a teacher?

Profile in Education Rafe Esquith

Rafe Esquith was beginning his third year of teaching in Los Angeles public schools. His class of 40 fifth-graders came from low-income homes where English rarely was spoken, and the best reader among them was two years below grade level. So he decided to teach them Shakespeare.

Five families agreed to let their children rehearse *Macbeth* for two hours after school. Within weeks, Esquith had kids gleefully soaking up the drama of blood and betrayal in medieval Scotland. They were learning words they had never heard before. Soon Esquith received a note from school leaders: "Mr. Esquith, it is not appropriate that you stay after school to teach Shakespeare. It would be better if you did something with the children that is academic."[a]

It would not be the last time that the narrow thinking of big-city school administration got in Esquith's way. And yet, he continues to teach, inspiring his fifth-graders to excel far beyond the low expectations often placed on poor, immigrant children. He has proved that a teacher who thinks big—harder lessons, larger projects, extra class time—can help disadvantaged children in ways most educators never imagine.

His students live in the heart of Central Los Angeles, a neighborhood better known for crime than for opportunity. Their school, Hobart Boulevard Elementary, has more than two thousand students; 90 percent live below the poverty level. Few expect any but the smartest and luckiest to rise beyond the limitations of their environment. Rafe Esquith does.

Esquith expects a lot from his 10-year-olds, and he gets it. They voluntarily arrive at school by 6:30 in the morning, work through recess, and stay until 5:00 P.M. And they come to class during vacations and holidays. Their hard work shows up in test scores, consistently scoring in the top 5 to 10 percent of the country.

"Like all real teachers, I fail constantly. I don't get enough sleep. I lie awake in the early-morning hours, agonizing over a kid I was unable to reach. Being a teacher can be painful." But Esquith finds hope and inspiration in his classroom, Room 56. "We've created a different world in Room 56. It's a world where character matters, hard work is respected, humility is valued, and support for one another is unconditional."[b]

With abiding faith and passion, Esquith leads his fifth-graders through a rigorous core curriculum of English, mathematics, geography, and literature. But he goes further, creating a real-world learning environment: Students must apply for a job, such as banker, office monitor, clerk, janitor, or police officer. Each child receives a monthly "paycheck" in classroom currency. They pay rent to sit at their desks—the closer to the front of the room, the higher the rent. Students can make extra money by getting good grades and participating in extracurricular activities; they can also be fined for breaking class rules or getting poor grades. The classroom motto is "Be nice, work hard. There are no shortcuts."

Though none of Esquith's students speaks English as a first language, they all read literature far above their fifth-grade level—*Catcher in the Rye, To Kill a Mockingbird, The Autobiography of Malcolm X,* and *Bury My Heart at Wounded Knee.* Esquith also takes his students beyond contemporary literature and into a world at the heart and soul of his teaching: an intensive immersion in Shakespeare—reading his plays, studying his life and times. This year-long study culminates in April, when students present a full-length, unabridged production of Shakespeare.

These student actors have been wildly successful. They have opened for the Royal Shakespeare Company, performed *A Midsummer Night's Dream* in Los Angeles, and appeared at the Globe Theater in London. At first, Esquith and his wife, Barbara Tong, funded his program out of their own pockets. Today, donations from major corporations and private individuals cover the cost of the class's travels and performances.

"If you're a young teacher or parent who has often wanted to break from the pack but has been afraid to do so, I can tell you that I've done so and am still standing. I have many scars and bruises, but I have, as Robert Frost tells us, taken the road less traveled. And it's made all the difference."[c]

[a] Rafe Esquith, *Teach Like Your Hair's on Fire* (New York: Viking), p. vi.
[b] Ibid., pp. vi–x.
[c] Rafe Esquith, "There are No Shortcuts." Copyright © 2003 by Rafe Esquith. New York, NY: Pantheon Books, a division of Random House, Inc.

REFLECTION: What characteristics do you admire in Rafe Esquith? Imagine your teaching career: What "road less traveled" might it take?

For additional sources of information, check with your university's placement office. You may want to begin reading professional education journals that include information about the employment picture. Websites are often the best source of up-to-date information, so you may want to visit sites sponsored by school districts, professional associations, placement services, or your university. You can also visit real sites, such as job fairs sponsored by school districts. Knowledge about the employment picture and the kind of candidate that is in demand can give you a powerful start on your teaching career.

Make sure your coursework is planned carefully.

Your first concern should be to enroll in courses that fulfill your certification and licensure requirements. We will explore certification and licensure in some depth later in the text, but for now it is worth remembering that in addition to earning your degree, you want to leave your program licensed to teach. A second consideration is to make yourself more marketable by going beyond minimum course requirements. For example, technology and special education skills are often in demand by schools, as are elementary teachers with special competence in math or any teacher with a proficiency in a second language. Plan to develop a transcript of courses that will reflect a unique, competent, and relevant academic background. Your transcript will be an important part of your overall candidacy for a teaching position.

Do not underestimate the importance of extracurricular activities.

Employers are likely looking for candidates whose background reflects interest and experience in working with children. A day care center or summer camp job may pay less than the local car wash, bank, or restaurant, but these career-related jobs may offer bigger dividends later on. Think about offering your services to a local public school or community youth group. Try to make your volunteer situation parallel the future job you would like to have. You want to build an inventory of relevant skills and experiences as well as personal contacts.

Begin networking.

Through both your coursework and your extracurricular activities, you will come into contact with teachers, administrators, and other school personnel. You should be aware that these people can function as an informal network for information about the local employment picture, as can your professors and even your classmates. Go out of your way to let these people know of your interests, your special skills, and your commitment to teaching. This does not mean that you should become such a nuisance that people will duck behind their desks when they see you coming. It does mean that, at the right times and in the right places, you can let them know what jobs you are looking for and your skills and experiences that qualify you for those jobs.

Begin collecting recommendations now.

Letters of recommendation can greatly influence employment decisions. Even if you find it difficult to request such letters, do not wait until you are student teaching to begin collecting them. Extracurricular activities, coursework, part-time employment, and volunteer work can all provide you with valuable recommendations. Your university placement office may be able to begin a placement folder for you, maintaining these recommendations and forwarding copies to potential employers at the appropriate time.

Ask for letters of recommendation while you are in a job or a course or immediately after leaving it. Professors, teachers, and past employers may move or retire, and, believe it or not, they may even forget you and just how competent and talented you are. You may be asked to help by drafting key points. Anything you can do to lighten the burden will be appreciated. Collecting letters of recommendation should be a continual process, not one that begins in the last semester of your teacher education program.

Develop a résumé and portfolio.

Traditionally, a résumé has been a central document considered during job applications, typically including a specific career objective and summarizing education, work experience, memberships, awards, and special skills. For example, a résumé might target a social studies teaching position in a particular area as your career objective, and it might report membership in the student National Educational Association (NEA) an office held in school government, fluency in Spanish, experience with a student newspaper, honors you have won, and any relevant jobs, such as summer camp counselor or aide in a day care center. Many software packages have résumé templates, there are scores of books and websites devoted to résumé writing, and advisers and counselors at your school should be able to assist.

Today, many colleges and school districts are moving beyond résumés and toward **portfolios,** a more comprehensive reflection of a candidate's skills. If you would like to do something a bit more innovative than simply preparing a dynamite résumé and providing sparkling letters of recommendation, or if your teacher education program is promoting more authentic and creative assessment strategies, then you might want to consider developing a portfolio. This text will help you in that process. You will find, cleverly placed between the major sections of this book, a special feature called *Reflective Activities and Your Portfolio (RAP).* The *RAP* activities will encourage you to reflect on your reading, undertake some interesting observations and activities, and begin collecting relevant materials for your portfolio. Even if you decide not to develop a portfolio, these *RAP* activities will be useful for developing professional materials that you can use in many different ways.

Make good first, second, third, and fourth impressions.

In many education courses, you will be asked to participate in local school activities. This participation may take the form of observing or of being a teacher's aide or student teacher. (You may find the Observation Handbook in the Online Learning Center of this book particularly useful for school visits.) Recording and thinking about your impressions can be a useful step in deciding on the kind of position you want. In each case, you will be making an impression on the school faculty and administration. Good impressions can lead to future job offers. Poor impressions can result in your name being filed in the *persona non grata* drawer.

Consider every visit to a school as an informal interview. Dress and act accordingly. Demonstrate your commitment and enthusiasm in ways that are helpful to school personnel. If you are viewed as a valuable and useful prospective member of the school community, you are a candidate with a head start for a current or future teaching position. Remember, known quantities are nearly always preferred to unknown quantities.

Visit the Online Learning Center for a range of contemporary videos with content related to this chapter.

www.mhhe.com/sadker10e

THE *TEACHERS, SCHOOLS, AND SOCIETY* READER WITH CLASSROOM OBSERVATION VIDEO CLIPS

Go to your *Teachers, Schools, and Society* Reader CD-ROM to:

READ CURRENT AND HISTORICAL ARTICLES

1. **Notes from an Accidental Teacher,** by Carol Ann Tomlinson, *Best of Educational Leadership* 2010–2011.

2. **Raising Teacher Quality Around the World,** by Vivien Stewart, *Educational Leadership*, December 2010/January 2011.

3. **Against the Current,** by Lisa Ann Williamson, *Teaching Tolerance*, Fall 2011.

4. **Metaphors of Hope,** Mimi Brodsky Chenfield, *Phi Delta Kappan*, December 2004.

5. **A New Professional: The Aims of Education Revisited,** by Parker J. Palmer, *Change* magazine, November/December 2007.

ANALYZE CASE STUDIES

1. **Megan Brownlee:** A parent visits her children's favorite elementary school teacher and is surprised to discover that the teacher does not encourage her to enter the teaching profession.

2. **Jennifer Gordon:** A mature woman beginning a second career as an elementary school teacher struggles during her student teaching experience with how to deal with her cooperating teacher, who treats her very badly and corrects her in front of the class.

OBSERVE TEACHERS, STUDENTS, AND CLASSROOMS IN ACTION

1. Classroom Observation: Teachers Discuss the Pros and Cons of Teaching

Deciding whether to enter the teaching profession is an important decision. As you've read in this chapter, there are many things to take into consideration when exploring teaching as a career. In this observation, you will observe experienced and new teachers as they discuss both the joys of teaching and their concerns with the profession, some of the surprises they discovered, and the advice they have for those considering a career in the classroom.

KEY TERMS AND PEOPLE

Esquith, Rafe, 20

Hall, Reverend Samuel, 11

Mann, Horace, 11

merit pay, 5

National Board for Professional
Teaching Standards (NBPTS), 12

normal school, 11

pay-for-performance, 5

pedagogy, 16

portfolio, 22

tenure, 8

DISCUSSION QUESTIONS AND ACTIVITIES

www.mhhe.com/sadker10e

CHAPTER REVIEW

Go to the Online Learning
Center to take a chapter self-
quiz, practice with key terms,
and review concepts from the
chapter.

1. This chapter introduces you to the importance of well-thought-out career decision making. You can read further on this decision-making process in one of the many career books now available. For example, Richard N. Bolles's *What Color Is Your Parachute?* contains many exercises that should help you clarify your commitment to teaching. Or you may want to visit Bolles's website at www.jobhunt-ersbible.com/. These resources, or a visit to your career center, can help you determine the best option for you.

2. Interview teachers and students at different grade levels to determine what they think are the positive and negative aspects of teaching. Share those interview responses with your classmates.

3. Suppose you could write an open letter to students, telling them about yourself and why you want to teach. What would you want them to know? When you attempt to explain yourself to others, you often gain greater self-knowledge. You might want to share your letter with classmates and to hear what they have to say in their letters. Perhaps your instructor could also try this exercise and share his or her open letter with you.

4. Check out teacher-related websites on the Internet. Schools and school districts, professional teacher organizations, and all sorts of interest groups sponsor not only websites but also listservs, chat groups, and other Internet activities. Seek out opportunities to interview practicing classroom teachers about their own classroom experiences. (Check out our websites at www.mhhe.com/sadker10e.)

5. Imagine that you are taking part in a career fair. Someone asks why you are exploring teaching. Briefly frame your answer.

Different Ways of Learning

CHAPTER 2

FOCUS QUESTIONS

1. How do multiple intelligences influence teaching and learning?
2. How does emotional intelligence influence teaching and learning?
3. How can teachers respond to students' different learning styles?
4. Is gender a learning style?
5. How are the needs of learners with exceptionalities met in today's classrooms?

It's not that I'm so smart, it's just that I stay with problems longer.

–ALBERT EINSTEIN

www.mhhe.com/sadker10e

CHAPTER PREVIEW

At the dawn of the twenty-first century, basic educational concepts are being redefined, reexamined, and expanded. What does "intelligence" really mean? How many kinds of intelligences are there? What is EQ (emotional intelligence quotient), and is it a better predictor of success than IQ (intelligence quotient)? What are learning styles and how should instruction respond to different learning styles?

Gender issues are a hot topic in schools as some argue that girls' and boys' learning differences create the need for separate schools. Are single-sex learning environments a good idea? Do girls and boys learn differently? We want you to begin thinking about how teachers can recognize differences in learning while avoiding the dangers of stereotypic thinking, and the current gender debate is a good place to begin.

Another educational transformation is the increasing numbers of schoolchildren now identified as learners with exceptionalities—students with learning, physical, developmental, and emotional/behavioral disabilities—all of whom deserve appropriate educational strategies and materials. Students with gifts and talents represent another population with special needs too often lost in the current educational system.

This chapter will broaden your ideas of how students learn, and how teachers can teach to the many different ways of knowing.

WHAT DO YOU THINK? Different ways of learning. Vote on eight classroom climate recommendations designed to improve academic performance.

25

Multiple Intelligences

Have you ever wondered what it really means to be a "genius"? How would you describe a genius? Have you ever met one? How would you rate your own intelligence? Above average? Average? Below average? Who decides, and what exactly is intelligence?

Traditional definitions of *intelligence* usually include mental capabilities, such as reasoning, problem solving, and abstract thinking. The Intelligence Quotient, called IQ, was developed early in the twentieth century to measure a person's innate intelligence, with a score of 100 defined as normal, or average. The higher the score, the brighter the person. Some of us grew up in communities where IQ was barely mentioned. In many cases, that lack of communication might have been a blessing. Others of us grew up with "IQ envy," in communities where IQ scores were a big part of the culture. Because the IQ was considered a fixed, permanent measure of intellect, like a person's physical height, the scores engendered strong feelings. Today, we know that one's environment and well-being can greatly affect intellectual development.

A growing number of researchers now view intelligence not as a fixed, predetermined entity, but as malleable, something we can control, at least in part. Stanford professor Carol Dweck describes it this way: *Entity theory* views intelligence as finite and determined at birth. An individual's IQ measures it, and it does not change. *Incremental theory,* on the other hand, suggests that rather than being fixed at birth, intelligence can be developed through life, if we exert effort. But here's the key: which view you hold about intelligence affects how you go about learning. On difficult tasks, students who believe intelligence is fixed give up more quickly, blaming their intelligence (or lack of) for their failure. But on those same difficult tasks, students who embrace an incremental view of intelligence are more likely to persevere and explore more inventive strategies to solve a problem. To this group, setbacks are not considered a permanent reflection of intelligence, rather opportunities to learn and grow.[1]

Traditional assessments of intelligence emphasize language and logical-mathematical abilities, another narrow view of intelligence. Harvard psychologist **Howard Gardner** has worked to broaden this concept of intelligence, defining intelligence as "the capacity to solve problems or to fashion products that are valued in one or more cultural settings."[2]

Gardner identified eight kinds of intelligence, not all of which are commonly recognized in school settings. Gardner believes that his theory of **multiple intelligences** more accurately captures the diverse nature of human capability. Consider Gardner's eight intelligences:[3]

1. *Logical-mathematical.* Skills related to mathematical manipulations and discerning and solving logical problems ("number/reasoning smart").

2. *Linguistic.* Sensitivity to the meanings, sounds, and rhythms of words, as well as to the function of language as a whole ("word smart").

3. *Bodily-kinesthetic.* Ability to excel physically and to handle objects skillfully ("body smart").

4. *Musical.* Ability to produce pitch and rhythm, as well as to appreciate various forms of musical expression ("music smart").

5. *Spatial.* Ability to form a mental model of the spatial world and to maneuver and operate using that model ("picture smart").

6. *Interpersonal.* Ability to analyze and respond to the motivations, moods, and desires of other people ("people smart").

FOCUS QUESTION 1

How do multiple intelligences influence teaching and learning?

www.mhhe.com/sadker10e

INTERACTIVE ACTIVITY

Multiple Intelligences
Label descriptions of different intelligences

Physical ability and body awareness are forms of kinesthetic intelligence.

7. *Intrapersonal.* Knowledge of one's feelings, needs, strengths, and weaknesses; ability to use this knowledge to guide behavior ("self smart").

8. *Naturalist.* (Gardner's most recently defined intelligence) Ability to discriminate among living things, to classify plants, animals, and minerals; ability to nurture animals and grow plants; a sensitivity to the natural world ("environment smart").

In regard to the last intelligence, young people spend 50 percent less time playing outside than they did a decade ago. Teachers and parents increasingly worry that today's children are at risk of developing "nature deficit disorder" and that the naturalist intelligence is being lost to video games, the Internet, academic pressures, and busy schedules.[4]

Gardner and his colleagues continue to conduct research, and this list is still growing. A possible ninth intelligence being explored by Gardner concerns an *existential intelligence,* the human inclination to formulate fundamental questions about who we are, where we come from, why we die, and the like. Gardner believes that we have yet to discover many more intelligences. (Can you can think of some?)

The theory of multiple intelligences goes a long way in explaining why the quality of an individual's performance may vary greatly in different activities, rather than reflect a single standard of performance as indicated by an IQ score. Gardner also points out that what is considered *intelligence* may differ, depending on cultural values. Thus, in the Pacific Islands, intelligence is the ability to navigate among the islands. For many Muslims, the ability to memorize the Koran is a mark of intelligence. Intelligence in Balinese social life is demonstrated by physical grace.

Gardner's theory has sparked the imaginations of many educators, some of whom are redesigning their curricula to respond to differing student intelligences. Teachers are refining their approaches in response to such questions as[5]

- How can I use music to emphasize key points?
- How can I promote hand and bodily movements and experiences to enhance learning?
- How can I incorporate sharing and interpersonal interactions into my lessons?
- How can I encourage students to think more deeply about their feelings and memories?
- How can I use visual organizers and visual aids to promote understanding?
- How can I encourage students to classify and appreciate the world around them?

GLOBAL VIEW
Describe the varied cultural, religious, or ethnic intelligences of your classmates.

Instructional Technology

Instructional technologies can open a wide door to the multiple intelligences. For instance, authoring tools such as PowerPoint enable students to create projects that incorporate text, animation, graphics, video, and sound, integrating several intelligences. The computer allows students to compose music or model art and science projects that enhance spatial learning. A physical education or dance teacher can videotape and then coach students on their techniques. Gardner suggests improving interpersonal intelligence by "recording tense interactions on video and having students choose the best human(e) means of reducing the tension; by involving students in chat rooms or discussion forums that include opportunities for helpfulness or deceit; or by creating cartoon simulations or virtual reality scenarios of human dilemmas where the student has options to interact in different ways."[6] Although Howard Gardner is impressed with the potential marriage of technology with his multiple intelligences approach, he has also voiced concern about teachers who get enamored with the technological wizardry and lose sight of the educational goal.

A Closer Look   Where Do the Mermaids Stand?

Giants, Wizards, and Dwarfs was the game to play.

Being left in charge of about eighty children seven to ten years old, while their parents were off doing parent things, I mustered my troops in the church social hall and explained the game. It's a large-scale version of Rock, Paper, and Scissors, and involves some intellectual decision making. But the real purpose of the game is to make a lot of noise and run around chasing people until nobody knows which side you are on or who won.

Organizing a roomful of wired-up grade schoolers into two teams, explaining the rudiments of the game, achieving consensus on group identity—all of this is no mean accomplishment, but we did it with a right good will and were ready to go.

The excitement of the chase had reached a critical mass. I yelled out: "You have to decide *now* which you are—a GIANT, a WIZARD, or a DWARF!"

While the groups huddled in frenzied, whispered consultation, a tug came at my pants leg. A small child stands there looking up, and asks in a small concerned voice, "Where do the Mermaids stand?"

A long pause: A *very* long pause. "Where do the Mermaids stand?" says I.

"Yes. You see, I am a Mermaid."

"There are no such things as Mermaids."

"Oh, yes, I am one!"

She did not relate to being a Giant, a Wizard, or a Dwarf. She knew her category, Mermaid, and was not about to leave the game and go over and stand against the wall where a loser would stand. She intended to participate, wherever Mermaids fit into the scheme of things. Without giving up dignity or identity. She took it for granted that there was a place for Mermaids and that I would know just where.

Well, where DO the Mermaids stand? All the "Mermaids"— all those who are different, who do not fit the norm and who do not accept the available boxes and pigeonholes?

Answer that question and you can build a school, a nation, or a world on it.

What was my answer at the moment? Every once in a while I say the right thing. "The Mermaid stands right here by the King of the Sea!" (Yes, right here by the King's Fool, I thought to myself.)

So we stood there hand in hand, reviewing the troops of Wizards and Giants and Dwarfs as they rolled by in wild disarray.

It is not true, by the way, that Mermaids do not exist. I know at least one personally. I have held her hand.

SOURCE: Robert Fulghum, *All I Really Need to Know I Learned in Kindergarten* (New York: Villard Books, 1989), pp. 81–83.

> **REFLECTION:** Was there ever a time when you did not fit neatly into a category—were you ever a mermaid? When and why? How will you make room for mermaids in your class?

Assessment

As instruction undergoes reexamination, so does evaluation. The old pencil-and-paper tests used to assess linguistic, math, and logical intelligences seem much less appropriate for measuring these new areas identified by Dweck Gardner, and others.[7] The **portfolio** approach as found in the *RAP*s in this text, is an example of a more comprehensive assessment, which includes student artifacts (papers, projects, videotapes, exhibits) that offers tangible examples of student learning. Some schools ask students to assemble portfolios that reflect progress in Gardner's various intelligences. In other cases, rather than A's and B's or 80s and 90s, schools are using descriptions to report student competence. In music, for example, such descriptions might include "The student often listens to music," "She plays the piano with technical competence," "She is able to compose scores that other students and faculty enjoy," and so on. Whether the school is exploring portfolios, descriptive assessment, or another evaluation method, Gardner's multiple intelligences theory is reshaping many current assessment practices.[8]

The Five Minds

Gardner's work on multiple intelligences has had a huge impact on how educators view teaching and learning. Now Gardner is at it again. In his book *Five Minds for the Future*, Gardner suggests new directions for schools. He points out that memorizing facts and cramming for standardized tests is not very useful in the twenty-first century. With huge amounts of information at our fingertips, with instant global communications, and with the growing intersections of cultures and countries, we have new lessons to learn. For schools to ignore these changes is self-defeating. So Gardner offers "five minds," really five ways of knowing, that he believes we need to develop and thrive in the twenty-first century. So, let go of the familiar, and let your imagination consider Gardner's "five minds."[9]

The Ethical Mind Did you ever notice how often we turn away from hard truths, as though ignoring them will make them disappear? We have become inured to dishonest behavior. For example, the majority of our students cheat on exams, copy homework from others, or plagiarize term papers. Depressing as that is, we still ignore it. In adult life, these unethical behaviors lead to grievous consequences on Wall Street, in corporations, in politics, and in our personal lives. Gardner believes that we must tackle this deceit head on and teach children to think reflectively about their behavior. He would like to see more young adults choose careers that advance society, rather than focus on accruing personal wealth at the cost of leading an ethical life.

The Respectful Mind How often do you listen to misogynist rap lyrics, combative talk radio, rude television commentators; laugh (even uncomfortably) at a racist joke; or witness road rage unfold before your eyes? Disrespectful behavior in our society has become commonplace, and Gardner believes we should teach children to develop respectful minds. This means honoring people with different ideas, different cultures, and different belief systems. In fact, we have much to learn from those who have experienced different lives. In an ever-shrinking world, the lack of respectful minds can have dire consequences.

The Disciplined Mind This mind may be the most familiar to you because it is part of today's school curriculum. The disciplined mind masters a field of study, such as literature, history, art, science, math, or even a craft. With a disciplined mind, one becomes a master of an area of work or a profession; without this mastery, one is destined to spend life simply following someone else's directions.

The Synthesizing Mind Today, we are inundated with information. Tomorrow, we will be inundated with even more information. We need to develop the ability to sort through this information, to figure out what is important and what is not so important, to see meaningful connections, and then to interpret how best we can use the data. In this information age, being able to eliminate the trivial while connecting the useful is key.

The Creating Mind Being creative is a timeless skill. A creative mind discovers new ways of looking at the world, offers new insights and a fresh way of thinking. Some believe that creativity may be America's greatest (and most underdeveloped) natural resource.

How do these five minds sound to you? Perhaps you have yet another mind that you think should be part of school life. We encourage you to continually consider new ways of looking at teaching and learning.

Emotional Intelligence

While the theories of multiple intelligences and the five minds raise fundamental questions about different ways students learn and use information, **EQ,** or the **emotional intelligence quotient,** offers another perspective on learning. In his book *Emotional Intelligence,* psychologist

---

IMAGINE...

Class Act

The Stuttgart, Arkansas, Junior High School varsity football team all shaved their heads so they could look more like teammate Stuart H., who lost most of his hair while undergoing chemotherapy. The coach explained: *They got together so he wouldn't feel weird, so they would all look weird together. These kids have got heart, and I love them all.*

SOURCE: *The American School Board Journal,* December 2009.

A Closer Look So What's Your EQ?

Like Daniel Goleman, Yale psychologist Peter Salovey works with emotional intelligence issues, and he identifies five elements of emotional intelligence. How would you rate yourself on each of these dimensions?

KNOWING EMOTIONS

The foundation of one's emotional intelligence is self-awareness. A person's ability to recognize a feeling as it happens is the essential first step in understanding the place and power of emotions. People who do not know when they are angry, jealous, or in love are at the mercy of their emotions.

Self-Rating on Knowing My Emotions *Always aware of my emotions__Usually aware__Sometimes aware__Out of touch, clueless.__*

MANAGING EMOTIONS

A person who can control and manage emotions can handle bad times as well as the good, shake off depression, bounce back from life's setbacks, and avoid irritability. In one study, up to half of the youngsters who at age 6 were disruptive and unable to get along with others were classified as delinquents by the time they were teenagers.

Self-Rating on Managing My Emotions *Always manage my emotions__Usually manage__Sometimes manage__ My emotions manage me.__*

MOTIVATING ONESELF

Productive individuals are able to focus energy, confidence, and concentration on achieving a goal and avoid anxiety, anger, and depression. One study of 36,000 people found that "worriers" have poorer academic performance than non-worriers. (A load off your mind, no doubt!)

Self-Rating on Motivation and Focus *Always self-motivated/focused__Usually self-motivated/focused__Sometimes self-motivated/focused__I can't focus on when I was last focused (and I don't care).__*

RECOGNIZING EMOTIONS IN OTHERS

This skill is the core of empathy, the ability to pick up subtle signs of what other people need or want. Such a person always seems to "get it," even before the words are spoken.

Self-Rating on Empathy *Always empathetic__Usually empathetic__Sometimes empathetic__I rarely "get it."__*

HANDLING RELATIONSHIPS

People whose EQ is high are the kind of people you want to be around. They are popular, are good leaders, and make you feel comfortable and connected. Children who lack social skills are often distracted from learning, and the dropout rate for children who are rejected by their peers can be two to eight times higher than for children who have friends.

Self-Rating on Relationships *I am rich in friendship and am often asked to lead activities and events.__I have many friends.__I have a few friends.__Actually, I'm pretty desperate for friends.__*

RATINGS

Give 4 points for each time you selected the first choice, 3 points for the "usual" or "many" second option, 2 points for the "sometimes" selection, and 1 point for the last choice.

18–20 points:	A grade—WOW! Impressive!
14–17 points:	B grade—You have considerable skills and talents.
10–13 points:	C grade—Feel free to read further on this topic.
5–9 points:	D grade—This may be a perfect subject to investigate in greater detail. Do you have a topic for your term project yet?

REFLECTION: Are you satisfied with your rating? If you earned a high rating, to what do you attribute your high EQ? If your rating was lower than you liked, how can you work on increasing your EQ? How will you develop the EQ of your students?

FOCUS QUESTION 2

How does emotional intelligence influence teaching and learning?

Daniel Goleman argues that when it comes to predicting success in life, EQ may be a better predictor than IQ. How does EQ work? The "marshmallow story" may help you understand:

> A researcher explains to a 4-year-old that he/she needs to run off to do an errand, but there is a marshmallow for the youngster to enjoy. The youngster can choose to eat the marshmallow immediately. But, if the 4-year-old can wait and *not* eat the marshmallow right away, then an extra marshmallow will be given when the researcher returns. Eat one now, or hold off and get twice the reward.

What do you think you would have done as a 4-year-old? According to the social scientists who conducted the marshmallow experiment, decisions even at this age foreshadow an emotional disposition characteristic of a successful (or less successful) adult. By the time the children in the study reached high school, the now 14-year-olds were described by teachers and parents in a way that suggested their marshmallow behaviors predicted some significant differences. Students who ten years earlier were able to delay their gratification, to wait a while and garner a second marshmallow, were reported to be better adjusted, more popular, more adventurous, and more confident in adolescence than the group who ten years earlier had gobbled down their marshmallows.

The children who gave in to temptation, ate the marshmallow, and abandoned their chances for a second one were more likely to be described as stubborn, easily frustrated, and lonely teenagers. In addition to the differences between the gobblers and the waiters as described by parents and teachers, there was also a significant SAT scoring gap. The students who, ten years earlier, could wait for the second marshmallow scored 210 points higher than did the gobblers. Reasoning and control, "the regulation of emotion in a way that enhances living," might be new, and perhaps better, measures of what we call smart, or intelligent.[10]

Emotional intelligence "is a type of social intelligence that involves the ability to monitor one's own and others' emotions, to discriminate among them, and to use the information to guide one's thinking and actions."[11] Goleman suggests that EQ taps into the heart, as well as the head, and introduces a new gateway for measuring intelligence, for children and adults.[12] By the way, how would you rate your EQ? (See A Closer Look on p. 30.)

Goleman and Gardner are toppling educational traditions, stretching our understanding of what schools are about. In a sense, they are increasing the range and diversity of educational ideas. The students you will teach will learn in diverse ways, and a single IQ or even EQ score is unlikely to capture the range of their abilities and skills. Your students will also bring to the classroom multiple learning styles that will further expand our grasp of how people learn.

www.mhhe.com/sadker10e

INTERACTIVE ACTIVITY

Emotional Intelligence Quotient Quiz Take an EQ quiz to determine your own emotional intelligence quotient.

Learning Styles

Many educators believe that students have different **learning styles**—diverse ways of learning, comprehending, and using information. Intriguing research suggests that learning styles may be as unique as handwriting. Some students do their best work late at night, but others set an early alarm because they are most alert in the morning. Many students seek a quiet place in the library to prepare for finals; others learn best in a noisy environment or with a crowd of people; still others study most effectively in a state of perpetual motion, constantly walking in circles to help their concentration.[13]

At least three types of factors—as diagrammed in Figure 2.1—contribute to each student's individual learning style:[14]

FOCUS QUESTION 3

How can teachers respond to students' different learning styles?

1. *Physiology.* Clearly, a student who is hungry and tired will not learn as effectively as a well-nourished and rested child. Other physiological factors are less obvious. Different body rhythms cause some students to learn better in the morning, whereas others excel in the afternoon. Some students can sit still for long periods of time; others need to get up and move around. Some students prefer to interact with material through touch; others like to take copious notes or doodle. Light, sound, and temperature are yet other factors to which students respond differently. How would you describe your physiological style?

2. *Affective (attitudes).* Individuals bring different levels of motivation to learning, and the intensity level of this motivation is a critical determinant of learning style. Other aspects of the **affective domain** include attitudes, values and emotions, factors that influence

FIGURE 2.1

Factors contributing to learning styles.

REFLECTION: Describe your own learning style by identifying at least one factor under the affective, physiological, and cognitive domains.

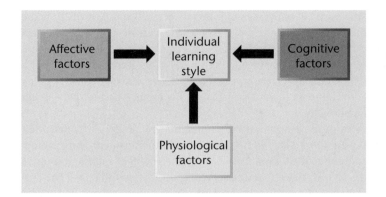

curiosity, the ability to tolerate and overcome frustration, a preference to learn in groups or individually, and the willingness to take risks. A fascinating aspect of the affective domain is a concept termed **locus of control.** Some learners attribute success or failure to external factors ("Those problems were confusing," "The teacher didn't review the material well," or "My score was high because I made some lucky guesses"). These learners have an external locus of control and do not take responsibility for their behavior. Others attribute performance to internal factors ("I didn't study enough" or "I didn't read the directions carefully"). These students have an internal locus of control because they have the sense that they control their fate, that they can improve their performance. How would you describe your affective style?

3. *Cognitive (information processing).* Individuals have different ways of perceiving, organizing, retaining, and using information, all components of the **cognitive domain.** Some students prefer to learn by reading and looking at material *(visual learners).* Others need to listen and hear information spoken aloud *(auditory learners).* Still others learn best using body movement, touch, and hands-on participation *(kinesthetic/tactile learners).* Some students are quick to respond; others are slower, preferring to observe and reflect. Some learners focus attention narrowly and with great intensity; others pay attention to many things at once. Some learners can master many concrete ideas; others excel at abstract thinking. How would you describe your cognitive style? (See Teaching Tip: Including Different Learning Styles on p. 33.)

Educators frequently try to shape their instruction to match a student's learning style. So if a student learns best visually, a teacher might focus instruction on photographs, videos, and drawings—but is this the best approach? Neuroscientists suggest that teachers should do more. They believe that learners benefit when teachers not only respond to a student's preferred learning style, but integrate it with other learning styles. Teaching to a single learning style may be comfortable for the student, but it does not enhance brain development as much as involving other ways of learning does. Why? When the brain is challenged, it can grow by developing new neural pathways. This process is called **neuroplasticity.**[15] As teachers integrate different learning styles into the classroom and push students out of their comfort zone, the brain grows new neural pathways, and students retain more deeply and can apply information more creatively.[16] Teachers are wise to explore a variety of learning styles in the classroom. Flexibility and variety are the keys: Don't assume that all students learn the way you do, and take care not to undervalue students just because their learning styles differ from yours.

Teaching Tip

INCLUDING DIFFERENT LEARNING STYLES

While not all educators agree that learning styles are important, many teachers are real advocates. Integrating different learning styles into instruction gives students a variety of learning experiences, builds new neural pathways, and has the added bonus of keeping instruction lively. Here are a few teaching tips you may want to consider:

VISUAL LEARNING

Learning with our eyes is common. Teachers can:

- Use textbooks, charts, course outlines, flash cards, videos, maps, and computer simulations as instructional aids.
- Ask students to highlight or color-code key lesson points.
- Note subheadings and illustrations before students read a chapter.
- Seat students up front, away from windows and doors (to avoid distractions).
- Use overheads, PowerPoints, flip charts, and whiteboards to list key points of the lesson.
- Use guided imagery and illustrations.

KINESTHETIC/TACTILE LEARNING

This is another popular learning style, which is also called *haptic* (Greek for "moving and doing") or *hands-on*. Teachers can:

- Plan student movement in class, as well as independent study time.
- Ask students to take notes and underline key points.

- Use skits and role-plays.
- Integrate hands-on lessons, observations, and field explorations.
- Create index or flash cards for students to manipulate.

AUDITORY LEARNERS

Auditory learning focuses on conversations and lecture; students often develop strong language skills. Teachers can:

- Encourage students to recite the main points of a book or lecture.
- Include group work into class activities so students can verbally share ideas.
- Audio-tape classroom activities or record key lesson ideas.
- Suggest that students read the text or any new vocabulary words out loud.

REFLECTION: Choose a subject or topic that you want to teach. Describe how you would integrate three learning activities in your lesson that incorporate three learning styles (visual, kinesthetic/tactile, auditory). Which of these learning styles appeals to you? Why? Which one takes you most out of your comfort zone?

Do Boys and Girls Learn Differently?

If your flying saucer arrived on Earth from another world and landed in a schoolyard, and you peeked through the schoolhouse windows, you might observe the following:

FOCUS QUESTION 4

Is gender a learning style?

- In a kindergarten class, the teacher decides to put a girl between two boys in order to "calm them down."
- Throughout the school, you sense excitement as students talk about the championship spelling bee, the one that will decide if the girls or the boys are the better spellers.
- Outside, the boys have three basketball games in progress while the girls are off to the side jumping rope.
- Over the public address system, the principal announces: "Good morning, boys and girls."

What are the assumptions inherent in boy-versus-girl competitions? Why are gender competitions still used, while school competitions based on race, religion, or ethnicity are seen as destructive?

It is all so obvious. You radio back to your home base: "Planet Earth dominated by two tribes: boys and girls. Will investigate further."

Brain Differences

Teachers' comments and behaviors often blindly reinforce a gender divide, yet if applied to race, religion, or ethnicity, teachers would quickly regain their vision. You will search long and hard to find a teacher who announces: "We will have a spelling bee today to see who will be the champion spellers, Jews or Christians!" Or imagine, "Good morning, blacks and whites." How about, "You two Hispanics are causing too much disruption, so I am placing a Native American between you!" Although sensitive to religious, ethnic, or racial affronts, we seem rather oblivious to gender comments. This is a situation with serious consequences.

Constant references to gender lead children to believe that teachers are intentionally signaling important differences between boys and girls. But are these differences significant, or are they stereotypes?

That's what Janet Hyde at the University of Wisconsin-Madison wanted to find out. Like most of us, she had heard that boys are more aggressive; better in math, science, and technology; and prefer an active and competitive male learning style. Girls, on the other hand, are seen as more nurturing and intuitive, preferring to personalize knowledge; they are more successful in the arts and languages, and more compliant than boys. This cooperative and personal approach to learning has been termed a female learning style. Hyde wanted to determine if these common gender assumptions were true.

Dr. Hyde evaluated all the studies on gender differences by using a sophisticated meta-analysis statistical procedure. What she found surprised many: there are precious few educationally relevant gender differences. So Hyde settled on a **gender similarities hypothesis:** rather than demonstrating separate learning styles and needs, males and females are actually more alike than different. According to Hyde's work, there are no important intellectual or psychological differences between females and males that require unique teaching approaches. In short, more educational differences exist *within* the genders than *between* the genders.[17] Other studies confirm Hyde's findings and show that the greatest challenges in educational achievement have less to do with gender and more to do with race, ethnicity, and economic status.[18] (However, some do not accept this idea and believe that boys and girls should be taught in separate schools. See A Closer Look: Single-Sex Education.)

Hyde's work did reveal a few exceptions to the gender similarities hypothesis. In some cases, her findings were counterintuitive: males overall exhibited slightly more helping behaviors than females, while self-esteem levels for adult men and women were quite similar. Hyde also found a couple of educationally relevant differences: boys are generally more aggressive and have better ability to rotate objects mentally.[19] But the reason for these few differences is not clear. Are they due to nature or nurture, or a combination of the two? After all, socialization plays a big role in our culture.

For example, researchers at the University of Michigan followed more than eight hundred children and their parents for thirteen years and found that traditional gender stereotypes greatly influence parental attitudes and behaviors related to children's interest in math. Parents provided more math-supportive environments for their sons than for their daughters, including buying more math and science toys. Parents, and dads especially, held more positive perceptions of their son's math abilities than of their daughters'.[20]

A Closer Look   Single-Sex Education

In classrooms across the country, educators are experimenting with single-sex education. Some schools do it to raise test scores because they believe that boys and girls learn differently. Others argue that dividing students removes sexual distractions and is a good behavior management strategy. Such notions fit easily into traditional belief systems, but are not supported by rigorous research.[a]

A Washington, DC middle school teacher shares his firsthand experience with single-sex education:

> At first, I felt there were some real advantages to separating the girls and boys. There was certainly less teasing, which had gotten out of hand the year before. So I saw the separation as having marginal advantages. But over time, each gender developed other discipline issues. Cliques of girls began teasing each other. They replaced the boys as the discipline problem. Boys really began acting out. They actually got goofier. Then there was a second problem: boys struggling with their sexual identity really lost out. Some of these boys had girls as their best friends, and when the separate classes began, they literally lost their best friends. They were now isolated in an alpha male environment. They were treated harshly and ridiculed. The third problem was sheer numbers: there were more girls in these classes than boys. The girls' classes got much bigger. The girls got less individualized attention. So what I thought at first would be a help for girls really failed them. It was not a good idea.
>
> I pride myself in not being an ideologue. I do not like it when people get stuck in one camp or the other. Show me something that works, and I want to find out why and how we can use it. But this did not work.[b]

[a] Diane Halpern, "The Pseudoscience of Single-Sex Schooling," *Education Forum* (September 22, 2011) pp. 1706–1707.
[b] David and Myra Sadker, and Karen Zittleman, *Still Failing at Fairness* (New York: Scribners, 2009), pp. 253–288.

REFLECTION: Support your views about single-sex schooling.

Lise Eliot, a neuroscientist at the Chicago Medical School, believes that such early socialization contributes to gender differences in learning. She describes how the many hours boys clock with Legos, baseball, and video games help develop spatial skills, like targeting and mental rotation, skills not taught in school. Such spatial skills figure prominently in subjects like physics, trigonometry, calculus, and engineering, subjects in which many boys excel. Girls, by contrast, are encouraged more than boys to read for pleasure outside school. Eliot contends that it is this practice, rather than any genetic or hormonal difference, that best predicts gender differences in reading achievement.[21] Clearly, socialization can be a powerful influence on academic success.

Importantly, our understanding of how nature and nurture influences gender roles is changing. We are reminded of this whenever we see quiet boys who love reading or music or girls who soar in math or on the athletic field. We typically view genetics and learning styles as pretty much fixed from birth, but research shows that it is more complicated than that.[22] The brain, for example, rather than being fixed, is like a muscle that can be developed and changed by our experiences. As we previously discussed, the ability of our brain to change itself and create new neural pathways is called *neuroplasticity*. For teachers, this is exciting news. It means that if we offer a variety of challenging and involving activities in our classes, we not only maintain student interest, but we can help students grow and cultivate their brains. On the other hand, if we teach to a single learning style or use stereotypes in our teaching, we limit the brain's possibilities. So teachers are wise to encourage all their students, girls and boys, to develop their brains by exploring different learning styles, incorporating both competitive and cooperative activities, integrating both personal connections and active learning, and focusing on the arts as well as traditional subjects.

Generalizing a pedagogy based on a student's gender will surely miss many students who do not fit neatly into a fixed gender mold. The same thing can be said of students with exceptional needs. We will end this chapter with a close look at teaching exceptional learners, from students with disabilities to gifted learners. Inclusion of these students may further broaden different learning styles and the range of teaching skills you will need.

GLOBAL VIEW

High female performance on international math tests correlates with high levels of gender equity in their home countries. Females in Iceland, Norway, and Sweden score highest on such measures, while women in the United States rank twenty-third out of sixty-nine nations. (Programme for International Student Assessment, 2011)

Exceptional Learners

FOCUS QUESTION 5

How are the needs of learners
with exceptionalities met in
today's classroom?

In a typical classroom, a teacher faces students with a great range of abilities, from students reading years behind grade level to students reading years ahead. Both these groups of students are described by the same broad term: **exceptional learners.** Integrating exceptional learners into the regular classroom is yet another aspect of teaching students with different learning styles.

Typically, learners with exceptionalities are categorized as students with

- Learning disabilities
- Developmental disabilities/intellectual disabilities
- Emotional disturbances or behavior disorders
- Hearing impairments
- Visual impairments
- Speech and communication disorders
- Attention deficit hyperactivity disorder
- Autism spectrum disorder
- Traumatic brain injury
- Orthopedic impairments
- Other health impairments
- Severe and multiple disabilities

And although it seems a very different kind of category, gifted and talented students are also considered exceptional learners.[23]

Teaching exceptional learners, from students with disabilities to gifted and talented learners, offers teachers the opportunity to stretch their imagination and creativity. Let's begin with a group many people believe need little, if any, special attention. How wrong they are.

The Gifted and Talented

> In Westchester County, a suburb of New York City, a 2½-year-old boy already emulates the language abilities of his parents. He speaks and reads English, French, Hebrew, Spanish, and Yiddish and he has mastered some Danish. He is studying music theory and is conducting scientific experiments. The parents, however, are unable to find any educational facility willing and able to educate their young, gifted child. A member of their local school board told them: "It is not the responsibility or function of public schools to deal with such children." As a result, the parents considered moving to Washington state, where there was an experimental preschool program for the gifted.[24]

If you are like most Americans, you may find it difficult to consider gifted and talented children to be in any way disadvantaged. After all, gifted learners are the lucky ones who master subject matter with ease. They are the ones who shout out the solution before most of us have a chance to write down the problem. Others may have perfect musical pitch, are athletic superstars, become the class leaders who inspire us, or demonstrate insights that amaze and inform us. Many exhibit endless curiosity, creativity, and energy.

Defining **giftedness** invites controversy.[25] To some, the traditional definition of giftedness includes those with an IQ of 130 or higher; to others, the label giftedness is reserved for those with an IQ score of 160 or higher. The National Association for Gifted Children defines five elements of giftedness: artistic and creative talents, intellectual and academic abilities, and leadership skills. (See Figure 2.2.) Noted psychologist Robert Sternberg has suggested that a new

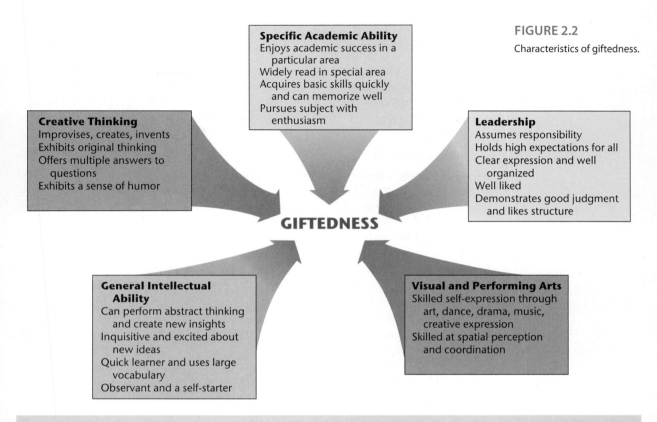

FIGURE 2.2

Characteristics of giftedness.

Specific Academic Ability
Enjoys academic success in a
  particular area
Widely read in special area
Acquires basic skills quickly
  and can memorize well
Pursues subject with
  enthusiasm

Creative Thinking
Improvises, creates, invents
Exhibits original thinking
Offers multiple answers to
  questions
Exhibits a sense of humor

Leadership
Assumes responsibility
Holds high expectations for all
Clear expression and well
  organized
Well liked
Demonstrates good judgment
  and likes structure

GIFTEDNESS

**General Intellectual
  Ability**
Can perform abstract thinking
  and create new insights
Inquisitive and excited about
  new ideas
Quick learner and uses large
  vocabulary
Observant and a self-starter

Visual and Performing Arts
Skilled self-expression through
  art, dance, drama, music,
  creative expression
Skilled at spatial perception
  and coordination

REFLECTION: Would you include Sternberg's concept of wisdom in this definition? How do these areas relate to Gardner's multiple intelligences?

area be included: wisdom. After years of researching what it means to be gifted, Sternberg now believes that giftedness is not just about how analytical and insightful you are, but also about how you use such skills. A clever business executive who uses his intelligence to earn a fortune, only to leave the company and stockholders in bankruptcy, may have been quite bright, but Sternberg argues that he should not be considered gifted. "The world is getting too dangerous. We have to train kids not just to be smart but to be wise."[26] Sternberg looks to Gandhi and Martin Luther King Jr. as examples of wisdom too often ignored in current definitions.

Although definitions of giftedness vary, only a small percentage of our population are identified with such high degrees of ability, creativity, motivation, pragmatic talent, or wisdom—making for a very exclusive club. The National Association for Gifted Children estimates that 6 percent, or 3 million students, are identified as academically gifted. A far greater number of gifted students may remain unidentified.[27] Intelligence testing often overlooks many students who are gifted. Students living in poverty, particularly those whose parents are uneducated or speak English as a second language, are less likely to develop the verbal skills measured by these traditional intelligence tests. Not surprisingly, students who are identified as gifted by such conventional tests are overwhelmingly White, Asian, and middle- or upper-class students. Assessments that measure spatial and mathematical intelligence as well as curiosity and leadership abilities identify a more diverse crop of gifted students.[28]

For those students who are identified as gifted, school can become an unfriendly place. Many do not succeed on their own. Gifted students may be haunted by a sense of isolation and loneliness, pressure to achieve, fear of failure, and negative peer pressure.[29] Gifted students talk often about their feelings of isolation and feeling different, of wanting to be "normal" and "like everyone else":

> *I just want to be a regular kid and not stick out so much all the time.*
>
> *I get taken advantage of. People ask to be my partner or work with me on a paper and I am stuck doing all the work. The only thing they do is make sure their name is on my paper or project. But I'm never asked to sit with them at lunch or hang out after school.*
>
> *I get scared for the world. Being smart allows me to see the world and what trouble we're really in.*[30]

Not surprisingly then, instead of thriving in school, too many gifted students drop out. The picture is especially dismal for gifted students from lower socioeconomic backgrounds and for gifted Hispanic and black children.[31] The result is that many of our nation's brightest and most competent students are lost to neglect and apathy, and some of our most talented youth do not succeed at school.

The challenges and opposition to providing special gifted programs and educational opportunities are many. To some it seems downright undemocratic to provide special services to children who already enjoy an advantage. Moreover, struggling with shrinking revenues and federal mandates that focus on improving the test scores of lower-achieving pupils, many school districts across the country are cutting programs for their most promising students. Consequently, there is often a lack of commitment to support curriculum and teachers for extremely advanced students. Only 20 states require public school services for gifted students, recognizing that—like other children with special needs—gifted students will not thrive without accommodations. And while the debate over school reform focuses on efforts to help low-performing students, no federal law offers a reward for raising the scores of high achievers and punishment if their progress lags—potentially leaving gifted students behind.[32]

Despite these challenges, many educators and parents believe that we need to do a better job of "gifted inclusion" by designing regular class activities that are more responsive to the needs of the gifted. How do teachers develop an instructional plan that will be challenging, enlightening, and intriguing to students of different abilities, and still maintain a sense of community within the classroom? The regular classroom can be a major instructional resource by providing enrichment activities such as independent projects, small-group inquiry and investigations, academic competitions, and learning centers that provide in-depth and challenging content beyond regular grade-level lessons.[33] A gifted student might also spend most of the day in a regular class and be pulled out for a part of the day, perhaps an hour or so, to receive special instruction. At the secondary level, high schools have augmented their offerings with challenging courses of study, such as the **Advanced Placement (AP)** program that offers college-level courses for high-achieving high schoolers and the **International Baccalaureate (IB)** program, an internationally recognized degree program that includes rigorous science, math, and foreign language requirements along with diverse cultural studies. Special high schools, such as the Bronx High School of Science and the North Carolina School for Mathematics and Science, have long and distinguished histories of providing educational opportunities for intellectually gifted students. Other special schools have focused on programs in acting, music, and dance.

Some school districts go beyond their own resources to meet the needs of gifted students, connecting gifted high school students with the local college or community college. These students spend part of their day enrolled in college-level courses, being intellectually challenged and receiving college credit while still enrolled in high school. Still other elementary, middle, and high school gifted students receive additional support through online instruction summer camps, or even special year-long programs that augment their regular courses. Johns Hopkins University, for example, has been sponsoring the Center for Talented Youth (CTY) in different parts of the nation for several decades. Many of these college programs are termed

accelerated programs because they allow gifted students from all grade-levels to skip grades or receive college credit early. Advanced Placement courses and exams (the APs) provide similar acceleration opportunities, permitting students to graduate before their chronological peers. Many gifted students report they feel just as comfortable, both academically and socially, with their intellectual peers as they do with their chronological peers, although cases of students who found acceleration to be a disaster are also plentiful.[34]

An important characteristic of effective gifted programs is the sense of community offered, a key step in reducing student anxiety and alienation. One student was relieved to find that "there are lots of people like me and I'm not a weirdo after all."[35] Teachers are also encouraged to help gifted students understand and manage the advantages and disadvantages that can come with their high intelligence and creativity. Moreover, when gifted students are placed in appropriate programs, they are often empowered to realize their full potential. As one 12-year-old girl said:

> I enjoy being smart because I am able to accomplish many things and I feel that being smart gives me more self-esteem. I love that I have unique interests and a place in school where I can pursue them. I enjoy challenging myself to always reach the next level.[36]

In the final analysis, it is not only the gifted who suffer from our national neglect and apathy; it is all of us. How many works of art will never be enjoyed? How many medical breakthroughs and how many inventions have been lost because of our insensitivity to the gifted?

Special Education

Perhaps you have read the book *Karen*. It is the story of a child with cerebral palsy, a child who persevered despite devastating obstacles. A formidable obstacle was an educational system that had no room for children with disabilities. The book was written by Karen's mother, who, like her daughter, refused the rejection of a hostile school and society. She wrote of her attempts to gain educational rights for her daughter and other children with disabilities:

> We constantly sought a remedy for this appalling situation which deprived so many of an education, and eventually we found a few doctors and educators who had made strides in developing valid testing methods for handicapped children. On one occasion, when I voiced a plea for the education of the handicapped, a leading state official retorted, "It would be a waste of the state's money. They'll never get jobs."
>
> We were frequently discouraged and not a little frightened as many of our "learned" men [sic] felt the same way.[37]

Such disparaging attitudes were common in our society for years and resulted in inadequate educational programs for millions of exceptional children.

Before the Revolutionary War, the most that was offered to exceptional children was protective care in asylums. The asylums made little effort to help these children develop their physical, intellectual, and social skills. Following the American Revolution, however, the ideals of democracy and the development of human potential swept the nation. Within this humanist social context, procedures were devised for teaching the blind and the deaf. Then, in the early 1800s, attempts were made to educate the "idiotic" and the "insane" children who today would be identified as having developmental disabilities or an emotional disturbance.

For many years, the legal system mirrored society's judgment that the best policy toward those with disabilities was "out of sight, out of mind." The courts typically saw education as a privilege rather than a right, and they ruled that children with disabilities should be excluded from schools. The notion was that the majority of children needed to be protected from those with disabilities: from the disruptions they might precipitate, from the excessive demands they might make, and from the discomfort their presence in classrooms might cause.

The years following World War II brought renewed hope and promise. Such pioneers as Grace Fernald, Marianne Frostig, and Heinz Werner—to name but a few—conducted research, developed programs, and gave new impetus to the field of **special education.** Their work was aided by the emergence of new disciplines, such as psychology, sociology, and social work. Parents also continued their struggle, individually and collectively, to obtain educational opportunities for children with disabilities. They took their cause to both the schools and the courts. Today, the educational rights of these children have been mandated by courts of law and are required practice in classrooms across the nation. Special education has broken away from the isolation and institutionalization so common in the late nineteenth century and has moved to mainstream exceptional children, as much as possible, into typical school settings.

Starting in the 1970s, Congress passed several landmark special education laws. In 1975, Public Law 94-142, the Education for All Handicapped Children Act, established the right of all students with disabilities to a "free and appropriate public education." Public Law 94-142 was replaced and expanded in 1991 by the **Individuals with Disabilities Education Act (IDEA),** which not only provides a more sensitive description of the act's purpose but also extends coverage to all disabled learners between the ages of 3 and 21, including individuals with autism and traumatic brain injuries. Recognizing the importance of early intervention, special education services were extended again in 2004 to include children from birth to 2 years old. The revised 2004 IDEA further requires that only a "highly qualified" state-certified special education teacher can work with special needs learners. IDEA also provides for rehabilitation and social work services. IDEA requires that each child with disabilities "have access to the program best suited to the child's special needs which is as close as possible to a normal child's education program."[38]

Six fundamental provisions are included in IDEA:

1. *Zero reject.* The principle of zero reject asserts that no child with disabilities may be denied a free, appropriate public education. Representatives of the disabled have asserted that excluding children with disabilities from public schools violates the constitutional interpretation behind the Supreme Court's *Brown* v. *Board of Education* (1954) decision, which put an end to claims of "separate but equal" schooling. The courts have responded with landmark decisions in Pennsylvania (*Pennsylvania Association for Retarded Children* v. *Commonwealth*) and in Washington, DC (*Mill* v. *D.C. Board of Education*) that mandate public schools in those jurisdictions to provide a free, appropriate education to all children with disabilities. Other federal and state decisions have followed suit.

2. *Appropriate education.* While the principle of zero reject ensures that children with disabilities will receive a public education, it is important to recognize that this principle goes beyond simply allowing children with disabilities to pass through the schoolhouse door. The term "appropriate education" implies that these children have the right to an education involving the accurate diagnosis of individual needs, as well as responsive programs targeted to those needs. Through IDEA, parents are mandated to become full partners in all stages of decision making, including curriculum and placements. Consequently, parents of students in special education have a greater say in their children's education than that held by parents of any other students.

3. *Nondiscriminatory education.* The principle of nondiscriminatory education, based on "due process" rights of the Fifth and Fourteenth Amendments of the U.S. Constitution, mandates that children with disabilities be fairly assessed so that they can be protected from inappropriate classification and tracking. Much of the court activity in this area has centered on the disproportionate number of children of color assigned to special education classes, a situation that some claim is the result of biased testing. In one case, a court ruled that IQ tests could not be used for placing or tracking students. Other courts have

Profile in Education   Sally L. Smith

Would you rather go to school or join a Secret Agents Club? Want to do both? Look no further than The Lab School of Washington and its colorful late leader **Sally L. Smith,** who started this "school modeled after a party" more than forty years ago. The school offers innovative programs for children and adults with learning disabilities, emphasizing experiential learning and the arts. Explained Smith, "I am in the business of saving lives." She started with her youngest son.

Gary Smith was born with severe learning disabilities. By the first grade, he struggled with the alphabet and math, yet easily solved puzzles and expounded on the similarities between Greek myths and Navajo rain dances. School officials quickly decided that Gary could not be taught. So Smith drew upon her background in psychology and cultural anthropology to create new approaches to teaching her son and tapping into his talents. Children's birthday parties provided initial clues.

> When I had birthday parties for the kids, I always picked a theme, whether it was Indians or secret agents or the Civil War. We made costumes, castles and tents, festive feasts; all were concrete activities with focused involvement. Suddenly it dawned on me that this kid couldn't tell you two plus two is four but through everything we did at birthday parties, he was learning. So I thought, what am I doing in these parties that is working?[a]

Her answer: "Total immersion of the senses." Smith discovered that children with learning disabilities are often visual thinkers and hands-on learners. The central nervous system of children with learning disabilities often scrambles information and impairs the orderly acquisition of knowledge. Smith calls it the "hidden handicap." Although students with learning disabilities struggle in learning environments focused on language and conformity, they can thrive in settings that use the arts as a gateway to learning.

In the summer of 1967, Smith received a telegram from a long-time friend and educator suggesting she start a school. She had twenty-five days to find volunteers, create a curriculum, and hire teachers. Recalls Smith, "I had the audacity, and perhaps naïveté, to design and direct a school for my son and others like him, when there was no such thing available." The seeds of the Lab School were sown. And after forty years, Smith remained a tireless champion of arts-based learning.

> The arts demand involvement. They counteract passivity. The arts ignite the whole learning process. The arts help organize knowledge. Our experience is that the arts hold children's attention and deal constantly with sequence and order—areas that cause the learning disabled so much trouble. The arts provide connections, linkages, and often clarify relationships.[b]

Smith designed the Academic Club Method, which encourages exploration and deep learning of academic content while building knowledge, language fluency, and critical thinking. The rigorous academic model combines various educational methods, including multisensory learning, cooperative education, discovery and project learning, and authentic assessment. Students study great thinkers, works of art, and literature in rooms decorated like ancient Egypt, a prehistoric cave, or a Renaissance hall. Students role-play to

learn the various stages of evolution. The Academic Clubs help students learn how to learn, not merely master facts.

Many students with learning disabilities are not comfortable in the world of words and are called stupid or lazy.

> They may look typical, but they don't learn typically. They are visual thinkers. They see shapes, forms, contours, colors, textures, movement. When imparting knowledge we need to paint pictures in their minds through hands-on-project learning and active learning. We see astonishing successes when we honor their different styles of learning.[c]

Yet, for many years, Sally Smith encountered doubts and derision. "Here comes the arts and crafts lady" the friendliest doubters said with a sneer. She didn't waver. Today her students' achievements speak volumes: More than 90 percent of Lab School students go on to college. And the success is spreading. Before her death in 2007, Smith opened arts-based schools in Baltimore and Philadelphia for students with learning disabilities. Our understanding of diverse ways of knowing continues to advance, in no small part because of the work and talents of Sally Smith.

[a]Sally Smith, *No Easy Answers* (Bantam Books, 1995).
[b]Sally Smith, *Learn It, Live It* (Brookes Publishing, 2005).
[c]Ibid, p. 21.

To learn more about Sally L. Smith, click on *Profiles in Education*.

www.mhhe.com/sadker10e

REFLECTION: Describe how the Academic Club Method could be used in regular classrooms. Do you believe that arts-based learning has a place in our standardized testing culture? Why or why not?

School learning environments need to accommodate a wide variety of student differences.

forbidden the use of tests that are culturally biased, and still others have ordered that testing take place in the children's native language.

4. ***Least-restrictive environment.*** The least-restrictive environment protects children with disabilities from being inappropriately segregated. Court decisions have urged that special needs students be educated in a setting that most closely resembles a regular school environment while meeting their special needs. **Mainstreaming** has traditionally referred to placing special needs students in regular classroom settings for at least part of the day. The more recent term, **inclusion,** sometimes called *full inclusion,* reflects an even stronger commitment to educate each student in a least-restrictive environment to the maximum degree possible. Separate classes and schools are to be avoided unless a child's disabilities are such that education in a regular classroom, even with the aid of special materials and supportive services, cannot be achieved. When to include and when to separate is a source of constant debate. (See Figure 2.3.)

5. ***Procedural due process.*** The principle of procedural due process upholds the right of students with disabilities to protest a school's decisions about their education. Due process entails the right of children with disabilities and their parents to be notified of school actions and decisions; to challenge those decisions before an impartial tribunal, using counsel and expert witnesses; to examine the school records on which a decision is based; and to appeal whatever decision is reached.

6. ***Individualized education program (IEP).*** Because of the diversity of disabilities, IDEA requires that a "free appropriate public education" be defined on an individual basis, using a written IEP. Each IEP must be reviewed and revised annually, ensuring that the educational goals designed for a child align with his or her learning needs and that these plans are actually delivered. Teachers shoulder the responsibilities of monitoring the needs of each child with disabilities placed in their classrooms. An IEP must include the following:

    -   A statement of the student's current performance, including long-term (annual) goals and short-term objectives.

    -   A description of the nature and duration of the instructional services designed to meet the prescribed goals.

    -   An overview of the methods of evaluation that will be used to monitor the child's progress and to determine whether the goals and objectives have been met.

    There is no specific IEP form that must be used, as long as goals, objectives, services, and evaluation are accurately reflected. In fact, hundreds of different IEP forms are currently in use; some run as long as twenty pages; others are only two or three pages New teachers should learn about their school district's norms and procedures for writing IEPs when they begin teaching. Remember, it is not the format that is important but, rather, whether or not the IEP accurately describes the educational needs and the related remedial plans. Even though writing these IEPs will undoubtedly consume a great deal of a teacher's time and energy, it often leads to better communication among the school staff, as well as between teachers and parents. Also, the practice of preparing IEPs will likely lead to more effective individualization of instruction for all children, not just those with disabilities.

    IDEA has been one of the most thoroughly litigated federal laws in history. Parents whose children qualify for special education services can and do sue the school district if they believe their children's needs are not being met. Local courts agreeing with parents' views have ordered public schools to hire extra teachers or specialized personnel or to spend additional dollars to

FIGURE 2.3

Appropriate education in the least restrictive environment for students with disabilities.

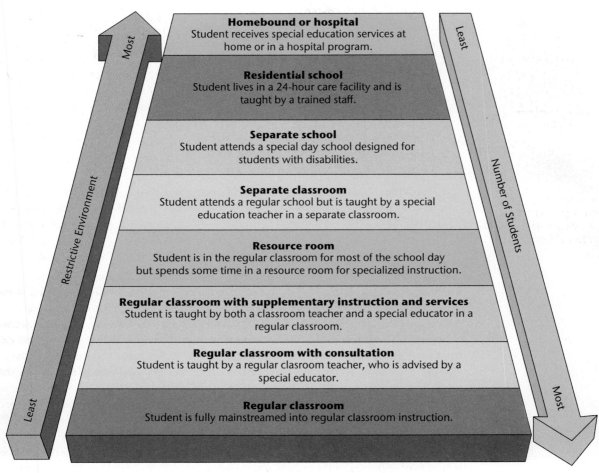

SOURCE: Adapted from: William Heward, *Exceptional Children: An Introduction to Special Education*, 10th ed. (Upper Saddle River, NJ: Macmillan/Prentice-Hall, 2012, p. 78.

REFLECTION: Why do some believe that all teachers are special education teachers?

provide an appropriate education. When judges believe that a school is unable to meet the special needs of a child, even with these additional resources, they can order and have ordered the public school to pay the tuition so that the student can attend a private school. However, parents will likely find it more difficult to demand better special education services for their children. The Supreme Court recently ruled that parents who disagree with a school's IEP for their child have the legal burden of proving that the plan will not provide the appropriate education. Disability advocates worry that school districts will now have little incentive to address parents' complaints or, even worse, to provide quality special education services.[39]

Today, nearly 7 million students (13 percent of the total public school population) are special needs. In a few areas, such as autism, growth has skyrocketed tenfold in only two decades.[40] **Learning disabilities** constitutes the largest group of special needs students. (See Figure 2.4.) Students with learning disabilities have difficulties with listening, speaking, reading, writing, reasoning, or mathematical skills. A student with a learning disability might

GLOBAL VIEW

More than 1 billion people worldwide live with disabilities. Mortality for children with disabilities is as high as 80 percent in many poor countries. Globally, less than 5 percent of children with disabilities have access to education.

FIGURE 2.4

Distribution of students served under idea (rounded to nearest percent).

SOURCE: U.S. Department of Education, *Condition of Education: Children and Youth with Disabilities* (2011).

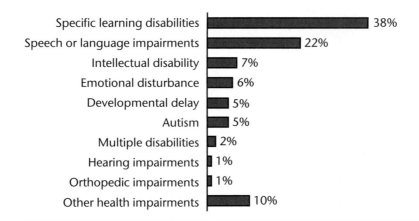

Specific learning disabilities	38%
Speech or language impairments	22%
Intellectual disability	7%
Emotional disturbance	6%
Developmental delay	5%
Autism	5%
Multiple disabilities	2%
Hearing impairments	1%
Orthopedic impairments	1%
Other health impairments	10%

REFLECTION: This distribution offers an insight into which special needs students teachers are most likely to have in regular classrooms. Suggest some of the accommodations a classroom teacher might consider for each of these special needs.

perform poorly in one area but extremely well in another. Uneven performance, hyperactivity, disorganization, and lack of follow-through are typical problems for these students. Educational literature reflects more than fifty terms to describe students with learning disabilities.

Meeting the growing needs of special needs students has strained education budgets nationwide.[41] Why the upsurge? The reasons are complex—and troubling. Some believe environmental pollutants increase children's disabilities. Others argue that special needs have always been common but in past years went undiagnosed. Some wonder if today we are over-diagnosing the problem. They point to affluent communities where parents hire private psychologists to ensure that their children are identified as having a learning disability. Why would they do this? In wealthy communities, such labels attract additional educational resources, smaller class size, and even extended time for taking high-risk tests such as the SATs.

But if special education means special privileges for the wealthy, the same diagnosis can mean fewer resources for the poor. Studies indicate that African American, Hispanic, and special education students from lower socioeconomic backgrounds are twice as likely to be educated in a more restrictive and separate setting than white and wealthier students. Poor parents struggle to make certain that the special education label is *not* attached to their children. In addition to poverty, cultural misunderstanding, low expectations, and the desire to remove "difficult" students from the classroom contribute to the high rate of African American and Hispanic students identified as having developmental disabilities or emotional disturbances.[42] And then there is gender. Boys tend to act out their frustrations and create classroom disturbances. Because their behavior gets noticed, boys are twice as likely as girls to be labeled with a disability. Girls are quieter in class, less likely to cause discipline concerns, and more likely to turn inwardly with problems and anxieties. As a result, their special education needs often go undetected and untreated.[43] So behind the growing numbers of special education students is a disturbing imbalance of boys, and an over-identification trend of students of color.

Once identified, attention focuses on how best to educate these students.[44] Students with mild disabilities typically attend regular classrooms for part of the day and leave for a period of time to receive special instruction in a resource room. These "pullout" programs have been criticized for stigmatizing students while failing to improve their academic performance. This concern has fueled the **regular education initiative,** which encourages schools to provide

You Be The Judge

STUDENTS WITH SPECIAL NEEDS

Should Be Mainstreamed Because . . .

WITHOUT INCLUSION, OUR DEMOCRATIC IDEAL IS HOLLOW

Segregating individuals with disabilities mirrors the historical seg-regation of African Americans and other groups, a segregation already rejected by the courts. Separate can never be equal, and all students quickly learn the stigma associated with those in "special" classrooms.

SOCIETY NEEDS THE TALENTS OF ALL ITS CITIZENS

Society needs the skills and economic productivity of all our citi-zens. Educating those with disabilities in a segregated setting decreases their opportunity for full and meaningful contributions later in life.

MAINSTREAMING IMPROVES ACADEMIC AND SOCIAL RELATIONS

Studies indicate that students with special needs perform better academically when mainstreamed in regular classes. Not surpris-ingly, their social adjustment is also improved.

THOSE WITHOUT DISABILITIES GAIN WHEN SPECIAL NEEDS STUDENTS ARE PRESENT

In our increasingly stratified society, students can spend years in school with peers just like themselves. Inclusion provides an oppor-tunity for children to appreciate and work with people who do not necessarily reflect their own experiences and viewpoints.

Should Not Be Mainstreamed Because . . .

MERELY SITTING IN REGULAR CLASSROOMS DOES NOT GUARANTEE A FITTING EDUCATION

A rallying cry like "democracy" sounds impressive, but we need to ensure that students with special needs receive a quality education, and the best place for that is not necessarily in a regular, main-streamed classroom.

PULLOUT PROGRAMS CAN OFFER STUDENTS WITH SPECIAL NEEDS THE RESOURCES THEY NEED TO SUCCEED

Pullout programs for children with special needs can offer an adjusted curriculum, special instructional techniques, and smaller class size. Students with special needs can soar in classrooms designed to meet their needs but flounder when they are inappro-priately placed in regular classes.

GIFTED AND TALENTED STUDENTS ARE AT PARTICULAR RISK

Gifted and talented students fall within the special needs category, and for them, mainstreaming is a disaster. If the gifted are not chal-lenged, they will be turned off from school, and the gifts of our most able students will be lost to society.

WHEN STUDENTS WITH SPECIAL NEEDS ARE MAINSTREAMED, STUDENTS WITHOUT DISABILITIES SUFFER

As teachers in regular classes adjust learning activities to accom-modate the special needs students, other students lose out. The extra time, special curriculum, and attention given to students with special needs amount to time and resources taken from others in the class.

SOURCE: Many of these arguments are found in greater detail in Jack L. Nelson, Stuart B. Palonsky, and Kenneth Carlson, *Critical Issues in Education: Dialogue and Dialectics* (New York: McGraw-Hill, 2009), pp. 441–67.

www.mhhe.com/sadker10e

YOU DECIDE . . .

What training would help you meet the special needs of students mainstreamed into your classroom? Can "separate" ever be "equal"? Whose needs are of most worth, those of students with special needs or those of "regular" students? Do their needs actually con-flict? As a teacher, would you want special needs children main-streamed or pulled out? Imagine yourself the parent of a special needs child. Would you want your child mainstreamed or pulled out?

special services *within* the regular classroom and encourages close collaboration between classroom teachers and special educators. Today, about half of the students with disabilities are mainstreamed for 80 percent or more of the school day in a regular classroom.[45]

Regular classroom teachers often express concerns about their ability to handle a mainstreamed classroom:

> They want us all to be super teachers, but I've got 33 kids in my class and it's really a job to take care of them without also having to deal with special needs kids too. I'm not complaining really— I wouldn't want to do anything other than what I'm doing—but it is demanding.[46]

Although classroom teachers are expected to meet many of society's obligations, including the education of special needs students, they are not always given adequate resources for the task. Frustration is often the result. To succeed, teachers need additional planning time, appropriate curricular materials, ongoing staff development programs, and sometimes, extra classroom assistance.

Despite the criticisms and problems of inclusion, one thing is certain: More students with disabilities are enjoying school life alongside their peers. Inclusion seems to thrive in schools that provide teachers with adequate planning time and resources; have open communication among teachers, administrators, and parents; promote a culture of innovation and reform; and encourage a commitment to funding the education of students with exceptional needs.

Assistive Technology

Technology-based devices for students with special needs, called **assistive or adaptive technology,** can provide a real boost for students in and beyond the classroom. Assistive technologies include wheelchairs, hearing aids, switches that respond to voice commands, and computer programs that read material for blind students. For example, blind students and their teachers can use Braille software that provides easy-to-use print-to-Braille and Braille-to-print translations. Students with visual or motor problems can use voice-activated software or specialized touch screens to direct the computer's actions. ERICA (Eyegaze Response Interface Computer Aid) allows students to control a computer's keyboard and mouse through eye movement alone, allowing even the most immobile learners to interact with teachers and peers. Those with learning disabilities report that computers (especially handheld computers) are useful for taking notes in class and keeping their schedules organized. And students with learning disabilities especially benefit from such tools as Spellcheck. Students with disabilities may use a variety of innovations to help achieve successful inclusion in regular classrooms, and the list of adaptive technology devices promises to grow in the years ahead.[47]

Technological advances have created new and exciting learning possibilities.

What are the pitfalls of such efforts, and can such "assistance" become too much? Some critics suggest that the use of spelling and grammar tools for special education students (as well as others) can short-circuit learning and that sending laptops home can lead to inappropriate use, from cyber-bulling to visiting pornography and hate-group websites to unsupervised Internet shopping excursions. In fact, the entire effort to include students with special needs has its critics, and even with technology and other resources, inclusion will not succeed unless teachers genuinely support the philosophy behind this approach. They must be committed to exploding stereotypes and able to recognize the essential value of helping all children to learn together. Their talents and commitment may be put to the test in communities such as San Francisco, where students unable to feed themselves, or speak, or even go

Teaching Tip

STUDENTS WITH SPECIAL NEEDS

Effective teaching of students with special needs can be a challenging—and rewarding—experience. Here are a few practical suggestions to create an engaged *and* equitable learning environment for special needs students. In fact, these strategies are likely to improve learning for *all* students!

- **Establish and frequently review classroom rules, procedures, and academic directions.**

  Some students with special needs can become frustrated when they want to do the right thing but get confused or forget. Repeating the rules keeps them—and all students—on track.

- **Set fair, yet challenging expectations for all students, and ask higher- as well as lower-order questions.**

  Students quickly pick up when the teacher lowers expectations. For example, a teacher should not ask easy questions just to students with special needs. Asking challenging as well as simpler ones to all students is one strategy that sets a more positive tone. How challenging can the question be? With experience you will learn how to continually challenge and not frustrate learners with exceptionalities.

- **Relate new learning to previous instruction and to students' backgrounds and experiences.**

  Seeing connections is central for learners with special needs because words alone are not always adequate. Think of connections that tie class learning to students' lives and to previous work.

- **Create high student engagement by using a variety of instructional strategies, including visual and auditory methods, hands-on activities, and shorter time segments for activities.**

  The more learning channels you open, the more engaged behavior you will encourage, and the more likely that students will connect with your academic goals.

- **Model skills and strategies, and always emphasize key words.**

  Be mindful that what you say and what you do are not incidental, casual, or secondary. Be purposeful and clear because your words and behaviors teach powerful lessons.

- **Closely monitor independent work, and provide precise and immediate feedback.**

  Unlearning a behavior is more difficult than learning it correctly the first time. Monitoring and offering clear feedback can eliminate the need to unlearn and relearn.

- **Include joy and success in learning.**

  Design activities that will give students a sense of accomplishment. Provide additional time if needed to complete assignments, and don't forget to put joy and smiles in your teaching and in your students' learning.

REFLECTION: Review these suggestions and consider how these strategies are likely to improve learning for non–special needs students as well.

---

to the bathroom, are mainstreamed.[48] These students are part of a first wave of severely impaired children placed in regular classrooms. Although a difficult situation for teachers, students, and parents, the belief is that they will do far better there than in a segregated and restricted environment. Inclusion is at its heart a moral issue, one that raises the timeless principles of equality, justice, and the need for all of us to learn to live and grow together—not apart. (See You Be the Judge: Students with Special Needs on p. 45.)

This chapter is all about the rich human diversity that graces our classrooms and enables all of us—teachers and students alike—to learn from one another. We will never know how many ideas, insights, inventions, and medical breakthroughs have been lost because of our inability to honor these different ways of knowing. But we can rededicate ourselves to honoring and nurturing the unique talents of each student.

ONLINE VIDEO ALBUM TO ACCOMPANY *TEACHERS, SCHOOLS, AND SOCIETY 10E*

Visit the Online Learning Center for a range of contemporary videos with content related to this chapter.

www.mhhe.com/sadker10e

THE *TEACHERS, SCHOOLS, AND SOCIETY* READER WITH CLASSROOM OBSERVATION VIDEO CLIPS

Go to your *Teachers, Schools, and Society* Reader CD-ROM to:

READ CURRENT AND HISTORICAL ARTICLES

6. **The Myth of Pink and Blue Brains,** by Lisa Eliot, *Best of Educational Leadership,* August 2011.

7. **Demystifying the Adolescent Brain,** by Laurence Steinberg, *Education Leadership,* April 2011.

8. **Inclusion in Two Languages: Special Education in Portugal and the United States,** by Margaret Inman Linn, *Phi Delta Kappan,* May 2011.

9. **Letters to My Younger Self,** by Emilie Shafto, *Educational Leadership,* September 2011.

ANALYZE CASE STUDIES

3. **Carol Brown:** A teacher, after socially integrating a diverse class, sees her efforts threatened when a child's pencil case disappears and is thought to have been stolen.

4. **Joan Martin, Marilyn Coe, and Warren Groves:** A classroom teacher, a special education teacher, and a principal hold different views about mainstreaming a boy with poor reading skills. The dilemma comes to a head over the method of grading him at the end of the marking period.

OBSERVE TEACHERS, STUDENTS, AND CLASSROOMS IN ACTION

2. Classroom Observation: A Multiple Inelligences Lesson in Action

As discussed in this chapter, Howard Gardner's multiple intelligences theory suggests that recognizing different types of intelligences can support students' learning. In this observation, you will observe an elementary teacher using Gardner's theory of multiple intelligences in her instruction through the creation of learning centers based on the different intelligences.

3. Classroom Observation: Including Students with Special Needs

As a classroom teacher, you will most likely have at least one student with special needs and more likely several. In this observation, you will observe an elementary teacher demonstrating how he makes accommodations for his students with special needs. Teaching techniques, classroom organization, professional assistance, and multiple instructional styles enable this instructor to reach ADHD, hearing-impaired, PDD, and other students with special needs.

4. Classroom Observation: Author David Sadker Identifies Classroom Bias through the Role Play

David Sadker (coauthor of *Teachers, Schools, and Society*) often works with school administrators and teachers to demonstrate, through a role play, several issues of gender bias that can overwhelm a classroom. In these two observations, you will observe David Sadker give one of these workshops.

KEY TERMS AND PEOPLE

accelerated programs, 39

Advanced Placement (AP), 38

affective domain, 31

appropriate education, 40

assistive or adaptive technology, 46

cognitive domain, 32

emotional intelligence quotient (EQ), 29

exceptional learners, 36

Gardner, Howard, 26

gender similarities hypothesis, 34

giftedness, 36

Goleman, Daniel, 30

inclusion, 42

individualized education program (IEP), 42

Individuals with Disabilities Education Act (IDEA), 40

International Baccalaureate (IB), 38

learning disabilities, 43

learning styles, 31

least-restrictive environment, 42

locus of control, 32

mainstreaming (inclusion), 42

multiple intelligences, 26

neuroplasticity, 32

nondiscriminatory education, 40

portfolio, 28

procedural due process, 42

regular education initiative, 44

Smith, Sally L., 41

special education, 40

zero reject, 40

www.mhhe.com/sadker10e

CHAPTER REVIEW

Go to the Online Learning Center to take a chapter self-quiz, practice with key terms, and review concepts from the chapter.

DISCUSSION QUESTIONS AND ACTIVITIES

1. Can you develop additional intelligences beyond the ones Gardner identifies? (This is often best accomplished in groups.)

2. How would you characterize your own learning style? Interview other students in your class to determine how they characterize their learning styles. Based on these interviews, what recommendations could you offer your course instructor about using learning styles in your class?

3. Do you believe that girls and boys have different gender learning styles? Brain differences? Provide some evidence to support your position.

4. Interview people who graduated from single-sex schools and ask them about their experiences. Did they find single-sex schools to be an advantage or not? In what ways? Do males and females have different assessments? What was lost by not attending a co-ed school? What was gained?

5. Investigate a special education program in a local school. Describe its strengths. What suggestions do you have for improving it? What is your position on "full inclusion"?

Teaching Your Diverse Students

CHAPTER 3

FOCUS QUESTIONS

1. In what ways are American schools failing culturally diverse students?
2. How do deficit, expectation, and cultural difference theories explain different academic performance among various racial, ethnic, and cultural groups?
3. How do phrases like "melting pot" and "cultural pluralism" both capture and mask American identity?
4. What are the political and instructional issues surrounding bilingual education?
5. What are the purposes and approaches of multicultural education?
6. Why is culturally responsive teaching important?
7. How can teachers use culturally responsive teaching strategies?

I think we have to own the fears that we have of each other, and then, in some practical way, some daily way, figure out how to see people differently than the way we were brought up to.

ALICE WALKER

www.mhhe.com/sadker10e

WHAT DO YOU THINK? Cultural diversity of students. Estimate the racial, ethnic, and social class backgrounds of today's students.

CHAPTER PREVIEW

The United States has just experienced the greatest immigration surge in its history. In the past few decades, newly minted Americans have arrived mainly from Latin America and Asia, but also from the Caribbean, the Middle East, Africa, and eastern Europe. Today, about one in ten Americans is foreign born, and the native language of well over 30 million Americans is a language other than English. Also, 2012 was the first year that minority births were greater than white births, and by 2030, half of all schoolchildren will be of color. These demographics create a remarkable and formidable challenge for the nation's schools.[1]

Some advocate a multicultural approach to education that recognizes and incorporates this growing student diversity into teaching and the curriculum. Others fret that disassembling our Eurocentric curriculum and traditional approaches to education may harm our U.S. culture. Many teachers struggle to teach students with backgrounds different from their own. How do teachers accomplish this? This chapter addresses that question directly, not only with breathtaking information and some astute (we hope) insights, but with practical suggestions as well.

Student Diversity

FOCUS QUESTION 1

In what ways are American schools failing culturally diverse students?

Since the 1960s, more immigrants have come to this country than at the beginning of the twentieth century, a time often thought of as the great era of immigration and Americanization. Today, about one in three Americans are of color. **Demographic forecasting**, the study of people and their vital statistics, predicts that by 2030 half the school population will be from non-European ethnic groups. You will teach in a nation more diverse and less Eurocentric than the one you grew up in.

So let's begin to explore our changing student population by defining some basic terms that are critical, but often used incorrectly. **Race** refers to a group of individuals sharing a common socially determined category often related to genetic attributes, physical appearance, and ancestry. Yet, racial categories can vary by society. For example, in the United States an individual with any known African ancestry is considered black. But in Caribbean and Latin American nations, race is often determined not by physical attributes, but by social class. In these countries, "money lightens": upward social mobility increases the likelihood of being classified as white. **Ethnicity** refers to shared common cultural traits such as language, religion, and dress. A sense of shared peoplehood is one of the most important characteristics of ethnicity. A Latino or Hispanic, for example, belongs to an ethnic group, but might belong to the Negro, Caucasian, or Asian race. **Culture** is a set of learned beliefs, values, symbols, and behaviors, a way of life shared by members of a society. There is not only a national culture, but also microcultures or subcultures. There are cultures related to class, religion, or sexual orientation, to offer but a few examples. These subcultures carry values and behaviors that differ from others in the same nation or the same community.[2] The willingness of people to understand and appreciate different cultures, races, and ethnicities is often at the heart of the diversity issue in the United States. The challenge for educators is to ensure that all our students achieve.

The 2000 Census added a new demographic by asking citizens to report if they were **multiracial**—that is, claiming ancestors from two or more races. Nearly 7 million Americans responded yes. Most of the respondents were under 18, and in at least ten states, more than a quarter of school-aged children were in the multiracial category, indicating that this group will grow in the years ahead. Few studies have investigated the specific challenges facing multiracial-multiethnic children, but we see some cultural inequities already emerging. Tiger Woods is considered by many to be our first great black golfer. Few refer to him as our first great Thai golfer. President Barack Obama is called our first black president, not our first half-white president. For them and others, any black heritage becomes shorthand for race identity. Teachers and schools have much to learn in honoring the full background of multiracial children and avoiding convenient and simplistic labels.

The United States is changing. Between 1980 and the first decade of the twenty-first century, the white population declined from 80 percent to 66 percent; the Hispanic population increased from 6 percent to 15 percent; the black population remained constant at about 12 percent; and the Asian/Pacific Islander population increased from less than 2 percent of the total population to 4 percent. During this period, that new category of multiracial children continued to grow as well.[3] (See Figure 3.1.)

Failing at Fairness

These population changes challenge our schools, as these statistics illustrate:[4]

- Hispanic, Native American, and African American students score consistently lower on standardized tests than do their Asian and white classmates.

- Almost half of the nation's historically under-resourced populations—Hispanic, African American, and Native American—are not graduating from high school.

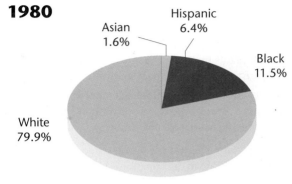

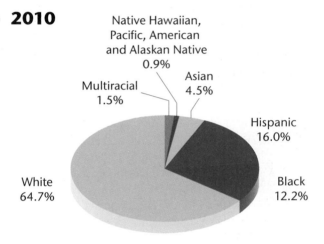

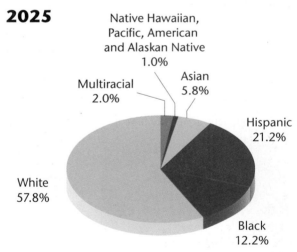

FIGURE 3.1
Resident population percentages in 1980, 2010, and projected to 2025.

SOURCE: U.S. Department of Education, National Center for Education Statistics, "Status and Trends in the Education of Racial and Ethnic Minorities," NCES 2010-015, July 2010.

REFLECTION: How can teachers best prepare to teach America's changing demographics?

- In Houston, Oakland, Cleveland, and New York, with large populations of poor students and students of color, between 50 and 70 percent of the students do not graduate high school.

- Black and Hispanic students are far more likely to be suspended or expelled from school, even when they violate the same rules as white students.

- The percentages of children who were living in poverty were higher for blacks (35 percent), American Indians/Alaska Natives (33 percent), Hispanics (27 percent), and Native Hawaiians or other Pacific Islanders (26 percent), than for Asians (11 percent) or whites (10 percent).

- The percentage of children living in poverty in the United States increased from 16.9 percent in 2006 to nearly 22 percent in 2010. In the UK and in France, the child poverty rate is well under 10 percent.

- Students from low-income families are six times more likely to drop out of school than are the children of the wealthy.

- In recent years, the achievement gap between white and minority students remains large, despite the focus of No Child Left Behind on increasing the test scores of African American and Hispanic students.

Most Americans do not blame schools for these achievement gaps, yet a majority (57 percent) feels it is up to the schools to close the gaps.[5] The Gallup Public Opinion poll suggests that Americans understand that issues outside of school affect what goes on in school. Even before children arrive at the schoolhouse door, poverty takes its toll. Lower birth weight, poor nutrition, and higher incidences of lead poisoning among children from low-income families contribute to academic and cognitive problems.[6] Preschool children from low-income households know fewer words, speak less, and have fewer, if any, books. And "poverty" is not a synonym for color, because most of the poor in the United States are white. Poverty affects students from all groups.

Race and ethnicity are, of course, well-publicized factors in academic performance. The test scores and graduation rates of African American and Hispanic American students lag behind those of white and Asian American students, in part because of a costly disconnect between school and home cultures. African American peers sometimes mock school achievement as "acting white," suggesting academic success is racial or cultural treason. Hispanic families may encounter not only cultural barriers, but also language barriers. In truth, the failure of our society to bridge and honor differences among ethnic and racial groups contributes to the weaker test scores and lower graduation rates of many students. The home–school disconnect has other dimensions: Jewish and Muslim children may encounter school obstacles to their religious practices, atheists encounter hostility to their nonreligious beliefs, American Indian tribes have seen schools attack their cultures and values, and even sexual orientation conflicts are now part of school life. In this chapter, we will explore many of these diversity dimensions. As a teacher and as a citizen, working to eliminate social and economic injustice is as important to academic success as anything you do in the classroom.

Lesbian, Gay, Bisexual, and Transgender Students (LGBT)

Being gay, lesbian, bisexual, or straight refers to a person's sexual orientation, an innate characteristic that determines who one is attracted to sexually and romantically. Being transgender refers to a person's gender identity—a person's innate sense of being male, female, or somewhere in between. Many school practices assume that all people are heterosexual and either male or female. A typical curriculum reflects this assumption in subtle and not so subtle ways. Literature like *Romeo and Juliet,* math word problems like "David bought Karen one dozen roses . . .", and electing a homecoming king and queen are obvious examples of assumed heterosexuality for all. However, some schools are altering these practices: inviting same-sex couples to the prom, providing gender-neutral or individual bathrooms and locker rooms for transgender students, and including LGBT people and perspectives in the curriculum.[7]

Being a good teacher in the years ahead will almost surely mean working with a culturally diverse population.

More and more gay students are coming out of the closet earlier, often in middle school, and are finding support among peers and teachers. Others find no support and liken school to a war zone. For Lawrence King, a 15-year-old in California who was shot and killed by a 14-year-old classmate, war zone is not an exaggeration. These different responses to LGBT students reflect our national division. A number of states have laws preventing teachers from even mentioning the word "homosexual"; some states mandate that homosexuality be presented in exclusively negative terms in the classroom.[8] Other school districts recognize LGBT people in their nondiscrimination policies, sending a clear message that no student, parent, or school employee will be discriminated against because of their sexual orientation or gender identity. There are more than 3,500 Gay-Straight Alliances (GSAs), student clubs that provide a safe space for LGBT students and their allies.[9] GSAs sometimes engender controversy, but the 1984 Federal Equal Access Act states that if schools allow any noncurricular clubs, they have to allow them all.

Depending on where you teach, you may or may not be able to include LGBT issues in your classroom. In California, for example, you will be required to include the contributions of gay and lesbian Americans in your teaching.[10] In other communities, you will be expected to be silent on this issue. But wherever you teach, you can ensure that democratic norms of equality are followed and that all students are respected regardless of individual differences. Students do not have to agree "It's okay to be gay," but they should understand that "It's not okay to discriminate against those who are gay." By providing a safe place for all students, teachers can create nurturing classrooms where every child can learn and every family is welcome.

SAFE ZONE

This space
RESPECTS
all aspects of people
including race, ethnicity,
gender expression, sexual orientation,
socio-economic background,
age, religion, body shape, size, and ability.

This SAFE ZONE poster is brought to you by your friends at Boulder County Public Health.
To request more posters, please call 303-678-6164.

Posters like this can be found in classrooms and school offices to ensure a safe zone for LGBT students and others.

Teaching Tip

SOME CONSIDERATIONS FOR TEACHING LGBT STUDENTS

Your visible support can help LGBT students achieve in school. You can do the following:

1. Post a "Safe Zone" sign in your classroom or office.
2. Don't tolerate intolerance. Immediately respond to comments like "fag" or "dyke" and explain that such bigotry is not acceptable.
3. Integrate the contributions of LGBT figures in science, history, athletics, the arts, and other areas of the curriculum.
4. Avoid assumptions about any particular student being gay. The range of behaviors and attitudes within each sex is enormous.
5. On the other hand, honor confidences shared with you by LGBT students.

6. Work to keep the school as a safe place for LGBT students. Think about becoming an adviser to the Gay-Straight Alliance.

SOURCE: Adapted from "Ally Yourself with LGBT Students," *Teaching Tolerance,* Fall 2010, p. 35.

REFLECTION: Why is being sensitive to LGBT issues a good classroom strategy, even if you do not think you have any LGBT students in your class?

Putting a Price on Racism

"Welcome to class," says the professor as you take your seat. "I want you to respond to the following case study. This, of course, is fictional, but suspend disbelief, read the parable, and tell me what you think."

As a student in this class, you think this sounds kind of interesting (and a good grade in this course would be really nice). So you settle down and read the brief scenario:

> You are a white person and are visited by an official who explains that a mistake has been made. You were actually born to black parents who live far from where you grew up. The error has to be rectified. At midnight, you will become black, acquiring a darker skin, and body and facial features that reflect your African heritage. Your knowledge and ideas, your "inside," however, will remain the same.
>
> Now this is an unusual and rare problem, the official explains, but the error was not yours, and the organization that he represents is ready and able to offer you appropriate recompense. His records indicate that you are likely to live another 50 years. How much financial recompense would you request?

You look around and see your classmates, each from their own unique perspective of race and ethnicity, settle into the task. You wonder: How much money will your white classmates ask for? How will the students of color respond to this controversial, some would say offensive, class exercise? Now the *big* question: How much money would *you* ask for?

Although the parable is not true, the scenario is. Professor Andrew Hacker at Cornell put this question to white students in his class and asked them to come up with a settlement figure: How much money would they want to offset the "error"? If you are wondering what figure Hacker's students came up with, most felt that a reasonable payment for the "mistake" would be $50 million, a million dollars for each coming black year.

That acclaimed study became the focus of a popular book, *Two Nations: Black, White, Separate, Hostile, Unequal* (1992), and while it raised some poignant questions, it left many unanswered.[11]

What if Professor Hacker had continued the experiment with other groups? How much money would a Hispanic American, an African American, and an Asian American request if a mistake were made and they had to live the rest of their lives as a member of another race or culture? Would they request less compensation for the "administrative" blunder? The same $50 million? Would they want more money?

Just posing the problem underscores the U.S. tendency to look to the courts to fix any mistake, no matter how bizarre. Of course, in this story, money is the all-American panacea, a salve for any social injury. But despite these confounding issues, the parable is fascinating, and the questions it raises are intriguing.

Why did Professor Hacker construct this strange story, and how did he interpret the payment? He believed that the story unmasks America's hidden racism. Professor Hacker considers white privilege to be so commonplace that most of us are no longer able to "see" it. He uses the parable because it makes visible the hidden advantage society gives to white Americans. In Hacker's estimation, the $50 million that his students thought was "fair" compensation represents the value that white people place on the color of their own skin.

When you hear the word *race,* what comes to your mind? Is it the image of a black man? Or perhaps you visualize an Asian woman? We would wager that most of you reading this

What do you see in this class? Hacker's anecdote unmasks the quiet racism that lurks in many adult minds as they view children's racial backgrounds as a predictor of future income and status. Could you predict what careers these students might have? How predominant was race in your prediction?

text do not visualize a white person. When "race" is mentioned in America, we tend to picture people of color, the ones who are not like the majority that dominate newspapers, books, and much of the media. For example, from time to time, a news commentator might point out how many African Americans are now in Congress. But when is the last time you heard a report of the number of whites in Congress? Like Andrew Hacker, author Peggy McIntosh helps us see the hidden privileges of being in the majority. She refers to these privileges as an "invisible knapsack," because those in the majority often do not even see their advantages. Here are a few examples of the invisible race knapsack, the hidden privileges of being white. As a white person:

- When I am cited for a traffic violation, I can be sure I have not been singled out because of my race.
- I can watch television or read the front page of the paper and see my race widely represented.
- If I walk into a meeting late, people don't assume that my lateness reflects on my race.
- I do not have to educate my children to be aware of systemic racism for their own daily physical protection.
- When I ask to talk to the "person in charge," I can feel confident that I will be talking to a person of my own race.
- I can take a job with an affirmative action employer without having my colleagues believe that I was hired because of my race and not my qualifications.
- I can walk into a stationery store and find a card to send with pictures of my race.
- People don't ask me to explain how my race feels about a topic.

Can you add to the list? If you'd like to see other examples, visit www.nymbp.org/reference/WhitePrivilege.pdf.

If you are white, or heterosexual, or Christian (and most teachers are), you also have a knapsack of hidden privileges, whether you know it or not.[12] But if your students come from other backgrounds, they bring fewer privileges to school. If teachers are to connect and communicate with the growing student diversity in their classroom, they will need to learn more about students whose backgrounds are different from their own. This chapter is intended to help you do just that.

Theories of Why Some Groups Succeed and Others Do Not

A number of theories have emerged to explain why some groups soar in school while others flounder. Some of the explanations are fatalistic, others are more hopeful. Here are three—deficit theory, expectation theory, and cultural difference theory. The argument for **deficit theory** is that certain students do poorly in school because they suffer some sort of deficit: cultural, social, economic, academic, linguistic, or even genetic. For instance, some studies indicate that as much as half the achievement gap can be predicted by economics. Even in wealthy suburbs, for example, black families are less wealthy than their white counterparts, and their children do less well in school. There are parenting differences as well, another line of reasoning among deficit theory advocates. Many black parents are not as academically oriented in raising their children as white parents. For example, in one study, only half as many black homes as white homes owned 100 or more books, and more white parents read to their children every day. Fewer books read, fewer vocabulary words used by parents, and little understanding of the relationship between education and careers contribute to the cultural deficit. Not that this is not an easy topic to discuss. When comedian Bill Cosby spoke about his desire to have African American parents more involved in their children's education, many black families were angered and felt that they were being blamed for the poorer academic performance of their children. Ronald Ferguson, an African American professor who has done much of this research, is well aware that these studies anger parents. He explains, "I don't want to be another one of those people lecturing black parents. I tell them we in the black community—we—need to build stronger intellectual lives at home."[13]

FOCUS QUESTION 2
How do deficit, expectation, and cultural difference theories explain different academic performance among various racial, ethnic, and cultural groups?

It should be noted that a nefarious branch of deficit theory moves beyond these behavioral and economic issues and argues that genetic and IQ deficiencies of certain groups, especially people of color, are the root cause of academic underachievement. Most deficit theory proponents today steer clear of such genetic claims and question the research advanced to make this case. But many believe that the academic and economic differences in life at home can contribute to poorer performance at school.

Those who subscribe to **expectation theory** believe that some children do poorly because their teachers do not expect much of kids from certain racial and ethnic groups. As a result, they teach these students differently, and the students' academic performance suffers. This insight was first made popular by a classic study done by Rosenthal and Jacobson, which is described in greater detail later in this text. In the study, students were randomly chosen and the teachers told these students would experience an intellectual growth spurt during the year. Lo and behold, over the year, their grades improved. Teacher expectations of improved performance led to improved performance. Now imagine the opposite, teachers who expect less from certain students, and you see how harmful this "self-fulfilling prophesy" can be.

A third explanation for student achievement argues for better cross-cultural understanding. **Cultural difference theory** asserts that academic problems can be overcome if educators study and mediate the cultural gap separating school and home. Let's consider a case in point:

> Polynesian children in a Hawaiian village are performing poorly on the school reading tests. They seem unresponsive to the extra time and effort made by teachers to improve their reading performance. Why is this happening, and how can the situation be improved?

In this example, educators studied the Polynesian culture and discovered that older children, rather than adults, play a major role in educating the young. Accordingly, the school established a peer-learning center to provide the opportunity for older children to teach younger ones. By recognizing and adopting cultural traditions, the school was able to dramatically improve students' reading scores.[14]

What role do these theories play in the classroom? Deficit theory teaches us that groups bring different experiences and values to the classroom, and some of these differences do not mesh with mainstream school culture. Mainstream society terms this mismatch a deficit. The economic poverty of some groups contributes to such deficits, an issue that many believe should be addressed by the larger society. Expectation theory teaches us the power of teacher attitudes, that the attitudes you bring to the classroom influence your students, for better or worse. Cultural difference theory teaches us the rich nature of the human experience and how much we can teach each other. This chapter is intended to do just that: help us appreciate each other.

From the Melting Pot to Cultural Pluralism

FOCUS QUESTION 3

How do phrases like "melting pot" and "cultural pluralism" both capture and mask American identity?

Start a discussion about cultural, racial, or ethnic differences at a social gathering—or even more challenging, in a work environment—and feel the tension grow as competing theories of group differences emerge. Introduce issues like affirmative action, immigration laws, classes being taught in Spanish or Laotian, or racial profiling, and some people become unglued. More than a few people will listen politely, carefully avoiding uttering a sound. Some might stay silent but wonder if the conversation is genuine or simply an attempt at "political correctness." Others, articulating beliefs they perceive as acceptable, may voice hopeful insights, but in their heart of hearts, they themselves do not believe them. A few may say things they will later regret, words that may spark an attack, or a charge of racism:

> "Why don't they learn to speak English? My grandparents had nothing, but they learned the language. Are people today too lazy or do they simply not care?"

> "I am fine with racial equality. I like it as a concept. I just wonder why all my friends are my race."

> "I treat all people the same, but some groups have a chip on their shoulder."

Provide Groups Separate Instruction By . . .

GENDER, TO FOCUS ON SPECIFIC ACADEMIC NEEDS

Same-gender classes help students focus on academics, not on each other. Girls can get extra encouragement in math and science; boys can get special assistance in reading and language arts.

COMMUNITY, TO PROMOTE RACIAL AND ETHNIC PRIDE

Let's eliminate the alienation caused by busing students out of their neighborhood. Students feel accepted and take pride in local schools, where they can study with friends and learn from a curriculum that reflects and honors their heritage.

RELIGION, TO ENCOURAGE SACRED OBSERVANCES

Secular American school norms and laws force all religious groups to make compromises. Some religious holidays are ignored, adult-led prayer in school is prohibited, school dress codes may conflict with religious requirements, and schools routinely ignore religious dietary law. By educating religious groups separately, different histories and beliefs can be honored and practiced. Students can pray as they like and pursue their religion without ridicule or taunting from peers, or interference from civil authorities.

NEED, TO PROTECT LGBT STUDENTS

Special schools can help LGBT students cope with their unique personal and academic circumstances. Being with LGBT students protects them from comparisons and ridicule that might exist elsewhere.

Teaching All Children Together Promotes . . .

GENDER EQUALITY

Learning and succeeding together in the classroom prepares boys and girls to live and work together as adults. Equitable instruction and curriculum will teach students how to eliminate traditional gender barriers in society.

CULTURAL AND RACIAL UNDERSTANDING

We must not allow our nation to be fractured along racial, ethnic, and class lines. Integrating children of different backgrounds mirrors our ideal of a democratic society. Cross-cultural classrooms enrich the learning experience.

RESPECT AND UNDERSTANDING OF RELIGIOUS DIFFERENCES

Religious practices are the domain of religious institutions and should not become the focal point of school life. Learning *about* different religions can help all of us to grow. Restricting each of us to one set of beliefs will eventually divide and separate Americans. By learning together, students gain valuable lessons as they prepare to live and work together as adults in a vibrant and diverse democracy. We see all too well in other countries how religion and government can create problems.

SAFETY AND HOPE FOR LGBT STUDENTS

Attending a regular school gives all students insight into more different lifestyles. Learning together as children can help us all live together as adults.

---

www.mhhe.com/sadker10e

YOU DECIDE . . .

Do you believe equal educational opportunity is best achieved in separate or integrated classrooms? Is your position consistent or does it vary depending upon the identified group? Extend this *You Be the Judge* feature by developing the arguments for either integrating or separating two other groups discussed in this chapter (or identify new groups).

Start a discussion about cultural, racial, or ethnic differences at a social gathering, and you may wish you never did.

Many of us continue to live in silence about race and ethnicity. As a nation, we have yet to come to terms with our multicultural society. Many believe that the United States is a wondrous melting pot where the Statue of Liberty opens her arms to all the world's immigrants. This was the image painted by Israel Zangwill in a 1910 play that coined the term *melting pot*.

> America is God's Crucible, the Great Melting Pot where all races of Europe are melting and reforming . . . Germans and Frenchmen, Irishman and Englishmen, Jews and Russians—into the Crucible with you all! God is making the American . . . The real American has not yet arrived. He is only in the Crucible, I tell you—he will be the fusion of all races, the coming superman.[15]

For many, "melting in" became a reality. Groups incorporated into the mainstream culture are said to have gone through **assimilation** or **enculturation.** Countless immigrants today cling to this idea of being transformed into a new citizen, a new person, an American. But the melting pot image, although enticing, describes only a part of the American reality.

Picture yourself traveling in another country and a person who has never been to America asks you to describe your country—how would you do it? Would you describe our great West, its majestic Rockies and mysterious deserts? Or perhaps you would choose South Beach in Miami, a city with a 1940s art deco feel and a beach at its doorstep. Or perhaps New York City catches your fancy, with its breathtaking skyscrapers, its world-class museums, and the wonders of Broadway theaters. Some of you might paint a picture of the magnificent Maine coast, or the rich Midwest farmlands, the pristine Alaskan wilderness, or perhaps the lush Hawaiian Islands. Okay, we will stop here because suddenly we are feeling an urge to travel. You probably already appreciate our point: A fair description of our nation would include all its diverse regions, from coast to coast.

Now, let's change the question, and imagine that you are asked not to describe America but to describe an American. How would you do it? Would you resort to the melting pot image: a white European, perhaps arriving penniless and now a rich American? Or perhaps you would take the question quite literally and describe our Native Americans, our many different Indian tribes. Or better yet, we hope that you have learned the lesson from the first question. Not only is our nation geographically diverse, our people are diverse as well. Americans live in communities called Germantown and Chinatown, maintaining traditions from their land of origin. Americans have dark skins, but they also have light skins, and every shade in between. They speak Spanish and Arabic, pray to Buddha and Christ, or perhaps look for spiritual answers in their own hearts, like the Quakers. What do we call this diversity? This is **cultural pluralism,** a recognition that some groups, voluntarily or involuntarily, have maintained their culture and their language. We now recognize that there are many kinds of Americans, and like geographic diversity, they make our nation diverse and beautiful. Different groups teach us different ways of seeing and understanding the world. As we learn to appreciate one another's experiences and viewpoints, our nation grows not only stronger but also wiser.

Schools are one of the portals where diverse Americans meet. It is a place where we can learn from one another. Teachers are the gatekeepers to that learning. If they are open to other cultures and peoples, they and their students will learn and grow.

Bilingual Education

What is going on in America? It is amazing, and disturbing, to ride on a road and see street signs that are printed not only in English but in other languages as well. What's more, even legal documents are now being written in foreign languages. How unnerving to walk down an American street and not understand what people are talking about. Maybe this isn't America. I feel like a stranger in my own land. Why don't they learn to speak English?

Sound like a stroll through today's Miami, or San Diego, or perhaps San Antonio? Good try, but you not only have the wrong city, you are also in the wrong century. Benjamin Franklin expressed this view in the 1750s.[16] He was disgruntled that Philadelphia had printed so many things, including street signs, in another language (German, in this case). Even the Articles of Confederation were published in German as well as English, and children were taught in Dutch, Italian, and Polish.

In some bilingual education programs, English is learned as a second language while the student takes other academic work in his or her native language.

Bilingual education in the United States is hundreds of years old, hardly a "new" issue. In 1837, Pennsylvania law required that school instruction be given on an equal basis in German as well as English. In fact, that example provides us with a fairly concise definition of **bilingual education**, the use of two languages for instruction. But, almost a century later, as the United States was being pulled into World War I, foreign languages were seen as unpatriotic. Public pressure routed the German language from the curriculum, although nearly one in four high school students was studying the language at the time. Individual states went even further. Committed to a rapid assimilation of new immigrants, and suspicious of much that was foreign, these states prohibited the teaching of *any* foreign language during the first eight years of schooling. (The Supreme Court found this policy not only xenophobic but unconstitutional as well, in *Meyer* v. *State of Nebraska,* 1923.)[17]

FOCUS QUESTION 4
What are the political and instructional issues surrounding bilingual education?

Despite the long history of bilingual education in this country, many school districts never really bought into the concept. In districts without bilingual education, students with a poor command of English had to sink or swim (or perhaps, more accurately, "speak or sink"). Students either learned to speak English as they sat in class, or they failed school, an approach sometimes referred to as **language submersion**. If submersion was not to their liking, they could choose to leave school. Many did. Congress responded with the Bilingual Education Act in 1968, providing financial incentives, what some people call "a carrot approach," to encourage schools to initiate bilingual education programs. Not all districts chased the carrot.

During the early 1970s, disillusioned parents initiated lawsuits. In 1974, the Supreme Court heard the case of ***Lau v. Nichols.*** This class action lawsuit centered around Kinney Lau and 1,800 other Chinese students from the San Francisco area who were failing their courses because they could not understand English. The Court unanimously affirmed that federally funded schools must "rectify the language deficiency" of students. Teaching students in a language they did not understand was not an appropriate education. The Court's decision in *Lau* v. *Nichols* prompted the U.S. Department of Education Office of Civil Rights to issue the "*Lau* Remedies," guidelines for school districts that specify that "language minority students should be taught academics in their primary language until they could effectively benefit from English language instruction."[18] Under this provision, school districts must take positive steps to eliminate language barriers to learning.

GLOBAL VIEW
Xenophobia generally means fear and hatred of strangers or foreigners. Worldwide xenophobic actions (by individuals, groups, and governments) are all too common. What contemporary or historic events can you name that demonstrate this worldwide xenophobia? How does xenophobia manifest in our nation?

Profile in Education   Carlos Julio Ovando

Why am I not allowed to speak Spanish at school? Why do Mexican students seem ashamed of speaking Spanish? Am I stupid for not learning English quickly so that I can do the assignments? Why are there no teachers who look like me and who share my culture and language? And why did my parents leave the warmth and comfort of Central America for the indifference and coldness of the United States?[a]

It was 1955. **Carlos Julio Ovando** had emigrated from Nicaragua and was anxious to show his teachers what he knew. But educationally disenfranchised by his linguistic and cultural background, he could not.

The promise of religious freedom and economic stability had motivated the Ovando family's move to Corpus Christi, Texas. In Nicaragua, the Somoza dictatorship opposed the vigorous attempts of Ovando's father, a former priest turned Protestant minister, to convert Catholics. The family was exiled. Yet, their Latin American heritage remained strong. Even after the Ovandos emigrated, Nicaraguan cultural traditions continued in the Ovando home and discussions of spiritual values were central to the family's daily life.

Whereas home was a cultural touchstone for Ovando, school was foreign territory. Unable to understand the lessons in English, he felt abandoned. At age 14, Carlos was placed in the sixth grade and wondered, "Why do teachers show little interest in who I am?" In Nicaragua, the family was entrusted with home life and the school took care of the academic lessons. But school was clearly not working for Carlos.

> I do not recall my parents ever asking to see my report cards or expressing interest in visiting my school to talk to my teachers about my progress. As in the case with many other newly arrived immigrants, it may be that while tacitly interested in my academic well-being, my parents did not know how or were afraid to approach the unfamiliar American schools.[b]

Disconnected from school and doubtful of his own abilities, Ovando was experiencing education that was not so much immersion as submersion, the classic "sink or swim" approach, and Ovando was sinking, looking at America from the bottom of the pool. Ironically, a different kind of pool, a pool hall, proved to be the turning point in his life.

> The turning point in my academic career began when somebody in the church congregation saw me coming out of a pool hall and told my father. Soon after that, in the hope of saving me from sin, my father sent me to a Mennonite high school in northern Indiana.[c]

At the new school, a teacher saw Ovando in an entirely different way. Not so much English challenged, as Spanish blessed. He affirmed Ovando's Latin American roots and championed his native linguistic talent. Spurred by his teacher's encouragement, Ovando rediscovered confidence in his academic abilities. Rather than being punished for speaking Spanish, he was acclaimed for his language talents. He won honors, including college scholarships. Ovando now reveled in the world of ideas. He taught Spanish in a Midwest high school before going on to college teaching and writing.

His work shows how language is much more than a set of words and grammar rules: It can be a cultural link for students, one that promotes academic achievement. Whereas critics see bilingual education as a threat to national identity, Ovando envisions a society built on the strengths of its diverse population. He challenges teachers to unlock each student's cultural touchstones: "Pedagogy that activates the student voice and embraces the local community provides a much richer environment for student understanding than pedagogy that treats students as if they were empty vessels into which knowledge is to be poured."[d]

[a] Adapted from Carlos J. Ovando and Virginia P. Collier, *Bilingual and ESL Classrooms: Teaching in Multicultural Contexts,* 2nd ed. (Boston: McGraw-Hill, 1998), p. 2.
[b] Ibid, p. 2.
[c] Ibid, p. 3.
[d] Ibid, p. 24.

To learn more about Carlos Julio Ovando, click on *Profiles in Education.*

www.mhhe.com/sadker10e

REFLECTION: How is the history of bilingual education in America reflected in Ovando's story? What is the downside of promoting a monolingual society? How do you explain the popularity of the effort to make English the "official language" in the United States? Why has the maintenance approach encountered so much difficulty? If you were to teach a student like Ovando, how could you tackle these linguistic and cultural challenges?

FIGURE 3.2

The Distribution of English Language Learners.

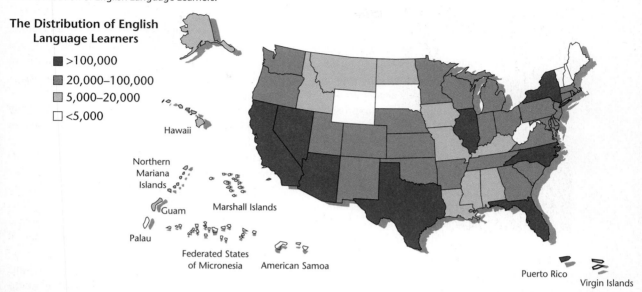

The Distribution of English Language Learners

- ■ >100,000
- ■ 20,000–100,000
- ▨ 5,000–20,000
- ☐ <5,000

Hawaii

Northern Mariana Islands

Guam

Palau

Marshall Islands

Federated States of Micronesia

American Samoa

Puerto Rico

Virgin Islands

SOURCE: U.S. Department of Education, OELA, www.ed.gov; National Clearinghouse for English Language Acquisition, Washington, DC, May 2010, www.ncela.gwu.edu/files/uploads/9/growingLEP_0708.pdf.

REFLECTION: What are the implications of this demographic on your life in the classroom? How can your teacher preparation help you prepare to teach ELL students?

Bilingual Education Models

More than 5 million **English language learners (ELLs)** are enrolled in public elementary and secondary schools (nearly 10 percent of school enrollment), and the number is steadily increasing (see Figure 3.2). About half of these non-English-speaking youngsters are from families that have recently come to the United States. Surprisingly, many ELL students were born in this country but have not yet learned English at home or in their community. About one in five school-age children speak a language other than English at home, with Spanish the most common.[19] As these non-English-speaking students enter schools, most will need to make sense of a new language, a new culture, and possibly new ways of interacting with teachers and classmates. Teachers can greatly assist this transition by creating a stable classroom environment.

English language learners typically work to master English and academic content. Several models of bilingual education help students reach these goals. These models vary in ease of implementation and effectiveness and often reflect the underlying philosophy of a local community or state. These philosophies fall along the continuum of cultural assimilation (immersion and ESL models) to cultural pluralism (maintenance and dual language methods).[20]

Typically in bilingual education programs, English language learners acquire English as a second language while taking other academic subjects in their native language. The **transitional approach** uses the native language as a bridge to English language instruction. Academic subjects are first taught using the native language, but progressively students transition to English, their new language. Cultural assimilation is often stressed. The goal is to prepare for English-only classrooms, typically within two to three years. The **maintenance** or **developmental approach** is designed to help children develop academic skills in both their native language and English.

Instruction occurs in both languages to create a truly bilingual student. An ideal maintenance program provides **dual-language instruction** from kindergarten through twelfth grade, although few exist at the secondary level. Students develop cognitively in both languages, learning about the culture and history of their ethnic group as well as that of the dominant culture. This two-way bilingual education adapts the maintenance approach to develop the language abilities of ELLs *and* their English-speaking peers. For example, children who speak Spanish are placed in the same class with children who speak English, and students learn each other's languages and work academically in both languages.

In the **immersion** approach, instruction is exclusively in English. Immersion cannot truly be considered bilingual but is used with ELLs nonetheless. Teachers using an immersion model often understand the students' native language but deliver lessons in a "sheltered" or simplified English vocabulary that attempts to familiarize students with English while learning academic content. **English as a Second Language (ESL)** supplements immersion programs by providing special pullout classes for additional instruction in reading and writing English. The goal is to assimilate learners into the English language as quickly as possible. While research suggests that English-only instruction is not as cognitively effective as sound bilingual programs, ESL instruction may work well for students highly motivated to be part of a mainstreamed English-only classroom.[21]

Language submersion is an extreme example of immersion. Submersion places students in classes where only English is spoken, and instruction is not modified at all. It is fundamentally a "sink or swim" approach.

The Bilingual Controversy

As schools struggle to meet the needs of ELL students, bilingual education continues to spark political controversy. Millions of students speak hundreds of languages and dialects, including not only Spanish but also Mandarin, French, Hmong, Urdu, Russian, Polish, Korean, Tagalog, and Swahili. Misunderstandings are multiplied when language barriers are accompanied by racial and ethnic differences, leading to even greater isolation and segregation for many ELL students. While some struggle to make bilingual education work, others believe that it never will.

Many people worry that bilingual education threatens the status of English as the nation's primary vehicle of communication. As a result, an **English-only movement** has emerged. (See Figure 3.3.) Those who support this movement feel that English is a unifying national bond that preserves our common culture. They believe that English should be the only language used or spoken in public and that the purpose of bilingual education should be to quickly teach English to ELL students. It is not surprising that the Bilingual Education Act of 1968 expired in 2002 and was not renewed, and many programs today emphasize rapid transition into English.

Bilingual education advocates argue that the United States is a mosaic of diverse cultures, that diversity should be honored and nurtured, and that mastery of several languages will pay economic dividends for our country in the competitive global economy.[22] One problem, they point out, is that we simply do not have enough competent bilingual teachers who can respond to the large numbers of ELL children now in our schools. They argue that it is unfair to blame bilingual education for the slow progress some students are making. Achieving proficiency in any second language can take years.[23] Bilingual advocates oppose the English-only movement, and they feel that it promotes intolerance, will turn back the clock, and may very well be unconstitutional. Education writer James Crawford points out, "It is certainly more respectable to discriminate by language than by race. . . . Most people are not sensitive to language discrimination in this nation, so it is easy to argue that you're doing someone a favor by making them speak English."[24]

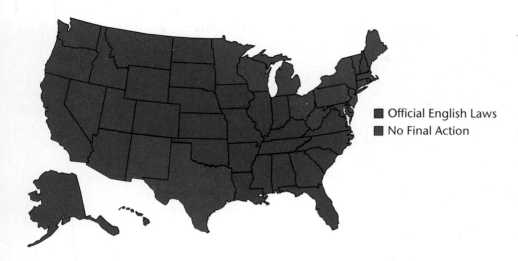

FIGURE 3.3
States with official English
language laws.

SOURCE: U.S. English, Inc. (2012),
Washington, DC.

REFLECTION: Do you
see any pattern in which
states have passed this
law? Does this influence
your decision as to
where you might want
to teach? Do you believe
such English-only laws
have any practical
impact?

- Official English Laws
- No Final Action

Alabama (1990)	Illinois (1969)	Nebraska (1920)
Alaska (1998)	Indiana (1984)	New Hampshire (1995)
Arizona (2006)	Iowa (2002)	North Carolina (1987)
Arkansas (1987)	Kansas (2007)	North Dakota (1987)
California (1986)	Kentucky (1984)	Oklahoma (2010)
Colorado (1988)	Louisiana (1812)	South Carolina (1987)
Florida (1988)	Massachusetts (1975)	South Dakota (1995)
Georgia (1986 & 1996)	Mississippi (1987)	Tennessee (1984)
Hawaii (1978)	Missouri (1998 & 2008)	Utah (2000)
Idaho (2007)	Montana (1995)	Virginia (1981 & 1996)
		Wyoming (1996)

Research on Bilingual Education

What does the research say about the effectiveness of bilingual education? Educators are just now beginning to analyze long-term data, and they are uncovering some useful findings. In one case, the researchers found that when language-minority students spend more time learning in their native language, they are more likely to achieve at comparable and even higher levels in English.[25] Another study found that the earlier a student starts learning a new language, the more effective that language becomes in an academic setting.[26] Yet another study showed that no single approach holds a monopoly on success, and different approaches to bilingual education can each be effective, suggesting that local school systems should carefully select the programs and teachers most appropriate for their communities.[27]

One major bilingual study, directed by Virginia Collier and Wayne Thomas, evaluated the experiences of 42,000 students over a thirteen-year period. Early findings suggested that students enrolled in well-implemented bilingual programs actually *outperform* students in monolingual programs. One successful approach assumed bilingual education to be a two-way street, one in which English speakers and ELL students would learn from each other. In this model, during the Spanish part of the day, the Spanish-speaking students explained the lessons to native-English peers, while during English instruction, the reverse took place. Collier and Thomas report that, by fourth grade, the students in these two-way classes had actually outperformed the native English speakers who attended English-only classes.[28] This study suggests that if our teachers could competently teach in two languages, academic achievement for all students might increase, along with all students becoming bilingual—now isn't that a remarkable possibility?

Teaching Tip

ENGLISH LANGUAGE LEARNERS

Here are several strategies for teaching English language learners:

- **Get to know your students, and when possible, use their backgrounds to make connections to the material being learned.** Creating a comfortable and safe classroom climate for your students despite the language and culture differences is an important first step. By connecting to their backgrounds, you will help ELL students feel that their new classroom culture is less alien and distant.

- **Give explicit directions, emphasize key words, and offer concrete examples to enhance the understanding of ELL students.** Simple strategies such as emphasizing key words, offering examples of your main points, and using visuals such as the chalkboard, flash cards, games, graphics, and puzzles can increase the understanding of ELL students.

- **Plan for and expect the active involvement of ELL students.** It is a good idea to call on all students to keep their attention and focus. ELL students are no exception. A preferred strategy is to ask a question before calling out a specific name so that all students have time to consider their answer. Feel free to use a variety of questioning strategies, but avoid rhetorical questions, because ELL students may not understand them. Waiting a bit longer for students to respond will give ELL students more time to process the question in their new language.

- **Do not depend simply on verbal, teacher-centered learning, but incorporate a variety of instructional strategies.** Hands-on activities, cooperative learning groups, and other strategies will help ELL students develop their language skills and learn new information through avenues other than teacher talk.

- **Always provide time to check for understanding and be sure to provide precise and immediate feedback.** Unlearning the wrong word or behavior is more difficult than learning it correctly the first time. Monitoring and offering clear feedback can eliminate the need to unlearn and relearn.

REFLECTION: Although these skills are designed for ELL students, how might they enhance your teaching effectiveness for all students?

More than two centuries ago, Ben Franklin expressed his fears about the multiple languages heard on America's streets. His concerns have echoed through the centuries, despite a world in which national borders seem to be blurring or even disappearing. In today's global community, Russians and Americans are working together in space, such international organizations as the United Nations and NATO are expanding their membership, and corporations are crossing national boundaries to create global mergers in an international marketplace. Moreover, technological breakthroughs, such as the Internet, have made international communications not just possible but commonplace. However, for most Americans, these international conversations are viable only if the other side speaks English. In this new international era, Americans find themselves locked in a monolingual society. How strange that, instead of viewing those who speak other languages as welcome assets to our nation, some seem eager to erase linguistic diversity.

Multicultural Education

GLOBAL VIEW

With English as the most common second language in the world (and the language of international business, air travel, and technology), why do today's educators need bilingual skills?

Students in many urban and suburban schools speak scores of languages. In some urban communities, students of color comprise 70 to more than 90 percent of school enrollment. A successful teacher in these communities will need to bridge possible racial, cultural, and language differences. In fact, even in very stable, overwhelmingly white school districts where all students share apparently similar backgrounds and are native speakers, cross-cultural knowledge is important. Many of these students will graduate, leave these communities, and work and live in more diverse areas. The success of their transition may depend on what they learned—or did not learn—in school. Moreover, communities that appear uniform and static may have differences in religion, social class, gender, and sexuality. The controversial question facing the nation: how best to teach our multicultural students?

FOCUS QUESTION 5

What are the purposes and approaches of multicultural education?

The Multiculturalism Debate

You enter teaching in a time of harsh and divisive "culture wars," as people argue about how diversity should be recognized in schools.[29] Some worry that overemphasizing diversity may pull us apart and fear that multiculturalism will lead to a Dis-United States. Adversaries of multiculturalism point to Yugoslavia and Czechoslovakia, nations dissolved by the power of ethnic differences. They argue for a uniform national identity and urge schools to promote one set of common beliefs based on our English and European traditions. In their eyes, time spent teaching about different cultures poses a double threat: pulling apart the national fabric while taking time from important academic subjects like math and reading. They would prefer that students focus on academic achievement and adopt what they see as core values of the United States.

Others claim that multiculturalism is the nation's future. They believe that schools can no longer ignore or devalue cultural and ethnic differences, either in this country or throughout the world. National demographics are changing, and schools must recognize these changes. They argue that current practices are failing in their mission to unite and educate all our students equitably and point to statistics like these to underscore their point:[30]

- Although schools were ordered to desegregate in the 1954 *Brown* decision, since the 1980s, schools have been resegregating.
- Since the 1990s, the segregation of students of every racial group has increased.
- Nationally, Asian Americans are more likely than students of other races to attend multiracial schools.
- White students are the least likely to attend multiracial schools and are the most isolated group.
- More than three-quarters of intensely segregated schools are also high-poverty schools.
- High school graduation rates are around 70 percent, and in many communities only 50 or 60 percent of Hispanic American, African American, and Native American students are graduating from high school.

Is multicultural education part of the answer to these troubling statistics? Perhaps multiculturalism itself, specifically Eastern thought, can offer an answer. A sacred belief of the Hindu religion is "We are one," that all humans are connected. A second Hindu truth is "Honor one another," emphasizing the importance of appreciating our differences. These Hindu beliefs are held simultaneously and are not viewed as mutually exclusive. Perhaps the key to moving ahead and avoiding yet another culture war is for us to learn balance, to honor our national commonalities as we celebrate our group and individual differences.

Approaches to Multicultural Education

When multiculturalism began, the focus was on fighting racism. Over time, these programs expanded to confront not only racism, but also injustices based on gender, social class, disability, and sexual orientation. Today, there are many dimensions to **multicultural education,** including (1) *expanding the curriculum* to reflect America's diversity; (2) *using teaching strategies* that are responsive to different learning styles; (3) *supporting the multicultural competence* *of teachers* so they are comfortable and knowledgeable working with students and families of different cultures; and (4) *a commitment to social justice,* promoting efforts to work and teach toward local and global equity.

Multiculturalism has come to mean different things to different educators.[31] Some focus on *human relations,* activities that promote cultural and racial understanding among different groups. Others teach *single-group studies,* which you may know as Black Studies, Hispanic Studies, or Women's Studies programs. Some educators believe multicultural education is all about creating close links between home and school so that minority children can succeed academically, an approach termed *teaching the culturally different.* Another tack, called simply *multicultural,* promotes different perspectives based on race, class, and culture; in a sense, developing new eyes through which students learn. And finally, the *multicultural reconstructionist* approach mobilizes students to examine and work to remediate social injustices. As you can see, multicultural education can mean different things to different people.

James Banks focuses specifically on developing a multicultural curriculum.[32] Banks believes that one way to achieve greater understanding and more positive attitudes toward different groups is to integrate and broaden the curriculum to make it more inclusive and action oriented. He defines four approaches to a multicultural curriculum that are related to several proposed by others[33] (Figure 3.4). As you read each description, consider if any of these approaches were used in your own schooling.

1. Multicultural education often begins with the *contributions approach,* in which the study of ethnic heroes (for example, Sacagawea, Rosa Parks, or Booker T. Washington) is included in the curriculum. At this superficial contributions level, one might also find "food and festivals" being featured or holidays such as Cinco de Mayo being described or celebrated.

2. In the *additive approach,* a unit or course is incorporated, often but not always during a "special" week or month. February has become the month to study African Americans, and March has been designated "Women's History Month." Although these dedicated weeks and months offer a respite from the typical curricular material, no substantial change is made to the curriculum as a whole.

3. In the *transformation approach,* the entire Eurocentric nature of the curriculum is changed. Students are taught to view events and issues from diverse ethnic and cultural perspectives. For instance, the westward expansion of Europeans can be seen as manifest destiny through the eyes of European descendants or as an invasion from the east through the eyes of Native Americans.

4. The fourth level, *social action,* goes beyond the transformation approach. Students not only learn to view issues from multiple perspectives, but also become directly involved in solving related problems. At this level, a school would address social and economic needs here and abroad, advocate human rights and peace, and work to ensure that the school building and activities did not harm the environment. Rather than political passivity, the typical by-product of many curricular programs, this approach promotes decision making and social action to achieve multicultural goals and a more vibrant democracy.

Multicultural education also seeks to help all students develop more positive attitudes toward different racial, ethnic, cultural, and religious groups. According to a 1990s survey of more than 1,000 young people between the ages of 15 and 24 conducted by People for the American Way, most respondents felt their attitudes toward race relations were healthier than those of their parents. Yet about half described the state of race relations in the United States as generally bad. Fifty-five percent of African Americans and whites said they were "uneasy" rather than "comfortable" in dealing with members of the other racial group.[34] If you are

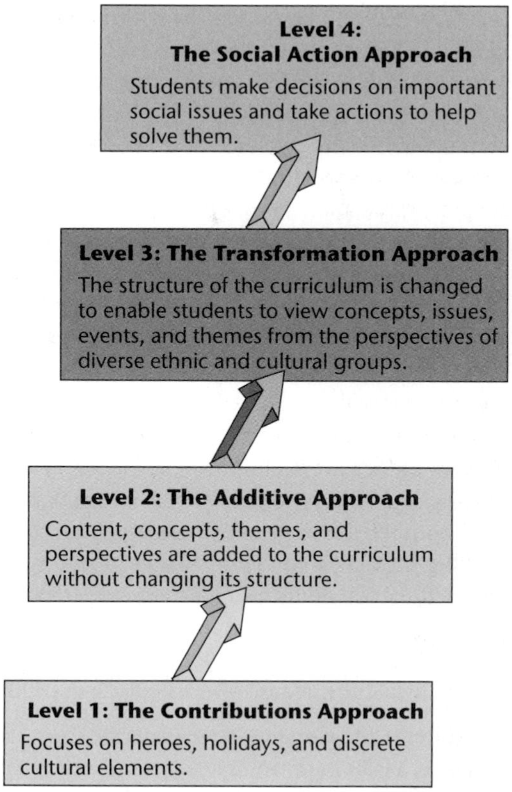

**Level 4:
The Social Action Approach**
Students make decisions on important social issues and take actions to help solve them.

Level 3: The Transformation Approach
The structure of the curriculum is changed to enable students to view concepts, issues, events, and themes from the perspectives of diverse ethnic and cultural groups.

Level 2: The Additive Approach
Content, concepts, themes, and perspectives are added to the curriculum without changing its structure.

Level 1: The Contributions Approach
Focuses on heroes, holidays, and discrete cultural elements.

FIGURE 3.4
Banks's approach to multicultural education.

> **REFLECTION:** Think back to your own schooling. At which of Banks's levels would you place your own multicultural education? Provide supporting evidence. As a teacher, which of these levels do you want to reach and teach? Explain.

thinking that the 1990s were a while ago, and perhaps things have changed since then, they have not. The 2008 presidential elections gave the entire nation a chance to talk about race, and perhaps learn more, but if the media is any indication, that conversation did not happen. Although most Americans took pride in electing a multiracial president, the media gave little in-depth coverage to race. "Black and white people have a different notion of the need to talk about race," notes *Chicago Tribune* reporter Clarence Page. Ninety-two percent of journalists reported that when it came to covering race relations, the media was not doing its job effectively.[35]

   Another indication of how slowly we are dealing with the race issue is school desegregation. Students are more segregated today than any time since the Civil Rights movement.[36] Segregated housing patterns and federal courts no longer willing to attend to this problem have left most American schoolchildren segregated by race and class, and ignorant of one another's cultures, languages, and experiences. How to encourage students to become more "comfortable" with one another depends at least in part on the skills and insights the teacher brings to the classroom, what some term *culturally responsive teaching.*

Culturally Responsive Teaching

A key assumption of multicultural education is that students learn in different ways and that effective teachers recognize and respond to these differences. **Culturally responsive teaching** focuses on the learning strengths of students and mediates the frequent mismatch between home and school cultures. **Gloria Ladson-Billings,** a professor at the University of Wisconsin, offers a powerful example of culturally relevant teaching. She wanted to find out what behaviors make some teachers successful with African American children, while others are not. She

FOCUS QUESTION 6
Why is culturally responsive teaching important?

asked parents and principals in four schools serving primarily African American students to nominate "excellent teachers," teachers they would rate as successful. As you might expect, principals chose teachers who had low numbers of discipline referrals, high attendance rates, and high standardized test scores. Parents, on the other hand, selected teachers who were enthusiastic, respectful, and understood that students need to operate in both the white world and their local community. Nine teachers, white and black, made both lists, and eight of them agreed to participate in her study. After several years of observations and interviews, she was baffled: their personalities, teaching strategies, and styles were entirely different; there seemed to be no common patterns. She was close to throwing in the towel when she finally saw the subtle, but striking, commonalities.

First, all of these eight teachers had chosen to teach in these more challenging schools and felt responsible for the academic success of each student. Second, they were sensitive to race discrimination in society; they actively fought bias and prejudice and wanted their students to do the same. For example, some of these teachers had students rewrite out-of-date textbooks or work on projects to improve their community. And finally, the teachers viewed both the home and school as connected and seized opportunities to learn from their neighborhoods. They honored the crafts and traditions in the community, inviting parents to share traditional cooking in the school. One teacher allowed students to use "home English" in class but required that students also master Standard English. Students were expected to learn both languages well. Teachers realized that they, too, were learners and needed to be open to new information. Gloria Ladson-Billings developed three promising culturally responsive principles for teaching not only African American children, but also others:[37]

1. **Students must experience academic success, which leads to a stronger self-esteem. Esteem is built on solid academic accomplishment.** We intuitively know that students who do not feel good about themselves have a tough time in (and beyond) school. But this is not enough. For school success, students' self-esteem needs to be built on solid academic accomplishment. Teachers must create lessons that are responsive to student learning styles *and* allow student mastery of the basic knowledge and skills necessary for success in today's society. The bottom line: Students feel good about themselves when there is real academic progress.

2. **Students should develop and maintain cultural competence, and the student's home culture is an opportunity for learning.** Too many teachers have been taught only about classroom teaching skills and not about community outreach possibilities. Ladson-Billings's research teaches us that we must expand our concept of the classroom to include the community. When there is friction between school and home, academic progress suffers. Put more positively, when teachers move beyond their classroom and integrate learning with the local community, they can create a more positive, seamless, and mutually supportive academic environment. For example, a local African storyteller can visit the class and relate an African folktale. Students could use the experience as a springboard for their writing or drawing. Or a local politician could be invited to class to share his or her public service work, challenging students to develop their own vision of community service and social activism. Following the presentation, students might do just that: organize a class project to improve the quality of community life. Identifying community resources and connecting classroom activities to those resources are key-stones to creating a fruitful academic climate for students.

3. **Students must develop critical consciousness and actively challenge social injustice.** A culturally relevant teacher needs to do more than connect with student needs and the local community; a culturally relevant teacher also works to improve the quality of life in the school and community. Do you remember the disconnect you may have felt among

life in school, the world you read about in textbooks, and "the real world" you lived in? Schools too often live in a sanitized bubble, separate from the world's problems. Culturally relevant teachers break that bubble and, along with their students, work to improve the quality of life. For instance, if school textbooks are weak and dated, a teacher might encourage students to rewrite them. The result would be more realistic and current texts, as well as student practice in writing. Or perhaps there are serious health problems in the community. Students might volunteer to attract additional resources to the community health clinic and in the process learn how local government works. Confronting and eliminating real social problems is the third component of a culturally relevant classroom.

As you prepare to teach, it is helpful for you to consider what it means to be a culturally responsive teacher, to broaden your view of what it takes to be successful in the classroom. Let's take a moment to think about what this means for your own teacher preparation. To be competent in each of Ladson-Billings's three points, you will need to acquire certain skills, attitudes, and knowledge. What teaching *skills* will you need to be a culturally responsive teacher for all your students? You will want to diagnose different student needs and plan for different learning styles. You will want to develop critical thinking skills and include all your students in an equitable manner. You will even want to make certain that you can be silent and listen to the answers that are volunteered by all the students (a skill called "wait time"). Studies show that even teachers with the best of intentions too often fail to use these skills. (We describe equitable teaching skills later in this text in Chapter 11, "Becoming an Effective Teacher.")

What *attitudes* will you need to be a culturally responsive teacher? How do you approach teaching students whose background may be quite different from your own? Because most of us have grown up in a segregated community, there is an excellent chance that most of your friends are similar to you in race, class, and ethnicity. You probably share a common set of values and opinions, seeing the world through a lens forged in your own socialization. As you prepare to teach, you may want to make an extra effort to move out of your familiar milieu and seek different views. The more voices you hear, the more likely you will be able to appreciate different life experiences and develop attitudes that are accepting of people who at first glance may seem very different from you.

Finally, as you prepare to teach, you will want to acquire *knowledge* about different group experiences in order to be a culturally responsive teacher. You already bring to the classroom some knowledge of other groups, but this knowledge is limited, and some of it may be inaccurate. You will want to educate yourself about your future students and the educational implications of their cultural backgrounds. This chapter helps you move down that path. For example, many African American communities often emphasize aural and participatory learning over writing. If you ignore this insight and use only writing activities in class, student performance may suffer.[38] As another example, research suggests that many girls and women personalize knowledge and prefer learning through experience and first-hand observation.[39] Creating personal connections and examples may increase the success of your female students. In fact, responding to all types of student diversity is simply good teaching. A Head Start teacher in Michigan, in this case teaching poor, white, rural students, shares her view of culturally responsive teaching:

> I believe that it is my responsibility to learn as much as I can about the child's family and their culture and then implement that into my classroom, so that the child can see his/her culture is a part of our classroom and that I respect them and their family and their culture. It can be hard; I don't want to present any new stereotypes to these kids, so I ask the parents a lot of questions. Sometimes I get the answers and sometimes I don't, but at least they see I am trying.[40]

The challenge for teachers is to acquire useful and accurate cultural insights that help connect classroom and the culture, while avoiding the trap of stereotypic thinking. What's the difference between a useful cultural insight and a damaging stereotype? That critical distinction is explored in the next section.

Stereotypes

The way we use the terms stereotype and generalization can be very confusing, so let's try to be more precise. **Stereotypes** are absolute beliefs that all members of a group have a fixed set of characteristics. The word *stereotype* originated in the print shop. It is literally a type—a one-piece plate that repeats a pattern with no individuality. Today's cultural stereotypes also ignore individuality and are repeatedly applied to all members of a group. People who use stereotypes try to save time by short-circuiting the thinking process, just like the original stereotype saved time in the printing process. A set of characteristics with no qualifiers is attributed to individuals based on their membership in a group. Simplistic sentences are used with words like "all Hispanics are" and are applied to every member of the group without distinction. Actually, stereotypes are examples of sloppy thinking that undermine the critical reflection that we want our students to develop. For example, a stereotype might naively proclaim that Hispanics are poor students, Asians are math geniuses, Jews are wealthy, and African Americans are great athletes. Stereotypes are impervious to contradictory information. Find a poor Jew, a Hispanic with a doctorate, an Asian dropping out of school, or an unathletic African American and each is thought to be an anomaly, the exception to the rule. The rule, the stereotype, endures. Stereotypes not only hurt people, they block learning. Stereotypic thinking obstructs a search for new information—not just "contradictory" information, but any information that might add to the complex, rich understanding of an individual or a group. Stereotypes ignore nuances, qualifiers, and subtleties that might more accurately characterize the group. This willingness to engage in complex thinking is what students need; unfortunately, stereotypes short-circuit thoughtful reflection.

Stereotype Threat

Let's look at an example of how damaging stereotypes can be. Opinion polls suggest that about half of white America endorses common stereotypes about blacks and Hispanics, such as the belief that they are not very intelligent. Such stereotypes influence expectations and behaviors not only of whites who hold them, but also of blacks and Hispanics who must live in a society marked by such beliefs. For example, an African American called on in class realizes that an incorrect answer may confirm the stereotype of inferior intelligence. For this student, speaking in class can be risky. As you might imagine, the risk intensifies on high-stakes tests. Consider the following studies: African American and white college students were asked to take a difficult standardized verbal examination. In the control group, the test was presented in a typical way, as a measure of intelligence. In the experimental group, the students were told that ability was not being assessed; rather, the psychology of their verbal problem-solving was being researched. The two groups were matched so that student abilities, time to take the test, and the test itself were similar. In the nonthreatening experimental groups, black test takers solved about twice as many problems as the ones in the control group; the white students solved the same number in both groups. In a similar study, researchers found that simply asking students to record their race before taking a test had a similar devastating impact on black performance.[41]

This dramatic outcome has been termed **stereotype threat,** a measure of how social context, such as self-image, trust in others, and a sense of belonging, can influence academic performance. When an individual is aware of a stereo-type, he or she is more likely to behave like the stereo-type than if it did not exist. Studies indicate that students who care the most about their academic per-formance are the most vulnerable to stereotype threat. Stereotype threat may explain in part why African Americans (and others) perform better in college than their SAT scores predict, and why standardized test scores can be so misleading. Nor are blacks alone. Lati-nos on English tests, females on math tests, and elderly people on short-term memory tests also fall victim to stereotype threat. In fact, even students with strong test scores can fall prey. White male engineering students with very high SAT scores were told that their perfor-mance on a test would help researchers understand the math superiority of Asians. Hearing about the comparison to strong Asian students, their scores fell. None of us is immune from stereotype threat.

Consider these three stu-dents. On the basis of this photo, what assumptions do you make about them? Are those assumptions based on stereotypes?

Stereotypes limit students by teaching them that intellect is a fixed trait, that some groups are naturally brighter than others, and that their future was determined at birth. The belief that group differences are unchangeable is not a helpful construct for teachers. A person's intellect, like a person's brain, grows and changes. Human potential is amazing. If students see their brain and their intellect as muscles that can be taught to grow and become stronger, stereotype threat is diminished, and test scores rise.[42] Imagine the impact of stereotypes not only on intellectual performance, but also on other characteristics. Teaching also deals with ethics, values, and character of students, and damaging stereotypes can inhibit this learning as well. Fortunately, stereotype threat can be overcome with proper instruction.[43]

You can diminish stereotype threat by ensuring that your curriculum represents diversity across race, ethnicity, gender, religion, and socioeconomic class. Or perhaps you prefer to confront the problem directly: Explain stereotype threat in class and explore with your stu-dents strategies to neutralize it. The one thing you do not want to do is ignore the damage done by stereotype threat.

Generalizations

Generalizations recognize that there are trends over large numbers of people. Members of religious, racial, or ethnic groups share certain experiences and may share certain similari-ties. Generalizations offer insights, not hard and fast conclusions like stereotypes, and unlike a stereotype, a generalization does not assume that everyone in a group has a fixed set of char-acteristics. So the generalization that many Japanese value and seek higher education still holds if one encounters a Japanese dropout who dislikes school. The generalization is never intended to be applied to all; it is open to modification as new information is gathered, and there are always exceptions. Note that generalizations use words like "many," "often," or "tend to." Moreover, whereas stereotypes view people in one group or another, generalizations rec-ognize that people belong to many groups simultaneously. Some Jews are Hispanic, some are Asian, and some are Arab, yet they are all Jews.

Generalizations offer us a hunch or clue about a group, and sometimes these clues are useful in planning for teaching. When you begin teaching you may know very little about your students, and a generalization offers a useful starting point. Think of it as an educated guess. As you learn more and more about each student, you will realize which generalizations are appropriate and which are not.

www.mhhe.com/sadker10e

INTERACTIVE ACTIVITY

Multicultural Literacy. Match multicultural terms with their descriptions.

How can we use generalizations to develop culturally responsive teaching? Let's assume that a teacher has many Native American students in class; the teacher does some research and discovers that most Native American students prefer to learn in a cooperative group, valuing community and family over individual competition. Rather than teaching in the familiar teacher-centered manner, she modifies her plan and creates student groups to work on several academic topics. Using open-ended questions, she asks the groups to share their experiences, and patiently waits for each group response, realizing that Native American children may prefer to carefully consider their comments and compose their thoughts. When she can, the teacher uses natural phenomena in her explanations, because Native Americans often value both natural and supernatural forces. She may also integrate Indian words, symbols, or legends as appropriate. By building the learning on sharing rather than competition, and on valuing tribal experiences and beliefs, the teacher is increasing her chance of connecting with most of her students.[44] Because generalizations are flexible, the teacher is free to use a different approach with some or all of her students if she later discovers that they prefer a different learning style.

As you become a more experienced teacher, you will become more skilled at confronting all kinds of limiting stereotypes, developing useful teaching generalizations, and becoming a more culturally responsive teacher. In fact, let's start that process right now.

Today's Classroom

Consider yourself a teacher working with the nation's diverse students. If you are teaching in a community that reflects the nation's population, your class of 40 students might include[45]

17 white children

6 Hispanic children

6 children who do not speak English at home

5 poor children

5 African American children

1 Asian American child

FOCUS QUESTION 7

How can teachers use culturally responsive teaching strategies?

The class might also include a Jewish, Native American, or Arab heritage child, not to mention multiracial or biracial students. Although we lack firm statistics concerning the number of gay, lesbian, bisexual, or transgendered children, estimates are that perhaps two or three of your students would fall into those categories. Planning for this class is quite a challenge!

The reality is that hyper-segregation of our schools makes it unlikely that you will be teaching students from all these groups in the same class at the same time. Unlikely, but not impossible. And certainly, over time, you may teach many if not all of them.

Meet Your Seventh-Grade Class

In this section, we profile eight students, students similar to ones you may some day teach. Each student is from a cultural, an ethnic, a racial, or some other group, bringing to your class a rich history and different learning preferences. It is important to keep in mind that each student is an individual and that any generalizations you make initially may change over time. But for now, let's take step one of culturally responsive teaching and learn about our students. For each student, we ask you to identify a generalization that might influence your teaching and enhance learning. As you read each student's description, you will encounter hints about potential generalizations. You may want to draw on your own knowledge as well. When you teach, you will want to learn more about your students through reading and personal interactions. But for now, let's establish your baseline, what you know about groups as you begin your teacher education program, and what you will want to learn in the future.

This exercise is not simple. You may be pushed beyond your comfort zone, and formulating generalizations will be a demanding task. If you are baffled, venture your best guess. At the end of the section, we shall provide you with sample generalizations that should help you think in new and constructive ways.

We will start you off by suggesting a few generalizations for the first student, Lindsey Maria Riley, who is Navajo. Then you are on your own. Try to identify at least one generalization for each of the other students. Later in the section, you can compare your responses with our suggestions.[46] Now, meet (and begin thinking about) your students.

Lindsey Maria Riley (Navajo)

Lindsey grew up in a small, poor town in the Southwest. Although Lindsey did not live on a reservation, her family adhered to traditional Navajo ways. Lindsey followed tradition when not at school and spent time mostly with girls and women learning to cook, make pottery, and weave at an early age. Navajo boys would hunt, make tools, and live more physical lives, quite separate from the girls. Lindsey's family did not have a lot of money and received assistance for her school supplies from Save the Children, a nonprofit organization. Lindsey enjoyed the school she attended that was run by the Bureau of Indian Affairs. But this year, her family moved to your community and she is a new student in your class.

Most of the other students in your class have seen Indians only in movies, such as *The Last of the Mohicans,* or on television. Some of Lindsey's classmates believe that Indians lived a long time ago on the frontier and are surprised to learn they still exist. Some have heard their parents say that Indians make a fortune running casinos. But neither casinos nor movies explain Lindsey. And Lindsey does not explain herself—she does not talk much. The students in your class like Lindsey, although they haven't really "figured" her out. To put it politely, Lindsey is a curiosity to them.

You recently asked the class to write a brief report on a president for Presidents' Day. Lindsey never handed in her report. When you asked her about it, she said that all the presidents had done bad things to her people and that she would rather report on a different topic. Today, she told you that the school mascot, an Indian chief, bothers her.

Potentially Useful Generalization: _____

_____

_____

Sample Response
[Note: Native Americans are not one group but hundreds of tribal nations with different languages and beliefs. Learning about tribal distinctions is a useful first step for teachers and students.] In this sample response, we will offer you a series of possible and well-accepted generalizations, but there are others as well. If we do not mention your generalization, you may want to research it to see if you are correct.

Potentially Useful Generalization: Many tribes revere modesty. Group, rather than individual, recognition is typically preferred, as is cooperation over competition and patience rather than immediate gratification (qualities too often lost in contemporary classrooms). Additionally, visual and artistic learning and "hands-on learning" are valued by many tribal cultures. Using American Indian cultural beliefs and insights during a lesson can help Native American students feel connected to the academic program. The supernatural, intuition, and spiritual beliefs are valued by many tribes and could also be incorporated in classroom instruction.

[In terms of the casino-to-riches stereotype mentioned in the profile, less than 1 percent of Indians work in casinos, and the casino profits often go to schools and community improvement projects.]

Marcus Griffin (African American)

Marcus is in your class because of your school district's policy to voluntarily bus African American students from across the county line, a rare event these days. He lives with his mother, who works at the post office, about ten miles from school. His older brother never attended this school; in fact, he never graduated from high school. You hear rumors that he is in and out of trouble. Marcus has only a few friends in class, a situation made worse by the bus schedule. After his last class, he hurries to catch his bus for the long ride home. Because of this schedule, he cannot participate in after-school activities, sports, and clubs. Marcus's neighborhood friends do not really talk much about school. They do not like the fact that Marcus chooses to bus to a white community instead of hanging out with them. Marcus feels that he is growing further and further away from his roots.

Marcus loves reading and writing, but feels like an alien in his new school. Virtually everything he sees or reads in school is about the history, accomplishments, and interests of whites. Only rarely are his people discussed, and then it is not in a very positive light. Marcus finds the teachers in your school pretty serious, and he decides not to rock the boat by suggesting different ideas in class. There is only one African American teacher in your school and only a few black students. Marcus would like to go to college, but his family's finances are limited. Some of the black kids talk about going to college on an athletic scholarship, but Marcus is not very athletic. You wish that you could connect with him, but when you try, he rarely looks at you. Like several other students in your school, he sometimes interrupts in class, a habit you find annoying. You hope for the best for Marcus, but you are not optimistic.

Potentially Useful Generalization: _____

_____

_____

Ana Garcia (Mexican American)

Ana Garcia is one of the warmest and most involved students in your class. She is one of those students who actually hugs people, including you! She loves to ask questions, works closely with her peers, and seems eager to explore new topics. Her favorite topic is history. Ana loves doing class projects, yet she is quite modest about her work.

Although Ana was born in the United States, her parents, who work as laborers, emigrated from Mexico. Ana is the only one in her family who speaks any English, but most of the time she speaks Spanish with friends and family. Unfortunately, despite her motivation, Ana's English language skills lag behind those of her peers, and the gap seems to be widening. Because you do not speak Spanish, you suggest that she participate in some of the after-school activities where she might have more opportunities to work on her English. Ana listens to your advice, but explains that she goes right home after school to care for her younger siblings. Although Ana loves school, you get the sense that she is getting frustrated and is already focusing on her future family responsibilities and becoming a mother.

Potentially Useful Generalization: _____

_____

_____

A Closer Look — Myths about Culturally Responsive Teaching

Myth 1—Culturally responsive teaching is a new approach intended to meet the needs of poor, urban students of color. Teaching has always been culturally responsive, but primarily responsive to the values of white, Euro-American, middle-class students. That is why schools historically have emphasized individual success more than group success, strict adherence to time schedules, knowledge valued through analytical reasoning, self-sufficiency, and even dress codes. More inclusive culturally responsive teaching embraces the values and experiences of other cultures as well.

Myth 2—Only teachers of color can actually be culturally responsive to students of color. Race is not an obstacle to culturally responsive teaching; ignorance is. Through teacher training, teachers of any cultural background can gain the knowledge, skills, and attitudes needed to teach children from diverse cultures. In turn, because most teachers are white, they can share important lessons about the dominant culture.

Myth 3—Culturally responsive teaching is little more than a collection of teaching ideas and practices to motivate students of color. Culturally responsive teaching offers a new way of looking at the roles of teachers and students. Culturally relevant teachers are committed to valuing the experiences of their students and working toward a more just society, far more profound goals than simply a collection of teaching ideas.

Myth 4—Culturally relevant teachers must master all the critical details of many cultures. It is unrealistic to expect teachers to master the intricacies of many cultures. But over time, thoughtful teachers will abandon simplistic, stereotypic thinking as they gain insights into cultural differences that influence behavior and learning.

Myth 5—Culturally relevant teaching categorizes children, which feeds stereotypic thinking. Actually, culturally relevant teaching reduces stereotypic thinking by asking teachers to be reflective. They must consider student experiences and backgrounds, create teaching opportunities that respond to student learning styles, hold high expectations for all students, and help students experience academic success.

SOURCE: Adapted from Jacqueline Jordan and Beverley Jeanne Armento, *Culturally Responsive Teaching* (Boston: McGraw-Hill, 2001).

REFLECTION: Why do you think these myths are so prevalent? What additional myths about culturally relevant teaching can you add? How has your understanding of culturally relevant teaching expanded by reading this chapter?

Kasem Pravat (Asian American from Thailand)

Kasem is a very pleasant student who seems content in your class. He is always respectful and calm. Kasem works very hard. His papers are done with great care, and his test grades are strong. The one skill you would like him to develop is speaking up in class. Sometimes, he seems painfully shy.

You met Kasem's family briefly before school started, and they impressed you as agreeable, patient, and hardworking people. Kasem reflects those values. His family came from Thailand only recently, but because Kasem studied English in Thailand, his language adjustment here was relatively smooth. His favorite subject is math, and he is already talking about majoring in engineering in college. Kasem is one of the few students in your middle school class who not only are talking about college, but also have already identified a major. Kasem is protective and caring of his younger sister, Keyo, who is in the neighboring elementary school.

Potentially Useful Generalization: _____

_____

_____

Ariel Klein (Jewish American)

Ariel is an excellent student, in part because she is so hard working. Ariel's family is originally from an Orthodox Jewish neighborhood in New York City. Your community does not have an Orthodox synagogue for observant Jews who want to strictly follow their faith, so the Kleins now practice the more secular Conservative Judaism. Maintaining a kosher home has proven too difficult for the family because the nearest kosher food store is almost two hours away. Ariel and her family still observe Rosh Hashanah and Yom Kippur, which caused a major disruption in September when those holidays kept her from taking your academic skills assessment test. It was very difficult scheduling a retest because the arranged make-up day was the following Saturday, her Sabbath. After several delays, she finally took the exam in the main office over two weekdays, but had to miss two more days of class, which troubled her.

Ariel is very outgoing. She can always be counted on to ask questions. Many questions. Her outspoken nature has turned some of the other students off, and to be honest, at times you too have found it irritating. Some call her "pushy." Lately, she seems to have more questions than you have answers. But she is a strong student who motivates others to work harder on school projects. She tells her friends that she would like to be a doctor some day, and if you were a betting sort, you would put your money on Ariel being just as hard working in medical school as she has been in middle school.

Potentially Useful Generalization: _____

_____

_____

Mary Goode (rural white)

Mary grew up in a small town tucked away in the mountains of West Virginia. She attended a local elementary school with an enrollment of only 120 students in grades 1–8. Mary went through the first six years of elementary school with pretty much the same close group of thirteen classmates. Her school had only nine classes and nine teachers. However, only a few teachers stayed during her entire time at the school. Because she helped out in the local food co-op, Mary knew virtually all the families in town. The few she missed during the weekdays at the co-op she would see at church on Sunday. Her parents talked about her brother doing well in high school and then perhaps opening a business. For Mary, the conversation revolved around potential suitors and someday converting her parents into grandparents.

When Mary moved to your much larger community, she was overwhelmed. She says that she was never with so many students in one school or in one class in her life, and you suspect this may be why she is overwhelmed. You also think she may be reacting to the fact that the children in this town are all so different from those in her old town. Mary is now quite introverted and rarely speaks, in part because some students make fun of her accent. She is self-conscious about her background and all the things she does not seem to know that everyone else knows. Her clothes draw special attention by the other girls, who explain how "yesterday" they are. When you finally meet her parents, they are very quiet and also a bit overwhelmed. They were reticent to come to school. Although Mary takes her schoolwork seriously and is doing fine right now, you are concerned that she may get lost in this new crowd, perhaps turn off from school, or worse yet, drop out.

Potentially Useful Generalization: _____

_____

_____

Ibrahim Mouawad (Arab American)

Although Ibrahim has lived in your community his entire life, many see him as a foreigner. His family was one of the few who invited you over for dinner, and you still recall how warm they were toward you. The food was wonderful, although the names of some of those dishes fled your mind quickly.

When students ask Ibrahim where he is from, he says the Middle East but avoids identifying a particular country. Since the September 11, 2001, attack and the war in Iraq, your community has been wary of the few Arab families living here. You can see that tension in the eyes and behaviors of some of your students. You find yourself paying a little more attention when Ibrahim and Ariel are in the same group or have extended interactions together. You too have been influenced by the Arab-Israeli conflict. Perhaps you are overreacting, but you wonder if Ibrahim's unnamed country is Palestine or Iraq.

Ibrahim enjoys school, and although quiet in class, he is extremely polite to you and his classmates. But it is clear that he does not always "fit in." During Ramadan, a Moslem religious time for fasting, for example, he avoided the cafeteria during lunch. No one talked much about it, but you wonder what it must be like to smell food and see everyone else eating while you are fasting. Lunchtime saw him sitting by himself for the whole month of Ramadan. Like Ariel, Ibrahim has real problems with cafeteria foods, which make no allowances for Jewish or Moslem dietary laws.

Potentially Useful Generalization: _____

_____

_____

Carlos Martinez (Gay)

Carlos always felt different from other boys. A year ago he realized that he was gay. His mom and dad had divorced when he was younger, and he is now estranged from his father, who is uncomfortable with Carlos's sexual orientation. His mother continues to accept him for who he is and relies on him to help care for his younger sister. Carlos is now in your class and he is doing well. Schoolwork has always been easy for him, but he and his friends are concerned about hateful comments, such as "fag," they sometimes hear in the hallways. They decided to start a Gay-Straight Alliance (GSA) to educate their peers.

The GSA was approved by the principal and began planning a fund-raiser to buy holiday gifts for underprivileged children in the community. When word reached a conservative community group, however, protests began pouring into the superintendent's office that the middle school has a "gay club that is promoting homosexuality."

The GSA was invited to speak at the school board meeting. Though a small group of parents complained about the GSA, the school board members were impressed with the maturity and compassion displayed by Carlos and the other students. The school board voted to affirm the right of the GSA, and other student clubs, such as the Bible Club, to meet in the school. You are excited that next month, Carlos will be speaking at the state capitol to testify before the House Education Committee in support of antibullying legislation. But you worry, and hope that no *backlash* will follow him here.

Potentially Useful Generalization: _____

_____

_____

So how did you do? Some of these scenarios may have been more challenging than others, and noting all the possible generalizations would be a Herculean task. Before we share our responses, look back at yours. Were some generalizations easier to identify than others? Or were all a challenge? What does that tell you about your own education, about what you have experienced and learned about other groups? Now you have an idea of what you need to learn to become more culturally knowledgeable. If you struggled with creating generalizations, you will want to learn more about different groups so that you can one day become a more effective culturally responsive teacher. Here are some generalizations for each student:

Marcus Griffin (African American)

Potentially Useful Generalizations: Research concerning African Americans indicates that many benefit from kinesthetic and activity-oriented learning; others have a strong oral language tradition—calling out in class may reflect interest and involvement, not rudeness; they tend to value imagination, imagery, and humor in learning; they also may value spirituality rather than a mechanistic approach to life. Also, not looking directly at an adult is often a sign of respect in this community.

Ana Garcia (Mexican American)

Potentially Useful Generalizations: One generalization is that many Mexican American students feel a loyalty and commitment to the family. Another, that many adhere to traditional gender roles in a patriarchal family. Mexican American students often prefer to work in peer groups rather than alone, and prefer structured learning environments; and the high school dropout rates of Latinos and Latinas are very high, with estimates ranging from 40 to 50 percent.

Kasem Pravat (Asian American from Thailand)

Potentially Useful Generalizations: [Note: Generalizations about Asian Americans are by nature a "broad brush," because Americans group Japanese, Indians, Chinese, Pakistanis, Indonesians, and Vietnamese—about half the world population—under the term "Asian." Learning about each unique culture and country is critical.] Thais typically honor their national independence, many are fatalistic, and they may be offended by someone touching their head, the most sacred part of their body. Many cast their eyes down as a sign of respect. Thais often value self-discipline and academic success, seek cooperation and reconciliation, can be quite modest, might work hard to avoid confrontation, are often quiet, and typically revere teachers.

Ariel Klein (Jewish American)

Potentially Useful Generalizations: Jewish families in general are strong supporters of education, and children are often academically diligent with high career expectations. Jewish holidays can conflict with school calendars, because schools are scheduled to conform to Christian holidays; observant Jews are unable to attend school functions on Friday nights and Saturdays and may not be able to eat in the cafeteria. Jewish-Gentile conflict has existed for centuries and provides a disturbing undercurrent of anti-Semitism in some communities, and most Jews live in urban communities and on the East and West coasts.

Mary Goode (rural white)

Potentially Useful Generalizations: About one in five students attends rural schools; they are more likely to graduate from high school than urban or suburban students, but less likely to attend college. Rural white students typically attend smaller schools and may struggle in a larger school community. Appalachian families are often traditional and patriarchal, with boys being favored.

Ibrahim Mouawad (Arab American)

Potentially Useful Generalizations: Arab homelands, rich heritage, and historical contributions are often discounted in the West and in the curriculum. Also, cultural, linguistic, religious, and national distinctions are typically ignored. (The word *Arabs* refers to different nationalities, religions, and ethnic groups connected by a common language and culture.) Close family relationships and respect for elders are common. Arabs are often generous and hospitable to friends and even strangers. Arabs often excel in math.

Carlos Martinez (Gay)

Potentially Useful Generalizations: LGBT students are often "overachievers" and show a high degree of creativity and energy. They are often committed to resolving social injustice. Some LGBT students, however, prefer to remain closeted.

And one last reminder that these generalizations offer you a starting point, a place where research suggests you are most likely to reach success. But once you get to know your students, each student becomes an individual and will not always "fit" the generalization. So after working with Ibrahim for several months, if you discover that despite the generalization about Arab proficiency in math, Ibrahim is struggling in that subject, then, of course, you would offer extra instruction in math. Individual needs always trump group tendencies.

Diversity Assets

Once you begin to formulate generalizations, you will realize that learning about students and their unique backgrounds can be a growth experience for the entire class, including the teacher. Even casual interactions can enhance learning for all, for each group brings rich and unique insights to school. These insights and experiences, these different ways of knowing and seeing the world, are *diversity assets.*

Let's visit those eight students in your class one more time. In each case, we will suggest a potential asset that the student's background may bring to your class, a way that this student's culture enriches learning.

Lindsey may be able to share her people's reverence for the earth and stewardship of the environment, their spiritual insights, artistic talents, oral traditions, and preference for cooperative learning. Perhaps her tribe's warm interpersonal relationships will help build the class community.

Marcus may offer a "lens" to help others see invisible white privilege. Perhaps Marcus will share a history of oral traditions and be another voice for cooperative learning.

Ana can contribute a second language, helping monolingual students broaden their linguistic horizons. Mexican American warmth and loyalty may also help create a class community.

Kasem can share yet another language and culture, a culture that may also enhance class cohesion. He may also model academic persistence for others.

Ariel may support Kasem in promoting an academic focus and class dialogue. She may also offer insights into one of the world's oldest religions and cultures, and help others see how Christian beliefs and practices shape "secular" practices in America.

Mary can offer insights into life in rural America, and may be particularly resourceful since growing up in a rural community often fosters independence. Rural life also encourages a closer community, sometimes lost in today's fast-paced lifestyles.

Ibrahim brings another language to class and may provide insights into the rich Arab culture and history, particularly crucial in today's world of ethnic and religious intolerance.

Carlos may be striving toward social justice and equality in the face of adversity. And in communities with little racial or ethnic diversity, Carlos may offer a diversity opportunity, a way to learn from the experiences and insights of others.

These students offer what a textbook or a curriculum cannot: a human connection to the world's diversity. Along with their backgrounds and insights, their individual choices must be honored. Some teachers fall into the trap of inviting a Navajo, an African American, or a Mexican American student to be the voice of their people. How do black Americans feel about this, or what do Hispanics think about this? Crowning a black or Hispanic student as a spokesperson is unwise; one student cannot and should not speak for an entire group, and such a request can make a student feel uncomfortable. But as students volunteer their stories and opinions, and communicate informally with one another, their diversity assets will enrich learning for all.

Teaching Skills

Diversity is a potential asset to every classroom.

Recognizing the experiences and histories of all your students is an important first step in creating a climate that honors and celebrates diversity. Your teaching behaviors should also reinforce your commitment to equity. All students benefit when they feel safe, their unique needs and interests are recognized, and they are part of classroom discourse. Teachers need to share their time and talent fairly, offering helpful feedback and encouragement to each student, and ensuring that the curriculum is meaningful. We will describe equitable teaching skills in Chapter 11, but here are some suggestions for effective and equitable teaching strategies. To help you remember them, we created the acronym *DIVERSE.*

Diverse Instructional Materials: Some say that an effective curriculum is both a window and a mirror. Are all your students able to see themselves in your curricular mirror? Are all parts of the world seen through your curricular window? Are diverse thoughts, views, and people woven into the curriculum? Do class and school displays reflect all the world's cultures and peoples?

Inclusive: Does your teaching provide opportunities for each student, especially those very quiet students, to participate in class discussions? Sometimes careful planning, thoughtful selection of particular students to respond, and patience can encourage even shy students to participate. Every student deserves a public voice and should be heard.

Variety: Using different teaching strategies—learning styles, sensory channels, and intelligences—can do wonders to involve all. Kinesthetic and artistic activities, cooperative learning, and other approaches honor different ways of learning and allow each student to experience success.

Exploration: Teachers should encourage students to explore new cultures and beliefs, and be open themselves to new ideas. Learning how different peoples view the world can unlock student (and teacher) minds.

Reaction: Often, teacher feedback is given too quickly, with little thought, and is of little help. Each student deserves the teacher's specific, timely, honest, and precise comments. With effective feedback, patience, encouragement, and high expectation, all children can learn, and can learn well.

Safety: Without safety and security, little learning is possible. Offensive comments about religion, race, ethnicity, or sexuality and verbal or physical bullying should be quickly confronted and stopped by the teacher.

Evaluation: Teachers often forget that the achievement tests, aptitude tests, and high-stakes tests are often designed for white, middle-class culture. Teachers should consider a variety of evaluation strategies to assess the unique strengths of each student. Evaluation can assist in student diagnosis and planning effective instruction. It can serve a more constructive purpose than simply ranking and rating students.

These skills should help you to reach out to all your students. While they promote equity, they also promote good teaching. How fortunate we are that equitable teaching skills are also effective teaching skills.

We Are One

In this chapter, we recognize that group differences offer a way of broadening our perspective on what it means to be truly educated. We should treat our wondrous diversity "as one of the most exciting parts of our education—an enormous opportunity to see the world in new ways and understand more about humanity. What is education about if not that?"[47]

As Hindu tradition reminds us, as we honor one another's differences, we need also to honor what we hold in common. So let's close this chapter by recognizing that we are all part of the human family. In his 1963 commencement speech at American University, John F. Kennedy said: "For in the final analysis, our most basic common link is that we all inhabit this small planet, we all breathe the same air, we all cherish our children's futures, and we are all mortal." Those words still ring true today. According to genome research, human beings are 96 percent alike, no matter where we live, no matter what experiences we have, no matter our color, our language, or our God.[48] Yes, we can do both: honor our common humanity and the richness of our differences.

An eighth-grade language arts teacher shared Langston Hughes's poem "I, Too, Sing America" with her students, and asked her students to create a similar poem based on their own experiences.[49] Her students wrote remarkable poems that underscored the continuing racism and sexism in society, as well as profound universal desires to accept and be accepted by others. We use this same activity in our teacher education classes, and each year we learn from our students. Here are two poems written by our teacher education students. You can find more poems on the text website, and we invite you to write and submit your own.

I, too, am an American
I am the trusting farm girl who grew up knowing no strangers
I ventured to the city, where they tell me I am too naïve
But I am not what my white, non-diverse, God-fearing, conservative roots suggest
I have experiences with the good and the bad this world has to offer
Yet, each day I choose to smile and look for the good

Maybe
I am the beginning of this cycle
One smile, one act of trust, one stranger turned friend at a time
I, too, am an American.

—*Lacey Rosenbaum*

I, too, am an original American.
But concealed by my blond locks
and ocean deep blue eyes,
Red Man's blood
courses through these veins.
Undetected.

The White Man joke about the gamble
they think they are safe
"I can spot an ingine a mile a way!"
They spout without a single thought.

Then I smile
and take their then trembling hand
"Rainwater, and yes, it's Cherokee"
is all I say
as I walk away.

I am an Original American.

—*Mandie Rainwater*

ONLINE VIDEO ALBUM TO ACCOMPANY *TEACHERS, SCHOOLS, AND SOCIETY, 10E*

Visit the Online Learning Center for a range of contemporary videos with content related to this chapter.

www.mhhe.com/sadker10e

THE *TEACHERS, SCHOOLS, AND SOCIETY* READER WITH CLASSROOM OBSERVATION VIDEO CLIPS

Go to your *Teachers, Schools, and Society* Reader CD-ROM to:

READ CURRENT AND HISTORICAL ARTICLES

10. **Learning from Latino Families,** by Susan Auerbach, *Educational Leadership,* May 2011.

11. **Understanding Unconscious Bias and Unintentional Racism,** by Jean Moule, *Phi Delta Kappan,* January 2009.

12. **The Threat of Stereotype,** by Joshua Aronson, *Educational Leadership,* November 2004.

13. **How Good Are the Asians: Refuting Four Myths About Asian-American Academic Achievement,** by Yong Zhao and Wei Qiu, *Phi Delta Kappan,* January 2009.

14. **I, Too, Am an American: Preservice Teachers Reflect upon National Identity,** by Nancy Gallavan, *Multicultural Teaching,* Spring 2002.

ANALYZE CASE STUDIES

5. **Helen Franklin:** A teacher who uses parents as volunteers to help with her unique classroom organization notices that a parent volunteer who has questioned the teachers' methods will work only with white students.

6. **Leigh Scott:** A teacher gives a higher-than-earned grade to a mainstreamed student on the basis of the boy's effort and attitude and is confronted by a black student with identical test scores who received a lower grade and who accuses her of racism.

OBSERVE TEACHERS, STUDENTS, AND CLASSROOMS IN ACTION

5. Classroom Observation: High School Students Discuss Issues They Face as Immigrant Students

A growing number of students in today's schools are immigrants. In this observation, you will hear several high school students talk about their experiences in school as immigrants. You will also hear a teacher who works with them discuss her role in helping them to adapt to their new community and achieve academic and social success.

KEY TERMS AND PEOPLE

assimilation (enculturation), 60

Banks, James, 68

bilingual education, 61

cultural difference theory, 58

cultural pluralism, 60

culturally responsive teaching, 69

culture, 52

deficit theory, 57

demographic forecasting, 52

dual-language instruction, 64

English as a Second Language (ESL), 64

English language learners (ELL), 63

English-only movement, 64

ethnicity, 52

expectation theory, 58

generalizations, 73

immersion, 64

Ladson-Billings, Gloria, 69

language submersion, 61

Lau v. *Nichols,* 61

maintenance (developmental) approach, 63

multicultural education, 67

multiracial, 52

Ovando, Carlos Julio, 62

race, 52

stereotypes, 72

stereotype threat, 72

transitional approach, 63

www.mhhe.com/sadker10e

CHAPTER REVIEW

Go to the Online Learning Center to take a chapter self-quiz, practice with key terms, and review concepts from the chapter.

DISCUSSION QUESTIONS AND ACTIVITIES

1. Observe a classroom, noting how many times teachers call on each student. Compare the amount of attention each student receives. Now determine group representation in the classroom. Does one group (boys or whites or native-English speakers) get more than its fair share of teacher attention? The online observation guide can be helpful in this activity.

2. How do you react to the various issues raised in this chapter? On a separate sheet of paper complete the following sentences as honestly as you can. If you wish, share your responses with your classmates.

   - To me, the phrase *invisible race privilege* means . . .
   - A great example of expectation theory is . . .

3. Given demographic trends, pick a region of the country and a particular community. Develop a scenario of a classroom in that community in the year 2030. Describe the students' characteristics and the teacher's role. Is that classroom likely to be affected by changing demographics? How are cultural learning styles manifested in the way the teacher organizes and instructs the class?

4. Choose a school curriculum and suggest how it can be changed to reflect one of the four approaches to multicultural education described by Banks. Why did you choose the approach you did?

5. Discuss the two main approaches to bilingual education in the United States: transitional and maintenance. Which do you favor, and why?

REFLECTIVE ACTIVITIES AND YOUR PORTFOLIO

Introduction

INTASC *Reflective Activities and Your Portfolio,* what we like to refer to as *RAP*s, give you a chance to explore your role as an educator by carefully considering what you have just read and tying it to your own experiences. *RAP*s are intended to help you decide if teaching is right for you. And if it is right, these very same *RAP*s will give you direction as you prepare for a career in teaching.

RAPs follow and connect each of the four sections of the textbook. Each *RAP* includes a(n):

Purpose—explains why this activity is useful, and what it is intended to accomplish.

Activity—allows you to apply your readings through observations, interviews, teaching, and action research.

Artifact—challenges you to collect and manage the items you will find useful for developing your portfolio.

Reflection—helps you think deeply and realistically about education and your place in it.

Portfolios

The term *portfolio* has traditionally been associated with artists and investors. Most artists maintain a showcase or portfolio of their best work to woo potential clients. Usually housed in a large portable attaché case, the portfolio is a pleasing way for clients to view an artist's best body of work. Similarly, investors keep track of their financial decisions with another type of portfolio. This portfolio tracks the gains and losses and helps determine short- and long-term investment strategies.

Although the concept of the portfolio is rooted in the worlds of art and investing, educators have embraced portfolios. For the teacher-in-training, portfolios can also serve as a powerful forum in which to showcase their best work, as well as demonstrate their professional growth over time.

Portfolios serve many purposes. They are used by states for licensure and licensure renewal, by school districts for merit pay increases, and by individual schools for hiring new staff. The National Board for Professional Teaching Standards (NBPTS) requires portfolios as part of the rigorous evaluation to reward and recognize high-achieving teachers with board certification. At the classroom level, teachers are using portfolios as an alternative evaluation method. Many teachers, students, and parents have found portfolios to be an authentic way to assess achievement.

As a teacher-in-training, you'll find that your portfolio will be a valuable asset in your teacher education program and in your eventual search for a teaching position. Questions to keep in mind as you assemble this showcase include:

1. What do I want my portfolio to say about me as a teacher?
2. What do I want my portfolio to say about me as a student?
3. What do I want my portfolio to say about my relationship with students?
4. How can my portfolio demonstrate my growth as an educator and a learner?
5. How can my portfolio demonstrate that I will be successful as a teacher?

Consider making your portfolio:[1]

- Purposeful—based on a sound foundation, such as the INTASC Standards for Licensing Beginning Teachers
- Selective—choosing only the appropriate materials for a specific purpose or circumstance, such as a job application
- Diverse—going beyond your transcript, student teaching critiques, and letters of recommendation to represent a broad array of teaching talent
- Ongoing—relaying your growth and development over time
- Reflective—both in process and in product, demonstrating your thoughtfulness
- Collaborative—resulting from conversations and interactions with others (peers, students, parents, professors, teachers, and administrators)

Getting Started on Your Portfolio—Collect, Select, and Reflect

In four places in this book, we have placed INTASC *RAP*s to help you through the process of creating your portfolio. The *RAP* activities in these sections are based on the INTASC standards and provide a springboard for your own creative portfolio artifacts. Read through the INTASC Core Teaching Standards included in this section (p. 89) to understand the sections your portfolio will include. Of course, you are encouraged to include material from other sources as well.

Building your portfolio is a three-step process—*collect, select, and reflect.*

1. *Collect* items for inclusion in your portfolio by completing *RAP*s and similar activities of your choosing.
2. *Select* items for inclusion in your portfolio from this pool of artifacts. You are encouraged to select at least one item from each of the ten INTASC Standards for Licensing Beginning Teachers.
3. *Reflect* on what was learned from each activity. This self-assessment should serve as a powerful learning tool, one you will be able to return to again and again.

Housing Your Portfolio—from Traditional Methods to the Electronic Portfolio

The choices of where and how to store your portfolio can be as diverse as the contents of the portfolio itself. Many teachers use portable plastic filing cases or crates. Others turn their portfolios into books for easy toting. Increasingly, teachers are employing a myriad of electronic tools to reach students. These can include video, the Internet, and computer activities such as PowerPoint presentations. How can teachers best include these artifacts in their portfolios? Through something called the *Electronic Portfolio* or *e-Portfolio.* Many software products exist to help in this process.

---

[1] Kenneth Wolf and Mary Dietz, "Teaching Portfolios: Purpose and Possibilities," *Teacher Education Quarterly,* Winter 1998, pp. 9–21.

The Learner and Learning
Standard 1: Learner Development

The teacher understands how children learn and develop, recognizing that patterns of learning and development vary individually within and across the cognitive, linguistic, social, emotional, and physical areas, and designs and implements developmentally appropriate and challenging learning experiences.

Standard 2: Learning Differences

The teacher uses understanding of individual differences and diverse cultures and communities to ensure inclusive learning environments that enable each learner to meet high standards.

Standard 3: Learning Environments

The teacher works with others to create environments that support individual and collaborative learning, and that encourage positive social interaction, active engagement in learning, and self-motivation.

Content Knowledge
Standard 4: Content Knowledge

The teacher understands the central concepts, tools of inquiry, and structures of the discipline(s) he or she teaches and creates learning experiences that make the discipline accessible and meaningful for learners to assure mastery of the content.

Standard 5: Application of Content Knowledge

The teacher understands how to connect concepts and use differing perspectives to engage learners in critical thinking, creativity, and collaborative problem solving related to authentic local and global issues.

Instructional Practice
Standard 6: Assessment

The teacher understands and uses multiple methods of assessment to engage learners in their own growth, to monitor learner progress, and to guide the teacher's and learner's decision making.

Standard 7: Planning for Instruction

The teacher plans instruction that supports every student in meeting rigorous learning goals by drawing upon knowledge of content areas, curriculum, cross-disciplinary skills, and pedagogy, as well as knowledge of learners and the community context.

Standard 8: Instructional Strategies

The teacher understands and uses a variety of instructional strategies to encourage learners to develop deep understanding of content areas and their connections and to build skills to apply knowledge in meaningful ways.

Professional Responsibility
Standard 9: Professional Learning and Ethical Practice

The teacher engages in ongoing professional learning and uses evidence to continually evaluate his or her practice, particularly the effects of his or her choices and actions on others (learners, families, other professionals, and the community), and adapts practice to meet the needs of each learner.

Standard 10: Leadership and Collaboration

The teacher seeks appropriate leadership roles and opportunities to take responsibility for student learning, to collaborate with learners, families, colleagues, other school professionals, and community members to ensure learner growth, and to advance the profession.

Part 1: Teachers and Students

1:1 Getting to Know Whom?

Purpose: Chapter 3, "Teaching Your Diverse Students," exposed some of life's heritage and happenings that influence who we are. Many of us have grown up in relatively homogeneous environments, knowing individuals of similar backgrounds and cultures. Meaningful conversations about how race, nationality, gender, religion, and socioeconomic status affect our own education are rare, especially when diverse backgrounds are missing. Yet such conversations could add important dimensions to your understanding of students.

Activity: Partner with a classmate, a campus colleague, or a friend, or someone new who comes from a background different from yours. Conduct an interview while being an active listener. Some opening questions might include:

- How do you identify your race or ethnicity?
- How would you describe your family heritage?
- How would you describe your family structure and patterns of daily life?
- How would you identify your social class?
- Do you have memories of bias and discrimination?
- What are your recollections of your education?
- Did your teacher make assumptions about you because of your background?
- Did your classmates?
- What are some things you wished your teachers knew about you that perhaps they didn't?
- What are some things teachers could do to help all groups get along better?
- What other concerns have you experienced that impeded your educational opportunity?

www.mhhe.com/sadker10e

FORM

Getting to know you

Artifact: "Diversity Insights for My Classroom." From your interview, cull answers that relate directly to the classroom. In about a paragraph, sum up ways that you can apply what you learned during the interview to your teaching.

Reflection: How are you and your interviewee different? How are you similar? How might this anecdotal information add to your understanding of child and human development? What aspects of your partner's cognitive, social, and emotional growth paralleled your own schooling? All in all, what words might describe your conversation: *insightful, laborious, superficial, intimate?* What words do you think your partner might use as a description? Will this paragraph and the information learned during the interview be useful when you enter the classroom? Why or why not? How has diversity influenced you own education or your commitment to teach?

1:2 Multiple Intelligence Bingo

Purpose: Educators are moving beyond the traditional IQ definition of intelligence. As the text discussed, Howard Gardner has identified at least eight intelligences—not all of which are commonly recognized in school settings—that he believes better define the unique nature of individual human capability. An effective teacher recognizes different types of intelligences and talents and adapts instruction accordingly. Although some teachers still tend to focus on the math and linguistic abilities, others enthusiastically incorporate Gardner's theory into their classrooms. In this activity, you will be challenged to identify intelligences and to see the theory applied in lessons.

Activity: Visit two classrooms. (If you can, try to include at least one with a teacher known for using a multiple intelligence approach.) You might want to include both an elementary and secondary classroom to see how MI is used at each level. Use the following chart to record examples of multiple intelligences, noting instructional strategies, curriculum, and even room displays. Reviewing the intelligences described in Chapter 2, and brainstorming with your peers before the observation will help you determine what might constitute evidence of a particular intelligence. See if your observation can fill every slot. Bingo!

Artifact: Use accompanying "Multiple Intelligence Bingo Card" to record your observations, and file the chart in your portfolio. Although this initial chart will help you to detect MI in action, in future years you may wish to use it for self-analysis, a way to make sure that you are including the multiple intelligences in your own teaching.

Classroom #_____ intelligence	Bingo Card Example During Instruction	Display or Material Example
Logical-mathematical		
Linguistic		
Bodily-kinesthetic		
Musical		
Spatial		
Interpersonal		
Intrapersonal		
Naturalist		
Others (your own)		

Reflection: What were the multiple intelligences emerging in these classrooms? After your observations, were there any intelligences missing? How might these missing intelligences be incorporated? Were some classes geared to only one or two intelligences? Which intelligences would be easier for you to use, and which more difficult? How did the class respond, in general, when the lessons involved intelligences other than the logical and linguistic? What can you apply to your own classroom?

www.mhhe.com/sadker10e

FORM

Multiple intelligences bingo

1:3 Why Teach?

Purpose: People may have already asked you why you are considering teaching. Sometimes they ask with reverent tones, other times in disbelief. (In either case, you are learning more about them than you are about your own potential teaching career.) Analyze your motivations so that you can provide a good answer to the person who matters most in this decision: you.

INTASC STANDARD 3
Learning
Environments

Activity: Write a letter to yourself detailing why you want to become a teacher. Draw on your experiences as a student. Perhaps you want to reflect on some of the teachers of your most memorable teachers and the types of learning environments they created (or didn't create).

How will your students benefit? How will society? How will you? This letter will help you better understand if and why you should become a teacher.

Artifact/Reflection: This "Why I Am Teaching" letter will serve as a mindful reflection and, if you choose, an artifact. Over the years, your reasons for becoming a teacher may change, becoming even stronger, or weaker, or different. You may well want to repeat this process in one, five or ten years and monitor your own inner motivation. The letter will provide you with a marker of your thinking as you first considered a teaching career.

1:4 Teacher Interview in Your Subject Area

Purpose: Teachers are expected to have knowledge of both the subject(s) they teach and the students they are teaching. Deciding what and how to teach are constant responsibilities. This activity gives you the opportunity to learn how teachers make these choices and to begin thinking how you might approach curricular and instructional decisions in your major subject area.

Activity: Interview a teacher in a subject area of special interest to you. Focus on how the teacher decides what content to teach and how best to teach it. Here are some curricular questions to ask, but feel free to add your own to this list:

- What factors contributed to your decision to teach this subject and at this grade level?
- What do you enjoy most about teaching this curriculum? What is most challenging?
- How do you go about selecting what content and skills to teach?
- Do you try to offer different perspectives (multidisciplinary, multicultural) on these topics?
- Are there areas of this subject that are controversial? How do you handle these controversial topics?
- How do you accommodate multiple intelligences in your classroom?
- How do you assess learning and record grades? Does your school or district require a certain format? Do you use grading software?
- When do you do your planning? The week before, the night before? Other?
- Do you integrate other subject areas into your program?
- How do the school district's official curriculum, national core standards, and the textbook shape your decisions?
- Can you make your own decisions as to what topics to teach, or are you confined to the official school curriculum?
- Are selections made by you alone or with others in your department or grade-level team?
- Do professional associations influence your decisions?
- Do parents or students participate in deciding what is taught?

Artifact: "Teacher: Interview: Subject Specialty." For your portfolio, you will want to include the interview questions you ask, the teacher responses, and eventually, your reflection. Make certain that you include the place and the date of the interview. You may want to re-read this artifact for some useful insights when you begin teaching. Or then again, you may want to read it in ten or twenty years, to see how much things have changed—or how much they haven't changed!

Reflection: What advice given by the teacher do you believe may influence your own decisions? How does the teacher's view of the content differ from your own? What role will standards, textbooks, and curricular guides likely play in our curricular decisions? Why are you interested in this subject area, and how do you anticipate your interest will affect your students and your teaching? What did you learn from this teacher that was surprising?

1:5 Creating a Career Information Document

Purpose: Applying for the right teaching position requires homework. You want to know where to apply, not only where the job openings are, but also where you will find the right school for you. Visiting schools and meeting with administrators will help you learn about the school culture and offer insights into the kinds of questions you should be asking as you investigate teaching. An informational interview with a school administrator is a useful rehearsal for you and could provide timely information on the job market and hiring procedures, and is a great way to begin your "Career Information" document.

Activity: Arrange an interview with a local school administrator (principal, personnel director). Consider going with a small group of peers (visitation team) so that your school administrator is not inundated with too many requests. Review information in this text and in your community about teacher supply and demand. Develop questions as a visitation team. The following list of suggestions will get you started.

- In regard to teacher openings, what grade levels, subject areas, or specialties will likely be needed this year? What do you anticipate will be needed in the next few years?
- What is the diversity breakdown of teachers in the district? How does this compare with the students in this school and district-wide? How do these factors affect screening and hiring?
- What is the application process for this district? Who else is involved in the hiring process? Do you require or recommend portfolios?
- If you could describe a perfect candidate, what traits would that teacher possess?
- What other questions should we ask concerning the educational job market and hiring process?
- What advice would you offer beginning teachers?
- Do you have specific suggestions for the interview process?

Artifact: Building a "Career Information" document can help you keep and build on this information. One section might be your geographic preferences, including city, suburbs, or rural areas. Another might be the kind of school you prefer, such as the school's educational philosophy, types of students, colleagues and administration, testing practices, diversity of staff, diversity of student body, salary/benefit package, community support, and so on.

This might be a good place to include job-seeking strategies, such as interviewing techniques. It is your document, so you decide what works for you. The purpose is to begin a process (that will be ongoing) that places you in the school that works best for you.

Reflection: Meet with your peers and compare interviews. Are certain trends evident in your locale? How do these realities influence your own decision making? What questions remain unanswered? Is a follow-up meeting or a phone call appropriate? Would it be a good idea to send a thank you note? Consider a similar interview during visits to other regions of the country. How does this information affect your teaching plans?

www.mhhe.com/sadker10e

FORM

Career Information Document

1:6 A Novel Read

Purpose: Great teachers have an incredible ability to care, really deeply, about children. Such teachers learn about their students, hold high expectations for them, and fully appreciate their diverse cultural perspectives and learning styles. One marvelous way to understand teachers and youngsters is to read about them in well written and powerful books. The right literature will not only inspire you, but also expand your awareness of diverse learners and teachers.

Activity: Let this activity be a change of pace from textbooks and research papers. Your education faculty will likely have additions to this book list. Pick a book and dig in:

Teacher, Sylvia Ashton-Warner

Warriors Don't Cry: A Searing Memoir of the Battle to Integrate Little Rock's Central High, Melba Patillo Beals

Mentors, Masters and Mrs. MacGregor: Stories of Teachers Making a Difference, Jane Bluestein

America Is in the Heart, Carlos Bulosan

Family Values: A Lesbian Mother's Fight for Her Son, Phyllis Burke

Black Ice, Lorene Cary

House on Mango Street, Sandra Cisneros

The Water Is Wide, Patrick Conroy

Reflections of a Rock Lobster: A Story about Growing Up Gay, Aaron Fricke

Up the Down Staircase, Bel Kaufman

Among Schoolchildren, Tracy Kidder

Coming of Age in Mississippi, Ann Moody

The Bluest Eye, Toni Morrison

900 Shows a Year, Stuart Palonsky

The Education of a WASP, Lois Stalvey

Native Son, Richard Wright

Artifact: "Lessons from Literature." After reading one of these selections, or a book of your choice with a school/education theme, write a review that focuses on lessons and themes from the book that can be applied to the classroom. The goal of your book review is not only to assess the book's strengths and weaknesses but also to extract lessons about effective and culturally responsive teaching practices.

Reflection: What did you learn from reading this book? Did you "unlearn" or abandon any misconceptions after your reading? Can you identify implications for your classroom? Would you assign this book to your students or suggest it for a faculty book club? How will you assess student learning? Your own understandings? Include your book review and reflection in your portfolio.

1:7 Planning for Diversity: A Lesson Plan

Purpose: This activity will give you an opportunity to plan for a lesson on diversity in society.

INTASC STANDARD 7
Planning for
Instruction

Activity: Develop a lesson plan related to a diversity topic (e.g., history of a group, cross-cultural understanding, a nontraditional hero, a religion that may not be familiar to many in your class, a social movement to create a more just society—you get the idea). Once you have selected a topic, begin to sketch out a lesson plan. Are you new to lesson planning? There are many approaches, but for this activity, let's use a design by educator Dr. Madeline Hunter. She recommends the following lesson plan elements:

Dr. Madeline Hunter's Seven-Step Lesson Plan

1. **Anticipatory Set** (focus)—Focus learners' attention on the instruction that is about to begin. This could be a teacher demonstration, a video, a story, a puzzle, or a handout before the actual lesson. This is also known as a "grabber," and it's a way to get your students' attention and interest.

2. **Purpose** (objective)—A clear explanation of what learners will understand and be able to do as a result of the lesson. This section should answer the question, "Why is this important to learn?"

3. **Instructional Strategy**—What content and skills need to be taught to accomplish this task? What are the best teaching strategies for this instructional task (lecture, activity, video, group work, etc.)?

4. **Modeling** (show)—Provide learners with examples or demonstrations of competencies associated with the lesson.

5. **Guided Practice**—Monitor learners as they apply new information.

6. **Check for Understanding**—Evaluate whether learners have the information needed to master the objective.

7. **Independent Practice**—Assign learners to work independently, without direct teacher assistance.

Now choose a topic related to diversity. It could be the history of a group, or current issues related to that group, or anything that speaks to your heart. Check out Chapter 3 for possible directions. Because you are planning for diversity, you may want to include some of the teaching strategies also described in Chapter 3. For example, include some of the tenets of culturally relevant teaching. Now outline your lesson using Hunter's outline.

Artifact: The artifact is your first lesson plan following Hunter's seven-step format. It will not be perfect, and you may well struggle with it. But there is learning in the struggle, and looking back at this lesson plan in the months and years ahead will provide you with a marker of how far you have come.

Reflection: What were your reactions in planning for instruction? What questions came up? What did this process teach you? What do you want to learn more about?

If you have had previous practice in writing a lesson plan, reflect on what you liked and did not like with the Hunter format. Compare this approach with your previous experience and share your assessment of different lesson planning strategies. What elements do you value in a good lesson plan?

1:8 If the Walls Could Speak

Purpose: It is human nature to surround oneself with familiarity, which brings a certain level of comfort. In the classroom, however, teachers can work to broaden students' vision and understanding of the world beyond their classroom and community. One way to achieve this goal is through classroom bulletin boards and other displays.

INTASC STANDARD 8
Instructional Strategies

Activity: On a poster board or in your classroom, create a bulletin board representing diverse sets of people and cultures. Perhaps you can choose groups related to historical holidays, recognition of leaders, anniversaries of special events, or current news developments. You can use Internet sources or magazines, newspapers, personal pictures, and so on. The walls of your class should reflect our world, the one that exists beyond your classroom and your community.

Seeing Diversity					
	Not at All				**Very**
	1	2	3	4	5
Clarity of Presentation					
Attractiveness					
Variety of Cultures Featured					
Equal Representation of Men and Women					
Mixture of Regular and Famous People					
Inclusion of Other Diversity Issues (Disability, Age, etc.)					
Overall Quality					
Overall Usefulness					

www.mhhe.com/sadker10e

FORM

Seeing diversity

INTASC STANDARD 9
Personal Learning
and Ethical Practice

Artifact: "Seeing Diversity." Take a photo of your display and, if appropriate, put it on your class web page or in the class newspaper. You could also include the photo in your portfolio. Then stand back and be an objective judge by rating your bulletin board for diversity, equality, and educational impact:

Reflection: What did you learn from this experience? What surprised you? Was it a challenge to create such a display? What part of this activity was easy? Did you learn how to improve this activity on your next try?

1:9 Nontraditional Hero

Purpose: We know that students can learn from inspiring figures—individuals who serve as role models and motivate students. Although heroes come from all backgrounds, curricular materials do not always reflect this diversity. The result is a disconnect between the growing diversity of America's students and the curriculum they study. You can enhance your curriculum by adding to the list of nontraditional champions in your texts. (Consider ethnicity, race, gender, age, class, lifestyle, disability, and circumstances as you select your hero.) You may also want to define different kinds of heroism as you tackle this project. Identifying such heroes has the additional advantage of broadening your own scholarship.

Activity: Select a unique individual or hero who has made a difference. Strive to select someone from a subject area that you will be teaching. Develop a lesson about this person. Make the language, content, and style relevant to the grade level you plan to teach. Develop visuals to enhance your presentation, perhaps a billboard or a poster of this person.

Artifact: "Nontraditional Hero Lesson." Save your lesson plan and supporting material for your portfolio, and for use when you begin teaching.

Bonus Artifact: Integrate technology with this activity by using video, PowerPoint, etc. Share the lesson with your college class. Afterward, tweak the presentation so that it is ready to be presented in your first classroom.

Reflection: What has this activity taught you about augmenting the curriculum? Was it a challenge to find a nontraditional hero—or a challenge to choose just one? Is it a teacher's professional and/or ethical responsibility to change instructional materials to better meet the needs of students? What are some of the arguments for and against modifying the curriculum? Will you consider modifying the curriculum in your own teaching? If you do make changes, what criteria will you use when altering the curriculum?

1:10 Special Education Services

Purpose: For many preservice teachers, the laws and services for students with special needs can be complex and confusing. Gaining a professional understanding of these concerns will help anyone with career plans in education. It might even motivate you to teach children with disabilities. Begin by reviewing the information in Chapter 2 that discusses special education.

INTASC STANDARD 10
Leadership and
Collaboration

Activity: Contact a local school district and identify the director of services for special education. Request a parent information packet that outlines the rights and responsibilities of the district regarding testing, resources, policy, practices, and all other information that would help you understand the Individuals with Disabilities Education Act (IDEA).

Highlight the key points in the literature, and take notes of what a teacher needs to do to meet the needs of special needs students.

Artifact: Create a document that will make this information more easily accessible to you when you begin teaching. The title might be "Special Needs Reminders" or something similar. This should be an easy-to-read piece, perhaps even a checklist, to help you fulfill your responsibilities and create the best possible educational climate for special needs learners.

Reflection: What more did you learn about IDEA? How does it feel to look at this information from a parent's perspective? How does it feel to look at this information from a student's perspective? How does it feel to look at this information from a teacher's perspective?

PART II

Schools and Curriculum

Chapter 4

Student Life in School and at Home *100*

Chapter 5

Purposes of America's Schools and the Current Reform Movement *133*

Chapter 6

Curriculum, Standards, and Testing *166*

Student Life in School and at Home

FOCUS QUESTIONS

1. What rituals and routines shape classroom life?
2. How does the teacher's gatekeeping function influence classroom roles?
3. What is tracking, and what are its advantages and disadvantages?
4. How do gender and peer groups influence children in elementary and middle school?
5. In what ways does the adolescent culture shape teenage perceptions and behaviors in high school?
6. What impact do changing family patterns and economic issues have on children and schools?
7. How can educators respond to social issues that place children at risk?

You will either step forward into growth, or you will step backward into safety.

–ABRAHAM MASLOW

CHAPTER PREVIEW

School is a culture. Like most cultures, it is filled with its own unique rituals and traditions, and its own set of norms and mores. In school, even the familiar, such as time, is made new. Time is told by subjects ("Let's talk before math") or periods ("I have bank seventh period"). Students are pinched into passive roles, following schedules created by others, sitting still rather than being active, and responding to teacher questions but seldom asking any of their own. Such a system challenges and confines both teachers and students. Peer groups create friendships and popularity, a strong subculture that makes winners and losers of us all—at least for a brief time. Adults pick up where children leave off, assigning students to what amounts to an academic caste system through *de facto* tracking or ability grouping. While adults focus on academics, many adolescents and preadolescents are focused on relationships and sexuality.

Economic and social factors are also powerful forces in today's classrooms, and have reshaped the family unit. New family patterns abound, challenging the traditional view of the mother, father, and two children (did we forget the dog?) as the "typical" American family. With these changes, economic and social problems threaten our children and challenge teachers. We will describe these challenges so that educators can work to create schools that are safe havens and institutions of hope.

www.mhhe.com/sadker10e

WHAT DO YOU THINK? **What was your school experience like?** See how it compares with that of your colleagues.

Rules, Rituals, and Routines

Schools create their own cultures, replete with norms, rituals, and routines. Even simple tasks, such as distributing textbooks, are clothed with cultural cues, but they are cues that differ for students and teachers.

"Come Right Up and Get Your New Books": A Teacher's Perspective

"Okay, class, quiet down, "said Mr. Thompson." The poetry books we've been waiting for have finally arrived. I'd like the first person in each row to come up, count out enough books for his or her row, and hand them out."

Six students charged to the front and made a mad grab for the books. In the ensuing melee, one stack of books went crashing to the floor.

"Hey, kids, take it easy. There are plenty of books to go around. When you get your texts, write your name and room number in the stamped box inside the cover." Mr. Thompson turned his attention to the several hands waving in the air.

"Yes, Jessica?"

"I can't fill in my name because my pencil just broke. Can I sharpen it?"

"Go ahead. Jamie?"

"My pencil's broken, too. Can I sharpen mine?"

"Yes, but wait until Jessica sits down. Let me remind you that you're supposed to come to class prepared. Now there will be no more at the pencil sharpener today.

After you get your books, turn to the poem on page 3. It's called 'Stopping by Woods on a Snowy Evening,' and it's by Robert Frost, one of America's most famous poets. Yes, Rosa?"

"I didn't get a book."

"Okay, Rosa, go down to the office and tell Mrs. Goldberg that we need one more of the new poetry anthologies. Now, as I was about to say, I'd like you to think about the questions that I've written on the board: How does the speaker in this poem feel as he looks at the snow filling up the deserted woods? Why does he wish to stop, and what makes him realize that he must go on? The speaker says, 'I have miles to go before I sleep.' He may be talking about more than going to bed for the night. What else may 'sleep' mean in this poem?

April! Maxine! This is not a time for your private chat room. This is a silent reading activity—and I do mean silent. Okay, class, I think most of you have had enough time to read the poem. Who has an answer for the first question? Jordan?"

"Well, I think the guy in this poem really likes nature. He's all alone, and it's private, with no people around to interrupt him, and he thinks the woods and the snow are really beautiful. It's sort of spellbinding."

"Jordan, that's an excellent response. You've captured the mood of this poem. Now for the second question. Maxine?"

"I think he wants to stop because . . ."

Maxine's answer was cut short by the abrasive ring of the fourth-period bell.

"For homework, I'd like you to answer the remaining questions. Alice?"

"Is this to hand in?"

"Yes. Any other questions? Okay, you'd better get to your next-period class."

As the last student left, Rick Thompson slumped over his desk and wearily ran his fingers through his hair. The whole lesson was a victim of the book brigade. He had been so busy getting the books dispensed and fielding all the interruptions that he had forgotten to give his brief explanation on the differences between prose and poetry. He had even forgotten to give his motivating speech on how interesting the new poetry unit was going to be. Well, no time for a postmortem now. Stampedelike noises outside the door meant the fourth-period class was about to burst in.

FOCUS QUESTION 1

What rituals and routines shape classroom life?

"Come Right Up and Get Your New Books": A Student's Perspective

From her vantage point in the fourth seat, fifth row, Maxine eyed the stack of new books on the teacher's desk. She knew they were poetry books because she had flipped through one as she meandered into the room. She didn't care that it wasn't "in" to like poetry; she liked it anyway.

Maxine settled into her seat and began the long wait for her book. "I suppose I can start my math homework or write some letters." Maxine got several of her math problems solved by the time her poetry anthology arrived, along with instructions to read the poem on page 3. She skimmed through the poem and decided she liked it. She understood how Robert Frost felt, watching the snowy woods and wanting to get away from all the hassles. It sure would be nice to read this poem quietly somewhere without listening to kids going on about pencil sharpeners and hall passes and seat changes. As she turned around to share her observation about hassles with April Marston, Mr. Thompson's sharp reprimand interrupted her. She fumed to herself, "Private chat room. What's with him? Half the class is talking, and old Eagle Eyes Thompson has to pick on me. And they're all talking about the football game Saturday. At least I was talking about the poem. Oh well, I'd better answer one of those questions on the board and show him that I really am paying attention."

Maxine waved her hand wildly, but Jordan got called for question 1. Maxine shot her hand in the air again for a chance at question 2. When Mr. Thompson called on her, she drew a deep breath and began her response. Once again, she was interrupted in midsentence, this time by the fourth-period bell.

"I really knew the answer to that question," she muttered under her breath. "Now we have to write all the answers out. Boring. Well, next period is science and we're supposed to be giving lab reports. Maybe we'll have a chance to finish the English homework there."

Watching the Clock

You have just read two replays of a seventh-grade English lesson, one from the vantage point of the teacher, the other from the vantage point of a student. Mr. Thompson and Maxine play different roles, which cause them to have very different experiences in this class. For example, Mr. Thompson was continually leapfrogging from one minor crisis to the next while Maxine was sitting and waiting.

In his book *Life in Classrooms,* Philip W. Jackson describes how time is spent in school.[1] He suggests that whereas teachers are typically very busy, students are often caught in patterns of delay that force them to do nothing. Jackson notes that a great deal of teachers' time is spent in noninstructional busywork, such as keeping time and dispensing supplies. In the slice of classroom life you just read, Mr. Thompson spent a substantial part of the class time distributing new texts. Indeed, most teachers spend a good deal of time giving out things: paper, pencils, art materials, science equipment, books, exam booklets, erasers, happy faces, special privileges—the list goes on and on. The classroom scene described also shows Mr. Thompson greatly involved in timekeeping activities. Within the limits set by school buzzers and bells, he determines when the texts will be distributed, when and for how long the reading activity will take place, and when the class discussion will begin.

What do students do while teachers are busy organizing, structuring, talking, questioning, handing out, collecting, timekeeping, and crisis hopping? According to Jackson's analysis, they do little more than sit and wait.[2] They wait for the materials to be handed out, for the assignment to be given, for the questions to be asked, for the teacher to call on them, for the teacher to react to their response, and for the slower class members to catch up so that

GLOBAL VIEW
U.S. public school students typically attend school for 180 days a year, much less than the school calendars in Europe (190–210 days) and Japan (240 days).

GLOBAL VIEW
"On-time behavior" is considered one of the most powerful cultural lessons in the school's hidden curriculum. Throughout the world however, people have a varied sense of time. Arriving 10 minutes after a scheduled appointment in the states might be considered "pretty much on time." Being an hour late in some other cultures is not at all impolite, and in fact arriving punctually at the exact appointment time might be seen as quite strange. How might you as a teacher cope with the differences between school time norms and cultural time norms students bring to your classroom?

the activity can change. They wait in lines to get drinks of water, to get pencils sharpened, to get their turn at the computer, to get to the bathroom, and to be dismissed from class. If students are to succeed in school, they must be able to cope with continual delay as a standard operating procedure.

One plea that is rarely granted is that of talking to classmates beyond controlled learning activities. Like the character from Greek mythology Tantalus, who was continually tempted with food and water but was not allowed to eat or drink, students are surrounded by peers and friends but are restrained from communicating with them. In other words, students in the classroom are in the very frustrating position of having to ignore social temptation, of acting as though they are isolated despite the crowd surrounding them. Furthermore, while trying to concentrate on work and to ignore social temptations, students are beset by frequent interruptions—the public address system blaring a message in the middle of an exam, the end-of-class bell interrupting a lively discussion, a teacher's reprimand or a student's question derailing a train of thought.

Consider how Maxine in Mr. Thompson's English class had to cope with delay, denial of desire, social distraction, and interruptions. She waited for the delivery of her new text. She waited to be called on by the teacher. Her attempt to concentrate on reading the poem was disturbed by frequent interruptions. Her brief communication with a classmate was interrupted by a reprimand. Her head was filled with ideas and questions. In short, there was a lot she would like to have said, but there was almost no opportunity to say it.

Educators concerned about school improvement have called attention to the inefficient use of time in school, claiming that we lose between one-quarter and one-half of the time available for learning through attendance problems, noninstructional activities (such as class changes and assemblies), administrative and organizational activities, and disruptions caused by student misbehavior. Knowing this, it becomes all the more crucial to maximize learning opportunities during the 1,260 hours or more students spend in the classroom each school year.[3]

Whereas the business world may suggest "time is money," for educators, time is learning. As one teacher points out,

> Time is the currency of teaching. We barter with time. Every day we make small concessions, small trade-offs, but, in the end, we know it's going to defeat us. After all, how many times are we actually able to cover World War I in our history courses before the year is out? We always laugh a little about that, but the truth is the sense of the clock ticking is one of the most oppressive features of teaching.[4]

There is a limited amount of time set aside for the school day. Research shows that when more time is allocated to subject-matter learning, student achievement increases.[5] When this valuable resource is spent handing out supplies or reprimanding misbehavior, it is lost for learning. Looked at from this perspective, Mr. Thompson's class not only was frustrating but also deprived students of a precious and limited resource—the time to learn.

What are the pluses and pitfalls of posting a schedule like this? Do you recall your own feelings as a student about the routine and regimentation of school life?

The Teacher as Gatekeeper

Philip Jackson reports that teachers are typically involved in more than one thousand verbal exchanges with their students every day.[6] Count the number of verbal exchanges Mr. Thompson had with his students during our abbreviated classroom scene and you will get some idea of how much and how often teachers talk. One of the functions that keeps teachers busiest is what Philip Jackson terms **gatekeeping.** As gatekeepers, teachers must determine who will talk, when, and for how long, as well as the basic direction of the communication.

FOCUS QUESTION 2

How does the teacher's gate-keeping function influence classroom roles?

Consider what effect patterns of classroom interaction have on both teachers and students:[7]

- Roughly two-thirds of classroom time is taken up by talk; two-thirds of that talk is by the teacher.
- While questioning signals curiosity, it is the teachers, not the learners, who do most questioning, asking as many as 348 questions a day. The typical student rarely asks an academic question.
- Most classroom questions require that students use only rote memory.
- Students are not given much time to ask, or even answer, questions. Teachers usually wait less than a second for student comments and answers.
- Teachers interact less and less with students as they go through the grades.

Ironically, although a major goal of education is to increase students' curiosity and quest for knowledge, it is teachers, not students, who most often dominate and manage classroom interaction (see A Closer Look: Patterns of the Classroom). Consequently, classroom interactions do not teach students to become active, inquiring, self-reliant learners. Students are expected to be quiet and passive, to think quickly (and perhaps superficially), to rely on

A Closer Look   Patterns of the Classroom

After observing in more than one thousand classrooms, *John Goodlad* and his team of researchers found that the following patterns characterize most classrooms:

- Much of what happens in class is geared toward maintaining order among twenty to thirty students restrained in a relatively small space.
- Although the classroom is a group setting, each student typically works alone.
- The teacher is the key figure in setting the tone and determining the activities.
- Most of the time, the teacher is in front of the classroom, teaching a whole group of students.
- There is little praise or corrective feedback; classes are emotionally neutral or flat places.
- Students are involved in a limited range of activities—listening to lectures, writing answers to questions, and taking exams.

- A significant number of students are confused by teacher explanations and feel that they do not get enough guidance on how to improve.

Goodlad concluded that "the emotional tone of the classroom is neither harsh and punitive nor warm and joyful; it might be described most accurately as flat."

SOURCE: John Goodlad, *A Place Called School* (New York: McGraw-Hill, 1984/2004).

REFLECTION: How many of these findings characterized your classroom life? How will you make learning more joyful and engaging?

You Be The Judge

HOMEWORK SHOULD BE

A Major Part of a Student's Life Because . . .

THERE IS TOO MUCH MATERIAL TO BE MASTERED ONLY DURING SCHOOL TIME

Given demands on students to learn more and to increase their test scores, much study and learning needs to take place at home. After all, students are in school for just five hours of a twenty-four-hour day.

IT BRINGS PARENTS INTO THE LEARNING PROCESS

School cannot accomplish its goals alone. Students achieve much more when academics are reinforced at home. By providing guidance and monitoring homework, parents demonstrate their support of learning, becoming true partners with teachers. Closing the school–home gap fosters competent and attentive students.

MANY STUDENTS DO NOT USE THEIR TIME WISELY

The average student comes home from school, talks on the phone with friends, "hangs out" at the mall, watches television for hours, and then plays a computer game or two before going to bed. Homework at least gives students something meaningful to do with their time.

Limited and Brief Because . . .

TOO MUCH STRESS IS PLACED ON STUDENTS AS IT IS

Schools have been taken over by this growing obsession with tests. The last thing we need to do is extend this angst to home life. Besides, homework is mostly busywork, unrelated to real learning.

IT FAVORS SOME STUDENTS AND PENALIZES OTHERS

Some children have highly educated parents, home computers, and the resources needed to produce quality homework. Other students have poor and uneducated parents, who may not even speak English, and who may be working two or more jobs. All too often, homework is simply a measure of family resources.

MANY STUDENTS DO NOT HAVE THE LUXURY OF EXTRA TIME

Many students go directly from school to their part-time job. Their families may need the money. Other students must care for younger siblings at home while parents are at work. Increasing homework would place an enormous burden on these families.

www.mhhe.com/sadker10e

YOU DECIDE . . .

How much homework do you think is appropriate? Do you have a plan to handle differences in family resources? What relationships do you see between homework and tracking/ability grouping?

---

memory, and to be dependent on the teacher. Not surprisingly, silent, disengaged students have less positive attitudes and lower achievement. Studies show that participating in class discussions, getting the opportunity to excel, and feeling that their schoolwork matters makes for an engaging education experience, regardless of the grade or age of students.[8] (See You Be the Judge: Homework Should Be) Perhaps the challenge new teachers should keep before them is finding a way to turn their gatekeeping role into a benefit for students, instead of a hindrance.

The Other Side of the Tracks

We have seen how teachers function as gatekeepers, controlling the amount and flow of student talk in the classroom. Let's step back a moment and consider an even more basic question: Which students sit in which classrooms? That very crucial decision falls on teachers, counselors, and administrators. Many believe that it is easier for students with similar skills and intellectual abilities to learn together, in same-ability, *homogeneous* classes. Educators following this belief test and sort students according to their abilities and, as a result, send them down different school paths, profoundly shaping their futures. Students of different abilities (low, middle, and high) are assigned to different *tracks* of courses and programs (vocational, general, college-bound, honors, and AP). **Tracking** is the term given to this process, and though some teachers believe that tracking makes instruction more manageable, others believe that it is a terribly flawed system. Either way, tracking is one of the oldest of school traditions.

FOCUS QUESTION 3
What is tracking and what are its advantages and disadvantages?

Sociologist Talcott Parsons analyzed school as a social system and concluded that the college selection process begins in elementary school and is virtually sealed by the time students finish junior high.[9] Parsons's analysis has significant implications, for he is suggesting that future roles in adult life are determined by student achievement in elementary school. The labeling system, beginning at an early age, determines who will wear a stethoscope, who will carry a laptop computer, and who will become a low-wage laborer.

Several researchers consider students' social class a critical factor in this selection system. Back in 1929, Robert and Helen Lynd, in their extensive study of Middletown (a small midwestern city), concluded that schools are essentially middle-class institutions that discriminate against lower-class students.[10] Approximately fifteen years later, W. Lloyd Warner and his associates at the University of Chicago conducted a series of studies in New England, the deep South, and the Midwest and came to a similar conclusion:

> One group [the lower class] is almost immediately brushed off into a bin labeled "nonreaders, first grade repeaters," or "opportunity class," where they stay for eight or ten years and are then released through a chute to the outside world to become hewers of wood and drawers of water.[11]

More recently, **Jeannie Oakes's** *Keeping Track* offered a scathing indictment of racial influence on tracking. She found that race, far more than ability, determines which students are placed in which tracks: Black, Hispanic, and Native American students with similar test scores as their white peers are three times more likely to be enrolled in low-track classes. Oakes also documented how these lower-tracked students have fewer learning opportunities and how teachers expect little from them. Their instruction covers less content, involves more drill and repetition, and places more emphasis on classroom management problems.[12]

Students in low-ability tracks have difficulty moving into higher tracks. Ray Rist observed a kindergarten class in an all-black urban school. By the eighth day of class, the kindergarten teacher, apparently using such criteria as physical appearance, socioeconomic status, and language usage, had separated her students into groups of "fast learners" and "slow learners."

Low teacher expectations and unchallenging courses may encourage student passivity and boredom.

She spent more time with the "fast learners" and gave them more instruction and encouragement. The "slow learners" got more than their fair share of control and ridicule. The children soon began to mirror the teacher's behavior. As the "fast learners" belittled the "slow learners," the low-status children began to exhibit attitudes of self-degradation and hostility toward one another. This teacher's expectations, formed during eight days at the beginning of school, shaped the academic and social treatment of children in her classroom for the entire year and perhaps for years to come. Records of the grouping that had taken place during the first week in kindergarten were passed on to teachers in the upper grades, providing the basis for further differential treatment.[13]

Profile in Education Jeannie Oakes

Jeannie Oakes never dreamed of being a schoolteacher. "It was just too ordinary. I wanted adventure, unconventionality." So she embraced her passion for reading, earned a degree in American Literature, married, and had children. "It turned out that I was a lot more conventional than I thought I was!" While raising her children at home in the 1960s, Oakes decided that, she would become a teacher for the "same old-fashioned reasons for which women have always taught—I wanted to be with my children when they came home from school every day."[a] But the unconventional spirit in Jeannie Oakes hadn't disappeared. She championed the Civil Rights movement and anti-Vietnam war activities. And she realized that teaching was a vehicle for social justice, that teaching could be far from ordinary.

Her first day in the classroom made a lasting impression. She didn't announce to students they were taking basic English but recalls how within five minutes they knew and announced, "Oh, we're in the dumb class!" During the seven years Oakes taught middle and high school English in suburban Los Angeles, she struggled to be as good a teacher to low-track classes as to the high ones and was astonished how her own instruction and expectations changed for students placed in honors, average, and basic classes. She also witnessed how tracking dictated disparate lives in schools. "In a very public way, adults make judgments about students' current and future abilities that take on a hierarchical nature: We talk about top groups and bottom groups. And in the culture of schools, the top group becomes the top kids and the bottom group the bottom kids in a very value-laden and defining way."[b]

Creating innovative classrooms that unlocked successful learning for diverse students became her challenge. Each new school year, Oakes developed new curriculum and instructional strategies, hoping to invigorate enthusiasm for learning in students and fellow teachers. Her calls for change met with administrative resistance and her voice was increasingly silenced.

Her voice was heard as a doctoral student at UCLA, as Oakes researched with John Goodlad the varied aspects of life in schools. Oakes specifically explored how tracking and ability grouping limit the school experiences of low-income students and students of color. Her landmark book *Keeping Track: How Schools Structure Inequality* (1985/2005) brings the inequities of tracking into the national spotlight, casting a riveting portrayal of how tracking creates segregation within schools and shortchanges quality learning and resources. Yet despite the attention, tracking remains one of the most entrenched school practices, relegating students to separate classrooms based less on ability and more on race and socioeconomic status.

Oakes believes the persistence is rooted in a cultural notion that intelligence is immutable and that there is virtually nothing schools can do to alter a student's fundamental capability. She doesn't buy such a limited view.

> Kindergartners show an enormous interest in learning, and this cuts across socioeconomic, racial, and ethnic lines. But as kids go through school, if they don't have successful experiences, they learn their efforts do not pay off. So by high school, we see disinterest unjustly interpreted by teachers as low ability.[c]

For Oakes, then, the fundamental goal of equalizing opportunity is not simply to detrack but also to increase the quality of curriculum and instruction for everybody in schools so that success is not limited to those in the high track. This requires a powerful shift in conventional norms, one that defines intellectual capacity as not fixed but learned through interaction, problem solving, and critical thinking.

Oakes recognizes that the process of detracking schools is not easy. School reform efforts are often met with resistance by those who benefit from the current system. This political dimension of inequality cannot be underestimated. Parents of high-achieving students exert considerable pressure to ensure that their children have access to honors and AP classes. Moreover, teachers of high-track students often resist efforts to detrack, enjoying the intellectual challenge and prestige that come from teaching these students. School administrators and teachers who have undertaken detracking efforts often tell her it is their most difficult undertaking—and most rewarding. Oakes understands why: "It's about fairness and creating better schools. And getting there is half the fun."[d]

A conventional career, perhaps. But Jeannie Oakes is an unconventional advocate for equity and change.

[a] Carlos Alberto Torres, *Education, Power, and Personal Biography: Dialogues with Critical Educators* (New York: Routledge, 1998), pp. 224–25.
[b] John O'Neill, "On Tracking and Individual Differences: A Conversation with Jeannie Oakes," *Educational Leadership* 50, no. 2 (October 1992), p. 18.
[c] Ibid, p. 20.
[d] Torres, *Education, Power, and Personal Biography*, p. 230.

To learn more about Jeannie Oakes, click on *Profiles in Education*.

www.mhhe.com/sadker10e

REFLECTION: How has Jeannie Oakes made teaching an act of social justice? Why does tracking persist? How have you experienced or witnessed the impact of tracking?

107

Consider some additional disturbing facts on race, socioeconomic status, and tracking:[14]

- Teachers with the least experience and the lowest levels of qualifications are assigned to students in the lowest tracks.
- Schools with predominately poor and minority populations offer fewer advanced and more remedial courses in academic subjects.
- Asian, White, and wealthy students are more likely than black, Hispanic, and poor students to be recommended for advanced classes and gifted programs, even with equivalent test scores.
- Low-track students are seldom required to take as many math and science classes as high-track students.
- Students are more likely to choose their friends from their tracked classes in elementary through high school. These social networks can further entrench racially segregated academic tracks.
- When parents intervene, counselors place middle- and upper-socioeconomic class students with low grades and test scores into higher tracked groups.

Such findings add momentum to the effort to *detrack,* or eliminate tracking practices from the nation's schools. But the task is not easy. Jeannie Oakes characterizes the tracking debate as symbolic of a larger struggle over the purpose of education:

> [A] norm that bolsters and legitimizes tracking is the American emphasis on competition and individualism over cooperation and the good of the community—a norm suggesting that "good" education is a scarce commodity available only to a few winners. Although the American system of public education was designed to promote the common good and to prepare children for participation in a democratic society, more recent emphasis has been placed on what a graduate can "get out" of schooling in terms of income, power, or status.[15]

"True," tracking advocates argue, "it would appear more democratic to put everyone in the same class, but such idealism is destined to fail." They contend that it is unrealistic to think everyone can or should master the same material or learn it at the same pace. Without tracking we have *heterogeneous,* or mixed-ability, classes. Tracking advocates are quick to point out that mixed-ability classes have their own set of problems: In heterogeneous classes, bright students get bored, slower students have trouble keeping up, and we lose our most talented and our most needy students. Teachers find themselves grading the brighter students on the quality of their work, and the weaker ones on their "effort," which is a big problem (especially with parents!). Teachers get frustrated trying to meet each student's needs, and hardly ever hitting the mark. Putting everyone in the same class simply doesn't work.[16]

Detracking advocates, as you might imagine, offer a different take on the issue: "No sorting system is consistent with equality of opportunity. Worse yet, the tracking system is not based on individual ability. It is badly biased in favor of white middle-class America. We must face the reality that poor children, often children of color, come to school far from being ready to learn. And the school, whose job it is to educate all our children, does little to help. The built-in bias in instruction, counseling, curricular materials, and testing must be overcome. Students get shoveled into second-rate courses that prepare them for fourth-rate jobs. Their track becomes 'a great training robbery,' and the students who are robbed may be ones with great abilities."

Whereas the social pitfalls of tracking have been well documented, tracking's efficacy has not. More than three decades of research documents how tracking fails to foster outcomes Americans value, such as academic excellence and educational equity. Tracking is especially inconsistent with today's national goal of having all students meet high academic standards. With little hard evidence supporting tracking, and a growing concern about its negative fallout, it is little wonder that the *term* "tracking" has fallen out of favor. Most schools now prefer the term "ability grouping."

Ability grouping sorts students based on capability, but the groupings may well vary by subject. Whereas tracks suggest permanence, ability grouping is more transitory. One year, a student might find herself in a high-ability math group and a low-ability English group. The following year, that same student might be reassigned to a new set of groups. Today, many middle and high schools talk about "ability grouping," but sometimes it is only the label that has been changed. Ability grouping can easily become *de facto* tracking. (You may want to think of school tracking as a take-off on the federal "witness protection program": a reality functioning under an assumed identity.)

Many educators believe that detracking can work, if it is implemented correctly. For example, detracked instruction is best offered through individualized, differentiated and cooperative learning (which we will discuss in-depth in Chapter 11), rather than the traditional approach of trying to teach all students simultaneously. Similarly, alternative assessments work far better than testing everyone with the same test. (Compare this view with the current emphasis on standardized tests.) In fact, although students arrive at school from very different backgrounds, learning from one another and together has great advantages. Detracked schools can be authentic places of learning, academically challenging to all while teaching a living lesson in democracy. What is needed is time, careful planning, and adequate training for teachers so that they can succeed and all students can learn.[17]

One of the ironies of tracking is that it simply builds on an already divided school culture. What educators do not do to divide students, students often do to themselves.

The Gendered World of Elementary and Middle Schools

In the first grade, when so much about school seems gigantic and fearful, children look to adults for safety: What am I supposed to do in the classroom? Where do I get lunch? How do I find the bus to ride home from school? Children go to their first-grade teacher not only for this practical information but also for hugs, praise, and general warmth and affection.[18] But by the second grade, a new world emerges, a world where gender shapes identities and relationships and intensifies during the school years. By the second grade, boys break away from teacher dependence and place more importance on their peer group—other boys. Boys claim their own territory on the athletic field and in the lunchroom, and sometimes even challenge the teacher. Male identity and entitlement are strengthened during elementary school years, but not for all boys, not for the boys considered sissies. Over time, many of these excluded males exhibit an increasing number of social, emotional, and academic problems.

Girls spend the first few elementary school years helping the teacher, behaviors that are rewarded, in part, with good report card grades. Girls also form best-friend relationships in which pairs of girls pledge devotion to one another. By the upper elementary grades, girls begin to fantasize about the "cute" boys in their class and about what being married and having a family would be like. Being a good student and having a pleasing personality are important to girls, but by the upper elementary grades, appearance often becomes the key to social status.

The *gender wall* blocking boys and girls from interacting is stronger than barriers to racial integration; there is more cross-race than cross-sex communication during the elementary school years. As one girl explains:

> If you say you like someone, other kids spread it all over the school and that's embarrassing. . . . If you even sit beside a boy in class, other kids say you like him. And they come to you in the bathroom and tease you about liking the boy. Once some of the girls put J. S. and B. B. on the bathroom walls. That was embarrassing.[19]

FOCUS QUESTION 4
How do gender and peer groups influence children in elementary and middle school?

FIGURE 4.1

Sociogram: A teacher's tool.

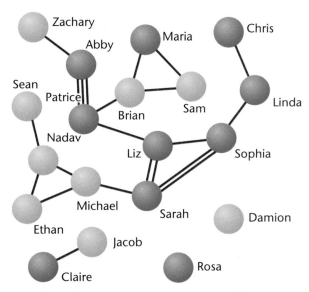

Sociograms provide insights into the social life of a class. In this sociogram, circles represent students, and colors indicate gender. Lines are drawn connecting circles when students interact with one another. Each line reflects a verbal communication: the more lines, the greater number of interactions. In this sociogram, it appears that Abby and Patrice are friends; Liz, Sarah, and Sophia may form a clique; while Damion and Rosa appear to be isolates. Charting several sociograms of these children over time would confirm or refute these initial perceptions.

> **REFLECTION:** Construct your own sociogram, drawing a circle for each person in your class or in a class that you are observing, or even in a lunchroom or during recess. Draw a line every time there is an interaction. Can you detect friends, cliques, and isolates? How does class seating affect relationships? What might you do as a teacher to influence these patterns?

Every day, teachers must work to create humane and caring classrooms. When students respond to questions designed to measure their friendship patterns, 10 percent of them emerge as not being anybody's friend (isolates). About half of these are just ignored. The other half become the victims of active peer group rejection and hostility. In fact, elementary school sociometric measures predict social adjustment better than most other personality and educational tests do.[20] These social preferences can be graphically presented in **sociograms.** (See Figure 4.1.) Most friendless children are aware of their problem and report feeling lonely and unsuccessful in relating to others. Rejection by the child's peer group is a strong indicator of future problems.

GUEST COLUMN: Haunted by Racist Attitudes

As graduation time approaches, I am supposed to get nostalgic about my community and my school. I should be thankful for how they have enriched my life, and I should expect to reminisce later on the "great things" about living here. Frankly, in my case, that will not be possible; I'll be trying to forget the bigotry here. Elementary school fostered my negative first impressions. One kid tried to insult me in the halls by calling me "African." My classmates told me to "go back where you came from." (Obviously they had no idea what country this was, but cultural education is another essay.) Often, I was used as an object in a "cooties" game. I was the contaminated one who had to touch all the other pure white-skinned kids. One day after school I was tied to a tree by some boys. The girls just stood around to laugh. They were the friendly ones because at least they did not inflict bodily pain. Wasn't I the naive buffoon to underestimate the burn of psychological humiliation?

Summer meant parks and recreation day camp, and that was hellish. Each day, I was depantsed by some fifth-grade boys in front of the amused campers. I was too embarrassed to tell my parents, and the counselors paid no attention to the foolish games all little boys play. Adult ignorance was by far the most agonizing injustice. In middle school, I sat in front of a boy who constantly whispered, "You f — nigger, black, disgusting" in my ear. Racism was intolerable. The teacher, I guess, disagreed. At least kids are honest. Isn't it amusing how they are little reflections of a community's attitudes? Today, the same people who tormented me as a child walk down the halls faceless. Once a racist reaches a certain age, he realizes that prejudice is not an outright verbal contract. It is subtle and "understood."

Social exclusion is a painful reality for many students from elementary to high school.

Just yesterday my five-year-old sister came home from her preschool and complained, "A girl said she didn't wanna play with me because I'm black." I said, "That's terrible! Did you tell the teacher?" My sister responded, "My teacher said, 'Just ignore her.' "

Yes, I'll have no trouble trying to forget this place.

—Student letter to the school paper[21]

An insightful teacher can structure a classroom to minimize negative and hurtful interaction and maximize the positive power of peer group relations. For instance, eliminating social cliques and race- and gender-based segregation is a precursor to successful cooperative groups. An intentional teacher often assigns students to seats or to group work to counter pupil favoritism and bias. A teacher's perceptiveness and skill in influencing the social side of school can mean a world of difference in the student's environment. These social needs only grow as students transition into middle school.

Was your transition from elementary to middle school smooth, filled with the excitement of new friends and independence? Or did the move spark angst as you navigated new buildings, teachers, and friendships? The transition is important because adolescence is a time of so much change: physical, psychological, and social.

Since the 1960s, many policymakers have advocated that middle school—generally grades 6, 7, and 8—should be a time when children have a chance to adjust to puberty. Attention to the emotional and physical developmental growth of adolescents is seen as the primary purpose of middle school life. However, some critics see middle schools as having gone "soft," overemphasizing self-esteem building at the expense of academic rigor. Describing the middle school years as the "Bermuda Triangle of American education," such critics call for a return to K–8 schooling and a more discipline-focused curriculum.[22] Because some adolescents can struggle with change, they argue that K–8 schools provide stability in neighborhood, building, peers, and staff for parents and students alike. Such efforts are supported by a recent study that found students moving into middle school frequently experience a sharp drop in math and language arts achievement in the transition year that plagues them as far out as tenth grade, even risking their ability to graduate high school and go on to college.[23] Yet, advocates

RELATED READING
Breaking Ranks in the Middle (2006) by Secondary School Principals

for middle schools argue that simply changing the grade configuration is no magic bullet. What happens in the classroom is what matters most. Noted one principal, "The challenge for us as middle-school educators in the age of high-stakes testing is to encourage teaching for understanding while addressing the myriad of social and emotional issues. Kids develop at their own rates; what's important is how you are personalizing that environment for them."[24] What do students believe is important to support their success in middle school? Five characteristics top their list:[25]

- Recognition for academic success
- Having the opportunity to do well
- Homework that is meaningful
- A best friend at school
- Feeling safe at school

While the future of middle schools is in doubt, one adolescent struggle remains omnipresent: the need to develop an identity, including what it means to be male or female:

> "I feel pressure from my parents and teachers to do well in school. But when I do, boys won't ask me to the school dance and even my girlfriends call me a 'nerd.' So now I talk less in class and don't study as much. The teasing hurts, so it's easier to hide being smart."

> "Boys joke around too much so teachers pay more attention by disciplining rather than helping them to learn."

> "Boys can't take music class without being called a fag. So I hide my musical talents, like playing Mozart on the keyboard."

> "Girls do everything for men in marriage."

Do these words sound like sexist artifacts of years ago? In fact, these are the voices of today's middle school students. Their words reveal how gender and peer relations play significant roles in their lives, expanding some options, but more often limiting academic and social development. When we asked more than four hundred middle schoolers to identify the "best and worst thing about being a boy or girl," their stories lifted the veil on the pervasive sexism in today's schools and society.[26] Students unequivocally had more positive things to say about being a boy than about being a girl. Male advantages focused on physical and athletic prowess, underscoring the central role physicality plays for boys. Students also described how boys "naturally" excel at sports: "Boys have more sports available and can play them better. It's fair to say that we are better athletes than girls."

Students also easily described male entitlements: They are listened to more, are naturally smarter, are allowed to do more, have the dominant role in marriage, and receive greater respect. More than one in ten students wrote that one of the best things about being a boy was not being a girl, citing the perils of periods, childbirth, pressures to be thin, and limited high-paying career options.[27] Yet middle school boys face challenges, too. When asked to describe the worst thing about being a boy, behavioral aggression and discipline topped the list, followed by poor grades and homophobia. Being a gay boy is now a challenge for middle schools because more gay children are "coming out" at a younger age. A survey of gay, bisexual, and transgender middle-schoolers from across the nation found that 81 percent were regularly harassed and 39 percent were physically assaulted. Only 29 percent said reporting these activities to authorities resulted in effective intervention.[28]

What are the joys for adolescent girls? Appearance was mentioned most often as the best reason for being a girl. Appearance comments included buying clothes, playing with hair styles, and taking beauty treatments, underscoring the need for females to seek approval outside themselves. One seventh-grade girl vividly captured this salience of appearance: "Clothes make it fun to be a girl. THE perfect outfit can make you feel pretty and worth something." Academic advantage was another "best" reason for being a girl and included two opposing sets of comments, one that spoke to undue favoritism given girls—the "teacher's pet" idea—and the other described the extra effort given by girls and the intellectual satisfaction derived from their higher grades.

Nearly one in five students wrote "nothing" to describe the best thing about being a girl, and students had little difficulty identifying negative aspects of being female. Relational aggression ranked highest with students describing a peer culture of gossip, rumors, and distrust among friends. Girls also noted their deliberate efforts to take easier courses, perform poorly on tests and assignments, and "act dumb" to gain popularity or have a boyfriend. Girls further expressed frustration at being the "second-class gender," describing limited career options, responsibility for domestic chores, and the fear of sexual harassment/rape. At the other end of the spectrum, girls also felt they need to be "supergirls"—everything to everyone all the time. Three-quarters of the girls described feeling "a lot of pressure" to please everyone. A ninth-grader shared her frustration: "There is way too much pressure to be skinny, popular, athletic, and have a boyfriend. Girls should be respected more as people than so-and-so's girlfriend."[29]

These experiences of middle-schoolers are similar for students in urban, suburban, and rural America; in wealthy and poor communities; in schools that are diverse as well as those that are homogeneous. Relational aggression and discipline, appearance, entitlement, and homophobia can create pressures that detract from both the academic emphasis and the social well-being of a school community. Schools that do not attend to these issues are placing a number of school goals at risk.

High School: Lessons in Social Status

More than 15 million students arrive at 20,000 public high schools every day. These schools run the gamut from decaying buildings plagued by vandalism and drugs to orderly, congenial places with modern technology and attractive facilities. They vary in size from fifty to five thousand students, who spend days divided into either six or seven 50-minute periods or perhaps fewer, longer blocks of time.[30] What happens in these schools greatly shapes the academic and social lives of millions of teenagers.

In his book *Is There Life After High School?* Ralph Keyes stirred up the pot of high school memories and asked many people, both the famous and the obscure, about their high school experiences. He was amazed at the vividness and detail with which their memories came pouring out—particularly about the status system, that pattern of social reward and recognition that can be so intensely painful or exhilarating. High school was remembered as a caste system of "innies" and "outies," a minutely detailed social register in which one's popularity or lack of it was continually analyzed and contemplated.

For many high school students, peer relationships, not academics, are central to school life. When asked to identify the one best thing about their high school, "my friends" usually ranks at the top of the list. Sports activities rank second. "Nothing" ranks higher than "classes I'm taking" and "teachers."[31] When asked to describe her school, one high school junior said,

> The classes are okay, I guess. Most of the time I find them pretty boring, but then I suppose that's the way school classes are supposed to be. What I like most about the place is the chance to be with my friends. It's nice to be a part of a group. I don't mean one of the clubs or groups the school runs. . . . But an informal group of your own friends is great.[32]

David Owen is an author who returned to high school undercover to study peer culture. He discovered first-hand how difficult it can be to navigate adolescent society. Posing as a

FOCUS QUESTION 5

In what ways does the adolescent culture shape teenage perceptions and behaviors in high school?

Peer groups tend to define the quality of students' school life.

student who had just moved into the area, he enrolled in what he calls a typical American high school, approximately two hours out of New York City. He was struck by the power of the peer group and how socially ill at ease most adolescents are. He likened adolescents to adults visiting a foreign country and a different culture. Experimenting with new behavior, they are terrified of being noticed doing something stupid:

> Being an adolescent is a full-time job, an all-out war against the appearance of awkwardness. No one is more attentive to nuance than a seventeen-year-old . . . When a kid in my class came to school one day in a funny-looking pair of shoes that one of his friends eventually laughed at, I could see by his face that he was thinking, "well, that does it, there goes the rest of my life."[33]

For those who remember jockeying unsuccessfully for a place within the inner circle of the high school social register, it may be comforting to learn that the tables do turn. Few studies show any correlation between high status in high school and later achievement as an adult. Those who are voted king and queen of the prom or most likely to succeed do not appear to do any better or any worse in adult life than those whose yearbook description is less illustrious. What works in that very insular adolescent environment is not necessarily what works in the outside world. One researcher speculates that it is those on the "second tier," those in the group just below the top, who are most likely to succeed after high school. He says, "I think the rest of our lives are spent making up for what we did or did not do in high school."[34]

In *A Tribe Apart: A Journey into the Heart of American Adolescence,* Patricia Hersch shares the story of three years she spent with seventh- through twelfth-graders in suburban Virginia.[35] What Hersch discovered was troubling: the development of an isolated, intense, and perilous adolescent culture, where drugs, alienation, and violence represent ongoing threats. It is a teenage society unknown to many parents. Contemporary adolescent friendships appear to be fluid: Teenagers may have one group of friends in a drama club, another from math class, and a third set from sports activities. Today cross-gender friendships are also more common as boys and girls do a better job of developing relationships without the need for a romantic attachment.

But even as the number of friendships grows, the quality of adolescent relationships remains a problem. Teenagers, both girls and boys, report that although they have many friends, they lack intimate, close friends and that being part of a meaningful group is challenging. Teenagers say that there is no one that they can really confide in, no one with whom to share their deepest thoughts. In the midst of a crowd, they feel alone. And increasingly under pressure.

> She has six exams in five days plus an analytical paper due. Her stomach hurts, she can barely eat. Some of her friends have panic attacks, while others study until 2 A.M. No, these are not law students; they are eleventh graders.

The academic pressure that engulfs teenage youth is palpable. Many adolescents spend their high school years in a seemingly endless contest for the best grades, highest test scores, and the most impressive collection of résumé-building accolades, all the tools they need to pry open the doors to a top college. Despite their tremendous abilities and stellar performances, many of these students succumb to the pressure. They experience a sense of purposeless, emptiness, and fear that emerge as mental health problems.[36] This stressful adolescent world is not sustainable.

With the best of intentions, adults can undermine the normal process of youthful growth and idealism, eliminating exploration, engagement, risk-taking, and the freedom to experiment. Overprotective and over-involved parents, sometimes referred to as "helicopter parents" for all their "hovering," contribute to a hyper-competitive teenage world where getting into the "right" college is not the most important thing; it's the only thing. These parents expect schools to teach-to-the-test, and even beyond school, they engage in an often costly and commercialized college admissions process. Youngsters caught in this pressure-cooker can suffer both physical and mental consequences, as their own interests and desires are submerged. Nearly 80 percent of adolescents feel they are not engaged in purposeful activities in school or other aspects of their lives.[37] While some parents recognize and rail against these unhealthy patterns, many others are swept into the prevailing cutthroat culture that craves academic status above all else. (Parental concerns often start early during elementary school years. See the Teaching Tip: How to Work with "Helicopter Parents", below.)

Teaching Tip

HOW TO WORK WITH "HELICOPTER PARENTS"

It was the day before my first year of teaching, my room was all set up, and I felt ready. But I hadn't much thought about one thing: the other adults involved with my students—their parents! I learned *very* quickly to focus on parent relationships. My first semester teaching, I learned these lessons.

BE PREPARED FOR ANYTHING

"Meet the Teacher Day" brought students with their parents, and I was taken by surprise. I had a parent yell at me for having an "inappropriate book series" in my classroom (even though this is a well-loved children's series that had been approved by our school board). I had a parent inform me that they had searched me on the Internet and knew where I'd gone to school, my past jobs, that I'd recently gotten married, my age, etc. Thankfully, there wasn't any negative information for her to find.

STAND YOUR GROUND

About two months after our first class science experiment, I had a parent e-mail me saying she was very unhappy with the grade her child received and wanted an explanation. The parent made it very apparent that she wanted me to change the grade and also threatened to pull the child from the school. This was demoralizing. However, I knew in my gut it wouldn't be fair to change the grade and it wouldn't help the student in the long run. Following an in-person meeting, the grade stayed, and so did the child. I learned that some parents just want to test their power.

COMMUNICATE REGULARLY

Each week I send home a brief newsletter with announcements, updates from the classroom, and a list of what we learned in each subject that week. Parents are e-mailed unless they request otherwise at Parent Night. It takes me about 15 minutes to put it together. Several parents have thanked me, as they didn't feel they had ever been so informed of their children's daily work. They also like feeling part of a team.

COMMUNICATE POSITIVELY

I wanted students to realize how much I value effort in class, so I came up with an "Honor Roll." All students have to do to earn a place on the Honor Roll is turn in all of their homework; they don't have to perform perfectly. When I posted my first honor roll, students were so excited and proud. What I think they valued even more was the note I sent home to their parents. I had many tell me that their son or daughter had never been recognized for any sort of effort or achievement, or that a positive note had ever been sent home.

By Amie Kemberling, an elementary school teacher in Tucson, Arizona

REFLECTION: Which of Amie's strategies resonate with you? Did any surprise you? Do you have a strategy to add?

But this need not be the case, and educators can make a difference. Studies indicate that unhealthy student stress can be alleviated by personal, caring relationships at school. In fact, positive teacher-student relationships are associated with:[38]

- Increasing student understanding and meaningfulness of what is being taught
- Feeling a sense of personal empowerment
- Decreasing incidences of depression
- Improving self-confidence
- Reducing student stress
- Developing resiliency
- Improving creativity

Caring school relationships build trust and a healthier academic and social climate for adolescents. Given the growing array of social challenges you are likely to confront in your classroom, stronger student–teacher relationships have never been more needed.

Social Challenges Come to School

Have you ever felt the cold slap of rejection because of your social class? Have you ever denied a family history that includes divorce or unplanned pregnancy? Has your life been touched by depression, an eating disorder, substance abuse, or bullying? Children across all racial, ethnic, and socioeconomic backgrounds may be plagued by such difficulties, affecting their academic and emotional well-being. Your students will likely carry these struggles and concerns with them as they walk through your classroom door. Although schools and teachers cannot completely solve these social issues (as much as we may try), education can bring purpose, hope, and empowerment to our most troubled youth.

Family Patterns

Not too many years ago, mothers stayed at home and fathers went to work. Interracial couples were shunned. Out-of-wedlock children and pregnant, unmarried women were hidden from the public's attention. Divorce was rare.

Today's family bears little resemblance to those images. Only two-thirds of children live in two-parent families, with children of color far less likely than their white peers to live with both parents (Figure 4.2). Nearly one in four children live only with their mothers, 3 percent live only with their fathers, and 4 percent live with neither parent. Half of those children living with no

FOCUS QUESTION 6

What impact do changing family patterns and economic issues have on children and schools?

FIGURE 4.2

The American family.

SOURCE: Federal Interagency Forum on Child and Family Statistics, *America's Children: Key National Indicators of Well-Being, 2011.*

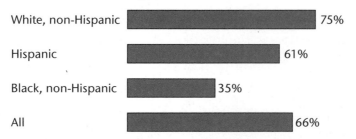

Children Living in Two-Parent Families

White, non-Hispanic — 75%
Hispanic — 61%
Black, non-Hispanic — 35%
All — 66%

REFLECTION: What factors might account for these family differences across racial groups?

parent are being raised by a grandparent.[39] Research shows that children from single-parent families are less likely to achieve academically and more likely to be expelled or suspended.[40]

Generally, our families are getting more smaller, older, and more diverse. Families most often have two children or fewer, and these children are born to increasingly older and more educated mothers. Today, one in seven children is born to a mother at least 35 years old, and more than 50 percent of new mothers have at least some college education.[41] More than half of American families are remarried or recoupled, including half of our children. Stepfamilies consist of biological and legal relationships with stepparents, stepsiblings, multiple sets of grandparents, and what often becomes a confusing array of relatives from old and new relationships.[42] Other families are created through cross-cultural and racial unions. It was only in 1967 that the Supreme Court overruled antimiscegenation laws, which had banned interracial marriage.

Although Americans still prefer marriage, the past two decades have seen the number of unmarried couples living together more than double, including both opposite- and same-sex partners. In fact, more than 40 percent of births today are to unmarried mothers, an increase of 30 percent since 1990.[43] *Nontraditional families* refers to family lifestyles other than a married male and female living with their children. Nontraditional families can consist of a single parent with children, stepparents and their children, biological parents who are not married, relatives or friends acting as child guardians, same-sex couples sharing parenting roles, nonmarried couples living as families, or serial relationships with continually changing partners. Yet, children in nontraditional families may feel discomfort as they learn from a curriculum that continues to feature the conventional family structure. Clearly, many schools have a way to go before they successfully integrate all family structures into family life.

Students often enjoy school life better when their families are supportive.

Wage Earners and Parenting

For the first time in our nation's history, women comprise half of all U.S. workers. In fact, women with children are the primary breadwinners or co-breadwinners in nearly two-thirds of American families. Back in 1960, a minority of women with children worked outside the home. Today, 80 percent of women with children between the ages of 6 and 17 work outside the home, and more than 60 percent of moms with children 6 or younger work in the salaried workforce. One trend that hasn't changed is paying women less. Although equal pay has been the law since 1963, employers still find ways to pay women less, even when education, skills, and experience are the same.[44]

Although parenting responsibilities still fall more on women (between sixteen and twenty hours a week), today more and more fathers are also assuming parenting responsibilities (about eight to ten hours a week). Working fathers and mothers desire more flexible work schedules, equal pay, redesigned family and medical leave, and comprehensive child care policies.[45]

Latchkey Kids

Jennifer unlocked her door quickly, raced inside, and shut it loudly behind her. She fastened the lock, dropped her books on the floor, and made her way to the kitchen for her usual snack. Within a few minutes, Jennifer was ensconced on the sofa, the television on. She tried not to spend too much time thinking about being lonely. She decided to do her homework later when her parents would be home. She turned her attention to the television, to spend the next few hours playing video games.

Jennifer is a latchkey kid, one of 5 million children left to care for themselves after school. The term **latchkey** was coined to describe children who carry a key on a cord or a chain around their necks to unlock their home door. These children are often from single-parent homes or families with two working parents, few extended family members, and no affordable, high-quality child care facilities nearby. Latchkey kids are found in all racial and socioeconomic groups, but the more educated the parents, the more likely they are to have a latchkey child. The average latchkey child is left alone two and a half hours per day, with most of that time devoted to watching television or playing video games. Unsupervised children are more likely to suffer with depression, smoke cigarettes and marijuana, and drink alcohol. They are also more likely to be the victims of crimes.[46]

Divorce

Although today divorce is common (more than half of new marriages end in divorce), it is hardly routine. The underlying stress can increase a child's anguish. Along with the emotional trauma of changing family dynamics, divorce can also create financial worries. The divorced mom often struggles with a severe loss of income; children living only with their mothers are five times more likely to live in poverty than children in a married household. Children who have experienced divorce may exhibit a variety of problem behaviors. Symptoms from depression to aggression diminish school performance. Children often go through a classic mourning process similar to that experienced after a death in the family. However, most children are resilient and can rebound from the trauma of divorce, with 80 to 90 percent recovering in about a year. Teachers should give children the chance to express their feelings about divorce and let them know they are not alone in their experience.[47]

Poverty

GLOBAL VIEW
Our child poverty rate is substantially higher—often two to three times higher—than that of most other major Western industrialized nations. For example, in 2011 the child poverty rate in the United States was 22 percent, in France and the United Kingdom it was well under 10 percent.

Today, children are the poorest group in our society, and current programs and policies are woefully inadequate to meet their growing needs. Stanford's Michael Kirst sums it up this way:

Johnny can't read because he needs glasses and breakfast and encouragement from his absent father. Maria doesn't pay attention in class because she doesn't understand English very well and she's worried about her father's drinking and she's tired from trying to sleep in her car. Dick is flunking because he's frequently absent. His mother doesn't get him to school because she's depressed because she lost her job. She missed too much work because she was sick and could not afford medical care.[48]

The more than one in five American children living in poor families are among the poorest in all developed nations. Poverty touches the lives of children across all diverse racial and ethnic backgrounds, and particularly jeopardizes the well-being of black, Hispanic, and Native American youth. Children in poverty often have to cope with issues that other children (and many adults) seldom, if ever, contemplate. Most parents of poor children work, but they don't earn enough to provide their families with basic necessities—adequate food, shelter, child care, and health care. When children are poor, they are more likely to drop out of school and be involved in violent crime, early sexual activity, and drugs. Children, with little voice and no votes, are among the first to lose services. Approximately 6 million children under age 18 have no medical coverage.[49] In short, poverty puts children at risk.

Poor children enter school with distinct disadvantages. Poor children are more often in single-parent families, typically receive less adult attention, have fewer books to read, and are not read to as often. As a consequence, they are not exposed to complex language or large vocabularies, a deficit when entering school. (See Figure 4.3.) Their neighborhoods usually have fewer adults with professional careers who can serve as role models. In fact, simply getting out of the neighborhood to visit museums or zoos or cultural activities is difficult. Such isolation deprives these children of experiences beyond the familiar and also chips away at their self-confidence. Their neighborhood reality is often filled with crime and drugs, so safety concerns can dominate daily existence. It is no surprise that research reveals how chronic stress from growing up poor can impair cognitive development. Each of these disadvantages makes only a small contribution to the educational struggles of poor children, but cumulatively they can easily overwhelm. Early childhood education can ease some of the challenges: children from low socioeconomic backgrounds who participate in these programs, such as Head Start, are four times more likely to graduate from college than their peers who do not participate. Access to such programs, however, remains problematic.[50]

How can teachers understand the unique needs of children living in poverty? We can start by considering that poverty itself may be a culture. The concept of the *culture of poverty* was coined by anthropologist Oscar Lewis and describes how people in poverty often have their own behavioral norms, communication skills, and even ways of viewing the world.[51] Because schools tend to reflect middle-class values, the culture of poverty can clash with school culture. This culture clash often alienates the poor from school, and school from the poor.

Here is an example of how class differences can hinder poor children even before they enter school. Researcher Shirley Brice Heath found that the number and the nature of verbal interactions in families varies according to socioeconomic status. In lower-class families, interactions between adults and children are fewer than in middle-class families, and the purpose is information driven. For example, a parent may ask a child, "Where is your sister?" or "Have you finished your homework?" For middle-class children, family interactions are more numerous and closely resemble school interactions. A parent may ask a child to identify

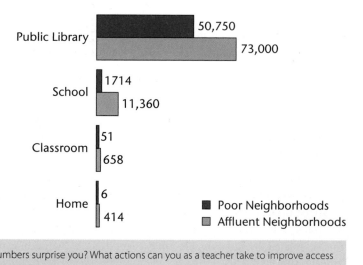

Public Library — 50,750 / 73,000
School — 1714 / 11,360
Classroom — 51 / 658
Home — 6 / 414

■ Poor Neighborhoods
□ Affluent Neighborhoods

FIGURE 4.3

Books and socioeconomic class.

SOURCE: Adapted from Royal Van Horn, *Bridging the Chasm between Research and Practice: A Guide to Major Educational Research* (Lanham, MD: Rowman and Littlefield Education, 2008), p. 32.

REFLECTION: Do these numbers surprise you? What actions can you as a teacher take to improve access to books for children from poverty?

an object or a word, share his or her opinion, or read together. Middle-class students who have had such interactions at home have in a sense been in training for school and arrive there better prepared.[52] It is not that poor children are less capable or intelligent; it is that what they bring to school is different. Students from poverty often lack the experiences and the strategies expected for success in school. Think about the struggle a middle-class child would have in a poor neighborhood.

Teachers need to avoid what has been termed "soft bias," the lowering of academic expectations for poor children. Strategies may differ, but academic goals and expectations should remain high. What kind of strategies might be useful? We discussed that poor children typically have a limited vocabulary, less than half the words of more affluent students, so working with poor children on expanding their vocabulary not only reduces the language deficit but also uses words to take the child beyond the local neighborhood to see a broader world perspective. Another teaching strategy is to involve poor students in after-school programs to expand their cultural, artistic, and athletic opportunities while keeping them in a safe environment for a longer part of the day. Extracurricular activities can also help forge new and constructive peer relationships.[53] In fact, you may want to check the culturally relevant teaching strategies described in Chapter 3, because many of those strategies also work with students living in poverty.

One of the most common misperceptions of the poor is that they do not value education. When poor parents do not attend a back-to-school night or miss a parent-teacher meeting, many in the middle or upper class simply assume that they are not committed to education. In reality, these absences may be due to working several jobs, struggling with unreliable transportation, or simply navigating the challenges of middle-class norms.

Karen Arnold and her colleagues have studied just how subtle and devastating the clash of norms can be when poor students are admitted to college but many end up never attending.[54] The world of postsecondary education and professional careers is a new one for low-income, first-generation college students, and they often lack the implicit knowledge that middle- and upper-class students take for granted. Counselors report that poor students "are gathering bits and pieces of information from people who don't really know anything." In one case, a student decided over the summer to apply to Northwestern University because he assumed it was the California branch of Northeastern University. Another senior reported: "I found a scholarship on eBay. Should I buy it?" After all, he said, "it was a $1,000 scholarship offer for only $500. Wasn't that a good deal?" In the absence of nuanced knowledge of colleges common to middle-class students, poor students sometimes make decisions that are based on misinformation.

Financial fears also loom large. As one counselor explained: "For them, $4,000 a year of loans is huge. Some parents and kids can't see debt as an investment. Even if they understand it, they don't believe it." As one student explained: "I don't think I want to go to college and be in debt the rest of my life." Families willing to take out loans may run into another problem: no creditworthy family member able to cosign a loan document. Even if college were free, it can be costly. Many students contribute a significant portion of their family's income; with them at college, the family can experience a painful financial setback.

Along with economic anxiety, safety concerns also emerge. As a daughter of a Dominican father explained, "They thought New York was too far, too dangerous, too expensive [Dad] was really strict. He didn't want me to go." For the poor, first-generation college student, going away to a four-year college may be a frightening prospect, and a local community college can be seen as a safer option. "Transferring is part of their plan," a counselor reported. As one student related the situation, his family suggested, ". . . 'why don't you go to a community college and transfer?' They don't see the importance, I guess, of going to a four-year. Going to a very nice school." Even positive family messages can imply failure far from home, as one student's grandmother advised: "If you don't do anything else, go to college. If you don't make it, at least you can say you went."

This shaky road to college need not be the case. Research suggests that to navigate the road into college, poor students need specific guidance on taking college entrance examinations and completing financial aid applications. It is also important to have counselors available during that critical summer as they transition to that brave new world called college. Counselors can reduce the fears and confusion about college. Clearly, treating lower-socioeconomic students as though they were middle class is a costly injustice.

Hidden America: Homeless Families

Homelessness may conjure up images of cardboard boxes, sleeping bags, and heating grates. The realities are more complex. By federal definition, "homeless child and youth includes minors living in shelters with or without family, doubling up with friends or extended family, settling into motels, campgrounds, trailer parks, or living in vehicles." The strain on families as they face declining fortunes can be soul draining. Survival needs such as food, safety, and shelter become daily struggles.

America's estimated 1.6 million homeless children (one in every forty-five children) are urban, suburban, and rural, and of every racial and ethnic background. Most experts agree that the true number of homeless children is much greater because official numbers do not count the indefinite number of families living on the edge of foreclosure and eviction.[55] These youth face significant school challenges. Although most attend school, there is constant turmoil and frequent transfers. Many arrive at school hungry, tired, distracted, and lacking even rudimentary study facilities. Add to this equation the drugs, crimes, violence, and prostitution often found in their lives, and it is clear that these children struggle against overwhelming odds. Children whose address has been in flux for more than a year are subject to developmental delays four times greater than their peers, are twice as likely to repeat a grade, and twice as likely to be identified as learning disabled.[56]

In 1987, Congress passed the **McKinney-Vento Homeless Assistance Act,** providing the homeless with emergency food services, adult literacy programs, access to schooling, job training, and other assistance. In the past, school districts had required proof of residency, birth certificates, and proof of immunization—simple tasks for most families, but enough to keep many homeless children out of school. Renewed in 2002, McKinney-Vento eliminated many such barriers, allowing students to enroll immediately without proof of a permanent address. Homeless students also have the right to participate in all extracurricular activities as well as all support programs, including meal services, before- and after-school care, special education, and gifted programs. School districts must provide transportation so that highly mobile students can stay in the same school, a place of familiar faces and stability. McKinney-Vento also mandates that school districts provide a homeless liaison to connect families to appropriate social and educational services. Importantly, illegal immigrant children, who are often homeless, have the right to attend public schools.[57] Despite this progress, and the potential of schools to be a stabilizing force, the educational needs of the nation's homeless children often go unmet.

Children: At Promise or at Risk?

It was not too long ago that teachers were concerned about students talking out of turn, chewing gum, making noise, running in the halls, cutting in line, and violating dress codes. More than half a century later, teachers' top student concerns reflect the devastating changes in the lives of their pupils: drug and alcohol abuse, pregnancy, suicide, bullying, low graduation rates, and weight issues.

Many teenagers smoke, do drugs (prescription and nonprescription), and engage in unprotected sex. Adolescents view this period between childhood and adulthood as a time for fun, and being adolescents, they feel protected by their own youth, by a sense of invulnerability. A second group of teenagers take similar risks for different reasons: They believe they have little to lose. Native American, Hispanic, black, and low-income teens may more often than whites view the future with a sense of hopelessness, a fatalistic belief that risky behavior is not so risky if life offers few options, if death may come at any time.[58]

Dropping Out

FOCUS QUESTION 7

How can educators respond to social issues that place children at risk?

Lamar was finishing junior high school with resignation and despair. He had just managed to squeak through with poor grades and no understanding of how this frustrating experience called school would help him. He wasn't good at schoolwork and felt that the classes he had to sit through were a waste of time. He wanted to end these long, boring days, get a job, and get a car. He'd had enough of school.

Lamar is a good candidate to join the nation's dropouts. In fact, students from low socioeconomic backgrounds are six times more likely to drop out than wealthy ones, and students whose parents do not value schooling are also on the "most-likely-to-drop-out" list. Students who eventually drop out often start struggling academically in the first grade, are likely to repeat a grade at least once, frequently transfer between different elementary and middle schools, and attend poor schools.[59] One teacher described the academic slide of dropouts like this: "Kids who fail math or English in sixth grade go on to start failing *everything* in ninth grade."[60]

GLOBAL VIEW

The United States is ranked tenth in the world in high school graduation rates.

Are you surprised to learn that nationwide only about 75 percent of students graduate from high school? Every day 2,500 students give up on school, resulting in more than 1 million American high school students who drop out every year. Racial, ethnic, and gender patterns offer an even more disturbing picture of educational attainment. (See Figure 4.4.) And not surprisingly, dropouts reflect a gap in socioeconomic status: students from families with

FIGURE 4.4

National high school graduation rates.

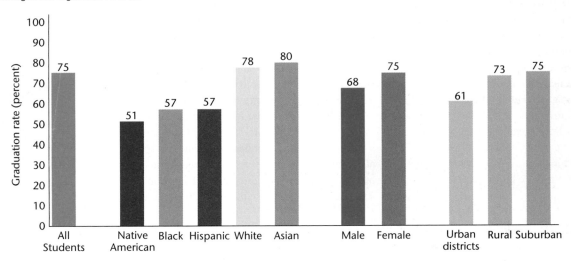

SOURCE: Education Week, *Diplomas Count 2012.*

REFLECTION: What strategies would you suggest to improve graduation rates? Do these strategies vary according to the race and gender of students? Socioeconomic status? Why or why not?

incomes in the lowest 20 percent of all family wealth are six times more likely as students from families in the top 20 percent to drop out of high school.[61]

Most students don't drop out because they can't do the work. In fact, nearly 90 percent have passing grades when they leave school. The major reason for opting out? Classes are too boring, and students feel academically disengaged. Others are more worried about pregnancy, family issues, or financial concerns. Indeed, the immediate monetary rewards of the workplace lure some students. Yet, dropouts earn on average $20,000 less a year than high school graduates, and are far more likely to need government assistance or end up in jail. Many educators believe that the dropout rate can be reduced through early intervention, early literacy programs, one-on-one instruction, mentoring and tutoring, more relevant curricular materials, service learning, and family involvement. Another growing effort, especially for low-income students, is a blended high school and college program with a career-focused curriculum that allows students to earn both a high school diploma and an associate's degree or credits toward a bachelor's degree.[62]

Sexuality and Teenage Pregnancy

Who can blame today's adolescents for being confused about sexuality? On the one hand, they see a "green light," as they are bombarded with suggestive advertising, graphic movies, bawdy television shows and sexualized cable channels. Contraceptives, including the morning-after pill, offer pregnancy safeguards that did not exist just a few years ago. Then students see a bright "red light" of morality standards preaching abstinence and the looming threat of sexually transmitted diseases (STDs). So how do schools respond to this conflict?

What students learn (or do not learn) in school about sex depends on the school they attend. More than a third of schools follow an "abstinence only" sex education curriculum, emphasizing no sex before marriage. Contraception in these programs is a non-topic, and these programs are not particularly effective. Teens' sexual behavior, pregnancy rates, and frequency of contracting STDs usually remain steady or increase following completion of abstinence-only courses.[63] Other school districts embrace a more comprehensive approach, stressing abstinence but also teaching about contraception. A national survey found that 90 percent of middle and high school students and their parents support such a comprehensive approach.[64] In 2010, the federal government reversed its decade-long policy of awarding funds only to abstinence-only sex education programs and began funding more comprehensive sex education in schools, ranging from abstinence to the use of contraception. Hopefully, this change will help ease staggering teen sexuality statistics: Rates of pregnancy and STDs in this nation are the highest in the industrialized world, and nearly half of high school students are sexually active.[65]

Substance Abuse

"You won't see the drug culture here unless you know what to look for. You'll get a lot of parent and school denial, but the reputation of this school is 'drug heaven.' "

"On an average week, I gross over $2,000 dealing drugs at this school."

These statements from high school students add a personal dimension to official reports indicating that the United States has the highest rate of teenage drug use of any industrialized nation in the world. Substance abuse ranges from alcohol and chewing tobacco to inhalants, cocaine, and LSD to food abuse, from dieting to obesity. Almost two-thirds of high school students say drugs are used, kept, and sold in their schools and are easily available.[66]

Although alcohol, cigarette smoking, and marijuana use among teenagers are at historic lows, they remain serious problems for our youth. Alcohol represents, by far, the most

GLOBAL VIEW

Teen pregnancy rates remain much higher in the United States than in many other developed countries—twice as high as in England and Wales or Canada, and nine times as high as in the Netherlands or Japan.

GLOBAL VIEW

Cigarette smoking and alcohol use are less prevalent for U.S. tenth-graders than in almost all European nations. The lifetime use of marijuana and other illicit drugs is higher in the United States than in any European country.

widespread form of substance abuse. More than two-thirds of high school seniors admit to drinking regularly. The pattern of abuse starts early: More than one third of eighth-graders report drinking within the last year. Cigarette smoking is down for the population as a whole, yet more than a million young people start smoking each year. Teens, though, understand that smoking is bad for their health, and very few believe the harmful effects of smoking have been exaggerated. Teens believe just the opposite about marijuana. The majority of students believe that marijuana is safe to regularly smoke, and use of the drug is growing. More than one in four teens used the drug at least once in the past year. More than half of all students will try an illicit drug, like acid, ecstasy, methamphetamine, cocaine, or heroin, by the time they finish high school.[67]

Researchers are discovering a cultural shift in drug abuse among teens with the increased use of inhalants, diet pills, sedatives, and prescription drugs. Although marijuana is the most popular choice for teens trying drugs for the first time, prescription drugs and inhalants are a close second and third. Today's youth grow up in a world where it is routine to reach for a prescription bottle to enhance performance, to focus better in school, and to stay awake or calm down. Not surprisingly, prescription painkillers such as Vicodin and Oxycontin are abused by one in ten high schoolers. One million teens have tried an inhalant—such as glue, paint, felt-tip markers, and air fresheners—to get high.[68]

What leads youth to substance abuse? Some blame the mixed messages children receive. Although parents and teachers may talk about the physical, emotional, and academic dangers, the media and pop culture often glorify alcohol and other drugs as methods for coping with stress and loneliness or to improve performance. Other contributing factors include family instability and the materialistic, success-driven nature of our culture that creates tremendous pressure on youth (and adults). Interestingly, social networking is linked to substance abuse. Every day, 70 percent of teenagers spend time on Facebook or other social networking sites, and these 17 million students are three to four more times more likely to abuse drugs, tobacco, and alcohol than their peers who are not regular social networkers.[69] (How many youth do you think are addicted to social networking?) Students who consider themselves popular are also more likely to use drugs, drink, and smoke than their unpopular peers. Yet, the problems of substance abuse are all too real for many students. When asked to describe their greatest concern, teens frequently cite the pressure to use drugs ahead of social and academic pressures.[70] We know all too well that substance abuse paves a risky, downward path:[71]

- Grades go down as alcohol consumption and drug use go up.
- The more teenagers drink, the more likely they are to be involved in violent crime, such as murder, rape, or robbery, either as victim or as perpetrator.
- Alcohol and drug abuse is associated with more unplanned pregnancies, more sexually transmitted diseases, and more HIV infections than any other single factor.
- Approximately 50 percent of all youth deaths from drowning, fires, suicide, and homicide are alcohol-related.

Schools often adopt programs such as Drug Abuse Resistance Education (D.A.R.E.) to help youth understand the facts about drugs and cope with peer pressures. Funded and run by local police departments, D.A.R.E. costs school districts very little and is popular in schools nationwide. Yet research reveals that D.A.R.E. and its "Just Say No" message are ineffective in curtailing drug use. Similar criticism has been leveled at the U.S. Department of Education's Safe and Drug-Free Schools program.[72] Given the poor track record of these national programs, many local schools choose to develop their own substance abuse curricula and policies.

FIGURE 4.5

Overweight and obese children.

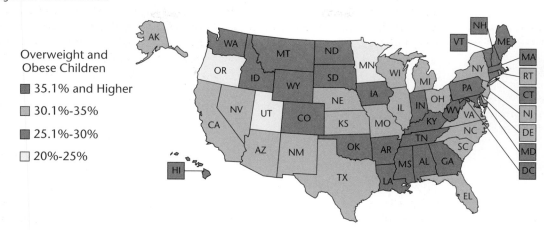

Overweight and
Obese Children

■ 35.1% and Higher

■ 30.1%-35%

■ 25.1%-30%

□ 20%-25%

SOURCE: U.S. Department of Health and Human Services (2012).

REFLECTION: What role, if any, should schools have in promoting a healthy lifestyle?

Obesity and Eating Disorders

What does forty hours a week watching television and playing video and computer games, and playing outside for only two hours a week and eating junk food get you? Pounds, lots of extra pounds. Nine million American children ages 6 to 19—one in three—are overweight or obese. (See Figure 4.5.) The trend starts early: Ten percent of children ages 2 to 5 are obese. At special risk are children from low socioeconomic backgrounds, as well as Hispanic, black, and Native American youth whose obesity rates are often 50 percent greater than those of their peers. The consequences of obesity are staggering. Besides potential health problems such as diabetes, arthritis, and heart disease, overweight children are more likely to have low self-esteem and be absent from school. Overweight students, particularly girls, are more likely to engage in sexual activity earlier and without protection and are less likely to attend college.[73]

Schools often make the problem worse. Faced with pressures to improve test scores, school leaders often try to increase academic classroom time by eliminating recess or physical education—despite evidence showing that exercise improves academic performance. Nationwide, only 4 percent of elementary schools, 8 percent of middle schools, and 2 percent of high schools provide daily physical education. (Only five states—Illinois, Iowa, Massachusetts, New Mexico, and Vermont—require physical education every year from kindergarten through twelfth grade.[74])

School meals often fail, too. The National School Lunch Program, signed into law by President Truman in 1946, was designed to feed hungry children who needed extra calories. Today, it serves 31 million kids, most of whom don't. Although school meals are subsidized by the government and should follow nutritional standards, that doesn't always translate into apples and cucumbers. Many schools do not offer any fresh fruits or raw vegetables on a daily basis. What's more, vending machines, some stocked with cookies and soda, can be found in nearly all middle and high schools. But these nutritional failings may change. The Healthy, Hunger-free Kids Act gives the federal government power to set new nutrition standards for all food served in schools, from lunchrooms to vending machines. Schools must serve up more fruits, vegetables, whole grains, and low-fat milk and less sodium.[75] (See Table 4.1.) We encourage you to see if your school follows these recommendations.

TABLE 4.1

What's in a meal?

SOURCE: United States Department of
Agriculture, Healthy, Hunger-free Kids
Act (2010), available at www.usda.gov.

REFLECTION: What are
your impressions about
the new school nutrition
guidelines? Who might
oppose these changes?

A Typical School Lunch Before and After the Passage of Healthy, Hunger-Free Kids Act.	
Old Menu	**Proposed New Menu**
Bean and cheese burrito (5.3oz) with mozzarella cheese (1 oz)	Sub sandwich (1 oz turkey, ½ oz low-fat cheese on whole wheat roll)
Applesauce (1/4 cup)	Refried beans (1/2 cup)
Orange juice (4 oz)	Jicama (1/4 cup)
Low-fat (1%) chocolate milk (8 oz)	Green pepper strips (1/4 cup)
	Cantaloupe wedges (1/2 cup)
	Low-fat ranch dip (1 oz)
	Reduced mayonnaise (1 oz)
	Low-fat (1%) milk (8 oz)
Old Menu	**Proposed New Menu**
Cheese pizza (1 slice)	Whole-wheat cheese pizza (1 slice)
Tater tots (1/2 cup)	Baked sweet-potato fries (1/2 cup)
Ketchup (2 tablespoons)	Grape tomatoes, raw (1/4 cup)
Canned pineapple (1/2 cup)	Applesauce (1/2 cup)
Low-fat (1%) chocolate milk (8 oz)	Low-fat (1%) milk (8 oz)
	Low-fat ranch dip (1 oz)

The good news? Some schools are stepping up to this challenge by planting organic gardens and harvesting the food that they use for school lunches and selling it at their own farmers' markets. Some ban vending machines completely, while others are filling them with low-sugar and low-salt snacks, juices, and water. Several major school food suppliers are doubling the amount of fresh produce they provide. First Lady Michelle Obama initiated the Let's Move campaign to encourage parents, school leaders, PTAs, food manufacturers, and elected officials to make physical activity and healthy foods an integral part of school life.

But obesity is not our only weight issue. Some children are taught by our culture that you cannot be too thin, and they take drastic measures to diminish their bodies. Eating disorders among youth are prevalent, and an estimated 11 million Americans struggle with anorexia and bulimia, 90 percent of whom are females and 10 percent males between the ages of 12 and 20. Anorexia is the third most common chronic illness among adolescents. For most kids, eating disorders typically start when they are 11 to 13 years old, but they can begin much earlier. Almost half (42 percent) of first- to third-grade girls want to be thinner, and 81 percent of 10-year-olds are afraid of being fat. The number-one wish of girls 11 to 17 years old is to lose weight.[76] Persistent, chronic dieting puts an enormous stress on youth, one that takes a toll on physical well-being and the energy needed to learn in school.

While movies, magazines, and television tell females that being thin is the ticket to success, males receive a different message: Bulk up those muscles and flatten those abs! Boys say, "I'm getting into shape," not, "I'm fat and need to go on a diet." Yet the fitness quest can quickly turn life-threatening. Males are about 10 percent of those struggling with anorexia, bulimia, or binge eating. The number may be much higher because males believe that food issues are "female issues" and are likely to deny or fail to recognize their own struggles with eating.

More than ever, American boys are trying to find perfect bodies not just by dieting or going to the gym but also from steroids. Nearly half a million boys are taking steroids, and boys as young as 10 are bulking up simply because they want to look good. Although steroids can guarantee a rack of rippling muscles, many of these substances can stifle bone growth and lead to cancer, hair loss, acne, and testosterone-driven rage.[77]

Americans of all ages have a long way to go themselves in freeing themselves from media images of one ideal body type. Healthy bodies come in many shapes, and it is not necessary for all females to be incredibly thin or all males to look like professional athletes.

Youth Suicide

A closely knit New Jersey community across the Hudson River from Manhattan was viewed as a model town. The high school frequently won the state football championship, the police department won awards for its youth-assistance programs, and the town was known for the beauty of its parks and the safety of its streets. On an early Wednesday morning in March, the community woke up to discover that four of their teenagers had locked themselves in a garage, turned on a car engine, and left a note requesting that they be buried together. The group suicide brought the total of teen suicides in the town to eight that year.

Suicide is the third most common cause of death among adolescents, and many health specialists suspect it is seriously underreported. Every day, eleven adolescents will take their own lives. Differences in suicidal behavior can vary across gender and ethnic groups. Native Americans have the highest suicide rate of all racial and ethnic groups. Females are three times more likely to attempt suicide, but males are four times more likely to die from an attempt. Particularly at risk are substance abusers, teens questioning their sexuality, victims of bullying, academic overachievers, and girls who have been physically or sexually abused.[78]

What should teachers look for? Depression often precedes suicide attempts. Manifestations include persistent sadness, boredom or low energy, loss of interests in favorite pastimes, irritability, physical complaints and illness, serious changes in sleeping and eating, and school avoidance or poor performance. To date, teachers and parents have not done well in preventing youth depression and suicide.

Bullying

Loser and *Fag* are scribbled on binders littering a classroom. A huddle of popular girls glare at the classmate they've chosen as outsider of the week. A broad-shouldered ninth-grade boy shoves his scrawny, bespectacled friend of yesterday into the stretch of lockers.[79]

Bullying. Though we bemoan such behavior, it's almost as if we expect it from adolescents, even young children. Although metal detectors and extra security measures have sharply reduced school violence, bullies still stalk. Cell phones, social networks, and online game rooms have joined playgrounds, hallways, cafeterias, and school buses as places where students interact informally with little adult supervision—prime areas for bullying. Bullies seek control over others by taking advantage of imbalances in perceived power, such as greater size, physical strength, or social status. Bullies can use physical force or threats, but sticks and stones aren't the only tools. Social weapons, such as taunts and teases, name-calling, gossip-mongering, and exclusion, can cut children much deeper. One-third to a half of America's children report being bullied at least once a month. In a typical classroom of twenty students, two or three come to school every day fearing being bullied, harassed, or worse. The most likely targets are gay students, or students perceived as gay.

IMAGINE...

Don't Be Like Me

When her 12-year-old daughter Miasha was suspended for bullying a classmate, a California mother took away the cell phone, banned television, and gave an unusual punishment: public humiliation. With the support of school officials, Miasha spent four days before and after school carrying a big sign that read "I Engaged in Bullying Behavior. I Got Suspended from School . . . Don't Be Like Me. Stop Bullying."

SOURCE: *Los Angeles Times*, May 18, 2009.

Although most youth describe bullying as harmful, a gap exists between that belief and students' behaviors. More than 40 percent of students admit to bullying a classmate at least once; more than half have witnessed bullying and not stopped or reported it.[80]

Bullying has been an accepted school tradition for decades, if not centuries, often because so many teachers accept the myths surrounding bullying: Only a small number of children are affected, students are just "tattling, it's a natural behavior," and "boys will be boys." But those myths are dangerous. Boys *and* girls engage in bullying, though often with different behaviors. Boys are more likely to engage in physical bullying, whereas girls often revert to relational bullying, such as gossip and exclusion. Both are likely to cyber-bully. Bullying is linked to academic difficulties, withdrawal from activities, depression, suicide, and eating disorders. And children who bully are more likely to get into fights, vandalize property, and drop out of school. Cyber-bullying is a relatively new phenomenon. The word didn't even exist a decade ago, but the problem is pervasive in children's lives today, with increasingly deadly consequences. Through e-mail, instant messaging, Internet chat rooms, and electronic gadgets such as camera cell phones, cyber-bullies forward and spread hurtful images and/or messages. Bullies use this technology to harass victims at all hours, in wide circles, and at warp speed. At least half of adolescents report being targeted by a cyberbully.[81] Noted one teacher:

> You can pass around a note to classmates making fun of a peer, and it stays in the room. But when you post that same note online, thousands can see it. The whole world becomes witness and is invited to participate. Wherever kids go with their computers or phones, which is nearly everywhere, the bullies come with them.[82]

Such experiences yield damaging consequences. Cyber-bullying victims are twice as likely to attempt suicide compared to students not targeted online.[83]

The cost of bullying is high, and officials—from the law to schools—are finally "getting it." Courts are declaring that bullying is *not* protected by freedom of expression, and more than forty states have laws against bullying in school. Massachusetts, for example, defines bullying as both cyber-bullying and any act that creates a "hostile learning environment." In that state, even bullying done away from the school can be punishable if the learning environment is affected. Teachers are required to report any instance of bullying to the school principal, who must take action. Every school in the state is required to provide age-appropriate anti-bullying instruction.[84]

Bullies in the schoolyard now have a new place to wield their punches—cyberspace.

School leaders are also stepping up, sending the message that bullying will not be tolerated and creating a climate where students know there are adults they can trust and to whom they can safely report information. Effective anti-bullying practices ask teachers to be involved and interested in students, set firm limits on unacceptable behavior, and act as authorities and positive role models. At one Illinois school district, students can call an anonymous tip line to report instances of bullying. The school system's policy handbook makes clear that staff members must report acts of bullying and protect students who report bullying from retaliation.[85]

Creating a safe classroom climate is the first step in effective teaching. Another is teaching empathy and community-building throughout the curriculum. Schools have devised some interesting ways of doing this. In one New York school, English classes discuss whether Friar Laurence was empathetic to Romeo and Juliet. In other schools, students share snacks and board games with autistic classmates or receive recognition for sitting with a new student at lunch or helping a panicked classmate on the rock-climbing wall. To help students better relate to life with a disability, a common assignment asks students to spend a day in a wheelchair and then write a short story or poem about the experience. Meditation and yoga are increasingly offered to promote compassion and kindness. Schools are also implementing peer mediation programs to help reduce bullying and school violence. Students are trained to help classmates peacefully solve problems, becoming empowered advocates against bullying.[86]

As our awareness of bullying increases, some educators are offering new ways to address the issues. For example, Colby College Professor Lyn Mikel Brown recommends a deeper look at the factors underlying bullying. Accordingly to Brown, educators need to:[87]

- *Talk accurately about behavior.* Bullying is a broad term. If it's sexual harassment, call it sexual harassment; if it's homophobia, call it homophobia. Calling behaviors what they are encourages more complex and meaningful solutions.

- *Move beyond the individual.* To understand why a child uses aggression toward others, it's important to understand what impact race, ethnicity, social class, gender, religion, and ability have on his or her daily experiences in school. How do these realities affect the kinds of attention and resources a child receives, where he fits in, or whether she feels marginal or privileged in school?

- *Stop labeling students.* Bully prevention programs typically put kids into three categories: bullies, victims, and bystanders. Labeling focuses on the child as the problem, downplaying the roles of parents, teachers, the school system, a powerful media culture, and societal injustices children experience every day. Labels also simplify the issue: We are all complex individuals with the capacity to do harm and to do good.

- *Accentuate the positive.* Instead of labeling kids, affirm their strengths and believe that they can do good, brave, remarkable things. The path to safer, less violent schools lies less in adults' control over children than in appreciating their need to have more control in their lives, to feel important, to be visible, to have an effect on people and situations.

We don't have to accept bullying as a part of growing up. Teaching acceptance and kindness toward others can be as much a part of schools as algebra or social studies.

ONLINE VIDEO ALBUM TO ACCOMPANY *TEACHERS, SCHOOLS, AND SOCIETY 10E*

Visit the Online Learning Center for a range of contemporary videos with content related to this chapter.

www.mhhe.com/sadker10e

THE *TEACHERS, SCHOOLS, AND SOCIETY* READER WITH CLASSROOM OBSERVATION VIDEO CLIPS

Go to your *Teachers, Schools, and Society* Reader CD-ROM to:

READ CURRENT AND HISTORICAL ARTICLES

15. **Bullying and the Culture of Peers,** by Philip C. Rodkin, *Educational Leadership,* September 2011.

16. **Challenging Assumptions: Helping Struggling Students Succeed,** by Lois Brown Easton and Michael Soguero, *Phi Delta Kappan,* February 2011.

17. **Keeping Youth in School: An International Perspective,** by Nancy Hoffman, *Phi Delta Kappan,* February 2011.

18. **The Engaged Classroom,** by Sam M. Intrator, *Educational Leadership,* September 2004.

19. **The Myth of the Culture of Poverty,** by Paul Gorski, *Educational Leadership,* April 2008.

ANALYZE CASE STUDIES

7. **Marsha Warren:** A teacher is overwhelmed by the problems created by her students, including eight children who have unique home problems and personal situations that are affecting their schooling.

8. **Anne Holt:** This case follows an experienced teacher through her morning routine with a diverse group of first-grade children. The case presents a detailed look at her organization and the climate she creates in the classroom.

OBSERVE TEACHERS, STUDENTS, AND CLASSROOMS IN ACTION

6. Classroom Observation: Three High School Girls Discuss Adolescent Self-Concept at Age 16

Understanding your students and the issues they face is an important part of being an effective teacher. Adolescents particularly struggle with self-esteem. In this observation, you will observe three adolescent girls as they discuss how their self-esteem fluctuates and is more influenced by the opinions of friends than of family.

7. Classroom Observation: Three High School Girls Talk about Drugs at Age 15

Understanding your students and the issues they face is an important part of being an effective teacher. Too many of today's adolescents will have some contact, direct or indirect, with illegal substances before they graduate from high school. In this observation, you will observe three teenage girls discussing drug use at their school and that fact that they believe that most of the kids in their school have at least experimented with marijuana

8. Classroom Observation: Characteristics of Children Who Bully

Being aware of the characteristics of bullying is an important first step in creating a safe classroom. In this observation, you will observe an interview with Dr. Espelage, an educational psychologist, in which bullying behavior and its characteristics are defined and the sex differences in bullying behavior are described.

KEY TERMS AND PEOPLE

ability grouping, 109
gatekeeping, 104
latchkey, 118

McKinney-Vento Homeless Assistance Act, 121
Oakes, Jeannie, 106, 107

sociograms, 110
tracking, 106

www.mhhe.com/sadker10e

CHAPTER REVIEW

Go to the Online Learning Center to take a quiz, practice with key terms, and review concepts from the chapter.

DISCUSSION QUESTIONS AND ACTIVITIES

1. Observe in a local elementary school. What are the rules and regulations that students must follow? Do they seem reasonable or arbitrary? Do students seem to spend a large amount of time waiting? Observe one student over a 40-minute period and determine what portion of those 40 minutes she or he spends just waiting.

2. Do you think that tracking is a valid method for enhancing student performance? Or do you think it is a mechanism for perpetuating inequality of opportunity based on social class, race, or sex? Debate someone in your class who holds an opposing point of view.

3. We have noted the vividness with which many people recall their high school years. Try to answer the following:

   • Who was voted most likely to succeed in your high school class? (Do you know what he or she is doing today?)

   • What was your happiest moment in high school? Your worst?

   • Name five people who were part of the "in crowd" in your class. What were they "like?"

   • Is there any academic experience in high school that you remember vividly? If so, what was it? If not, why?

4. Research the issue of adolescent alienation. Make some recommendations on how secondary schools could get students to become more involved in academic and extracurricular activities.

5. What can schools do to address each of the following issues?

- Poverty
- Different family structures
- Parental income
- Substance abuse
- Dropping out
- Obesity and eating disorders
- Bullying

Purposes of America's Schools and the Current Reform Movement

CHAPTER 5

FOCUS QUESTIONS

1. What are the goals of America's schools?
2. What school goals are important to you?
3. What are the characteristics of effective schools?
4. Why has school reform become a top national priority?
5. What new school options are replacing the traditional neighborhood public school?
6. What is the role of teachers and students in reforming our schools?

To educate the peasantry, three things are needed: schools, schools and schools.

—LEO TOLSTOY, *ANNA KARENINA*

CHAPTER PREVIEW

Although most of us take school for granted, the proper role of this institution continues to evoke heated debate. Are schools here to prepare students for college and a vocation—or perhaps to achieve high scores on standardized tests? Should schools also be responsible for developing effective interpersonal relationships, and patriotism, or even changing our society?

In this chapter, you will have the opportunity to examine the major purposes assigned to schools as well as voice your views on appropriate school goals. We will also look at what research indicates is needed for a school to be effective. Defining the place, purpose, and effectiveness of schools has never been more challenging. From charter schools to virtual schools, education in America is being reshaped. The priorities of today's schools have been greatly influenced by the economy, but too often the views of teachers and students are not heard. Many wonder if school options, such as charter schools, hold the key to better schools. We conclude this chapter with a fundamental question: Is the reform movement headed in the right direction?

For inspirational stories about people who have had a powerful impact on the lives of others, go to the Online Learning Center and read the "Class Acts."

www.mhhe.com/sadker10e

WHAT DO YOU THINK? What do you think schools and students are like today? Check off what you think and see how others respond.

What Is the Purpose of School?

FOCUS QUESTION 1
What are the goals of
America's schools?

It sounds like a complaint many of us have uttered after a bad day at school, but it is more than that: It is a deceptively complex question. Although we all agree that students go to school to learn things, we do not agree on just what those things are. Quite popular today is the idea that the nation's financial well-being depends on an educated workforce, one that can compete in the global economy. On a personal level, you have heard this purpose targeted to you: "If you want to get a good job, you better get a good education!" Politicians and businesspeople are on the same page but with even more focus: They want schools to emphasize science, math, and technology so we can compete with countries such as India and China. The emphasis has been on achieving high scores on international tests, expecting American students to rank number one (instead of lower down the list, where we often score). Some traditionalists believe that schools should focus on the basics, the "three Rs": reading, 'riting, and 'rithmatic (although spelling might be a good addition). There are a few voices who argue that given all the corruption in business, the improper conduct of politicians, the cheating in school, white-collar crime, and society's ethical dilemmas, perhaps schools should focus on making us all better people, more honest, kinder, and compassionate. Some schools call this character development, and many Americans believe that is the most important goal any school can have. There is always a small but energized group that believes schools should promote creativity in the arts and develop the individual skills and talents within each of us. New York City's High School of Performing Arts does just that, and became famous in the movie *Fame.* Who wouldn't want to go to a school like that? There is always a group that believes schools must focus on graduating loyal Americans, while others see patriotism as educating Americans to question and even challenge their government. How would you define a good citizen? We will stop here, but you get the idea. This simple question is not so simple. Our views of what schools should be doing are diverse, sometimes superficial, and even contradictory. Let's spotlight what many see as the two fundamental, yet somewhat antithetical, purposes of all schools.

Purpose 1: To Transmit Society's Knowledge and Values (Passing the Cultural Baton)

GLOBAL VIEW
Japan's Hiroshima memorial
explains that "the situation in
Pearl Harbor hurtled Japan
into the Pacific war." There is
no mention of Japan's surprise attack on Pearl Harbor
and no explanation of the
Japanese invasion and occupation of China years earlier.
Can you cite examples of how
other nations (as well as our
own) "whitewash" history?

Society has a vital interest in what schools do and how they do it. Schools reflect and promote society's values. There is a world of knowledge out there, more than any school can possibly hope to teach, so one of the first tasks confronting the school is to *select* what to teach. This selection creates a cultural message. Each country chooses the curriculum to match and advance its own view of history, its own values, its self-interests, and its own culture. In the United States, we learn about U.S. history, often in elementary, middle, and high school, but we learn little about the history, geography, and culture of other countries—or of America's own cultural diversity, for that matter. Even individual states and communities require schools to teach their own state or local history, the "culture" of Illinois or of New York City. By selecting what to teach—and what to omit—schools are making clear decisions as to what is valued, what is worth preserving and passing on.

   Literature is a good example of this selection process. American children read works mainly by U.S. and British writers, and only occasionally works by Asian, Latin American, and African authors. This is not because literary genius is confined to the British and U.S. populations; it is because the keepers of the culture and creators of the curriculum see to it that certain authors are to be taught, talked about, and emulated while others are not. Similar decisions are made concerning which music should be played, which art viewed, which dances performed, and which historical figures and world events studied. As each nation makes these cultural value decisions, it is the role of the school to transmit these decisions to the next generation.

As society transmits its culture, it also transmits its values. Being American means valuing certain things and judging countries and cultures from that set of values. Democratic countries that practice religious tolerance and respect individual rights are generally viewed more positively by Americans than repressive societies. By transmitting culture, schools breathe values into a new generation, molding its view of the world.

But molding is also limiting. In transmitting culture, schools provide students with a world view that does not allow much deviation or perspective. Cultural transmission may contribute to feelings of cultural superiority, a belief that "we are the best, number one!" Such chauvinistic views may decrease tolerance and respect for other cultures and peoples.

Purpose 2: Reconstructing Society (Schools as Tools for Change)

If society were perfect, transmitting the culture from one generation to the next would be all that is required of schools. But our world, our nation, and our communities are far from ideal. Poverty, hunger, injustice, pollution, overpopulation, racism, sexism, and ethical challenges—and, of course, the dark clouds of terrorism, economic turmoil, nuclear, chemical, and biological weapons—are just some of our problems. To **reconstructionists,** society is broken, it needs to be fixed, and the school is a perfect tool for making the needed repairs. Reconstructionists see successful students as citizens ready to make change by transforming injustices and improving the world.

To prepare students for such engagement, *social democratic reconstructionists* believe that civic learning—educating students for democracy—needs to be on par with other academic subjects. Yet knowing how to achieve this goal is not easy. Some believe that students should be made aware of the ills of society; study these critical, if controversial, areas; and equip themselves to confront these issues as they become adults.[1] Other reconstructionists are more action-oriented and believe that schools and students shouldn't wait until students reach adulthood. They call for a *social action curriculum,* in which students actively involve themselves in eliminating social ills. For example, to gain public and government support for increased school construction and repairs, high school students in Baltimore, Maryland, organized a photo exhibit of their decaying school buildings. State legislators received a guided tour of the photos, which showed broken heaters, moldy walls, library shelves with no books, cockroaches, a stairwell filled with garbage, and broken windows.[2] As another example, students of all ages can learn about poverty and hunger in their communities and then organize a food drive or work in a soup kitchen.

This idea of students contributing to society is not unique. The Carnegie Foundation for the Advancement of Teaching recommends that every student be required to earn a **service credit,** which might include volunteer work with the poor, the elderly, or the homeless. The idea behind a service credit is not only to reduce social ills but also to provide students with a connection to the larger community, to develop a sense of personal responsibility for improving the social condition.[3] In 1992, Maryland became the first state requiring students to perform community service before they would be granted their high school diploma, and service learning became more popular nationwide throughout the 1990s.[4] More than half of students in grades 6 through 12 participate in service learning, although who participates and what they do to gain service credits is somewhat erratic. Girls are more likely to participate than are boys, and whites outnumber students of color. Participation increases when schools take an active role in setting up the service opportunities and when they require it

GLOBAL VIEW
Should the values that U.S. schools practice and promote be disseminated abroad? Is the equal treatment of women a U.S. value, or a universal value? Do we only have an economy that is global, or is promoting human rights part of our role in the world?

A Closer Look What's in a Name?

Ever wonder how schools get their names—and which names are the most popular? The National Education Resource Center researched the most popular proper names for U.S. high schools: Washington, Lincoln, Kennedy, Jefferson, Roosevelt (both Franklin and Teddy), and Wilson. (Presidents do well.) Lee, Edison, and Madison round out the top ten names. But proper names are not the most common high school names. Directions dominate: Northeastern, South, and Central High School are right up there. Creativity obviously is not a criterion, but politics is. Citizens fight over whether schools should be named after George Washington or Thomas Jefferson—who, after all, were slaveholders—and over why so few African Americans, Hispanics, and people of non-European ancestry are honored by having a school named after them. And, considering how many women are educators, it is amazing that so few schools are named to honor women—Eleanor Roosevelt, Amelia Earhart, Christa McAuliffe, and Jacqueline Kennedy are exceptions. Some schools have honored writers (Bret Harte, Walt Whitman, and Mark Twain) or reflect local leaders and culture. (In Las Vegas, you will find schools named Durango, Silverado, and Bonanza, which some complain sound more like casinos than western culture.)

> **REFLECTION:** What choices do you think educators might make if they were responsible for school names? If students were in charge, would schools be named after sports figures or music and media stars? How do our school names reflect the power and culture in a society? What's in a name?

IMAGINE...

A Very Close School Community

There are 61 other one room schools in rural Montana, but Sunset School District #30 is special: it has only one student: Amber Leetch, age 11. Amber attended another school eight miles away, but left after four years because of bullying. So now she is back and the only student in the school.

The schoolroom is quite up-to-date with a Smartboard, and three computers. But technology is not people. Ms. Hatten, a first year teacher herself, is Amber's lunch buddy, [her] P.E. buddy, and recess buddy. For theater productions, teacher and student take multiple parts. For sports, teacher and student drive 21 miles for Amber to play volleyball at another elementary school.

"The hardest part is getting through the day without feeling too lonely," said Amber. To help with the loneliness, the school found Baylee, a 3-month-old husky, who is now the official school dog. But being the only student can have its advantages. "If she doesn't get something, we'll work on it longer," Ms. Hatten said. "That's the beauty of one student."

SOURCE: Jim Robbins, "One-Room School Also One-Student School," *New York Times*, January 30, 2012, p. A11.

for graduation. And student participation increases with the educational level of their parents.[5]

Social democratic reconstructionists are reform-minded, but *economic reconstructionists* hold a darker view of society's ills. They believe that schools generally teach the poorer classes to accept their lowly stations in life, to be subservient to authority, to unquestioningly follow rules while laboring for the economic benefit of the rich. To economic reconstructionists, schools are tools of oppression, not institutions of learning. They believe that students should be taught to reform economic realities. For example, one such curriculum project targets a popular and highly visible athletic company, one that produces incredibly expensive sport shoes. This company manufactures its products in developing nations, maintaining horrid working conditions. Children in these poor countries are sold into labor bondage by their impoverished families. As young as 6, they work twelve or more hours a day, enduring cruelty and even beatings as they earn only pennies an hour. Although the companies defend themselves by saying that they cannot change local conditions, economic reconstructionists believe that companies intentionally select such locations because of cheap labor. Economic reconstructionists point out that American children play with products made through the agonizing toil of other children. Educators who focus on economic reform have developed materials, websites, and social action projects that not only teach children about such exploitation but also provide them with strategies to pressure companies into creating more humane and equitable working conditions.[6]

Is the purpose of schools just academic learning, or might the goals include fostering an awareness of the benefits of community service, such as volunteering to tutor others?

GLOBAL VIEW

Numerous press stories report child labor law violations and the sexual abuse of girls and boys in foreign factories that provide the products we use. From computers to cell phones, working conditions in overseas factories often harm workers, many of whom are quite young. How can teachers help children to understand the sacrifices made by families and children in other countries? Should U.S. children take action to stop such oppression?

Perhaps the most noted contemporary economic reconstructionist was **Paulo Freire,** author of *The Pedagogy of the Oppressed,* a book about his efforts to educate and liberate poor, illiterate peasants in Brazil.[7] In his book, Freire describes how he taught these workers to read and identify how they were being kept poor and powerless. From this education, they were able to analyze their problems—such as how the lack of sanitation causes illness—and what they could do to solve specific problems and liberate themselves from their oppressive conditions. Freire highlighted the distinction between schools and education. Schools often miseducate and oppress. But true education liberates. Through education, the dispossessed learned to read, to act collectively, to improve their living conditions, and to reconstruct their lives. (See the education *Hall of Fame* in Chapter 7 for more about Freire.)

Public Demands for Schools

Preserving the status quo and promoting social change represent two fundamental directions available to schools, but they are not the only possible expectations. When you think about it, the public holds our schools to a bewildering assortment of tasks and expectations.

John Goodlad, in his massive study, *A Place Called School,* examined a wide range of documents that tried to define the purposes of schooling over three hundred years of history. He and his colleague found four broad goals:

1. *Academic,* including a broad array of knowledge and intellectual skills
2. *Vocational,* aimed at readiness for the world of work and economic responsibilities
3. *Social and civic,* including skills and behavior for participating in a complex democratic society
4. *Personal,* including the development of individual talent and self-expression[8]

Goodlad included these four goal areas in questionnaires distributed to parents, and he asked them to rate their importance. (See Figure 5.1.) Parents gave "very important" ratings to all

FIGURE 5.1

Goals of schools.

> **REFLECTION:** Under each goal, list specific efforts a school could make to reach the goal. How would you prioritize these goals? Explain.

Vocational

Personal

Academic

Social, civic

four. When Goodlad asked students and teachers to rate the four goal areas, they rated all of them as "very important." When pushed to select one of these four as having top priority, approximately half the teachers and parents selected the intellectual area, while students spread their preferences fairly evenly among all four categories, with high school students giving a slight edge to vocational goals. When it comes to selecting the purpose of schools, both those who are their clients and those who provide their services resist interpreting the purpose of schools narrowly.

What do Americans want from their schools? Evidently, they want it all! As early as 1953, Arthur Bestor wrote, "The idea that the school must undertake to meet every need that some other agency is failing to meet, regardless of the suitability of the schoolroom to the task, is a preposterous delusion that in the end can wreck the educational system."[9]

Then, in the 1980s, Ernest Boyer conducted a major study of secondary education and concluded,

> Since the English classical school was founded over 150 years ago, high schools have accumulated purposes like barnacles on a weathered ship. As school population expanded from a tiny urban minority to almost all youth, a coherent purpose was hard to find. The nation piled social policy upon educational policy and all of them on top of the delusion that a single institution can do it all.[10]

Three decades later, the public continues to hold schools to a myriad of high expectations: More than two-thirds of Americans believe that schools are responsible for the academic as well as behavioral, social, and emotional needs of all students.[11]

Where Do You Stand?

Identifying school goals seems to be everyone's business—parents, teachers, politicians, and a variety of experts. Over the years, many reform reports have been written, each enumerating goals for schools—sometimes too many goals, or conflicting goals, or short-sighted goals, or unrealistic ones. Let's see what you believe schools should be doing. The following goals have been advocated by different groups at different times. How do you feel about each goal? Write down your responses, and we will show you how your priorities mesh with others.

Circle the number that best reflects how important you think each school goal is.

www.mhhe.com/sadker10e

INTERACTIVE ACTIVITY

How Important Are These School Goals? Do this exercise online. See how others responded to each statement.

1 Very unimportant

2 Unimportant

3 Moderately important

4 Important

5 Very important

	Very Unimportant				Very Important
1. To transmit the nation's cultural heritage, preserving past accomplishments and insights	1	2	3	4	5
2. To encourage students to question current practices and institutions; to promote social change	1	2	3	4	5
3. To prepare competent workers to compete successfully in a technological world economy	1	2	3	4	5
4. To develop healthy citizens aware of nutrition, exercise, and good health habits	1	2	3	4	5
5. To lead the world in creating a peaceful global society, stressing an understanding of other cultures and languages	1	2	3	4	5
6. To provide a challenging education for America's brightest students	1	2	3	4	5
7. To develop strong self-concept and self-esteem in students	1	2	3	4	5
8. To nurture creative students in developing art, music, and writing	1	2	3	4	5
9. To prevent unwanted pregnancy, AIDS, drugs, addiction, alcoholism	1	2	3	4	5
10. To unite citizens from diverse backgrounds (national origin, race, ethnicity) as a single nation with a unified culture	1	2	3	4	5
11. To provide support to families through after-school child care, nutritional supplements, medical treatment, and so on	1	2	3	4	5
12. To encourage loyal students committed to the United States; to instill patriotism	1	2	3	4	5
13. To teach students our nation's work ethic: punctuality, responsibility, cooperation, self-control, neatness, and so on	1	2	3	4	5
14. To demonstrate academic proficiency through high standardized test scores	1	2	3	4	5
15. To provide a dynamic vehicle for social and economic mobility, a way for the poor to reach their full potential	1	2	3	4	5
16. To prepare educated citizens who can undertake actions that spark change	1	2	3	4	5
17. To ensure the cultural richness and diversity of the United States	1	2	3	4	5
18. To eliminate racism, sexism, homophobia, anti-Semitism, and all forms of discrimination from society	1	2	3	4	5
19. To prepare as many students as possible for college and/or well-paid careers	1	2	3	4	5
20. To provide child care for the nation's children and to free parents to work and/or pursue their interests and activities	1	2	3	4	5

Now, think about your three most valued goals for school and write those goals below:
Three valued goals:

_____, _____, _____

Do your responses to these items and your three priority goal selections cast you as transmitter of culture or as change agent for restructuring society? To help you determine where your beliefs take you, record your scores on the following selected items:

Purpose of Schools

Transmitting Culture		Reconstructing Society	
Focused Item		*Focused Item*	
1	_____	2	_____
3	_____	5	_____
10	_____	9	_____
12	_____	15	_____
13	_____	16	_____
19	_____	18	_____
Total	_____	*Total*	_____

REFLECTION: Do your responses reflect the school experiences you had, or the ones you had hoped for? Which camp are you in: transmitting culture or reconstructing society?

Let's investigate how your choices reflect your values. The current emphasis on standards, tests, and academic performance is reflected in items 1, 13, and especially 14. Are you in agreement with this contemporary educational priority? If you scored high on items 1 and 10, then you value the role schools serve in preparing Americans to adhere to a common set of principles and values. This has been a recurrent theme in schools as each new group of immigrants arrives. Some people called this the melting pot, more formally termed **acculturation,** or **Americanization** (replacing the old culture with the new American one). Others believe that it is a mistake to try to forge a singular definition of an American. Given our nation's diversity, they want schools to honor cultural pluralism, to learn and honor our different cultural and ethnic traditions, and to gain different insights on our world. Look at how you responded to item 17 to see the degree of your support for cultural pluralism. Item 17, along with items 2 and 18, also suggests a commitment to civil rights and student empowerment, hallmarks of the 1960s and 1970s, and because history often runs in cycles, perhaps those goals will resurface in the not-too-distant future. Do you like the Horatio Alger folklore: hard work and a little elbow grease, and the poor become wealthy? Agree with this folklore and you probably rated items 15 and 19 pretty high. Take a little time and see where you stand on the other items. And while you look them over, consider item 20, which may seem a bit odd. After all, few people see schools as babysitters, but without this "service," most parents would be overwhelmed. And consider the impact of millions of adolescents applying for jobs; unemployment would skyrocket and wages would tumble. By minding the children, schools provide parents with time and keep our workforce down to a manageable size.

What did your ratings teach you about your values and your view of schools? Were your goals popular during particular periods of our past, or are you more future-oriented? You may want to compare your goals for education here with your philosophical preferences as identified in Chapter 8.

Once you settle on an answer to what's a school for, you are ready for the next question: What makes a school effective? So let's look at what we know (and don't know) about effective schools.

What Makes a School Effective?

Consider the following situation: Two schools are located in the same neighborhood and are considered "sister schools." They are approximately the same size and serve the same community, and the student populations are identical. However, in one school, state test scores are low and half the students drop out. In the other school, student test scores exceed the state average and almost all students graduate. Why the difference?

Puzzled by such situations, researchers attempted to determine what factors create successful schools. Several studies have revealed a common set of characteristics, a **five-factor theory of effective schools.**[12] Researchers say that effective schools are able, through these five factors, to promote student achievement. Let's take a look at these classic five factors, and then move on to some more-recent studies.

FOCUS QUESTION 3

What are the characteristics of effective schools?

www.mhhe.com/sadker10e

INTERACTIVE ACTIVITY

What Makes Schools Effective? Rate what you think makes schools effective. Compare your responses with those of your colleagues.

Factor 1: Strong Leadership

In her book *The Good High School,* Sara Lawrence Lightfoot drew portraits of six effective schools.[13] Two, George Washington Carver High School in Atlanta and John F. Kennedy High School in the Bronx, were inner-city schools. Highland Park High School near Chicago and Brookline High School in Brookline, Massachusetts, were upper-middle-class and suburban. St. Paul's High School in Concord, New Hampshire, and Milton Academy near Boston were elite preparatory schools. Despite the tremendous difference in the styles and textures of these six schools, ranging from the pastoral setting of St. Paul's to inner-city Atlanta, they all were characterized by strong, inspired leaders, such as Robert Mastruzzi, principal of John F. Kennedy High School.

When Robert Mastruzzi started working at Kennedy, the building was not yet completed. Walls were being built around him as he sat in his unfinished office and contemplated the challenge of not only his first principalship, but also the opening of a new school. During his years as principal of John F. Kennedy, his leadership style has been collaborative, actively seeking faculty participation. Not only does he want his staff to participate in decision making, but he also gives them the opportunity to try new things—and even the right to fail. For example, one teacher made an error about the precautions necessary for holding a rock concert (eight hundred adolescents had shown up, many high or inebriated). Mastruzzi realized that the teacher had learned a great deal from the experience, and he let her try again. The second concert was a great success. "He sees failure as an opportunity for change," the teacher said. Still other teachers describe him with superlatives, such as "he is the lifeblood of this organism" and "the greatest human being I have ever known."[14]

Mastruzzi seems to embody the characteristics of effective leaders in good schools. Researchers say that students make significant achievement gains in schools in which principals

- Articulate a clear school mission.
- Are a visible presence in classrooms and hallways.
- Hold high expectations for teachers and students.
- Spend a major portion of the day working with teachers to improve instruction.
- Are actively involved in diagnosing instructional problems.
- Create a positive school climate.[15]

Factor 2: A Clear School Mission

In effective schools, even extremely busy principals somehow find time to develop and communicate a vision of what that school should be. Successful principals clearly articulate the

Teaching Tip

CONNECTING TEACHERS AND FAMILIES

Research shows that when a school mission is clear and communicated effectively, students do better academically and socially. With some thoughtful actions, teachers can be a critical link to families, insuring effective communication of school goals and expectations. Here are a few ways teachers can connect with families:

1. *Create a listserv to send messages to families.* You can fill them in on assignments and projects, current and future activities, test dates, and other reminders. If you are more tech savvy, develop a class web page with similar information. If your families are not online, send home a brief newsletter, an informational outline of the week's objectives and activities.

2. *Encourage participation.* Send a questionnaire home to families asking if they can contribute to the class. Is someone artistic? Can someone help in class or on a field trip? Perhaps there is a special interest or expertise, and a family member can be a guest speaker.

3. *Homework help.* In the earlier grades especially, you can help monitor homework by asking parents to sign the homework assignment sheet each day.

4. *Share good news.* A message from the teacher need not be a negative sign. Make positive phone calls about student progress and insights.

5. *Assessment understanding.* Share test results with families, explaining both the purpose and the results of the assessment, as well as how they can help their child in future assessments. Be specific. Provide parents with the materials and insights to assist their child.

6. *Visit homes and get to know families.* A good source of information for this is the parent–teacher home visit project at www.pthvp.org/.

It is essential that the principal share his or her vision so that teachers understand the school's goals and all work together for achievement. Unfortunately, surveys indicate that more than 75 percent of teachers say that they have either no contact or infrequent contact with one another during the school day. In less effective schools, teachers lack a common understanding of the school's mission, and they function as individuals charting their own separate courses. Extending that mission communication not only to teachers but to parents as well is important. When school and parents are connected with the school's mission, the children are more likely to achieve academic success.

---

school's mission, and stress change, innovation and improvement. In contrast, less effective principals are vague about their goals and focus on maintaining the status quo. They make such comments as, "We have a good school and a good faculty, and I want to keep it that way."[16]

Good schools have safe environments.

Factor 3: A Safe and Orderly Climate

Certainly, before students can learn or teachers can teach, schools must be safe. An unsafe school is, by definition, ineffective. Despite those horrific headlines reporting student shootings, today's schools in fact are safer than they have been in years.[17] The vast majority of teachers (96 percent) and students (93 percent) report feeling safe in school (thank goodness).[18] LGBT students represent an exception to this general rule; they are three times more likely to feel unsafe in school than their peers.[19]

Safe school learning environments are created by more than metal detectors and school guards. Safe schools focus on academic achievement, the school mission, involving families and communities in school activities, and creating an environment where teachers, students, and staff are treated with respect. Student problems are identified early, before they deteriorate into violence. School psychologists, special education programs, family social workers, and school-wide programs increase communication and reduce school tension.

In some of America's most distressed neighborhoods, safe schools provide a much needed refuge. Sara Lawrence Lightfoot tells of the long distances that urban students travel to reach John F. Kennedy High School in the Bronx. One girl, who did not have money to buy a winter coat or glasses to see the chalkboard, rode the subway 1 hour and 40 minutes each way to get to school. She never missed a day, because for her school was a refuge—a place of hope where she could learn in safety.[20]

Factor 4: Monitoring Student Progress

As the researcher walked through the halls of a school we will call Clearview Elementary School, she noted attractive displays of student work mounted on bulletin boards and walls. Also posted were profiles clearly documenting class and school progress toward meeting academic goals. Students had a clear sense of how they were doing in their studies; they kept progress charts in their notebooks. During teacher interviews, the faculty talked about the individual strengths and weaknesses of their students. Teachers referred to student folders that contained thorough records of student scores on standardized tests, as well as samples of classwork, homework, and performance on weekly tests.

A visit to Foggy Bottom Elementary, another fictitious school with a revealing name, disclosed striking differences. Bulletin boards and walls were attractive, but few student papers were posted, and there was no charting of progress toward academic goals. Interviews with students showed that they had only a vague idea of how they were doing and of ways to improve their academic performance. Teachers also seemed unclear about individual student progress. When pressed for more information, one teacher sent the researcher to the guidance office, saying, "I think they keep some records like the California Achievement Tests. Maybe they can give you what you're looking for."

Following the visit, the researcher wrote her report: "A very likely reason that Clearview students achieve more than Foggy Bottom students is that one school carefully monitors student progress and communicates this information to students and parents. The other school does not."

Effective schools carefully monitor student progress with:

- **Norm-referenced tests** compare individual students with others in a nationwide norm group (e.g., the Stanford, the Iowa Test of Basic Skills, or the SAT).

- **Objective-referenced tests** measure whether a student has mastered a designated body of knowledge (e.g., state assessment tests used to determine who has "mastered" the material).

- Teacher tests are an important (and often overlooked) measure of student progress. Some teachers ask students to track their own progress in reaching course objectives as a way of helping them assume more responsibility for their own learning.[21]

- Homework is another strategy to monitor students. Researcher Herbert Walberg and colleagues found that homework increases student achievement scores from the 50th to the 60th percentile. When homework is graded and commented on, achievement is increased from the 50th to nearly the 80th percentile. Although these findings suggest that graded homework is an important ingredient in student achievement,[22] how much homework to assign and what kinds of homework tasks are most effective continue to be points of contention.

Factor 5: High Expectations

The teachers were excited. A group of their students had received extraordinary scores on a test that predicted intellectual achievement during the coming year. Just as the teachers had expected, these children attained outstanding academic gains that year.

Now for the rest of the story: The teachers had been duped. The students identified as gifted had been selected at random. However, eight months later, these randomly selected children did show significantly greater gains in total IQ than did another group of children, the control group.

In their highly influential 1969 publication, **Pygmalion in the Classroom,** researchers Robert Rosenthal and Lenore Jacobson discussed this experiment and the power of teacher expectations in shaping student achievement. They popularized the term *self-fulfilling prophecy* and revealed that students may learn as much—or as little—as teachers expect.[23] Although methodological criticisms of the original Rosenthal and Jacobson study abound, those who report on effective schools say that there is now extensive evidence showing that high teacher expectations do, in fact, produce high student achievement, and low expectations produce low achievement.[24] Too often, teacher expectations have a negative impact. An inaccurate judgment about a student can be made because of error, unconscious prejudice, or stereotype. For example, good-looking, well-dressed students are frequently thought to be smarter than their less attractive peers. Often, male students are thought to be brighter in math, science, and technology, and girls are given the edge in language skills. Students of color are sometimes perceived as less capable or intelligent. A poor performance on a single standardized test (perhaps due to illness or an "off" day) can cause teachers to hold an inaccurate assessment of a student's ability for months and even years. Even a casual comment in the teachers' lounge can shape the expectations of other teachers. When teachers hold low expectations for certain students, their treatment of these students often differs in unconscious and subtle ways. Typically, they offer such students

- Fewer opportunities to respond
- Less praise
- Less challenging work
- Fewer nonverbal signs (eye contact, smiles, positive regard)

In effective schools, teachers hold high expectations that students can learn, and they translate those expectations into teaching behaviors. They set objectives, work toward mastery of those objectives, spend more time on instruction, and actively monitor student progress. They are convinced that students can succeed.

Do high expectations work if students do not believe they exist? Probably not, and that is too often the case. Whereas a majority of secondary school principals believe that their schools hold such expectations for their students, only 39 percent of teachers believe this to be true, and, even more discouraging, only one in four students believes their school holds high expectations for them.[25] We need to do a better job of communicating these expectations to students and making certain that these expectations truly challenge students.

It is not only students who benefit from high expectations. In *The Good High School,* Sara Lawrence Lightfoot reported that when teachers hold high expectations for their own performance, the entire school benefits. At Brookline High School, "star" teachers were viewed as models to be emulated. Always striving for excellence, these teachers felt that no matter how well a class was taught, next time it could be taught better.

Beyond the Five Factors

New effective-schools findings offer us insights beyond these original five factors of effective schooling:[26]

- *Early start.* The concept that there is a particular age for children to begin school needs to be rethought. The earlier schools start working with children, the better children do. High-quality programs during the first three years of life include parent training, special screening services, and appropriate learning opportunities for children. Such programs are rare, but those that are in operation have significantly raised IQ points and have enhanced language skills. It is estimated that $1 spent in an early intervention program saves school districts $7 in special programs and services later in life.

- *Focus on reading and math.* Children not reading at grade level by the end of the first grade face a one-in-eight chance of ever catching up. In math, students who do not master basic concepts find themselves playing catch-up throughout their school years. Effective schools identify and correct such deficiencies early, before student performance deteriorates.

- *School size.* Some studies find that students in small schools learn more, are more likely to pass their courses, are less prone to resort to violence, and are more likely to attend college than those attending large schools. Studies also show that disadvantaged students in small schools outperform their peers in larger schools, and many large schools have responded to these findings by reorganizing themselves into smaller units, into schools within schools. But this may be a bit simplistic, because students in some very large schools do very well also. More research is needed to clarify the importance of school size.

- *Smaller classes.* Although the research on class size is less powerful than the research on school size, some studies indicate that smaller classes are associated with increased student learning, especially in the earlier grades. Children in classes of fifteen outperform students in classes of twenty-five, even when the larger classes have a teacher's aide present.

- *Increased learning time.* Though not an amazing insight, research tells us what we already suspect: More study results in more learning. Longer school days, longer school years, more efficient use of school time, and more graded homework are all proven methods of enhancing academic learning time and student performance.

- *Teacher training.* Researcher Linda Darling-Hammond reports that the best way to improve school effectiveness is by investing in teacher training. Stronger teacher skills and qualifications lead to greater student learning. Conversely, students pay an academic price when they are taught by unqualified and uncertified teachers.

- *Trust.* Trusting relationships among parents, students, principals, and teachers are a necessary ingredient to govern, improve, and reform schools. As trust levels increase, so does academic performance.

- *Parental involvement.* Learning is a cooperative venture, and a strong school–home partnership can build a more positive attitude toward academic achievement and social well-being and the trust needed for greater success Not surprisingly, teachers' expectations for student success also rise as parents become more engaged in school life.

- *Parent education and support.* Unfortunately, a growing economic gap in our nation has created not only a widening achievement gap between rich and poor children, but also a parenting gap between the wealthy and poor. Wealthy parents invest more time and money in their children, while poor families, often single-working-parent families, are stretched for time and resources. It may be that schools and society need to take a more active role in enriching the educational and social experiences that poor American children receive outside of school, or we risk the creation of a two class educational society, one for the wealthy, and a second-rate system for the poor.

From working with parents to monitoring student progress, research and experience will continue to offer insights into that pressing question, "What makes a school effective?" But the effort to reform American education is not waiting for all those questions to be answered.

Educational Reform and School Choice

FOCUS QUESTION 4

Why has school reform become a top national priority?

Today's headlines of poor student test scores and a faltering economy underscore the need for a more educated workforce. Fears of an increasingly competitive global economy have fueled today's race to "fix" America's schools, but behind the headlines is another story: school reform is not new. A century ago, reforming schools was all about preparing students for a life on the assembly line. Decades later, we were still reforming schools, this time to enforce compulsory high school attendance. Our current reform effort can be traced to a 1983 government report, *A Nation at Risk,* calling for a more rigorous curriculum. Eventually, that led to *No Child Left Behind (NCLB)* and a testing culture that still permeates the nation's schools. (More about *NCLB* in Chapter 6.) Tests were equated with educational success. If students tested poorly, the school, the principal, and the teachers was considered "failing." Failing schools were code blue, in need of critical care, and were threatened with being closed.

The foundation of today's reform movement can be traced back to the economist **Milton Friedman.** He believed that weak local public schools existed because neighborhood families were a "trapped" clientele. There was no incentive to improve because everyone had to go to their local public school, whether or not it was a good school—everyone but the rich, that is. Wealthy parents could move to a better neighborhood or choose a private school. Friedman believed that if all families could choose their schools, weak public schools would surely lose their students and be forced to close. His voucher plan, which we will discuss shortly, would give every family the same choice that the wealthy enjoyed. For Friedman, choice and competition were the keys to improving schools.

In a 1981 study, *James Coleman* found that private schools were doing a better job of educating students than were the neighborhood public schools. Private school students were better behaved and scored higher on tests. In 1993, another study found that Catholic schools were particularly effective for inner-city students of color and were less costly and more racially integrated than the neighboring public schools.[27] So now we had two arguments for giving parents a choice in school selection. One was Friedman's marketplace idea—competition creates better schools—and the other that private schools were doing better than public schools.

By the late 1980s, a third, even more persuasive, argument emerged: Many public schools, especially inner-city schools, were disasters. In these under-resourced schools, teacher turnover was high, the buildings were in disrepair (and often rodent infested), test scores were abysmal, and dropout rates high. Rather than finding open doors to promising futures, many students in these schools did not even make it to graduation. To require parents, typically poor parents, to send their children to such troubled neighborhood public schools seemed both cruel and unfair. The neighborhood public school, once sacrosanct, was now vulnerable.

By the early 2000s, national figures such as Bill Gates were telling the nation that if we were to compete on the world stage, more than the neighborhood elementary schools needed to be fixed; high schools were also failing. Gates argued that our high schools were "obsolete," designed to prepare students for a world that has not existed for decades. "Only one-third of our students graduate from high school ready for college, work and citizenship . . . In 2001,

India graduated almost a million more students from college than did the United States; China graduates twice as many students with bachelor's degrees as the United States, and they have six times as many graduates majoring in engineering."[28] The Bill and Melinda Gates Foundation committed several billion dollars to strengthening America's high schools.

The prestigious consulting firm McKinsey & Company voiced a similar concern in a report titled *The Economic Impact of the Achievement Gap in America's Schools.* This report examined the dimensions of four distinct achievement gaps in education: (1) between the United States and other nations, (2) between black and Latino students and white students, (3) between students of different income levels, and (4) between similar students schooled in different systems or regions. The report actually put a monetary cost on these gaps. It concluded that the nation's gross domestic product, or GDP (that is, the total value of all goods and services produced each year), would be $1.3 to $2.3 trillion higher if these achievement gaps did not exist. If educational reform had been successful after *A Nation at Risk* was initially published in 1983, our nation's economy today would be far stronger. The slow pace of educational reform has led to the economic equivalent of a permanent national recession, with lower earnings, poorer health, and higher rates of incarceration. One author of the report put it this way: "We waste 3 to 5 billion dollars a day by not closing these achievement gaps. This is not simply an issue about poor kids in poor schools; it's about most kids in most schools." Our lagging education system is costing us all.[29]

For over a decade, reforming schools and giving parents and students educational options has been a top national priority. As we describe each of these school options, consider which sound attractive to you, perhaps places where you would like to teach. Let's begin with charter schools, an option that has greatly influenced public education. (See Figure 5.2.)

Charter Schools

In the early 1990s, Minnesota created the first charter school, launching an idea that has mushroomed into more than 5,000 charter schools creating new competition for neighborhood public schools. While Arizona, California, Texas, and Florida have created the most charter schools, other states have been more cautious. (To check on the charter schools in your state, visit www.uscharterschools.org.)

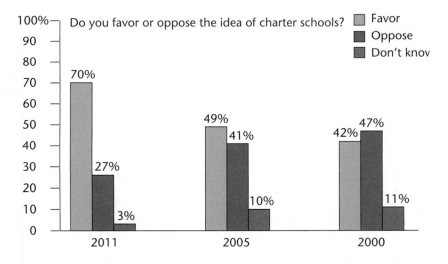

FIGURE 5.2

Do you favor or oppose the idea of charter schools?

SOURCE: Highlights of the *2011 Phi Delta Kappa/Gallup Poll:* "What Americans said about Public Schools." http://www.pdkintl.org/ kappan/ docs/2011_ Poll_Report.pdf

REFLECTION: Given the evaluations that many charter schools are in fact weak, why do you think the public is attracted to this option?

FOCUS QUESTION 5

What new school options are replacing the traditional neighborhood public school?

What is a charter school? The concept is simple. A **charter school** is a tax-supported public school that has legal permission (called a charter or a contract) from a local or state school board to operate a school, usually for a fixed period of time with the right to renew the charter if the school is successful. So if you and a group of your friends wanted to create a school, you would apply for a charter. If the school board accepted your plan, you could begin your school. You would look for a building to rent, perhaps an unused school building, or if you were really lucky, find a benefactor to help finance your school. (Charter schools have drawn some very wealthy benefactors.) You would create your budget, develop your curriculum, hire your teachers and staff, and solicit parents to enroll their students. For each student who enrolled in the school, you would receive a certain amount of money from the state. Enroll enough students, and you will have the money you need to fund your school. Your charter school curriculum could be as creative or as traditional as you like because it is your school. You would be exempt from most state and local regulations, although you would have to follow health, safety, and civil rights rules. In effect, charter schools "swap" regulations for greater freedom and the promise that they will be effective and their students will do well. After a certain period of time, perhaps five years, your school would be evaluated to make certain that students were performing well.

A charter school typically

- Allows for the creation of a new school, the conversion of an existing building, or is a virtual school

- Prohibits admission tests

- Is nonsectarian

- Requires a demonstrable improvement in performance

- Can be closed if it does not meet expectations

- Does not need to conform to most state rules and regulations

- Receives public funding based on the number of students enrolled (with additional private funding possible and not uncommon)

Okay, because you are taking what might be your first education class, perhaps it is a bit premature for you to open a charter school, but you might be wondering who would take on such a task. Tom Watkins, director of the Detroit Center for Charter Schools, describes three types of charter advocates: reformers, zealots, and entrepreneurs. *Reformers* are those who want to expand public school options, create a positive option for parents and children, and perhaps promote a specific approach, such as a more student-centered institution. Reformers engender positive reports in the press. Watkins also describes *zealots,* who want to promote more conservative schools and who typically do not like teacher unions. Often, these charters model private schools and emphasize traditional curricular ideas and teacher-centered classrooms. The final group consists of *entrepreneurs,* businesspeople who believe that efficiency can convert schools into untapped profit centers. This last group believes that you can have effective charter schools that teach students well and make a profit for investors. We will take a closer look at these educational entrepreneurs a bit later.[30]

Some charter schools offer new teachers more freedom than the traditional neighborhood school, allowing you to create your own standards and curriculum, establish rules for discipline, plan programs with your colleagues, and even make budget decisions. (See *A Closer Look: Teaching at a Charter School.*) But other charters offer you less teacher freedom. KIPP schools (which stands for Knowledge Is Power Program) were begun by two graduates of Teach for America who had some very firm ideas about what it takes to make inner-city

A Closer Look   Teaching at a Charter School

Casey Mason, 28, teaches ninth grade social studies at Amy Biehl High School (ABHS), a charter school in New Mexico. Casey is also one of two certified special education teachers at the school. Her interests in social justice and special education led to her current position teaching inclusive classes at the small school of 250 students.

Casey is intensely collaborative with her fellow teachers.

I have not once planned a class in isolation. Our curriculum is planned with our colleagues; we decide what is enduring and important about New Mexico history, the quadratic equation, and biology. We have academic discussions where we explore what we will teach our students. At times I feel as though I'm still in college. It's wonderful. I chose ABHS because I knew creative lessons that value critical thinking and differentiation would be expected here.

After teaching in a more traditional middle school for two years, Casey finds that she enjoys a different kind of school. "Through the luxury of a small learning community, I am able to build more personal relationships with my students and really get to know their learning needs. At traditional public schools I would teach 150 students per day, with up to 35 students in each class. At ABHS, I have no more than 20 students in a class." ABHS is a public high school and any student can attend; because of the limited enrollment, students are picked by lottery. How do students chosen by lottery become so special? Casey's answer: being part of an intimate community.

There are no prerequisites for attending ABHS, it is a public school. I have wonderful students not because they are the highest achievers, the most talented, or the best behaved. At our small school, my students get to be who they are without fear of being the other. The size of ABHS allows for and mandates this. You can't hide in a small school. The same goes for the teachers. The power of small personal communities is what makes my school magical.

Casey Mason has a BA in women's studies and African American studies and an MA in special education from the University of New Mexico.

schools work. Unlike Casey's experience at Amy Biehl High School, KIPP teachers have less autonomy, following specific rules and five core principles:

1. *More time.* KIPP schools have longer school days and a longer school year. For example, school days may run 7:30–5:00 Mondays through Fridays, and three hours at least one Saturday a month. School also continues for two or three weeks in the summer. Teachers earn a higher salary (typically 15 to 20 percent more than a typical teacher's salary) to compensate for this additional time. This longer school day and year is a KIPP practice that is gaining popularity in other schools as well.

2. *High expectations.* Students, parents, teachers, and staff work to create a culture of achievement and support. Parents sign contracts guaranteeing their involvement in monitoring their children's work and participating in school activities.

3. *Choice and commitment.* Everyone in a KIPP school chooses to be there and to put in the time and the effort required to succeed.

4. *Power to lead.* The principals of KIPP schools have control over their school budget and personnel and are held accountable for learning. There is no central bureaucracy. Principals are expected to achieve results, or they are replaced.

5. *Focus on results.* What are those results? Certainly, high student scores on standardized tests are a KIPP priority. Students are expected to achieve a level of academic performance that will enable them to graduate and go on to the nation's best high schools and colleges.

There are more than 100 KIPP schools in twenty states, usually grades 5 through 8 but expanding to other grades as well. They are often in major cities, some in rural areas as well, serving children from low income backgrounds. These students typically attain stronger test scores than students in local public schools and continue on to college-preparatory high schools. Sounds pretty good, but there is a catch: KIPP, like many inner-city public schools, has a dropout problem. The urban environment has many distractions, and when a KIPP

Shimon Waronker's New American Academy illustrates that people of different backgrounds can thrive in a school based on trusting relationships.

student cannot keep up with the academics, the student does not graduate. So although KIPP graduates do well, the challenge is keeping students in school long enough to graduate.[31] (For more information, visit www.kipp.org/.)

The New American Academy takes a very different approach than highly structured KIPP. Big open rooms with sixty students and four teachers allow students to work in different areas and on different activities. Teachers float between groups of students, attending to one student, then the next. Students are less likely to sit at individual desks than around big tables. It is less like a learning factory and more like a family, a trusting family, and that is just what Shimon Waronker, the headmaster, intended.

Waronker dislikes the American education model, which he believes was based on twentieth-century Prussian schools, schools intended to create docile subjects and workers. Waronker created a school to function more like today's collaborative world, focusing on nurturing relationships. In fact, teachers "graduate" with the same children year after year, so relationships are long term.

Shimon Waronker is no ordinary headmaster. He grew up speaking Spanish in South America, became a U.S. Army intelligence officer, and is an observant Jew. Although he studied at Columbia, Harvard, and the New York City Leadership Academy, many doubted that a bearded Jew wearing a yarmulke and dressed in a black suit would be able to relate to the poor minority students in New York. But after he revitalized one of the most violent junior high schools in New York, all doubts were put to rest, and he has gone on to create a very different kind of charter school, The New American Academy (http://thenewamericanacademy.org/).[32]

We started our discussion of charters by suggesting that you could open one yourself—which is not so far-fetched. In 2010, after three years in the classroom, a group of six young teachers in Newark, New Jersey, were frustrated with seeing so much failure, so they asked for and received their own K–8 charter school. They became the teacher-leaders who decided what to teach and how long the school day or school year should be. In teacher-led schools from Los Angeles to New York, studies show that there is higher morale, less turnover, and greater motivation.[33] So there's an option for you to consider.

Although there are some wonderful charter schools, the majority of them do not appear to be any better than local public schools, and many are weaker. A Stanford University study found that about one in five charter schools offered a better education than local schools, almost half offered a similar quality of education, and more than a third, 37 percent, were "significantly worse."[34] Many charters struggle to find appropriate facilities, retain qualified teachers, the resources for computers or library books.[35] The funds for charter schools may be inadequate, but those dollars would have otherwise gone to the local public school, so neighborhood schools lose out.[36] Charter school enrollments also tend to be more racially isolated than local public schools.[37]

Like neighborhood public schools, some charter schools do well, while others struggle; more time is needed before the final verdict is in. What is exciting about charter schools is that they offer an opportunity to experiment, to try new schooling options and approaches. Will the charter school movement eventually improve American education? Time will tell.

Full Service Schools for the Whole Child

When Mayor Michael Bloomberg was asked to identify the most important person living in New York City, he did not name a famous New York actor, billionaire, renowned artist, or scientist; he named Geoffrey Canada. Geoffrey Canada, educator and community advocate, created the Harlem Children's Zone, a nearly 100-block area in the Harlem section of New York City where his community based organization and charter schools serve 17,000 children. If you visit one of his schools, you would encounter more than teachers and principals working with children; you would find dentists, nutritionists, drivers to help with transportation, and counselors helping both the parents and the children create productive lives. Canada explains, "In communities where kids are failing in record numbers, you can't just do one thing. . . . We start with children at birth and stay with them until they graduate from college. . . . In the end, you have to create a series of supports that really meet all of their needs." Like KIPP schools, his are open most of the day and 11 months a year, recognizing that children cannot learn when they come to school tired, hungry, or abused, or if their families are in distress.[38] Such schools are rare. Called **full-service schools,** they can be public or charter, and both types are often impressive.

Vouchers

Although the charter school movement has greatly affected public education, this is not at all what economist Milton Friedman had in mind when he first promoted school choice more than half a century ago. Friedman was encouraging competition through vouchers, not charters. What's a voucher? You might think of an educational **voucher** as an admission ticket to any school, public or private. The government gives parents an educational voucher, a ticket for each child, and then the family would go "shopping" for the best school. After a school was chosen, the parent would give the voucher to the school administrator, the school would turn it over to the local or state government, and the government would pay the school a fixed sum for each voucher. In Friedman's mind, good schools would collect many vouchers, convert them into cash, and thrive, perhaps even expand, while weak schools would find it difficult to attract "customers" and would go out of business. Competition would do the work of reforming schools by simply eliminating weak schools and expanding the good ones. But this sounds better in theory than fact.

In 1990, Milwaukee became the site of the first publicly financed voucher program. Wisconsin lawmakers approved a plan for Milwaukee students to receive about $3,000 each to attend nonsectarian private schools and then, in 1995, amended the law to allow students to attend religious schools as well. The inclusion of religious schools, first in the Milwaukee voucher plan, then in a similar plan in Cleveland, sparked a heated controversy and a round of lawsuits. The reason that religious schools are so closely involved in the voucher dispute is that they are the prime beneficiaries, receiving upward of 90 percent of the students using such vouchers. Why is this? Two reasons: First, most private schools are religious schools, and second, most religious schools have low tuition rates. Voucher plans offer only modest financial support, too little for elite private schools but adequate to cover the cost of many parochial schools.[39] So perhaps you might be thinking: How can vouchers—public taxpayer money—be used to send children for religious instruction? Doesn't the First Amendment of the Constitution ensure the separation of church and state—or has all that changed?

In fact, the legal picture is in flux. Back in 1971 in ***Lemon* v. *Kurtzman*** and in 1973 in the *Nyquist* case, the Supreme Court constructed clear walls limiting the use of public funds to support religious education. What became known as the *Lemon* test provided three criteria to determine the legality of government funds used in religious schools. According to *Lemon,* the funds (1) must have a secular purpose, (2) must not primarily advance or prohibit religion, and (3) must not result in excessive government entanglement with religion. So the wall separating church and state seemed pretty high, until 2002, when a more conservative court

FIGURE 5.3

Americans view vouchers.

SOURCE: *The 2011 Phi Delta Kappa/ Gallup Poll of the Public's Attitudes toward the Public Schools*

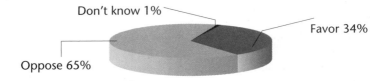

Do you favor or oppose allowing students and parents to choose private schools at public expense?

Don't know 1%

Favor 34%

Oppose 65%

REFLECTION: Why do you believe the public is more reticent to support vouchers than charter schools?

revisited the issue. In ***Zelman* v. *Simmons-Harris*** (2002), a narrow 5–4 Supreme Court majority ruled that publicly funded vouchers could be used to send children to Cleveland's private religious schools. Chief Justice William Rehnquist wrote that such vouchers permit a "genuine choice among options public and private, secular and religious." Justice John Paul Stevens dissented, writing, "Whenever we remove a brick from the wall that was designed to separate religion and government, we increase the risk of religious strife and weaken the foundation of our democracy."[40] Even though this Supreme Court decision allowed the use of vouchers, some state constitutions restrict public aid to private and religious institutions.[41] Many Americans oppose public funds going to promote religious doctrine.[42] (See Figure 5.3.) Moreover, evaluations of the few voucher programs that do exist indicate that they have not been particularly effective.[43] Little surprise that vouchers are used in just a handful of states, while charter schools remain popular in many parts of the country.

Magnet Schools

Although few people thought of it as a reform more than seventy years ago, for talented students, magnet schools were a school choice option. You may have heard of magnet schools, or perhaps you even attended one. A **magnet school** offers one or more special programs, perhaps in math or science or the arts, programs so highly regarded that, like a magnet, they draw students from near and far. In large school districts such as New York City, some very fine magnet schools have been serving students for a very long time. In 1936, New York City Mayor Fiorello H. LaGuardia founded the High School of Music & Art for students gifted in the arts. Today, it is the LaGuardia School of Arts, a public magnet school open to students who pass a rigorous audition. Among its hundreds of well-known graduates are Jennifer Aniston, Ellen Barkin, Al Pacino, and Wesley Snipes. Stuyvesant High School, also in New York, is a magnet school for mathematics, science, and technology. As many as 20,000 students each year are tested for admission to Stuyvesant, but only 800 or so are accepted. Stuyvesant proudly announces on its website that four of its graduates went on to become Nobel Laureates.

Although magnets like these were created to offer high-quality programs for talented students in metropolitan areas, the magnet idea gained additional momentum in the 1960s and 1970s as a method to voluntarily racially desegregate schools. A magnet school with a strong specialized program would be established in a school in a predominantly African American community. White students would voluntarily travel to attend these special programs, and the result would be an integrated school. But it is important to remember that though the school was integrated, many of the classrooms were not. Most of the African American students in the school attended the regular high school classes, whereas most of the white students attended the special magnet classes. About half of today's magnet schools have helped racial desegregation, but as today's cities and communities become ever more racially segregated, the ability of magnet schools to desegregate communities is diminished.

More than 2 million students attend magnet schools today. Unlike charter schools, magnet schools are not in the spotlight, and many suffer from underfunding, especially when it comes to paying for transportation costs, but that is not to say they are not doing an effective job. Often, magnet schools are more effective and racially integrated than public neighborhood or charter schools.[44]

Magnet schools offer specialized programs that build student talent.

Open Enrollment

In 1988, Minnesota instituted **open enrollment,** which eliminated the requirement that students must attend the closest public school. Like the magnet schools, open enrollment encouraged parents to choose a school, but it greatly increased the number of public schools from which to choose. Any public school with available space became eligible. Arkansas, Iowa, Nebraska, and other states soon followed Minnesota's lead and introduced open enrollment legislation. Today, more than forty states allow open enrollment within school districts. However, even more radical proposals are available that may redefine, if not eliminate, the neighborhood school.[45]

Schools.com

One of the most unusual schools we shall look at (well, perhaps not exactly "look at" because you cannot really see it) is a school that has no building and no parking lot, and no one actually goes there. (Some might call it a "dream school.") But before you get carried away, **virtual schools** provide a wealth of learning, usually through technology. Actually, a virtual school is a form of **distance learning,** or learning provided over long distances by means of television, the Internet, and other technologies. Conceived as a way to teach augment homeschooling, virtual education is now an alternative to traditional public schools for an increasingly wide range of students, including high achievers, home-bound, special needs, teenage parents, and victims of bullying. Today, K–12 online learning programs exist in about half of the states, with more than 700,000 students enrolled in more than 1 million courses. Recognizing the importance of online literacy, in 2006 Michigan became the first state to require high school students to complete one online course to graduate.[46] Rather than taking cars or buses to school, more students now ride the Internet, attending class when they want with students from their own community, or from across the country, or even from around the world. Although many virtual high schools offer specific courses for students, some have been organized as full-time charter high schools, offering an entire high school curriculum online. Some students find online learning to be quite personal, interactive, and individualized, and others point out that virtual schools may hold the answer to a growing teacher shortage.[47] While some believe virtual schools are filling an important need, others criticize the quality of

How would you feel about teaching in a virtual school? What are the advantages and disadvantages?

Profile in Education   Jonathan Kozol

A Harvard graduate and Rhodes scholar, **Jonathan Kozol** had no idea "what it was like to be a poor kid in America." He quickly learned. In 1964, the Klu Klux Klan in Mississippi murdered three young civil rights workers. The injustice ignited a need to act.

> I'd never been involved with racial issues. I was not particularly political. In fact, I wasn't political at all. But this event had an extraordinary effect. I volunteered to spend the summer teaching at a black church which had set up a freedom school. When September came, I walked into the Boston school department and said, "I'm going to be a teacher."[a]

He was assigned to the fourth grade of an urban school in Boston, a school so impoverished he didn't have a classroom. Kozol and his disenfranchised students camped out in an auditorium. In an effort to resuscitate their interest in learning, he shared his favorite poetry. Students recited lines, asked questions, even cried as they identified with the words of Langston Hughes. Although the words of the black poet may have inspired students, the author was not on the school's approved reading list. Kozol was fired. He chronicled his first year teaching in *Death at an Early Age* (1967), which alerted the nation to the wrenching injustices found in impoverished schools and the resiliency of their students.

For almost four decades, Kozol's compassionate spirit has given voice to the poor. In his best-selling book, *Savage Inequalities* (1991), he describes life in destitute schools from East St. Louis to the Bronx. Kozol writes of schools so overcrowded that students get desks only when other students are absent. Of students who go for part, most, or all of the year without textbooks. While decrying this tragedy, Kozol does not find an answer in voucher programs.

> [T]he idea behind choice (within the district), basically, is that if you let people choose, everybody will get the school they want. [But] people very seldom have equal choices, and even when they theoretically have equal choices, they rarely have equal access.
>
> People can't choose things they've never heard of, for example. And lots of the poorest folks in our inner cities are functionally illiterate. In many of our inner cities, as many as 30 percent of our adults cannot read well enough to understand the booklets put out by school systems delineating their choices.
>
> Even if they can understand and even if the school system is sophisticated enough to print these things in five different languages for all the different ethnic groups in cities like New York or Chicago, there's a larger point that those who hear about new schools, good schools, first are almost always the well connected.
>
> And so, what often happens is that while everybody theoretically has the right to choose any school, the affluent, the savvy, the children of the academics, the children of the lawyers, the children of the doctors, the children of the school superintendent tend to end up in the same three little boutique elementary schools. And I call them boutique schools because they're always charming, and the press loves them, and they always have enough racial integration so it looks okay for the newspaper or the TV camera. But, in fact, they are separated by both race and class, and more and more by class.
>
> What happens is that the poorest of the poor often do not get into these schools or very small numbers get in. Large numbers of the kids who nobody wants end up concentrated in the schools that no one chooses except by default . . .
>
> Now the dark, terrifying prospect of vouchers or a choice agenda, of a so-called market basis for our public schools, is that rather than encourage a sense of common loyalties among people, choice will particularize loyalties. It will fragmentize ambition, so that the individual parent will be forced to claw and scramble for the good of her kid and her kid only, at whatever cost to everybody else. There's a wonderful quote from John Dewey. He said "What the best and wisest parent wants for his own child, that must the community want for all its children. Any other ideal for our schools is narrow and unlovely. Acted upon, it destroys our democracy."
>
> . . . The best known voucher advocate, John Chubb, of the Brookings Institute, in Washington, says something—I'm paraphrasing him— like this: "Democratic governance of schools is what's wrong with schools. We need a voucher plan in order to break the bonds of democratic education, because it hasn't worked." That's what he says.
>
> When I hear that, I think to myself, "Wait a minute. We've never tried democratic education." We haven't yet given equal, wonderful, innovative, humane schools—at the level of our finest schools—to all our children. . . . I think we should try it first, see how it might work.[b]

[a] Mardell Raney. Interview with Jonathan Kozol. *Technos* 7, no. 3 (Fall 1998), pp. 4–10.
[b] Reprinted with permission of *Educational Leadership* 50, no. 3 (November 1992), pp. 90–92.

To learn more about Jonathan Kozol, click on *Profiles in Education.*

www.mhhe.com/sadker10e

REFLECTION: In your opinion, what American values are reflected—or undermined—in school choice?

education being provided. They argue that distance education isolates students and deprives them of important social interactions (one reason there are far fewer virtual schools at the elementary level). (For more information, visit "Welcome to the Virtual High School" at www.govhs.org.)

Schools for Profit

The charter school movement opened the door for private companies to establish and run K–12 schools for a profit. **Privatization** is the term used to describe this process of transferring a public service, like education or police protection, to a private, for-profit business. The Edison Schools Inc. is an example. Started in 1992, the company claimed that it could run public schools for less money, improve student achievement, and do both while making a profit for its shareholders. Several cities hired Edison to run their schools, but Edison schools did not do well. Studies found their students did no better than regular public school students, and sometimes worse.[48] Edison still exists, but now it is called Edison Learning and focuses only on managing charter schools, moving away from teaching, curriculum development, or being responsible for student test scores.[49]

www.mhhe.com/sadker10e

INTERACTIVE ACTIVITY
Virtual High School
Click on the Virtual High School Collaborative website to learn more.

While Edison floundered, privatization itself is thriving. Advantage Schools, a Boston-based company, focuses on urban school districts, hires nonunion teachers, and promotes intense teacher–student interactions. Sylvan Learning Systems provides after-school instruction for students who are performing below expectations. K12 Inc. is the largest provider of full-time public virtual schools. If Sylvan were a school district, it would rank among the thirty largest districts in the nation, reaching 95,000 students in twenty-nine states and the District of Columbia. Revenues exceed half a billion dollars a year, earning its chief executive millions of dollars a year.

While some applaud the role of business in education, others worry that the profit motive will shortchange students' academic and social needs and that profits and learning are a bad mix. The practices of some private firms are attracting increased scrutiny.[50] (See "You Be the Judge: For-Profit Schools.")

Home Schools

Thirteen-year-old Taylor is working at the kitchen table, sorting out mathematical exponents. At 10, Travis is absorbed in *The Story of Jackie Robinson,* while his brother Henry is practicing Beethoven's Minuet in G on his acoustic guitar. The week before, the brothers had attended a local performance of a musical comedy, attended a seminar on marine life, and participated in a lively debate about news reports concerning corporal punishment in Singapore. What makes their homeschooling story somewhat unusual is that their father is unable to fully participate, since he spends much of his time teaching other children at a local public high school.[51]

Homeschooling is also a choice—a decision not to send a child to the neighborhood school, or any school, but to educate the child at home. Only a few decades ago, a mere 12,500 students were homeschooled; today close to 2 million children are taught at home.[52] Why the huge increase?

Although concerns about the school environment, such as safety, drugs, and peer pressure, motivate some families to homeschool, most parents opt for homeschooling to ensure specific religious and moral instruction, usually evangelical Christian beliefs. Researcher Van Galen divides parents who homeschool as ideologues or pedagogues. *Ideologues* focus on imparting certain values. They create a homeschool where they choose the curriculum, create the rules, enforce a schedule, and promote their beliefs, usually religious beliefs. *Pedagogues* are motivated to offer a more effective education than what is available in a public

You Be The Judge
FOR-PROFIT SCHOOLS

Are a Good Idea Because . . .

COMPETITION LEADS TO BETTER SCHOOLS

For-profit schools will break down the public school monopoly by creating competition and choice. As schools compete, parents (particularly poor parents) will finally have a choice, and not be forced to place their children in the neighborhood school. Just as in business, the weak schools will lose students and declare "bankruptcy." The stronger schools will survive and prosper.

SCHOOLS WILL BE ABLE TO REWARD GOOD TEACHERS, AND REMOVE WEAK ONES

The current public school bureaucracy protects too many incompetent teachers through the tenure system, and does not recognize teaching excellence. Using sound business practices, for-profit schools will reward superior teachers through profit-sharing incentives, retain competent teachers, and terminate ineffective teachers.

BUSINESS EFFICIENCY WILL IMPROVE SCHOOL PERFORMANCE

Education needs the skills and know-how of the business community. For-profit schools will implement the most effective educational strategies in a business culture. The top-heavy management of today's schools will be replaced by only a handful of administrators, and teachers will be driven to greater productivity through the profit incentives.

FOCUSED PROGRAMS AND INVESTOR OVERSIGHT LEAD TO ACADEMIC SUCCESS

For-profit schools will do a better educational job because they provide a focused and proven instructional plan. These schools avoid the public school pitfall of trying to offer "something-for-everyone." And if they falter and profits disappear, investor pressure will put them back on track.

Are a Bad Idea Because . . .

COMPETITION LEADS TO WEAKER SCHOOLS

Transplanting businesslike competition into the education arena would be a disaster. Competition is not all that business brings: false advertising, "special" promotions, a "feel-good" education—all the hucksterism of the marketplace to mislead students and their parents. Worse yet, the local public school, which holds a community together, will be lost.

TEACHERS WILL LOSE THEIR INFLUENCE AND ACADEMIC FREEDOM

Teachers who speak out against the company, or teach a controversial or politically sensitive topic, will have a brief career. The business community is quite vocal about teachers sharing in the profits but strangely silent about what will happen during economic hard times.

PROFITS AND EDUCATION DO NOT MIX

For-profit schools are exactly that, "for profit," and when the interests of children and investors clash, investor interests will prevail. If investors demand better returns, if the stock market drops, if the economy enters hard times, the corporate executives will sacrifice educational resources. After all, while students enjoy little leverage, stockholders can fire business executives.

FOCUSED PROGRAMS MEANS KEEPING SOME STUDENTS OUT

Their one-size-fits-all approach practiced by these schools might be good for efficiency, but it is bad for students. The more challenging students, those with special needs, nonnative speakers of English, or those who need special counseling, will be left to the underfunded public schools to educate.

www.mhhe.com/sadker10e

YOU DECIDE . . .

Do you believe that business and schools are a good or a bad match? Explain. Do you believe that profits can be made in schooling the nation's children? As a teacher, would you want to work for a for-profit school? Now here is your chance to be the author! What additional advantages and disadvantages of for-profit schools can you add to these lists?

school (like the opening description of Taylor, Travis, and Henry homeschooling).[53] States vary in how tightly they monitor and support homeschooling, and today, technology can provide a big boost for homeschools. (You can visit www.hslda.org/laws/default.asp for specific state information.)

Here is a snapshot of homeschool families:[54]

- The median annual income is between $75,000 and $80,000.
- The majority of homeschooling parents have a college degree.
- Homeschool families typically have three or more children.
- More than 91 percent of homeschooling children are white and non-Hispanic.
- More than 80 percent of homeschool mothers do not work outside the home.

Is homeschooling effective? In fact, homeschooled children do quite well on school achievement tests and earn higher GPAs in college than conventionally schooled students. Professors describe them as more self-directed and willing to take risks than the traditional student.[55] But critics express concern about what homeschoolers are taught. Science and history subjects are often heavily influenced by religious doctrine, and concepts like evolution are disparaged. Most homeschooling families want a Bible version of the earth's creation, and not a scientific one.[56] Other critics are concerned about homeschool isolation, learning in an environment where diverse beliefs and backgrounds are absent. Because public schools were intended to meld a single nation from people with differing backgrounds, critics fear the impact of disparate homeschools on the nation's cohesion.[57]

Green Schools

Schools have become a focal point of the green movement; the very health of teachers and students depends upon the quality of the school environment. About half of all schools have unsatisfactory indoor environmental conditions, one in five schools has unhealthy air quality, and about a third of all school buildings are in need of extensive repair. Many of the 60 million students, teachers, administrators, and staff spend their days in unhealthy school buildings. Green schools, on the other hand, offer healthier environments with clean air and water, nourishing and natural foods, nontoxic cleaners, and promote outdoor activities. As you might have guessed, when schools become green, incidences of illness and teacher and student sick days decrease.

Green schools also promote energy efficiency and sustainability through recycling, the use of solar and wind energy sources, and alternative means of transportation. The Earth Day Network has the goal of greening all America's schools within a generation. A school that does exemplary work in promoting environmental and sustainable education, effectively using energy, and creating a healthy school climate can be recognized as a **green ribbon school** by the U.S. Department of Education. Maryland joined the green school movement early on by requiring that all high school graduates be environmentally literate. Maryland schools have a great deal of independence in designing interdisciplinary programs to promote environmental understanding and action. Sustainability, smart growth, and the health of our natural world are now part of core subjects like science and social studies. (For more information, visit www.earthday.net/education.)[58]

Environmentally friendly schools like this one in Denmark can enhance teaching and learning.

A green school also uses its "greenness" to provide relevant learning opportunities. At Whitmore Lake High School in Michigan, students design shoebox-size cars that work on solar power, and investigate wind power as part of their "Green Tech" program.[59] The Chesapeake Bay Foundation created the No Child Left Inside program to overcome "nature deficit disorder."[60] No Child Left Inside works with schools to develop a green curriculum and more active learning. Most students (and teachers) embrace the green movement, and teacher retention and student test scores are higher in the healthier environment of green schools.

Teachers, Students, and Reform

GLOBAL VIEW
What country is doing the most to green its schools? Where is the lack of green schools particularly problematic?

In the mid- and late 1980s, leading educators such as Theodore Sizer, John Goodlad, and Ernest Boyer called for teachers to assume a greater role in educational reform. Alarmed at the loss of teacher autonomy in what too often felt like oppressive school climates, they believed that teachers should be given more responsibility to reshape their schools, a process called *empowering teachers.* These educators believed that schools managed by teachers would reduce bureaucracy, create a better-trained and better-paid teacher faculty, practice local decision making, and be able to study subjects in greater depth. They saw teachers as the focal point of reforming America's schools. Today, many in the public and the media view teachers as quite the opposite, as an obstacle to school reform. This has been a monumental turnaround.

The rise of charter schools is one indicator of public dissatisfaction with the familiar neighborhood public school, especially if that school is a poor-performing inner-city school. Many attribute ineffective schools to ineffective teachers—that is, ineffective tenured teachers who are difficult to replace.[61] Beyond tenure, salaries are determined by seniority and degrees, years of teaching experience and advanced degrees add up to a bigger paycheck. But seniority does not equal teaching effectiveness. Both Democratic and Republican presidents have challenged teacher seniority, as well as teacher unions. "To say that we're under attack is an understatement," explained a Los Angeles union leader.[62]

FOCUS QUESTION 6
What is the role of teachers and students in reforming our schools?

The focus of teacher evaluation has become less about experience and degrees, and more about classroom performance. The federal program called Race to the Top rewards states with extra money if they reform their teacher evaluations and include how much student test scores improved—or do not improve—with a teacher.[63] This approach is called **value added**—that is, how much value did each teacher add to the student's education? Value added would determine which teachers would be rewarded (with extra pay, for example) and which teachers would be replaced. But sometimes, simple ideas sound better in the description than in reality.

Despite its popularity, depending on student test scores to measure teachers is fraught with problems. After all, teachers are not the only factor influencing student scores, not all students test well regardless of what they had learned, and even if tests were perfect measures, test scores represent only one dimension of a person's education. So it is encouraging that teacher associations, administrators, researchers, and politicians are working together to develop a more comprehensive and equitable system, one that includes student test scores along with other factors such as videotaped samples of teaching.[64]

Blaming teachers is a new and discomforting part of the reform movement, and while few actually ask teachers for their opinions about how to improve schools,[65] the nonprofit Education Sector did just that. They surveyed more than 1,000 teachers on how they view the reform movement.[66] The survey found that most teachers support reform and change. Teachers in the survey reported that they do not feel comfortable in a system that rewards longevity rather than competence, and this is especially true for younger teachers. Older teachers or teachers with graduate credits are not necessarily the most skilled. Let's take tenure as an example, a job protection you may already know a bit about. Historically, if you teach well for your first three years or so, you will earn **tenure,** an expectancy of continued employment. Tenure protects teachers from arbitrary dismissal because they are teaching an inconvenient fact, have an unpopular idea, or have a personality conflict with an administrator—a job protection called academic freedom. But tenure also has been used to protect teachers who are incompetent. (Perhaps you have had such a teacher, which is not a pleasant experience.) Many teachers report that they know at least one colleague who should be fired, but they fear that firing an incompetent teacher might put all teachers at risk. Why? No tenure protection sets fear in motion for teachers, and they have doubts that changing tenure protections will be fair. But in an effort to improve schools, many states have done just that, raised the bar for receiving tenure, and in some cases, they have eliminated tenure entirely.[67]

To bring more accountability to teaching, in addition to changes in the tenure laws, many advocate **merit pay,** a system that bases a teacher's pay on performance. Merit pay certainly sounds fairer than seniority, but basing salary solely on student test scores does not sit well with many teachers. So how can we determine which teachers deserve merit pay?[68] Let's listen in on a hypothetical (but incredibly realistic) faculty meeting to get a sense of teachers' concerns:

PRINCIPAL MOORE: "As you may have heard, our school board is now promoting a merit plan for our district. I have outlined four different approaches to merit pay, and I'd like to hear your reactions to them."[69] Dr. Moore turns to her PowerPoint presentation:

- *Teacher performance.* This plan sends observers into your classroom to measure your teaching effectiveness, and merit is determined by these observations.

- *Individualized productivity.* Do you remember the professional goals each of you wrote for this school year? This plan would ask you to write more detailed goals for what you would like to accomplish this year, including new skills you will be working on and any additional assignments you agree to take on. You would receive financial bonuses based on how much of your plan school administrators believe you have accomplished.

- *Teaching assignment.* With this plan, compensation is related to market demands. Our math, science, and special education teachers would probably receive the greatest bonuses if we were to adopt this plan.

- *Student performance—Value added.* This plan is the one supported by many political leaders and if made into law, it will be the one we need to follow. Teacher salary raises will be tied to student gains on standardized tests. As you know, test scores are very important to the school board and to our parents. So if your students score well, you will get merit pay. If they do not, you will not.

As the PowerPoint shuts down, the teachers jump in:

"This sounds great! I can finally get that bonus I deserve for all my extra hours."

"Does only the teacher with all the smart kids get merit when they do well on tests?"

"I don't think I'd feel comfortable if other people found out that I was getting extra money. Teaching is supposed to mean working as a team, not competing for bonuses."

"Dr. Moore, you try to be fair, but not everyone does. What about supervisors who give merit pay to their friends? Or don't know how to evaluate teachers?"

"What if I teach well and the students bomb the test? There is not a lot of research backing this 'value added' model."

"Kids' scores are influenced by their home situation, their stresses, their health; why should I be the only one held accountable?"

"I teach special ed kids how to take a bus, dress for work, and hold a job. I think that is incredibly valuable, but nobody tests that. What happens to me?"

"I'm in the same boat. I teach art."

"In my grade, students have nine teachers. How do you tell which teacher is most responsible for a good—or bad—test score? And what if they all contribute to strong student test performance?"

"Why can't we all get merit pay? We all do a tough job."

"I don't think we all deserve merit pay. I think some of us are stronger teachers than others, and it is well past time that we recognize that. When kids don't learn, we need to bear at least some of the responsibility."

As you can hear from these comments, merit pay can strain relationships among teachers, raise serious questions about measuring classroom success, fan the fear of "playing politics," and create a sense of being manipulated by outside forces. But many teachers, particularly young ones, are excited about the possibility of a higher salary and feel that too many weak teachers are paid the same as stronger ones. The Education Sector survey reported that almost 80 percent of teachers express a desire for a stronger teacher evaluation system, as well as financial incentives for superior teachers, but they want one that is fair. Influential teacher organizations are also supportive, but cautious, and more likely to support a merit plan if it is not based solely on student test scores, if local teachers are involved in planning, and if the plan does not penalize teachers who work in under-resourced schools.[70] (We will discuss the challenges of teacher assessments and merit pay in Chapter 12.)

History suggests that teachers may be right and that linking teacher pay to student performance may not be a successful long-term strategy. When merit pay was first tried, back in 1710 in England, teacher salaries were tied to student test scores. You can probably predict the results: Schools became all about test preparation.[71] Historians David Tyack and Larry Cuban write: "The history of merit performance-based salary plans has been a merry-go-round" as districts initially embrace such plans, only to drop them after a brief trial. But in spite of these failures, school officials keep "proposing merit pay again and again."[72] Will merit pay work this time? Will tenure become a thing of the past? Will skeptical teachers join the reform movement? It may all depend on something too few talk about: trust.

The Importance of Trust

After almost a decade of studies of the Chicago public schools, researchers came to a conclusion that was both startling and obvious: Meaningful school improvement and reform depend on trust.[73] Teachers in schools without trust naturally cling to tenure for protection and are unlikely to feel comfortable trying new strategies. If teachers are expected to reform their schools, they need to feel safe and to be part of the process. Teachers in trusting schools thrive, and so do their students. The researchers uncovered that when trust is present in a school, student academic performance improves.

You probably already know what a trusting school looks like. People respect one another, even when they disagree, and rude behavior is not tolerated. Teachers and parents listen carefully to each other, and they keep their word. Tenure is not used to protect weak teachers, and competent teachers are recognized for their talents. Educators are willing to reach out to students, parents, and one another, and nothing is more important than the welfare and education of the students. We hear a great deal about school reform but too little about creating trust in schools. Clearly, if reform is going to work, teachers need to be a central part of the effort—trusted partners. To date, their voices are not heard.

Students and School Reform

If teachers feel left out of decision making in school reform, just imagine how students feel. Their opinions are rarely sought; their voices rarely heard. Elementary students, asked to draw pictures of typical learning situations, sketch teachers and chalkboards and books in their drawings, but not themselves. Their drawings show how disengaged elementary students feel from traditional classroom instruction. But when asked to draw learning activities they like, they draw themselves as central in those activities.[74] When they enjoy learning, they are not drawing teachers and classrooms.

Nor do things improve at the high school level, where one in four students frequently arrives at school without paper, pencil, or homework.[75] Some call this "pretend attend," a situation where student bodies are in school but their minds and their interests are elsewhere. Many college students also are disengaged. A YouTube video titled "A Vision of Students Today" is based on a survey of two hundred college students. The video depicts the survey results by showing students sitting in a large lecture hall taking turns holding up signs: "My average class size is 115." "18% of my teachers know my name." "My neighbor paid for this class, but never comes." "I spend two hours a day on my cell phone." "I Facebook through most of my classes." And then a close-up of a question written on the back of a chair: "If students learn what they do, what are they learning sitting here?" The video, made by students and their professor in an anthropology class at Kansas State University, is a stunning example of college student alienation. (Ironically, the students who made the tape were probably very engaged in their activity.)

Many college students feel disengaged from classroom instruction. Visit "A Vision of Students Today" on YouTube to get a sense of their alienation.

SOURCE: http://mediatedcultures.net/ksudigg/?p=188

Statistics suggest that students drop out of school more from boredom than from academic failure.[76] If students had a voice in educational reform, what changes would they envision? Middle and high school students throughout the United States and Canada were asked that question, and here are some of their suggestions:[77]

- Take me seriously.
- Challenge me to think.
- Nurture my self-respect.
- Show me I can make a difference.
- Let me do it my way.

- Point me toward my goal.
- Make me feel important.
- Build on my interests.
- Tap my creativity.
- Bring out my best self.

Some schools do listen to students, and trust is strong.[78] In these schools, students participate in textbook selection, in writing school behavior policies, and even in designing new school buildings. In some high schools, students participate in hiring the principal, teaching others how to use technology, researching their dream careers, and organizing school forums. Unfortunately, these schools are far too few.

Affective needs, students' social, emotional, and psychological development, although important, are often ignored. The Carnegie Council on Adolescent Development report, *Turning Points: Preparing American Youth for the 21st Century* warns that one in four adolescents does not have caring relationships with adults, guidance in facing sometimes overwhelming biological and psychological changes, the security of belonging to constructive peer groups, and the perception of future opportunity. Students report that when they are feeling sad or depressed, overwhelmingly they turn for help to friends (77 percent) or family (63 percent); far less frequently do they seek out educators (33 percent).[79] Educational researcher Sara Lawrence Lightfoot describes the following incident, which took place in an elite school in a wealthy suburb in the Midwest:

> A student with a history of depression . . . had been seeing a local psychiatrist for several years. For the last few months, however, she had discontinued her psychotherapy and seemed to be showing steady improvement. Since September, her life had been invigorated by her work on *Godspell*—a student production that consumed her energies and provided her with an instant group of friends.
>
> After *Godspell*, her spirits and enthusiasm declined noticeably. After a visit to her psychiatrist, she killed herself.
>
> The day after, the school buzzed with rumors as students passed on the gruesome news—their faces showing fear and intrigue. . . . But I heard only one teacher speak of it openly and explicitly in class—the drama teacher who had produced *Godspell*. Her words brought tears and looks of terror in the eyes of her students. "We've lost a student today who was with us yesterday. We've got to decide where our priorities are. How important are your gold chains, your pretty clothes, your cars? . . . Where were we when she needed us? Foolish old woman that I am, I ask you this because I respect you. . . . While you still feel, damn it, feel . . . reach out to each other."[80]

Rethinking Reform

We said at the beginning of this text that from time to time, your authors would share their views on a topic. Now is one of those times, and we would like to share some of our thoughts on the current reform efforts. History teaches us that past education reform efforts have fizzled, and we believe that this one is not doing well. Today's schools look remarkably like the schools of a century ago. (Okay, not the neat technology part, but pretty much everything else.) The current reform movement is based on some fundamental assumptions about public education and how it can be improved, assumptions that we believe deserve more scrutiny:[81]

Charter schools will improve education.

Some charter schools are indeed impressive and successful. But families and students who make that extra effort to attend charter school are among the most motivated in a community, which explains a big part of the success of some charters. However, charters are no panacea. National studies of charter schools strip much of their glamour, documenting that in fact about 80 percent of charters are performing at a level comparable to or "significantly" weaker than local public schools. We do not believe that charter schools by themselves are likely to improve the nation's schools.

Merit pay will improve teaching and learning.

A number of high profile business and political leaders advocate teacher evaluations and merit pay as the path to better schools, and many states have taken this path. But the research on merit pay does not support the idea that it leads to better student achievement. In fact, most teachers are drawn to teaching for reasons other than money (although we believe that teachers deserve better pay!) and prefer cooperating rather than competing with colleagues. Later in the text, we will explore what really motivates teachers and students—and it is not merit pay.

Unions protect weak teachers.

When teacher unions protect incompetent teachers, they are at fault. But most teachers are competent and working hard to promote student achievement. Teachers are critical to student success, but there are other factors at work here too. Some schools are in terrible shape, lacking basic facilities, adequate heat, plumbing, and insulation and without appropriate instructional materials. To add to this, students bring a

A Closer Look A World without Schools

In *Descooling Society,* Ivan Illich compared schools to a medieval church, performing more a political than an educational role. The diplomas and degrees issued by schools provide society's "stamp of approval," announcing who shall succeed, who shall be awarded status, and who shall remain in poverty. By compelling students to attend, by judging and labeling them, by confining them, and by discriminating among them, Illich believed that schools harm children. He would replace schools with learning "networks," lifelong and compulsory. To Illich, the notion of waking up to a world without schools would be a dream fulfilled.

Education reformer John Holt agreed, and coined the term "un-schooling" to describe an education where kids, not parents or teachers, decide what they will learn. Holt believed that children do not need to be coerced into learning; they will do so naturally if given the freedom to follow their own interests and a rich assortment of resources. For unschooled kids, there are no mandatory books, no curriculum, no tests, and no grades. Children are given complete freedom to learn and explore whatever they choose—from Chinese to aesthetic mathematics to tuba lessons to the Burmese struggle for civil rights.

SOURCE: Ivan Illich, *Descooling Society* (New York: Harper & Row, 1973); John Holt, *Instead of Education* (New York: Dutton, 1976).

REFLECTION: How are schools more a political than an educational institution? What would your community be like if it were de-schooled?

myriad of dilemmas to school, including neglect, hunger, medical and mental problems, and linguistic and economic difficulties. It takes more than teachers to resolve these fundamental social, economic, and infrastructure predicaments. Most teachers are doing an admirable job, sometimes under difficult circumstances. It is true that teacher unions exist in some of the nation's weakest school districts; but they also exist in the nation's strongest school districts. On the world stage, many nations scoring the highest on international tests also have the strongest unions. Finland, for example, a nation at the top of international testing, puts its teachers at the center of education decision making. It is illogical to cast unions as the culprit.

Schools are in deep decline.

As we discussed in Chapter 1, America's schools have not entered a new age of dramatic deterioration, despite the media headlines. For three decades, the percentage of Americans earning a high school diploma has risen. On international tests, U.S. students, especially poor and English language learners, lag behind students in many Asian nations, and we can certainly do better. But many U.S. schools are performing well on the world stage, and since 1995, the typical U.S. elementary and middle school student scores have improved.

Test scores tell us which students, teachers, and schools are doing well.

Are the scores on high stakes standardized tests the measure of an education? We believe that this measure of a person's education is short-sighted. An education should also honor a student's unique gifts, talents, creativity, and insights (more about this in the next chapter).

We must train workers to successfully compete in the world economy.

This goal brings us back to the beginning of this chapter, and the central question we asked you to consider: What is the purpose of schools? The current reform movement assumes a single, overarching purpose: to prepare workers to compete in a global economy. This is certainly a goal, but should it push aside all other goals? There is no shortage of challenges facing our nation, from the growing gap between the rich and the poor to national discord, all deserving the school's attention, all pieces of the answer to the question: What's a school for?

ONLINE VIDEO ALBUM TO ACCOMPANY *TEACHERS, SCHOOLS, AND SOCIETY, 10E*

Visit the Online Learning Center for a range of contemporary videos with content related to this chapter.

www.mhhe.com/sadker10e

THE *TEACHERS, SCHOOLS, AND SOCIETY* READER WITH CLASSROOM OBSERVATION VIDEO CLIPS

Go to your *Teachers, Schools, and Society* Reader CD-ROM to:

READ CURRENT AND HISTORICAL ARTICLES

20. **Fire and Water, Reflections on Teaching in the City,** by Gregory Miche in *Burned In: Fueling the Fire to Teach,* by Audrey E. Friedman and Luke Reynolds (eds.), 2011, New York: Teachers College Press.

21. **Tackling the Toughest Turnaround—Low-Performing High Schools,** by Daniel L. Duke and Martha Jacobson, *Phi Delta Kappan,* February 2011.

22. **The Power of Personal Relationships,** by Thomas S. Mawhinney and Laura L. Sagan, *Phi Delta Kappan,* February 2007.

23. **Questionable Assumptions about Schooling,** by Elliot Eisner, *Phi Delta Kappan,* May 2003.

24. **Teaching against Idiocy,** by Walter Parker, *Phi Delta Kappan,* January 2005.

ANALYZE CASE STUDIES

9. **Amy Rothman:** A high school resource room teacher is confronted by a parent during a staffing meeting about a gifted, autistic student in her resource room for whom the parent wants a service not provided by the school district.

10. **Chris Kettering:** A teacher finds to his dismay that his white, middle-class students are not interested in social activism and that he is unable to promote awareness and openmindedness in them.

OBSERVE TEACHERS, STUDENTS, AND CLASSROOMS IN ACTION

9. Classroom Observation: Tour of a Boston Charter School

You may one day want to explore teaching in a charter school. In this observation, you will observe the faculty and administrators of the Match charter school, who provide insights into daily life and teaching in a charter school. A number of comparisons with typical public schools are made.

10. Classroom Observation: Family-to-School Connection

Positive relationships between families and teachers help build connections that enrich students' performance and create a home and school bond. In this video, an elementary school principal, a middle school principal, and a middle school guidance counselor discuss various successful strategies they have used to involve parents in their children's education.

KEY TERMS AND PEOPLE

A Nation at Risk, 146

acculturation, 140

Americanization, 140

charter school, 148

distance learning, 153

five-factor theory of effective schools, 141

Freire, Paulo, 137

Friedman, Milton, 146

full-service school, 151

Goodlad, John, 137

green ribbon school, 157

homeschooling, 155

Kozol, Jonathan, 154

Lemon v. *Kurtzman,* 151

magnet school, 152

merit pay, 159

norm-referenced tests, 143

objective-referenced tests, 143

open enrollment, 153

privatization, 155

Pygmalion in the Classroom, 144

reconstructionists, 135

service credit, 135

tenure, 158

value added, 158

virtual schools, 153

voucher, 151

Zelman v. *Simmons-Harris,* 151

www.mhhe.com/sadker10e

CHAPTER REVIEW

Go to the Online Learning Center to take a chapter self-quiz, practice with key terms, and review concepts from the chapter.

DISCUSSION QUESTIONS AND ACTIVITIES

1. Discuss your list of school goals that you recorded with your classmates. Which goals seem to be most important to your peers? to your instructor? Which do you consider most important? Give reasons for your priorities.

2. Congratulations! You have been put in charge of designing the next charter school in your district. Describe the charter school that you would design. Be sure to include the research on effective schools in your description. Going beyond the current research, what unique factor(s) would you make part of your school because you believe they would contribute to an effective school?

3. Reform movements are not new, but the current one has been under way for a quarter of a century, and still has a great deal of momentum. How would you describe the strengths and the weaknesses of this movement? Explain whether you believe it will succeed and strengthen America's schools—or come up short.

4. What do you think of private businesses contracting to run schools? What factors would cause you to seek or avoid teaching for a corporation? Would you feel secure in your job, even without tenure?

5. Does your local public school district have an official (or unofficial) policy concerning homeschooling? Do homeschooled students participate in any school activities or receive any school resources? How do you feel about these (un)official policies?

Curriculum, Standards, and Testing

FOCUS QUESTIONS

1. What is the formal curriculum taught in schools?
2. How does the invisible curriculum influence learning?
3. What is the place of the extracurriculum in school life?
4. What forces shape the school curriculum?
5. How do textbook publishers and state adoption committees "drive" the curriculum?
6. How has No Child Left Behind influenced America's schools?
7. What are common core state standards?
8. What problems are created by high-stakes testing, and what are the testing alternatives?
9. How are cultural and political conflicts reflected in the school curriculum?
10. How has technology affected the curriculum?
11. What are some potential directions for tomorrow's curriculum?

The difference between school and life? In school, you're taught a lesson and then given a test. In life, you're given a test that teaches you a lesson.

TOM BODETT

www.mhhe.com/sadker10e

WHAT DO YOU THINK? What books did you read in high school English? Compare what you read with what others read for a larger view of the high school canon.

CHAPTER PREVIEW

"We shape our buildings and afterwards our buildings shape us," said Winston Churchill. Had the noted statesman been a noted educator, he might have rephrased this epigram, substituting curriculum for buildings, for what children learn in school today will affect the kind of adults they will become and the kind of society they will eventually create. In fact, it is the power of curriculum to shape students, and ultimately society, that takes curriculum development out of the realms of philosophy and education and into the political arena. Children learn through the formal curriculum, made up of objectives and textbook assignments, and through the more subtle lessons of the hidden, null, and extracurriculum. This chapter will explore the process of deciding what should be taught in the nation's schools.

Several trends are pushing schools toward a similar curriculum: the indomitable textbook, technology in schools, and the recent emphasis on national standards and testing. Protests (perhaps better titled "anti-tests") have been growing against the increasing influence of standardized tests in general, and the testing legacy of No Child Left Behind in particular. The assumptions and problems of the Common Core Standards and high-stakes tests are explored in this chapter, as are more positive and creative ways of looking at curriculum and testing.

The Saber-Tooth Curriculum

New-Fist was a brilliant educator and thinker of prehistoric times. He watched the children of his tribe playing with bones, sticks, and brightly colored pebbles, and he speculated on what these youngsters might learn that would help the tribe derive more food, shelter, clothing, security, and, in short, a better life. Eventually, he determined that to obtain food and shelter, the people of his tribe must learn to fish with their bare hands and to club and skin little woolly horses; and to live in safety, they must learn to drive away the saber-tooth tigers with fire. So New-Fist developed the first curriculum. It consisted of three basic subjects: (1) "Fish-Grabbing-with-the-Bare-Hands," (2) "Woolly-Horse-Clubbing," and (3) "Saber-Tooth-Tiger-Scaring-with-Fire."

New-Fist taught the children these subjects, and they enjoyed these purposeful activities more than playing with colored pebbles. The years went by, and by the time New-Fist was called by the Great Mystery to the Land of the Setting Sun, all the tribe's children had been systematically schooled in these three skills. The tribe was prosperous and secure.

All would have been well and the story might have ended here had it not been for an unforeseen change—the beginning of the New Ice Age, which sent a great glacier sliding down upon the tribe. The glacier so muddied the waters of the creeks that it was impossible for people to catch fish with their bare hands. Also, the melted water of the glacier made the ground marshy, and the little woolly horses left for higher and drier land. They were replaced by shy and speedy antelopes with such a scent for danger that no one could get close enough to club them. And finally, as if these disruptions were not enough, the increasing dampness of the air caused the saber-tooth tigers to contract pneumonia and die. The tigers, however, were replaced by an even greater danger: ferocious glacial bears, who showed no fear of fire. Prosperity and security became distant memories for the suffering tribe.

Fortunately, a new breed of brilliant educators emerged. One tribesman, his stomach rumbling with hunger, grew frustrated with fruitless fish-grabbing in cloudy waters. He fashioned a crude net and in one hour caught more fish than the whole tribe could have caught had they fish-grabbed for an entire day. Another tribesman fashioned a snare with which he could trap the swift antelope, and a third dug a pit that captured and secured the ferocious bears.

As a result of these new inventions, the tribe again became happy and prosperous.

Some radicals even began to criticize the school's curriculum and urged that netmaking, snare-setting, and pit-digging were indispensable to modern life and should be taught in the schools. But the wise old men who controlled the schools objected:

> With all the intricate details of fish-grabbing, horse-clubbing, and tiger-scaring—the standard cultural subjects—the school curriculum is too crowded now. We can't add these fads and frills of net-making, antelope-snaring, and—of all things—bear-killing. Why, at the very thought, the body of the great New-Fist, founder of our Paleolithic educational system, would turn over in its burial cairn. What we need to do is to give our young people a more thorough grounding in the fundamentals. . . . The essence of true education is timelessness. It is something that endures through changing conditions like a solid rock standing squarely and firmly in the middle of a raging torrent. You must know that there are some eternal verities, and the saber-tooth curriculum is one of them.[1]

The Saber-Tooth Curriculum was written in 1939, but it still resonates. How do educators avoid a curriculum

FOCUS QUESTION 1
What is the formal curriculum taught in schools?

programmed for obsolescence? What in today's curriculum is "Saber-Tooth-Tiger-Scaring-with-Fire," and what skills are we not teaching that we should be? Those are just some of the questions that you should be thinking as you read this chapter.

The Visible Curriculum

If you ask a teacher for a copy of the curriculum, you will likely be handed a curriculum guide, a description of courses offered, or perhaps some syllabi describing what the students are supposed to be learning at each grade level and in each subject. A **curriculum** refers to the set of courses, and their content, offered at a school or university. (It derives from the Latin, referring to a race course, an understandable origin because students are expected to progress or "run" along this path of courses, this curriculum.) If you ask the teacher for a more detailed curriculum, you might receive specific lesson plans, the classroom activities that will enable students to meet those objectives. Educator Hilda Taba emphasized the importance of a school curriculum: "Learning in school differs from learning in life in that it is formally organized. It is the special function of the school to arrange the experiences of children and youth so that desirable learning takes place."[2] While many would call arranging classroom experiences for learning, like creating a lesson plan, the *curriculum,* it is more accurately called the **formal or explicit curriculum.** And if you could go back in time (and in this text, you can!), you soon realize that the formal curriculum changes with the values of the time. If you were a student in colonial America in the 1660s, your formal curriculum would focus on religion and reading, the "two Rs." If you were a student in the 1960s, you would explore exciting new electives like Multicultural Education, Peace Studies, Ecology, and Women's Studies. But by the 1980s, schools were eliminating many of these electives and increasing the number of required basic courses, sometimes referred to as a **core curriculum.** Support for clear academic standards and frequent testing increased, topics we will explore later in this chapter.

GLOBAL VIEW
"Educational isolationism" is the term used to describe a lack of knowledge or interest in how others approach education. How can you avoid being an educational isolationist and learn about the curriculum in other schools, states, and nations?

The Invisible Curriculum

Let's face it, some of the most powerful curricular lessons taught in school are not to be found in the formal curriculum at all. This "invisible curriculum" has two parts, and by describing each we hope to make it more visible for you. Let's start with what educators sometimes call the **implicit or hidden curriculum**—learnings that are not always intended but emerge as students are shaped by the school culture, including the attitudes and behaviors of teachers. Here is an example offered by Jules Henry, an anthropologist who has analyzed the hidden curriculum of the elementary school. Henry described a fourth-grade spelling bee. Team members were chosen by two team captains. When a student spelled a word correctly on the board, a "hit" was scored. When three spelling errors were made, the team was "out." Students cheered or groaned, depending on the outcome for their team. Did you see the hidden curriculum?

According to Henry, these students were learning powerful lessons: the importance of winning, the pain of losing, how competition can turn a friend into an adversary, the joy of being chosen early for a team, and the embarrassment and rejection when you are not. Some of the more thoughtful students may have seen the absurdity of a spelling lesson being taught as a baseball game.[3] Schools teach many powerful but hidden lessons, from the importance of punctuality to following the rules, from social conformity to respecting authority. Although some hidden lessons are useful, others can be destructive. The first step in evaluating the appropriateness of the hidden curriculum is to actually see it.

Let's remove the veil from another part of the invisible curriculum, all the material that you do not learn in school. When someone or some group decides that a topic is unimportant or

FOCUS QUESTION 2
How does the invisible curriculum influence learning?

too controversial, inappropriate or not worth the time, that topic is never taught and becomes part of the **null curriculum.** If your American History class never went beyond World War II, your null curriculum included the Korean, Vietnam, and two Gulf Wars; the fall of communism; the civil rights and women's rights movements; an assassination and an impeachment; the disaster in Somalia; widespread corporate corruption; the technology revolution; the September 11, 2001, attack, and the economic recession of the past few years. When a school board decides not to teach about the theory of evolution or sex education, they have made a decision that these topics will become part of the null curriculum. The null curriculum is rich but invisible. (It would be fascinating to witness what students would learn if some enterprising educators created a charter school to focus on the null curriculum.)

The Extracurriculum

Now let's look at one last curriculum, a vibrant ingredient of school life but often not thought of as a curriculum at all. The **extracurriculum** teaches the lessons students learn in school activities such as sports, clubs, governance, and the student newspaper, places where a great deal of learning occurs, without tests or grades. A majority of students participate in at least one extracurricular activity, with students from smaller schools and with stronger academic records the most likely to be involved.[4] In high school, varsity sports attract more than half of the boys and about 40 percent of the girls, reducing behavior problems and increasing positive attitudes toward school while teaching lessons in leadership, teamwork, persistence, diligence, and fair play.[5] Though it may surprise some, the fastest-growing high school sport for both girls and boys is bowling, defying the perception that it is a sport of a bygone era.[6] About one student in four participates in music and drama, and about the same percentage joins academic clubs in science, languages, computers, debate, and the like—clubs that enhance not only academic learning but social skills as well. High school seniors involved in school activities are less likely to cut class, three times as likely to have a GPA of 3.0 or higher, and more likely to attend college when compared to students who are not involved in school activities.[7] Nationwide programs such as Odyssey of the Mind, National Forensics Study, and Scholars Bowl promote cross-curricular interests and creative problem-solving skills. Advocates see these activities as so important that they refer to them not as the extracurriculum but as the *co-curriculum,* and believe that their value goes far beyond the high school years. Participation in the extracurricular activities has been connected with:

FOCUS QUESTION 3
What is the place of the extracurriculum in school life?

- Enriched student life and learning
- Higher student self-esteem, school completion, and civic participation
- Improved race relations
- Higher SAT scores and grades
- Better health and less conformity to gender stereotypes
- Higher career aspirations, especially for boys from poor backgrounds[8]

But the extracurriculum is not without problems. The underrepresentation of low-socioeconomic students is evident in many programs, as are gender differences in participation in performing arts, athletics, school government, and literary activities.[9] Skeptics suggest that the best we can say "is that the effects of extracurricular participation on secondary school students' personal development and

Extracurricular activities enrich student life and learning.

academic achievement are probably positive, but very modest, and are definitely different among students with different social or intellectual backgrounds."[10] Given the current emphasis on test scores and academic standards, the extracurriculum is sometimes viewed as little more than a distraction.[11] In Texas and other states, "no pass, no play" rules deny students in poor academic standing the right to participate in varsity sports. In other communities, budget tightening has led to "pay to play" rules, in which a fee is required for sports participation, posing a serious problem for low-income families and students. Such policies raise puzzling questions and issues. Should academic performance and financial constraints be factors in deciding who participates in extracurricular activities? The top academic students, more likely to be wealthy and white, already dominate the extracurriculum, so will "pay to play" and "pass to play" regulations make this curriculum even more exclusive, driving deeper divisions between the haves and the have-nots and further segregating racial and ethnic groups?

Who and What Shape the Curriculum?

FOCUS QUESTION 4

What forces shape the school curriculum?

Although all three curriculums are powerful forces, the public and the press typically focus on the most visible—the formal or official curriculum—when evaluating schools. Given the current emphasis on standards and testing, and the recurrent controversies over the teaching of evolution or the place of religion in the curriculum, the formal curriculum is constantly in the news. It makes a lot of sense for you, as a future teacher, to begin thinking about who decides what you should teach. In fact, what you teach is decided by competing interest groups, and the product sometimes feels as though it was created in a pressure cooker. (See Figure 6.1.) Anyone, from the president of the United States to a single parent, can have an impact on what is taught in your classroom. Let's take a brief tour of some of the chefs at work on the curricular pressure cooker.

Teachers

Teachers develop curriculum both formally and informally. They may serve on textbook selection committees that determine what texts the school will purchase, or they may actually work on writing a district's curriculum. In a less formal but no less powerful way, classroom teachers interpret and adapt whatever official text or curriculum guide has been assigned, stressing certain points in a text while giving scant attention to others and supplementing with teacher-made materials or directing students to the Internet.

FIGURE 6.1

A pressure cooker of groups shapes the curriculum.

REFLECTION: What groups today exert the most influence on the curriculum? Do you see all these groups as a mark of democratic participation, or an inappropriate intrusion in curricular decision making?

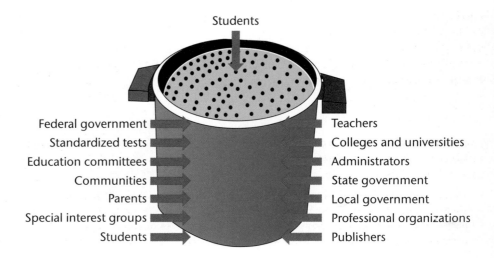

Students

Federal government	Teachers
Standardized tests	Colleges and universities
Education committees	Administrators
Communities	State government
Parents	Local government
Special interest groups	Professional organizations
Students	Publishers

Parental and Community Groups

Parents can be quite forceful in influencing the curriculum. They might advocate for more rigorous academic courses, may be concerned about poor student performance on standardized tests, or may desire more practical vocational training, such as an increase in computer science courses. Banning certain books or videos from the curriculum is also not unusual. In conservative communities, religious fundamentalists have objected to the absence of Christian values, and liberal communities have objected to books that use racial, ethnic, or gender slurs and stereotypes.

Students

During the 1960s and 1970s, students demanded curricular relevance. Although students have not seemed particularly interested in influencing curriculum policy recently, they have been active in protests against standardized testing. Typically, students are given some freedom to select topics for independent projects, research papers, book reviews, and even authentic learning.

Administrators

Principals, in their role as instructional leaders, can wield substantial influence in shaping the curriculum. For example, a principal announces at a faculty meeting that the school's scores on the state standardized test in mathematics were disappointing, and this year's priority is to raise those scores. The result might well be a math curriculum that "teaches to the test." Sometimes central-office personnel, such as a language arts coordinator or a social studies supervisor, might create a new or revised school or district curriculum.

GLOBAL VIEW
Perestroika, a Brazilian school, has placed student personal experiences, societal needs, and an emphasis on doing at the heart of its education programs, allowing students to shape their own learning. Visit www.perestroika.com.br/.

State Government

States are now assuming a larger role in education, and their interest in curriculum matters has sharpened through state standards and tests, curriculum guides, and frameworks for all schools to follow. In some states, religion and evolution are hot-button issues. In other states, instructional materials are expected to include, or exclude, cultural diversity.

Local Government

Local school boards make a variety of curriculum decisions, requiring courses from sex education to financial literacy to technology. Supporters feel that local school boards should have a strong voice in the curriculum, because they are closest to the needs of the local community and the interests of the students. Others feel that school board members lack training to make curricular decisions.

Colleges and Universities

Institutions of higher learning influence curricula through their entrance requirements, which spell out courses high school students must take to gain admittance. As A. Bartlett Giamatti noted when he was president of Yale University:

> The high schools in this country are always at the mercy of the colleges. The colleges change their requirements and their admissions criteria and the high schools . . . are constantly trying to catch up with what the colleges are thinking. When the colleges don't seem to know what they think over a period of time, it's no wonder that this oscillation takes place all the way through the system.[12]

Standardized Tests

The results of state and national tests, from the state subject matter tests needed for graduation to the SATs, influence what is taught in the school. If students perform poorly in one or more areas of these standardized tests, the government or public pressure pushes school officials to strengthen the curriculum in these weak spots.

Schools of education are not immune from the current focus on test performance. Because an increasing number of states are requiring new teachers to take qualifying tests, such as the Praxis Series, these tests influence what is covered in teacher education programs. For example, if Benjamin Bloom's Taxonomy of Educational Objectives is emphasized on such tests, teacher education colleges will teach more about Bloom in their own programs.

Education Commissions and Committees

From time to time in the history of U.S. education, various committees, usually on a national level, have been called upon to study an aspect of education. Their reports often draw national attention and influence elementary and secondary curricula. In 2010, for example, the Council of Chief State School Officers and the National Governors Association developed common core state standards, identifying the skills and content students should master at each grade level in math and English from kindergarten to grade 12. More than forty states adopted these standards.

Professional Organizations

Professional organizations publish journals and hold conferences that emphasize curriculum developments. Their programs and materials help teachers in a number of areas, from technology to authentic learning. Teachers receive these curricular updates from the National Education Association (NEA), the American Federation of Teachers (AFT), the National Association for the Education of Young Children (NAEYC), and numerous subject area associations (teacher groups in English, math, science, and the like).

Special Interest Groups

Today's students are tomorrow's customers, so it is not surprising that businesses and interest groups offer teachers free (and attractive) curricular materials promoting their view of the world. A student-friendly magazine on protecting the environment looks wonderful at first glance, but how do you handle Company X's self-promoting distortion of its own environmental policies that may be part of the narrative? A month's supply of free newspapers for all students is appealing, but does acceptance mean that you are endorsing the editorial opinions of the paper? Teachers need to examine materials and products carefully to present a fair and accurate view.[13]

Publishers

The major goal of textbook publishers is—not surprisingly—to sell books. That is why textbooks are attractively packaged and chock full of terms and names deemed important at the time (including this text!). Unfortunately, most elementary and secondary texts rarely provide in-depth coverage of topics and avoid unpopular points of view (unlike this text). Teachers need to remember that textbooks are published to meet market demands, and not necessarily objective or complex viewpoints.

Federal Government

The federal government influences the curriculum through judicial decisions, financial incentives, and legislation. In 2001, No Child Left Behind was a major piece of legislation that significantly altered the curricular landscape. (We will look closer at this law a little later in this chapter.)

The Reign of the Textbook

The textbook may be our *de facto* national curriculum. Students around the nation study from the same books, do the same exercises, and are expected to master the same material. Studies reveal that students spend as much as 95 percent of classroom time using textbooks. Teachers base more than 70 percent of their instructional decisions and as much as 90 percent of homework assignments on the text.[14] No wonder some believe that textbooks rule.

Before 1850, there were no textbooks. Instructional materials consisted of what teachers and their students could bring to class. Picture yourself trying to teach a class with random materials children had in their homes. Despairing teachers appealed for common texts so that all students could be on the same page (literally). Local legislators responded by requiring schools to choose specific books—and then requiring parents to buy them. Today, this process continues with school districts buying the textbooks, but the quality of those textbooks has come under increasing criticism:

> Imagine a public policy system that is perfectly designed to produce textbooks that confuse, mislead, and profoundly bore students, while at the same time making all the adults in the process look good, not only in their own eyes, but in the eyes of others. Although there are some good textbooks on the market, publishers and editors are virtually compelled by public policies and practices to create textbooks that confuse students with non sequiturs, that mislead them with misinformation, and that profoundly bore them with pointedly arid writing.
>
> None of the adults in this very complex system intends this outcome. To the contrary, each of them wants to produce good effects, and each public policy regulation or conventional practice was intended to make some improvement or prevent some abuse. But the cumulative effects of well-intentioned and seemingly reasonable state and local regulations are textbooks that squander the intellectual capital of our youth.[15]

Why are so many people frustrated with the quality of textbooks? The story starts with textbook adoption states. About half the states, located mainly in the South and the West, are **textbook adoption states.** (These states are indicated in Figure 6.2.) Local school districts in these states must select their texts from an official, state-approved list. This system creates a common, statewide curriculum, and because of the large numbers of books purchased, the hope is that the per-book cost is kept relatively low. The other states do not provide a state approved list of texts to their schools, so teachers in these states can select whatever text they want.

So far so good. The problem begins with the power that a few of the textbook adoption states have to shape the content of the nation's texts. Here's how it works: Four states (Texas, California, North Carolina, and Florida) because of their large student populations, exert an enormous influence on what is included in—or omitted from—these textbooks. Publishers view them as critical markets where profits are made or lost. When these states adopt standards for what they would like to see in a textbook, publishers listen. In a typical year, American schools spend upward of $7 billion on textbooks, and the lure of such profits has created a corporate feeding frenzy among the four publishing giants. Powerful adoption states, such as these four, have reduced the choices further by dictating to these companies what content to include—and sometimes what topics, words, or names to exclude. The remaining publishers cannot afford to lose the sales of these major adoption states, and so they comply, too. As a result, there is little competition about what should be included in the textbook, and all

FOCUS QUESTION 5

How do textbook publishers and state adoption committees "drive" the curriculum?

FIGURE 6.2

Textbook adoption states. Although some school districts are free to choose any text, others are limited to state-approved textbooks.

SOURCE: Association of American Publishers, Washington, DC, 2011.

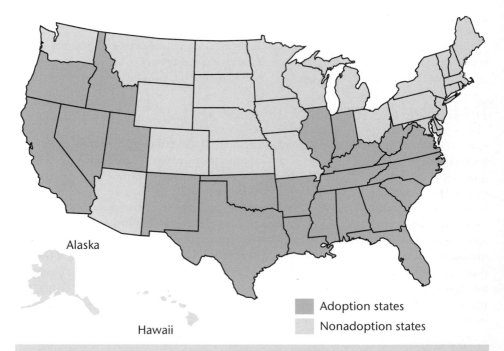

Alaska

Hawaii

Adoption states

Nonadoption states

REFLECTION: What patterns do you notice in the states that require texts be selected from an approved list? Would such state adoption procedures be a factor in deciding where you might teach? Visit the site for updates at www.publishers.org.

textbooks become quite similar. School districts in other states find themselves selecting from the texts that these four states prefer, especially the largest adopters, Texas and California. So if you are thinking that pre-K through grade 12 textbook authors, experts, and publishers decide what should be in these books, you need to rethink that idea.

In some of these textbook adoption states, deciding on what should be taught becomes more political than educational. In recent years, Texas has required very fundamental changes in its texts and has exerted a great deal of influence on publishers. In 2009, Texas voters elected a very politically conservative board of education that decided that the science curriculum should accept neither evolution nor climate change. In 2010, the social studies standards were up for review, and the Texas State Board of Education approved more controversial changes. The new Texas guidelines required publishers to write texts that included Phyllis Schlafly, the Contract with America, the Heritage Foundation, the Moral Majority, and the National Rifle Association. The standards also required teachers to describe the Judeo-Christian influences of the nation's Founding Fathers, but avoid emphasis on the rationale for the separation of church and state. Publishers were to alter references to American "imperialism" in favor of American "expansionism." Margaret Sanger, the birth-control pioneer, would be omitted because she "and her followers promoted eugenics." Also dropped from the Texas standards were Ralph Nader, Edward Kennedy, and Ross Perot (and for a time, Thomas Jefferson, before the board reconsidered). Stonewall Jackson, the Confederate general, was to be described as a role model for effective leadership, and the ideas in Jefferson Davis's inaugural address were to be presented alongside Abraham Lincoln's speeches. The board also tweaked the history of the civil rights movement and removed references to race, sex, or religion in talking about how different groups have contributed to the national identity.[16]

Will the Texas version of history be the national version of history, as it so often was in the past? It is not clear. At least one publisher claims that with the arrival of digital publication technology, Texas social studies texts will be restricted to Texas. (It is interesting to speculate

GLOBAL VIEW

How does the peopling of America affect schools? Visit the *Americans All* website at www.americansall.com/ to see its large and inclusive electronic database on our immigration history.

what publishers will do if other school districts want the Texas version of American history.) In the current trend to create a national set of core standards for all states, discussed in the next section, Texas is one of several states not partici- pating. As we go to press, so do the new texts in Texas.[17]

When those selecting a text have a choice, they can be influenced not only by the content, but by superficial quali- ties such as the cover, the graphics, and the design. Although visual attractiveness can enhance learning, it is no substitute for well-written and accurate content, and texts are increas- ingly criticized for their lack of originality or accuracy.[18] (This textbook, of course, is an exception!)

Because some states will buy texts only if they have a specified reading level, publishers are under pressure to develop books that meet this crite- rion. Often, authors avoid difficult words and long sentences so that, for example, esophagus becomes food tube and protoplasm becomes stuff. The result is the *dumbing down* of the textbook. Ironically, dumbing down can make books harder, not easier, to read. When authors simplify vocabulary, they replace precise and clear terminology with less precise, even ambig- uous words. Shorter sentences often leave out the connective tissue—and, but, therefore— words that clarify the relationships between events and ideas. Shortening sentences to make reading simple can make understanding challenging ideas even more difficult.

Critics also are frustrated by the *mentioning phenomenon,* the attempt of publishers to include as many topics and names as possible to show how comprehensive their texts are, and why schools should buy them. But the result is so superficial that students do not really understand what is going on.[19] Nor are publishers alone to blame. State adoption commit- tees, as we have just seen in Texas, sometimes delineate in minute detail all the names, dates, and places they want included and what skills they want students to attain. In-depth analysis and clarifying examples are lost in favor of mentioning all the required names, places, and dates. Researchers have also found that basal readers and other texts, in attempting to be inof- fensive to potential purchasers, include only a limited range of story types, often devoid of interpersonal and internal conflict.[20]

Textbooks offer an inviting target, but before we banish them from schools, let's consider some of their strengths and some ways that teachers can use them effectively. With a clear narrative, informative graphics, and exercises that develop skills, students can learn a great deal from a textbook. And if a teacher is fortunate to be working with a well-crafted text, research suggests that the text can actually motivate the teacher to try new ideas in the class- room.[21] At its best, a good text is a catalyst for change. Even when a text is less well crafted and floods the reader with too much information, the teacher can make critical choices on how best to use it. One simple idea is to be selective: Choose certain chapters while skipping oth- ers; assign a few of the better exercises in the book rather than require that all be done. Even a weak text can be used effectively. Texts can be supplemented, either online or with other books, to provide more depth or other points of view. Here's one final idea: Although blatant stereotypes of the past are rarely found in today's texts, subtle bias persists. Rather than ignore this bias, teach your students how to see the inequity, offer examples of how bias appears in texts, and then ask your students to evaluate their own books. This approach empowers stu- dents to become critical readers. (For more on this, see "A Closer Look: Seven Forms of Bias.")

While texts make their mark on America's classrooms, politicians were concerned with the quality of American education, so they created No Child Left Behind, a law that was intended to monitor learning and hold schools accountable. Although criticism of this law has led to changes, it still casts a long shadow not only over the curriculum, but over American education as a whole. Let's take a look at what the law required, and how it continues to influence the curriculum.

IMAGINE...

New Afghan Texts

The Afghan government has published new textbooks for schoolchildren that shun the country's history of conflict in an effort to promote national unity. "In the past four decades we have had some topics that were controversial," education ministry spokesman Amanullah Iman said—referring to Soviet occupation, civil war, the rise of the Taliban and a US-led invasion. "We have decided not to include them in the new curriculum."

SOURCE: *Agence France-Presse,* February 7, 2012.

INTERACTIVE ACTIVITY
What Is the Bias? Match scenarios with the bias being displayed.

A Closer Look   Seven Forms of Bias

Although yesterday's stark racist and sexist texts are thankfully gone, subtle bias persists. Here are descriptions of seven forms of bias that emerge in today's texts. These categories can identify bias toward racial and ethnic groups, the elderly, English language learners, females, and gays and lesbians (and others). By teaching your students about the forms of bias, you can help them to become critical readers, an important skill they can take into adulthood.

Invisibility: Before the 1960s, African Americans, Latinos, Asian Americans, women, and Native Americans were largely invisible; that is, not even included in texts. Today, those with disabilities or gays and lesbians are often invisible.

Stereotyping: When rigid roles or traits are assigned to all members of a group, a stereotype is born. Examples include portraying all African Americans as athletes, Mexican Americans as laborers, and women only in their family roles.

Imbalance and Selectivity: Texts can perpetuate bias by presenting only one side of an issue, such as describing how women were "given" the vote. In fact, women endured physical abuse and other sacrifices in their struggle to gain their civil rights.

Unreality: Curricular materials often paint a Pollyanna picture of the nation. (And that goes for any nation!) Our history texts often ignore class differences, the lack of basic health care for tens of millions, as well as ongoing racism, classism, and sexism.

Fragmentation and Isolation: Have you ever seen a chapter or a section focusing on one group, perhaps titled "Ten Famous Asian Americans"? When texts isolate groups in this way, they are subtly suggesting that those groups are not part of society's mainstream.

Linguistic Bias: Using words such as "roaming" and "wandering" to describe Native Americans suggests nondirected behavior and relationships, language that implicitly justifies the seizure of native lands by white Americans who "settled" the lands. Other examples are word choices that place men in primary roles and women in family roles: "men and their wives."

Cosmetic Bias: Cosmetic bias offers the "illusion of equity" to lure educators into purchasing books that appear current, diverse, and balanced. A science textbook brandishes a female scientist on the cover, but alas, there is almost no content on female scientists in the text content.

SOURCE: The forms of bias were developed by Myra Sadker and David Sadker for Title IX equity workshops.

REFLECTION: These forms of bias emerge in more than just textbooks. Choose a television program, a website, a movie, or a news show, and see how many of these biases you can identify.

The Testing Legacy of No Child Left Behind

FOCUS QUESTION 6

How has No Child Left Behind influenced America's schools?

The bipartisan 2001 **No Child Left Behind Act (NCLB)** was described as "the most significant change in federal regulation of public schools in three decades."[22] NCLB changed the face of American education, creating a high-stakes testing culture and labeling thousands of schools as underperforming. A decade after passage, with the fear that most of the nation's schools would be labeled as failing, the law was changed, but not the testing culture it created.[23] Here is a snapshot of what was required under NCLB:

- *Annual testing in reading, math, and science in grades 3–8 and once in high school.* Schools needed to report not only individual student test scores, but also student scores by race, ethnicity, disability, social class, and limited English proficiency. States created their own tests and their own passing grades, some easy, and some more demanding. By 2013–2014, all students were supposed to be proficient in reading and mathematics, an unattainable goal.

- *States and school districts received "report cards" and underperforming schools were closed.* School test results would be made public, a kind of report card, and if the school did not do well on the state exams for five years, the school was closed and either reconstituted by the state or reopened as a charter school.

Opponents argued that deciding if a school is successful or not based on a single test (typically a multiple choice test) is fundamentally unsound, especially when there are huge resource differences between wealthy and poor schools.[24] Parents, politicians, and educators complained that the law was, in fact, leaving many children behind. Once a supporter of NCLB, Diane Ravitch, a former undersecretary of education in the first George W. Bush administration, became an outspoken critic. She called NCLB "corporate reform," funneling money from public schools to private companies that sell tests or run charter schools, without any evidence that this will improve education. She railed against creating test-takers, rather than improving real learning, and lamented the elimination of arts, physical education, foreign language, and history in the curriculum. She no longer believed that high-stakes tests led to improved schools.[25] While No Child Left Behind has waned, high stakes standardized testing continues.[26]

Common Core State Standards

In recent years, state governors and superintendents, encouraged by the federal government, have established standards-based education in their states. **Standards-based education** specifies precisely what students should learn, focuses the curriculum and instruction on meeting those standards, and provides assessment to see if the standards are achieved. But here's what's new: Almost all states and the District of Columbia have agreed to abide by the *same* set of standards, a dramatic departure from different standards in different states. Today, **Common Core State Standards** identify the skills and content a student should master at each grade level from kindergarten to grade 12, providing "a consistent, clear understanding of what students are expected to learn."[27] (Visit www.corestandards.org for more information.) Eventually, the standards will include many subjects, but at this early point in their development, the focus is on core math concepts with an emphasis on writing and nonfiction reading (the later to help students better understand the information in textbooks). While the specifics of how to reach these standards will differ from community to community or state to state, the standards themselves are intended to reflect a national consensus on what all American students should learn.

FOCUS QUESTION 7

What are common core state standards?

Many are excited that these Common Core Standards focus on fewer topics, require greater depth, and no longer expect students to race through subjects with only a superficial understanding of what they are studying. This change is a sign that U.S. schools are adopting the less-is-more approach used in countries like Finland and South Korea, countries where students go deeper into topics and score higher on international achievement tests. Others are pleased that as a nation we are finally identifying a common thread of what all American students should be learning. But it is important to remember that we are talking only about standards, not a national curriculum, so no one is dictating precisely what courses or books every student should read. Each state will define the curriculum and identify the books appropriate for its own students in attaining these standards. Supporters also point out that these Common Core Standards will graduate students better prepared for college and careers, allow more accurate state-to-state comparisons of how schools are performing, and ease the transition for students moving from one state to another.[28] Okay, let's take a breath here and be thankful that we are moving in a direction of a more coherent, nationwide approach to improving our schools. But you know that life is rarely this simple, and there are real doubts that core standards offer the best path for school improvement. So let's take a closer look at some of these concerns.

Is there consensus on a single set of core standards for all states? While we have a general agreement on math, reading, and writing standards, the remaining subjects will present a bigger challenge. In the science standards, for example, the early drafts address climate change and evolution, controversial topics in some states (we will discuss the evolution–intelligent design debate a bit later in this chapter). There is no consensus on what should be included in the history standards, or whether subjects like psychology or anthropology should even be included. And even the math, reading, and writing standards adopted thus far have been criticized. Opponents fear that the emphasis on nonfiction reading will devalue

A Closer Look   Common Core Standards

What do these mathematics and English standards look like? They can be quite broad, allowing room for teachers, publishers, and school districts to develop a curriculum to meet them. Here's a sample:

MATHEMATICS

- Make sense of problems and persevere in solving them.
- Reason abstractly and quantitatively.
- Construct viable arguments and critique the reasoning of others.
- Attend to precision.
- Use appropriate tools strategically.
- Look for and make use of reasoning.

ENGLISH AND LANGUAGE ARTS

- Read and comprehend why complex individuals, events, and ideas develop and interact over the course of a text.
- Read and comprehend complex literary and informational texts independently and proficiently.
- Integrate and evaluate content presented in diverse formats and media, including visually and quantitatively, as well as in words.
- Develop and strengthen writing as needed by planning, revising, editing, rewriting, or trying a new approach.
- Use technology, including the Internet, to produce and publish writing and to interact and collaborate with others.

REFLECTION: How do you feel about the idea of teaching to national standards? What is lost, and what is gained? For more information, visit www.corestandards.org.

first-rate fiction, while others have noted that the common core math standards are actually weaker than math standards that were used in some states.[29]

Are all states onboard? While the majority of states are onboard, not all are, and even among those supporting the common core, enthusiasm varies. (See Figure 6.3.) Some states have invested little time or resources into preparing their schools and teachers. Common Core Standards are intended for implementation and assessment in 2014–2015, and at the current pace, it is unlikely that all teachers, districts, or states will be ready.[30]

Do the standards reflect an appropriate direction for schools? The relatively quick agreement on math, reading, and writing standards underscores that they were developed with a clear goal: meeting the expectations of employers and colleges. But should preparation for college admission or employment be the only focus of K–12 schooling?[31] The arts, social sciences, active citizenship, physical education, caring human relations, creativity, and health concerns, among other goals, are all important dimensions of a well-rounded education, and they are once again being submerged in this very narrow view of the purpose of schools.

Is a single set of Common Core Standards desirable? Critics like Alfie Kohn (see Profiles in Education) wonder if requiring all students—from different states, different backgrounds, and with different skills and talents—to meet the same standards is a wise move. He fears that common standards will not lead to quality education, but simply to standardization. He is not alone.[32]

Are Common Core Standards the right direction for America's schools? Any new innovation, like common core standards, ushers in great expectations, but as Stanford University professor Linda Darling-Hammond points out, a common set of standards is no panacea. Students from Finland, for example, have no such detailed standards, yet do strikingly well on international tests. In fact, Finland improved its students' test scores by doing quite the opposite, shifting "to a more localized system in which highly trained teachers design curriculum around very lean national standards."[33] Students from countries with national standards scored at the bottom as well as the top on international tests in math and science. So the standards movement, although popular, is no guarantee of better schools.

What will testing be like for these standards? How testing will be done in this new world of Common Core Standards is not yet clear and may well differ from state to state, but testing done poorly can do a great deal of damage. Early reports indicate that several states are exploring computer-driven assessments rather than multiple-choice tests, perhaps to avoid

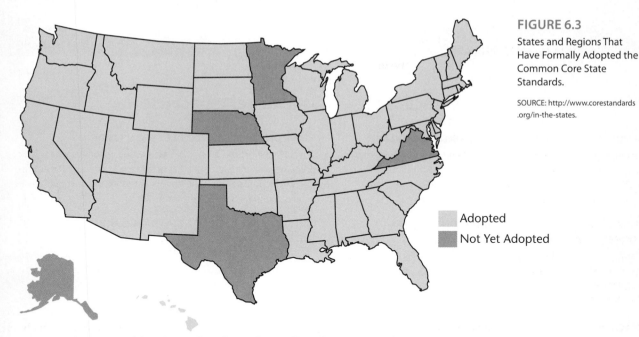

FIGURE 6.3

States and Regions That Have Formally Adopted the Common Core State Standards.

SOURCE: http://www.corestandards .org/in-the-states.

Adopted

Not Yet Adopted

States and Regions that have formally adopted the Common Core State Standards as of August 2012

Alabama	Louisiana	Ohio
Arkansas	Maine	Oklahoma
Arizona	Maryland	Oregon
California	Massachusetts	Pennsylvania
Colorado	Michigan	Rhode Island
Connecticut	Mississippi	South Carolina
Delaware	Missouri	South Dakota
District of Columbia	Montana	Tennessee
Florida	New Hampshire	U.S. Virgin Islands
Georgia	New Jersey	Utah
Hawaii	New Mexico	Vermont
Idaho	Nevada	
Kentucky	Northern Mariana Islands	

REFLECTION: Do you think that the remaining states will eventually sign on? Or is it more likely that some of the states that have signed on will eventually back out?

some of the testing problems of No Child Left Behind. Our recent experience with standardized tests offers a clear warning that any innovation, including standards-based education, can be torpedoed by a testing culture.[34]

The Problem with Standardized Tests

Although it may sound as if we are anti-testing, this is not the case. Standardized tests can help educators analyze the curriculum and teaching methods to see what's working—or what needs to be changed, as well as identify students who need additional help. Tests can point out problems that need to be corrected. The problem is with *high-stakes* standardized tests— the kind used to determine the fate of students, teachers, and schools—because these tests

GLOBAL VIEW

The Council of Foreign Relations issued a report in 2012 that warned the failure of the nation's schools to produce quality graduates "undermine American security" and economic well being in the future. Do you agree?

FOCUS QUESTION 8

What problems are created by high-stakes testing, and what are the testing alternatives?

You Be The Judge

A COMMON CORE OF STANDARDS

Is Desirable Because . . .

SCHOOLS AND EDUCATORS WILL BE HELD ACCOUNTABLE

Testing all students in all schools on the same standards will enable us to compare school effectiveness in different regions of the country. We will discover who is really learning and who is not.

IT MAKES US EDUCATIONALLY AND ECONOMICALLY COMPETITIVE

Many of today's high school graduates lack basic literacy skills, a result of weak standards and poor accountability. To compete in world markets, we must have strong national standards and tests to ensure a first-class labor force.

TEACHERS WORK COLLABORATIVELY RATHER THAN IN ISOLATION

A common set of standards promotes cooperation. Teachers and principals work together to identify problems, develop instructional solutions, and collaborate as a professional team working to ensure that all the standards are met.

IT BINDS OUR CITIZENS

Common Core Standards unify students in our common heritage. One set of standards will coalesce the nation's diverse ethnic and cultural communities.

Is a Mistake Because . . .

STANDARDIZED TESTS DETRACT FROM LEARNING

Schools taking time away from interesting learning activities to prepare for a high-stakes test flies in the face of an authentic education and ignores all that we have learned about multiple intelligences and individual differences.

FOR SOME, THE NATIONAL STANDARDS ARE A STEP BACKWARD

Standards in the nation's best school districts exceed this common core, so for these schools to focus on weaker core standards actually lowers the quality and excellence of their students' education.

TEACHERS WORK COMPETITIVELY RATHER THAN COOPERATIVELY

Student test scores are used to evaluate teachers, so many teachers feel that test preparation is necessary to ensure that their students score well and they are evaluated as effective. Survival of the fittest becomes the norm.

IT WILL DIVIDE THE NATION

In the end, it is unlikely that all states will agree on a single set of standards in subjects like history and science. The futile effort to create core standards will make it apparent to all that we are a divided people.

www.mhhe.com/sadker10e

YOU DECIDE . . .

Where do you stand on the core standards and testing? Can you separate standards from testing? How might you determine if standards are being met—without using a standardized test? Some educators assert that test development should precede standards development. Do you agree or disagree? Why?

are more likely to create than solve problems. When people's careers, salaries, and futures rely on a single test score, havoc and hurt can be the results.[35]

Take the case of a New York City middle school where the principal asked teachers to spend fifteen minutes a day with students practicing how to answer multiple-choice math questions in preparation for the state-mandated test. One teacher protested, explaining that she taught Italian and English, not math. But the principal insisted, because he, the school, the teachers, and the students would all be measured by this high-stakes test. As you might suspect, the plan failed, and fewer than one in four of these students passed the exam. All this test preparation taught students some powerful lessons about the school's hidden curriculum: test scores mattered more than English or Italian, teachers did not make the key instructional decisions, principals and teachers feared tests, and the most important thing going on in school was improving test scores.

(It was a powerful lesson, because once the test was over, one-third of the students in the protesting teacher's class stopped attending school, skipping the last five weeks of the school year.[36])

Upscale Scarsdale, New York, had a different response to high stakes testing: a student boycott. Two-thirds of the students did not show up for the exam.[37] In Massachusetts, some local school boards defied the state and issued their own diplomas to students they believed were being unfairly denied graduation because of the state-mandated test.[38] Why are teachers, students, and parents protesting? What's wrong with measuring academic progress through such tests? Here are some reasons high-stake tests are problematic:

1. *Poorer students are at greater risk.* Using the same tests for all students—those in well-funded posh schools along with students trying to learn in underfunded, ill-equipped schools—is grossly unfair, and the outcome is predictable. Because students do not receive equal educations, holding identical expectations for all students places the poorer ones at a disadvantage. For example, one year in Georgia, two out of every three low-income students failed the math, English, and reading sections of the state's competency tests. No students from well-to-do counties failed any of the tests, and more than half exceeded standards. Even moderate income differences could result in major test score differences.

   Wealthy students grow up with the intellectual advantages at home, such as books, travel, and technology, and are more likely to arrive at school with many of the academic skills commonly measured on standardized tests. For them, teachers can focus on valuable higher-level thinking skills. Poor and minority children, on the other hand, lack these home resources and must learn basic academic skills at school. The assets that minorities and the poor do bring to school—other languages, knowledge of other cultures, oral storytelling, unique music, and artistic experiences—are not honored or developed, much less tested.[39]

   There was a standard that received little attention in No Child Left Behind: the opportunity-to-learn standard. *Opportunity-to-learn standards* were created to ensure a level playing field by providing all students with appropriate educational resources, competent teachers, and modern technology. Differences in student learning styles were to be accommodated and additional time provided for students to relearn material if they failed the test. Teachers were to be given quality in-service training. Yet most states did not allocate enough resources to remedy dramatic educational differences among school districts, and real barriers to achievement—racism, poverty, sexism, low teacher salaries, language differences, and inadequate facilities—were lost in the sea of testing and inadequate funding. Although the rhetoric of the standards movement is that a rising tide raises all ships, in fact, without the adequate resources, some ships do not rise.[40]

2. *Lower graduation rates.* If testing of these standards is linked to promotion and graduation, school dropouts will likely increase. A Harvard University study found that students in the bottom 10 percent of achievement were 33 percent more likely to drop out of school in states that required graduation tests. The National Research Council found that low-performing elementary and secondary school students who are retained in grade do less well academically, are much worse off socially, and are far likelier to drop out than equally weak students who are promoted. Retention in grade is the strongest predictor of which students will drop out—stronger even than parental income or mother's education level. Ironically, when a weak student drops out, the school's average score rises, giving a picture of success when the real picture is failure.[41]

   With limited resources, schools create a triage. The strong students do not need special attention to pass the tests. They might be excellent students, but the tests are geared to measure minimal skills, not excellence. The weakest students can also be ignored, because they need more time and resources than most schools have. The students who do get the attention are

IMAGINE...

The Posse

In 1988, Deborah Bial ran into a former student, a smart kid, a successful student who had won a scholarship to an elite college. But he had dropped out and was now back home in the Bronx. "I never would have dropped out of college if I had my posse with me," he told her.

So Deborah started the Posse Foundation. About 600 students a year from eight different cities are grouped into posses of ten students who support each other as they attend an elite college. Most Posse Scholars would not have qualified for these colleges on their SAT scores alone, but they showed leadership qualities and other assets not measured by the test. Ninety percent of Posse Scholars graduate, and half make the dean's list. Many become campus leaders. Bryn Mawr college had only 40 Posse scholars among its 1,300 students, but these 40 have won the best all-around student award three times in seven years. The Posse shows colleges that success can be achieved when the schools look beyond SAT scores.

SOURCE: Tina Rosenberg, "Beyond SATs, Finding Success in Numbers," *New York Times*, February 15, 2012.

called "bubble kids," because they are closest to a passing grade. A Texas teacher poignantly captures this dilemma:

> Ana's got a 25 percent. What's the point in trying to get her to grade level? It would take two years to get her to pass the test, so there's really no hope for her. I feel like we might as well focus on the ones there's hope for.[42]

3. *Higher test scores do not mean more learning.* To many, teaching has become test preparation, and learning is measured by test scores. But this is not how teachers see it. Only 28 percent of teachers see standardized tests as an essential or very important gauge of student achievement, and only one in four teachers believe that these tests accurately reflect student learning. About half of the teachers believe that students do not take these tests seriously, and therefore do not try to do their best.[43] Consider these findings:

   - A study of eighteen states compared trends in state test scores with long-term trends on national standardized tests. When state tests were given, performance went down on the ACT, the SAT, and the math test of the National Assessment of Educational Progress (NAEP). The study concluded that higher state test scores were most likely due to direct test preparation rather than increased student learning.[44]

   - Three-quarters of fourth-grade teachers surveyed by RAND in Washington State, and the majority of principals, believed that better test preparation (rather than increased learning) was responsible for most of the score gains.[45]

GLOBAL VIEW

A World-Class Education: Learning from International Models of Excellence and Innovation by Vivien Stewart offers some insights and good ideas for discussion about school practices around the world and how the United States might do schooling differently.

4. *Standardized testing shrinks the curriculum.* Educator Alfie Kohn advises parents to ask an unusual question when a school's test scores increase: "What did you have to sacrifice about my child's education to raise those scores?"[46] Many teachers believe that their schools give less attention to subjects that are not on the state test. One teacher had this to say about how the timing of state tests drives teaching: "At our school, third- and fourth-grade teachers are told not to teach social studies and science until March."[47] Indeed, a study by the Center on Education Policy found that about 62 percent of school districts increased the amount of time spent in elementary schools on English/language arts or math, and 44 percent of districts cut time on science, social studies, art and music, physical education, lunch, or recess.[48] Such a narrow view of the curriculum is self-defeating. In schools where the arts are part of the core curriculum, one finds self-motivated students, improved social and emotional development, greater parental involvement, intensified student and teacher engagement, stronger collegiate aspirations, greater civic engagement, and respect for cultural differences. While the global economy demands innovation, schools view the world through a traditional and narrow perspective.[49]

5. *When tests fail.* Tests themselves are often flawed, and high-stakes errors become high-stakes disasters. Stories continue to mount as the crush of millions of new tests overwhelms the handful of testing companies. In Massachusetts, a senior spotted an alternative answer to a math question, and the scores of 449 students were suddenly propelled over the passing mark. A flawed answer key incorrectly lowered multiple-choice scores for 12,000 Arizona students, erred in adding up scores of essay tests for students in Michigan, and forced the re-scoring of 204,000 essay tests in Washington. Another error resulted in nearly 9,000 students in New York City being mistakenly assigned to summer school, and $2 million in

Profile in Education Alfie Kohn

One day in 1967, fifth-grader **Alfie Kohn** received a class assignment. As expected, he wrote his name and the date at the top of the paper. The title he chose, though, was unanticipated: "Busywork." He doesn't remember the announced purpose of the assignment. He does remember that it was busywork. Over three decades later, Alfie Kohn still discriminates between genuine learning and mindless school routine. As a teacher, researcher, and journalist, his work carries a common theme: Educational excellence comes from personalized learning, from recognizing the uniqueness of each student, not from a lockstep curriculum. As a teacher, he remembers:

> I lovingly polished lectures, reading lists, and tests. I treated the students as interchangeable receptacles—rows of wide-open bird beaks waiting for worms.

Finally I realized I was denying students the joy of exploring topics and uncovering truths on their own.[a]

In his own education, Kohn adopted this personalized approach to learning. As an undergraduate at Brown University, he created an interdisciplinary major, and dubbed it normativism. He again took an unbeaten path at the University of Chicago, writing his graduate thesis on humor. "Learning was meaningful because I started with the question and then drew from whatever fields were useful in exploring it, rather than being confined to the methods and topics of a particular discipline."[b] When he visits classrooms today, Kohn is often disheartened. Rarely does he witness such engaged learning. Instead, he sees students usually learning just to pass a test.

Kohn challenges today's popular clamor for higher standards and increased testing. "Standardized testing has swelled and mutated, like a creature in one of those old horror movies, to the point that it now threatens to swallow our schools whole."[c] He passionately warns educators, policymakers, and parents that raising standardized test scores is completely different from helping students to learn. And the pressurized culture of testing exacts a high cost. Every hour spent on such exam preparation is an hour not spent helping students to think creatively, to tackle controversial issues, and to love learning.

Common standards often begin with "all students will be able to . . ." and Kohn sees a harmful message in such wording: Individual differences don't exist or are unimportant. Often justified in the name of accountability or rigor, standards turn schools into fact factories. Students may recite Civil War battles, distinguish between phloem and xylem, and memorize prime numbers in hopes of meeting predetermined standards of excellence. Will they? Kohn doesn't think so.

With a focus on standards of outcome rather than standards of opportunity, real barriers to achievement—racism, poverty, low teacher salaries, language differences, inadequate facilities—are lost in the sea of testing. "[A]ll students deserve a quality education. But declaring that everyone must reach the same level is naïve at best, cynical at worst, in light of wildly unequal resources."[d] Equally troublesome is testing's unbalanced reward system. As a bonus for good scores, more money is often given to successful schools and less to those already deprived. Callous is how he describes such a retreat from fairness and the implication that teachers and students need only be bribed or threatened to achieve.

Alfie Kohn also knows that change in schools can be slow. Standardized curriculum and testing are fueled by concerns of competition in our global economy and reinforced by a tradition of teacher-centered instruction. "I am not a utopian. I am as aware as anyone of the difficulties of creating schools that are genuinely concerned about learning and about meeting children's needs, but that causes me to redouble my efforts rather than throw up my hands."[e]

[a] Jay Matthews, "Education's Different Drummer," *The Washington Post*, January 9, 2001, p. A10.
[b] Ibid.
[c] Alfie Kohn, "Standardized Testing and Its Victims," *Education Week*, September 27, 2000.
[d] Alfie Kohn, "One-Size-Fits-All Education Doesn't Work," *Boston Globe*, June 10, 2001, p. C8.
[e] Matthews, "Education's Different Drummer."

To learn more about Alfie Kohn, click on *Profiles in Education.*

www.mhhe.com/sadker10e

REFLECTION: Do you agree with Kohn that standardized testing undermines learning? In the next decade, do you think schools in the United States will become more or less reliant on standardized tests? Justify your answer.

Both teachers and students often find that a testing culture diminishes education to a test score.

achievement awards being denied to deserving students in Kentucky.[50] The National Board on Educational Testing and Public Policy reported that fifty high-profile testing mistakes had occurred in twenty states from 1999 through 2002; and in 2006, rain fell on some SAT answer sheets, affecting the test scores of 4,000 college hopefuls, most in a negative direction.[51] Many question the wisdom of rewarding and punishing students, teachers, and schools on the basis of the flawed history of the testing industry.[52]

6. *Teacher stress.* Although teachers support high standards, they object to learning being measured by a single test.[53] Not surprisingly, in a national study, nearly seven in ten teachers reported feeling test stress, and two out of three believed that preparing for the test took time from teaching important but nontested topics.[54] Fourth-grade veteran teachers were requesting transfers, saying that they could not stand the pressure of administering the high-stakes elementary exams, and teachers recognized for excellence were leaving public schools, feeling their talents were better utilized in private schools where test preparation did not rule the curriculum.[55] When eighty Arizona teachers and teacher educators were asked to visually depict the impact of standardized tests, their drawings indicated test-driven classrooms where boredom, fear, and isolation dominate. Teachers feel that they are shortchanging schoolchildren from a love for learning. Figure 6.4 presents one of those drawings.

7. *What's worth knowing?* The fact that history, drama, the arts, and a host of subjects are given less attention in the current testing movement raises intriguing curricular questions: What is really important to teach? What is worth knowing? Although it may sound obvious, thinking beyond the obvious is often a good idea. Much of what is taught in schools is tradition and conventional wisdom, curricular inertia rather than careful thought. To see how society's notion of what is important can change, try your hand

FIGURE 6.4

A teacher's impression of the testing movement.

SOURCE: http://ganesh.ed.asu.edu/ aims/view_image.php?image_ id572&grade_range_id53. See also Tirupalavanam Ganesh, "Held Hostage by High-Stakes Testing: Drawing as Symbolic Resistance," *Teacher Education Quarterly* (2002).

REFLECTION: Try your own hand at drawing an image of how you feel when you are about to take a high-stakes test.

at the test questions below that were used to make certain that eighth-graders in Kansas knew "important information." We have shortened the exam, but all these questions are from the original. (Hint: Brush up on your orthography.) See if you would qualify to graduate from elementary school in 1895.[56]

8th Grade Examination Graduation Questions
Saline County, Kansas
April 13, 1895

Reading and Penmanship—The Examination will be oral and the Penmanship of Applicants will be graded from the manuscripts.

Grammar

1. Give nine rules for the use of Capital Letters.
2. Define Verse, Stanza, and Paragraph.
3. What are the Principal Parts of a verb? Give Principal Parts of do, lie, lay, and run.

Arithmetic

1. District No. 33 has a valuation of $35,000. What is the necessary levy to carry on a school seven months at $50 per month, and have $104 for incidentals?
2. What is the cost of a square farm at $15 per acre, the distance around which is 640 rods?
3. Write a Bank Check, a Promissory Note, and a Receipt.

U.S. History

1. Give the epochs into which U.S. History is divided.
2. Tell what you can of the history of Kansas.
3. Describe three of the most prominent battles of the Rebellion.

Orthography

1. What are the following, and give examples of each: Trigraph, subvocals, diphthong, cognate letters, linguals?
2. Give four substitutes for caret "u."
3. Mark diacritically and divide into syllables the following, and name the sign that indicates the sound: card, ball, mercy, sir, odd, cell, rise, blood, fare, last.

Geography

1. Name and describe the following: Monrovia, Odessa, Denver, Manitoba, Heela, Yukon, St. Helena, Juan Fernandez, Aspinwall, and Orinoco.
2. Name all the republics of Europe and give capital of each.
3. Describe the movements of the earth. Give inclination of the earth.

Physiology

1. How does nutrition reach the circulation?
2. What is the function of the liver? Of the kidneys?
3. Give some general directions that you think would be beneficial to preserve the human body in a state of health.

How did you do? Well, if you bombed it, don't feel too badly; few of today's PhDs would pass. So what does this teach us? Are today's schools far weaker than earlier ones? If we failed, are we not truly educated? Or perhaps what we consider "important knowledge" is less enduring than we believe. How much of today's "critical" information will be a curious and unimportant footnote in the years ahead?

Evaluating Teachers by Student Test Scores

In recent years, policymakers have taken the testing culture to another level, using student test scores to evaluate not only students, but teachers as well. We talked about *value added* earlier in the book, the notion that students can be tested from year-to-year to measure their annual educational growth. Many districts are using these year-to-year test results, this value added, to evaluate a teacher's skills. Find the teachers adding the most (and the least) value to a student's education, and bingo, you can determine which teachers to reward, and which to penalize. Or can you?

Take the case of five fifth-grade teachers at Public School 146 in Brooklyn, one of the highest-achieving elementary schools in New York. These five teachers were quite talented, having won grants to study in Ghana, Mexico and Peru and a Guggenheim Museum arts award and had worked for Columbia University to help educate other teachers. They often stayed until 7 or 8 at night to work with students, and their principal believed them to be among the most gifted and hard-working fifth-grade teachers she ever had on staff. There was no surprise when in 2009, 96 percent of their fifth-graders tested proficient in English, and 89 percent in math, scores near the top in New York City. The surprise was that because of these test scores, these teachers received negative evaluations. In the value-added system, students are measured by testing improvement, and their students actually scored a bit higher the year before, so these gifted teachers were penalized.[57]

Using students' test scores to assess teachers is a flawed approach, not only because of the imperfect value-added concept, but also because one test score is an inadequate measure of student growth, much less teacher effectiveness. Yet one student test score can become 40 or 50 percent of a teacher's evaluation, as it is in some states.[58] In fact, these test scores often tell us more about a student's world than the teacher's. Student achievement is influenced by health issues, home life, class size, curriculum materials, school attendance, other teachers, peers, parenting at home, and of course, the wealth or poverty of the student and the school. So it is not surprising that teachers' ratings vary from year to year, depending on students, classes, tests, and other factors. Teachers who rank at the top one year are often rated as only average or worse in following years. As one Houston teacher put it: "I teach the same way every year. [My] first year got me pats on the back. [My] second year got me kicked in the backside. And for year three, my scores were off the charts. I got a huge bonus. What did I do differently? I have no clue."[59]

Sometimes even test score improvements lead to despair. Because of its remarkable test turnaround, Noyes Elementary in the District of Columbia was one of 264 public schools nationwide named a blue ribbon school by the U.S. Department of Education in 2009. The school was touted as an example of how a once-low-performing school can be transformed. In 2010, each teacher won an $8,000 bonus, and the principal won $10,000.[60] A closer look at Noyes, however, raised questions about its test scores. An investigation revealed an extraordinarily high numbers of erasures on the tests, with wrong answers being consistently changed to right ones. Noyes was not alone. In 2008 and 2009, 109 schools in Atlanta were under suspicion for test tampering. When Georgia officials investigated, they identified at least 180 principals, teachers, and staff were involved in test-tampering. By 2012, the *Atlanta Journal* found that 196 of the nation's 3,125 largest school districts had suspicious test results suggesting adult tampering. For thirty-three of these districts, the odds of their test scores occurring naturally were greater than one in a million.[61]

Why is cheating happening? Statisticians have an answer: **Campbell's law.** Donald T. Campbell, a social scientist, wrote: "The more any quantitative social indicator is used for social decision-making, the more subject it will be to corruption pressures and the more apt it will be to distort and corrupt the social processes it was intended to monitor." In other words, the more important test scores become, the more likely cheating. So when such tests are used

GLOBAL VIEW

Singapore's minister of education explains that his country would never evaluate teachers by student test scores because doing so would create bad incentives and undermine collaboration. In Portugal, when merit pay was based on test results, that is exactly what happened: teacher collaboration decreased. Why do you think that American policymakers so rarely consider the impact of their decisions on teacher collaboration?

for firing, tenure, and merit decisions in any field, sometimes quite inappropriately, a few will rebel and break the rules.[62]

Changing test answers is pretty egregious, but what we call "cheating" does not always have such a clear line. If a teacher focuses her class not on learning all kinds of things, but on learning just what the test calls for, and then has her students spend many hours practicing for the test, is that cheating? Such practice is now commonplace. Students learn less content in this scenario, but the standardized test results suggest that they are learning more. As one teacher explains, "Teaching to the test is still third-degree [cheating] in my mind."[63]

So what's the alternative? As in any profession, evaluation of teachers should be ongoing and done by experts. Most teachers agree that student progress over the year should be considered in their evaluations, along with other measures. Classroom observations and evidence of student learning from both classroom work and other exams should also be taken into account, not only to evaluate the teacher, but to help the teacher improve. Assessment of students should move beyond standardized, fill-in-the-bubble tests; we should consider a variety of ways to measure learning.

Alternatives to High-Stakes Testing

Standardized tests are popular because they are relatively inexpensive compared with other assessments, offer clear results, and can be rapidly implemented. But, as we have seen, high-stakes standardized tests are plagued with problems. In fact, testing guidelines issued by the American Psychological Association specifically prohibit basing any consequential decisions about individuals on a single test score.[64] Most educational organizations, measurement experts, and teachers believe that a better gauge of student performance is multiple assessments: tests, class participation, portfolios, formal exhibitions, independent student projects, and teacher evaluations. **Authentic assessment** (also called alternative or performance-based assessment) captures actual student performance, encourages students to reflect on their own work, and is integrated into the student's whole learning process. Such tests usually require students to synthesize and use information. The student might demonstrate what has been learned through a portfolio (like the ones we encourage you to develop in the *RAPs* found in this text) or a journal or by undergoing an interview, conducting an experiment, or giving a presentation. Authentic assessment offers a focused and intense insight into what the student has learned and requires evidence quite different from what is required by responding to questions on a typical high-stakes test.[65] Comparisons are often made to sports, in which participants are expected to demonstrate in a game what they have learned in practice. A tennis player works on her backhand so that she can demonstrate mastery in a game; similarly, when students know that they will be called on to demonstrate and use their knowledge, they are more motivated to practice their academic skills. Many states are exploring authentic methods of assessment.[66]

Authentic assessment is used in the Coalition of Essential Schools, founded by prominent educator Theodore Sizer. The coalition encourages schools to define their own model for successful reform, guided by nine basic principles that emphasize the personalization of learning.

IMAGINE...

A Test of Goodwill

Colman McCarthy teaches high school Peace Studies but has never given a test. In his own words, he prefers giving "tons of homework." His assignments include: Tell someone you love her or him. Do a favor for someone who will not know you did it. Thank the people who drive the school bus, cook the food, and clean the toilets. If students don't do the homework, McCarthy explains, they will fail. Worse than failing a standardized test, they will fail their better selves; they will fail to make the world a better place.

SOURCE: *The Washington Post*, March 18, 2006.

These principles include the requirement that students complete "exhibitions," tasks that call on them to exhibit their knowledge concretely. The high school curriculum is structured around these demanding, creative tasks, which may include:

- Completing a federal Internal Revenue Service Form 1040 for a family whose records you receive, working with other students in a group to ensure that everyone's IRS forms are correct, and auditing a return filed by a student in a different group
- Designing a nutritious and attractive lunch menu for the cafeteria within a specified budget and defending your definitions of nutritious and attractive
- Designing and building a wind instrument from metal pipes, then composing and performing a piece of music for that instrument
- Defining one human emotion in an essay, through examples from literature and history, and in at least three other ways (through drawing, painting, or sculpture; through film, photographs, or video; through music; through pantomime or dance; or through a story or play that you create)[67]

An increase in authentic assessment may contribute to a greater classroom focus on critical thinking and personal development. Authentic assessments may help us go beyond the current dependence on high-stakes standardized tests in determining the competence of students and the success of schools.

Tension Points

FOCUS QUESTION 9

How are cultural and political conflicts reflected in the school curriculum?

You can read a curriculum the way you read the day's newspaper, because in it you can see the fractures and tensions in our society. Often, the curriculum becomes a battleground for competing political and cultural ideas. Here are some examples.

Intelligent Design versus Evolution

In colonial New England, the Bible was the major text, and religious instruction was the center of the curriculum. But the new nation's constitution changed all that. Or did it? From prayer in school to sex education, courts continually debate the role of religion in school. Here are two examples of too much religious influence.

The following questions were assigned to students in a public school in Virginia:

1. List six proofs that the Bible is God's word.
2. God is supreme ruler and has given man free choice. This shows that God is:
   A. Omniscient B. Good   C. Sovereign   D. Merciful[68]

A California public school system was using textbooks that taught that God helped Columbus discover America, that Native American accomplishments were "worthless" because they had no knowledge of the "true" God, described non-Christian religions as "cults," and asked students to punctuate a sentence that read: "The Hebrew people often grumbled and complained."[69]

These examples were clearly religious instruction and illegal, because the First Amendment does not allow schools to promote or denigrate any religion. (See Chapter 8 for a detailed discussion on the role of religion in schools.) According to the Supreme Court, also illegal is the teaching of **creationism,** the position that God created the universe in six 24-hour periods as described in the Bible. But does that mean that the theory of evolution should be taught as the only explanation of life's origin? **Evolution,** as put forth by Charles Darwin, is a keystone of modern biological theory and postulates that animals and plants have their origin in other preexisting types and that there are modifications in successive generations. Christian fundamentalists (also referred to as religious fundamentalists or the religious right) do not believe that this explains the origin of human life, and they are not alone. They support the teaching of *intelligent design,* which credits an unnamed intelligence or designer for aspects of nature's complexity still unexplained by science, and support the concept that evolution is simply a theory, not a fact. While civil rights attorneys and many scientists argue that intelligent design is religious and unscientific, polls indicate that a large segment of the public is comfortable with the notion that students deserve to hear competing theories.[70] More than a dozen states (a number likely to grow) are either considering passing or have already passed legislation requiring that when evolution is taught, criticism be included, or alternative explanations of the origins of humans, including the supernatural, be taught as well. Tennessee, for example, provides guidelines for teachers on how to answer student questions that challenge evolution, global warming, and other scientific subjects, and the state guarantees that teachers won't be disciplined for ignoring the tenets of science.[71] Other states and school districts have actually removed the word *evolution* from the curriculum. Compared with people in other countries, Americans are far less likely to believe in evolution.[72] (See Figure 6.5.)

The subtlety of language is partially responsible for this tension point, because "theory" has two separate meanings. In common language, "theory" means an idea or a hunch. In science, a theory is a thoroughly tested belief unlikely to change, such as the theory of gravitation or cell theory or evolutionary theory.[73] Scientific theories are the result of decades or centuries of insights drawn on many interconnected observations and ideas. The theory of evolution is more than a hunch and needs to be understood as a well-founded scientific explanation. But that does not mean that evolution exists in a vacuum. Science refutes a literal interpretation of the Bible as a measure of the age of the earth, but it does not refute a spiritual or higher intelligence at work. Perhaps intelligent design works through evolution. The bottom line is that we still have much to learn. It is unfortunate that such debates create pro- and anti-science camps.

These controversies frighten some teachers, and this is unfortunate. Teaching should be about opening minds, not indoctrination. Teaching the theory of evolution is important; teaching *about* different religions is important. Promoting or disparaging religious or scientific beliefs is inappropriate. Unfortunately, many teachers, fearful of the consequences, avoid teaching about religion or evolution.[74] Teaching spirituality is even more rare. *Spirituality,* a

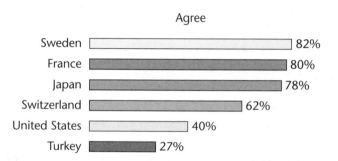

Agree

Sweden 82%
France 80%
Japan 78%
Switzerland 62%
United States 40%
Turkey 27%

FIGURE 6.5

Do you believe in evolution?

SOURCE: "Trend Lines: Acceptance of Evolution," *Washington Post,* January 16, 2007.

REFLECTION: Why do you think the percentage of Americans who believe in evolution is so much lower than many other countries?

personal and pluralistic view of life's meaning, is broader than any particular religion. Spirituality encompasses many ideas common to all religions; activities that renew, lift up, comfort, heal, and inspire both ourselves and others. Religion, science, and spirituality need not be in conflict. Religious intolerance, scientific hostility, and spiritual ignorance do not move the world forward, but they do inhibit learning.

Censorship and the Curriculum

Ruth Sherman lived just outside New York City, in a Long Island neighborhood known for its Italian community and its easy commute to the city. Although she traveled only a short distance to P.S. 75, where she taught third grade, she might as well have been teaching in another country. P.S. 75 was in the Bushwick section of Brooklyn, a graffiti-filled neighborhood populated by poor black and Hispanic families living in the midst of a rampant drug culture. "Why there?" her friends asked her. "Because I want to turn things around," she responded. She was that kind of teacher. But, in just three months, it was Ruth Sherman, and not her students, who was turned around.

Her problems started in September, although she did not learn about it until later, when she assigned a book called *Nappy Hair,* by African American author Carolivia Herron. Her students loved the book, about a little black girl with "the nappiest, fuzziest, the most screwed up, squeezed up, knotted hair," and clamored for copies to take with them. By Thanksgiving, the parents in Ruth Sherman's class had also discovered the book, which they considered racially insulting. At a parents' meeting, she was confronted by fifty parents (most of them parents of children not in her class), who shouted racial epithets and eventually threatened her. The superintendent sent Ruth home for her own protection. A review of the book followed. The review brought only praise for a book that promoted positive images for children and presented stories that appealed to them. Within a few days, the superintendent wrote her a letter, commending her performance, inviting her back to the school, and promising security escorts to protect her. But, by then, it was too late. Ruth Sherman, the teacher who wanted to make a difference, did not want to work in a climate that required "escorts" to ensure her safety. She transferred to another school.[75]

This incident occurred in New York, but it could occur anywhere, anytime. Nearly everyone—teachers, parents, the general public, and various special interest groups—wants some say as to what is and is not in the school curriculum. No matter what content is found in a particular textbook or course of study, someone is likely to consider it too conservative or too liberal, too traditional or too avant-garde, racist, sexist, anti-Semitic, violent, un-Christian, or pornographic.[76] When this happens, pressure to censor the offending materials soon follows.

There is no such thing as a totally safe, acceptable, uncontroversial book or curriculum. Each of the following has been subjected to censorship at one time or another:

- Mary Rodgers's *Freaky Friday:* "Makes fun of parents and parental responsibility"
- Plato's *Republic:* "This book is un-Christian"
- Jules Verne's *Around the World in Eighty Days:* "Very unfavorable to Mormons"
- William Shakespeare's *Macbeth:* "Too violent for children"
- Fyodor Dostoyevsky's *Crime and Punishment:* "Serves as a poor model for young people"
- Herman Melville's *Moby Dick:* "Contains homosexuality"
- Anne Frank's *Diary of a Young Girl:* "Obscene and blasphemous"
- E. B. White's *Charlotte's Web:* "Morbid picture of death"
- J. R. R. Tolkien's *The Hobbit:* "Subversive elements"
- Roald Dahl's *Charlie and the Chocolate Factory:* "Racist"

- Mark Twain's *The Adventures of Huckleberry Finn:* "Racism, insensitivity, and offensive language"
- *Webster's Dictionary:* "Contains sexually explicit definitions"[77]

According to the American Library Association, more than 500 books are challenged in a typical year.[78] But the incidences of **self-censorship,** which some term **stealth censorship,** are considered much higher. Stealth censorship occurs when educators or parents quietly remove a book from a library shelf or a course of study in response to an informal complaint—or to avoid controversy. Teachers practice the same sort of self-censorship when they choose not to teach a topic or not to discuss a difficult issue. Numbers on the frequency of self-censorship are impossible to obtain. Tallying up the number of books that were officially removed or placed on restricted-access shelves in libraries is far easier. Frequently challenged authors include J. K. Rowling, John Steinbeck, Judy Blume, Robert Cormier, Mark Twain, Phyllis Reynolds Naylor, Stephen King, Lois Duncan, Maya Angelou, J. D. Salinger, and Toni Morrison. On today's list of challenged books, you will find:

- *To Kill A Mockingbird* by Harper Lee for offensive language, racism, and being unsuited to age group
- *Twilight* (series) by Stephenie Meyer for religious viewpoint, being sexually explicit, and being unsuited to age group
- *It's Perfectly Normal* by Robie H. Harris for homosexuality, nudity, sex education, religious viewpoint, and abortion
- *Forever* by Judy Blume for sexual content and offensive language
- *The Catcher in the Rye* by J. D. Salinger for sexual content and offensive language
- *The Chocolate War* by Robert Cormier for sexual content and offensive language
- *And Tango Makes Three* by Justin Richardson and Peter Parnell for being anti-ethnic and anti-family, homosexuality, religious viewpoint, and being unsuited to age group
- *His Dark Materials* trilogy by Philip Pullman for political viewpoint, religious viewpoint, and violence
- *Scary Stories* by Alvin Schwartz for occult/satanism, religious viewpoint, and violence
- *It's So Amazing! A Book about Eggs, Sperm, Birth, Babies, and Families* by Robie H. Harris for sex education and sexual content[79]

At the heart of the case against censorship is the First Amendment, which guarantees freedom of speech and of the press. Those who oppose censorship say that our purpose as educators is not to indoctrinate children but to expose them to a variety of views and perspectives. The case for censorship (or, perhaps in a more politically correct phrase, *mature judgment and selection*) is that adults have the right and obligation to protect children from harmful influences. But "harmful influences" are in the eye of the beholder. For instance, challenges to books that include homosexuality have become commonplace. Critics say that these books promote homosexuality, and that is not acceptable in school. Others believe that such books teach tolerance, arguing that reading about different sexual orientations is not promoting any particular sexual outlook.[80]

Deciding what students should be able to read, and at what age, continues to be a difficult challenge for teachers and parents. It has been made even more difficult by the Internet, which has opened wide the schoolhouse door. While some school Internet access is now filtered or blocked, technology has made all types of information available in homes, libraries, and hot spots.[81] Censorship challenges at school will undoubtedly continue in the years ahead. For helpful advice in dealing with such challenges in your classroom, visit www.ala.org/offices/oif/ifissues/censorshipschools.

Cultural Literacy or Cultural Imperialism?

Both George Orwell and Aldous Huxley were pessimists about the future. "What Orwell feared were those who would ban books," writes author Neil Postman. "What Huxley feared was that there would be no one who wanted to read one."[82] Perhaps neither of them imagined that the great debate would revolve around neither fear nor apathy but, rather, deciding which books are most worth reading.

Proponents of **core knowledge,** also called **cultural literacy,** argue for a common course of study for all students, one that ensures that an educated person knows the basics of our society. Allan Bloom's *The Closing of the American Mind* (1987) was one of several books that sounded the call for a curricular canon. *Canon* is a term with religious roots, referring to a list of books officially accepted by the church or a religious hierarchy. A curricular *canon* applies this notion to schools by defining the most useful and valued books in our culture. Those who support a curricular canon believe that all students should share a common knowledge of our history and the central figures of our culture, an appreciation of the great works of art and music and, particularly, the great works of literature. A shared understanding of our civilization is a way to bind our diverse people. Some of the reasons for Common Core Standards can be seen in these concerns.

Allan Bloom, professor of social thought at the University of Chicago, took aim at the university curriculum as a series of often-unrelated courses lacking a vision of what an educated individual should know, a canonless curriculum. He claimed that his university students were ignorant of music and literature and charged that too many students graduate with a degree but without an education.[83]

E. D. Hirsch, Jr., in his book *Cultural Literacy,* was more successful than Bloom in including the contributions of various ethnic and racial groups, as well as women. This is a rarity among core curriculum proponents. In fact, Hirsch believes children from poverty and children of color will benefit most from a cultural literacy curriculum. According to Hirsch, a core curriculum will teach them the names, dates, places, events, and quotes that every literate American needs to know to succeed. In 1991, Hirsch published the first volume of the core knowledge series, *What Your First Grader Needs to Know.* Other grades followed in these mass-marketed books directed not only at educators but at parents as well.[84]

Not everyone is enamored with the core curriculum idea. A number of educators wonder who gets included in this core and, just as interesting, who gets to choose? Are Hirsch, Bloom, and others to be members of a very select committee, perhaps a blue-ribbon committee of "Very Smart People"? Why are so many of these curricular canons so white, so male, so Eurocentric, and so exclusionary?

Many call for a more inclusive telling of the American story, one that weaves the contributions of many groups and of women as well as of white males into the textbook tapestry of the American experience. Those who support **multicultural education** say that students of color and females will achieve more, will like learning better, and will have higher self-esteem if they are reflected in the pages of their textbooks. (In Chapter 3, we discuss multicultural education in depth.) And let's not forget white male students. When they read about people other than themselves in the curriculum, they are more likely to honor and appreciate their diverse peers. Educator and author James Banks calls for increased cultural pluralism:

> People of color, women, and other marginalized groups are demanding that their voices, visions, and perspectives be included in the curriculum. They ask that the debt Western civilization owes to Africa, Asia, and indigenous America be acknowledged. . . . However, these groups must acknowledge that they do not want to eliminate Aristotle and Shakespeare, or Western civilization, from the school curriculum. To reject the West would be to reject important aspects of their own cultural heritages, experiences, and identities.[85]

The Technology Revolution

In the twentieth century, education was forever changed. Human beings serving as teachers, the core of schooling for centuries if not millennia, were made technologically obsolete. The new invention was used at home and then in the more affluent schools. Eventually, all schools were connected. Slowly but surely, the classroom teacher was replaced. These new machines took students where they had never been before, did things no human could do, and shared an unlimited reservoir of information. Clearly, this technological breakthrough had potential to teach more effectively at a far lower cost than human teachers. Predictions varied from the replacement of all teachers to the replacement of most teachers. Some even predicted the replacement of schools themselves.

FOCUS QUESTION 10
How has technology affected the curriculum?

Sound familiar? Although today's computer revolution has sparked those sorts of predictions, the developments just described had nothing to do with computers or the Internet, or even the twenty-first century. Those predictions were made in the 1950s about television. The popular perception back then was that educational television would reshape the classroom and revolutionize schools, and perhaps put a few million teachers out of work. That never happened. Although television has reshaped much of the cultural landscape (and not all for the good), predictions about its impact on schools were greatly exaggerated. Americans are quick to see a brave new world with each new invention. Consider the following soothsayers:

"The motion picture is destined to revolutionize our educational system, and . . . in a few years it will supplant largely, if not entirely, the use of textbooks."

—**Thomas Edison**

"The time may come when a portable radio receiver will be as common in the classroom as is a blackboard."

—**William Levenson, director of
Cleveland Public School's radio station**[86]

It should not be surprising, then, that the large investments in computer-based technologies have not been matched by significant gains in student achievement. In fact, researchers are divided on the academic benefits of computers. Evidence suggests that drills and tutorials in science, social science, and math may be effective in helping students show increased performance on standard multiple-choice tests, but more advanced simulations, such as virtual dissections, are not. Perhaps with more sophisticated uses of technology in the future, more effective learning will occur—or perhaps not.[87] For some students, including home schooled, technology offers a tremendous assist. But there are downsides as well. Students who become too dependent on calculators before understanding mathematical concepts can see their mathematics test scores tumble.[88] Word processing has produced longer, higher-quality writing by students, but teachers complain about the spelling and grammatical shortcuts of students' e-texting.[89] Technology has created some ethical dilemmas as well. Nearly 40 percent of college students use the cut-and-paste function on their computers to lift text from the Internet. Text-messaging on cell phones has been used to share information during exams. High-tech cheating is rarely reported by students.[90]

Technology brings students instant information, but educators wonder about its ultimate impact on learning.

Ways Technology Is Used in the Classroom

Although computers have not proved to be the silver bullet that magically improves student achievement, most adults believe that computers offer essential workplace skills. The public sees computers in the classroom as a sign of educational progress, and increasingly, teachers view technology as a central part of classroom life. What technology? When asked to rank their needs, teachers listed a computer station with access to e-mail at the top of the list, followed by the Internet, a telephone (yes, a telephone!), an encyclopedia and other reference materials on CD, and at least one computer for every four students. Presentation and multimedia authoring programs were also mentioned.[91] The interactive whiteboard is a technology in about 15 percent of classrooms in 2010, and growing rapidly.

In the curriculum, teachers use technology in some exciting ways:

- *Simulations* re-create events, such as elections, cross-cultural meetings, and historical events, with amazing realism that pulls students into another time or place. Science simulations allow modeling of natural concepts like molecular activity to help students understand concepts that would otherwise remain abstract.

- *Data sensors* allow students to use scientific tools to collect data measurements in real time on phenomena they are studying. The use of real data helps move student understanding from abstract to concrete.

- *Virtual field trips* transport students to the ocean depths; to outer space on NASA's shuttle site; and to the National Zoo, where zookeepers share their knowledge of the animals and students can talk with the experts. The technology can also create reverse field trips where the expert is brought into the class electronically to serve as a guest speaker.

Expanding the classroom is now commonplace with the Internet resources available to teachers:

- First People's Project provides a site, in Spanish and English, for students from indigenous cultures. The goal is for students to learn about different cultures and perhaps become involved in humanitarian efforts (see www.iearn.org.au/fp/). More than 6,000 schools in Mexico, the United States, and Canada participate in wildlife migration studies in the Western Hemisphere by recording sightings in their areas.

- "Journey North: A Global Study of Wildlife Migration" teaches students to care for wildlife by creating or protecting habitats (see www.learner.org/jnorth).

- At the Holocaust/Genocide Project, students produce a magazine called *An End to Intolerance* (see www.iearn.org/hgp/).

- World Wise Schools is a Peace Corps project where classrooms can partner with Peace Corps volunteers and follow them as they do their work during the course of a year (see www.peacecorps.gov/wws).

- Podcasting lectures and discussions are a way of teaching students even when they are not in class. Although teachers now podcast information to students, schools also are encouraging students to produce their own podcasts in various subjects.

Distance learning, the technology-enabled outgrowth of correspondence courses, provides opportunities for students to experience courses and earn credits and degrees without a brick-and-mortar building. Estimates range between 1 and 2 million such learners are already enrolled online. While Michigan became the first state to require an "online learning experience" before high school graduation back in 2006, today more than half of the states provide a state virtual education program.[92] Virtual education opens new opportunities for homebound students, homeschooling families, student athletes with rigorous practice schedules, students who have problems in traditional schools, or students wanting to access courses not available in their schools, such as Advanced Placement courses. For older adults, virtual education offers opportunities to those working unusual or unpredictable hours, commuters who would rather travel the Internet than the interstate, and individuals who simply like learning on their own time and in their own place. (What kinds of distance learning experience have you had?)

The next big growth area for technology-enabled education is the hybrid course. Hybrid or blended courses are delivered neither entirely online nor entirely face-to-face in the classroom. Many teachers already use podcasting lectures and discussions, and as they learn more about virtual possibilities, their courses are likely to become more clearly hybrid, blending the best of both worlds.[93]

The federal government's National Educational Technology Plan calls for a "revolutionary transformation" of the educational system and a twenty-first-century model of learning powered by technology.[94] They view technology as the lever for real educational change, eventually increasing the percentage of both high school and college graduates.

But Stanford University professor Larry Cuban, looking beyond even these positive signs, sees problems on the horizon. When academic advances do not follow technological advances, we often blame teachers for not adequately embracing new technology. If teachers are not to blame, we place our criticism on the doorstep of an unresponsive school bureaucracy unable to manage change. If that does not work, then we attribute failure to insufficient resources, a public unwilling to fund costly technology. Rarely do Americans question the technology itself. Cuban points out that we know little about using technology to enhance instruction, that the problem may not be teachers, administrators, or funding; it may be America's unbridled faith in technology.[95] How do you view technology's potential?

The Digital Divide

Technology offers hope to many, but it does not always offer opportunity to everyone. The gap between technology haves and have-nots has been termed a **digital divide.** For years, African American, Hispanic, and female students had fewer computers and less access to or interest in the Internet, a technology gap with educational implications.[96] But in recent years, this gap has been closing because of the falling price of laptops, new cell phone technology, and the increasing number of school computers (although at the college level, whites, Asians, and males continue to constitute the majority of computer science majors and professionals).[97]

Although nearly all public schools have Internet access, the digital divide has not disappeared. For instance, every classroom in wealthier communities is more likely to have sufficient up-to-date technology with high-speed broadband Internet connections than are poorer communities. And although most students can be e-connected at school, differences emerge at home.[98] (See Figure 6.6.) Geography matters, because running fiber-optic cables to rural communities is often an expense that telecommunications companies avoid. The Internet connections are left to acoustic modems that are slow, making it almost impossible for students participating in online classes. Even in schools with high-speed Internet access to the building, an inadequate school network may create a digital divide that has its own title: the **last mile problem.**[99]

Finally, let's focus on a more subtle digital divide: *how* technology is used.[100] You probably have some friends who struggle with technology and others who are wizards. There is more to technology than simply access. Some schools use technology to promote drill and practice, whereas other schools use technology to challenge students. Professor Henry Jay Becker warns, "Efforts to ensure equal access to computer-related learning opportunities at school

FIGURE 6.6

Students using computers at home.

SOURCE: National Center for Education Statistics, Digest of Education Statistics, 2009 (issued April 2010).

REFLECTION: Do you believe that teachers should work with disadvantaged families to improve computer use at home? If so, how might this be accomplished?

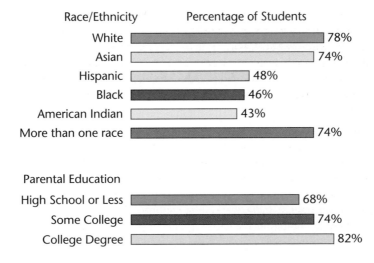

GLOBAL VIEW

Eighty-five percent of European youth agreed with the statement that they "would rather spend a great day outside than a great day online." Would American students agree? Would you? The Internet is not necessarily a way of life but a useful tool and an interesting diversion.

FOCUS QUESTION 11

What are some potential directions for tomorrow's curriculum?

must move beyond a concern with the numbers of computers in different schools toward an emphasis on how well those computers are being used to help children develop intellectual competencies and technical skills."[101] Although technology can awe us, in the end it is how well we use the technology that matters.

It is unlikely that education will be redefined completely in the near future, yet it is also clear that technology's influence is growing. Consider technology mastery as part of your professional development. Attend relevant courses and workshops, and observe colleagues applying technology, but do not lose your skepticism. Be wary of "magic bullets"—simple solutions to complex educational problems.

Suggestions for Tomorrow's Curriculum

Now let's take a moment and do some critical thinking of our own. Imagine that you are in charge of taking the schools down an educational path. What path would you trail blaze? What content or skills do you see as most critical?

Tough question, and it's not fair to ask you such a question if we are not ready to answer it ourselves. So here are some of our ideas:

Using and evaluating information. Technology brings us so much information, that the challenge is not for teachers to impart information that student should memorize, but to teach students to separate the useful from the unnecessary, the accurate from the inaccurate. We would like to see a curriculum that helps students effectively use and evaluate all that digital information, a curricular challenge in our age of technology.

Critical thinking skills. Have you noticed that students seem to do a lot of memorizing in school, but far less comparing, interpreting, observing, summarizing, classifying, decision making, creating, and criticizing? Using more of these critical-thinking skills in subjects from mathematics to history increases our higher-order thinking, our ability to think clearly.[102]

Financial literacy. Today's economic challenges remind us that passing algebra, geometry, and calculus is one thing, but balancing a checkbook or keeping a credit card under control is quite another. Nearly 20 states have added financial literacy to school curriculums in an effort to reach children and young adults before debt and credit-card companies do.[103]

Physical fitness. Too many of our children confront obesity, diabetes, and coronary disease in their lifetimes. You don't have to be an athlete to be physically active. Lifelong fitness activities—yoga and Pilates, how to climb a rock wall or kickbox, ice skate, dance, or golf—can be enjoyed today and promote health for many years. As one student explained: "I love it [lifelong fitness activities] because it's fun. I'm not an athlete, so I used to dread P.E. Now I am learning new activities that I enjoy and keep me healthy and I am not embarrassed about my body."[104]

Civics education. It is not too much to say that American democracy is in trouble. Political gridlock, the influence of money in politics, a divided citizenry, television networks that have become propaganda mills, all this and more weakens the nation. More than 80 percent of eighth-graders are not proficient in civics knowledge and skills. "Ultimately, schools are the guardians of democracy," and we advocate a more robust civics education throughout the curriculum. The price of not doing this is high indeed.[105]

Creativity. We are a people who have created art, media, and countless inventions. Yet with all the focus on education, few are talking about how to promote and honor creativity in schools.

Collaboration and human relations. Too often we see a world marked by misunderstanding and anger; cultural, class, and religious warfare; widespread poverty; physical deprivation; and interpersonal and international conflicts. Here is a sample of what we would add to the curriculum.

- *Human Relations 1: Understand Yourself.* Often we learn only a few salient aspects of our backgrounds, such as personal and family history, cultural and religious beliefs, gender challenges, and a single view of our national heritage. But these are incomplete lessons. We lack a healthy appreciation of how our backgrounds have shaped our lives and our worldview. Only through greater self-insight can we begin to understand our perceptions and motivations, our strengths and weaknesses, our limits and strengths, and why we behave and think as we do.
- *Human Relations 2: Celebrate Others.* After we understand ourselves, we can seek insights from other peoples and cultures. Although some have called this *tolerance,* tolerance falls woefully short. We believe that diversity should be celebrated. Cultural, racial and ethnic, and religious differences offer us wondrous insights into the human experience. We can learn so much from one another. Our challenge is to learn from our differences, not fear them.
- *Human Relations 3: Encourage Individual Talents.* Schools should prepare students to live purposeful and satisfying lives. To do this, students need to learn and develop their own unique interests and abilities, skills, and talents. By measuring all students against the same yardsticks of literacy and numeracy, individual creativity and talents are lost or denigrated. We would like to see more individualization in the curriculum.
- *Human Relations 4: Promote Purposeful Lives.* At the Antioch College commencement in 1859, Horace Mann advised the graduates, "Be ashamed to die until you have won some victory for humanity." The real measure of an education is not what a student receives as a grade or even does while in school; the real measure is what people do after graduation. Are students living and working ethically? Are adults caring for one another, treating their children, families, colleagues, and even strangers with love, compassion, and forgiveness? The way we choose to live our lives as adults, and not our test scores, will be the true measure of our schooling, and our society.

Those are some of the keystones to our curriculum. What are the keystones to yours?

Teaching Tip

STUDENTS ON MY MIND

One of the things that has been most important to me in my daily work is to remember that I am not teaching a subject, but that I am teaching students. In these days of standards, clearly defined and often prescribed teaching objectives, it is hard to remember sometimes that the most important thing isn't the "standard"—it is the student. When I remember this, it calls me to use skills that aren't always written in my lesson plan. I have to be open-minded in my approach to students, remembering that their knowledge, experiences, and concerns are not what I might expect or predict. Remembering to teach to the student, I also call on the gifts of humor, patience, and creativity. While these are not written into any of my daily lesson plans, they are critical to reaching the students that I teach in authentic and transforming ways.

Diane Petteway is the International Baccalaureate Middle Years Program coordinator at East Millbrook Magnet Middle School in Raleigh, North Carolina.

REFLECTION: Can you construct a different kind of standard for your own teaching? Build your standard not around content, but on your connection with your students.

ONLINE VIDEO ALBUM TO ACCOMPANY *TEACHERS, SCHOOLS, AND SOCIETY, 10E*

Visit the Online Learning Center for a range of contemporary videos with content related to this chapter.

www.mhhe.com/sadker10e

THE *TEACHERS, SCHOOLS, AND SOCIETY* READER WITH CLASSROOM OBSERVATION VIDEO CLIPS

Go to your *Teachers, Schools, and Society* Reader CD-ROM to:

READ CURRENT AND HISTORICAL ARTICLES

25.   **Worthy Texts: Who Decides?** by Barry Gilmore, *Educational Leadership,* March 2011.

26.   **Curriculum Theory and Practice: What's Your Style?** by Donna L. Miller, *Phi Delta Kappan,* April 2011.

27.   **Why Has High-Stakes Testing So Easily Slipped into Contemporary American Life?** by Sharon Nichols and David Berliner, *Phi Delta Kappan,* May 2008.

28.   **International Education: What's In a Name?** by Walter Parker, *Phi Delta Kappan,* November 2008.

29.   **All Our Students Thinking,** by Nel Noddings, *Educational Leadership,* February 2008.

ANALYZE CASE STUDIES

11. **Elaine Adams:** A student teacher near the end of her assignment observes her cooperating teacher give the students help while administering the district-mandated standardized tests. She finds herself unsure how to deal with the situation.

12. **Melinda Grant:** A teacher who has developed an innovative curriculum is concerned because another teacher continually warns her that she will be held responsible for her students' end-of-year standardized test scores.

OBSERVE TEACHERS, STUDENTS, AND CLASSROOMS IN ACTION

11. Classroom Observation: High-Stakes Testing

As we discussed in this chapter, No Child Left Behind has ushered in a period of high-stakes testing. In this observation, teachers and principals discuss the benefits and the disadvantages of high-stakes testing. What are some of the advantages and some of the disadvantages of high-stakes testing?

KEY TERMS AND PEOPLE

authentic assessment, 187

Campbell's law, 186

Common Core State Standards, 177

core curriculum, 168

core knowledge, 192

creationism, 189

cultural literacy, 192

curriculum, 168

digital divide, 195

evolution, 189

extracurriculum, 169

formal or explicit curriculum, 168

implicit or hidden curriculum, 168

Kohn, Alfie, 183

last mile problem, 195

multicultural education, 192

No Child Left Behind Act (NCLB), 176

null curriculum, 169

standards-based education, 177

stealth or self-censorship, 191

textbook adoption states, 173

www.mhhe.com/sadker10e

CHAPTER REVIEW

Go to the Online Learning Center to take a chapter self-quiz, practice with key terms, and review concepts from the chapter.

DISCUSSION QUESTIONS AND ACTIVITIES

1. For some students, the hidden curriculum and the extracurriculum are most central to their school experience. Define the roles of these unofficial curricular experiences in your own education. If you were placed in charge of a school today, how would you change these hidden and extracurricular experiences? How might your changes be evident in elementary, middle, and high schools? Why?

2. What subject areas spark the greatest debate and controversy over creating a single, national curriculum? Are there strategies to help reach a consensus on these issues? How might a national history curriculum written today differ from one written a century from now? a century ago? Why?

3. Collect textbooks from your local elementary and secondary schools, and analyze them according to the following criteria:

    - Do they include instructional objectives? Do these require students to use both recall of factual information and analytical and creative thinking skills?

    - Were readability formulas used in the preparation of the textbooks? If so, did this appear to have a negative or a positive impact on the quality of the writing?

    - Are under-represented group members included in the textbooks' narrative and illustrations? Are individuals with disabilities included?

    - When various individuals are included, are they portrayed in a balanced or a stereotyped manner?

4. If you were given the job of developing a standards-based curriculum with assessment tools, where would you go to identify standards? What kinds of tests would you use? What kinds of tests would you avoid? What subjects and skills do you consider crucial? Why?

5. Do you believe that children's educational materials should be censored? Are there any benefits to censorship? Any dangers? What kinds of materials would you refuse to let elementary school students read? Middle or high school students? Postsecondary students?

REFLECTIVE ACTIVITIES AND YOUR PORTFOLIO

Part II: Schools and Curriculum

2:1 Scoping School Culture

Purpose: Have you ever wanted to "stop the world" and, rather than get off, take the time to really observe people's behavior? Here's your chance with an experience that will help you better understand your future teaching environment. Curiosity, coupled with some directed observations, can offer a rich opportunity to study the growth and development of students.

Activity: Visit an elementary, middle, or high school, preferably at the level you envision teaching one day. Set yourself up to the side of the major thoroughfares with notepad, laptop, or sketchbook and make "notes." Consider public and informal spaces: cafeteria, hallways, open space quad, blacktop/field, or recess areas.

Artifact: Create a "School Observation Diary" by taking notes on what you observe. Here are some questions to guide you. Feel free to add your own thoughts, questions, and observations.

INTASC STANDARD 1
Learner Development

School Observation Diary

- What does the "scene" look like? How are individuals and groups dressed? What else do you see?
- Focus on students and their body language. Who's talking, touching, or teasing? Describe the behavior. Are groups divided along racial, gender, and/or economic lines?
- Focus on staff or faculty in the area. What are their roles? Are they detached, integrated, or "in charge"? Describe their actions. What is the ratio of male teachers to female teachers?
- What noise is evident—music, varied languages, general chatter, or "sounds of silence"?
- Compare and contrast school geography to see if cliques dominate certain areas or activities?
- What other behaviors, in general, do you observe?

---

www.mhhe.com/sadker10e

FORM:

School Observation Diary

Reflection: Did the students' behavior appear to vary by such factors as gender, race, physical size, language fluency, and clothing? What insights did you have about this student body and individual pupils? How did their use of time and space in the halls, cafeteria, and open areas interest and inform you? What insights about student and teacher behavior might you draw from your observations? How might these observations help you understand human development? Has this observation experience influenced your opinion about a career in teaching? Attach your reflection to the "School Observation Diary," and include both in your portfolio.

2:2 Curriculum Bias Detectors

Purpose: The way curricular materials portray different groups can promote either knowledge or stereotypes. In this activity, you will refine your skills for detecting bias. As a teacher, once you recognize this problem, you can select or adapt materials to counter such biases.

Activity: Review the seven forms of bias discussed in Chapter 6. Borrow a K–12 textbook (appropriate for your subject major or grade level) from your college's curriculum resource center, a local school, or a teaching friend. Look for an example of each form of bias.

Bias Busters		
Book Title/Author/Reference Information: Brief description of text:		
Type of Bias	**Page #**	**Example**
1. Invisibility		
2. Stereotyping		
3. Imbalance and selectivity		
4. Unreality		
5. Fragmentation and isolation		
6. Linguistic bias		
7. Cosmetic bias		

Reflection: What did you learn from this experience? Was there more or less evidence of bias than you thought? What surprised you about this activity? Will this experience influence how you use materials in your classroom? Why or why not? How will you teach your students to become "Bias Detectors"?

2:3 Effective Schools

Purpose: Chapter 5 detailed five factors of effective schools: strong leadership, a clear school mission, a safe and orderly climate, the monitoring of student progress, and high expectations.

Activity: Visit one or more elementary, middle, or high schools in an effort to find evidence of these factors. Walk the halls of these schools and spend time in classrooms. Look for examples of how each of these five factors affects students' learning environment. Use the following chart to record your observations.

Artifact:

Effective Schools Observation	
	Learning Environment Examples
Strong leadership	
Clear school mission	
Safe and orderly climate	
Monitoring of student progress	
High expectations	
Other	

Reflection: Were some of the five factors easier to spot than others? Were you able to see examples associated with each of these five factors that influenced students' learning environments? Describe. What did you learn from your school observations? What do you recall of how the learning environment motivated (or did not motivate) you when you were a student? What types of learning environments did you envision creating as a teacher?

2:4 State and National Curricular Standards

Purpose: Many of today's schools are immersed in standards and testing, and being familiar with these policies can be enormously helpful. Knowledge of standards and testing can influence you in deciding where to teach, or once in the classroom, helping you craft effective lessons.

Activity: Perform an Internet search of "Common Core Standards" and "curriculum standards" at both the national and the state level. For state curriculum standards, choose a particular state that interests you. (If you are thinking of several states as possible places where you might want to teach, compare the standards for each of these states.) Standards are typically broken into curricular areas, so choose at least one subject area for your focus. A useful resource for this activity is: www.educationworld.com/standards.

Artifact: "Venn Diagram: Curricular Standards" After reading through the curriculum standards at both the national and the state level, complete the following Venn diagram. Venn diagrams are useful for examining similarities and differences. They help us to compare the elements of one or more items. Compare and contrast at least three standards.

Venn Diagram

Subject and Standard (*example* Math—numbers and operations grades 3–5):

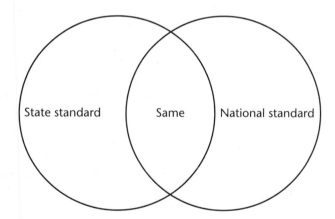

Reflection: What did you learn from this activity? Any surprises? In your opinion, are these standards realistic? Useful? Support your opinion. What kind of similarities and differences do you find between the national Common Core Standards and the state-level curriculum standards? Are most of the state standards mirroring the national ones, or are there differences? If you investigated more than one state, how do these standards differ from state to state? How do you envision using curriculum standards in planning lessons? Attach your reflections to your Venn diagram and include in your portfolio.

2:5 A Public Service Announcement: The Purpose of School

Purpose: Chapter 5 details two diverse purposes of education: to transmit society's knowledge and values (passing the cultural baton) and to reconstruct society (schools as tools for change). Your ability to formulate and express your vision for education can guide your formal application for a teaching position. Communicating your goals (content) clearly and creatively is a foundation of effective instruction.

Activity: Develop a public service announcement (PSA) supporting one of these purposes of education. Think of it as a radio spot (thirty to forty-five seconds long) that tells the listening public just what *they* need to know.

Artifact: "Public Service Announcement for Schools." Write, edit, and practice your script. Rewrite, edit again, and rehearse until you think it is the most persuasive and informative. You may not always be able to practice and tighten your lessons this thoroughly, but the strategies you use to develop and refine the content of your PSA are a necessary part of your communication repertoire. *Challenge:* Develop a second PSA supporting the other purpose of education. If possible, deliver your PSAs during class.

Reflection: What did you learn from this activity? How were your peers' messages similar or different? Which PSAs appealed to you the most? Did you find yourself supporting the other purpose of education? Is it really possible to support only one of these purposes of education? Attach your PSA artifact to your reflection and include in your portfolio.

2:6 Memoirs of a Time-Tested Student

INTASC STANDARD 6
Assessment

Purpose: National, state, and district tests are a huge part of school culture, yet few teachers analyze their own role in the current testing climate. The following activity will help you define that role.

Activity: Think about the quizzes and tests you took as a student. Looking back, would you rate your teachers as helpful or not so helpful? Either through your own journal entry or a conversation with a partner (live, recorded, or online), consider the following questions as you explore your testing experiences.

- What's an early memory of a "big deal" test? (Sharpening your number 2 pencil? Unsealing special pamphlets in elementary school? Being tucked in a cardboard "cubby" for privacy? Proctors milling about looking for cheating?) Solicit some experiences from your classmates and see if more recollections are sparked.
- What did the teacher do that encouraged and supported you during the test?
- Do you remember any words or behaviors that distracted or annoyed you during the test?

www.mhhe.com/sadker10e

FORM:

You Be the Judge: "Testing Do's and Don'ts"

Artifact: Review the *You Be the Judge* format that you find in this text, and create two columns that would be useful for your teacher-testing role. Prepare a *You Be the Judge* feature on testing by brainstorming what teachers can do to ensure a positive climate for student testing in one column, and list actions teachers should definitely avoid in the other.

You Be the Judge: "Testing Do's and Don'ts"	
What Teachers SHOULD Do . . .	**What Teachers Should NOT Do . . .**
1. Describe the purpose of the test[*]	1. Leave the room[*]
2.	2.
3.	3.
etc.	etc.

[*]Sample items.

204

Reflection: What have you learned from this activity? Based on your analysis, what are some of the most critical factors in a testing climate? How can you remember to implement effective testing practices?

2:7 A Real In-service Program

Purpose: Many districts and states, along with independent schools, require community service as a high school graduation requirement. The intent is to instill a contributory ethic in students. Although an ongoing service requirement may be one way to meet this principled goal, you as a teacher can help by integrating this "service ethic" in your lessons.

INTASC STANDARD 7
Planning for
Instruction

Activity: Recall a lesson or a unit you have seen. Brainstorm how you might add a service component.

Artifact: "A Service Component." Briefly outline a lesson or a unit that you will be teaching, and then describe in (about 150 words) how you would integrate a service project or activity into your lesson. The following sample chart offers some suggestions.

Service Integration Ideas	
Lesson	**Sample Service Component**
Language arts	Read with special population students, children, or seniors
Science	Assist with student health appraisal
Math	Be a homework helper, one on one, with a student
Social studies	Work on a community project ensuring that citizens' rights are protected
Technology	Teach computer skills at a local shelter
Physical education	Referee or supervise a children's sport event or recess
Health	Bring the Great American Smoke Out to a local high school
Vocational and career	Review career materials for bias
Foreign language	Assist bilingual parents with school visits and conferences
Arts	Volunteer with children in theater, art, dance, or music

Reflection: This reflection might better be called a projection. Project yourself into the future, actually teaching your lesson. Describe your service component. What goals do you hope to accomplish? Your service component teaches "higher lessons" about honoring one another and developing a caring community. How can you integrate these lessons of caring and compassion with your official curriculum? Attach your reflection to the artifact and include in your portfolio.

2:8 Visit a "Choice" School

Purpose: Public education is moving beyond the neighborhood school. An abundance of school choices now exist: magnet schools, charter schools, for-profit schools, voucher programs, and homeschooling, to name a few. If you choose to become a teacher, you may find yourself working in a very different setting from the one you attended. For this reason, it is important that you become familiar with the changing face of America's public schools, and how instructional strategies may differ in different schools.

INTASC STANDARD 8
Instructional
Strategies

Activity: Arrange to visit at least one "choice" school. Spend time in the classrooms and observe the school culture. If possible, speak with administrators, teachers, students, and parents. What is the educational environment like? What instructional strategies are used? Are any of these strategies new to you? How are the instructional strategies different from or similar to those of public schools in your area?

Artifact: Create a "Choice School Instruction Diary" that includes your notes and observations about these teaching strategies and practices. Include your assessments of these strategies. Create a Venn diagram comparing this school's instructional practices with those in a non-choice school. You can compare it with the school you attended as a student or one you recently visited.

Venn Diagram

Type of Choice School (*example* charter):

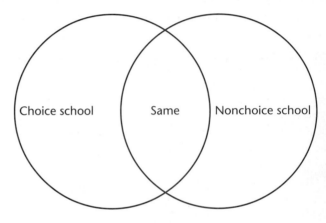

Reflection: What did you learn from observing these instructional strategies? Would you want to adopt or adapt some of these strategies? Why or why not? Attach your notes and Venn diagram to your reflection and include in your portfolio.

2:9 Reflections of a High School Yearbook

INTASC STANDARD 9
Personal Learning
and Ethical Practice

Purpose: Part II of this text looked at all aspects of the school scene, from the student role to a teacher's reality. Although you may have shifted perspective as you walked away from your high school graduation ceremony, the purpose of this activity is to look back and assess some of your choices and actions. Your high school yearbook symbolizes a snapshot of your school and a view of yourself in the social system. What does it show you about your school, yourself, and others?

Activity: Dig out your high school yearbook or see if it is available online. Read through the questions below before starting the artifact.

- Find yourself. Are you included? What is the caption under your senior photo? Did you get caught in candid shots? Are you with clubs, in activities, and on teams? Are you surrounded by your friends or often on your own? Which images recall emotions: pride, embarrassment, sadness? Did your school have an organization like FTA (Future Teachers of America)? Were you pictured with them, or were you exploring another career? Were your school strengths evident by achievements, awards, and participation? In what ways are you the same or different today?

- Find your friends. In what ways were you similar to or different from them? When and where do they appear?

- Find lesser-known faces. Stop and really stare at students you may have walked by for years. What of their stories do you suspect or know? What groups were they in? What labels described their lives?
- Who is invisible or missing? Are there students who appear only in their "mug shot" and never as part of the campus culture? Do female or male students, from varied racial and ethnic groups, dominate particular activities or campus locales?

Artifact: Write a brief essay titled "My High School Days" or "The Story Behind the Story" describing what really was going on with you socially, physically, and psychologically during this year in high school. Include both positive and negative experiences and feelings. (You can even compose a song or a poem to share your high school years.)

Reflection: What do you notice about your school and yourself? How do your experiences compare with the student cultures described in this text? Would you want to teach at a school like the one you attended or at a very different school? Why? What stories from your yearbook pages would be valuable to share with classmates? Attach your reflection to your artifact and store in your portfolio.

2:10 Support Staff Interview

Purpose: When you have a teaching job, you become part of a learning community. Knowing about the roles and the responsibilities of support personnel will enhance your understanding of the way schools work. Nonteaching employees contribute significantly to a well-functioning school. Bus drivers, clerical personnel, media and custodial staff, instructional aides, playground and lunch supervisors, resource specialists, medical and psychological professionals, and security and safety personnel all do their part. They befriend alienated kids, clean up after trashy nutrition breaks, reset chairs in an auditorium as many as eight times a day, protect students from physical threats, make lunchrooms smell like fresh cookies, and find curricular resources for both teachers and students. Support personnel see students and the school through some very different lenses than teachers. Fostering collaborative relationships with these colleagues is a way to create a valuable extension of your classroom community and school trust.

INTASC STANDARD 10
Leadership and
Collaboration

Activity: Try to schedule a twenty-minute interview with one of the nonteaching employees at a local school. Here are some questions to ask, but feel free to add your own to the list.

- Describe your job duties.
- What do you like best about your job?
- What is the most challenging aspect of your job?
- How do students, teachers, and administrators affect your job?
- What is one thing about your job that you would like students to know about?
- What is one thing about your job that you would like teachers to know about?
- How can teachers help you to do your job?
- What is one thing about your job that you would like administrators to know about?
- Recount your best day on the job.

Artifact: Write a brief description titled "A Day in the Life of _____." How do teachers support the support personnel, and more specifically, what can you do to create a positive, collaborative relationship with school support personnel?

Reflection: What did you learn from this experience? How might this interview affect your rapport and behavior with support staff?

PART III

Foundations

Chapter 7

The History of American Education *210*

Chapter 8

Philosophy of Education *245*

Chapter 9

Financing and Governing America's Schools *273*

Chapter 10

School Law and Ethics *302*

The History of American Education

FOCUS QUESTIONS

1. What was the nature and purpose of colonial education?
2. How did the Common School Movement promote universal education?
3. What developments mark the educational history of Native Americans?
4. How did teaching become a "gendered" career?
5. How did secondary schools evolve?
6. What were the main tenets of the Progressive Education movement?
7. What role has the federal government played in American education?
8. How did history shape the educational experiences of African Americans, Hispanics, Asian Americans/Pacific Islanders, and Arab Americans?
9. What educational barriers and breakthroughs have girls and women experienced?
10. Who are some of the influential educators who have helped fashion today's schools?

For inspirational stories about people who have had a powerful impact on the lives of others, go to the Online Learning Center and read the "Class Acts."

www.mhhe.com/sadker10e

WHAT DO YOU THINK? How much do you already know about the history of education? Before reading the chapter, take a quiz that includes some "basics" and fun facts.

Education then, beyond all other devices of human origin, is the great equalizer of the conditions of men, the balance-wheel of the social machinery.

–HORACE MANN

CHAPTER PREVIEW

In this chapter, we will trace American education from colonial times to the present. You will discover how social class, race, ethnicity, gender, and religion influenced American education throughout history. Education during the colonial period was intended to further religious goals and was offered primarily to white males—typically, wealthy white males. Over time, educational exclusivity diminished and learning goals changed, but even today, wealth, race, and gender continue to have an impact on educational quality. In this chapter, we share the story of America's struggle to honor its commitment to equality by opening the schoolhouse door to more of our diverse citizens.

Understanding the history of America's schools offers you perspective—a sense of your place in your new profession. Your classroom is a living tribute to past achievements and sacrifices. We will begin by looking into the classroom of Christopher Lamb, a New England teacher in one of the earliest American schools, more than three centuries ago.

Christopher Lamb's Colonial Classroom

The frigid wintry wind knifed through Christopher Lamb's coat, chilling him to the bone as he walked in the predawn darkness. The single bucket of firewood that he lugged, intended to keep his seventeenth-century New England schoolroom warm all day, would clearly not do the job. Once the fire was started, Christopher focused on his other teaching tasks: carrying in a bucket of water for the class, sweeping the floor, and mending the ever so fragile pen points for the students. Margaret, who loved school, was the first student to arrive. Like most girls, she would stay in school for only a year or two to learn to read the Bible so that she could be a better wife and mother. With any luck, she might even learn to write her name before she left school. But that was really not important for girls. The other students found their way to either the boys' bench or the girls' bench, where, in turn, they read their Testament aloud.

Christopher was amazed at how poorly some students read, tripping over every other word, whereas others read quite fluently. The last student to finish, Benjamin, slowly rose from the bench, cringing. Christopher called out, "Lazy pupil," and a chorus of children's voices chimed in: "Lazy pupil. Lazy pupil. Lazy pupil." Benjamin, if not totally inured to the taunts, was no longer crushed by them, either. After the recitation and writing lessons, all the children were lined up and examined, to make certain they had washed and combed. For ten minutes, the class and the teacher knelt in prayer. Each student then recited the day's biblical lesson.

FOCUS QUESTION 1
What was the nature and purpose of colonial education?

Christopher Lamb had been an apprentice teacher for five years before accepting this position. He rejected the rod approach used so frequently by his master teacher. Using the children to provide rewards and punishments was far more effective than welts and bruises, marks left by a teacher's rod. Yes, Christopher was somewhat unorthodox, perhaps even a bit revolutionary, but the challenges of contemporary seventeenth-century society demanded forward-thinking educators, such as Christopher Lamb.

Colonial New England Education: God's Classrooms

One of the striking differences between Christopher Lamb's colonial classroom and today's typical public school is the role of religion in education. The religious fervor that drove the Puritans to America also drove them to provide religious education for their young, making New England the cradle of American education. In Christopher Lamb's time, school was meant to save souls. Education provided a path to heaven, and reading, writing, and moral development all revolved around the Bible.

Early colonial education, both in New England and in other colonies, often began in the home. (Today's home-schooling movement is not a *new* approach.) The family was the major educational resource for youngsters, and the first lessons typically focused on reading. Values, manners, social graces, and even vocational skills were taught by parents and grandparents. Home instruction eventually became more specialized, and some women began to devote their time to teaching, converting their homes into schools. These "dames" taught reading, writing, and computation, and their homes became known as **dame schools.**

This colonial recitation lesson includes a boy sitting in the corner with a dunce cap. By today's standards, "time out" back then was quite humiliating.

A "dame," or well-respected woman with an interest in education, became (for a fee) the community's teacher.

An *apprenticeship* program rounded out a child's colonial education. While boys, sometimes as young as 7 years of age, were sent to live with masters who taught them a trade, girls typically learned homemaking skills from their mothers. Apprenticeship programs for boys involved not only learning skilled crafts but also managing farms and shops. Many colonies required that masters teach reading and writing as well as vocational skills. The masters served *in loco parentis*—that is, in place of the child's parent. The competencies of the masters guiding apprentices varied greatly, as did the talents of family members, dames, ministers, and others fulfilling the teaching role. Not surprisingly, this educational hodgepodge did not always lead to a well-educated citizenry; a more formal structure was needed.

Twenty-two years after arriving in the New World, the Puritans living in the Commonwealth of Massachusetts passed a law requiring that parents and masters of apprentices be checked periodically to ensure that children were being taught properly. Five years later, in 1647, Massachusetts took even more rigorous measures to ensure the education of its children. The Massachusetts Law of 1647, more commonly known as the **Old Deluder Satan Law**—the Puritans' attempt to thwart Satan's trickery with Scripture-reading citizens—required that

- Every town of fifty households must appoint and pay a teacher of reading and writing.

- Every town of one hundred households must provide a (Latin) grammar school to prepare youths for the university, under a penalty of £5 for failure to do so.[1]

By 1680, such laws had spread throughout most of New England. The settlement patterns of the Puritans, who lived in towns and communities rather than scattered throughout the countryside, made establishing schools relatively uncomplicated. After learning to read and write, most girls returned home to practice the art of housekeeping. Boys who could afford to pay for their education went on to a **Latin grammar school.** In 1635, only fifteen years after arriving in America's wilderness, the Puritans established their first Latin grammar school in Boston. The Boston Latin Grammar School was not unlike a "prep" school for boys and was similar to the classical schools of Europe. The Boston Latin Grammar School was a rather exclusive school for boys of wealth, charging tuition to teach boys between the ages of 7 and 14. (Within a year of the founding of the Boston Latin Grammar School, Harvard College was established specifically to prepare ministers. Founded in 1636, Harvard was the first college in America, the jewel in the Puritans' religious and educational crown.)

Many consider the Boston Latin Grammar School to be the first step on the road to creating the American high school, although the school's curriculum reflected European roots. Students were expected to read and recite (in Latin, of course) the works of Cicero, Ovid, and Erasmus. In Greek, they read the works of Socrates and Homer. (Back to basics in colonial times meant back to the glory of Rome and Greece.) By the eighteenth century, the grammar school had incorporated mathematics, science, and modern languages. Classes started at 7 a.m., recessed at 11 a.m., and picked up from 1 p.m. until 5 p.m. Graduates were expected to go on to college and become colonial leaders, especially ministers.

For attendance at exclusive schools, such as Boston Latin Grammar, or at college, wealth was critical. The least desirable educational and apprenticeship opportunities were left to the poor. Some civic-minded communities made basic education in reading and writing more available to the poor, but only to families who would publicly admit their poverty by signing a "Pauper's Oath." Broadcasting one's poverty was no less offensive in colonial times than today, and many chose to have their children remain illiterate rather than sign such a public admission. The result was that most poor children remained outside the educational system.

Blacks, in America since 1619, and Native Americans were typically denied educational opportunities. In rare cases, religious groups, such as the Quakers, created special schools for children of color.[2] But those were the exceptions. Girls did not fare much better. After they had learned the rudiments of reading and writing, girls were taught the tasks related to their future roles as mother and wife. They were taught handicrafts. Girls memorized the alphabet and then learned to stitch and display their accomplishments. They also learned to reproduce and attractively display religious sayings, on the road to becoming good Christian wives and mothers. Much as we value these beautiful samplers today, they are a sad reminder of a time when they marked the academic finish line for girls, the diploma of a second-rate education, a depressing denial of equal educational rights. Later in this chapter, we will describe in more detail the barriers separating many Americans from a quality education.

Location greatly influenced educational opportunities. The northern colonies were settled by Puritans, who lived in towns and communities relatively close to one another. Their religious fervor and proximity made the creation of community schools dedicated to teaching the Bible a predictable development.

In the middle colonies, the range of European religious and ethnic groups (Puritans, Catholics, Mennonites, the Dutch, and Swedes) created, if not a melting pot, a limited tolerance for diversity.[3] Various religious groups established schools, and apprenticeships groomed youngsters for a variety of careers, including teaching. In the middle colonies, the development of commerce and mercantile demands promoted the formation of private schools devoted to job training. By the 1700s, private teachers and night schools were functioning in Philadelphia and New York, teaching accounting, navigation, French, and Spanish.

The first city in North America was St. Augustine, Florida, where there is evidence that the Spanish settlers established schools. The southern English colonies trailed behind in education. The rural, sparsely populated southern colonies developed an educational system that was responsive to plantation society. Wealthy plantation owners took tutors into their homes to teach their children not only basic academic skills but also the social graces appropriate to their station in life. Plantation owners' children learned the proper way to entertain guests and "manage" slaves, using such texts as *The Complete Gentleman*. Wealthy young men seeking higher education were sent to Europe. Poor white children might have had rudimentary home instruction in reading, writing, and computation. Black children made do with little if any instruction and, as time went by, encountered laws that actually prohibited their education entirely.[4]

Education has come a long way from colonial days and from Christopher Lamb's class—or has it? Consider the following:

1. The colonial experience established many of today's educational norms:
    - Local control of schools
    - Compulsory education
    - Tax-supported schools
    - State standards for teaching and schools

2. The colonial experience highlighted many of the persistent tension points challenging schools today:
    - What is the role of religion in the classroom?
    - How can we equalize the quality of education in various communities?

- How can the barriers of racism, sexism, religious intolerance, and classism be eliminated so that all children receive equal educational opportunity?
- How can we prepare the most competent teachers?

A New Nation Shapes Education

The ideas that led to the American Revolution revolutionized our schools. European beliefs and practices, which had pervaded America's schools, were gradually abandoned as the new national character was formed. Importantly, none of these European beliefs had been more firmly adhered to than the integration of the state and religion.

In sixteenth- and seventeenth-century England, the Puritans' desire to reform the Church of England was viewed as treason. The Puritans encountered both religious and political opposition, and they looked to the New World as an escape from persecution. However, they came to America *not* to establish religious freedom, as our history books sometimes suggest, but to establish their own church as supreme, both religiously and politically. The Puritans were neither tolerant of other religions nor interested in separating religion and politics. Nonconformers, such as the Quakers, were vigorously persecuted. The purpose of the Massachusetts colony was to establish the "true" religion of the Puritans in America. Schools were simply an extension of the religious state, designed to teach the young to read and understand the Bible and to do honorable battle with Satan.

In addition to serving two terms as president of the United States, Thomas Jefferson was the colonial era's most eloquent spokesperson for education and was the founder of the University of Virginia.

During the 1700s, American education was reconstructed to meet broader, nonsectarian goals. Such leaders as **Thomas Jefferson** wanted to go beyond educating a small elite class or providing only religious instruction. Jefferson maintained that education should be more widely available to white children from all economic and social classes. Public citizens began to question the usefulness of rudimentary skills taught in a school year of just three or four months. They questioned the value of mastering Greek and Latin classics in the Latin grammar schools, when practical skills were in short supply in the New World.

In 1749, **Benjamin Franklin** penned *Proposals Relating to the Youth of Pennsylvania,* suggesting a new kind of secondary school to replace the Latin grammar school—the **academy.** Two years later, the *Franklin Academy* was established, free of religious influence and offering a variety of practical subjects, including mathematics, astronomy, athletics, navigation, dramatics, and bookkeeping. Students were able to choose some of their courses, thus setting the precedent for elective courses and programs at the secondary level. The Franklin Academy accepted both girls and boys who could afford the tuition, and the practical curriculum became an attractive innovation. Franklin's Academy sparked the establishment of six thousand academies in the century that followed. The original Franklin Academy eventually became the University of Pennsylvania.[5]

Jefferson's commitment to educating all white Americans, rich and poor, at government expense and Franklin's commitment to a practical program of nonsectarian study offering elective courses severed American educational thought from its European roots. Many years passed before these ideas became widely established practices, but the pattern for innovation and a truly American approach to education was taking shape. (For a description of texts that shaped early American education, see A Closer Look: Early Textbooks).

A Closer Look   Early Textbooks

As a teacher, you will come across references to some of the limited but influential curriculum materials of the past. Here is a brief profile of the best-known instructional materials from yesterday's schools.

HORNBOOK

The most common teaching device in colonial schools, the **hornbook** consisted of an alphabet sheet covered by a thin, transparent sheet made from a cow's horn. The alphabet and the horn covering were tacked to a paddle-shaped piece of wood and often hung by a leather strap around the student's neck. Originating in medieval Europe, the hornbook provided colonial children with their introduction to the alphabet and reading.

NEW ENGLAND PRIMER

The first real textbook, the **New England Primer** was a tiny 2½- by 4½-inch book containing 50 to 100 pages of alphabet, words, and small verses accompanied by woodcut illustrations. First published in 1690, it was virtually the only reading text used in colonial schools until about 1800. The Primer reflected the religious orientation of colonial schools. A typical verse was

> In Adam's Fall
> We sinned all.
> Thy Life to mend,
> This Book attend
> The idle fool
> Is whipt at School.

AMERICAN SPELLING BOOK

The task undertaken by Noah Webster was to define and nourish the new American culture. His **American Spelling Book** replaced the *New England Primer* as the most common elementary textbook. The book contained the alphabet, syllables, consonants, rules for speaking, readings, short stories, and moral advice. The bulk of the book was taken up by lists of words. Royalty income from the sale of millions of copies of this book supported Webster in his other efforts to standardize the American language, including his best-known work, which is still used today, the *American Dictionary*.

MCGUFFEY READERS

William Holmes McGuffey was a minister, professor, and college president who believed that clean living, hard work, and literacy were the virtues to instill in children. He wrote a series of readers that emphasized the work ethic, patriotism, heroism, and morality. It is estimated that more than 100 million copies of *McGuffey Readers* educated several generations of Americans between 1836 and 1920. **McGuffey Readers** are noteworthy because they were geared for different grade levels and paved the way for graded elementary schools.

> **REFLECTION:** Can you detect the morals and traditional values being promoted in today's texts? Can you cite any examples?

The Common School Movement

During the early decades of the nineteenth century, the democratic ideal became popular as many "common people"—immigrants, small farmers, and urban laborers—demanded greater participation in the democracy. With the election of Andrew Jackson in 1828, the voices of many poor white people were heard, particularly their demands for educational access. Many more decades would pass before additional voices—particularly those of people of color—would also be heard.

Horace Mann became the nation's leading advocate for the establishment of a **common school** open to all. Today, we know this common school as the public **elementary school**. Historians consider Horace Mann to be the outstanding proponent of education for the common person (the Common School Movement), and he is often referred to as "the father of the public school." Mann helped create the Massachusetts State Board of Education and in 1837 became its secretary, a position similar to today's state superintendent of schools. In this role, Mann began an effort to reform education, believing that public education should serve both practical and idealistic goals. In practical terms, both business and industry would benefit from educated workers, resulting in a more productive economy. In idealistic terms, public schools should help us identify and nurture the talents in poor as well as wealthy children, and schools should ameliorate social disharmony.[6] Mann decried the rifts between rich and poor, Calvinists

FOCUS QUESTION 2
How did the Common School Movement promote universal education?

and religious reformers, new Irish immigrants and native workers. A common school instilling common and humane moral values could reduce such social disharmony (a popular belief today as well). Mann attempted to promote such values, but he encountered strong opposition when the values he selected revealed a distinct religious bias, one that offended Calvinists, atheists, Jews, Catholics, and others. His moral program to create a common set of beliefs had the opposite impact, igniting a dispute over the role of religion in school.

The idea of public education is so commonplace today that it seems difficult to imagine another system. But Horace Mann, along with such allies as Henry Barnard of Connecticut, fought a long and difficult battle to win the acceptance of public elementary schools. The opposition was powerful. Business interests predicted disaster if their labor pool of children were taken away. Concerned taxpayers protested the additional tax monies needed to support public education. There was also the competition. Private schools and religious groups sponsoring their own schools protested the establishment of free schools. Americans wondered what would become of a nation in which everyone received an elementary education. Would this not produce overeducated citizens, questioning authority, and promoting self-interest? The opposition to public elementary schools was often fierce, but Horace Mann and his allies prevailed.

GLOBAL VIEW
The United States has not ratified the *Convention on the Rights of the Child* (1990), which requires free compulsory primary education and equal treatment regardless of gender, race, or cultural background for children worldwide.

As he fought for public schools for all, Mann also waged a battle for high-quality schools. He continually attempted to build new and better schools, which was a problem, because so many Massachusetts schools were in deplorable condition. By publicly disseminating information about which communities had well-built or poorly built schools, he applied public pressure on districts to improve their school buildings. He worked for effective teacher training programs as well and promoted more stringent teacher licensing procedures. As a result of his efforts, several **normal schools** were founded in Massachusetts, schools devoted to preparing teachers in pedagogy, the best ways to teach children. He opposed the routine practice of corporal punishment and sought ways to positively motivate students to learn. Mann emphasized practical subjects useful to children and to adult society, rather than the mastery of Greek and Latin. Mann saw education as a great investment, for individuals and for the country, and he worked for many years to make free public education a reality. He worked for the abolition of slavery, promoted women's educational and economic rights, and even fought alongside the temperance movement to limit the negative impact of alcohol. He was not only a committed educator but a committed reformer as well.

By the time of the Civil War, this radical notion of the public elementary school had become widespread and widely accepted. Educational historian Lawrence Cremin summarized the advance of the common school movement in his book *The Transformation of the School:*

> A majority of the states had established public school systems, and a good half of the nation s children were already getting some formal education. Elementary schools were becoming widely available; in some states, like Massachusetts, New York, and Pennsylvania, the notion of free public education was slowly expanding to include secondary schools; and in a few, like Michigan and Wisconsin, the public school system was already capped by a state university. There were, of course, significant variations from state to state and from region to region. New England, long a pioneer in public education, also had an established tradition of private education, and private schools continued to flourish there. The Midwest, on the other hand, sent a far greater proportion of its school children to public institutions. The southern states, with the exception of North Carolina, tended to lag behind, and did not generally establish popular schooling until after the Civil War.[7]

Native American Tribes: The History of Miseducation

FOCUS QUESTION 3
What developments mark the educational history of Native Americans?

While the notion of universal education, especially at the elementary level, spread slowly among Americans of European ancestry, many who lived here were not European. In fact, Europeans were the late arrivals. It is estimated that 50 to 100 million Native Americans occupied both

You Be The Judge
SCHOOL MASCOTS

Should Change with the Times Because . . .

MASCOT NAMES CAN BE HURTFUL

A pep rally featuring chanting "Indians" shaking rubber tomahawks trivializes meaningful rituals and cultural differences. Names such as the "Lady Navajos" or "Tigerettes" perpetuate an image of female inferiority and the second-class status of their sports.

MASCOT NAMES PROMOTE VIOLENCE

Stands filled with "Redskins" wielding tomahawks and chanting insults bring us all closer to potential violence and injury. Mascots should build a positive climate, not a destructive one.

WE SHOULD SET AN EXAMPLE FOR STUDENTS

We must teach by example, and changing offensive mascot names gives us that opportunity. By adopting names like "Freedom" or "Liberty," we teach our children how names can model our historical best, not our historical bigotries, and how adults can learn from past mistakes.

Should Not Change over Time Because . . .

IT'S JUST A NAME

There are more important issues to address than changing names of athletic teams. Exaggerated complaints about mascot names consume hours of school board meetings—and only show how political correctness is driving the times.

MASCOT NAMES BUILD SCHOOL SPIRIT

Proud mascot names like the "Warriors" highlight courage and bravery. Mascot names instill school spirit, a trait sorely needed by today's young people.

TRADITION MATTERS

Some things really do need to stay the same. Building a positive and stable school community is hard enough with people constantly moving and families splitting. School mascot names provide stability, and do not mindlessly mirror every passing fad.

www.mhhe.com/sadker10e

YOU DECIDE . . .

You and your classmates may want to share your own experiences on this hot-button issue. Should any mascot names be changed?

Which names and why (or why not)? Brainstorm positive team names and mascots. This may be more challenging than you think. To understand more about mascots and American Indians, visit www.racismagainstindians.org.

North and South America before Columbus arrived.[8] Within a relatively brief time following European arrival, more than 90 percent of them would be dead from disease, starvation, and conquest. The survivors in the United States would soon experience what many describe as an attempt to kill their culture through education. Church missionaries educated Native peoples to abandon their history and language to become "civilized Christians." Native beliefs, customs, and languages were systematically ridiculed and repressed.[9] (Do today's school mascots continue the denigration of Native culture? See You Be the Judge: School Mascots.)

Despite adverse conditions, Native Americans achieved some extraordinary educational accomplishments. For example, when their oral traditions and beliefs were discredited, Sequoyah invented a Cherokee syllabary in 1822. This permitted the Cherokee language to be written. Books were published in Cherokee; Cherokee schools became bilingual; and the Cherokee nation wrote, edited, and published the *Cherokee Phoenix,* a bilingual weekly newspaper. However, as federal interventions became more systematic, the tribes' control over their own education diminished.

In 1824, the federal government established the Bureau of Indian Affairs (BIA) and began placing whole tribes of Native peoples on reservations. The BIA continued to use education as a tool of cultural conquest. Indian reservations saw more white superintendents, farm agents, teachers, inspectors, and missionaries. Indian boarding schools were established to assimilate young Native Americans into the dominant European American values: veneration of property, individual competition, European-style domesticity, toil, and European standards of dress. Many Native Americans refused to send their children to reservation schools. Arrest and kidnapping were common practices in forcing Native American children to attend. Rations were often withheld from parents as a means of compelling them to send their children to school.

Today, more than half of the Native Americans in this country do not live on reservations. The vast majority of Native children are educated in public schools where they have lost their "critical mass," which is often associated with higher achievement. Native American students have the highest dropout rate of all students and are more likely to struggle with alcohol and drug addiction.[10]

In an effort to improve the lives of Native people, recent decades have witnessed continued efforts by Native Americans to win control of the reservations, including the schools. Tribes feel strongly that such control will maintain cultural identity, as well as increase the academic achievement of their children.

The following Ancient Digger Indian proverb captures the last two centuries of Indian tribal education:

> In the beginning, God gave to every people a cup of clay, and from this cup they drank their life. They all dipped in the water, but their cups were different. Our cup is broken now. It has passed away.

Spinsters, Bachelors, and Gender Barriers in Teaching

Although today's perception is that teaching is predominantly a female career, in fact, men dominated teaching well into the mid-nineteenth century. Teaching was a **gendered career,** and it was gendered "male." Although a few women taught at home in *dame schools,* the first women to become teachers in regular school settings, earning a public salary, were viewed as gender trespassers, "unsexed" by their ambition, and considered masculine. Concerned by this negative characterization, early feminists such as Catherine Beecher implored female teachers to accentuate their feminine traits, highlight their domestic skills, and continue their preparation for marriage.[11] Despite the national reluctance to allow women into the workforce, and despite the perception that teachers should be male, the demand for more and inexpensive teachers created by common schools made the hiring of women teachers inevitable.

FOCUS QUESTION 4

How did teaching become a "gendered" career?

By the early part of the twentieth century, women constituted upward of 90 percent of teachers. But not all women were equally welcome. School districts preferred "spinsters," women unmarried and unlikely to marry. Such women would not suffer the dual loyalties inherent in "serving" both husband and employer. Unmarried women were hired so frequently in the late nineteenth and early twentieth century that teaching and spinsterhood became synonymous. Cartoonists, authors, and reporters made the spinster schoolteacher a cultural icon. Boarding and rooming houses, and eventually small apartments, sometimes called *teacher-ages,* were built to provide accommodations for this new class of workers. Teaching was gendered again, but now it was gendered "female."

As women came to dominate teaching, the gender tables were turned, and a new concern arose: the fear that female teachers were "feminizing" boys. There were demands to bring men back to teaching and to halt the "feminization" of young schoolboys. President Theodore Roosevelt added a touch of racism to the debate, arguing that because so many white women were choosing teaching over motherhood, they were committing "race suicide," and the continuance of the white race was in jeopardy.[12] School districts responded by actively recruiting male teachers, and male educators carved out their own niches in school systems. Administration, coaching, vocational education, and certain high school departments, specifically science and math, became male bastions.

For women, teaching meant economic and financial liberation. But not without cost. The dedicated teaching *spinsters* of the nineteenth century became the object of ridicule in the twentieth century. Women choosing teaching over motherhood were considered unnatural by a mostly male cadre of psychologists, physicians, and authors. Articles and books began to appear early in the twentieth century arguing that being unmarried caused women to be spiteful, hateful, and disgusting. The eminent psychologist G. Stanley Hall wrote an article entitled "Certain Degenerative Tendencies among Teachers," explaining why unmarried women were frustrated, bitter, and otherwise unpleasant. Stage shows and movies picked up the theme, portraying lesbian relationships in and beyond school settings. The National Education Association reacted by campaigning for school districts to drop their ban against hiring married women. But when the depression hit in the 1930s, the idea of hiring wives and creating two-income families was anathema: The scarce jobs were to be funneled to women living alone or to men, the family "breadwinners." It was not until the end of World War II that most school districts even employed married women.

Men who remained in teaching also paid a price. Conventional wisdom early in the twentieth century held that effeminate men were gay men and that gay men were naturally drawn to teaching. Worse yet, gay men were considered to be a teaching time bomb, because they would be poor role models for children. All male teachers became suspect, and few were drawn to teaching. School districts avoided hiring men who did not possess a clearly masculine demeanor. (Married men with children were preferred.) The Cold War and the accompanying McCarthy anti-Communist scare of the 1950s declared war on liberal ideas and unconventional choices: Homosexuality was seen as a threat to America. "There was a list of about twenty-one things that you could be fired for. The first was to be a card-carrying Communist, and the second was to be a homosexual."[13] Single teachers declared their "healthy" heterosexuality, and gay teachers stayed hidden. During this time, the number of married teachers doubled.

Although recent years have witnessed a loosening of gender straitjackets, sex stereotypes, myths, and bigotry against gays continue to restrict and confine both women and men. Men drawn to teaching young children and women seeking leadership roles confront both barriers and social sanctions. Gay and lesbian teachers (and students) frequently endure hurtful comments and discriminatory treatment. As long as these gender and sexual barriers persist, we are all the poorer.

The Secondary School Movement

With Horace Mann's success in promoting public elementary schools, more and more citizens were given a basic education. In 1880, almost 10 million Americans were enrolled in elementary schools, and, at the upper levels of schooling, both private and public universities were established. But the gap between the elementary schools and the universities remained wide.

Massachusetts, the site of the first tax-supported elementary schools and the first college in America (Harvard), was also the site of the first free secondary school. Established in Boston in 1821, the **English Classical School** enrolled 176 students (all boys); shortly thereafter, 76 students dropped out. The notion of a public high school was slow to take root. It was not until 1852 that Boston was able to maintain a similar school for girls. The name of the boys' school was changed to The English High School and, even more simply, Boys' High School, to emphasize the more practical nature of the curriculum.

As secondary schools spread, they generally took the form of private, tuition-charging academies. Citizens did not view the secondary schools as we do today, as a free and natural extension of elementary education. A major stumbling block to the creation of free high schools was public resistance to paying additional school taxes. (Sound familiar?) But, in a series of court cases, especially the **Kalamazoo, Michigan, case** in 1874, the courts ruled that taxes could be used to support secondary schools. In Michigan, citizens already had access to

FOCUS QUESTION 5

How did secondary schools evolve?

A Closer Look

The Development of American Schools

ELEMENTARY SCHOOLS

Dame Schools (1600s) These private schools taught by women in their homes offered child care for working parents willing to pay a fee. The dames who taught here received meager wages, and the quality of instruction varied greatly.

Local Schools (1600s–1800s) First started in towns and later expanded to include larger districts, these schools were open to those who could afford to pay. Found generally in New England, these schools taught basic skills and religion.

Itinerant Schools (1700s) and Tutors (1600s–1900s) Rural America could not support schools and full-time teachers. As a result, in sparsely populated New England, itinerant teachers carried schooling from village to village; they lived in people's homes and provided instruction. In the South, private tutors taught the rich. Traveling teachers and tutors, usually working for a fee and room and board, took varying levels of education to small towns and wealthy populations.

Private Schools (1700s–1800s) Private schools, often located in the middle colonies, offered a variety of special studies. These schools constituted a true free market, as parents paid for the kind of private school they desired. As you might imagine, both the curricula and the quality of these schools varied greatly.

Common Schools (1830–present) The common school was a radical departure from earlier ones in several ways. First, it was free. Parents did not have to pay tuition or fees. Second, it was open to all social classes. Previously, schools usually taught either middle-class or upper-class children. Horace Mann's common school was intended to bring democracy to the classroom. By the mid-nineteenth century, kindergarten was added. In the past few decades, many common schools, now called *elementary schools,* have added Head Start and other prekindergarten programs.

SECONDARY SCHOOLS

Latin Grammar Schools (1600s–1700s) These schools prepared wealthy men for college and emphasized a classical curriculum, including Latin and some Greek. From European roots, the curriculum in these schools reflected the belief that the pinnacle of civilization was reached in the Roman Empire.

English Grammar Schools (1700s) These private schools moved away from the classical Latin tradition to more practical studies. These schools were viewed not as preparation for college but as preparation for business careers and as a means of instilling social graces. Some of these schools set a precedent by admitting white girls, thus paving the way for the widespread acceptance of females in other schools.

Academies (1700s–1800s) The academies were a combination of the Latin and English grammar schools. These schools taught English, not Latin. Practical courses were taught, but history and the classics were also included. Some academies emphasized college preparation, and others prepared students to enter business and vocations.

High Schools (1800s–present) These secondary schools differed from their predecessors in that they were free; they were governed not by private boards but by the public. The high school can be viewed as an extension of the Common School Movement to the secondary level. High schools were open to all social classes and provided both precollege and career education.

Junior High Schools (1909–present) and Middle Schools (1950s–present) Junior high schools (grades 7–9) and middle schools (grades 5–8) were designed to meet the unique needs of preadolescents and to prepare them for the high school experience.

Charter Schools (1991–present) Charters are tax-supported elementary and secondary schools that are free from some of the rules and regulations that apply to other public schools. A type of choice school, charters are created with unique missions, instructional strategies, or curriculum designs.

REFLECTION: If you were responsible for creating a new school based on contemporary needs, what kind of school would you create?

GLOBAL VIEW Choose any country in the developing world. Discover how gender, race, class, and geography affect educational opportunities.

free elementary schools and a state-supported university. The courts saw a lack of rationality in not providing a bridge between the two.[14] The idea of public high school slowly took hold.

During the last half of the nineteenth century, the nation moved from agrarian to industrial, from mostly rural to urban, and people viewed the elementary school as inadequate to meet the needs of a more sophisticated and industrialized society. More parents viewed the high school as an important stepping stone to better jobs. With the gradual decrease in demand for teenage workers, high school attendance grew. Half a century earlier, the public elementary school had reflected the growing dreams and aspirations of Americans and their changing economy. Now the public high school was the benchmark of those changes. The high school became a continuation of elementary education, a path to public higher education, and an affirmation of democracy. (See A Closer Look: The Development of American Schools.)

Although the high school grew in popularity, it did not meet the needs of all its students. The junior high school, first established in 1909 in Columbus, Ohio, included grades 7, 8, and 9, and was designed to meet the unique needs of preadolescents. More individualized instruction, a strong emphasis on guidance and counseling, and a core curriculum were designed to respond to the academic, physiological, social, and psychological characteristics of preadolescents. The junior high school concept was further refined in the middle school, which included grades 5 through 8.

During the last decades of the twentieth and into the twenty-first centuries, the academic effectiveness of public schools was being questioned, and sparked calls for reform.

A Brief History of Educational Reform

Our Nation is at risk. Our once unchallenged prominence in commerce, industry, science, and technological innovation is being overtaken by competitors through-out the world. . . . If an unfriendly foreign power had attempted to impose on America the mediocre educational performance that exists today, we might well have viewed it as an act of war. . . . We have, in effect, been committing an act of unthinking, unilateral educational disarmament.[15]

So began the 1983 report of the National Commission on Excellence in Education, *A Nation at Risk: The Imperative for Educational Reform.* The report cited declining test scores, the weak performance of U.S. students compared with students in other industrialized nations, the fear that the United States is losing ground economically to other countries, and the high number of functionally illiterate Americans. *A Nation at Risk* put school reform in the national spotlight. In response to the report, states increased the number of course requirements needed for graduation and required more testing of both students and teachers. Today, decades later, even more importance has been given to these tests. (See Chapter 5 for a detailed discussion on current reform efforts.) Although low international test scores and the global economy fuel the demand for better schools, reforming schools actually began more than a century ago.

At the end of the nineteenth century, the United States was undergoing profound economic and social transformations. Vast new industries and giant corporations were being formed and factory labor was being exploited; massive numbers of immigrants were arriving, the population was surging, and urban America was growing; traditional agrarian life was disappearing. How should schools respond? In 1892, the National Education Association (NEA) established the *Committee of Ten* to develop a national policy for high schools. The Committee, composed for the most part of college presidents and professors, wanted consistency and order in the high school curriculum for an easier transition into college. The committee report required that high schools teach certain required courses four or five times a week for one year and that student progress be measured by *Carnegie Units*. Now it became easier for colleges to decide which students were prepared to do college-level work.

The NEA repeated the process in 1918, but this time committee members included education professors, high school principals, the U.S. commissioner of education, and others focused not on transition to college but on preparing adults for their life roles. The truth is, very few Americans went on to college at that time; most went on to work and family. The committee wanted to know: What can high school do to improve the daily lives of citizens in an industrial democracy? This committee's report, *Cardinal Principles of Secondary Education,* identified seven goals for high school: (1) health, (2) worthy home membership, (3) command of fundamental academic skills, (4) vocation, (5) citizenship, (6) worthy use of leisure time, and (7) ethical character. The high school was seen as a socializing agency, an opportunity to improve all aspects of a citizen's life. (Almost a century later, those 1918 goals still sound balanced and useful.)

John Dewey and Progressive Education

FOCUS QUESTION 6

What were the main tenets of
the Progressive Education
movement?

John Dewey was possibly the most influential educator of the twentieth century—and probably the most controversial one. Some saw him as a savior of U.S. schools; others accused him of nearly destroying them. Rather than become engrossed in the heated controversy surrounding Dewey, however, let us look at *progressivism,* the movement with which he is closely associated and, in the next chapter, explore the philosophy behind progressivism.

As early as 1875, Francis Parker, superintendent of schools in Quincy, Massachusetts, introduced the concepts of progressivism in his schools. But it was not until the 1920s and 1930s that the progressive education movement became more widely known. During the 1920s and 1930s, the Dalton and Walden schools in New York, the Beaver Country Day School in Massachusetts, the Oak Lane Country Day School in Pennsylvania, and laboratory schools at University of Chicago and Columbia began to challenge traditional practices. The progressive education approach soon spread to suburban and city public school systems across the country. Elements of progressive education can still be found in many schools.

Progressive education includes several components. First, it broadens the school program to include health concerns, family and community life issues, and a concern for vocational education. Second, progressivism applies new research in psychology and the social sciences to classroom practices. Third, progressivism emphasizes a more democratic educational approach, accepting the interests and needs of an increasingly diverse student body.

This model of education assumes that students learn best when their learning follows their interests. Progressivists believe that knowledge is not an inert body of facts to be committed to memory; rather, it consists of experiences that should be used to help solve present problems. Passively listening to the teacher, according to the progressive movement, is not the most effective learning strategy. Students' interests should serve as a springboard to understanding and mastering contemporary issues. The role of the teacher is to identify student needs and interests and provide an educational environment that builds on them. In fact, progressive education shares some characteristics with problem-based and authentic learning, popular innovations in some of today's schools.

John Dewey, in many minds, is the personification of progressive education, as well as its most notable advocate. In no small part, this is due to the tens of thousands of pages that Dewey wrote during his long life. (Dewey was born on the eve of the Civil War in 1859 and died during the Korean War in the early 1950s.) Toward the end of Dewey's life, both he and progressive education came under strong attack.

The criticism of Dewey and progressive education originated with far-right political groups, for it was the era of Senator Joseph McCarthy and his extremist campaign against communism. Although McCarthy's hunt for communists was directed primarily at the government and the military, educators were not immune. Some viewed progressive education as an atheistic, un-American force that had all but destroyed the nation's schools. Because students were allowed to explore and question, many critics were able to cite examples of how traditional values were not being taught. Although these critics were generally ignorant of Dewey's ideas and progressive practices, a second group was more responsible in its critique.

This second wave of criticism came from individuals who felt that the school curriculum was not academically sound. Hyman Rickover, a famous admiral and developer of the nuclear submarine, and Arthur Bestor, a liberal arts professor, were among the foremost critics decrying the ills of progressive education. They called for an end to "student-centered" and "life-adjustment" subjects and a return to a more rigorous study of traditional courses. While the arguments raged, the launching of *Sputnik* by the Soviet Union in 1957 put at least a temporary closure on the debate. The United States was involved in a space race with the Soviets, a race to educate scientists and engineers, a race toward the first moon landing. Those arguing for a more rigorous, science- and math-focused curriculum won the day. Although many still argued vociferously over the benefits and shortcomings of progressive education, traditionalists were setting the direction for the nation's curriculum.

Before leaving progressive education, however, it will be beneficial to examine one of the most famous studies of the progressive movement. The Progressive Education Association, formed in 1919, initiated a study during the 1930s that compared almost three thousand graduates of progressive and of traditional schools as they made their way through college. The study, called the Eight-Year Study, was intended to determine which educational approach was more effective. The results indicated that graduates of progressive schools:

1. Earned a slightly higher grade point average

2. Earned higher grades in all fields except foreign languages

3. Tended to specialize in the same fields as more traditional students

4. Received slightly more academic honors

5. Were judged to be more objective and more precise thinkers

6. Were judged to possess higher intellectual curiosity and greater drive

The Federal Government

As World War II drew to a close, the United States found itself the most powerful nation on earth. For the remainder of the twentieth century, the United States reconstructed a war-ravaged global economy while confronting world communism. In fact, the United States viewed education as an important tool in accomplishing those strategic goals. When the Soviets launched *Sputnik,* for example, the government enlisted the nation's schools in meeting that new challenge. Consequently, Congress passed the **National Defense Education Act (NDEA)** in 1958 to enhance "the security of the nation" and to develop "the mental resources and technical skills of its young men and women." The NDEA supported the improvement of instruction and curriculum development, funded teacher training programs, and provided loans and scholarships for college students that allowed them to major in subjects deemed important to the national defense (such as teaching). However, looking back in history, it is not at all clear how the federal government was legally able to do that. After all, the framers of the Constitution made their intentions clear: Education was to be a state responsibility, and the federal government was not to be involved. How did the NDEA and other federal acts come to pass?

Many people are unaware that the responsibility for educating Americans is not even mentioned in the Constitution. Under the **Tenth Amendment,** any area not specifically stated in the Constitution as a federal responsibility is automatically assigned to the states. Why was education a nontopic? Some historians believe that because the individual colonies had already established disparate educational systems, the framers of the Constitution did not want to create dissension by forcing the states to accept a single educational system. Other analysts believe that education was deliberately omitted from the Constitution because Americans feared control of the schools by a central government, any central government, as had been the case in Europe. They saw central control as a possible threat to their freedom. Still others suggest that the framers of the Constitution, in their haste, bartering, and bickering, simply forgot about education. (What a depressing thought!) Whatever the reason, distinct colonial practices continued as each state created its own educational structure—its own approach for preparing teachers and funding schools.

FOCUS QUESTION 7

What role has the federal government played in American education?

A Closer Look Selected Federal Legislation

The following is a partial list of legislation indicating the long history of federal involvement in education.

1. *Land Ordinance Act* and *Northwest Ordinance* (1785 and 1787). These two ordinances provided for the establishment of public education in the territory between the Appalachian Mountains and the Mississippi River. In these new territories, one square mile out of every thirty-six was reserved for support of public education, and new states formed from these territories were encouraged to establish "schools and the means for education."

2. *Morrill Land Grant College Acts* (1862 and 1890). These acts established sixty-nine institutions of higher education in the various states, some of which are among today's great state universities. These acts were also called simply the *Land-Grant College Acts,* because public land was donated to establish these colleges.

3. *Smith-Hughes Act* (1917). This act provided funds for teacher training and program development in vocational education at the high school level.

4. *Servicemen's Readjustment Act* (G.I. Bill of Rights, 1944). This act paid veterans' tuition and living expenses for a specific number of months, depending on the length of their military service.

5. *National Defense Education Act* (1958). In response to the Soviet launching of *Sputnik,* the NDEA provided substantial funds for a variety of educational activities, including student loans, the education of school counselors, and the strengthening of instructional programs in science, mathematics, and foreign languages.

6. *Elementary and Secondary Education Act* (1965). This law provided financial assistance to school districts with low-income families, to improve libraries and instructional materials, and to promote educational innovations and research. In the 1970s, this legislation was expanded to include funding for bilingual and Native American education, drug education, and school lunch and breakfast programs.

7. *Project Head Start* (1964–1965). This act provides medical, social, nutritional, and educational services for low-income children 3 to 6 years of age.

8. *Bilingual Education Act* (1968). In response to the needs of the significant number of non-English-speaking students, Congress authorized funds to provide relevant instruction to these students. The primary focus was to assist non-English speakers, particularly Spanish-speaking students, almost 70 percent of whom were failing to graduate from high school. Although many other languages besides Spanish are included in this act, a relatively limited percentage of non-English-speaking students participate in these programs because of funding shortfalls.

9. *Title IX of the Education Amendments* (1972). This regulation prohibits discrimination on the basis of sex. The regulation is comprehensive and protects the rights of both males and females from preschool through graduate school, in sports, financial aid, employment, counseling, school regulations and policies, admissions, and other areas. Title IX enforcement has been lax, and many schools violate one or more parts of the regulation.

10. *Individuals with Disabilities Education Act* (1975, 1991, 1997, 2004). This act provides financial assistance to local school districts to provide free and appropriate education for the nation's 8 million children with disabilities who are between 3 and 21 years of age.

11. *No Child Left Behind Act* (2001). This act revises the Elementary and Secondary Education Act (ESEA, 1965) and calls for standards and annual testing of math, reading, and science. Schools that test poorly face the possibility of being closed and teachers being fired. Parents are given greater freedom to select schools, with increased federal support for charter schools. By 2011, the federal government responded to a backlash against NCLB by granting exceptions to underperforming schools and by giving states more freedom to hold schools and teachers accountable.

REFLECTION: Current federal initiatives promote standards and testing. How is this a departure from the general history of federal legislation?

Over time, however, the federal government discovered ways to influence education. (A Closer Look: Selected Federal Legislation offers a snapshot of some federal education roles.) As early as the revolutionary period, the new nation passed the **Land Ordinance Act** of 1785 and the **Northwest Ordinance** of 1787. These acts required townships in the newly settled territories bounded by the Ohio and Mississippi rivers and the Great Lakes to reserve a section of land for educational purposes. The ordinances contained a much-quoted sentence underscoring the new nation's faith in education: "Religion, morality, and knowledge being necessary to good government and the happiness of mankind, schools and the means of education shall forever be encouraged."

The federal government also exerted its influence through targeted funding, or categorical grants. By using federal dollars for specific programs, the government was able to create new colleges and universities, to promote agricultural and industrial research efforts, and to provide schools for Native Americans and other groups. During the Great Depression of the 1930s, the federal government became even more directly involved with education, constructing schools, providing free lunches for poor children, instituting part-time work programs for high school and college students, and offering educational programs to older Americans. With unemployment, hunger, and desperation rampant in the 1930s, states welcomed these federal efforts. More and more Americans were coming to realize that some educational challenges were beyond the resources of the states. But federal involvement in education was sometimes resisted by states and local communities. In the case of African American education, it took nearly a century for the federal government to move forcefully to end racial segregation. And then, a few decades later, most students found themselves once again racially segregated.

Black Americans: The Struggle for a Chance to Learn

Much of the history of African American education in the United States has been one of denial. The first law prohibiting education of slaves was passed in South Carolina in 1740. During the next hundred years, many states passed similar and even stronger compulsory-ignorance laws. For example, a 1823 Mississippi law prohibited six or more Negroes from gathering for educational purposes. In Louisiana, a 1830 law imposed a prison sentence on anyone caught teaching a slave to read or write. However, because education has always been integral to African Americans' struggle for equal opportunity, they risked the penalties of these laws and even the dangers of violence for a chance to learn. They formed clandestine schools throughout most large cities and towns of the South. Suzie King Taylor described what it was like to attend one of those secret schools in Savannah, Georgia:

> We went every day about nine o'clock with our books wrapped in paper to prevent the police or white persons from seeing them. We went in, one at a time, through the gate, into the yard to the L Kitchen which was the schoolroom.[16]

The Civil War brought an end to policies of compulsory ignorance and an affirmation of black people's belief in the power of education. Most of the schooling of African Americans immediately following the Civil War was carried out by philanthropic societies. These associations worked with the Freedmen's Bureau, a federal agency established to provide various services, including the establishment of schools. School staffs were usually a mixture of instructors from the North, blacks of Caribbean island heritage, and formerly enslaved literate blacks.

Many white Southerners responded to the education of blacks with fear and anger. Sometimes there was terrorism against black schools. State after state passed laws that explicitly provided for segregated schools. With the 1896 **Plessy v. Ferguson** Supreme Court decision, segregation became a legally sanctioned part of the American way of life. In this landmark case, the Court developed the doctrine of **separate but equal.** Separate but equal initially legalized separate railway passenger cars for black and white Americans and was also used to justify a legally segregated school system, which in many states lasted for more than half a century.

"Separate but equal" was not equal. In 1907, Mississippi spent $5.02 for the education of each white child but only $1.10 for each black child. In 1924, the state paid more than $1 million to transport whites long distances to schools. No money was spent for blacks, and for them a daily walk of more than twelve miles was not out of the question. Attending schools

FOCUS QUESTION 8

How did history shape the educational experiences of African Americans, Hispanics, Asian Americans/Pacific Islanders, and Arab Americans?

Scenes like this one became commonplace all across America in the years following the landmark *Brown* v. *Board of Education of Topeka* decision in 1954 and the passage of the Civil Rights Act in 1964.

without enough books, seats, space, equipment, or facilities taught African American children the harsh reality of "separate but unequal." In the South, a dual school system based on race was in existence. This was **de jure segregation**—that is, segregation by law or by official action.

In the North, school assignments were based on both race and residence. **De facto (unofficial) segregation** occurred as the result of segregated residential patterns, patterns that were often prompted by discriminatory real estate practices. As housing patterns changed, attendance zones were often redrawn to ensure the separation of white and black children in schools. Even in schools that were not entirely segregated, black children were routinely placed in special classes or separate academic tracks, counseled into low-status careers, and barred from extracurricular activities. Whatever the obstacle, however, African Americans continued their struggle for access to quality education. As W. E. B. DuBois noted: "Probably never in the world have so many oppressed people tried in every possible way to educate themselves."[17]

Political momentum for civil rights reform grew with the participation of African Americans in World War II and the 1954 Supreme Court decision that schools must desegregate "with all deliberate speed." In ***Brown* v. *Board of Education of Topeka*** (Kansas), the court ruled unanimously that "in the field of public education the doctrine of 'separate but equal' has no place. Separate educational facilities are inherently unequal." Yet a decade after *Brown,* almost 91 percent of all African American children in the South still attended all-black schools.

In 1964, President Johnson and Congress moved boldly to eradicate racial segregation. The Civil Rights Act gave the federal government power to help local school districts desegregate (Title IV) and, when necessary, to initiate lawsuits or withhold federal school funds to force desegregation (Title VI). The Civil Rights Act produced more desegregation in the next four years than the Supreme Court's *Brown* decision had in the preceding decade. All branches of the federal government now moved in concert to desegregate the nation's schools.

During the late 1960s and early 1970s, the Supreme Court also attacked de facto segregation stemming from racially imbalanced neighborhoods. Courts supported busing, racial quotas, and school pairing to eradicate school segregation in both the North and the South. But opposition to these measures grew, and school districts began to experiment with magnet schools, choice plans, and voluntary metropolitan desegregation—remedies more acceptable to many school families.

Even as some schools became more racially balanced, a new barrier to equality appeared. In the same school building, black and white students found themselves separated by tracking, treated differently by teachers and administrators, and even gravitating to different areas of the school.[18] (See Chapter 4 for more on tracking) This within-school segregation was termed **second-generation segregation.** In the 1960s, the Kerner Commission warned: "Our nation is moving toward two societies, one black, and one white—separate and unequal." The commission charged that white society must assume responsibility for the black ghetto. "White institutions created it, white institutions maintain it, and white society condones it."[19]

IMAGINE...

Private Proms

Although the 2009 graduating class at Montgomery County High School in Georgia had only fifty-four seniors, an old tradition continued: White and black students went to separate proms on different nights. Throughout the South, although schools are racially integrated, many proms continue the history of segregation. When film star Morgan Freeman offered to pay for a first-of-its-kind integrated prom at his old high school in Mississippi, the students embraced the idea. However, white parents rejected the offer and sponsored a "private, whites-only" prom.

SOURCE: *The New York Times Magazine,* May 24, 2009.

But the Kerner Commission's warning was not heeded. As the century drew to a close, affirmative efforts such as busing were abandoned, and in the *Hopwood* (1996) and the *University of Michigan* decisions (2003), firm racial set-asides for college and law school admissions were eliminated. Although the courts said that race could be a factor in promoting student diversity, it could not be a major factor. In a 2007 ruling, the Supreme Court further backed away from desegregation efforts by striking down plans in Seattle and Louisville that used race to assign K–12 students to public schools.[20]

The consequences of these actions are now evident in the nation's schools, as residential patterns and the diminished legal pressures have re-segregated the nation's schools. Today's students are more segregated than they were four decades ago, with white students experiencing the most segregated educational environment.[21] Should desegregation still be a goal? Has its time passed? Some believe that even the idea that African American or Latino children can learn effectively only when they sit next to a white student is demeaning. Others see segregation as a way to protect African American and Latino cultures.

Researcher Gary Orfield of the UCLA Civil Rights Project does not agree. His research suggests that students who attend integrated schools are more comfortable with peers from diverse racial, cultural, and socioeconomic backgrounds and more understanding of different points of view. As schools re-segregate, those benefits are lost. Others argue that racial isolation puts minority children in poorer schools with less experienced teachers, weaker precollegiate courses, and lower achievement and graduation rates.[22] As one advocate for desegregation decried, "[African Americans] who favor resegregation are doing whites the great favor of relieving both their guilty conscience and their pocketbooks."[23]

Hispanics: Growing School Impact

More than 50 million Hispanics live in the United States, most as U.S. citizens. Hispanics constitute 16 percent of the nation's population, the largest minority group in the nation. Only Mexico has a larger Hispanic population than the United States.[24] Ongoing legal and illegal immigration (often to escape economic and political repression) together with high birthrates for young families in their childbearing years, have made Hispanics the youngest and fastest growing school-age population in the United States. Hispanic children are 20 percent of the school-aged population and often confront numerous educational barriers as they work to master English. As early as kindergarten, many Hispanic students are less able than their white peers to identify colors, recognize letters, count to fifty, or write their first name. More than half of Hispanics drop out of school.[25]

Hispanics consist of several subgroups, which share some characteristics, such as language, but differ in others, such as race, location, age, income, and educational attainment. The three largest Hispanic subgroups are Mexican Americans, Puerto Ricans, and Cuban Americans. There is also significant representation from other Latin American and Caribbean countries, such as the Dominican Republic, El Salvador, Nicaragua, and Honduras. (See Figure 7.1.) In contrast to these new immigrants, many from war-torn or poverty-stricken countries, there is also an "old" population of Mexican and Spanish descent living in the Southwest with a longer history on this continent than those who trace their ancestors to the New England colonies. Let's briefly look at some of the groups that make up the Hispanic community.

Mexican Americans

At the end of the United States' war with Mexico (1846–1848), the Mexicans who decided to stay in the new U.S. territories were guaranteed full citizenship. By 1900, approximately 200,000 Mexican Americans were living in the Southwest, having built the cities of Los

FIGURE 7.1

U.S. Hispanic Subgroups.

SOURCE: *Hispanic Americans by the Numbers* U.S. Census Bureau, 2011.

REFLECTION: Although many refer to Hispanics as a homogeneous community, they are not. What distinctions can you make for each of these subgroups? What similarities have you observed or studied?

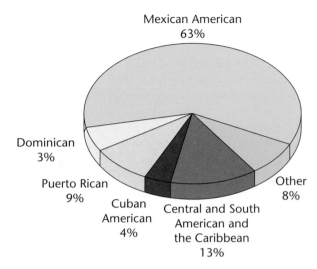

U.S. Hispanic subgroups

Angeles, San Diego, Tucson, Albuquerque, Dallas, and San Antonio. The devices that were used to deny educational opportunity to Mexican Americans were similar to those imposed on African Americans. By 1920, a pattern of separate and unequal Mexican American schools had emerged throughout the Southwest.

A significant number of Mexican American families migrated once or twice a year, exploited as a source of cheap labor in rural, agricultural communities. With constant transitions, children's learning suffered. One superintendent in Texas, reflecting deeply engrained prejudice, argued that education was actually dangerous for Mexican Americans:

> Most of our Mexicans are of the lower class. They transplant onions, harvest them, etc. The less they know about everything else, the better contented they are . . . so you see it is up to the white population to keep the Mexican on his knees in an onion patch. . . . This does not mix well with education.[26]

In the late 1960s, César Chávez led the fight of migrant Mexican American laborers to organize themselves into a union and to demand a more responsive education that included culture-free IQ tests, instruction in Spanish, smaller classes, and greater cultural representation in the curriculum.

Today, families continue to cross the border every day, hoping to improve their economic lives. More than one in three public schools enroll migrant and immigrant students, mostly Mexican Americans. The greatest numbers are in California, Illinois, Texas, Arizona, and Florida.[27]

Puerto Ricans

During the nineteenth century, many of the Puerto Ricans in the United States were highly respected political exiles striving for the independence of their homeland. But all that changed in 1898, when Puerto Rico was acquired from Spain and became a territory of the United States. Citizenship, through the Jones Act in 1917, provided free movement between the continent and the island. Migration to the mainland peaked during the 1950s, with the majority of Puerto Ricans settling in New York City. Currently, about half the Puerto Rican population lives within the fifty

states, and the other half lives in Puerto Rico.[28] The frequent passage between the island and the United States, as families search for a better economic life, makes schooling all the more difficult for Puerto Rican children.

Cuban Americans

Following the Castro-led revolution in the 1950s, Cuban immigration to the United States increased significantly. During the 1960s, Cubans who settled in the United States were primarily well-educated, professional, and middle- and upper-class. By 1980, 800,000 Cubans—10 percent of the population of Cuba—were living in the United States. For the most part, Cubans settled in Miami and other locations in southern Florida, but there are also sizable populations in New York, Philadelphia, Chicago, Milwaukee, and Indianapolis. Cubans, considered one of the most highly educated people in American immigration history, tend to be more prosperous and more conservative than most of the other Latino groups.[29] In the second immigration wave, during the 1980s, there were many more black and poor Cubans, who have not been accepted as readily into communities in the United States.

GLOBAL VIEW

The very high 96 percent adult literacy rate in Cuba is often tied to policies of former President Fidel Castro. Go to UNICEF's website (www. unicef.org/statistics) to find out other international literacy rates.

Asian Americans and Pacific Islanders: The Magnitude of Diversity

The term "Asian Americans and Pacific Islanders" embraces peoples from nations as diverse as India, Vietnam, China, Pakistan, Korea, Samoa, Japan, and Native Hawaii, about half the world's population. More than 17 million Americans have roots in Asia, although demographers predict that this figure will increase to more than 40 million in the upcoming years. As a group, these Americans have attained a high degree of educational and economic success. This section will describe the differing experiences of four of the largest Asian immigrant groups—Chinese, Filipinos, Asian Indians, and Japanese—as well as problems faced by refugees from Southeast Asia.[30]

Many of these cultures hold education in high esteem, and well-mannered, respectful, and studious Asian American students have earned themselves the moniker of *model minority*. In kindergarten, Asian American children consistently outscore their peers in reading and math.[31] More than 50 percent of Asian American/Pacific Islanders students graduate from college. One year after graduation, they have a higher starting salary than any racial or ethnic group. However, diversity within the Asian community is often overlooked, and as with many stereotypes, misconceptions abound. Fewer than half of Vietnamese and Samoan Americans graduate from high school. Asian New Wavers reflect the current countercultural pattern, with baggy pants, combat boots, and dyed hair, challenging the model minority stereotype.[32]

The United States is a nation of immigrants. Our country's motto, *E Pluribus Unum*, means "from many, one." How to educate and honor the individual while creating a unified nation is a long-standing tension for American schools.

Chinese Americans

When the Chinese first began immigrating to the West Coast in the 1850s, they were mostly young, unmarried men who left China, a country ravaged by famine and political turmoil, to seek their fortune in the "Golden Mountains" across the Pacific and then take their wealth back to their homeland. The California gold mines were largely depleted by the time they arrived, and the completion of the transcontinental

railroad signaled a loss of jobs for Chinese laborers. Many found that the hope of taking fortunes home to their families in China was an impossible dream.

By 1880, approximately 106,000 Chinese had immigrated to the United States, fueling a vicious reaction: "The Chinese must go." With the passage of the Immigration Act of 1882, along with a series of similar bills, further Chinese immigration was blocked. The Chinese already in this country responded to increasing physical violence by moving eastward and consolidating into ghettos called Chinatowns. Inhabited largely by male immigrants, these ghettos offered a grim and sometimes violent lifestyle, one with widespread prostitution and gambling. Chinatowns, vestiges of century-old ghettos, can still be found in many of America's cities.

In 1949, the institution of a Communist government in mainland China caused Congress to reverse more than a century of immigration quotas and naturalization and anti-miscegenation laws and grant refugee status to five thousand highly educated Chinese in the United States. Despite facing active prejudice and discrimination, Chinese Americans today have achieved a higher median income and educational level than that of white Americans. And the Chinese language Mandarin is the second most popular foreign language in U.S. schools, second only to Spanish.

Filipino Americans

After the 1898 Spanish-American War, the United States acquired the Philippines. Filipinos, viewed as low-cost labor, were recruited to work in the fields of Hawaii and the U.S. mainland. Thousands left the poverty of their islands to seek economic security.

With a scarcity of women (in 1930, the male–female ratio was 143 to 1) and the mobility of their work on farms and as field hands, the Filipinos had difficulty establishing cohesive communities in the United States. Like other Asian immigrants, they came with the goal of taking their earnings back to their homeland; like other Asian immigrants, most found this an impossible dream. Finding acceptance in the United States also proved a struggle.

The Tydings-McDuffie Act of 1934 was a victory for those who wanted the Filipinos excluded from this country. Promising independence to the Philippines, this act limited immigration to the United States to fifty per year. All that changed in 1965, when a new immigration act allowed a significant increase in Filipino immigration. Between 1970 and 1980, the Filipino population in the United States more than doubled. The earlier presence of the U.S. military in Manila generated an educated elite who spoke English, studied the American school curriculum, and moved to the United States with professional skills, seeking jobs commensurate with their training. Concentrated in urban areas of the West Coast, Filipinos are the second-largest Asian American ethnic group in the United States.[33]

Asian Indian Americans

Traders from India arrived in New England in the 1880s, bartering silks and spices. Intellectuals Henry David Thoreau, Ralph Waldo Emerson, and E. M. Forster (*Passage to India*) gravitated to the culture, religion, and philosophy of the Eastern purveyors. On the West Coast, Indians from Punjab migrated to escape British exploitation, which had forced farmers to raise commercial rather than food crops. With farming conditions in California similar to those in India, Punjabees became successful growers and landowners. They were destined to lose their lands, however,

GLOBAL VIEW
From 1910 to 1940, Chinese immigrants were detained and interrogated at Angel Island station in San Francisco Bay. For further information on U.S. immigration history, visit the Angel Island website at www.angelisland.org. Ellis Island was the New York gateway for European immigration from 1900 to 1920 (www.ellisisland.com). An extensive collection of primary resource photographs and immigration history for educators can be found at *Americans All* (www.americansall.com).

Although often grouped together, Asian Americans and Pacific Islanders reflect great ethnic and cultural diversity.

and even their leasing rights, under the California Alien Land Law, which recalled the ownership of land held by Indians and Japanese.

In addition to legal restrictions, Indian laborers were attacked by racist mobs in Bellingham, Washington, in 1907, triggering other riots and expulsions throughout the Pacific region. U.S. government support for British colonial rule in India became the rationale to further restrict Indian immigration. It was not until 1946 that a law allowing Indian naturalization and immigration was passed. During the past three decades, tens of thousands of Indians arrived in America. Most Indians are extremely well educated, and many are professionals. Their educational and income levels are the highest of any group in the United States, including other Asians.[34]

Japanese Americans

Only when the Japanese government legalized emigration in 1886 did the Japanese come to the United States in significant numbers. For example, in 1870, records show only 50 Japanese in the United States, but by 1920, the number had increased to more than 110,000.

With immigration of the Chinese halted by various exclusion acts, Japanese immigrants filled the need for cheap labor. Like the Chinese, the early Japanese immigrants were males who hoped to return to their homeland, an unfulfilled dream. Praised for their willingness to work when they first arrived in California, the Japanese began to make other farmers nervous with their great success in agriculture and truck farming. Anti-Japanese feelings became prevalent along the West Coast. Such slogans as "Japs must go" and warnings of a new "yellow peril" were frequent. In 1924, Congress passed an immigration bill that halted Japanese immigration to the United States.

After Japan's attack on Pearl Harbor on December 7, 1941, fear and prejudice about the "threat" from Japanese Americans were rampant. On February 19, 1942, President Franklin Roosevelt issued Executive Order No. 9006, which declared the West Coast a "military area" and established federal *relocation camps*. Approximately 110,000 Japanese, more than two-thirds of whom were U.S. citizens, were removed from their homes in the "military area" and were forced into ten *internment (relocation) camps* in California, Idaho, Utah, Arizona, Wyoming, Colorado, and Arkansas. Located in geographically barren areas, guarded by soldiers and barbed wire, these internment camps made it very difficult for the Japanese people to keep their traditions and cultural heritage alive. Almost half a century later, the U.S. government officially acknowledged this wrong and offered a symbolic payment ($20,000 in reparations) to each victim.

Despite severe discrimination in the past, many of today's Japanese Americans enjoy both a high median family income and educational attainment. Their success is at least partially due to traditional values, a heritage some fear may be weakened by increasing assimilation.

Southeast Asian Americans

Before 1975, the United States saw only small numbers of immigrants from Southeast Asia, including Vietnam, Laos, and Kampuchea/Cambodia. Their arrival in greater numbers was related directly to the end of the Vietnam War and resulting communist rule. The refugees came from all strata of society. Some were wealthy; others were poverty stricken. Some were widely traveled and sophisticated; others were farmers and fishing people who had never before left their small villages. Most came as part of a family, and almost half were under age 18 at the time of their arrival. Refugee camps were established to dispense food, clothing, medical assistance, and temporary housing, as well as to provide an introduction to U.S. culture and to the English language.

By December 1975, the last refugee camp had closed and the U.S. government had reset-tled large numbers of Southeast Asians across the nation without too high a concentration in any one location. This dispersal was well intentioned but often left the refugees feeling lonely and isolated. In fact, many moved from original areas of settlement to cities where large num-bers of Asian Americans were already located.

A second wave of Southeast Asian refugees followed in the years after 1975. Cambodians and Laotians migrated to escape poverty, starvation, and political repression in their home-lands. Many tried to escape in small fishing boats not meant for travel across rough ocean seas. Called *boat people* by the media, almost half of them, according to the estimates, died before they reached the shores of the United States.

Similar to war refugees from Latin America, these children brought memories of terrible tragedy to school. For example, a teacher in San Francisco was playing hangman during a lan-guage arts lesson. As the class was laughing and shouting out letters, she was shocked to see one child, a newcomer, in tears. The girl spoke so little English she could not explain the prob-lem. Finally, another child translated. The game had triggered a traumatic memory. In Cam-bodia, the girl had watched the hanging of her father.[35] Since the fall of Saigon in 1975, more than 1.4 million Southeast Asians have resettled in the United States. Their struggle to find a place in this society remains conflicted, because most Americans associate Vietnam with war.

Arab Americans: Moving beyond the Stereotype

Misunderstanding and intolerance have been all-too-common facts of life for 3 million Amer-icans of Arab descent. Arab Americans' quality of life is often influenced by events taking place in other parts of the world. The Iraq wars, assaults on the terrorist camps in Taliban-ruled Afghanistan, the September 11, 2001, attacks on the World Trade Center and the Penta-gon, and the continuing conflict between Israelis and Palestinians create tension and anxiety for Americans of Arab descent. These news events are troubling enough, but media portrayals can exacerbate the problem. Books and movies depict a strange mélange of offensive Arab caricatures: greedy billionaires, corrupt sheiks, immoral terrorists, suave oil cartel magnates, and even romantic, if ignorant, camel-riding Bedouins. Nor are children's books immune from such characterizations. Caroline Cooney's *The Terrorist* (1999), a popular book for chil-dren in grades 5 through 10, is the fictional tale of an American teenager who tries to find the Arab terrorist responsible for her younger brother's death. It is not surprising that polls taken as far back as the 1980s reveal that most Americans perceive Arabs as anti-American, violent, wealthy from oil, and oppressive of women.[36] The challenge to educators could not be clearer. Students and teachers need to learn about Arab Americans, as well as the Arab world.

GLOBAL VIEW

Friendship through Education is a consortium of groups linking U.S. students and stu-dents in countries with Arab populations. www.Friendship ThroughEducation.org

The first wave of Arab immigrants, mostly from Syria and Lebanon, came to America at the end of the nineteenth century for the same reasons that have driven so many immigrants: political freedom and economic opportunity. Toledo, Ohio, and Detroit, Michigan, became important centers of Arab immigration, and business became the economic mainstay of this first wave. Other waves of immigration followed, one just after World War II, and the third as a result of the Palestinian–Israeli conflict. Arabs arrived from over a score of countries, typically settling in major urban centers. (See Figure 7.2.)

Many Americans confuse Arabs and Muslims, mistaking Islam, a religion, with Arabs, a cultural group. Although Islam is the predominant religion of the Middle East, and most Arabs living there are Muslims following Islam, there are also millions of Christian Arabs (as well as those who are Jewish or Druse). In the United States, the vast majority of the 3 million Arab Americans are Christian. And, in contrast, the majority of America's 8 million Muslims are not Arab. Although Arabs practice different religions, they do share the same language and cul-ture, a culture that is at times in conflict with Western values.[37]

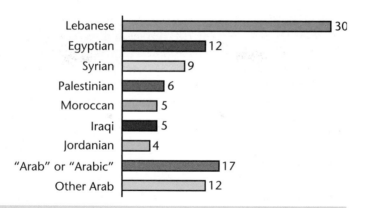

FIGURE 7.2

Arab Americans by Ancestry.

Note: Other Arab (12 percent) includes Yemeni, Kurdish, Algerian, Saudi, Tunisian, Kuwaiti, Libyan, Berber, Emirati (United Arab Emirates), Omani, Bahraini, Alhuceman, Bedouin, Rio de Oro, and the general terms Middle Eastern and North African.

SOURCE: Arab American Institute, "Demographics" 2011, www.aaiusa.org.

REFLECTION: As a teacher, what steps can you take to help your students appreciate the diversity obscured by broad labels such as "Arab American"?

Such differences can create friction, in and beyond school. For example, Arabs enjoy close social proximity, and members of the same sex often walk arm-in-arm or hold hands, behaviors at odds with American practice. Features of the Arabic language, including loudness and intonation, may be perceived in America as too loud and even rude. Whereas punctuality is considered a courtesy in the United States, being late is not considered a sign of disrespect in Arab culture. In addition to these cultural disconnects, more profound differences emerge, such as the disparity between the role of women in Arab society and the role of women in Western society. Many Arab nations cast women in an inferior position, denying them education, inheritance, and power. Saudi Arabia, for example, still prohibits coeducation and requires that women wear veils in public. Arranged marriages and polygamy are practiced in several Arab nations. Whereas the birth of a son is celebrated in conventional Arab families, the birth of a daughter may be met with silence. Yet, change is also sweeping part of the Arab world. Several Arab states have opened schools and the workplace to women, with dramatic results.

Today, students of Arab heritage can be found in all fifty states and, as a group, do well in American schools. The proportion of Arab Americans who attend college is higher than the national average, and Arab Americans earn postgraduate degrees at a rate nearly double the national average. Yet, they still face challenges. They learn from textbooks that have little if anything to say about their history or experiences. American teachers lack basic information about Arab culture, which may present problems. For example, a traditional Arab student may be troubled or confused in an American school where women can be both teachers and principals. In a similar way, an American teacher who criticizes an Arab student in public may have unintentionally erected a wall of hard feelings. Arabs put a lot of emphasis on personal and family honor, and public ridicule is a serious matter.[38]

If an Arab student happens to be of Muslim faith, additional issues emerge. Muslims discover that although schools typically celebrate Christmas, they ignore Muslim holidays. For instance, during Ramadan, Muslims fast for a month during daylight hours, yet few schools recognize this observance, much less make provisions for it. In terms of dietary restrictions, school cafeterias serve, but do not always label, pork products, a food Muslims are prohibited from eating. Clearly, Arab and Muslim American students are all but invisible in the official and hidden curriculum of most American schools. Teacher training, curricular revision, and a greater understanding of these cultural and religious issues are needed if equal educational opportunities are to become a reality for these Americans.

Teaching Tip

ELUSIVE HISTORY

Napoleon said that history is a myth that we agree to believe; Henry Ford thought history was "bunk"; Mark Twain was even more cynical, characterizing the very ink used to write history as "fluid prejudice." History always has a bias because only one side writes it, and more often than not, it is the side of power.

When you teach history, as well as some other subjects, you may want to leave your pre-learned ideas outside the classroom, and start fresh along with your students. Primary sources like original letters, correspondence, eyewitness reports, and print and media accounts will likely offer a more complete and accurate perspective than a single textbook version. (Even this one!)

Let's take the Civil War as an example. Most of us were taught that the Civil War was fought over states' rights, or slavery, or two colliding economic systems. (Which one were you taught?) But in *A People's History of the Civil War* (2005) by David Williams, we learn a very different story, a story of greed and class warfare. Poor southern farmers and northern factory workers were exploited and drafted to fight and often die in a war many opposed. Wealthy southerners and

northerners were protected from the bloodshed by law, but used the war as an opportunity to grow their fortunes. Northern factory owners gladly bought southern cotton to make uniforms, because trading with the enemy to make a profit was fine for both sides. But profits did not mean quality products. In fact, the word "shoddy" comes from the Civil War. Back then, shoddy was a grade of cotton, the lowest quality cotton. When used to make uniforms, the uniforms would quickly disintegrate. It wasn't long before "shoddy" was applied to the poor quality of most things sold to the governments, north and south. This may not be the Civil War history many of us learned, but Williams provides an abundance of primary source documents to support his findings.

REFLECTION: What are the advantages of working with primary sources to help students reach their own insights? What are the downsides of this kind of learning?

Women and Education: A History of Sexism

FOCUS QUESTION 9

What educational barriers and breakthroughs have girls and women experienced?

GLOBAL VIEW

Even in the twenty-first century, the schoolhouse door remains closed to far too many. About 100 million primary-school aged children in developing countries do not attend school. About one-fifth of the world's adult population still cannot read or write. Around the world (including the United States) students who are poor, female, or live in rural areas face an uphill battle for equal educational opportunities.

The peopling of America is a story of voluntary immigration and forced migration. The story of women's struggle for educational opportunity may be just as hard to uncover but equally important to reclaim.

For almost two centuries, girls were barred from America's schools. Although a woman gave the first plot of ground for a free school in New England, female children were not allowed to attend the school. In 1687, the town council of Farmington, Connecticut, voted money for a school "where all children shall learn to read and write English." However, the council quickly qualified that statement by explaining that "all children" meant "all males." In fact, the education of America's girls was so limited that fewer than a third of the women in colonial America could even sign their names.[39] For centuries, women fought to open the schoolhouse door.

In colonial America, secondary schools, called female seminaries, appealed to families financially able to educate their daughters beyond elementary school. **Emma Hart Willard** wrote and disseminated her views on opening higher education to women and won favorable responses from Thomas Jefferson, John Adams, and James Monroe. Eventually, with local support, she opened the Troy Female Seminary, devoted to preparing professional teachers, thus providing a teacher education program years before the first normal (teacher training) school was founded. In Massachusetts, Mary Lyon created Mount Holyoke, a seminary that eventually became a noted women's college. Religious observance was an important part of seminary life in institutions such as Mount Holyoke. Self-denial and strict discipline were considered important elements of molding devout wives and Christian mothers. By the 1850s, with help from Quakers such as Harriet Beecher Stowe, Myrtilla Miner established the Miner Normal School for Colored Girls in the nation's capital, providing new educational opportunities for African American women. While these seminaries sometimes offered superior educations, they were also trapped in a paradox they could never fully resolve: They were educating girls for a world not ready to accept educated women. Seminaries sometimes went to extraordinary lengths to reconcile this conflict. Emma Willard's Troy Female Seminary was devoted to "professionalizing motherhood." (And who could not support motherhood?) But, en route to reshaping motherhood, seminaries reshaped teaching.

For the teaching profession, seminaries became the source of new ideas and new recruits. Seminary leaders, such as Emma Hart Willard and Catherine Beecher, wrote textbooks on how to teach and on how to teach more humanely than was the practice at the time. They denounced corporal punishment and promoted more cooperative educational practices. Because school was seen as an extension of the home and another arena for raising children, seminary graduates were allowed to become teachers—at least, until they decided to marry. More than 80 percent of the graduates of Troy Female Seminary and Mount Holyoke became teachers. Female teachers were particularly attractive to school districts—not just because of their teaching effectiveness but also because they were typically paid one-third to one-half of the salary paid to male teachers.

By the end of the Civil War, a number of colleges and universities, especially tax-supported ones, were desperate for dollars. Institutions of higher learning experienced a serious student shortage because of Civil War casualties, and women became the source of much-needed tuition dollars.

Female funding did not buy on-campus equality. Women often faced separate courses and hostility from male students and professors. At state universities, male students would stamp their feet in protest when a woman entered a classroom.

In *Sex in Education* (1873), Dr. Edward Clarke, a member of Harvard's medical faculty, argued that women attending high school and college were at risk because the blood destined for the development and health of their ovaries would be redirected to their brains. The stress

> Low teacher salaries can be traced back to the late nineteenth century, when communities found that they could hire capable women teachers for approximately 60 percent of what men teachers were paid.

of study was no laughing matter. Too much education would leave women with "monstrous brains and puny bodies . . . flowing thought and constipated bowels." Clarke recommended that females be provided with a less demanding education, easier courses, no competition, and "rest" periods so that their reproductive organs could develop. He maintained that allowing girls to attend such places as Harvard would pose a serious health threat to the women themselves, with sterility and hysteria potential outcomes.

M. Carey Thomas, future president of Bryn Mawr and one of the first women to earn a PhD in the United States, wrote in her diary about the profound fears she experienced as she was studying: "I remember often praying about it, and begging God that if it were true that because I was a girl, I could not successfully master Greek and go to college, and understand things, to kill me for it."[40] In 1895, the faculty of the University of Virginia concluded

that "women were often physically unsexed by the strains of study." Parents, fearing for the health of their daughters, often placed them in less-demanding programs reserved for females, or kept them out of advanced education entirely. Even today, the echoes of Clarke's warning resonate, as some people still see well-educated women as less attractive, view advanced education as "too stressful" for females, or believe that education is more important for males than for females.

In the twentieth century, women won greater access to educational programs at all levels, although gender-segregated programs were the rule well into the 1970s. Even when females attended the same schools as males, they often received a less valuable education. Commercial courses prepared girls to become secretaries, and vocational programs channeled them into cosmetology and other low-paying occupations. After World War II, it was not unusual for a university to require a married woman to submit a letter from her husband, granting her permission to enroll in courses, before she would be admitted. By the 1970s, with the passage of Title IX of the Education Amendments of 1972, females saw significant progress toward gaining access to educational programs, but not equality. The opening section of Title IX states

> No person in the United States shall, on the basis of sex, be excluded from participation in, be denied the benefits of, or be subjected to discrimination under any education program or activity receiving federal financial assistance.

The law is straightforward, but misperceptions are common. For example, many equate Title IX only with athletics; yet, the law prohibits gender discrimination in admissions, treatment of students, counseling, financial aid, employment, and health benefits, to name but a few. Nor is Title IX only about females; males are protected from gender discrimination as well. Ignorance of the law is widespread, one reason it is so rarely enforced. In fact, in almost four decades since Title IX became law, no school has ever been financially penalized by the federal government for violating Title IX.[41]

Unfortunately, sexism still thrives in today's classrooms, affecting attitudes and careers. Nursing, teaching, library science, and social work continue to be predominantly female while engineering, physics, and computer science are male domains. Even in medicine and law, where women have made progress, they find themselves channeled into the least prestigious, least profitable specialties.[42] A "glass wall" still divides the sexes, and some call for the glass wall to become permanent, believing that males and females are so different that the nation should return to single-sex schools, an idea that was popular in colonial America, bringing us full circle in this chapter.

At the beginning of the chapter, we peeked into Christopher Lamb's colonial classroom to watch our school traditions take root. Unfortunately, one such tradition was that education was reserved for some and denied to others. We still struggle to create fair schools. In a sense, today's teachers stand on the shoulders of Christopher Lamb and other educators as each generation makes its own contribution to creating fairer, more effective schools. We have chosen to conclude this chapter with a Hall of Fame, a small tribute to those whose shoulders we stand on.

www.mhhe.com/sadker10e

INTERACTIVE ACTIVITY

When Did That Happen?
Place important educational events on a timeline to test your knowledge.

Hall of Fame: Profiles in Education

FOCUS QUESTION 10
Who are some influential educators who helped fashion today's schools?

A "hall of fame" recognizes individuals for significant contributions to a field. Football, baseball, rock and roll, and country music all have halls of fame to recognize outstanding individuals. We think education is no less important and merits its own forum for recognition. In fact, Emporia State University in Kansas houses a Teachers' Hall of Fame. Following are the nominations we would offer to honor educators who we believe should be in a hall of fame.

A Closer Look Education Milestones

SEVENTEENTH CENTURY

Informal family education, apprenticeships, dame schools, tutors

1635	Boston Latin Grammar School
1636	Harvard College
1647	Old Deluder Satan Law
1687–1890	*New England Primer* published

EIGHTEENTH CENTURY

Development of a national interest in education, state responsibility for education, growth in secondary education

1740	South Carolina denies education to blacks.
1751	Opening of the Franklin Academy in Philadelphia
1783	Noah Webster's *American Spelling Book*
1785, 1787	Land Ordinance Act, Northwest Ordinance

NINETEENTH CENTURY

Increasing role of public secondary schools, increased but segregated education for women and minorities, attention to the field of education and teacher preparation

1821	Emma Willard's Troy Female Seminary opens, first endowed secondary school for girls.
1821	First public high school opens in Boston.
1823	First (private) normal school opens in Vermont.
1827	Massachusetts requires public high schools.
1837	Horace Mann becomes secretary of board of education in Massachusetts.
1839	First public normal school in Lexington, Massachusetts
1855	First kindergarten (German language) in United States
1862	Morrill Land Grant College Act
1874	Kalamazoo case (legalizes taxes for high schools)
1896	*Plessy* v. *Ferguson* Supreme Court decision supporting racially separate but equal schools

TWENTIETH CENTURY

Increasing federal support for educational rights of under-achieving students; increased federal funding of specific (categorical) education programs

1909	First junior high school in Columbus, Ohio
1919	Progressive education programs
1932	New Deal education programs
1944	G.I. Bill of Rights
1950	First middle school in Bay City, Michigan
1954	*Brown* v. *Board of Education of Topeka* Supreme Court decision outlawing racial segregation in schools
1957	*Sputnik* leads to increased federal education funds.
1958	National Defense Education Act funds science, math, and foreign language programs.
1964–1965	Job Corps and Head Start are funded.
1972	Title IX prohibits sex discrimination in schools.
1975	Public Law 94-142, Education for All Handicapped Children Act (renamed Individuals with Disabilities Education Act, 1991), is passed.
1979	Cabinet-level Department of Education is established.
1990–present	Increased public school diversity and competition through charter schools, for-profit companies, open enrollment, and technological options. Promotion of educational goals, standards and testing.

TWENTY-FIRST CENTURY

Increasing focus on standards, testing, and accountability

2001	Passage of No Child Left Behind Act.
2011-present	Federal government modifies NCLB, allowing states greater freedom in evaluating students and teachers.

SOURCE: Joel Spring, *American Education,* 15th ed. (New York: McGraw-Hill, 2011).

REFLECTION: What milestones do you believe may occur in the years ahead?

Obviously, not all influential educators have been included in these brief profiles, but it is important to begin recognizing significant educational contributions. Indirectly or directly, these individuals have influenced your life as a student and will influence your career as a teacher.

For establishing the kindergarten as an integral part of a child's education—

Friedrich Froebel (1782–1852). Froebel frequently reflected on his own childhood. Froebel's mother died when he was only 9 months old. In his recollections, he developed a deep sense of the importance of early childhood and of the critical role played by teachers of the young. Although he worked as a forester, chemist's assistant, and museum curator, he eventually found his true vocation as an educator. He attended Pestalozzi's institute and extended Pestalozzi's ideas. He saw nature as a prime source of learning and believed that schools should provide a warm and supportive environment for children.

In 1837, Froebel founded the first **kindergarten** ("child's garden") to "cultivate" the child's development and socialization. Games provided cooperative activities for socialization and physical development, and such materials as sand and clay were used to stimulate the child's imagination. Like Pestalozzi, Froebel believed in the importance of establishing an emotionally secure environment for children. Going beyond Pestalozzi, Froebel saw the teacher as a moral and cultural model for children, a model worthy of emulation. (How different from the earlier view of the teacher as disciplinarian.)

In the nineteenth century, as German immigrants came to the United States, they brought with them the idea of kindergarten education. Margaretta Schurz established a German-language kindergarten in Wisconsin in 1855. The first English-language kindergarten and training school for kindergarten teachers were begun in Boston in 1860 by Elizabeth Peabody.

For her integrity and bravery in bringing education to African American girls—

Prudence Crandall (1803–1889). Born of Quaker parents, Prudence Crandall received her education at a school in Providence, Rhode Island, founded by an active abolitionist, Moses Brown. Her upbringing within Quaker circles, in which discussions of abolition were common, may have inspired her interest in racial equality, an interest that led her to acts of personal courage as she strove to promote education among people of all colors.

After graduating from the Brown Seminary about 1830, Crandall taught briefly in Plainfield, Connecticut, before founding her own school for girls in the neighboring town of Canterbury. However, her decision to admit a black girl, Sarah Harris, daughter of a neighboring farmer, caused outrage. Although African Americans in Connecticut were free, a large segment of the white population within Canterbury supported the efforts of the American Colonization Society to deport all freed blacks to Africa, believing them to be inherently inferior. Many were adamant that anything but the most basic education for African Americans would lead to discontent and might encourage interracial marriage. The townspeople voiced fears that Crandall's school would lead to the devaluation of local property by attracting a large number of blacks to the area. Prudence Crandall was pressured by the local population to expel Sarah Harris. However, she was determined to defy their wishes. When the wife of a prominent local clergyman suggested that if Harris remained, the school "could not be sustained," Crandall replied, "Then it might sink then, for I should not turn her out."

When other parents withdrew their children, Crandall advertised for pupils in *The Liberator*, the newspaper of abolitionist William Lloyd Garrison. A month later, the school reopened with a student body comprising fifteen black girls. However, the townspeople made life difficult for Crandall and her students. Supplies were hard to obtain, and Crandall and her pupils faced verbal harassment, as well as being pelted with chicken heads, manure, and other objects. Nonetheless, they persisted.

In 1833, only one month after Crandall had opened her doors to African American girls, the Connecticut legislature passed the notorious "Black Law." This law forbade the founding of schools for the education of African Americans from other states without the permission of local authorities. Crandall was arrested and tried. At her trial, her counsel advised the jury, "You may find that she has violated an act of the State Legislature, but if you also find her protected by higher power, it will be your duty to acquit." Her conviction was later overturned on appeal, but vandalism and arson continued. When a gang stormed the school building with clubs and iron bars, smashing windows and rendering the downstairs area uninhabitable, the school finally was forced to close.

Prudence Crandall's interest in education, racial equality, and women's rights continued throughout her life. Several of her students continued her work, including her first African American student, Sarah Harris, who taught black pupils in Louisiana for many years.

For her work in identifying the educational potential of young children and crafting an environment in which the young could learn—

Maria Montessori (1870–1952). Montessori was no follower of tradition, in her private life or in her professional activities. Shattering sex-role stereotypes, she attended a technical school and then a medical school, becoming the first female physician in Italy. Her work brought her in contact with children regarded as mentally handicapped and brain damaged, but her educational activities with these children indicated that they were far more capable than many believed. By 1908, Montessori had established a children's school called the Casa dei Bambini, designed to provide an education for disadvantaged children from the slums of Rome.

Montessori's view of children differed from the views held by her contemporaries. Her observations led her to conclude that children have an inner need to work at tasks that interest them. Given the right materials and tasks, children need not be rewarded and punished by the teacher. In fact, she believed that children prefer work to play and are capable of sustained periods of concentration. Young children need a carefully prepared environment in order to learn.

Montessori's curriculum reflected this specially prepared environment. Children learned practical skills, including setting a table, washing dishes, buttoning clothing, and displaying basic manners. They learned formal skills, such as reading, writing, and arithmetic. Special materials included movable sandpaper letters to teach the alphabet and colored rods to teach counting. The children developed motor skills as well as intellectual skills in a carefully developed sequence. Montessori worked with each student individually, rather than with the class as a whole, to accomplish these goals.

The impact of Montessori's methods continues to this day. Throughout the United States, early childhood education programs use Montessori-like materials. A number of early childhood institutions are called *Montessori schools* and adhere to the approach she developed almost a century ago. Although originally intended for disadvantaged students, Montessori's concept of carefully preparing an environment and program to teach the very young is used today with children from all social classes.

For her contributions in moving a people from intellectual slavery to education—

Mary McLeod Bethune (1875–1955). The first child of her family not born in slavery, Bethune rose from a field hand, picking cotton, to an unofficial presidential adviser. The last of seventeen children born to South Carolina sharecroppers, she filled the breaks in her fieldwork with reading and studying. She was committed to meeting the critical need of providing education to the newly freed African Americans, and when a Colorado seamstress offered to pay the cost of educating one black girl at Scotia Seminary in Concord, New Hampshire, she was selected. Bethune's plans to become an African missionary changed as she became more deeply involved in the need to educate newly liberated American blacks.

With $1.50, five students, and a rented cottage near the Daytona Beach city dump in Florida, Bethune founded a school that eventually became Bethune-Cookman College. As a national leader, she created a number of black civic and welfare organizations, serving as a member of the Hoover Commission on Child Welfare, and acting as an adviser to President Franklin D. Roosevelt.

Mary McLeod Bethune demonstrated commitment and effort in establishing a black college against overwhelming odds and by rising from poverty to become a national voice for African Americans.

For her creative approaches placing children at the center of the curriculum—

Sylvia Ashton-Warner (1908–1984). Sylvia Ashton-Warner began her school career in her mother's New Zealand classroom, where rote memorization constituted the main avenue for learning. The teaching strategies that Ashton-Warner later devised, with their emphasis on child-centered learning and creativity in the classroom, stand in opposition to this early experience.

Ashton-Warner was a flamboyant and eccentric personality; throughout her life, she considered herself to be an artist rather than a teacher. She focused on painting, music, and writing. Her fascination with creativity was apparent in the remote New Zealand classrooms, where she encouraged self-expression among the native Maori children. As a teacher, she infuriated authorities with her absenteeism and unpredictability, and in official ratings she was never estimated as above average in her abilities. However, during the peak years of her teaching career, between 1950 and 1952, she developed innovative teaching techniques that influenced teachers around the world and especially in the United States.

Realizing that certain words were especially significant to individual pupils because of their life experiences, Ashton-Warner developed her "key vocabulary" system for teaching reading to young children. Words drawn from children's conversations were written on cards. Using these words, children learned to read. Ashton-Warner asserted that the key to making this approach effective lay in choosing words that had personal meaning to the individual child: "Pleasant words won't do. Respectable words won't do. They must be words organically tied up, organically born from the dynamic life itself. They must be words that are already part of the child's being."

Bringing meaning to children was at the center of Ashton-Warner's philosophy. This belief provided the foundation of several reading approaches and teaching strategies used throughout the United States. Her work brought meaning to reading for millions of children. In her best-selling book, *Teacher,* she provided many future teachers with important and useful insights. Her emphasis on key vocabulary, individualized reading, and meaningful learning is evident in classrooms today in America and abroad.

For his work in identifying the crippling effects of racism on all American children and in formulating community action to overcome the educational, psychological, and economic impacts of racism—

Kenneth Clark (1914–2005). Kenneth Clark attended schools in Harlem, where he witnessed an integrated community become all black and felt the growing impact of racism. He attended Howard University, was the first African American to receive a doctorate in psychology from Columbia University, and in 1960 became the first black to be tenured at City College of New York. His concern with the educational plight of African Americans generally, and the Harlem community in particular, was always central in his professional efforts.

Beginning in the 1930s, Clark and his wife, Mamie Phipps Clark, assessed black children's self-perceptions. They bought black dolls for 50 cents each at a store in Harlem, one of the few places where black dolls could be purchased. They showed black and white children two white dolls and two black dolls, and asked the children to pick out the "nice" doll, the "pretty" doll, and the "bad" doll. Both groups tended to pick the white dolls as nice and pretty, and the black doll as bad. He repeated the study in the 1950s in South Carolina, where white students received far more funds for education than black children. The results were similar. He concluded that the lesson of black inferiority was so deep in society that even young black children understood it and believed it. As Clark noted, "A racist system inevitably destroys and damages human beings; it brutalizes and dehumanizes blacks and whites alike." In *Brown* v. *the Topeka Board of Education* (1954), the Supreme Court cited Clark's "doll" study in deciding that "separate was inherently unequal."

For his global effort to mobilize education in the cause of social justice—

Paulo Freire (1921–1997). Abandoning a career in the law, Brazilian-born Freire committed himself to the education of the poor and politically oppressed. His efforts moved literacy from an educational tool to a political instrument.

Freire denounced teacher-centered classrooms. He believed that instructor domination denied the legitimacy of student experiences and treated students as secondary objects in the learning process. Freire championed a *critical pedagogy,* one that places the student at the center of the learning process. In Freire's pedagogy, student dialogues, knowledge, and skills are shared cooperatively, legitimizing their experiences. Students are taught how to generate their own questions, focus on their own social problems, and develop strategies to live more fruitful and satisfying lives. Teachers are not passive bystanders or the only source of classroom wisdom. Freire believed that teachers should facilitate and inspire, that teachers should "live part of their dreams within their educational space." Rather than unhappy witnesses to social injustice, teachers should be advocates for the poor and agents for social change. Freire's best-known work, ***Pedagogy of the Oppressed,*** illustrated how education could transform society.

www.mhhe.com/sadker10e
INTERACTIVE ACTIVITY
Who Am I? Using hints, determine the identity of famous educational figures.

Freire's approach obviously threatened the social order of many repressive governments, and he faced constant intimidation and threats. Following the military overthrow of the Brazilian government in 1964, Freire was jailed for "subversive" activities and later exiled. In the late 1960s, while studying in America, Freire witnessed racial unrest and the antiwar protests. These events convinced Freire that political oppression is present in "developed nations" as well as third world countries, that economic privilege does not guarantee political advantage, and that the pedagogy of the oppressed has worldwide significance.

We invite you to read about some additional hall of famers in the Profiles in Education section in Chapter 7 on the Online Learning Center.

Comenius (1592–1670), profiled for his pioneering work in identifying developmental stages of learning and his support of universal education.

Jean-Jacques Rousseau (1712–1778), profiled for his work in distinguishing schooling from education and for his concern with the stages of development.

Johann Heinrich Pestalozzi (1746–1827), profiled for his recognition of the special needs of the disadvantaged and his work in curricular development.

Johann Herbart (1776–1841), profiled for his contributions to moral development in education and for his creation of a structured methodology of instruction.

Emma Hart Willard (1787–1870), profiled for opening the door of higher education to women and for promoting professional teacher preparation.

Horace Mann (1796–1859), profiled for establishing free public schools and expanding the opportunities of poor as well as wealthy Americans, and for his vision of the central role of education in improving the quality of American life.

Booker T. Washington (1856-1915), profiled for his contributions to the vocational education of black Americans and for establishing Tuskegee University.

John Dewey (1859–1952), profiled for his work in developing progressive education, for incorporating democratic practices in the educational process.

W. E. B. DuBois (1868–1963), profiled for cofounding the National Association for the Advancement of Colored People (NAACP) and for his efforts to encourage black Americans to pursue higher education.

Jean Piaget (1896–1980), profiled for his creation of a theory of cognitive development.

Burrhus Frederick (B. F.) Skinner (1904–1990), profiled for his contributions in altering environments to promote learning.

ONLINE VIDEO ALBUM TO ACCOMPANY *TEACHERS, SCHOOLS, AND SOCIETY, 10E*

Visit the Online Learning Center for a range of contemporary videos with content related to this chapter.

www.mhhe.com/sadker10e

THE *TEACHERS, SCHOOLS, AND SOCIETY* READER WITH CLASSROOM OBSERVATION VIDEO CLIPS

Go to your *Teachers, Schools, and Society* Reader CD-ROM to:

READ CURRENT AND HISTORICAL ARTICLES

30. **My Pedagogic Creed,** by John Dewey, *School Journal,* January 1897.

31. Text excerpts from ***Narrative of the Life of Frederick Douglass: An American Slave,*** by Frederick Douglass, 1845.

32. Text excerpts from ***The Education of Free Men,*** by Horace Mann, 1846.

33. **Reviving the Goal of An Integrated Society: A 21st Century Challenge,** by Gary Orfield, *The Civil Rights Project,* January 14, 2009.

ANALYZE CASE STUDIES

13. **Hamilton High:** From the 1950s through the 1980s, this case presents how a school has changed in reaction to societal and educational changes.

OBSERVE TEACHERS, STUDENTS, AND CLASSROOMS IN ACTION

12. Classroom Observation: Progressivism in Action: A Classroom Lesson

John Dewey believed in learning by doing, one of the keystones of progressive education. In this observation, you will observe students in an American civics class learning about the law by role-playing different legal cases. In this instance, the students are arguing the Pledge of Allegiance case.

KEY TERMS AND PEOPLE

KEY TERMS

academy, 214

American Spelling Book, 215

A Nation at Risk, 221

Brown v. Board of Education of Topeka, 226

common school, 215

dame schools, 211

de facto segregation, 226

de jure segregation, 226

elementary school, 215

English Classical School, 219

gendered career, 218

hornbook, 215

in loco parentis, 212

Kalamazoo, Michigan, case, 219

kindergarten, 238

Land Ordinance Act, 224

Latin grammar school, 212

McGuffey Readers, 215

National Defense Education Act (NDEA), 223

New England Primer, 215

normal schools, 216

Northwest Ordinance, 224

Old Deluder Satan Law, 212

Pedagogy of the Oppressed, 241

Plessy v. *Ferguson,* 225

progressive education, 222

second-generation segregation, 226

separate but equal, 225

Tenth Amendment, 223

www.mhhe.com/sadker10e

CHAPTER REVIEW

Go to the Online Learning Center to take a quiz, practice with key terms, and review concepts from the chapter.

KEY PEOPLE

Ashton-Warner, Sylvia, 240

McLeod Bethune, Mary, 239

Clark, Kenneth, 240

Comenius, 241

Crandall, Prudence, 238

Dewey, John, 222, 242

DuBois, W. E. B., 242

Franklin, Benjamin, 214

Freire, Paulo, 241

Jefferson, Thomas, 214

Mann, Horace, 215, 242

Froebel, Friedrich, 238

Herbart, Johann, 242

Montessori, Maria, 239

Pestalozzi, Johann Heinrich, 241

Piaget, Jean, 242

Rousseau, Jean-Jacques, 241

Skinner, Burrhus Frederick (B. F.), 242

Washington, Booker T., 242

Willard. Emma Hart, 234, 242

DISCUSSION QUESTIONS AND ACTIVITIES

1. In the colonial period, a number of factors influenced the kind of education you might receive. Describe how the following factors influenced educational opportunities:

   - Geography
   - Wealth
   - Race/ethnicity
   - Gender

2. Progressive education has sparked adamant critics and fervent supporters. Offer several arguments supporting the tenets of progressivism, as well as arguments against this movement.

3. In what ways are terms such as African Americans, Asian Americans, Hispanic Americans, or Arab Americans helpful? In what ways are these labels misleading?

4. Identify the contributions made by the following educators, whom some might consider candidates for the Hall of Fame: Septima Poinsette Clark, Madeline C. Hunter, Johnetta Cole, and Henri Mann.

5. Some teacher preparation programs do not consider or discuss the history of education, whereas other programs devote courses reviewing and analyzing educational history. Set up a debate arguing the pros and cons of the following proposition. Resolved: Teacher preparation programs should focus on current issues and not consider the history of education.

Philosophy of Education

CHAPTER 8

FOCUS QUESTIONS

1. What is a philosophy of education, and why should it be important to you?
2. How do teacher-centered philosophies of education differ from student-centered philosophies of education?
3. What are some major philosophies of education in the United States today?
4. How are these philosophies reflected in school practices?
5. What are some of the psychological and cultural factors influencing education?
6. What were the contributions of Socrates, Plato, and Aristotle to Western philosophy, and how are their legacies reflected in education today?
7. How do metaphysics, epistemology, ethics, political philosophy, aesthetics, and logic factor into a philosophy of education?

> *The paradox of education is precisely this: that as one begins to become conscious one begins to examine the society in which he is being educated.*
>
> –JAMES BALDWIN

CHAPTER PREVIEW

The root for the word **philosophy** is made up of two Greek words: *philo,* meaning "love," and *sophos,* meaning "wisdom." For thousands of years, philosophers have been wrestling with fundamental questions: What is most real—the physical world or the realm of mind and spirit? What is the basis of human knowledge? What is the nature of the just society? Educators must take stances on such questions before they can determine what and how students should be taught.

Because educators do not always agree on the answers to these questions, different philosophies of education have emerged. Although there are some similarities, there are also profound differences in the way leading educators define the purpose of education, the role of the teacher, the nature of the curriculum and assessment, and the method of instruction.

This chapter is intended to start you on a path of thoughtfully considering your values and beliefs. Five influential philosophies will be described, and you will see how each can shape classroom life. We invite you to consider how psychological and cultural beliefs can also affect schools. We then revisit the roots of Western philosophy with three ancient Greeks as our guides: Socrates, Plato, and Aristotle. Finally, we briefly examine the building blocks of philosophy, the divisions within philosophy that focus on questions pertinent to educators: What is of worth? How do we know what we know? The ideas in this chapter will spark some very basic questions about your role in the classroom, and the school's role in society. Your answers to these questions will help you frame your philosophy of education.

www.mhhe.com/sadker10e

WHAT DO YOU THINK? What is your philosophy of education? Take an electronic version of the quiz on pages 247–249. Then, submit your responses to see how they compare with those of your colleagues.

Finding Your Philosophy of Education

What is a philosophy of education? Do you have one? Do you think it matters? If you are like most people, you probably have not given much thought to philosophy, in education or elsewhere. Being a practical person, you may be more concerned with other questions: Will I enjoy teaching? Will I be good at it? How will I handle discipline problems? Believe it or not, underlying the answers to those practical questions *is* your philosophy of education.

FOCUS QUESTION 1

What is a philosophy of education, and why should it be important to you?

At this point, your philosophy may still be taking shape (not a bad thing). Your beliefs may reflect an amalgam of different philosophies. Unfortunately, they may also be filled with inconsistencies. To help shape a coherent and useful educational philosophy, you must consider some basic—and very important—questions, such as:

What is the purpose of education?

What content and skills should schools teach?

How should schools teach this content?

What are the proper roles for teachers and students?

How should learning be measured?

Still not sure what a philosophy of education is all about, or how it shapes classroom and school life? Let's listen to some teachers discussing the direction a new charter school should take. You'll see that each teacher has very clear ideas about what schools are for, what students should learn, and how teachers should teach.

Hear that noise coming from the faculty room down the hall? Your potential colleagues sometimes get a bit loud as they debate the possible directions for the new charter school. As you listen in, try to sort out which of these educational directions appeals to you.

JACOB POLLACK: I am so excited! This new charter school can be just what we need, a chance to reestablish a positive reputation for the quality of public education! Let's face it, we are competing in a global economy, against nations whose students outscore ours on all the standardized tests that matter. It's embarrassing. I'd love to see a school with a strict code of conduct and core courses, like literature, history, math, and science, and no silly electives. It's all about rigorous standards.

MYRA MILLER: Jacob, you and I both would like to teach in a more rigorous school, but the truth is I'm fed up with testing. I'll tell you a secret: I don't much care whether South Korean kids or those at Country Day School score better than us on a multiple-choice test. Kids thirst for meaningful ideas. The school I envision would focus on classic works of literature and art. How about a school where we discuss Great Books like *Moby Dick, The Old Man and the Sea,* Plato's *Republic,* and Homer's *Iliad.* Maybe we can re-invent the all-but-extinct American student: One who knows not only how to read, but a student who actually *wants* to read, *enjoys* reading, and best of all, knows how to *think.*

MARCUS WASHINGTON: I agree with Myra that we need to move beyond today's tyranny of testing, but Hemingway and Homer are not the answers. Our job as teachers is to make certain that our students can do well in the real world. When I was in eighth grade, my class took a three-week trip around the Midwestern states by train. We researched and planned where to go; figured out how to read train schedules; used maps; and ended up learning math, history, geography, and writing. Talk about an integrated curriculum! We learned by doing. I want students to learn how to solve real-world problems, not just answer test questions or discuss books.

TED GOODHEART: At last, reality! But there are more pressing issues than a train trip. I want students to do more than simply fit into society; I want them to leave the world a better place than they found it. Behind our community's pretty façade are people in pain. Rather than insulate them from real-world concerns like poverty, violence, pollution, bigotry, and injustice, we should help our kids develop a social conscience and the political skills needed to improve our society. Teaching in a socially responsible charter school would be my dream.

CARA CAMUS: Everyone in this room has been trying to design a charter school backwards. Let's set aside what we as teachers want and consider a revolutionary idea: building a school based on what students want. Students must assume primary responsibility for their own learning. I would like our charter school staffed by teachers who are skilled in facilitating children to reach their personal goals. Believe it or not, I trust students, and I would give every child (even the youngest or least able) an equal voice in decision making. We have forgotten the purpose of schools: to help students find their way.

These teachers are not only discussing different approaches to a proposed charter school, but are also shedding light on five major educational philosophies. Do any of these diverse views sound attractive to you? Do any sound particularly unappealing? If so, note which of these teachers you thought reflected your own beliefs, and which were really off the mark. If you found that you had strong opinions—pro or con—about one or more of these ideas, then you are beginning to get in touch with your educational philosophy. Let's leave the faculty-room conversation and take a closer look at your own philosophical leanings. The following inventory can help you sort out tenets of your educational philosophy.

Inventory of Philosophies of Education

As you read through the following statements about schools and teaching, decide how strongly you agree or disagree. We will help you interpret your results. Write your response to the left of each statement, using the following scale:

5   Agree strongly

4   Agree

3   Neither agree nor disagree

2   Disagree

1   Disagree strongly

_____   1.   A school curriculum should include a common body of information that all students should know.

_____   2.   The school curriculum should focus on the great ideas that have survived through time.

_____   3.   The gap between the real world and schools should be bridged through field trips, internships, and adult mentors.

_____   4.   Schools should prepare students for analyzing and solving the social problems they will face beyond the classroom.

_____   5.   Each student should determine his or her individual curriculum, and teachers should guide and help them.

_____ 6. Students should not be promoted from one grade to the next until they have read and mastered certain key material.

_____ 7. Schools, above all, should develop students' abilities to think deeply, analytically, and creatively, rather than focus on transient concerns like social skills and current trends.

_____ 8. Whether inside or outside the classroom, teachers must stress the relevance of what students are learning to real and current events.

_____ 9. Education should enable students to recognize injustices in society, and schools should promote projects to redress social inequities.

_____ 10. Students who do not want to study much should not be required to do so.

_____ 11. Teachers and schools should emphasize academic rigor, discipline, hard work, and respect for authority.

_____ 12. Education is not primarily about workers and the world economic competition; learning should be appreciated for its own sake, and students should enjoy reading, learning, and discussing intriguing ideas.

_____ 13. The school curriculum should be designed by teachers to respond to the experiences and needs of the students.

_____ 14. Schools should promote positive group relationships by teaching about different ethnic and racial groups.

_____ 15. The purpose of school is to help students understand themselves, appreciate their distinctive talents and insights, and find their own unique place in the world.

_____ 16. For the United States to be competitive economically in the world marketplace, schools must bolster their academic requirements to train more competent workers.

_____ 17. Teachers ought to teach from the classics, because important insights related to many of today's challenges and concerns are found in these Great Books.

_____ 18. Students learn effectively through social interaction, so schools should plan for substantial social interaction in their curricula.

_____ 19. Students should be taught how to be politically literate, and learn how to improve the quality of life for all people.

_____ 20. The central role of the school is to provide students with options and choices. The student must decide what and how to learn.

_____ 21. Schools must provide students with a firm grasp of basic facts regarding the books, people, and events that have shaped the nation's heritage.

_____ 22. The teacher's main goal is to help students unlock the insights learned over time, so they can gain wisdom from the great thinkers of the past.

_____ 23. Students should be active participants in the learning process, involved in democratic class decision making and reflective thinking.

_____ 24. Teaching should mean more than simply transmitting the Great Books, which are replete with biases and prejudices. Rather, schools need to identify a new list of Great Books more appropriate for today's world, and prepare students to create a better society than their ancestors did.

_____ 25. Effective teachers help students to discover and develop their personal values, even when those values conflict with traditional ones.

_____ 26. Teachers should help students constantly reexamine their beliefs. In history, for example, students should learn about those who have been historically omitted: the poor, the non-European, women, and people of color.

_____ 27. Frequent objective testing is the best way to determine what students know. Rewarding students when they learn, even when they learn small things, is the key to successful teaching.

_____ 28. Education should be a responsibility of the family and the community, rather than delegated to formal and impersonal institutions, such as schools.

Interpreting Your Responses

Write your responses to statements 1 through 25 in the columns provided here; then tally up your score in each column. (We will return to items 26 to 28 in a bit.) Each column is labeled with a philosophy and the name of the teacher who represented that view in this chapter's opening scenario (the charter school discussion). The highest possible score in any one column is 25, and the lowest possible score is 5. Scores in the 20s indicate strong agreement, and scores below 10 indicate disagreement with the tenets of a particular philosophy.

A Essentialism (Jacob)	B Perennialism (Myra)	C Progressivism (Marcus)	D Social Reconstructionism (Ted)	E Existentialism (Cara)
1. ___	2. ___	3. ___	4. ___	5. ___
6. ___	7. ___	8. ___	9. ___	10. ___
11. ___	12. ___	13. ___	14. ___	15. ___
16. ___	17. ___	18. ___	19. ___	20. ___
21. ___	22. ___	23. ___	24. ___	25. ___
Scores ___	___	___	___	___

Your scores in columns A through E, respectively, represent how much you agree or disagree with the beliefs of five major educational philosophies: essentialism, perennialism, progressivism, social reconstructionism, and existentialism. Check back to see if your scores reflect your initial reactions to these teachers' points of view. For example, if you agreed with Jacob's proposal to create an "Academy," then you probably agreed with a number of the statements associated with essentialist education, and your score in this column may be fairly high.

www.mhhe.com/sadker10e

INTERACTIVE ACTIVITY
Where Do You Stand on
the Philosophy Spectrum?
Note where you think your
philosophy of education
falls, and compare with
your colleagues.

Compare your five scores. What is your highest? What is your lowest? Which three statements best reflect your views on education? Are they congruent and mutually supporting? As you look at the statements that you least support, what do those statements tell you about your values? You may notice that your philosophical leanings, as identified by your responses to statements in the inventory, reflect your general outlook on life. For example, your responses may indicate whether you generally trust people to do the right thing, or if you believe that individuals need supervision. How have your culture, religion, upbringing, and political beliefs shaped your responses to the items in this inventory? How have your own education and life experiences influenced your philosophical beliefs?

Now that you have begun to examine varying beliefs about education, you may even want to lay claim to a philosophical label. But what do these philosophical labels mean? In the following pages we will introduce you to all five of these educational philosophies and look at their impact in the classroom.

Five Philosophies of Education

Essentialism, perennialism, progressivism, social reconstructionism, and existentialism. Taken together, these five schools of thought do not exhaust the list of possible educational philosophies you may consider, but they present strong frameworks for you to refine your own educational philosophy. We can place these five philosophies on a continuum, from teacher-centered (some would say "authoritarian") to student-centered (some would characterize as "permissive").

Let's begin our discussion with the teacher-centered philosophies.

Teacher-Centered Philosophies

FOCUS QUESTIONS 2–4

How do teacher-centered philosophies of education differ from student-centered philosophies of education?

What are some major philosophies of education in the United States today?

How are these philosophies reflected in school practices?

Traditionally, *teacher-centered philosophies* emphasize the importance of transferring knowledge, information, and skills from the older (presumably wiser) generation to the younger one. The teacher's role is to instill respect for authority, perseverance, duty, consideration, and practicality. When students demonstrate through tests and writings that they are competent in academic subjects and traditional skills, and through their actions that they have disciplined minds and adhere to traditional morals and behavior, then both the school and the teacher have been successful. (If you recall from Chapter 5, these philosophies view the primary purpose of schools as "passing the cultural baton.") The major teacher-centered philosophies of education are essentialism and perennialism.

Essentialism

Essentialism strives to teach students the accumulated knowledge of our civilization through core courses in the traditional academic disciplines. Essentialists aim to instill students with the "essentials" of academic knowledge, patriotism, and character development. This traditional or **back-to-basics** approach is meant to train the mind, promote reasoning, and ensure a common culture among all Americans.

American educator **William Bagley** popularized the term *essentialism* in the 1930s,[1] and essentialism has been a dominant influence in American education since World War II. Factors such as the launching of *Sputnik* in 1957, the 1983 report *A Nation at Risk,* standardized testing mandated by *No Child Left Behind,* intense global economic competition, and increased immigration into the United States have all kept essentialism at center stage. Some educators refer to the present period as neoessentialism because of the increased core graduation requirements, stronger standards and more testing of both students and teachers.

Not all essentialists are the same. Author Allan Bloom, *The Closing of the American Mind,* contends that immigration and multiculturalism threaten the traditional "American" identity. He advocates for a time-honored, Anglo-Saxon curriculum reflecting European traditions. On the other hand, **E. D. Hirsch Jr.** advocates for a more inclusive curriculum that offers all students a shared knowledge, a common cur-

The current emphasis on pen-and-paper testing is an example of essentialism in action.

riculum (not unlike Horace Mann's idea of a common school). Hirsch wrote *Cultural Literacy: What Every American Needs to Know* and *The Knowledge Deficit,* and he suggests facts and ideas that might be included in his curriculum. Although people refer to his work by the popular title of his book, cultural literacy, he prefers to call it "core knowledge," a knowledge that would be shared by all Americans.[2] (See Chapter 6 for an in-depth discussion on the works of Bloom and Hirsch.)

Most of you reading this chapter have been educated in essentialist schools. You were probably required to take many courses in English, history, math, and science. Such a program would be typical in an essentialist school.

The Essentialist Classroom Essentialists urge that traditional disciplines such as math, science, history, foreign language, and literature form the foundation of the curriculum, which is referred to as the **core curriculum.** Essentialists frown upon electives that "water-down" academic content. Elementary students receive instruction in skills such as writing, reading, measuring, and computing. Even when studying art and music, subjects most often associated with the development of creativity, students master a body of information and basic techniques, gradually moving to more complex skills and detailed knowledge. Only by mastering the required material are students promoted to the next higher level.

Essentialists maintain that classrooms should be oriented toward the teacher, who should serve as an intellectual and moral role model for the students. The teachers or administrators decide what is most important for the students to learn and place little emphasis on student interests, particularly when such interests divert time and attention from the academic curriculum. Essentialist teachers rely on achievement test scores to evaluate progress. Essentialists expect that students will leave school possessing not only basic skills and an extensive body of knowledge but also disciplined, practical minds, capable of applying schoolhouse lessons in the real world.

Essentialism in Action: Rancho Elementary School Rancho Elementary School in Marin County, California, proudly promotes its essentialist philosophy, and announces on its web page that "students will participate in a highly enriched environment exposing them to rigorous academics, foreign language, citizenship/leadership opportunities, and grade appropriate technology." Its mission is the acquisition of basic skills through direct instruction in the core academic areas, including reading through phonics. As a testament to its success, the school boasts high test scores. Beyond academics, the school also emphasizes "firm, consistent discipline" and close parent-teacher relationships.

If you do not live in Marin County, you may not have heard of Rancho, but you may have heard of a school belonging to The Coalition of Essential Schools, as two hundred schools nationwide are members. But don't be misled by the name. Although these schools promote intellectual rigor, test students for mastery of information, and emphasize strong thinking skills across subjects, they are not pure examples of essentialism. The schools do not share a fixed core curriculum, they emphasize the study of single topics or issues in depth, and they incorporate components of perennialism, which brings us to the other teacher-centered philosophy.

Perennialism

Perennialism is a cousin to essentialism. Both advocate teacher-centered classrooms. Both tolerate little flexibility in the curriculum. Both implement rigorous standards. Both aim to sharpen students' intellectual powers and enhance their moral qualities. So what are the differences?

Perennialists organize their schools around books, ideas, and concepts and criticize essentialists for the vast amount of factual information they require students to absorb in their push for "cultural literacy." Perennial means "everlasting"—a perennialist education focuses on enduring themes and questions that span the ages. Perennialists recommend that students learn directly from the **Great Books**—works by history's finest thinkers and writers, books as meaningful today as when they were first written.

Perennialists believe that the goal of education should be to develop rational thought and to discipline minds to think rigorously. Perennialists see education as a sorting mechanism, a way to identify and prepare the intellectually gifted for leadership, while providing vocational training for the rest of society. They lament the change in universities over the centuries from institutions where a few gifted students (and teachers) rigorously pursued truth for its own sake, to a glorified training ground for future careers.

Those of you who received a religious education might recognize the perennialist philosophy. Many parochial schools reflect the perennialist tradition with a curriculum that focuses on analyzing great religious books (such as the *Bible,* the *Talmud,* or the *Koran*), discerning moral truths, and honoring those moral values. In the classroom description that follows, we will concentrate on secular perennialism as formulated in the twentieth-century United States by such individuals as Robert Hutchins and Mortimer Adler.

In a perennialist classroom, primary sources rather than textbooks are the center of learning.

The Perennialist Classroom   As in an essentialist classroom, students in a perennialist classroom spend considerable time and energy mastering the three "Rs," reading, 'riting, and 'rithmetic. Greatest importance is placed on reading, the key to unlocking the enduring ideas found in the Great Books. Special attention is given to teaching values and character training, often through discussion about the underlying values and moral principles in a story. High school marks an increase in academic rigor as more challenging books are explored, including works of Darwin, Homer, and Shakespeare. Few elective choices are allowed. In an extreme example, **Mortimer Adler** proposed in his *Paideia Proposal* (1982) a single elementary and secondary curriculum for all students, with no curricular electives except in the choice of a second language.

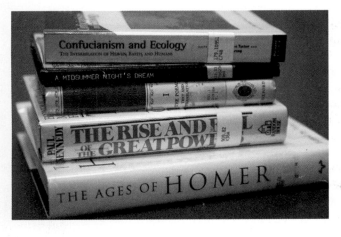

Electives are not the only things perennialists go without. Critics chastise perennialists for the lack of

A Closer Look

Essentialists and Perennialists: Different Core Curricula

Although both essentialism and perennialism promote a traditional approach to education, these teacher-centered philosophies draw their curricula from different sources. The first column includes excerpts from a typical essentialist list (we included a few of the words and phrases under the letter "c"); the second column provides selections from the perennialists' *Great Books* curriculum. Remember, these are only a few suggestions from very long lists!

The List (Essentialism)

centigrade	Caesar Augustus
center of gravity	*Candide*
cerebellum	cast pearls before swine
Calvary	Cascade Mountains
capital expenditure	carbon dioxide
Cèzanne	carte blanche
Canberra	Caruso, Enrico
Cain and Abel	cathode ray tube

Great Books (Perennialism)

Aristotle, *Sense and Sensible*	*The Koran*
The Bible	Karl Marx, *Das Kapital*
Geoffrey Chaucer, *Canterbury Tales*	Herman Melville, *Moby Dick*
Charles Darwin, *On the Origin of Species*	Thomas Paine, *Common Sense*
Charles Dickens, *Oliver Twist*	Plato, *Charmides*
F. Scott Fitzgerald, *The Great Gatsby*	Jonathan Swift, *Gulliver's Travels*
Homer, *The Iliad*	Virginia Woolf, *Night and Day*
James Joyce, *Ulysses*	Leo Tolstoy, *War and Peace*

REFLECTION: Does this list make you feel culturally literate—or illiterate? Do you believe that lists like this one should be important? Why or why not?

women, people of color, and non-Western ideas in the Great Books they teach, but many perennialists are unmoved by such criticism. To them, "training the mind" is ageless, beyond demographic concerns and transient trends. As Mortimer Adler wrote,

> The Great Books of ancient and medieval as well as modern times are a repository of knowledge and wisdom, a tradition of culture which must initiate each generation.[3]

You also find few if any textbooks in a perennialist class. **Robert Hutchins,** who as president of the University of Chicago introduced the Great Books program, once opined that textbooks "have probably done as much to degrade the American intelligence as any single force."[4] Because perennialist teachers see themselves as discussion seminar leaders and facilitators, lectures are rare.

Perennialism in Action: St. John's College The best-known example of perennialist education today takes place at a private institution unaffiliated with any religion: St. John's College, founded in 1784 in Annapolis, Maryland (www.sjcsf.edu). St. John's College uses the Great Books as a core curriculum and assigns readings in the fields of literature, philosophy and theology, history and the social sciences, mathematics and natural science, and music. Students write extensively and attend seminars twice weekly to discuss assigned readings. They also complete a number of laboratory experiences and tutorials in language, mathematics, and music, guided by the faculty, who are called *tutors*. Seniors take oral examinations at the beginning and at the end of their senior year and write a final essay that must be approved before they are allowed to graduate.

Although grades are given to facilitate admission to graduate programs, students receive their grades only upon request and are expected to learn only for learning's sake. Because the St. John's experience thrives best in a small-group atmosphere, the college established a second campus in 1964 in Santa Fe, New Mexico, to handle additional enrollment.

Student-Centered Philosophies

Student-centered philosophies are less authoritarian, less concerned with the past and "training the mind," and more focused on individual needs, contemporary relevance, and preparing students for a changing future. Progressivism, social reconstructionism, and existentialism place the learner at the center of the educational process: Students and teachers work together on determining what should be learned and how best to learn it. School is not seen as an institution that controls and directs youth, or works to preserve and transmit the core culture, but as an institution that works with youth to improve society or help students realize their individuality.

Progressivism

Progressivism organizes schools around the concerns, curiosity, and real-world experiences of students. The progressive teacher facilitates learning by helping students formulate meaningful questions and devise strategies to answer those questions. Answers are not drawn from lists or even Great Books; they are discovered through real-world experience. Progressivism is the educational application of a philosophy called pragmatism. According to **pragmatism,** the way to determine if an idea has merit is simple: Test it. If the idea works in the real world, then it has merit. Both pragmatism and progressivism originated in America, the home of a very practical and pragmatic people. John Dewey refined and applied pragmatism to education, establishing what became known as progressivism.

John Dewey was a reformer with a background in philosophy and psychology who taught that people learn best through social interaction in the real world. Dewey believed that because social learning had meaning, it endured. Book learning, on the other hand, was no substitute for actually doing things. Progressivists do not believe that the mind can be disciplined through reading Great Books, rather that the mind should be trained to analyze experience thoughtfully and draw conclusions objectively.

Dewey saw education as an opportunity to learn how to apply previous experiences in new ways. Dewey believed that students, facing an ever-changing world, should master the scientific method: (1) become aware of a problem, (2) define it, (3) propose various hypotheses to solve it, (4) examine the consequences of each hypothesis in the light of previous experience, and (5) test the most likely solution. (For a biography of John Dewey, see the online "Hall of Fame: Profiles in Education" in Chapter 7.)

Dewey regarded democracy and freedom as far superior to the political ideas of earlier times. Dewey saw traditional, autocratic, teacher-centered schools as the antithesis of democratic ideals. He viewed progressive schools as a working model of democracy. Dewey wrote:

> To imposition from above is opposed expression and cultivation of individuality; to external discipline is opposed free activity; to learning from texts and teachers, learning through experience; to acquisition of isolated skills and techniques by drill is opposed acquisition of them as means of attaining ends which make direct vital appeal; to preparation for a more or less remote future is opposed making the most of the opportunities of present life; to statistics and materials is opposed acquaintance with a changing world.[5]

The Progressive Classroom   Walk into a progressivist classroom and you will not find a teacher standing at the front of the room talking to rows of seated students. Rather, you will likely see children working in small groups, moving about and talking freely. Some children might be discussing a science experiment while another group works on a model volcano and a third prepares for a presentation. Interest centers would be located throughout the room, filled with books, materials, software, and projects designed to attract student interest on a wide array of topics. Finally you notice the teacher, walking around the room, bending over to talk with individual students and small groups, asking questions and making suggestions. You sense that the last thing on her mind is the standardized state test scheduled for next week.[6]

Learning by doing is a touchstone of progressivism.

Progressivists build the curriculum around the experiences, interests, and abilities of students, and encourage students to work together cooperatively. Teachers feel no compulsion to focus their students' attention on one discrete discipline at a time, and students integrate several subjects in their studies. Thought-provoking activities augment reading, and a game such as Monopoly might be used to illustrate the principles of capitalism versus socialism. Computer simulations, field trips, and interactive websites on the Internet offer realistic learning challenges for students and build on students' multiple intelligences.

Progressivism in Action: The Laboratory School In 1896, while a professor at the University of Chicago, Dewey founded the Laboratory School as a testing ground for his educational ideas. Dewey's writings and his work with the **Laboratory School** set the stage for the progressive education movement. Based on the view that educators, like scientists, need a place to test their ideas, Dewey's Laboratory School eventually became the most famous experimental school in the history of U.S. education, a place where thousands observed Dewey's innovations in school design, methods, and curriculum. Although the school remained under Dewey's control for only eight years and never enrolled more than 140 students (ages 3 to 13) in a single year, its influence was enormous.

Dewey designed the Lab School with only one classroom but with several facilities for experiential learning: a science laboratory, an art room, a woodworking shop, and a kitchen. Children were likely to make their own weights and measures in the laboratory, illustrate their own stories in the art room, build a boat in the shop, and learn chemistry in the kitchen. They were unlikely to learn through isolated exercises or drills, which, according to Dewey, students consider irrelevant. Because Dewey believed that students learn from social interaction, the school used many group methods such as cooperative model-making, field trips, role-playing, and dramatizations. Dewey maintained that group techniques make the students better citizens, developing, for example, their willingness to share responsibilities.

Children in the Laboratory School were not promoted from one grade to another after mastering certain material. Rather, they were grouped according to their individual interests and abilities. For all its child-centered orientation, however, the Laboratory School remained hierarchical in the sense that the students were never given a role comparable to that of the staff in determining the school's educational practices.

Social Reconstructionism

Social reconstructionism encourages schools, teachers, and students to focus their studies and energies on alleviating pervasive social inequities and, as the name implies, reconstruct society into a new and more just social order. Although social reconstructionists agree with progressivists that schools should concentrate on the needs of students, they split from progressivism in the 1920s after growing impatient with the slow pace of change in schools and in society. **George Counts,** a student of Dewey, published his classic book, *Dare the Schools Build a New Social Order?*, in which he outlined a more ambitious, and clearly more radical, approach to education. Counts's book, written in 1932, was no doubt influenced by the human cost of the Great Depression. He proposed that schools focus on reforming society, an idea that caught the imagination and sparked the ideals of educators both in this country and abroad.

Social challenges and problems provide a natural (and moral) direction for curricular and instructional activities. Racism, sexism, climate change and environmental pollution, homelessness, poverty, substance abuse, homophobia, and violence are rooted in misinformation and thrive in ignorance. Therefore, social reconstructionists believe that school is the ideal place to begin ameliorating social problems. The teacher's role is to explore social problems, suggest alternative perspectives, and facilitate student analysis of these problems. Although convincing, cajoling, or moralizing about the importance of addressing human tragedy would be a natural teacher response, such adult-led decision making flies in the face of reconstructionist philosophy. A social reconstructionist teacher must model democratic principles. Students and teachers are expected to live and learn in a democratic culture; the students themselves must select educational objectives and social priorities.

The Social Reconstructionist Classroom A social reconstructionist teacher creates lessons that both intellectually inform and emotionally stir students about the inequities that surround them. A class might read a book and visit a photojournalist's exhibit portraying violent acts of racism. If the book, the exhibit, and the class discussion that follows move the students, the class might choose to pursue a long-term project to investigate the problem. One group of students might analyze news coverage of racial and ethnic groups in the community. Another student group might conduct a survey analyzing community perceptions of racial groups and race relations. Students might visit city hall and examine arrest and trial records to determine the role race plays in differential application of the law. Students might examine government records for information about housing patterns, income levels, graduation rates, and other relevant statistics. The teacher's role would be as facilitator: assisting students in focusing their questions, developing a strategy, helping to organize visits, and ensuring that the data collected and analyzed meet standards of objectivity. Throughout, the teacher would be instructing students on research techniques, statistical evaluation, writing skills, and public communications.

In a social reconstructionist class, a research project is more than an academic exercise; the class is engaged in a genuine effort to improve society. In this case, the class might arrange to meet with political leaders, encouraging them to create programs or legislation to respond to issues the students uncovered. The students might seek a *pro bono* attorney to initiate legal action to remedy a social injustice they unmasked. Or the students might take their findings directly to the media by holding a press conference. They might also create a web page to share their findings and research methods with students in other parts of the country, or other parts of the world. How would the teacher decide if the students have met the educational goals? In this example, an objective, well-prepared report would be one criterion, and reducing or eliminating a racist community practice would be a second measure of success.

Social Reconstructionism in Action: Paulo Freire **Paulo Freire** believed that schools were just another institution perpetuating social inequities while serving the interests of the dominant group. Like social reconstructionism itself, Freire's beliefs grew during the Great

GLOBAL VIEW
The Council on Global Education is dedicated to the development of a new model of education for the child in the twenty-first century. Its four building blocks are universal values, global understanding, excellence in all things, and service to humanity. www.globaleducation.org

Depression of the 1930s, when he experienced hunger and poverty firsthand. Influenced by Marxist and neo-Marxist ideas, Freire accused schools of perpetuating the status quo views of the rich and powerful "for the purpose of keeping the masses submerged and content in a culture of silence."[7] Schools were endorsing **social Darwinism,** the idea that society is an ingenious "sorting" system, one in which the more talented rise to the top, while those less deserving find themselves at the bottom of the social and economic pecking order. The conclusion: Those with money deserve it, those without money deserve their lot in life, and poverty is a normal, preordained part of reality.

In social reconstructionism, students not only learn by doing, they learn to make the world a better, more just place to live.

Freire rejected this conclusion. He did not believe that schools should be viewed as "banks," where the privileged deposit ideas such as social Darwinism to be spoon-fed into the limited minds of the dispossessed. He envisioned schools as a place where the poor can acquire the skills to regain control of their lives and influence the social and economic forces that locked them in poverty in the first place. Freire engaged the poor as equal partners in dialogues that explored their economic and social problems and possible solutions. Freire believed in **praxis,** the doctrine that when actions are based on sound theory and values, they can make a real difference in the world. (It is no accident that the term *praxis* is also the name given to the teacher competency tests required by many states.) Freire's ideas took hold not only in his native Brazil but in poor areas around the globe. As poor farmworkers became literate and aware, they organized for their self-improvement and began to work for change. It is not surprising that the autocratic leaders of his country eventually forced him into exile, for he had turned schooling into a liberating force. (For a biography of Paulo Freire, see the "Hall of Fame: Profiles in Education" in Chapter 7.)

Existentialism

Existentialism, the final student-centered philosophy we shall discuss, places the highest priority on students directing their own learning. **Existentialism** asserts that the purpose of education is to help children find the meaning and direction in their lives, and it rejects the notion that adults should or could direct meaningful learning for children. Existentialists do not believe that "truth" is objective and applicable to all. Instead, each of us must look within ourselves to discover our own truth, our own purpose in life. Teaching students what adults believe they should learn is neither efficient nor effective; in fact, most of this "learning" will be forgotten. Instead, each student should decide what he or she needs to learn, and when to learn it. As the Buddhist proverb reminds us: When the student is ready, the teacher will appear.

There is little doubt that for many readers this is the most challenging of all the philosophies, and schools built on this premise will seem the most alien. We are a culture very connected to the outside world, and far less connected to our inner voice, or as an existentialist might say, our essence. We compete with one another for material goods, and we are distracted by hundreds of cable channels, iPads, smartphones, and a constant array of external stimuli. Thinking about why we are here and finding our purpose in life is not what schools typically do, but existentialists believe it is precisely what they should do. Schools should help each of us answer the fundamental questions: Why am I here? What is my purpose?

Profile in Education   Jane Roland Martin

"Domephobia," the fear of things domestic, is **Jane Roland Martin**'s word for gender bias in schools and in society. She coined the term when she compared the distinct educations Jean-Jacques Rousseau designed for his fictitious students Emile and Sophie. Martin was frustrated that whereas the boy, Emile, was said to revel in intellectual exploration, Sophie was to receive second-rate training—to be a wife and a mother.

Martin deplores the disconnect between intellectual development and the development of abilities to love and care for a family. She recognizes that today's schools continue to craft different expectations for males and females. In fact, she knows this inequity firsthand. Teaching philosophy at the University of Massachusetts at Boston for more than thirty years, Martin found herself fighting to have her intellectual voice heard in a traditional male discipline. Her experience of bias fueled her anger that equal-opportunity education is still so far from reality.

Yet, Jane Roland Martin knows "women are barometers of change." Feminism today, like Sophie's education three hundred years ago, gives men and women a special gift—a new perspective on gender roles. Women's roles at work and in the family are indeed changing. Not only are women wives and mothers, they are corporate CEOs, medal-winning soccer players, and Supreme Court justices. Yet even

as society may champion the greater earning power and talents of women, we are seeing a backlash against the more liberated roles of women. The trouble? The changes have cast as fiction the rosy Norman Rockwell portrait of the American family: More than half of all mothers work outside the home and single-parent homes number one in four. These numbers stir concern that day care is bad, working mothers are neglectful, and the well-being of the nation's children is threatened.

What society may see as problematic, Jane Roland Martin envisions as opportunity. Historically, the physical, emotional, and social needs of children have been met by family, primarily mothers. Today, women are drawn by economic need and personal desire to enter the workforce. Martin sees these changes as a defining moment for schools, a chance to re-create within schools the nurturing tasks traditionally performed at home.

Martin's critics say no, schools should focus only on intellectual development. Not Martin. A social reconstructionist, she challenges schools to open their doors to what she calls the 3Cs—caring, concern, and connection. As more children are cared for outside the home, she fears the 3C curriculum is in danger of being lost. And American society has paid a heavy price for ignoring such domestic needs. Social inequalities continue and children are often the victims. Martin has an antidote: Transform schoolhouses into "schoolhomes."

The schoolhome is far different from traditional "factory-model schooling, which views children as raw material, teachers as workers who process their students before sending them on to the next station on the assembly line, [and] curriculum as the machinery that forges America's young into marketable products."[a] Instead, Martin's schoolhome focuses on students' individual emotional and cognitive needs. It embraces the experience of all

learners and welcomes racial, cultural, and gender diversity. Martin's vision of schools reflects her vision of American society as everyone's home:

> Instead of focusing our gaze on abstract norms, standardized tests, generalized rates of success, and uniform outcomes, the ideas of the schoolhome direct action to actual educational practice. Of course a schoolhome will teach the 3Rs. But it will give equal emphasis to the 3Cs—not by designating formal courses in these but by being a domestic environment characterized by safety, security, nurturance, and love. In the schoolhome, mind and body, thought and action, reason and emotion are all educated.[b]

The schoolhome will incorporate the 3Cs into our very definition of what it means for males and females to be educated. Creating such nurturing and equitable schools will require "acts of both great and small, strategic and utterly outrageous. The cause demands no less, not one whit less."[c]

[a]Jane Roland Martin, *The Schoolhome: Rethinking Schools for Changing Families* (Cambridge, MA: Harvard University Press, 1992), p. 41.
[b]Jane Roland Martin, "Women, School, and Cultural Wealth." In Connie Titone and Karen Maloney (eds.), *Thinking Through Our Mothers: Women's Philosophies of Education* (Upper Saddle River, NJ: Merrill, 1999), pp.161–62.
[c]Jane Roland Martin, *Coming of Age in Academe: Rekindling Women's Hopes and Reforming the Academy* (New York: Routlege, 2000), p. 182.

To learn more about Jane Roland Martin, click on *Profiles in Education.*

www.mhhe.com/sadker10e

REFLECTION: Do you agree with Jane Roland Martin that the 3Cs should be an integral part of the curriculum? Explain. Describe what a 3C curriculum might look like in schools today.

The Existentialist Classroom Existentialism in the classroom is a powerful rejection of traditional, and particularly essentialist, thinking. In the existentialist classroom, subject matter takes second place to helping the students understand and appreciate themselves as unique individuals. The teacher's role is to help students define their own essence by exposing them to various paths they may take in life and by creating an environment in which they can freely choose their way. Existentialism, more than other educational philosophies, affords students great latitude in their choice of subject matter and activity.

The existentialist curriculum often emphasizes the humanities as a means of providing students with vicarious experiences that will help unleash their creativity and self-expression. For example, existentialists focus on the actions of historical individuals, each of whom provides a model for the students to explore. Math and the natural sciences may be de-emphasized because their subject matter is less fruitful for promoting self-awareness. Career education is regarded more as a means of teaching students about their potential than of teaching a livelihood. In art, existentialism encourages individual creativity and imagination more than it does the imitation of established models.

Existentialist learning is self-paced and self-directed and includes a great deal of individual contact with the teacher. Honest interpersonal relationships are emphasized; roles and "official" status are de-emphasized. According to philosopher Maxine Greene, teachers themselves must be deeply involved in their own learning and questioning: "Only a teacher in search of his freedom can inspire a student to search for his own." Greene asserts that education should move teachers and students to "wide awakeness," the ability to discover their own truths.[8]

Although elements of existentialism occasionally appear in public schools, this philosophy has not been widely disseminated. In an age of high-stakes tests and standards, only a few schools, mostly private, implement existentialist ideas. Even Summerhill, the well-known existentialist school founded in England by A. S. Neill in 1921, struggles to persevere with its unusual educational approach.

Existentialism in Action: The Sudbury Valley School Visit Sudbury Valley School just outside Boston, Massachusetts, look around, look closely, and you still may not see the school. The large building nestled next to a fishing pond on a ten-acre campus looks more like a mansion than a school. Walk inside and you will find students and adults doing pretty much as they please. Not a "class" in sight. Some people are talking, some playing, some reading. A group is building a bookcase over there, a student is working on the computer in the corner, another is taking a nap on a chair. All ages mix freely, with no discernible grade level for any activity. In fact, it is even difficult to locate the teachers. If there is a curriculum, it is difficult to detect. Instead, the school offers a wide variety of educational options, including field trips to Boston, New York, and the nearby mountains and seacoast, and the use of facilities that include a laboratory, a woodworking shop, a computer room, a kitchen, a darkroom, an art room, and several music rooms.

Sudbury Valley provides a setting, an opportunity, but each student must decide what to do with that opportunity. Students are trusted to make their own decisions about learning. The school's purpose is to build on the students' natural curiosity, based on the belief that authentic learning takes place only when students initiate it. The school operates on the premise that all its students are creative, and each should be helped to discover and nurture his or her individual talents.

Sudbury Valley is fully accredited, and the majority of Sudbury Valley's graduates go on to college. The school accepts anyone from 4-year-olds to adults and charges low tuition, so as not to exclude anyone. Evaluations or grades are given only on request. A high school diploma is awarded to those who complete relevant requirements, which mainly focus on the ability to be a responsible member of the community at large. More than thirty schools follow the Sudbury model, including schools in Canada, Europe, Israel and Japan.[9]

You Be The Judge
TEACHER-VERSUS STUDENT-CENTERED APPROACHES TO EDUCATION

Teacher-Centered Approaches Are Best Because . . .

AFTER CENTURIES OF EXPERIENCE, WE KNOW WHAT TO TEACH

From Plato to Orwell, great writers and thinkers of the past light our way into the future. We must pass our cherished cultural legacy on to the next generation.

TEACHERS MUST SELECT WHAT IS WORTH KNOWING

The knowledge explosion showers us with mountains of new, complex information on a daily basis. Selecting what students should learn is a daunting challenge. Teachers, not students, are trained and best equipped to determine what is of value. To ask students to choose what they should learn would be the height of irresponsibility.

SCHOOLS MUST BE INSULATED FROM EXTERNAL DISTRACTIONS

Students can be easily distracted by the "excitement" of contemporary events. Although academic and rigorous school-based learning may be less flashy and less appealing, in the long run, it is far more valuable. Once schoolwork has been mastered, students will be well prepared to leave the sanctuary of learning and confront the outside world.

DISCIPLINED MINDS, RESPECTFUL CITIZENS

Students who listen thoughtfully and participate respectfully in classroom discussions learn several important lessons. For one, they learn the worth and wisdom of Western culture. They also learn to appreciate and to honor those who brought them this heritage, the guardians of their freedom and culture: their teachers.

Student-Centered Approaches Are Best Because . . .

GENUINE LEARNING ORIGINATES WITH THE LEARNER

People learn best what they want to learn, what they feel they should or need to learn. Students find lessons imposed "from above" to be mostly irrelevant, and the lessons are quickly forgotten.

THEY BEST PREPARE STUDENTS FOR THE INFORMATION AGE

The knowledge explosion is actually a powerful argument for student-directed learning. Teachers can't possibly teach everything. We must equip students with research skills, then fan the flames of curiosity so they will want to learn for themselves. Then students can navigate the information age, finding and evaluating new information.

EDUCATION IS A VITAL AND ORGANIC PART OF SOCIETY

The most important lessons of life are found not on the pages of books or behind the walls of a school but in the real world. Students need to work and learn directly in the community, from cleaning up the environment to reducing violence. Social action projects and service learning can offer a beacon of hope for the community while building compassionate values within our students.

HUMAN DIGNITY IS LEARNED IN DEMOCRATIC CLASSROOMS

Democracy is learned through experience, not books. Students flourish when they are respected; they are stifled when they are told what and how to think. As students manage their own learning, they master the most important lessons any school can teach: the importance of the individual's ideas and inner motivation.

www.mhhe.com/sadker10e

YOU DECIDE . . .

Do you find yourself influenced more by the arguments supporting teacher-centered approaches or student-centered approaches? Are there elements of each that you find appealing? How will your classroom practices reflect your philosophy?

Can Teachers Blend These Five Philosophies?

Some of you might be drawn to (and let's face it, sometimes resistive to) one or more of these philosophies. A social reconstructionist idea such as students learning as they work to improve the world sounds perfect to some of us, whereas a more traditional approach focused on reading and discussing great books is a dream come true to others. For many, elements from both of these approaches are appealing. So you might be wondering if this is an either/or proposition; must we be purists and choose one philosophy, or can we mix and match, blending two or more philosophies?

As you probably have guessed, people differ on the answer, which means you get to think it through and come to your own conclusion. Some schools blend philosophies. For example, the YES College Preparatory School in Houston and Wakefield High School in Maryland mix several philosophies in their programs. There is both traditional academic emphasis on content mastery, with many AP tests being offered, as well as a more progressive approach as students create independent senior projects. And the faculty and students seem to appreciate the blending. But others are not so sure this is a good idea.

Advocates of a purist model argue that although blending sounds like a comfortable and reasonable compromise, much is lost. For example, if we want children to be independent problem solvers, then we must promote that approach. Blending independent problem solving with a traditional philosophy of teachers telling students what they are to learn might not work. Either students are taught how to think for themselves, or they are told what to think, and compromise is not an option. More traditional teachers fear that much of progressive education, although replete with lofty goals, actually leads to little real learning. They claim that blending student-centered philosophies with a demanding traditional curriculum actually dilutes learning.[10] As you consider where you want to teach geographically, you might also want to consider where you want to teach philosophically. Are you comfortable with the school's educational philosophy? If you have some freedom in structuring your classroom, which philosophy or philosophies will you follow? Are you a purist, or will you be blending several philosophies? (See Table 8.1. on p. 262)

Psychological Influences on Education

Essentialism, perennialism, progressivism, social reconstructionism, and existentialism are influential philosophies of education, but they are far from the only forces shaping today's schools. The following descriptions offer a glimpse into some other forces guiding current school practices.

FOCUS QUESTION 5
What are some of the psychological and cultural factors influencing education?

Constructivism

Constructivism, like progressivism, social reconstructionism, and existentialism, puts the learner at the center of the educational stage. **Constructivism** asserts that knowledge cannot be handed from one person to another (from a teacher to a learner) but must be *constructed* by each learner through interpreting and reinterpreting a constant flow of information. Constructivists believe that people continually try to make sense of and bring order to the world.

Built on the work of Swiss and Russian psychologists, Jean Piaget and Lev Vygotsky, constructivism reflects cognitive psychologists' view that the essence of learning is the constant effort to assimilate new information. In a constructivist classroom, the teacher builds knowledge in much the same way, gauging a student's prior knowledge and understanding, then carefully orchestrating cues, penetrating questions, and instructional activities that challenge

TABLE 8.1   Five philosophies of education.

	Focus of Curriculum	Sample Classroom Activity	Role of Teacher	Goals for Students	Educational Leaders
Student-Centered Philosophies					
Progressivism	Flexible; integrated study of academic subjects around the needs and experiences of students	Learning by doing—for example, students plan a field trip to learn about history, geography, and natural science	Guide and integrate learning activities so that students can find meaning	To become intelligent problem solvers, socially aware citizens who are prepared to live comfortably in the world	John Dewey, Nel Noddings
Social Reconstructionism	Focus on social, political, and economic needs; integrated study of academic subjects around socially meaningful actions	Learning by reconstructing society—for example, students work to remove health hazards in a building housing the poor	Provide authentic learning activities that both instruct students and improve society	To become intelligent problem solvers, to enjoy learning, to live comfortably in the world while also helping reshape it	George S. Counts, Jane Roland Martin, Paulo Freire, bell hooks
Existentialism	Each student determines the pace and direction of his or her own learning	Students choose their preferred medium—such as poetry, prose, or painting—and evaluate their own performance	One who seeks to relate to each student honestly; skilled at creating a free, open, and stimulating environment	To accept personal responsibility; to understand deeply and be at peace with one's own unique individuality	A. S. Neill, Maxine Greene
Teacher-Centered Philosophies					
Essentialism	Core curriculum of traditional academic topics and traditional American virtues	Teacher focuses on "essential" information or the development of particular skills	Model of academic and moral virtue; center of classroom	To become culturally literate individuals, model citizens educated to compete in the world	William Bagley, E. D. Hirsch, Jr.
Perennialism	Core curriculum analyzing enduring ideas found in Great Books	Socratic dialogue analyzing a philosophical issue or the meaning of a great work of literature	Scholarly role model; philosophically oriented, helps students seek the truth for themselves	To increase their intellectual powers and to appreciate learning for its own sake	Robert Hutchins, Mortimer Adler

REFLECTION: How many of these philosophies have you experienced in your own education? Describe the circumstances. Would you like to encounter others as a student? a teacher? Explain.

A Closer Look   Voices of Five Philosophies

YESTERDAY'S VOICES

William Bagley (1874–1946) *Essentialism* Bagley believed that the major role of the school is to produce a literate, intelligent electorate; argued against electives while stressing thinking skills to help students apply their academic knowledge.

Robert M. Hutchins (1899–1979) *Perennialism* During the sixteen years he served as president of the University of Chicago, Hutchins abolished fraternities, football, and compulsory attendance, and introduced the Great Books program.

John Dewey (1859–1952) *Progressivism* A founder of progressivism, Dewey not only worked to democratize schools but also fought for women's suffrage and the right of teachers to form unions.

George S. Counts (1907–1974) *Social Reconstructionism* Counts viewed education as an important tool to counter social injustices, and, if educators questioned their own power to make critical decisions, Counts's plea was to "Just do it!"

A. S. Neill (1883–1973) *Existentialism* Neill's attitude toward education stemmed from his own problems as a student, problems that fueled his creation of Summerhill, a school that encouraged youngsters to make their own decisions about what and when to learn.

TODAY'S VOICES

E. D. Hirsch Jr. (1928–) *Essentialism* He established the Core Knowledge Foundation to develop a prescribed curriculum in subject areas. Visit your local bookstore and browse through his books delineating what educated people should know.

Mortimer Adler (1902–2001) *Perennialism* He renewed interest in perennialism with the publication of *The Paideia Proposal* (1982). Adler advocated that all students be educated in the classics and that education be a lifelong venture.

Nel Noddings (1929–) *Progressivism* She believes that an ethic of care can best be cultivated when the curriculum is centered on the interests of students. Schools are challenged to nourish the physical, spiritual, occupational, and intellectual development of each child.

bell hooks (1952–) *Social Reconstructionism* Her theory of education, *engaged pedagogy,* helps students and teachers develop a critical consciousness of race, gender, and class biases. A prolific writer, her books include *Ain't I a Woman: Black Women and Feminism* (1981) and *Teaching to Transgress: Education as the Practice of Freedom* (1994).

Maxine Greene (1917–) *Existentialism* She believes that it is crucial for students and teachers to create meaning in their lives. Greene sees the humanities and the arts as catalysts for moving people to critical awareness and conscious engagement with the world.

REFLECTION: How do historical and political events influence whose voices are heard? Whose voices are being heard in education today, and why?

and extend a student's insight. Teachers can use **scaffolding,** that is, questions, clues, or suggestions that help a student link prior knowledge to the new information. The educational challenges facing students in a constructivist classroom could be creating a new way to handle a math problem, letting go of an unfounded bias about an ethnic group, or connecting the role of religion in political movements. In a constructivist classroom, students and teachers constantly challenge their own assumptions. (If you check back to the philosophy inventory, see how you responded to item 26, which captured this aspect of constructivism.)

Although constructivism runs counter to the current emphasis on uniform standards and testing, it is enjoying popularity, especially among school reformers. Perhaps part of the reason for its growing acceptance is that constructivism dovetails with authentic learning, critical thinking, individualized instruction, and project-based learning, ideas popular in reform circles.

Behaviorism

In stark contrast to constructivism, **behaviorism** is derived from the belief that free will is an illusion and that human beings are shaped entirely by their environment. Alter a person's environment and you will alter his or her thoughts, feelings, and behavior. People act in response to physical stimuli. We learn, for instance, to avoid overexposure to heat through the impulses of pain our nerves send to our brain. More complex learning, such as understanding the material in this chapter, is also determined by stimuli, such as the educational support you have received from your professor or parents and the comfort of the chair in which you sit when reading this text.

Harvard professor **B. F. Skinner** became the leading advocate of behaviorism, and he did much to popularize the use of positive reinforcement to promote desired learning. (For a biography of B. F. Skinner, see the online "Hall of Fame: Profiles in Education" in Chapter 7.) Behaviorists urge teachers to use a system of reinforcement to encourage desired behaviors, to connect learning with pleasure and reward (a smile, special privilege, or good grades). In a program termed **behavior modification,** extrinsic rewards are gradually lessened as the student acquires and masters the targeted behavior. By association, the desired behavior now produces its own reward (self-satisfaction). This process may take minutes, weeks, or years, depending on the complexity of the learning desired and on the past environment of the learner. The teacher's goal is to move the learner from extrinsic to intrinsic rewards. (If you check the inventory at the chapter's opening, behaviorism was represented by statement 27. How did you respond?)

Critics of behaviorism decry behaviorists' disbelief in the autonomy of the individual. They ask, Are people little more than selfish "reward machines"? Can clever forces manipulate populations through clever social engineering? Are educators qualified to exert such total control of students? Those who defend behaviorism point to its striking successes. Behaviorism's influence is apparent in the joy on students' faces as they receive visual and auditory rewards via their computer monitor, or in the classroom down the hall where special needs learners make significant progress in a behaviorist-designed curriculum.

Cultural Influences on Education

Most of the ideas and philosophies discussed in this chapter are drawn from Western culture. As a nation, we rarely identify or reflect on the ideas that derive from many parts of Asia, Africa, Eastern Europe, and Latin America. We are guilty of **ethnocentrism,** the tendency to view one's own culture as superior to others and (perhaps worse) to fail to consider other cultures at all. Let's broaden our view and examine education as practiced in other cultures.

www.mhhe.com/sadker10e

INTERACTIVE ACTIVITY

What Philosophy or Approach Is This?
Read scenarios and match the philosophy or approach being exhibited.

In much of the West, society's needs dictate educational practices, with statewide standards, national goals, and high-stakes testing. In the rest of the world, that is to say, in most of the world, the child's education is primarily a concern of the family, not the society. A child's vocational interests, for example, might mirror the occupation of a parent or be built around the unique interest or talent of the child, rather than respond to the broader employment market or societal priorities. Family and community are foremost; the nation is a weaker influence.

In Western society, formal schools, formal certification and degrees are valued; in other societies, more credence is placed on actual knowledge and mastery rather than educational documentation. The notion of *teachers* and *nonteachers* is foreign in many cultures, since all adults and even older children participate in educating the young. Children learn adult roles through observation, conversation, assisting, and imitating, all the while absorbing moral, intellectual, and vocational lessons. This shared educational responsibility is called **informal education.**[11] What does calling this practice "informal education" reveal about Western values and assumptions? Would someone in a culture practicing this integrated education call it "informal education"? In the process, adults also learn a great deal about the children in the community. Strong bonds are forged between the generations. (As you probably already concluded, item 28 on our opening inventory describes informal education. You might want to check your answer to that statement.)

Oral traditions enjoy particular prominence in many parts of the world, even in literate societies where reading and writing are commonplace and valued. In the **oral tradition,** spoken language becomes a primary method for instruction: Word problems teach reasoning skills; proverbs instill wisdom; and stories, anecdotes, and rhymes teach lessons about nature, history, religion, and social customs. The oral tradition refines communication and analytical skills, and reinforces human connections and moral values. Not infrequently, religious and moral lessons are passed on initially through oral communication, only later to be written.

The practices and beliefs of peoples in other parts of the world offer useful insights for enhancing—or questioning—our own educational practices, but they are insights too rarely considered, much less implemented. Perhaps this will change in the years ahead as immigration, the global economy, and technology continue to bring all world cultures closer together. For now, however, our education philosophies are rooted in the ideas and thoughts of Western thinkers. Let's visit some of these powerful thinkers and their influential, enduring contributions.

The Three Legendary Figures of Classical Western Philosophy

To understand Western philosophy, we must look back to its birthplace—ancient Greece. Specifically, we must begin with a trio of philosopher-teachers: Socrates, Plato, and Aristotle. Together they laid the foundation for most of Western philosophy. It is likely that you are familiar with at least their names. Let's review their lasting contributions to the world of philosophy.

The name **Socrates** is practically synonymous with wisdom and the philosophical life. Socrates (469–399 B.C.E.) was a teacher without a school. He walked about Athens, engaging people in provocative dialogues about questions of ultimate significance. Socrates is hailed as an exemplar of human virtue whose goal was to help others find the truths that lie within their own minds. In that regard, he described himself as a "midwife." By repeatedly questioning, disproving, and testing the thoughts of his pupils on such questions as the nature of "love" or "the good," he helped his students reach deeper, clearer ideas. Today we call his approach the **Socratic method.**

GLOBAL VIEW

William. G. Sumner introduced the cultural concept of *ethnocentrism* early in the 1900s. Culture captures the concepts of national character, perception, time and space, thinking, language and nonverbal communication, values, behavior (norms, rules, manners), social groupings and relationships.

GLOBAL VIEW

The word *Qur'an (Koran)* is often translated as "the Recitation."

FOCUS QUESTION 6

What were the contributions of Socrates, Plato, and Aristotle to Western philosophy, and how are their legacies reflected in education today?

A Closer Look   The Socratic Method in Action

TEACHER: Today we will try to understand what we mean by the concepts of right and wrong. What are examples of conduct you consider wrong or immoral?

STUDENT: Lying is wrong.

TEACHER: But what if you were living in Germany around 1940 and you were harboring in your house a certain Jewish man named Nathan Cohen, who was wanted by the Nazis? If asked by a Nazi if you knew the whereabouts of that Mr. Cohen, wouldn't it be acceptable, even obligatory, to lie?

STUDENT: I suppose so.

TEACHER: So could you rephrase what you meant when you said that lying is wrong or immoral?

STUDENT: I think what I meant is that it is usually wrong to lie. But it is true that there are times when lying is acceptable, because the overall effects of the lie are good. Look at how much your Mr. Cohen was helped; the lie about where he was may have saved his life.

TEACHER: So you are saying that it is okay to lie, as long as the consequences of the lie are positive. But consider this hypothetical situation: I am a business tycoon who makes millions of dollars selling diamonds to investors. I sell only to very rich people who can afford to lose the money they invest in my diamonds. I tell my customers that my diamonds are worth $10,000 each, but they really are fakes, worth only $2,000 each. Rather than keeping the profits myself, I give all the money to the poor, helping them obtain the food and shelter they need to live. If you look at the obvious consequences of my business—the rich get slightly poorer and the needy are

helped out immensely—you may conclude that my business has a generally positive effect on society. And, yet, because the business is based on fraud, I find it immoral. Do you agree?

STUDENT: Yes, I find it immoral. I suppose I was wrong in saying that whenever a lie has generally good results it is morally acceptable. In your diamond example, unlike the Nazi example, the lie was directed at innocent people and the harm done to them was significant. I want to change my earlier statement that a lie is acceptable whenever it has generally good results. What I want to say now is that you should never lie to innocent people if that would cause them significant harm.

As is typical of Socrates' dialogue, this one could go on indefinitely, because there is no simple, "correct" solution to the issues being discussed—the meaning of right and wrong and, more specifically, the contours of when a lie is morally acceptable. By asking questions, the teacher is trying to get the student to clarify and rethink his or her own ideas, to come eventually to a deep and clear understanding of philosophical concepts, such as right and wrong.

REFLECTION: Have you ever experienced the Socratic Dialogue as a student? What were your reactions? Would you like to develop this teaching technique? Why or why not?

Socrates' method did not just promote intellectual insights in his students; it also challenged the conventional ideas and traditions of his time. Socrates offended many powerful people and was eventually charged with corrupting the youth of Athens. Even in that, Socrates provides a lesson for today's teachers: Challenges to popular convention may lead to community opposition and sanctions. (Luckily, sanctions today are less severe than those meted out to Socrates, who was condemned to death for his "impiety.")

We know about Socrates and his teachings through the writings of his disciples, one of whom was **Plato** (427–347 B.C.E.). Plato's writing is renowned for its depth, beauty, and clarity. His most famous works were dialogues, conversations between two or more people that present and critique various philosophical viewpoints. Plato's dialogues feature Socrates questioning and challenging others and presenting his own philosophy. After Socrates was put to death, Plato became disillusioned with Athenian democracy and left the city for many years. Later, he returned to Athens and founded the **Academy,** considered by some to be the world's first university.

Plato held that a realm of eternally existing "ideas" or "forms" underlies the physical world. In Plato's philosophy, the human soul has three parts: intellect, spirit, and appetite (basic animal desires). Plato believed that these faculties interact to determine human behavior. Plato urged that the intellect, the highest faculty, be trained to control the other two. For a look at Plato's famous "Allegory of the Cave," from *The Republic,* setting out his political philosophy—he

Why We Remember Socrates, Plato, and Aristotle

- **Socrates.** His philosophical lifestyle; the Socratic method, in which students are provocatively questioned so that they can rethink what they believe; his noble death
- **Plato.** Discussions of philosophy through eloquent dialogues; the theory of "forms," or "ideas," that exist in an eternal, transcendent realm
- **Aristotle.** The breadth of his knowledge; the synthesis of Plato's belief in the eternal "forms" and a scientist's belief in the "real" world that we can see, touch, or smell; the theory of the Golden Mean (everything in moderation)

Many of the ideas first formulated by Socrates, Plato, and Aristotle have long been integrated into Western culture and education.

REFLECTION: How might your current classroom instruction change if your education professor was Dr. Socrates, Plato, or Aristotle? Detail aspects of a "typical" lesson.

envisioned a class of philosopher-kings that would rule over the warriors and the common people—visit the Online Learning Center.

Just as Plato studied under Socrates, **Aristotle** (384–322 B.C.E.) studied under Plato. Aristotle entered Plato's Academy at age 18 and stayed for twenty years! In 342 B.C.E., Aristotle went to northern Greece and, for several years, tutored a young boy named Alexander, later known as Alexander the Great. After educating Alexander, Aristotle returned to Athens to set up his own school, the *Lyceum,* adjacent to Plato's Academy.

The depth and breadth of Aristotle's ideas were unsurpassed in ancient Western civilization. In addition to tackling philosophical questions, Aristotle wrote influential works on biology, physics, astronomy, mathematics, psychology, and literary criticism. Aristotle placed more importance on the physical world than did Plato. Aristotle's teachings can, in fact, be regarded as a synthesis of Plato's belief in the universal, spiritual forms, and a scientist's belief that each animal, vegetable, and mineral we observe is undeniably real.

Aristotle also won renown for his ethical and political theories. He wrote that the highest good for people is a virtuous life, fully governed by the faculty of reason, with which all other faculties are in harmony. Aristotle promoted the doctrine of the **Golden Mean,** or the notion that virtue lies in a middle ground between two extremes. Courage, for example, is bordered on the one side by cowardice and on the other side by foolhardiness.

Basic Philosophical Issues and Concepts

Philosophy has many subdivisions that are of particular significance to educators: metaphysics, epistemology, ethics, political philosophy, aesthetics, and logic. (See Figure 8.1.) These fields are where key educational questions are raised, including: How do we know what we know? What is of value? What is education's role in society? As you ponder these questions, you should find elements of your philosophy of education coming into sharper focus.

FOCUS QUESTION 7

How do metaphysics, epistemology, ethics, political philosophy, aesthetics, and logic factor into a philosophy of education?

Metaphysics and Epistemology

Metaphysics deals with the origin and the structure of reality. Metaphysicians ask: What really is the nature of the world in which we live? **Epistemology** examines the nature and the origin of human knowledge. Epistemologists are interested in how we use our minds to distinguish valid from illusory paths to true knowledge. It may be easiest to remember the scope of these closely related disciplines by considering that epistemology and metaphysics address *how* we know (epistemology) *what* we know (metaphysics) about reality.

FIGURE 8.1
Branches Of Philosophy

REFLECTION: This view of philosophy is like a tree. Are any of these branches new to you?

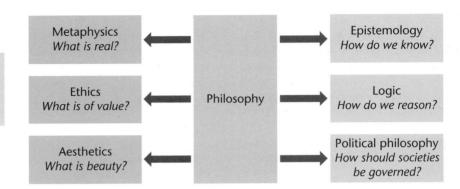

Is Reality Composed Solely of Matter? One of the most basic metaphysical issues is whether anything exists other than the material realm that we experience with our senses. Many philosophers assert the existence only of the physical, affirming fundamentally the existence of matter, a philosophy called **materialism.** By emphasizing in their curriculum the study of nature through scientific observation, modern public schools clearly deem that the material world is real and important. Other philosophers contend that the physical realm is but an illusion. They point out that matter is known only through the mind. This philosophy is called spiritualism or **idealism.** The physical world exists to teach us higher principles and meaningful lessons, and life is far more than a drive to acquire physical things. Educators focused on idealism might teach students the importance of finding their place and purpose in the world, the importance of helping one another, and the need to protect the environment. A third group of philosophers asserts that reality is composed of materialism and idealism, body and mind, a belief associated with French philosopher René Descartes and called **Cartesian dualism.**

Is Reality Characterized by Change and Progress? Metaphysicians question whether nature is constantly improving through time. The belief that progress is inevitable is widely held in the United States. On the other hand, some philosophers hold that change is illusory and that a foundation of timeless, static content underlies all reality. Still others believe that change is cyclical, swinging widely from one side of center to the opposing side.

Teachers who believe in the inevitability of progress seek new approaches to teaching and new subjects to be taught, thereby "keeping up with the times." Other teachers pay little heed to current trends and technologies. They may prefer to teach everlasting, timeless truths described in the Great Books or discussed by great thinkers, such as Plato and Aristotle. Finally, some teachers suggest that, with change such a constant, it is pointless to try to keep pace. They choose to ignore these cycles and to simply select the teaching methods they find most comfortable.

What Is the Basis of Our Knowledge? **Empiricism** holds that sensory experience (seeing, hearing, touching, and so on) is the source of knowledge. Empiricists assert that we experience the external world by sensory perception; then, through reflection, we conceptualize ideas that help us interpret that world. For example, because we have seen the sun rise every day, we can formulate the belief that it will rise again tomorrow. The empiricist doctrine that knowledge is gained most reliably through scientific experimentation may be the most widely held belief in Western culture. People want to hear the latest research or be shown documentation that something is true. Teachers expect students to present evidence before drawing conclusions. Even children demand of one another, "Prove it."

Rationalism emphasizes the power of reason—in particular, logic—to derive true statements about the world, even when such realities are not detected by the senses. Rationalists point out that the field of mathematics has generated considerable knowledge that is not based on our senses. For example, we can reason that 7 cubed equals 343 without having to count 7 times 7 times 7 objects to verify our conclusion experientially. Whereas educational empiricists would support hands-on learning activities as the primary source for discovery and validation of information, rationalists would encourage schools to place a greater emphasis on teaching mathematics, as well as such nonempirical disciplines as philosophy and logic.

Logic

Logic is the branch of philosophy that deals with reasoning. Logic focuses on how to move from a set of assumptions to valid conclusions and examines the rules of inference that enable us to frame our propositions and arguments. Whereas epistemology defines reasoning as one way to gain knowledge, logic defines the rules of reasoning.

Schools teach children to reason both deductively and inductively. When teaching **deductive reasoning,** teachers present their students with a general rule and then help them identify particular examples and applications of the rule. Inductive reasoning works in the opposite manner. When teaching **inductive reasoning,** teachers help their students draw tentative generalizations after having observed specific instances of a phenomenon.

A teacher who explains the commutative property of addition (a + b = b + a) and then has the student work out specific examples of this rule (such as 3 + 2 = 2 + 3) is teaching deductive reasoning. Contrast this with a teacher who begins a lesson by stating a series of addition problems of the form 3 + 2 = 5 and 2 + 3 = 5, then asks, "What do you notice about these examples?" If students can draw a generalization about the commutative property of addition, they are reasoning inductively. Whereas math is a natural field to isolate examples of deductive and inductive reasoning, logic equips students to think more precisely in virtually any field.

Ethics, Political Philosophy, and Aesthetics

Whereas metaphysics focuses on what "is," ethics, political philosophy, and aesthetics are concerned with what "ought to be." In these disciplines, philosophers grapple with the issue of what we should value. As you read on, consider the place of ethics, political philosophy, and aesthetics in the classroom.

Ethics is the study of what is "good" or "bad" in human behavior, thoughts, and feelings. It asks, What is the good life? and How should we treat each other? (What should schools teach children about what is "good" and what is "bad"?)

Political philosophy analyzes how past and present societies are arranged and governed and proposes ways to create better societies in the future. (How might schools engage in an objective evaluation of current governments, including our own?)

Aesthetics probes the nature of beauty. It asks, What is beauty? Is beauty solely in the eyes of the beholder? Or are some objects, people, and works (music, art, literature) objectively more beautiful than others? (How can teachers help students understand how their personal experiences, peer group values, and cultural and ethnic history shape their standards of what is beautiful?)

Teaching Tip

WRITING YOUR PHILOSOPHY STATEMENT

Writing your philosophy of teaching statement can feel like a daunting experience, but it's a lot more manageable when you do it one step at a time. Here a few ideas to help you get started.

1. Review the philosophies described in this chapter. Which one(s) most closely aligns with your beliefs about education? Why?

2. Now, ask yourself some specific questions about learning, teaching, and schools:

   - What qualities do good teachers have?
   - What is the role of a teacher?
   - The role of a student?
   - What adjectives describe your teaching style?
   - What is the most effective way to motivate students?
   - What should students learn in school?
   - What is the most effective way to assess student learning?
   - What is the purpose of school?

Your answers to these questions are the beginning of your philosophy statement! A philosophy of teaching statement might be just one or two typed pages, but collecting your thoughts into a single document helps you reflect on how you will apply your knowledge and insights to your actual teaching practice. Your philosophy is a work in progress. As your teaching experience grows and reflections deepen, see how much your ideas change, or stay the same.

REFLECTION: What new insights did you learn about yourself, teaching or learning from drafting your philosophy statement?

Your Turn

> [I]n modern times there are opposing views about the practice of education. There is no general agreement about what the young should learn either in relation to virtue or in relation to the best life; nor is it clear whether their education ought to be directed more towards the intellect than towards the character of the soul. . . . [A]nd it is not certain whether training should be directed at things useful in life, or at those conducive to virtue, or at nonessentials. . . . And there is no agreement as to what in fact does tend towards virtue. Men [sic] do not all prize most highly the same virtue, so naturally they differ also about the proper training for it.[12]
>
> *Aristotle*

More than 2,300 years later, we still find that reasonable people can come to entirely different points of view on all kinds of issues in education. (Remember the charter school discussion in the faculty room at the beginning of the chapter?) If everyone agreed on what should be taught, and how to teach it, there might be just one philosophy of education. But it is not so simple.

Re-reading the inventory statements at the beginning of this chapter can help you determine if one of the five major philosophies speaks for you. You may be more eclectic in your outlook, picking and choosing elements from different philosophies. Your responsibility as an educator is to wrestle with tough questions, to bring your values to the surface and to forge a coherent philosophy of education.

You might say a clear philosophy of education is to a teacher what a blueprint is to a builder—a plan of action, reassurance that the parts will fit together in a constructive way. With a clear philosophy of education, you will not ricochet from one teaching method to another and will not confuse students, parents, and administrators with conflicting messages about the role of students and teacher in the classroom. If you have a well-honed philosophy of education, you will be better able to assess whether you will find a comfortable fit in a school and a community. Simply put, a philosophy brings purpose and coherence to your work in the classroom.

ONLINE VIDEO ALBUM TO ACCOMPANY *TEACHERS, SCHOOLS, AND SOCIETY, 10E*

Visit the Online Learning Center for a range of contemporary videos with content related to this chapter.

www.mhhe.com/sadker10e

THE *TEACHERS, SCHOOLS, AND SOCIETY* READER WITH CLASSROOM OBSERVATION VIDEO CLIPS

Go to your Teachers, Schools, and Society Reader CD-ROM to:

READ CURRENT AND HISTORICAL ARTICLES

34. **The Humanities: Why Such a Hard Sell?** by David J. Ferrero, *Educational Leadership,* March 2011.

35. Text excerpts from ***Experience and Education***, by John Dewey, copyright 1938, 1998 by Kappa Delta Pi.

36. Text excerpts from ***Escape from Childhood,*** by John Holt, 1974, New York: E.P. Dutton. The excerpt is taken from *Taking Sides* (2009).

ANALYZE CASE STUDIES

14. **Brenda Forester:** A preservice education student is concerned that one of her methods classes will not prepare her for teaching. Her philosophy of education is challenged when she observes a writing process classroom.

15. **Michael Watson:** A teacher finds that the assistant principal's evaluation of his class calls into question his teaching style as well as his philosophy of education. The evaluation suggests that his style and rapport with the students are getting in the way of his being more demanding.

OBSERVE TEACHERS, STUDENTS, AND CLASSROOMS IN ACTION

13. Classroom Observation: Essentialism in Action: A Classroom Lesson

It is hard to visualize how different philosophies might manifest themselves in the classroom. In this observation, you will observe essentialism in action as an elementary teacher organizes an exciting class competition based on a television game. The involvement and excitement of the students is apparent.

KEY TERMS AND PEOPLE

www.mhhe.com/sadker10e

CHAPTER REVIEW

Go to the Online Learning Center to take a quiz, practice with key terms, and review concepts from the chapter.

KEY TERMS

Academy, 266

aesthetics, 269

back-to-basics, 250

behaviorism, 264

behavior modification, 264

Cartesian dualism, 268

constructivism, 261

core curriculum, 251

deductive reasoning, 269

empiricism, 268

epistemology, 267

essentialism, 250

ethics, 269

ethnocentrism, 264

existentialism, 257

Golden Mean, 267

Great Books, 252

idealism, 268

inductive reasoning, 269

informal education, 265

Laboratory School, 255

logic, 269

materialism, 268

metaphysics, 267

oral tradition, 265

perennialism, 252

philosophy, 245

political philosophy, 269

pragmatism, 254

praxis, 257

progressivism, 254

rationalism, 269

scaffolding, 264

social Darwinism, 257

social reconstructionism, 255

Socratic method, 265

KEY PEOPLE

Adler, Mortimer, 252, 263

Aristotle, 267

Bagley, William, 250, 263

Counts, George, 256, 263

Dewey, John, 254, 263

Freire, Paulo, 256

Greene, Maxine, 263

Hirsch Jr., E. D., 251, 263

hooks, bell, 263

Hutchins, Robert, 253, 263

Martin, Jane Roland, 258

Neill, A. S., 263

Noddings, Nel, 263

Plato, 266

Skinner, B. F., 264

Socrates, 265

DISCUSSION QUESTIONS AND ACTIVITIES

1. Suppose that you are a student who must choose one of five schools to attend. Each reflects one of the five major philosophies. Which would you choose and why? Which school would you choose to work in as a teacher? Why?

2. Interview a teacher who has been teaching for several years. Find out what that teacher's philosophy was when he or she started teaching and what it is today. Is there a difference? If so, try to find out why.

3. Re-read the five statements by the teachers in the faculty room at the beginning of the chapter. In what areas do you think these teachers agree? In what areas are their philosophies different? What do you predict will be the result of their meeting? Which of the statements by the five teachers do you agree with most?

4. How would you describe your own philosophy of education? Imagine you are a teacher. Create a three-minute talk that you would give to parents on back-to-school night that outlines your philosophy of education and identifies how it would be evident in the classroom.

5. The key terms and people in this chapter could be dramatically expanded by including Far Eastern and Middle Eastern philosophy. Consider the following additions: Buddhism, Confucius, Hinduism, Islam, Jainism, Judaism, Mohammed, Shinto, Taoism, Zen Buddhism. Research and briefly describe each of these. What has been (or might be) the impact of these religions, principles, and individuals on our present school philosophy?

Financing and Governing America's Schools

CHAPTER 9

FOCUS QUESTIONS

1. Why do teachers need to know about finance and governance?
2. How is the property tax connected to unequal educational funding?
3. What is the distinction between educational equity and educational adequacy?
4. What are the sources of state revenues?
5. How does the federal government influence education?
6. How does commercialization at home and in school affect children?
7. What current trends are shaping educational finance?
8. How do school boards and superintendents manage schools?
9. What is the "hidden" government of schools?
10. How does the business community influence school culture?
11. How are schools being made more responsive to teachers and the community?

The school is that last expenditure upon which Americans should be willing to economize.

—FRANKLIN D. ROOSEVELT

www.mhhe.com/sadker10e

CHAPTER PREVIEW

Do you know who pays for U.S. schools, and how? You might be surprised. In this chapter, we introduce you to the decentralized, politically charged systems of school funding and school governance in the United States. You will become familiar with the sources of financial inequity in schooling and the attempts to keep effective education within the reach of all, not just the very wealthy. Both the formal structure of power in school governance (school boards, school superintendents, and the like) and the informal, hidden government will affect your life in the classroom. By understanding the mechanics behind school finance and governance, you will be more empowered as a classroom teacher and better able to influence decisions that shape the education of our nation's children.

Local and state governments have long grappled with the difficult proposition of raising enough public funds to adequately support education while dodging taxpayer ire over high taxes. Students in wealthy neighborhoods attend modern, well-equipped schools; poorer children make their way to decaying, ill-equipped school buildings in impoverished communities. Courts have forged solutions aimed at reducing these glaring disparities and bringing a measure of fairness to education. Many states are now focusing on guaranteeing that every student receives an adequate and appropriate education, but a first-class education is often hampered by hard economic times, tight budgets, and funding controversies among public, charter, and private schools.

Day-to-day classroom life is influenced not only by economic issues but also by the ways in which schools are governed. In this chapter, you will learn how schools are managed, officially and unofficially. Your knowledge of educational decision making can be a powerful ally in shaping a successful teaching career. We will also give you a quick look at what Finland has done to construct a successful educational system.

WHAT DO YOU THINK? There are three governments involved in funding education, federal, state, and local. Each must decide how much of its budget to spend on education versus other items. Try your hand at estimating what percentage of each government's budget is spent on education.

Follow the Money: Financing America's Schools

Why Should Teachers Care Where the Money Comes From?

Why should a teacher be concerned about school finance? (Put another way, why should I want to read this chapter?) Doesn't a teacher's responsibility pretty much start and end at the classroom door?

FOCUS QUESTION 1

Why do teachers need to know about finance and governance?

Sounds reasonable, but here is where the authors jump in. We believe that it is unwise, and even dangerous, for teachers to invest their time and talent in a career in which the key decisions are considered beyond their knowledge or influence. Educational finance may well determine not just the quality of life you experience as a teacher but also the very futures of the students you teach. Common sense tells us that the amount of money spent in a school is directly related to how well students learn, but not everyone agrees. What is the wisest way to invest educational dollars—and who should decide?

We believe that teachers should be major participants in financial and governance policy decisions. The current trend toward testing teachers and developing school standards is an example of what happens when teachers are left out of policy circles. The emphasis on standards and testing too often casts the teacher in the role of a technician, implementing other people's goals with the resources other people decide they should have. And in the end, other people evaluate how well teachers (and students) perform. We believe that this system serves neither teachers nor students well. We see teachers as advocates for children, children who themselves are excluded from policy decisions. Teachers and students find themselves the victims of rising educational expectations but limited educational resources. Too many teachers are forced to dig into their own pockets, spending an average of $475 a year buying classroom materials.[1]

Teachers should have a voice, and be a voice for children as well. Consider this chapter a step in that direction, and a primer on both the economics and the governance of schools.

The Property Tax: The Road to Unequal Schools

> The method of financing public schools . . . can be fairly described as chaotic and unjust.
>
> *(Supreme Court Justice Potter Stewart)*

To someone from another country, the way the United States funds its schools must seem bizarre, and certainly unfair. Unlike many other nations, which use a centralized funding system, we have a decentralized system. In fact, we have three levels of government—local state, and federal—all raising and distributing funds. Currently, the local and state governments share the biggest burden of funding schools, with the federal government responsible for just 6 to 8 percent of the total. What a tangled web we weave when fifty states, 14,000 local governments, and one enormous federal government become involved in funding and managing 100,000 schools.

FOCUS QUESTION 2

How is the property tax connected to unequal educational funding?

How did this financial hodgepodge begin? In colonial America, schools were the concern of local communities. Then, at the birth of our nation, the Constitution did not designate a federal role in education, effectively leaving it the responsibility of the states. "Local control" of schools became a well-established tradition, one that still holds sway today.

GLOBAL VIEW

Most poor countries spend more on servicing foreign debt than on educating their own children. See Oxfam International at www.oxfam.org.

In the agrarian society of colonial times, wealth was measured by the size of people's farms. So to raise money for schools, colonial towns and districts assessed a **property tax.** Although today only 2 percent of Americans still work the land, the property tax continues to be the major source of school revenue. Today's property taxes are levied on real estate (homes and businesses) and sometimes personal property (cars and boats). Whether a school district will find itself rich in resources or scrambling to make ends meet depends largely on the wealth of the community being taxed. Not surprisingly, a tax on a Beverly Hills mansion raises many more thousands of dollars than a tax on a house in South Central Los Angeles. Communities blessed with valuable real estate can easily raise funds for their schools. Impoverished communities are not so fortunate. Urban areas struggle the most, suffering not only from lower property values but also from the need to use those limited resources to fund more police officers, hospitals, subways, and other services than their suburban counterparts, a phenomenon known as *municipal overburden.*[2]

Reforming Education Finance

Unequal school funding results in stark differences. In 1968, 48-year-old sheet-metal worker Demetrio Rodriguez looked with despair at his children's school in a poor Latino section of San Antonio, Texas. Not only did Edgewood Elementary School lack adequate books and air conditioning, the top two floors were condemned, and barely half the teachers were certified.[3] Ten minutes away, in affluent Alamo Heights, children were taught by certified teachers, in comfortable surroundings with ample materials. The educational cards were stacked against Rodriguez and his neighbors: even though Edgewood residents paid one of the highest tax rates on their property of any Texas community, their property was not worth much. Edgewood raised only $37 per student; Alamo Heights raised $412 per student. Rodriguez went to court, claiming that the system violated the U.S. Constitution's guarantee for equal protection under the law.

In a landmark decision, **San Antonio v. Rodriguez** (1973), the Supreme Court ruled against Rodriguez, deferring to the long history of local communities funding neighborhood schools. The Court declared that education was not a "fundamental right" under the U.S. Constitution and that preserving local control was a legitimate reason to use the property tax system. Although the Court recognized that educational funding through the property tax was a seriously flawed system, it was left up to the states to change it. It took sixteen more years before the Texas Supreme Court would act on the Rodriguez case. By the mid-1980s, Edgewood had neither typewriters nor a playground, but affluent Alamo Heights had computers and a swimming pool. Throughout Texas, per-pupil expenditures ranged from $2,112 in the poorest community to $19,333 in the wealthiest. In *Edgewood* v. *Kirby* (1989), the Texas Supreme Court issued a unanimous decision that such differences violated the Texas constitution and ordered Texas to devise a fairer plan.

Reformers had more courtroom success under state constitutions' equal protection clauses. The California Supreme Court, in **Serrano v. Priest** (1971), struck down the state's financing system as unconstitutional. The court, faced with the glaring differences between Beverly Hills, spending $1,232 per student, and nearby Baldwin Park, spending only $577 a student, declared that education was a fundamental right under the California constitution and that the property tax system violated equal protection of that right. The court found that heavy reliance on the local property tax "makes the quality of a child's education a function of the wealth of his parents and neighbors. . . . Districts with small tax bases simply cannot levy taxes at a rate sufficient to produce the revenue that more affluent districts produce with a minimum effort." *The Serrano* v. *Priest* decision ushered in both a wave of litigation in other states and an increase in the state share of school funding[4] (see Figures 9.1 and 9.2). **Robin Hood reformers,** as they were called, won a victory as they took funds from wealthy districts and redistributed the monies to the poorer districts, much like the Robin Hood hero of Sherwood Forest fame. States have used different programs to try to equalize funding. In the foundation program, the state provides funds to ensure that each student receives a minimal or "foundation" level of educational services. Unfortunately, the established minimum is frequently far below actual expenditures. Another approach is the guaranteed tax base program, which adds state funds to poorer districts, helping to reduce economic inequities.

Profile in Education Marian Wright Edelman

Growing up in South Carolina (vintage 1940s), **Marian Wright Edelman** learned to counter the summer heat with a swim. African American children were not allowed in the public pool, so Marian and her friends did their summer swimming, diving, and fishing in the creek, even though it was polluted with hospital sewage. One of her friends decided that the bridge spanning the creek would be a good diving platform, but that decision turned out to be fatal: He broke his neck on impact. His death was one of several tragedies that taught Edelman early lessons on the deadly impact of race segregation. In recalling those tragedies, Edelman says: "You never, ever forget."[a]

Marian Wright Edelman's family provided a refuge from this racial hatred. Her father was a Baptist minister, her mother a devout Sunday School teacher, and both instilled a sense of service. Sharing a bed, a meal, or a pair of shoes with foster children or neighbors in need was a common event for Edelman and her four siblings. Because public playgrounds were closed to black children, her parents made Shiloh Baptist Church a community resource center for black sports teams, Boys Scouts, and Girl Scouts. Edelman learned that "[s]ervice is the rent we pay for living. It is the

very purpose of life and not something you do in your spare time."[b]

During the 1960s, Edelman worked as a volunteer at the National Association for the Advancement of Colored People (NAACP), campaigning for passage of the Voting Rights Act as well as finding legal assistance for students jailed during sit-ins and demonstrations. As she sorted through requests for NAACP assistance from poor black citizens, Edelman realized that law could be a vehicle to social justice. She attended Yale University Law School and became the first black woman to pass the bar exam in Mississippi. Although she practiced civil rights law, Edelman's work with poor children helped her to see that they were the most vulnerable and voiceless group in our society. Children "had no one to speak out on their behalf—no one to make sure that there were laws and government policies in place to protect them."[c] During the next four decades, Marian Wright Edelman became their voice.

Edelman founded the Children's Defense Fund (CDF) in 1973, with the mission to "Leave No Child Behind." The CDF works to ensure that every child has a Healthy Start, a Head Start, a Fair Start, a Safe Start, and a Moral Start in life. The CDF strives to protect all children—and particularly children of low-income and minority families—through research, community organization, federal and state government lobbying, and public education. Among those who worked for the CDF was a young Wellesley graduate named Hillary Rodham, who continued to advocate for children's rights later when she became the First Lady and then U.S. Senator from New York.

CDF also sponsors Freedom Schools that recruit college students to serve as mentors to more than 12,000 students both after school and during the summer. Edelman understands the

lasting influence mentors give students, and she has a message for all teachers:

Teaching is a mission, not just a task or a job. I don't care how fancy the school, how low the student-teacher ratio (which I believe should be lower), how high the pay (which I think should be higher): If children don't feel respected by adults who respect themselves, and don't feel valued, then they lose and all of us lose. Make it a reality that all children, especially poor children, are taught how to read, write, and compute so they can have happy and healthy options in their future. We need to understand and be confident that each of us can make a difference by caring and acting in small as well as big ways."[d]

[a]Marian Wright Edelman, *The Measure of Our Success: A Letter to My Children and Yours* (Boston: Beacon Press, 1992), p. 8.
[b]Ibid, p. 6.
[c]Marian Wright Edelman, *Lanterns: A Memoir of Mentors* (Boston: Beacon Press, 1999), p. 28.
[d]Ibid, p. 22.

To learn more about Marian Wright Edelman, click on *Profiles in Education*.

www.mhhe.com/sadker10e

REFLECTION: Go to the Children's Defense Fund website at www.childrensdefensefund.org and click on State Data. Compare the social problems and needs of children in your state with national averages. Which statistics surprised you? What responsibilities do you believe teachers have to ensure equal educational opportunity for children in poverty?

FIGURE 9.1

The public education dollar: Where the money comes from.

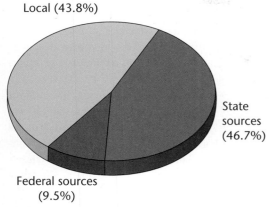

Local (43.8%)

State sources (46.7%)

Federal sources (9.5%)

SOURCE: *Public Education Finances, 2009,* U.S. Census Bureau, issued May 2011.

> **REFLECTION:** Is the proportion of revenue spent by local, state, and federal governments on education different from your initial perceptions? If you were able to suggest changes in this pie graph, what would they be? Why?

FIGURE 9.2

The public education dollar: Where the money goes.

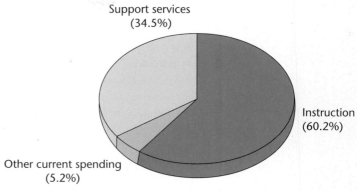

Support services (34.5%)

Instruction (60.2%)

Other current spending (5.2%)

SOURCE: U.S. Census Bureau, February, 2009 Annual Survey of Local Government Finances—School Systems. Issued May 2011.

> **REFLECTION:** Does the distribution of educational funds surprise you? Are there changes that you would suggest?

The *Serrano* victory in California was short-lived. Many voters feared tax increases, and wealthy voters revolted as their tax dollars were transported from their own children's schools to faraway poor schools. Proposition 13 was passed to limit the property tax. With decreased tax revenue, California saw its schools go into a rapid decline. California schools were finally becoming equal, but equally bad.

From Robin Hood to Adequacy

As the effort to equalize funding disparities grew, so did the opposition. In New Jersey, for example, the legislature was dominated by wealthy interests and middle-class communities who fought the Robin Hood idea. The state court shut down the schools to force the legislature to distribute more funds to poorer districts. In *Abbott* v. *Burke* (1990, 1998), the state court identified twenty-eight failing districts (known as "Abbott districts") where the rights of poor students were being denied. The court mandated that significantly greater funds be spent to transform their students into "productive members of society."[5]

The *Abbott* cases in New Jersey contributed to a new line of litigation focusing on *educational outcome* (student achievement) rather than *financial input* (per-pupil expenditures). State constitutions do not guarantee that every student is entitled to either an equal education or equal funding, but they do guarantee a basic education to all. States use different words to express this right. Some states require that every student receives an "efficient" education, others a "sound basic" education or a "thorough" education, or that all schools need to be "free and uniform."[6] Together, these constitutional clauses are referred to as **adequate education** guarantees, intended to ensure that all students have the basic skills they need to be effective citizens and compete in the labor market.[7]

States differ dramatically in how they interpret adequate education, and how effective or ineffective their responses are.[8] In Kentucky, the court ruled that the state's "entire system of common schools was infirm."[9] The Kentucky state legislature launched a new curriculum, statewide performance tests, preschool programs for at-risk students, multiple grades in the

FOCUS QUESTION 3

What is the distinction between educational *equity* and educational *adequacy*?

same class, and economic incentives for educational progress. New York initially took a mini-malist approach, but eventually went much further.[10] States from Wyoming to Ohio endured years of litigation as they struggled to define adequate education.

Perhaps the purest example of the adequacy approach is found in Maryland. Historically, states decided how much money they could afford to spend on education and then decided how best to distribute those funds. Maryland turned that approach upside down. The state appointed a commission that defined adequate education, then computed how much money was needed to achieve it. Adequate education was defined as a school with at least 94 percent student attendance, less than a 4 percent dropout rate, and 70 percent or more of the students passing state achievement tests. Then the state commission studied successful schools that were meeting those goals and found that they were spending about $6,000 per pupil. At the other end of the spectrum, low-performing schools had high numbers of poor children, non-English speakers, and children with special needs. Maryland determined that those schools would require an additional $4,500 per pupil to reach the goals of an adequate education: Maryland would need to add more than a billion education dollars. The state tackled the problem voluntarily, and without litigation.[11] Maryland calls its program "The Bridge to Excellence" and invests about 80 percent of the additional funds for teacher salaries and hiring, particularly teachers working with poor and special education students, as well as English Language Learners. *Education Week* ranks the state's schools first in the nation.[12]

Maryland is making a big investment in its schools. Is it worth it? When one economist calculated the impact of effective schools on a community, in this case Virginia Beach, Virginia, he found that the school district produced about $1.53 of community value for every $1 spent. On a national scale, the cost of poor achievement is beyond the imagination. In 2009, the consulting firm McKinsey & Co. estimated that the under education of poor and minority students costs the United States' between $1.3 trillion and $2.3 trillion (yes, trillion!) in gross domestic product a year.[13] When communities and nations cut back their educational spending, they lose far more than they save.

Adequate Education in Difficult Times

While adequate education has become the new rallying cry for more equitable school funding, the worst economic decline since the Great Depression began in 2008 and tested whether adequate education will be sustained. The recession caused most states to make deep cuts to school budgets, often affecting the neediest students.[14] New York, for example, had just created a new formula to ensure adequate education, increasing school funding by billions of dollars, and then the recession hit. At first, the plan was frozen; then it was abandoned as a new round of cut backs began. New York was not alone.[15] Other states made even more devastating cuts. The Center on Budget and Policy Priorities surveyed twenty-four states and found that twenty-one of them were spending less on education in 2012 than they did in 2011; when the rate of in inflation was considered, seventeen of the twenty-four were actually spending less than they did in 2008, even though costs for education and other services had risen. In California, the average per-pupil expenditure dropped by about $1,500, causing many school districts, including Los Angeles, to cut eight to ten days from the school year. Class size grew to thirty students, and more than forty students in some high schools. Hawaii furloughed teachers and canceled classes for seventeen Fridays in a row. Texas terminated preschool services for 100,000 (mostly at-risk) children.

When local and state budgets get tight, school budgets become a ready target for cuts.

You Be The Judge
"EQUITY" OR "ADEQUACY"

We Should Seek Educational "Equity" Because . . .

MONEY TALKS

The gap between wealthy and poor communities makes a mockery of democracy and fairness. Poor students attend schools with leaking roofs and uncertified teachers; wealthy students learn in schools with computers, swimming pools, and well-paid and qualified teachers. No real democracy can ignore such glaring inequities.

EQUALIZING INPUT IS CRUCIAL

Isn't it strange that those who advocate business values like choice and competition ignore the most fundamental business value of all: money. Wealth creates good schools; poverty creates weak ones. Invest money wisely over a period of time, and watch those once-poor schools thrive.

EQUITY IS POWERFUL

Democracy and equity are powerful words representing powerful ideals. Adequacy is a feeble word subject to interpretation and compromise. What's adequate? Is it the ability to read at a high school level, or at an eighth-grade level? Does an adequate education lead to a minimum wage job? Only "Equity" can serve as a rallying cry.

We Should Seek Educational "Adequacy" Because . . .

MONEY DIVIDES

Robin Hood is dead. Wealthy communities are not going to fund poor ones, happily sending their hard-earned dollars to fund someone else's school. The cornerstone of democracy is local control, and trying to redistribute wealth is fundamentally unfair, and smacks of the approach used by communists (another failed system).

EQUALIZING INPUT IS INEFFECTIVE

We will never make schools more effective by throwing dollars at them. When California moved toward equitable input, the quality of its public schools deteriorated. Our goal is not to increase school budgets and per-pupil expenditures, but to increase student achievement.

ADEQUACY IS ATTAINABLE

Equity is a powerful dream, but adequacy is an attainable one. We are unlikely to achieve a completely equitable school system, but we can demand reasonable and reachable educational standards. Moreover, we are on firmer legal footing, because state constitutions guarantee not identical expenditures but an adequate education for all.

www.mhhe.com/sadker10e

YOU DECIDE . . .

Do you believe that adequacy or equity provides the best foundation for reforming schools? Explain. Can these approaches be blended, or are they mutually exclusive?

Not surprisingly, it is back to the courts as school districts sued states for their promised funding. As we go to press, we do not know the outcomes of these lawsuits. Some believe that it is likely that the courts will once again require these states to honor their constitutions and fully fund schools. Others wonder if these difficult economic times may force the courts to reinterpret "adequate education" in a more limited way, requiring fewer resources from states that today seem to have fewer resources.[16]

Why are states poorer today than in the past? The national economy continues to struggle, and the anti-tax movement is starving both federal and state governments of revenues. Senior citizens are consuming more of the shrinking government budget, the national debt remains high, and all this at a

IMAGINE...

School Superintendent Gives Back $800,000

Fresno County School Superintendent Larry Powell is returning $800,000 in compensation. Powell manages 325 schools and thirty-five school districts with 195,000 students and will now earn less than a starting California teacher earns. He wants to fund projects close to his heart that were destined to be eliminated through budget cuts. Those projects include kindergarten and preschool, the arts, and a project that steers B and C students into college by teaching them how to take notes and develop learning strategy skills.

"Our goal has never been to have things," Powell said of himself and his wife. "We want to give back."

SOURCE: The Associated Press, August 28, 2011.

279

time when there are fewer households with school-age children. It is likely that schools will be forced to find new ways of educating children. Perhaps class sizes will grow, because research reports that smaller class size benefits really affect students only in the early years. Rather than base salary on teacher seniority, it may be that young and less experienced teachers with strong teaching ratings will be given increased salaries, increased responsibilities, and larger classes. Greater use of online courses and other technological advances could well reduce school costs. Consolidation is likely to continue, eliminating even more rural and small schools into larger ones considered more cost-effective.[17] Services that were once free, like school supplies, bus transportation, after-school clubs, or course materials, are in some districts already being charged to parents as "fees," a trend likely to grow.[18] Other changes are more difficult to predict. Just as charter schools are making longer school days and years more commonplace, budget tightening is having the opposite effect. It is difficult to forecast whether the school day and year will be lengthened or shortened. It is even difficult to foresee the future of adequate education laws themselves, because some question whether this approach is working.

The Camden, New Jersey experience raises doubts about using funds to improve achievement. After tens of millions of additional dollars were spent there, academic performance did not improve. Some argued that the reason for the failure was that additional funds were not used wisely. Other districts had similar experiences: court-ordered increases in school funding did not improved academic performance.[19] Perhaps it is time to rethink adequate education, and ask the question: Does money matter?[20]

Does Money Matter?

> To my knowledge, the U.S. is the only nation to fund elementary and secondary education based on local wealth. Other developed countries either equalize funding or provide extra funding for individuals or groups felt to need it.[21]

Why do Americans tolerate such dramatic inequities in school funding? Here are a few explanations:[22]

1. *Local control.* In colonial times, it was left to individual communities in rural America to support their local schools. The Constitution codified this practice, and even after urbanization and suburbanization, Americans continue to believe that local taxes should be used to educate neighborhood children.

2. *Horatio Alger.* The rags-to-riches story of fictional Horatio Alger symbolizes the strongly held American belief that wealth and success are the fruits of individual effort, and that an individual's circumstances are merely obstacles to be overcome. It stands to reason, therefore, that if hard work and motivation alone are responsible for success, poverty comes from a lack of effort and a lack of talent. Individualism absolves communities from any collective responsibility for the poverty of others.

3. *Genetics.* For centuries, genetic differences have been used to explain why some succeed and others fail. The notion that certain groups are genetically deficient is a recurring theme and often promoted in books such as Richard Hernstein and Charles Murray's *The Bell Curve*.

4. *Culture of poverty.* Some believe that poor people live in and are shaped by the problems inherent in impoverished communities, problems that cannot be remedied through additional school funding.

5. *Flawed studies.* Back in the 1960s, the classic Coleman study reported that school quality and funding had less of an effect on student achievement than family background or peer groups, that schools mattered very little. (Note: Such studies have been cited for major methodological flaws.)

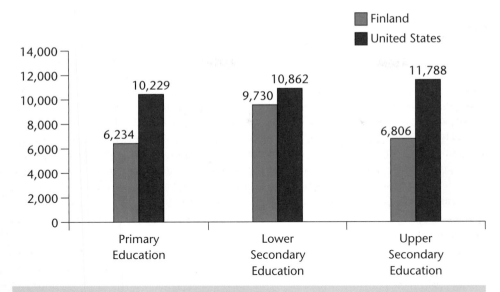

FIGURE 9.3

Comparison of per student expenditures in the United States and Finland.

SOURCE: Adapted with permission from Annual Expenditure by Educational Institutions per Student for All Services. CIEB: Finland. http://www.ncee.org/programs-affiliates/center-on-international-education-benchmarking/top-performing-countries/finland-overview/finland-system-and-school-organization/

REFLECTION: How does the way schools are managed affect the impact of the effectiveness of funding? Why is collaboration working in Finland, but not being used here?

6. *Previous funding increases have not resulted in achievement gains.* Critics point out that although education spending has increased, test scores have not. However, most new funds were not for increasing scores, but for specific educational needs, like special education, dropout prevention, expanded school lunch programs, and higher teacher salaries.

7. *Unaware of how other nations fund and manage schools.* Other countries fund and manage schools quite differently, and we can learn much from their methods. Later in this chapter, we will discuss Finland, a nation that approaches education with great freedom and flexibility, spends far less money, and often scores at the very top on international tests. In Finland, the federal government assumes about 57 percent of the costs of education, the local government the remaining 43 percent. Teachers are given great autonomy to decide the direction of education, and the key approach in schools is collaboration: successful schools, managed differently and costing far less. (See Figure 9.3.)

Does money matter? Trick question: It depends on how it is spent. Wealthier schools can attract better prepared teachers and create smaller classes, factors that make a difference.[23] Poorer schools cannot afford this.[24] In Illinois, for example, one wealthy district spends about $20,000 more per student (not $20,000 per student, which is amazing, but $20,000 *more* per student) than a poor district in that state.[25] All across America, schools with educational everything continue to exist alongside schools struggling to keep the heat in and the rats out. Research suggests that well-spent funds can reduce the achievement gap, but adequate education does not even attempt to equalize spending; it simply tries to ensure a fundamental level of learning for all students.[26] Despite the Horatio Alger "rags-to-riches" myth, studies show that children born into poor families in the United States are less likely to rise out of poverty than those in other industrialized nations.[27] Schools disappoint the poor, and states need the money to reform them.

IMAGINE...

That Will Cost You $36.13

In Scotts Valley, California, children who take a day off from school have to pay up. Students typically skip two days a year for nonillness reasons, such as family vacations. Each of those missed school days costs the local district $36.13 in lost state aid. In a typical year, that is about $250,000. The school district is asking families to make up the difference, $36.13 for each non–sick day the student skips school.

SOURCE: *Mercury News*, February 14, 2007.

States Finding the Money

FOCUS QUESTION 4

What are the sources of state revenues?

Let's assume that you have been asked by your (choose one or more of the following) (a) education professor, (b) teacher association, (c) favorite political candidate, or (d) spouse to find out where states find the money for our schools. Here are some common sources:

1. *Sales tax* (a charge added to all sales). Consumers pay a few extra pennies for small purchases or a few extra dollars for large purchases. The sales tax accounts for 30 percent of the typical state's income[28] More than 40 states use a 2 percent to 8 percent sales tax. Sounds easy, but there are problems: Some people avoid the tax by taking their business to a neighboring state. The tax is regressive; that is, it hurts poor families more than rich ones because the poor spend most of their income buying necessities, so most of their money is being taxed.

2. *Personal income tax* (used in more than 40 states). The personal income tax brings in more than 25 percent of state revenues.[29] The personal income tax is collected through payroll deductions, money deducted even before you receive your paycheck. The tax is a percentage of income, and each state determines how equally, or unequally, the tax burden falls on the poor, the middle class, and the rich.

3. *Other revenue sources.* Other common state sources of funding include excise taxes (on tobacco, gasoline, and liquor, sometimes known as a *sin tax*), severance tax (based on the state's mineral wealth), motor vehicle license fees, estate or gift taxes, and state lotteries. Although state lotteries offer holders of winning tickets the chance to collect millions in prize money, a disproportionate higher percentage of the poor purchase these long-shot lottery tickets. Most states use lottery revenues to supplement, not fund, parts of an established education budget.[30]

Your brief course in "State Finance 101" is over. You can see some of the limits of state revenue sources. For extra credit, can you devise an entirely new scheme to raise state funds? As you can tell from Figure 9.4, states vary widely in how much money is invested in education.

FIGURE 9.4

State per-pupil expenditures for elementary and secondary schools: 2009–2010

SOURCE: Public Education Finances, 2010, U.S. Census Bureau, Issued June 2012.

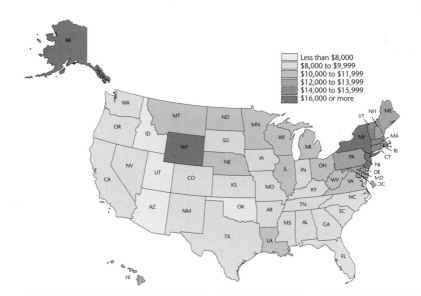

Less than $8,000
$8,000 to $9,999
$10,000 to $11,999
$12,000 to $13,999
$14,000 to $15,999
$16,000 or more

REFLECTION: Do your teaching plans include any of the states that spend the most or least amount per-pupil? Will this spending information influence your decision on where to teach? For more information on how different states respond to the needs of children, visit www.childrendefense.org.

The Federal Government's Role in Financing Education

At this point, some of you might be thinking: Even if every state provided every school district with adequate funding and a great education plan, the economic gaps among the states would still be enormous. If you thought about that, congratulations; you have put your finger on a systemic problem. For instance, students in New York or Connecticut typically receive far more education dollars than students in Mississippi or Arizona, regardless of the state's revenue plan. Because of the Constitution, this is a problem the United States seems unable to correct.

If the Constitution had assigned education as a federal responsibility, we might expect to see the federal government close the economic gap between states. U.S. schools might be centrally financed and governed; or at the very least, the Supreme Court might rule funding inequities among states unconstitutional. But this is not the case. The Supreme Court has ruled that education is not a "fundamental right" under the U.S. Constitution and has left education to the states. Accordingly, the federal government's role in the financing of education is relatively small. In fact, the federal government typically pays only 6 to 9 percent of the nation's educational costs, a very small part of its overall budget.[31] (See Figure 9.5.)

However, the federal government still manages to influence schools. How does it do this? One way has been through **categorical grants**—funds directed at specific categories and targeted educational needs. Categorical grants have provided funding for preschool programs for poor children, library construction, acquisition of new technology, educational opportunities for veterans, the training of teachers and administrators, educational reform, lunches for low-income youth, and loans to college students. By targeting funds, federal aid, although limited, has had a significant impact in schools.

The federal government also funds schools through **block grants,** large sums of money given directly to the states with few strings attached. Block grants reduce the obligations, rules, and even competition associated with seeking federal dollars. You can see that each type of grant has strengths and weaknesses. Categorical grants give the federal government influence by identifying how federal money should be used. Block grants give the states the power to make those spending decisions.

The federal government also influences education through the courts. For example, the 1954 Supreme Court's *Brown* decision desegregated the nation's schools, a monumental

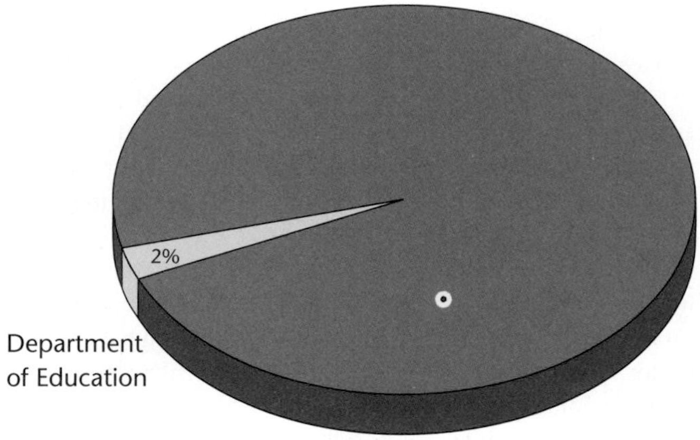

FOCUS QUESTION 5
How does the federal government influence education?

2%

Department
of Education

FIGURE 9.5
Federal budget and education. Within the federal budget, education expenditures remain quite small. This 2 percent includes elementary, secondary, vocational and higher education, as well as research and educational assistance.

SOURCE: Office of Management and Budget, fiscal year 2013.

REFLECTION: Can you think of an area of the federal budget that receives fewer dollars than education?

IMAGINE...

Investing in Teachers Pays Off

What is the financial impact of a good teacher on a student? A teacher in the top 15 percent of teachers can, *in one year,* add more than $20,000 to a student's lifetime earnings. For a class of twenty, that's $400,000 of additional earning. And that's just one teacher. Closing the achievement gap of U.S. students on international assessments would have an enormous economic impact, increasing the annual growth rate of the United States by 1 percent of GDP. Over a lifetime, this achievement gain would increase U.S. economic output at least $112 trillion. (That's trillion, not billion.)

SOURCE: Eric A. Hanushek, *Education Next*

change that affected every state in the union. The civil rights laws that followed increased educational opportunities for students of color, limited speakers of English, students with disabilities, and females. Federal courts matter, and so do targeted federal laws such as No Child Left Behind (2001), which ushered in an era of high-stakes testing that persists today. When the 2008 recession put the nation in the midst of the most profound economic crisis since the Great Depression, the federal government initiated the American Recovery and Revitalization Act (ARRA), preventing the firing of hundreds of thousands of teachers and professors.[32] But the bottom line is that the federal government's role is limited. If schools are to improve, it will be local communities and state governments that will make that happen.[33]

Schools, Children, and Commercialism

FOCUS QUESTION 6

How does commercialism at home and in school affect children?

This section is about the impact of businesses on children and schools, and we want to tell you up front that we are not neutral on this topic. Business dollars are shaping our children, and not in good ways. Along with other writers and educators, the authors of this text have deep reservations about what happens to children when they are targeted by commercial interests and when schools are used for marketing products. We believe that the goal of public education should be to open minds, not turn a profit, and children should be off limits for advertisers and business interests. So as you read this section, you should be aware of our values. But as always, we do present the arguments of those on the other side of this issue in a You Be the Judge feature in Chapter 5, where we explore for-profit schools. We invite you to read both sides of the argument and form your own opinion.

Commercializing Childhood

> We have become a nation that places a lower priority on teaching its children how to thrive socially, intellectually, even spiritually, than it does on training them to consume. The long-term consequences of this development are ominous.[34]

Just a few decades ago, the children's advertising industry spent $100 million selling products to kids, mainly through television ads. By 2006, food companies alone spent $1.6 billion marketing carbonated beverages, fast-food restaurants, and breakfast cereals to children.[35] Today, marketing is not just television ads. Computer games, cell phones, MP3 players, DVDs, and even school itself have become advertising hubs. Children are the target for 20 billion advertising dollars annually.

Why the surge in commercializing childhood? Politics, changing lifestyles, and electronic innovation all contribute to this problem. In the 1970s, corporate pressure moved Congress to prohibit the Federal Trade Commission (FTC) from banning television marketing to children under 8 years old. In the 1980s, children's television was deregulated even further, and television programs focused on selling products directly to children. As single-parent and two-working-parent families increased, so did the number of children watching television. Today, almost half of 3-month-old babies regularly watch television, and 10 percent of babies under 1 year of age have a television in their bedroom. The recent surge in personal electronic gadgets means that companies now target ads directly to children on iPods and other devices.[36]

Advertisers influence children through product placement (in movies and computer games), brand licensing (a company's brand name placed on other products), viral marketing (advertising done on pre-existing social networks), and guerrilla marketing (selling things in unconventional and unexpected places).

Today's children spend a trillion consumer dollars annually. Their allowances, their paychecks, and the influence they exert on parents' spending make them prime targets for advertisers. Marketing experts film children at play, study their behaviors, and analyze their tastes. Based on that research, sophisticated and effective sales pitches are created, and children are persuaded to buy products from fast food to cosmetics.

Are children a legitimate target for advertisers?

Here is one example of how this research shapes the buying habits of children: Advertisers have learned that younger children want to be like older children, so *aspirational marketing* was born. Advertisers intentionally market older products to younger children. Young girls are targeted for sexy adolescent clothes, although they lack the maturity to understand the strong social messages wearing such clothes sends. Abercrombie and Fitch sells thong underpants to 8-year-olds with slogans such as "wink wink" and "eye candy," and girls under 5 go to "spas" such as Sak's Fifth Avenue's Club Libby Lu to get "makeovers."[37] Rather than developing their creativity and self-expression, young girls emulate the older girls they see in *High School Musical* and *Hannah Montana*. The result is that young girls become consumers of weight-reduction products, makeup, clothes, and dating.

For young boys, it is about emulating the physical strength and toughness of older boys, so rough competitions are valued. Young boys watch wrestling matches on television, play violent video games, and sometimes experiment with steroids. The Federal Trade Commission has criticized the entertainment industry for continuing to market R-rated movies, M-rated video games, and explicit-content recordings on television shows and websites with substantial teen audiences.[38] For both genders, sex-role stereotyping is emphasized at the expense of authentic relationships. Creative play, innocence, and connecting with nature, all healthy childhood activities, are lost to commercialism.

Other industrialized nations do not let this happen. Television marketing to children is banned in Norway and Sweden, junk-food ads for the young are banned in Britain, and Greece never allows war toys to be advertised. America's children are virtually defenseless in the face of sophisticated marketing, and they pay a price. Allen Kanner, a clinical child psychologist, finds that children now talk about making money and their friends' clothes and designer labels, but "not the person's human qualities."[39]

Commercialism promotes self-gratification: "It's about me, and I want it now." Happiness is achieved by acquiring things, and one can never have enough things. Such values have led to assaults, as students attacking each other to steal designer jackets or Nike shoes. Marketing to the young teaches all kinds of lessons, few if any of them good. When the marketing occurs at school, the costs are even greater.

Brand Name Education: Should Schools Be Open for Business?

To increase attendance, some schools are offering prizes, paid for by local businesses, just for showing up. For example, in Hartford, Connecticut, a 9-year-old won a raffle for students with perfect attendance and was given the choice of a new Saturn Ion or $10,000. (His parents chose the money.) At Oldham County High School in Kentucky, a high school senior was awarded a canary yellow Ford Mustang. Krispy Kreme doughnuts awards students in Palm Beach County, Florida, a free doughnut for every report card A. Describing his quest for additional school funds, one high school principal noted, "My approach is Leave No Dollar Behind."[40]

Schools also promote specific products by entering "exclusive agreements" so that no competitive products are sold on school grounds. About 75 percent of high schools have signed exclusive soft drink contracts. Coca-Cola promised Oakland, California, half a million dollars to support a community youth program in return for a ten-year agreement banning the sale of competing soft drinks on city property. Such exclusive contracts may turn out to be a very bad business deal if schools are sued for contributing to America's obesity epidemic,[41] while keeping vendors of healthy snacks and drinks from selling on school grounds.[42]

GLOBAL VIEW

Investigate how other countries handle marketing to children.

Branding schools does not stop with products; school districts now sell the naming rights of athletic facilities, school buildings, and offer companies the opportunity to put their corporate logos on textbooks. Sometimes the corporation pays the school for getting students and parents to buy their products. General Mills donates funds to schools according to the number of boxtops turned in or other coupons showing proof of purchase. Channel One broadcasts commercials in school and on school time. Students admit they are more likely to remember the ads than the educational programs. If children grow up with Nike and McDonald's in school, they are likely to stay with those companies as adult consumers. As one critic noted, if you teach business values early enough, children accept it as truth.[43]

Schools and teachers can be persuaded to echo the tactics of advertisers. Tom Farber, an advanced-calculus teacher in San Diego, decided that a good way to pay the cost of photocopying tests was to sell advertising space to local businesses and parents. He charges $10 for an ad on a quiz, $20 for an ad on a test, and $30 for an ad on the final exam. He raised $625 and explained, "When money is tight, you really have to be creative."[44]

These are overt examples of commercialism, but it is wise to remember that the influence of business can be far more subtle. Everyday school practices that seem so familiar also teach students corporate values such as neatness, conformity, and punctuality. As educator Linda Darling-Hammond has noted:

> The short segmented tasks stressing speed and neatness that predominate in most schools the emphasis on rules from the important to the trivial, and the obsession with bells, schedules, and time clocks are all dug deep into the ethos of late nineteenth-century America, when students were being prepared to work in factories on predetermined tasks that would not require them to figure out what to do.[45]

Commercial interests can overwhelm schools, but we are not helpless. When the Seminole County, Florida, school district was paid by McDonald's to put student report cards in envelopes covered by McDonald's advertising and offering free Happy Meals, almost 2,000 parents protested. The county was forced to stop the practice. *Scholastic* magazine promoted Bratz items at their book clubs and book fairs. (Bratz is the brand for provocative and sexualized dolls made under suspect labor conditions in China.) More than 5,000 e-mails persuaded *Scholastic* to stop the practice. Massachusetts and Vermont have introduced legislation to prohibit marketing in school, and citizens and organizations continue to lobby the federal government to regulate childhood commercialization in and beyond school.

Teachers can make an enormous difference as well. Teaching media literacy empowers children to understand and confront the market messages that manipulate them. Classrooms can be places where children discuss the underlying values implicit in consumerism and its impact on the planet and themselves. Rather than sitting by as young lives become focused on consuming, educators can help children connect with healthy alternatives, such as exploring nature, developing creative talents, discovering the joys of community service, and forming authentic relationships. For those who want to learn more about confronting childhood commercialism, we recommend the Campaign for a Commercial Free Childhood as a helpful resource.

What the Future May Hold for School Finance

Today, we are in a period of shifting governmental responsibility for the financing of schools. Reformers are focusing less on financial inequity and more on educational inadequacy. What are some other trends in educational finance, issues that are likely to surface in the years ahead?

FOCUS QUESTION 7

What current trends are shaping educational finance?

Accountability

The public wants to see academic progress for their tax dollars—in short, **accountability.** Schools are often ranked by their students' standardized test scores, as the testing culture persists. Teachers find that student test scores can influence their pay and careers, while tenure itself has become more difficult to obtain, or retain.

Choice Programs and the Neighborhood School

The neighborhood school, long a mainstay of public education, is being challenged by school competition and the growth of charter schools. Many neighborhood schools are disappearing or being reconstituted. (See Chapter 5.)

Longer School Day and School Year

A number of charter schools have extended their school day and their school year as one tangible way to improve student performance. Some public schools are now following this trend, but it is difficult to determine what will happen when longer school days and years collide with shrinking educational budgets.[46]

The Economy's Impact on School Budgets

When the economy takes a downturn, state and local budgets are cut, and education suffers. This means fewer teachers, larger class sizes, and the elimination of sports, extracurricular activities, art, and music. Few state and local governments maintain the financial reserves necessary to avoid such cutbacks. This may become a steady pressure in the years ahead.[47]

The Rich–Poor School Divide Is Likely to Grow

While poor schools struggle, wealthier districts are developing creative strategies to ensure that their schools are not endangered by funding redistribution plans. Through Parent-Teacher Association donations, online fund-raisers, cooperative agreements with local business endowments, unequal local funding that gives more to schools that have more experienced teachers, and tax-sheltered private educational foundations, additional educational dollars find their way to schools in wealthier neighborhoods. Wealthy communities defend such practices as a way to prevent parents from fleeing "to private school if they don't perceive the public education to be excellent."[48]

Century-old inner-city schools are sad examples of the decaying infrastructure.

Decaying Infrastructure

Here we are in the twenty-first century, using schools that were built in the nineteenth century. When local governments need to replace these aging buildings, they usually resort to issuing bonds. A **bond** is a certificate of debt issued by a government guaranteeing payment of the original investment plus interest by a specified future date. Bonds give the local communities the money they need to build the schools and fifteen to twenty years to pay off the debt.

But for most schools, repair, not replacement, is the remedy for antiquated buildings. Although rewiring for computer and Internet installation is needed, teachers and principals give higher priority to "adequate" heating, lighting, acoustics, ventilation, and air conditioning. The Department of Education estimates that tens of thousands of schools need major repairs, repairs that range from $279 billion to $500 billion.[49] In a nationwide survey of elementary and secondary public school principals, more than 40 percent reported that poor building conditions were impairing teacher instruction and student learning.[50]

www.mhhe.com/sadker10e
INTERACTIVE ACTIVITY
Know Your School Finance Lingo! Match economic terms with educational definitions.

Commercializing Children and Schools

Many educators and psychologists believe that marketing to the nation's children, especially in school, has an adverse affect on their health and the quality of their lives. Sophisticated marketing techniques create a thirst for consumption and selfishness that replaces healthy, caring, and creative childhood activities. Although other nations protect their young from marketers, the United States does not.

Governing America's Schools

School Governance Quiz

The following quiz should help you focus on how schools are governed. If you are stumped by some of these questions, fear not; the remainder of the chapter is organized around a discussion of these questions and their answers.

1. Most school board members are (Choose only one.)
   a. White, male, and middle or upper class.

b. Middle-class women, about half of whom have been or are teachers.

c. Middle of the road politically, about evenly divided between men and women, and representing all socioeconomic classes.

d. So diverse politically, economically, and socially that it is impossible to make generalizations.

www.mhhe.com/sadker10e

INTERACTIVE ACTIVITY

School Governance
Quiz Take an electronic version of this quiz.

2. State school boards and chief state school officers are
   a. Elected by the people.
   b. Elected by the people's representatives.
   c. Appointed by the governor.
   d. Appointed by officials other than the governor.
   e. All of the above.
   f. None of the above.

3. During the past two decades, the influence of local school boards has
   a. Increased.
   b. Decreased.
   c. Remained unchanged.

4. Local school district superintendents are (You may choose more than one.)
   a. Often mediating conflicts.
   b. Civil service–type administrators.
   c. Elected officials.
   d. Sometimes powerless figureheads.

5. Who might be considered part of the "hidden school government"? (You may choose more than one.)
   a. The school principal.
   b. The state school superintendent.
   c. The U.S. secretary of education.
   d. The school secretary.
   e. Parents.
   f. The Teacher Arbitration and Labor Relations Board.

6. The influence of the business community in U.S. schools can best be characterized as
   a. Virtually nonexistent.
   b. Felt only in vocational and commercial programs.
   c. Extensive and growing.
   d. Usually illegal.

7. In most schools, teachers are expected to
   a. Design the policies guiding their schools.
   b. Collaborate with principals and district officials to create policies to suit their schools.
   c. Comply with policies made by principals and by district and state officials.
   d. Comply with policies that seem appropriate and change those that do not.

School Governance Answer Key

1. a   2. e   3. b   4. a, b, d   5. d, e   6. c   7. c

0 to 1 wrong: You receive the Horace Mann Award.

2 wrong: You may want to run for school board.

3 wrong: Read the rest of the chapter carefully.

4 or more wrong: Take detailed notes on this part of the chapter; become a frequent visitor to the text web page; find a friend to quiz you; and whatever you do, stay away from TV quiz shows.

The Legal Control of Schools

The following sections review and discuss the quiz you have just taken, beginning with the first two questions:

1. Most school board members are . . . *white, male, and middle or upper class.*

2. School boards and chief state school officers are . . . *elected by the people, elected by the people's representatives, appointed by the governor, or appointed by officials other than the governor.*

FOCUS QUESTION 8

How do school boards and superintendents manage schools?

GLOBAL VIEW

The World Data on Education (WDE) website provides access to information for 144 national education systems.

School boards, whether at the state or local level, determine educational policy, and their members tend to be male (more than 60 percent), white (more than 85 percent), and not young (most are 50 years of age or older). In short, many school board members look like the leaders we find in corporate America or government.[51] As for the second question, in some states, school boards and chief state school officials are elected; in others, they are appointed. Even the name for the chief state school officer differs from place to place: superintendent, commissioner, or even secretary of education. Why the differences? The **Tenth Amendment** reminds us: "The powers not delegated to the United States by the Constitution, nor prohibited by it to the States, are reserved to the states, respectively, or to the people." More than 200 years ago, the authors of the Constitution did not discuss education, so each state was free to create its own school system. While most nations have a national ministry of education to determine what and how all students will be taught, in our country, each of the fifty states, the District of Columbia, and several U.S. territories make those decisions.

The governor, legislature, state superintendent, or the state school board consider different ideas for improving education. One state might require that all schools have a certain number of computers, and another state might decide that all high school students must pass four years of science. Suppose you apply for a position in a state that passed a new requirement: all new teachers must pass a course in "Instructional Strategies for Improving Student Test Performance." The state superintendent and the state department of education would inform all teacher candidates (including you) of the new course requirement. If you applied to teach in the state, someone in the state department of education would review your transcript to make certain that you had successfully completed the new course on improving test scores before issuing you a teacher's license. If you took that course and completed all the state's requirements, voilá, you will be issued your teacher's license. But (nothing personal) don't expect the state to hire you.

Although states issue teacher licenses, hiring and firing of teachers is done by the local school district, about 14,000 of them across the country. So you don't apply to the state for a teaching position, but to the local district. The district will check to make certain that you have your teacher's license, and then consider you for a position. Figure 9.6 describes these levels of school governance:

State Board of Education   The **state board of education** is responsible for formulating educational policy. The members are usually appointed by the governor, but sometimes they are chosen in a statewide election.

Chief State School Officer   Called *superintendent, commissioner, secretary of education,* or *director of instruction,* the **chief state school officer** is responsible for overseeing, regulating,

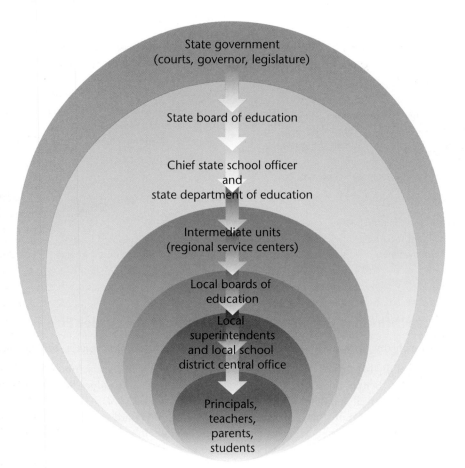

FIGURE 9.6
Structure of a typical state school system.

REFLECTION: What are some of the difficulties in these many levels of governance? Do you favor elected or appointed school boards? Why?

and planning school activities, as well as implementing the policies of the board of education. The state superintendent is usually selected by the board of education but sometimes campaigns for the position in an election.

State Department of Education The **state department of education** performs the administrative tasks needed to implement state policy. This includes licensing teachers, testing student progress, providing information and training to teachers, distributing state and federal funds, seeing that local school systems comply with state laws, and conducting educational research and development. The state superintendent usually manages state department of education activities.

School Districts—Local School Boards and Superintendents All states except Hawaii have delegated much of the responsibility for local school operations to local school districts. (Hawaii treats the entire state as a single school district.) School districts vary in size from those serving only a few students to those with more than a million. Most local school districts mirror the state organization, with a local school board that is usually elected, a superintendent, and an office of education. Local school districts may be responsible for school construction, taxing, budgeting, the hiring of school personnel, curriculum decisions, and local school policy. Although school districts operate at the local level, their authority derives from the state, and they must operate within the rules and regulations specified by the state. (A Closer Look: Who Controls What? Levels of Educational Power, summarizes the relationships between state and local control of schools.)

A Closer Look

Who Controls What? Levels of Educational Power

STATE GOVERNMENTS

- Levy taxes
- License teachers and other educators
- Set standards for school attendance, safety, etc.
- Outline minimum curricular and graduation standards (sometimes including specific textbooks to be used and competency tests for student graduation and teacher certification)
- Regulate the nature and size of local school districts

LOCAL SCHOOL DISTRICTS

- Implement state regulations and policies
- Create and implement local policies and practices for effective school administration

- Hire school personnel
- Provide needed funds and build appropriate facilities
- Fix salaries and working conditions
- Translate community needs into educational practice
- Initiate additional curriculum, licensing, or other requirements beyond state requirements
- Create current and long-range plans for the school district

REFLECTION: As a classroom teacher, offer some examples of the issues that would lead you to deal with state government. Which issues would send you down a path to the local government?

State Influence Grows as School Boards Come under Fire

3. During the past two decades, the influence of local school boards has . . . *decreased.*

Forged in the hamlets of colonial New England, school boards have symbolized small-town democracy. School board meetings evoke the essence of Americana—the kind painted by Norman Rockwell and made into a Frank Capra movie titled *Mr. Deeds Elected to the School Board* (starring Jimmy Stewart as the beleaguered school board president). But Americana aside, many criticize school boards as unresponsive and entrenched bureaucracies.

Part of the problem is that there is little consensus on how school boards should operate.[52] Most school board members view themselves as *trustee representatives,* selected to serve because of their educational expertise and good judgment. But others, including many voters, see school board members as *delegate representatives,* responsible for implementing the will of the public (or being voted out of office if they do not). The type of elections used to select school board members can shape the kind of school board that will emerge. When school boards are selected through "at-large" elections, in which the entire school district votes for all the members of the school board, the school board is expected to represent the interests of the entire community (trustee representatives). But some school districts choose board members to represent the interests of specific neighborhoods (delegate representation).

District-wide, at-large elections typically result in more elite, politically conservative, and upper-class individuals being elected to school boards. After all, it is the well-established individual who is likely to have the financial resources and educational and business background needed to win a big, district-wide election. Poorer citizens, people of color, and women are less likely to find themselves on at-large school boards. Unfortunately, many citizens feel disenfranchised when it comes to school board elections.

Other criticisms include the following:

- School boards have become *immersed in administrative details,* at the expense of more important and appropriate policy issues. One study of West Virginia school boards showed that only 3 percent of all decisions made concerned policy.

- School boards are *not representing local communities,* but only special interest groups. Elections to the school board receive little public support. In a New York City school board election, for instance, only 7 percent of the voters participated.

- The *politics of local school board elections* have a negative impact on attracting and retaining superintendents and lead to conflict with state education agencies.

- The composition of the boards is *not representative,* with individuals of color, women, the poor, and the young unrepresented or underrepresented.

- School boards have been in the *backseat when it comes to educational change and reform.* As a matter of fact, many school boards do not support current educational reform proposals, and members have lagged behind public opinion on such issues as school choice and charter schools.

- The education of children goes beyond school issues to include health, social, and nutritional concerns. School boards are *too limited in scope* to respond to all the contemporary concerns of children.

- If schools continue to be *financed less from local funds and more from state funds,* local boards could become less influential.

- Many of the new reforms call for *new governance organizations,* site-based management, or choice programs that relegate the school board to a less important, perhaps even unnecessary, role.[53]

Although these criticisms suggest a dismal future for school boards, preparing their obituary may be premature. School boards have endured a long time and may be around long after many of the reform recommendations are forgotten.

The School Superintendent and Principal

4. Local school district superintendents are . . . *often mediating conflicts, civil service–type administrators, sometimes elected and sometimes powerless figureheads.*

The first superintendents were hired to relieve school boards of their growing administrative obligations. The year was 1837, and these new superintendents worked in Buffalo and Louisville. As the nineteenth century progressed, more communities followed this example. Superintendents were expected to supervise and hire teachers, examine students, and buy supplies, which had become too burdensome for the school boards themselves. Superintendents also kept school records, developed examinations, chose textbooks, and trained teachers.

By the twentieth century, the superintendent's role had changed from the board's administrative employee to its most knowledgeable educational expert—from helper to chief executive officer. Today, the superintendent is the most powerful education officer in the school district, responsible for budgets, buildings, new programs, daily operations, long-term goals, short-term results, and recruiting, hiring, demoting, and firing personnel. When things are going well, the superintendent enjoys great popularity. But when things are going poorly, or school board members are not pleased, or local community groups are angry, or teacher organizations turn militant, or . . . you get the picture. When there is a problem, it is usually the head of the system, the superintendent, who gets fired. The superintendent lives and works in a fishbowl, trying to please various groups while managing the school district. It is a very insecure existence of sidestepping controversies, pleasing school board members, responding to critics, juggling many different roles and goals, and living with conflict. In many urban school districts, superintendents serve only a few years before they are fired, resign, or retire.[54] Many believe that this high-visibility, high-stress position is also subject to subtle forms of racism and sexism. About 80 percent of superintendents are male, and more than 90 percent are white.

One need not look hard for the reasons for this turnover. Successful superintendents must win and maintain public support and financing for their schools. This involves forming political coalitions to back their programs and to ward off attacks from those more concerned with rising taxes than with the school budget. In an era in which most citizens in many communities do not have children in schools, this becomes a real test of political acumen. Superintendents find themselves serving on a number of civic committees, speaking to community groups, and being the public relations spokesperson for the school district. Yet, despite feeling high levels of stress, nine out of ten superintendents find their work rewarding and believe they made the right career choice.[55]

School superintendents who survive and thrive are the politically savvy administrators who can "read" their school board. In *The School Managers: Power and Conflict in American Public Education,* Donald McCarty and Charles Ramsey provide a useful classification system that matches school board types with different superintendent styles.[56]

School Boards in Communities That Are . . .	*Prefer Superintendent Style That Is . . .*
Dominated: School boards run by a few local elite who dominate community and school policies	*Functionary:* Follows wishes of the board
Factional: Divided community, competing factions	*Political:* Balances often opposing concerns, avoids appearance of favoritism
Pluralistic: Competition among interest groups	*Adviser:* Moves cautiously as adviser among shifting community coalitions
Inert: No visible power structure, little interest in schools	*Decision maker:* Board relies on superintendent for leadership and decision making

An effective superintendent must be an effective manager, and a number of new superintendents of large school districts have been selected for their management skills rather than their educational expertise. New York City, San Diego, Seattle, and Los Angeles have chosen generals, lawyers, and a former governor to lead their schools.[57] Although well-known figures may bring visibility and hope, there is no superman to "fix" the problem. An effective superintendent is a good manager who builds solid relationships and persists at the job for more than a few years.[58] And good management is essential. Superintendents have been terminated when textbooks or school buses arrive late. In fact, some school districts have adopted performance-based contracts that link superintendent compensation directly to student performance.[59]

While the superintendent is the focal point of district pressures, the principal bears the brunt of school pressure. "Stress, testing, and social problems are all in the schools now: AIDS education, security, parenting classes, language programs. There are so many things that they are responsible for that they might not have control over, and it's led to concern about principal burnout."[60] Even at the elementary level, where many consider the stress most tolerable, a typical elementary principal supervises thirty teachers, fourteen other staff members, 425 students, and works an average of nine or ten or more hours a day, sixty or even seventy hours a week.[61] When budget cuts reduce support staff, they juggle roles as teachers, community liaisons, nurses, athletic directors, crisis managers and budget managers. Amazingly, 20 percent of principals report spending five to ten hours a week in efforts aimed at a single

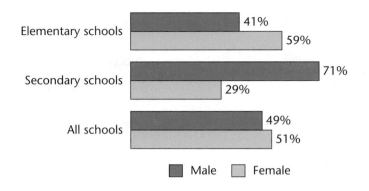

Elementary schools
41%
59%

Secondary schools
71%
29%

All schools
49%
51%

■ Male   □ Female

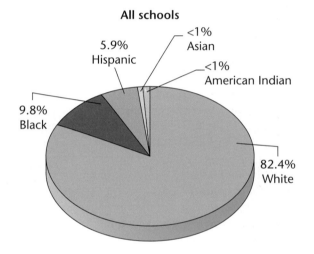

All schools

<1%
Asian

5.9%
Hispanic

<1%
American Indian

9.8%
Black

82.4%
White

FIGURE 9.7

Elementary and secondary principals.

SOURCE: National Center for Educational Statistics, "Public and Private School Principals by Selected Characteristics," *Condition of Education, 2011*, for latest available data 2007–2008.

REFLECTION: Why are more women principals at elementary rather than secondary schools? What are the potential challenges for schools with white principals and a majority of students of color?

purpose: avoiding lawsuits.[62] Principal recruiters struggle to overcome persistent racial and ethnic imbalances as well.[63] (Figure 9.7 provides insight into principal demographics.) Because of the central role of the school principal, it is not a surprise to learn that their competence is second in importance only to teacher quality in improving schools.[64]

These statistics underscore the tough challenges that superintendents and principals face, and you may be wondering, "Why would anyone want these jobs?" Here's one reason: Talented educational leaders take satisfaction from making a real difference in the lives of thousands of students. If you are considering teaching, then making a positive difference in the lives of the students in your class is a motivator for you. Magnify that and you can see why some are drawn to administration. School districts committed to serious reform know that principals and superintendents can make a difference, and New York City is a case in point. The city established its own Leadership Academy to prepare a new generation of administrators. Once they graduate, these new principals manage schools that have been made smaller to increase their effectiveness. The new principals exert greater authority, control their own budget, and hire their faculty. They also shoulder a greater responsibility for the academic performance of their students and take home a larger paycheck than past administrators. Many of these new principals are only in their 30s. In fact, more than half of New York City's principals are now under 50. Why does the city seek younger (and less experienced) leaders? "I wanted to change the old system," former Schools Chancellor Joel Klein said. "New leadership is a powerful way to do that."[65]

Covert Power in Schools

FOCUS QUESTION 9

What is the "hidden" government of schools?

5. Who might be considered part of the "hidden school government". . . *the school secretary and parents.*

So you think that the school principal is the only one responsible for school personnel decisions, including hiring and firing? Think again. Parents, vocal individuals, the school secretary, and community groups have **covert power** and can bring significant pressure to bear on which teachers stay in a school, and which leave. These unofficial but highly involved people and groups constitute the **hidden government** of schools.[66]

The concept of hidden government is not unique to schools. In fact, most of our institutions, including the White House, have developed their own unique forms of hidden government. There, decision making is often influenced more by old colleagues back home (the "kitchen cabinet") than by the president's official advisers and cabinet members.

How does hidden government operate in schools? Following are some examples.

Example 1 A first-year teacher in a New England junior high school spent long hours after school preparing lessons and working with his students. Admirable as all this appeared, the school secretary, Ms. Hand, advised the teacher not to work with female students after school hours, because "You may get your fingers burned." The teacher smiled, ignored the secretary's advice, and continued providing students with after-school help.

Within a week, the principal called the teacher in for a conference and suggested that the teacher provide extra help to students only if both male and female students were present. The teacher objected to the advice and to the secretary's complaining to the principal. The principal responded, "You're new here, and I can understand your concern. But what you have to learn is that Ms. Hand is more than a secretary. She knows this school better than I do. Follow her advice and you'll do just fine."

Lesson: You can't always tell which people hold the real power by their official position.

Lesson: The school secretary is often the eyes and ears of the principal. In some cases, the secretary manages the day-to-day operations of the school.

The school secretary holds a position that can exert significant covert power in his or her pivotal role as the principal's "eyes and ears".

Example 2 A young teacher in an elementary school in the Midwest was called into the principal's office for a conference. The principal evaluated her teaching as above average but suggested that she maintain greater discipline. Her classroom was simply too noisy, and the students' chairs were too often left in disarray. The conference was over in ten minutes.

The teacher was offended. She did not feel her classroom was too noisy, and the chairs were always arranged in a neat circle. Moreover, the principal had visited her class for only five minutes, and during that time the students had said hardly a word.

The next day, in the teacher's lounge, all became clear when she discussed the conference with another teacher. The teacher nodded, smiled, and explained:

"Mr. Richards."

"The custodian?"

"Yup. He slowly sweeps the halls and listens for noisy classrooms. Then he tells the principal. He also hates it when the chairs are in a circle, since it makes sweeping harder. Nice straight rows are much easier. Just make sure your classroom is quiet when he's in the halls and have your students put the chairs in neat, straight rows at the end of the day. That's the ticket for getting a good evaluation!"

Lesson: School custodians are often a source of information for principals and of supplies for teachers. They make very helpful allies and powerful adversaries.

Example 3 An elementary school teacher in a rural southern community was put in charge of the class play. Rehearsals were under way when the teacher received a note to stop by the principal's office at 3:00 P.M.

The principal had received a call from a parent who was quite disappointed at the small part her daughter had received in the play. The principal wanted the teacher to consider giving the child a larger part. "After all," he explained, "her mother is influential in the PTA, and her father is one of the town's most successful businessmen. It's silly for you to alienate them. Give her a bigger part. Life will be easier for both of us."

Lesson: Parents can also be influential in school decisions by applying pressure on principals, school boards, and community groups. When you decide to make a stand in the face of parental pressure, choose a significant issue and be able to substantiate your facts.

Business and Schools

6. The influence of the business community in U.S. schools can best be characterized as . . . *extensive and growing.*

Business values have long influenced school practices, and decades ago educators adopted a business vocabulary. *Superintendent,* the title originally given to a factory supervisor, was assigned to the school district leader. Both a factory and a school have been called a *plant. Quality control, accountability, management design,* and *efficiency* were also expropriated. Little surprise that a growing number of superintendents come from the business sector. School values often mirror those of business: hard work, competition, dependability, punctuality, neatness, conformity, and loyalty.[67] Companies that formalize a relationship with a school, by dedicating personnel or products or signing exclusive rights contracts, are said to have formed an **educational partnership.** A number of educators express concerns about these developments, an issue we explored earlier in this chapter. But whether we are comfortable or uncomfortable with this trend, "the most far-reaching initiative in education to emerge in recent years is the growing corporate interest in public schools."[68]

Making Schools More Responsive

7. In most schools, teachers are expected to . . . *comply with policies made by principals and by district and state officials.*

While parents, community groups, and the business sector carve out their roles in schools, teachers traditionally have been omitted from meaningful involvement in school governance.

Teachers, as a rule, do not participate in hiring new teachers, in developing criteria by which their teaching will be evaluated, in setting graduation requirements, or in scheduling classes. One reason is sheer size: Over the past centuries, schools and school districts have continued to grow. Larger districts are

FOCUS QUESTION 10
How does the business community influence school culture?

FOCUS QUESTION 11
How are schools being made more responsive to teachers and the community?

Corporate influence in schools can be seen in the emphasis on competition, punctuality, and the growing trend to advertise to children.

Teachers, who know more than most people in the educational chain about the needs and interests of individual students, have often been excluded from school management and policy making.

considered more cost-effective because they lower the per-pupil expenses, from preparing food to building maintenance, and bigger school districts are able to offer more courses, extracurricular activities, and sports programs.[69] Merging smaller schools and districts into larger ones is called **consolidation.** In 1940, more than 117,000 school districts existed in the United States. Today there are about 14,000.[70] Larger schools and school districts also mean more red tape, greater student alienation, and reduced parent-teacher involvement; in other words, less responsive schools.[71] Many districts are now reversing the trend, creating smaller schools and smaller districts, a process called **decentralization,** or creating charter schools operating without central office involvement.[72]

In addition to size, top-down decision making by principals and superintendents also contributes to a sense of teacher powerlessness.[73] Efforts to empower teachers include site-based or school-based management and collaborative decision making. **Site-based or school-based management** shifts decision making from the central district office to individual schools, and **collaborative decision making** creates teacher committees to share power between the principal and the faculty. If you find yourself teaching in a school using one or both of these approaches, keep in mind that the results have been mixed. Some teachers enjoy making curricular and budgetary decisions, but others feel such participation simply becomes "just another meeting you've got to go to." To complicate these efforts even further, federally mandated tests have preempted many local decisions.[74] One of the challenges facing you as a teacher or an administrator will be to create more responsive and humane school climates, both for yourself and your students.

Education in Finland

American students have been struggling on the international stage for decades. While many bemoan the sad state of our test scores, few take the time or make the effort to discover why students in other countries do so much better. For the past decade, for example, 15-year-old Finnish students have consistently tested at or near the top in reading, mathematics, and science. (See Figure 9.8.) Why is Finland doing so well? We will conclude this chapter by taking a brief look at how Finland manages its schools, and see what lessons it may offer us.[75]

In the early 1970s, Finland had much in common with the United States today: an underperforming education system. Their economy was in dire straits, dependent on a quickly disappearing natural resource, lumber. The Finns knew that to compete in the world economy, they would have to make fundamental changes to their schools and rebuild their economy. But unlike our reform efforts (discussed in Chapter 5), Finland did not focus on competition, school choice, merit pay, or standardized testing: Finland focused on teachers. First teacher education was revamped and turned into a five-year program of study, research, and practice. Finnish teachers were prepared to work with all students with learning disabilities and given more time to study their subject fields; when they completed their preparation, they received a master's degree. Now they were ready to begin teaching. This high-quality preparation led to a highly honored career: teaching. A career in teaching is now highly selective; nine out of every ten people who apply to become teachers are rejected. People who go into teaching enjoy their careers, and few leave.

Finland has a national curriculum not unlike our current effort to create national core standards. But in Finland, the curriculum is quite general, and teachers are given great autonomy in designing and teaching their own lessons. Unlike the United States, there are no national tests, and no emphasis on test preparation. In fact, most Finnish students take their

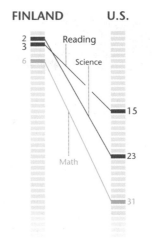

FIGURE 9.8

Rankings on international PISA tests.

SOURCE: Programme for International Student Assessment, 2009 (most current data available).

REFLECTION: What lessons do you take away from how Finland manages its schools, and how its students score on international tests?

first standardized test when they graduate high school. The few tests given before then are used for school comparisons and are not for public consumption.

Now you have the key clues to Finland's success (as well as Japan's and Singapore's educational success): *trusting teachers.* Parents trust teachers because they are professionals, and teachers trust one another and regularly collaborate to solve mutual problems. Trust is seen every day as teachers work in teams, continually improving their curriculum and each other's teaching. Their motto is "Trust Through Professionalism." The evidence indicates that trust is far more effective in raising test scores than test preparation.

Some might point out that Finland and the United States are too different to make useful comparisons. Certainly, there are differences, and those differences are worth pointing out. For one, Finland is less diverse than the United States, but it is far from a homogenous nation. Fifteen percent of the population speaks a second language, and 45 languages are spoken in Helsinki schools. Another difference favors the United States: we are wealthier. But our willingness to tolerate one out of five Americans living in poverty detracts from school achievement. Less wealthy Finland has a poverty rate of only 3 to 4 percent, but their poor receive more services than the poor here, and poverty is far less crushing. Finland's national policies to mitigate the impact of poverty are evident in school performance: The difference between the highest performing school and the lowest performing school in Finland is less than 4 percent. When one compares Finland to individual U.S. states, comparisons are even easier to make. Finland is the size and population of about thirty-three states, but it outperforms all of them on international tests.

U.S. schools are managed and to some degree financed with an eye to high-stakes testing, competition, and school choice. When Finnish educators view the way we run our schools, they are astonished. The idea of merit pay, teacher competition, and evaluating teachers by students' test scores make no sense to them. The very idea of promoting teacher competition rather than teacher collaboration is alien. Students feel less pressure, have frequent breaks for physical activity during their relatively short school day, and don't begin school until they are 7 years old. Every Finnish child gets a free school meal and a free education—even at the university level.

By focusing on quality teaching rather than testing, Finland regularly attains the highest test scores in the Western world, and its economy is rated among the most innovative, creative, and successful. It is a nation that respects its educators and gives them the autonomy to design and measure each student's education without working under the fearful shadow of testing and competition. We have much to learn from Finland.

ONLINE VIDEO ALBUM TO ACCOMPANY *TEACHERS, SCHOOLS, AND SOCIETY, 10E*

Visit the Online Learning Center for a range of contemporary videos with content related to this chapter.

www.mhhe.com/sadker10e

THE *TEACHERS, SCHOOLS, AND SOCIETY* READER WITH CLASSROOM OBSERVATION VIDEO CLIPS

Go to your *Teachers, Schools, and Society* Reader CD-ROM to:

READ CURRENT AND HISTORICAL ARTICLES

37. **Finding Fairness for Rural Students,** by Marty Strange, *Phi Delta Kappan,* March 2011.

38. **Respect—Where Do We Start?** by Marie-Nathalie Beaudoin, *Educational Leadership,* September 2011.

39. **School Funding's Tragic Flaw,** by Kevin Carey and Marguerite Roza, *Education Sector Reports,* May 15, 2008.

40. **Where Have All the Strong Poets Gone?** by Alan C. Jones, *Phi Delta Kappan,* April 2007.

ANALYZE CASE STUDIES

16. **Kate Sullivan:** A principal faces the problems endemic to the students served by her school, which is located in a very low socioeconomic area. Issues of drugs, poverty, neglect, hunger, and homelessness are compounded by the underfunding for the school.

17. **Jane Vincent:** A teacher is asked by her principal to reconsider her grading of a student whose numerical average for the marking period is just below the department's cutoff score for that grade.

OBSERVE TEACHERS, STUDENTS, AND CLASSROOMS IN ACTION

14. Classroom Observation: School Board Meeting to Discuss and Analyze Application for Jaime Escalante Charter School

As a teacher, you will be affected by decisions made by your local school board. In this observation, you will observe an actual Montgomery County (MD) School Board meeting during which officials struggle with a proposal for the district's first charter school.

KEY TERMS AND PEOPLE

accountability, 287

adequate education, 277

block grants, 283

bond, 288

categorical grants, 283

chief state school officer, 290

collaborative decision making, 298

consolidation, 298

covert power, 296

decentralization, 298

Edelman, Marian Wright, 276

educational partnership, 297

hidden government, 296

property tax, 274

Robin Hood reformers, 275

San Antonio v. *Rodriguez,* 275

school boards, 290

Serrano v. *Priest,* 275

site-based (school-based) management, 298

state board of education, 290

state department of education, 291

Tenth Amendment, 290

www.mhhe.com/sadker10e

CHAPTER REVIEW

Go to the Online Learning Center to take a quiz, practice with key terms, and review concepts from the chapter.

DISCUSSION QUESTIONS AND ACTIVITIES

1. Create a plan for (a) raising funds for education and (b) distributing funds equitably to all school districts within a state.

2. What is your opinion of the "adequacy" argument? Do you have any reservations about this approach? Do you believe that educational expenditures and educational quality are directly related? Support your position.

3. Research the average costs of educating a student in a local district. Discuss with classmates as you compare district programs, tax base, facilities, and student achievement.

4. Which of the four types of school boards would you prefer to serve on, or work for? Why? Which of the four types of school superintendents would you prefer to be, or to work for? Why?

5. Have you had any personal experience in an organization that had both a formal and a "hidden" government? Explain how these governments operated.

CHAPTER 10

School Law and Ethics

FOCUS QUESTIONS

1. What are your legal rights and responsibilities as a teacher?
2. What legal rights do students enjoy (and do they have legal responsibilities)?
3. What are the ethical responsibilities of teachers and students?

Ethics is knowing the difference between what you have a right to do and what is right to do.

—POTTER STEWART

CHAPTER PREVIEW

- An honors student sues the school district after being randomly strip-searched.
- A teacher is reprimanded for allowing a first-grader to read a Bible story to the class.
- A teacher is suspended for texting a student.
- A student complains that peer grading of assignments is a violation of privacy.
- A homosexual teacher sues a school district for discrimination.

In this chapter, you will have the opportunity to respond to actual legal situations that have confronted teachers and students. (Get ready to determine your RQ—rights quotient.) Also included are some pragmatic steps for your legal self-defense, steps that you can take to avoid potential problems. But, beyond the nitty-gritty of these legal case studies, we will ask more penetrating questions about right and wrong, questions that go beyond the law, such as: How should teachers deal with ethical issues that emerge in school? Should teachers take positions on moral issues? To handle these important but difficult ethical dilemmas, we will offer some suggestions for ways teachers can organize their classrooms, and themselves.

www.mhhe.com/sadker10e

WHAT DO YOU THINK? What is your rights quotient? Take an electronic version of the quiz starting on page 303.

Classroom Law

You have probably heard it before: The United States is a litigious society. "Take them to court," "I'll sue," and "Have your lawyer call my lawyer" are phrases that have worked their way into the American lexicon. And actions match words. People sue companies. Companies sue people. Governments sue companies. Companies and people sue governments. Today, parents sue teachers. Students sue teachers. Teachers sue schools. Lawyers and judges are increasingly a part of school life. Such a litigious world has an impact on instruction. Four out of five teachers and nearly that many principals in urban, suburban, and rural areas describe "defensive teaching"—meaning that their educational decisions are motivated by a desire to avoid legal challenges. Educators believe that fewer laws would reduce their legal concerns and improve the quality of education.[1]

Despite the growing concern over legal issues, many educators are still unaware of their basic legal rights and responsibilities.[2] This can be a costly professional blind spot. What rights do you have in the classroom? Consider this exchange between a college professor and a former associate superintendent of public instruction for California:

> SUPERINTENDENT: "Teaching is a privilege, not a right. If one wants this privilege, he or she has to give up some rights."
>
> PROFESSOR: "Just what constitutional rights do people have to give up in order to enter teaching?"
>
> SUPERINTENDENT: "Any right their community wants them to give up."[3]

Although such simplistic attitudes still exist, recent years have seen extraordinary changes in the legal rights of both teachers and students. Once the victims of arbitrary school rules and regulations, today's teachers and students can institute legal action if they believe that their constitutional rights are being threatened.

As a classroom teacher, what can you legally say and do? Can you "friend" students on Facebook? What disciplinary methods are acceptable? How does your role as teacher limit your personal life? Knowing the answers to these questions *before* you step into a classroom can help you avoid costly mistakes.

While teachers would like to know definitively what is legal and what is not, courts often set forth standards with such terms as "reasonable care" or "appropriate under the circumstances." Courts try to balance legitimate concerns that can be raised on both sides of an issue and to keep their options open. Staying legally up-to-date is an ongoing professional task.

What Is Your Rights Quotient?

The following case studies focus on court cases or federal law.[4] The vignettes are divided into two parts: teachers' rights and students' rights. In each case, an issue is identified, a situation is described, and you are asked to select an appropriate (legal) response. After your selection, the correct response and relevant court decisions or laws are described. Keep track of your rights and wrongs; a scoring system at the conclusion will help you determine your RQ (rights quotient). Good luck!

FOCUS QUESTION 1

What are your legal rights and responsibilities as a teacher?

A Closer Look — School Law Basics

Federal, state, and local governments all have a voice in education, although they don't necessarily speak in unison. To help you navigate the legal landscape, here's a brief look at how the different branches and levels of government influence school law.

THE U.S. CONSTITUTION

Although the Constitution does not mention education, it does guarantee to individuals basic rights, rights that are of concern in schools. Three Constitutional Amendments are of special interest to teachers and students.

- The **First Amendment** protects freedom of religion and speech. An important part of this Amendment is the **establishment clause,** which prohibits government (including school) advancement of religion.
- The **Fourth Amendment** protects basic privacy and security.
- The **Fourteenth Amendment** protects the right to due process and equal protection.

FEDERAL LAWS

Many federal laws influence education. The Civil Rights Act of 1964 bars discrimination on the basis of race, color, or national origin. Title IX prohibits discrimination on the basis of sex. The Individuals with Disabilities Education Act expands educational opportunities to persons with disabilities. By funding certain programs, and withholding funds from others, from elementary school through college, the federal government exerts a significant influence on education.

STATE AND LOCAL LAWS

State constitutions as well as state and local laws influence education, so there are significant local differences throughout the nation. State and local laws (also known as statutes) often deal with school financing, collective bargaining, teacher certification, and compulsory attendance.

THE COURTS

A dual judicial system of state and federal courts exists in the United States. State courts initially hear most legal issues in education. Only cases challenging the U.S. Constitution or federal laws are heard in federal courts, including the U.S. Supreme Court.

SOURCE: Michael LaMorte, *School Law: Cases and Concepts,* 10th ed. (Upper Saddle, NJ: Prentice Hall 2011).

REFLECTION: What are the advantages and the disadvantages of these different government jurisdictions determining school law?

I. Teachers' Rights and Responsibilities

Issue	*Situation 1*
Applying for a position	You did it! You finished student teaching (you were great!) and the school district you most want to teach in has called you for an interview. Mr. Thomas, from the personnel office, seems impressed with your credentials and the interview is going well. He explains that the school district is very committed to its teachers and invests a great deal of resources in training. He wants to make certain that this investment makes sense, so he asks you for your long-range plans with such questions as: "Do you see yourself teaching in this system for a long time?" and "Are you planning to get married or have children in the near future?"

_____ You answer the questions realizing that the district is entitled to know about your long-range plans.

_____ You avoid answering the questions. You think it's none of his business, but you are worried that you won't get the position.

Legal Decision Not too long ago, school districts regularly considered marital and parenthood status in employment decisions. For women these were critical factors in being offered a job, and the "right" answer was: "No, I am not going to get married or have children." For male candidates, the question was less important and rarely asked. Now a variety of federal and state laws and court decisions make such inquiries illegal. Interview questions must be related to the job requirements. Questions about race, creed, marital status, sex, religion, age, national origin, and physical or other disabilities and even a request for photographs along with an application are generally illegal. **Title IX of the Education Amendments (1972)** and **Title VII of the Civil Rights Act (1964)** are two federal laws that prohibit many of these practices. In situation 1, the questions are inappropriate and illegal, and you need not answer them. The challenge, of course, is how you could answer such questions without ruining your chances of being offered a position—that is, if you still want the job.[5]

Issue	*Situation 2*
Sexual harassment	After surviving the gender discriminatory interview, you are offered a teaching position and decide to take it. After all, you like the community and the children. You are very excited as you prepare for your first day. You enter the school, feeling hopeful and optimistic. You enjoy and respect your new colleagues, but you feel strange around Mr. Gray, the custodian. You spend the next year dodging his lewd comments, his unwanted touches, and his incessant propositions. You share your concerns with the other teachers, but you are alone in your experience. Finally you approach the school principal, who assures you that Mr. Gray means no harm, but promises to have a chat with the custodian. You feel good about giving voice to the problem but soon realize the only thing that has changed is that Mr. Gray no longer empties your classroom trashcan. The harassment continues. At the end of the year, you find yourself emotional drained and contemplating a leave of absence. You decide that

_____ Your emotional well-being is at risk. You will resign before things get worse.

_____ Enough is enough. You sue the district for damages.

Legal Decision Anita Hill's charges against Supreme Court nominee Clarence Thomas, as well as similar charges against former President Clinton, a stream of senators, and other officials have awakened millions of Americans to the issue of sexual harassment. The custodian's behavior, both verbal and physical, is clearly an example of this problem. The Supreme Court ruled that under Title IX, victims of sexual harassment are also victims of sex discrimination and can recover monetary damages. Keeping a record of the custodian's behavior and having witnesses will strengthen your case. You certainly can sue, and, if you are successful, you may be awarded significant monetary damages.[6]

Along with protecting teachers from sexual harassment and sex discrimination in employment, Title IX prohibits sex discrimination in many areas of education for employees and students, males and females. The law covers federally funded institutions—schools, colleges, vocational training centers, public libraries and museums—and ensures fairness in athletics, employment, counseling, financial aid, admissions, and treatment in classrooms.

Issue	*Situation 3*
Personal lifestyle	After your first few months, your reputation is established: You are known as a creative and effective teacher and are well liked by students and colleagues. (Isn't that wonderful!) But your life outside the classroom is not appreciated by school officials. You are single and living with your "significant other." Several school officials have strong feelings about this and believe that you are a poor role model for the students. The school system publicly announces that your cohabitation is having a negative influence on your elementary-aged students and suspends you.

_____ You are the victim of an illegal action and should sue to be reinstated.

_____ The school board is within its rights in dismissing you and removing a bad role model from the classroom.

Legal Decision This case hinges on how much personal freedom an individual abandons as a teacher and role model for students. Although court decisions have varied, the following general standard should be kept in mind: Does your behavior significantly disrupt the educational process or erode your credibility with students, colleagues, or the community? If the school district can demonstrate that you have disrupted education or have lost credibility, then you may be fired.

In the case outlined here, the teacher sued the school district (*Thompson* v. *Southwest School District*). The court indicated that until the school district took action to suspend the teacher on grounds of immorality, the public was generally unaware of the teacher's cohabitation with her boyfriend. The court decided that it was unfair of the board of education to make the issue public to gain community support for its position. Furthermore, the court ruled that the teacher's behavior had not interfered with her effectiveness in the classroom. With neither a loss of credibility nor a significant disruption of the educational process, the board lost its case and the teacher kept her job.

Do you believe that a teacher's sexuality is a legitimate consideration for employment?

What if the teacher's "significant other" was of the same sex? Whether gay and lesbian teachers need legal protection from dismissal based on sexual orientation is a divisive and unsettled debate. Although there is no federal law prohibiting this discrimination, a growing number of states and nearly two hundred cities and counties prohibit sexual orientation discrimination in employment. Even in places without specific laws protecting gay and lesbian teachers, it is unlikely that they can be dismissed without direct evidence showing that a homosexual lifestyle negatively affects their teaching.

Court decisions regarding the personal lifestyles of teachers have differed from state to state. Driving while intoxicated or smoking marijuana was found to be grounds for dismissal in one state but not in another, depending on whether the behavior resulted in "substantial disruption" of the educational process. On the other hand, an attempt to dismiss a teacher because she did not attend church was not upheld by the court.

What about your personal appearance? What can a school district legally require in regard to personal grooming and dress codes for teachers? Courts have not been consistent in their decisions, although the courts may uphold the legality of dress codes for teachers if the dress requirements are reasonable and related to legitimate educational concerns.[7] (See A Closer Look: How Private Is Your Personal Life?)

A Closer Look   How Private Is Your Personal Life?

Courts are constantly asked to draw the line between a teacher's personal freedom and the community's right to establish teacher behavior standards. Although each case must be judged on its own merits, some trends do emerge. Courts have ruled that the community has the right to fire a teacher for

- Making public homosexual advances to nonstudents
- Incorporating sexual issues into lessons and ignoring the approved syllabus
- Inciting violent protest among students
- Engaging in sex with students
- Encouraging students to attend certain religious meetings
- Allowing students to drink alcohol
- Drinking excessively
- Using profanity and abusive language toward students
- Stealing school property (even if it is returned later)
- Not living within his or her district if that is listed as a condition of employment
- Wearing inappropriate clothing, such as short skirts or jeans

On the other hand, courts have ruled that teachers should not be fired for

- Unwed cohabitation
- Private homosexual behavior

- Obesity (unless it inhibits teaching performance)
- Adultery
- Use of vulgar language outside school
- AIDS or disability

Why are teachers dismissed in some cases and not in others? Often, the standard the courts use is whether the behavior under question reduces teacher effectiveness. Public behavior, or behavior that becomes public, may compromise a teacher's effectiveness. In such cases, the courts find it reasonable and legal to terminate the teacher. If the behavior remains private, if the teacher shows discretion, the teacher's "right to privacy" often prevails.

SOURCE: Nathan L. Essex, *School Law and the Public Schools: A Practical Guide for School Leaders,* 5th ed. (Boston: Allyn & Bacon, 2011).

REFLECTION: Courts have disagreed on whether the following three situations constitute grounds for dismissal of a teacher. If you were the judge, how would you rule on the following issues?
- Sex-change operation
- Unwed parenthood
- Conviction for shoplifting

Issue

Teachers' academic freedom

Situation 4

As a social studies teacher, you are committed to teaching about the futility of hate and discrimination. You assign your middle school students the fictional mystery *The Terrorist,* a novel that evokes strong feelings on ethnic and religious issues. Class discussions and activities focus on challenging stereotypes and creating peaceful responses to violence. Your students find the novel engaging, and class discussions are lively and respectful. But in the post–9/11 climate, some parents are upset, and the school board asks you not to teach such a controversial lesson. Committed to your beliefs, you persist. At the end of the school year, you find that your teaching contract is not renewed.

www.mhhe.com/sadker10e

INTERACTIVE ACTIVITY

What Can a Teacher Be Fired For? Test your knowledge of teacher's rights.

_____ Because you think your academic freedom has been violated, you decide to sue to get your job back.

_____ You realize that the school board is well within its rights to determine curriculum, that you were warned, and that now you must pay the price for your indiscretion.

Legal Decision The right to **academic freedom** (that is, to teach without coercion, censorship, or other restrictive interference) is not absolute. The courts will balance your right to academic freedom with the school system's interests in its students' learning appropriate subject matter in an environment conducive to learning. Courts look at such factors as whether your learning activities and materials are inappropriate, irrelevant to the subjects to be covered under the syllabus, obscene, or substantially disruptive of school discipline. In this case, the lesson related to ethnic and religious differences appears to be appropriate, relevant, and neither obscene nor disruptive. If you were to sue on the grounds of academic freedom, you would probably get your job back.[8]

Legal Decision In recent years, litigation against teachers has increased dramatically. The public concern over the quality of education, the bureaucratic and impersonal nature of many school systems, and the generally litigious nature of our society have all contributed to this rising tide of lawsuits. Negligence suits against teachers are common. In the cafeteria example, you would be in considerable jeopardy in a legal action. A teacher who is not present at his or her assigned duty might be charged with negligence unless the absence is "reasonable." The courts are very strict about what is "reasonable." (Leaving your post to put out a fire is reasonable, but going to the telephone to make a call is unlikely to be viewed as reasonable.) It is a good practice to stay in your classroom or assigned area of responsibility unless there is an emergency.

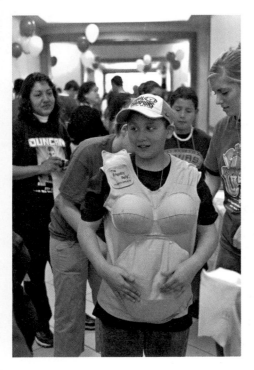

Academic freedom protects a teacher's right to teach about sensitive issues, such as sex education topics, as long as the topic is relevant to the course, is not treated in an obscene manner, and is not disruptive of school discipline.

Issue

Legal liability (negligence)

Situation 5

You are assigned to cafeteria duty. Things are quiet, and you take the opportunity to call a guest speaker and confirm a visit to your class. While you are gone from the cafeteria, a student slips on some spilled milk and breaks his arm. His parents hold you liable for their son's injury and sue you for damages.

_____ You will probably win, because you did not cause the fall and were on educational business when the accident occurred.

_____ The student's parents will win, because you left your assigned post.

_____ The student who spilled the milk is solely responsible for the accident.

_____ No one will win, because the courts long ago ruled that there is no use crying over spilled milk. (You knew that was coming, right?)

Teacher liability is an area of considerable concern to many teachers. Courts generally use two standards in determining negligence: (1) whether a reasonable person with similar training would act in the same way and (2) whether or not the teacher could have foreseen the possibility of an injury. Following are some common terms and typical situations related to teacher liability:

- **Misfeasance.** Failure to conduct in an appropriate manner an act that might otherwise have been lawfully performed; for example, unintentionally using too much force in breaking up a fight is misfeasance.
- **Nonfeasance.** Failure to perform an act that one has a duty to perform; for example, the cafeteria situation is nonfeasance, since the teacher did not supervise an assigned area of responsibility.

- **Malfeasance.** An act that cannot be done lawfully regardless of how it is performed; for example, starting a fistfight or bringing marijuana to school is malfeasance.

So what is your "take-away" from this case? Here are some reasonable precautions you can take to avoid liability:

- Establish safety rules for students.
- Try to anticipate and avoid dangerous situations.
- Warn students of any potential dangers.
- Provide proper supervision.
- If an accident does occur, document the specifics and how you helped the victim.

What is not on this list is liability coverage. It is wise to check with your district's personnel office to determine the limits of professional liability protection. Teacher associations and organizations usually offer additional and voluntary liability policies for you. One common risk that teachers unwittingly take is to offer rides to their students for school events. You might want to check your district's liability policy about autos before doing this. Remember, your personal insurance policy may not cover student injuries.[9]

Although liability usually involves physical injury to students because of what a teacher did or failed to do, a new line of litigation, called **educational malpractice,** is concerned with "academic damage." Some students and parents have sued school districts for failing to provide an adequate education. Many courts have rejected these cases, pointing out that many factors affect learning and that failure to learn cannot be blamed solely on the school system.

Issue	*Situation 6*
Teachers' freedom of speech	As a teacher in a small school district, you are quite upset with the way the school board and the superintendent are spending school funds. You are particularly troubled about all the money being spent on high school athletics, because these expenditures have cut into your proposed salary raise. To protest the expenditures, you write a lengthy letter to the local newspaper criticizing the superintendent and the school board. After the letter is published, you find that the figures you cited in the letter were inaccurate.
	The following week, you are called into the superintendent's office and fired for breaking several school rules. You have failed to communicate your complaints to your superiors and you have caused harm to the school system by spreading false and malicious statements. In addition, the superintendent points out that your acceptance of a teaching position obligated you to refrain from publicizing critical statements about the school. The superintendent says although no one can stop you from making public statements, the school system certainly does not "have to pay you for the privilege." You decide to

_____ Go to court to win back your position.

_____ Chalk it up to experience, look for a new position, and make certain that you do not publish false statements and break school rules in the future.

Legal Decision This situation is based on a suit instigated by a teacher named Marvin Pickering. (*Pickering v. Board of Education*) After balancing the teacher's interests as a citizen in commenting on issues of public concern against the school's interests in efficiently providing public services, the Supreme Court ruled in favor of the teacher. It found that the disciplined operation of the school system was not seriously damaged by Pickering's letter and that the misstatements in the letter were not made knowingly or recklessly. Moreover, there was no special need for confidentiality on the issue of school budgets. Hence, concluded the Court, prohibiting Pickering from making his statements was an infringement of his First Amendment right to freedom of speech. You, too, would probably win in court if you were to issue public statements on matters of public concern, unless your statements were intentionally or recklessly inaccurate, disclosed confidential material, or hampered either school discipline or your performance of duties.[10]

A teacher's freedom of speech often involves gray areas and may not always come out in the teacher's favor. Consider these two cases. A federal judge ruled that a Southern California public high school history teacher violated the First Amendment when he made disparaging statements during a classroom lecture about Christians and their beliefs and called creationism "religious, superstitious nonsense." The First Amendment prohibits teachers from displaying religious hostility.[11] Can a teacher wear a political button in the classroom? During the 2008 presidential campaign, many New York City public school teachers wore buttons to school in support of their candidate. Critics argued that the buttons created an environment of intimidation and hostility toward students who did not share their teacher's opinion. The teachers insisted that the students were able to distinguish between personal and institutional views. A federal judge ruled against the teachers.[12]

Issue	*Situation 7*
Copying published material	You read a fascinating two-page article in *The New York Times Magazine,* and, because the article concerns an issue your class is discussing, you duplicate the article and distribute it to your students. This is the only article you have distributed in class, and you do not bother to ask either the author or the magazine for permission to reprint it. You have

_____ Violated the copyright law, and you are liable to legal action.

_____ Not violated any copyright law.

Legal Decision A teacher's ability to freely reproduce and distribute published works is determined by **copyright laws.** Such laws provide guidelines for using someone else's intellectual property, such as written material, original audio and visual work, and computer programs. Teachers may use copyrighted materials in class under three conditions:

- Written permission is obtained from the author or publisher.
- Material is in the public domain (it is more than 75 years old or is published by the government).
- Reproduction of material is considered *fair use.*

Fair use is legal principle that allows the limited use of copyrighted materials without written permission or payment. Teachers must observe three criteria in selecting the material: brevity, spontaneity, and cumulative effect.

1. *Brevity.* A work can be reproduced if it is not overly long. It is always wise to contact publishers directly, but typical limits might include the following cri⁀   Poems or excerpts from poems must be no longer than 250 words. Articles, stories, and essays of less than 2,500 words may be reproduced in complete form. Excerpts of any prose work may be reproduced only up to 1,000 words or 10 percent of the work, whichever is less. Only one illustration (photo, drawing, diagram) may be reproduced from the same book or journal. The brevity criterion limits the length of the material that a teacher can reproduce and distribute from a single work. If you were the teacher in this example and you reproduced only a two-page article, you probably would not have violated the criterion of brevity.

2. *Spontaneity.* If a teacher has an inspiration to use a published work and there is simply not enough time to receive written permission, then the teacher may reproduce and distribute the work. The teacher in our vignette has met this criterion so is acting within the law. If the teacher wishes to distribute the same article during the next semester or the next year, written permission would be required because ample time exists to request such permission.

3. *Cumulative effect.* The total number of works reproduced without permission for class distribution must not exceed nine instances per class per semester. Within this limit, only one complete piece or two excerpts from the same author may be reproduced and only three pieces from the same book or magazine. Cumulative effect limits the number of articles, poems, excerpts, and so on that can be reproduced, even if the criteria of spontaneity and brevity are met. The teacher in our vignette has not reproduced other works and therefore has met this criterion also.

What are the three criteria for fair use of copyrighted materials in your classroom—and can you answer this without peeking at the text?

Under the fair use principle, single copies of printed material may be copied for your personal use. Thus, if you want a single copy for planning a lesson, that is not a problem. Whenever multiple copies are made for classroom use, each copy must include a notice of copyright.

What about DVD recordings, computer software, mixed media, and the vast amount of material published online? These resources, like printed materials, are considered *intellectual property* and are copyrighted. Text, graphics, web page code, online videos (including YouTube), multimedia materials, and even e-mail and Facebook postings are copyright protected. Therefore, teachers must follow fair use guidelines when using videos, photos, and information obtained from the Internet and gleaned from e-mail attachments. With so much information at our fingertips, both teachers and students need to be aware that all work posted on the Internet is copyright protected, whether or not a specific notice is included. It is always advisable to check with your local school district officials to determine school policy and procedures.[13]

Issue	*Situation 8*
Labor rights	Salary negotiations have been going badly in your school district, and at a mass meeting teachers finally vote to strike. You honor the strike and stay home, refusing to teach until an adequate salary increase and benefits are provided. During the first week of the strike, you receive a letter from the school board, stating that you will be suspended for fifteen days without pay at the end of the school year, owing to your participation in the strike. You decide

_____ To fight this illegal, unjust, and costly suspension.

_____ To accept the suspension as a legal action of the school board.

Legal Decision State courts vary in upholding teachers' right to strike. In some states, courts have determined that teachers provide a vital public service and cannot strike. Although more than 30 states have laws that prohibit strikes, many communities choose not to prosecute striking teachers.[14] You need to understand your state laws and community norms to know if you are breaking the law by honoring the strike. The decision to strike is a difficult one. Under what circumstances, if any, you would choose to strike?

In a number of cases, courts have recognized the right of teachers to organize, to join professional organizations, such as the NEA (National Education Association) and the AFT (American Federation of Teachers), and to bargain collectively for improved working conditions. You cannot legally be penalized for these activities. Yet, even though membership in teacher organizations and the right to collective bargaining have been upheld by the courts, some states and communities are adamantly opposed to such organizations and refuse to hire or to renew contracts of teachers who are active in them. Such bias is clearly illegal; nevertheless, it is very difficult to prove in court and, consequently, it is very difficult to stop.[15]

In summary, law and reality do not always coincide. Legally speaking, teachers may be prohibited from striking by state law but are rarely prosecuted or penalized. In some places, active involvement in teacher organizations (albeit legal) may result in discriminatory school board actions. If you choose to strike, join a union, or participate in collective bargaining, do so with the realization that such activity may make you liable to legal sanctions or, at the very least, community hostility.[16]

II. Students' Rights and Responsibilities

FOCUS QUESTION 2

What legal rights do students enjoy (and do they have legal responsibilities)?

Issue	*Situation 9*
Student records	You are a high school teacher who has decided to stay after school and review your students' records. You believe that learning more about your students will make you a more effective teacher. As you finish reviewing some of the folders, Brenda, a 16-year-old student of yours, walks in and asks to see her folder. Because you have several sensitive comments recorded in the folder, you refuse. Within the hour, the student's parents call and ask if they can see the folder. At this point, you

_____ Explain that the information is confidential and sensitive and cannot be shared with nonprofessional personnel.

_____ Explain that the parents can see the folder and describe the procedure for doing so.

Legal Decision *The Family Rights and Privacy Act,* commonly referred to as the **Buckley Amendment,** allows parents and guardians access to their children's educational records. The amendment also requires that school districts inform parents of this right and establish a procedure for providing educational records on request. Moreover, written parental permission is needed before these records can be shared with anyone other than professionals connected with either the school the student attends or another school in which the student seeks to enroll, health or safety officials, or individuals reviewing the student's financial aid applications. If the student has reached 18 years of age, he or she must be allowed to see the folder and is responsible for granting permission for others to review the folder.

The Buckley Amendment was recently tested by the common teacher practice of asking students to exchange and grade others' papers. In *Owasso Independent School District*

Profile in Education   Morris Dees

"Flight delayed." For most, those two words evoke frustration and impatience. But for **Morris Dees,** a delayed flight was a life-changing event. At the airport bookstore, he bought a used copy of Clarence Darrow's *The Story of My Life*. Although he had long admired Darrow for his defense of John Scopes in the famous "Monkey Trial," Dees had not known of Darrow's decision to leave the security and success of corporate litigation to practice civil rights law. Darrow's choice inspired Dees. "[A]ll the pulls and tugs of my conscience found a singular peace. It did not matter what my neighbors would think or the judges, the bankers, or even my friends. I had found an opportunity to return to my roots, to fight for racial equality."[a] He sold the profitable book company that he had started with a friend and began to practice civil rights law full-time.

Dees had earned a law degree from the University of Alabama and had become quite successful, both at his small law firm and at his book company, Fuller & Dees, which became one of the country's largest publishing houses. The company was based in Montgomery, Alabama. While Dees turned profits, Martin Luther King Jr. was in the same city, focused on turning hearts. As Dees points out, back then, he didn't pay much attention to

King. "The Movement happened all around me, but I was oblivious, too caught up in the finesse of business . . . until [that] stormy night in 1967 at a Cincinnati airport."[b]

Not that Dees was new to the racial struggle of the South. Growing up in Alabama, Morris Dees worked with black laborers in the cotton fields his father owned, an unusual partnership in the deeply segregated South of the 1940s. As he worked alongside them, he learned about the scars of prejudice, both physical and emotional. The seeds of his career in civil rights advocacy were sown on those Alabama cotton fields but needed time to take root.

In 1969, Dees sued the YMCA. Fifteen years after *Brown* v. *Board of Education*, the YMCA still refused to admit African American youth to its summer camp. Dees filed a class action suit to stop the YMCA's policy of racial discrimination. The suit was a long shot. Private organizations were considered beyond the scope of civil rights law—the business and social stalwarts untouchable. Morris Dees didn't flinch, and because of *Smith* v. *YMCA,* the Montgomery YMCA was forced to desegregate.

Lawyer Joe Levin, another Alabamian, followed *Smith* v. *YMCA* closely, impressed with the imagination and dogged determination of Dees. In 1971, the two joined forces to create a small civil rights firm, the Southern Poverty Law Center (SPLC). Today, the SPLC is a national nonprofit organization known for its legal victories against white supremacist groups, tracking of hate groups, and sponsorship of the Civil Rights Memorial.

Dees's call for justice and understanding can be heard in the classroom

as well. Dees has created Teaching Tolerance, a collaboration between the SPLC and teachers across the country. The project features a magazine, videos, and curriculum to help teachers and students collectively tackle issues of racial, religious, class, and gender bias.

After completing a study that showed an increase of hate websites, Dees realized that hate had a new home. The Internet. He wanted to recapture the wonder of the Internet and use it to spread fairness. Dees and Teaching Tolerance created Tolerance. org, an interactive site of anti-bias lessons and classroom activities. After more than thirty years of litigation and education, Morris Dees has adopted this latest tool in his quest for social justice. "To everything there is a season. There will be a season of justice."[c]

[a]Morris Dees, *A Season for Justice: The Life and Times of Civil Rights Lawyer Morris Dees* (New York: Charles Scribner, 1991).
[b]Ibid.
[c]Ibid.

To learn more about Morris Dees, click on *Profiles in Education*.

www.mhhe.com/sadker10e

REFLECTION: Will you choose to confront discriminatory attitudes and behavior in your classroom? in yourself? (Yes, we all have biases.) How? Take a tour of http://tolerance .org. Submit an original anti-bias teaching idea to Tolerance.org.

v. *Falvo,* the Supreme Court ruled that students can grade their peers' academic work and even announce the results in class without violating the privacy act. The Court determined that under the Buckley Amendment, grades do not become private and part of students' educational records until they are recorded in a teacher's grade book.

Under this law, you should have chosen the second option, for it is the parents' right to see this information.[17]

Issue	**Situation 10**
Suspension and discipline	You are teaching a difficult class, and one student is the primary source of trouble. After a string of disorderly episodes on this student's part, the iPads for the entire class mysteriously disappear. You have put up with more than enough, and you send the student to the principal's office to be suspended. The principal backs you up, and the student is told not to return to school for a week. This action is

_____ Legal and appropriate (and probably long overdue!).

_____ Illegal.

Legal Decision Although troublesome and disorderly students can be disciplined, suspension from school represents a serious penalty, one that should not be taken lightly. When considering suspension, the Supreme Court has ruled (**Goss v. Lopez**) that teachers and administrators are required to follow certain procedures to guarantee the student's **due process** rights granted by the **Fourteenth Amendment.** In this case, the student must be informed of the rule that has been broken and of the evidence. The student is also entitled to tell his or her side of the story in self-defense. For suspensions in excess of ten days, the school must initiate more formal procedures. School officials can be held personally liable for damages if they violate a student's clearly established constitutional rights (*Wood* v. *Strickland*).

If you look back at this vignette, you will notice that you do not know for sure that this student is responsible for the missing iPads, nor is the student given the opportunity for self-defense. If you selected "illegal," you chose the correct response.

Many schools have adopted zero-tolerance policies in an attempt to create safe schools. A **zero-tolerance policy** typically sets out predetermined consequences or punishment for specific offenses, regardless of the circumstances or disciplinary history of the student involved. Many schools have zero-tolerance policies covering possession of firearms, alcohol, drugs, and tobacco, as well as incidents of violence. Courts have generally ruled that students' constitutional right to due process is not violated by zero-tolerance policies. However, opponents point out that zero-tolerance policies are inherently unfair and can backfire. For example, one 6-year-old was expelled for bringing a weapon into school. His grandmother had placed a "weapon" in his lunch sack—a plastic knife for spreading peanut butter. The American Bar Association has denounced zero-tolerance policies that mandate expulsion or referral to juvenile court for minor offenses that do not compromise school safety. Others worry that zero-tolerance policies contribute to a "schools-to-prisons" pipeline that overwhelmingly hurts more minority than white children. Hispanic and African American students make up nearly three-quarters of students involved in school-related arrests or incidents involving police. Black students are three times more likely than their white peers to be suspended or expelled. Revealing another pattern of discrimination, gay, lesbian, and bisexual youth are more likely to be punished than their straight peers. Are minority students committing more infractions, or are they receiving tougher punishment for similar incidents?[18]

While considering discipline, let us look at the legality of **corporal punishment.** In *Ingraham* v. *Wright* (1977), the Supreme Court ruled that physical punishment may be authorized

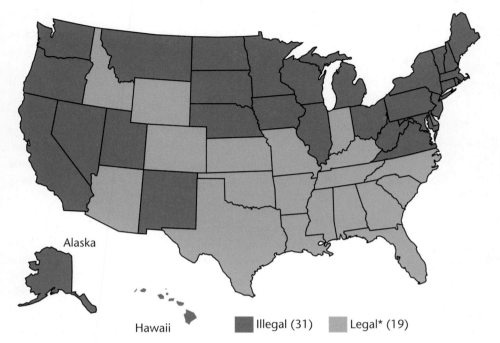

FIGURE 10.1

Corporal punishment.

*In states where corporal punishment is legal, not all school districts implement the policy.

SOURCE: Center for Effective Discipline, "States Banning Corporal Punishment," April 2012, www.stophitting.com.

Alaska

Hawaii   ■ Illegal (31)   ■ Legal* (19)

REFLECTION: Knowing whether corporal punishment is legal in your state and in your school is only part of the issue; sorting out your philosophy on this issue is more to the point. As a teacher, would you use physical punishment against a student? Explain your reasoning.

by the states. The Court ruled that the corporal punishment should be "reasonable and not excessive," and such factors as the seriousness of the student offense, the age and physical condition of the student, and the force and attitude of the person administering the punishment should be considered. Although the courts have legalized corporal punishment, many states and school districts do not believe in it and have prohibited the physical punishment of students; other districts and states provide very specific guidelines for its practice. You should be familiar with the procedures and norms in your district before you even consider this disciplinary strategy.[19] (See Figure 10.1.)

Issue	**Situation 11**
Freedom of speech	During your homeroom period, you notice that several of your more politically active students are wearing T-shirts with a red line drawn through a cell phone. You call them to your desk and ask them about it. They explain that they are protesting the new school board policy that prohibits cell phone use and texting during school hours. You tell them that you share their concern but that wearing the protest T-shirts is specifically forbidden by school rules. You explain that you will let it go this time because they are not disturbing the class routine, but that if they wear them again, they will be suspended.
	Sure enough, the next day the same students arrive at school still wearing the T-shirts, and you send them to the principal's office. The students tell the principal that although they understand the rule, they refuse to obey it. The principal suspends them. The principal's action is

_____ Legally justified, because the students were given every opportunity to understand and obey the school rule.

_____ Illegal, because the students have the right to wear T-shirts if they so desire.

Courts have upheld students' freedom of speech in a number of cases, so long as the protests were not disruptive of other students' right to learn and were not obscene.

GLOBAL VIEW

Free the Children gives young people a powerful and legitimate voice in the creation of their own future. Children study and redesign education, family environments, business, and politics. www.freethechildren.org

Legal Decision In December 1965, three students in Des Moines, Iowa, demonstrated their opposition to the Vietnam War by wearing black armbands to school. The principal informed them that they were breaking a school rule and asked that they remove the armbands. They refused and were suspended.

The students' parents sued the school system, and the case finally reached the Supreme Court. In the landmark *Tinker* v. *Des Moines Independent Community School District* case, the Court ruled that the students were entitled to wear the armbands, as long as the students did not substantially disrupt the operation of the school or deny other students the opportunity to learn. Because there was no disruption, the Court ruled that the school system could not prohibit students from wearing the armbands or engaging in other forms of free speech.[20] The school system in this vignette acted illegally; it could not prevent students from wearing the protest T-shirts.

Hate speech is another matter. For example, a California high school prevented a student from wearing a T-shirt with the slogan "Homosexuals are shameful." The student argued that such a dress code policy violated his First Amendment right to free speech. But a federal court ruled that "demeaning of young gay and lesbian students in a school environment is detrimental not only to their psychological health and well-being, but also to their educational development" and that students should feel safe from attacks based on sexual orientation, race, religion, and gender while at school.[21]

In *Morse* v. *Frederick,* limits were again placed on student speech, this time when the message might promote drug use. What does "Bong Hits 4 Jesus" mean to you? Is it offensive, or nonsensical? An Alaskan high schooler, Joseph Frederick, displayed the banner with the phrase as the Olympic torch passed by his school. Frederick explained: "I wasn't trying to say anything about religion. I wasn't trying to say anything about drugs. I was just trying to say *something.* I wanted to use my right to free speech." Rather than display the banner on school grounds, he crossed the street, but the school principal also crossed the street and confiscated the banner. Although the student was not on school property, the Supreme Court supported the principal's action and opined that though the student was not disruptive, his speech was promoting an illegal activity.[22]

Does *Tinker* apply in cyberspace? Maybe.

Although the courts have not definitely resolved the issue, several "cyberTinker" decisions support First Amendment rights. One of the first lawsuits arose after a Missouri high school suspended a student for creating an Internet homepage that criticized his school administration. The student, Brandon Buessink, created the homepage outside school on his home computer. The website caused no documented disturbance at this school, and a federal district court reversed the suspension, citing the principal's simple dislike of the content as "unreasonable justification for limiting it."[23]

Yet tech-savvy students are increasingly paying a price, including criminal arrest, for parodying their teachers on the Internet. A study by the National School Boards Association found that more than one in four teachers has been targeted with online pranks by their students. Tired of jokes and false accusations, teachers and schools are fighting back against digital ridicule by their students, often with lawsuits and long-term suspensions or permanent expulsions.[24]

The issue of allegedly "obscene" student speech has been considered by the Supreme Court. In *Bethel School District* v. *Fraser,* the Court evaluated the First Amendment rights of a high school senior, Matthew Fraser. Fraser presented a speech at a school assembly that contained numerous sexual innuendoes, though no explicit, profane language. After Fraser was suspended for his speech and told that he was no longer eligible to speak at his class's graduation, his father sued the school district. The Court upheld the suspension on the grounds that the language in the speech was indecent and offensive and that minors should not be exposed to such language.[25]

Issue	*Situation 12*
School prayer	A student in your class objects to the daily prayer recitation. You are sensitive to the student's feelings, and you make certain that the prayer is nondenominational. You also tell the student that he may stand or sit silently without reciting the prayer. As a teacher, you have

_____ Broken the law.

_____ Demonstrated sensitivity to individual needs and not violated the law.

Legal Decision You were sensitive, but you violated the law. Teachers are not allowed to lead a class in prayer. The Supreme Court has ruled that educators must be completely neutral with regard to religion and may neither encourage nor discourage prayer (***Engel v. Vitale***). Public schools can, however, offer courses on comparative religion, and teachers may read from the *Bible,* the *Koran,* or any religious text as an example of literature, as long as no religious doctrine is promoted or defamed.

Although the First Amendment prevents educators from promoting religious activities, the issue varies for students. For example, students may engage in private prayer and religious discussion during school and form religious clubs on school property if other, nonreligious clubs are also given school space. Although "official" prayers given by school personnel are not permitted at graduation ceremonies (where they frequently are heard despite the law), state laws vary on whether a student can give a graduation speech when the speech includes prayer. However, the Court has declared that student-led public prayers at athletic events constitute school sponsorship of religion, a violation of the establishment clause of the First Amendment.

The Pledge of Allegiance also sparks controversy in public schools. Though many state and local school districts often champion the need for patriotism when requiring students to recite the pledge, students cannot be compelled to salute the flag. Finally, a moment of silence can be observed in schools as long as its purpose is secular and does not encourage prayer over any other quiet, contemplative activity. Students can, however, voluntarily choose to pray during this time.[26] (See A Closer Look: Religion and Public Schools for a detailed review of religion in schools.)

> **IMAGINE...**
>
> **Religious Freedom for All?**
>
> In Alabama, a family of Jewish children was repeatedly harassed after complaining about the promotion of Christian beliefs in their public schools. One of the students was forced to write an essay on "Why Jesus Loves Me." At a mandatory school assembly, a Christian minister condemned to hell all people who did not believe in Jesus Christ.
>
> SOURCE: Anti-Defamation League, May 19, 2006, www.adl.org/issue_ religious_freedom/separation_cs_primer_violations_schools.asp.

Issue	*Situation 13*
Search and seizure	The drug problem in your school is spreading, and it is clear that strong action is needed. School authorities order a search of all student lockers, which lasts for several hours. Trained police dogs are brought in, and each classroom is searched for drugs. The school principal randomly chooses several students, who are taken to the locker rooms and strip-searched.

The First Amendment guarantees freedom of religion in our nation. It also requires *a separation of church and state* so that one religion is not preferred over any other in government institutions. What does this mean for public schools? The following United States Supreme Court decisions offer some guidance.

Yes...	Yes...	No...	No...
Parents can enroll their children in a private, religious school instead of a public school. *Pierce* v. *Society of Sisters* (1925)	Schools must provide equal access to public facilities to all groups, including religious organizations. *Board of Education* v. *Mergens* (1990)	Teachers cannot require students to recite prayers in class. *Engel* v. *Vitale* (1962)	Schools cannot require a moment of silence for silent prayer. *Wallace* v. *Jaffree* (1985)
Students can refuse to salute the American flag. *West Virginia State Board of Education* v. *Barnette* (1943)	Students may say public prayers at school athletic events. *Santa Fe Independent School District* v. *Jane Doe* (2000).	Schools cannot ban religious clothing and symbols. *Tinker* v. *Des Moines School District* (1969)	Teachers cannot teach creation science instead of evolution. *Edwards* v. *Aguillard* (1987)
Students may be excused from public school to attend religious classes away from school property. *Zorach* v. *Clauson* (1952)	Parents can use public money (vouchers) to send their children to private religious schools. *Zelman* v. *Simmons-Harris* (2002)	Schools cannot post a copy of the Ten Commandments. Stone v. Graham (1980) *Stone* v. *Graham*	Teachers and school leaders cannot lead prayer at public school graduation ceremonies. *Lee* v. *Weisman* (1992)

REFLECTION: What place, if any, do you believe religion has in school?

_____ School authorities are well within their rights to conduct these searches.

_____ Searching the lockers is legal, but strip-searching is inappropriate and illegal.

_____ No searches are called for, and all these activities present illegal and unconstitutional violation of student rights.

Legal Decision Courts have ruled that school authorities have fewer restrictions than do the police in search-and-seizure activities. Moreover, the school has a parent-like responsibility (termed ***in loco parentis***) to protect children and to respond to reasonable concerns about their health and safety. Courts have indicated that school property, such as lockers or cars parked in the school lot, is actually the responsibility of the school. A student's locker may be searched by a school official if there is *reasonable suspicion* that the locker contains something illegal or dangerous. At the same time, courts have determined that randomly conducting strip searches or spot-checking lockers for drugs, weapons, or other illicit materials violates students' rights under the Fourth Amendment. (The **Fourth Amendment** protects basic individual privacy and ensures due process.)

In this situation, the locker search is legal because the lockers were not randomly searched and the increased drug problem at the school gave the school principal reasonable suspicion. However, the strip search is illegal, because students were randomly selected with no grounds for suspicion.

The second choice is the correct response. Although school personnel have great latitude in conducting school search and seizures, educators should be familiar with proper legal procedures and should think carefully about the related ethical issues.[27]

Issue	*Situation 14*
Freedom of the press	*The Argus* is the official student newspaper, written by students as part of a journalism course, but it has run afoul of school administrators. First, the student newspaper ran a story critical of the school administration. In the next edition, the paper included a supplement on contraception and abortion. With their patience worn thin, school administrators closed the publication for the remainder of the school year.

_____ Closing the student newspaper is a legal action.

_____ Closing the student newspaper is an illegal action.

Legal Decision The Supreme Court ruled in ***Hazelwood School District* v. *Kuhlmeir*** that student newspapers may be censored under certain circumstances. The Court held that student newspapers written as part of a school journalism course should be viewed as part of the official school curriculum. School administrators, according to the Court, can readily censor such a paper. In situation 14, because the publication is part of a journalism course, closing the school newspaper would be legal.

On the other hand, if the newspaper were financed by the students and not associated with an official school course, the students would enjoy a greater degree of freedom. Additional grounds for censoring a school newspaper include obscenity, psychological harm, and disruption of school activities.[28]

Issue	*Situation 15*
HIV-infected students	As you enter school one morning, you are met by a group of angry parents. They have found out that Randy, one of your students, is HIV positive. There is no compromise in the voices of the parents confronting you. Either Randy goes, or they will keep their children at home. You listen sympathetically but find your mind wandering to your own contact with Randy. You worry that you, too, may be at risk. In this case, you decide

_____ It's better to be safe than sorry, so you ask Randy to return home while you arrange a meeting with the principal to discuss Randy's case. There is no cure for AIDS and no reason to put every child's life in jeopardy.

_____ AIDs treatments have greatly improved. It's probably okay for Randy to attend school, so you check with your principal and try to calm down the parents.

Legal Decision In *Bragdon* v. *Abbott,* the Supreme Court determined that HIV-infected students are protected under the Individuals with Disabilities Education Act and cannot be denied a public education. The Court concluded that the loss of a student's education is more harmful that the remote chance of other students contracting AIDS. If some AIDS children present more of a public risk (for example, biting behavior, open sores, and fighting), more restrictive school environments may be required. To date, however, HIV-infected students and teachers are not viewed as a significant risk to the health of the rest of the population and cannot be denied their educational rights.[29]

Issue	*Situation 16*
Sexual harassment	Christina, an eleventh-grader, confided in her guidance counselor: "I didn't do too well on a pop quiz in Mr. Armando's algebra class. Mr. Armando suggested I repeat the quiz after school in his office. I thanked him for the second chance, especially since I want to make highest honors this year. But before I began the quiz, he started stroking my hair and whispering that I'd have to be nice to him if I really wanted to bring up my grade. I felt really uncomfortable." Sexual harassment?

_____ This is a clear example of an unwanted sexual request.

_____ While the teacher's behavior is suggestive, sexual harassment cannot be proven based on a student's uncomfortable feelings. Without witnesses or evidence, this is a classic "he said–she said" scenario.

Legal Decision Educators wrestle every day with the challenge of helping students feel safe in schools, and have both a legal and an ethical responsibility to prevent and respond to harassment. What is **sexual harassment**? Is it what happens if a male student or teacher accidentally bumps into a girl in the hallway? Does it mean teachers can't hug students? That hand-holding between students is wrong? Absolutely not! These are popular misconceptions. Sexual harassment *is not* an accidental jostle on the way to class, an encouraging hug, or a show of affection. Sexual harassment *is* unwelcome behavior of a sexual nature that occurs in person or electronically. Harassment ranges from sexual comments and gestures, to inappropriate touching, to rape—and the consequences are troubling. Sadly, sexual harassment is a pervasive, harrowing part of everyday school life for both males and females that interferes with students' and teachers' abilities to learn, study, work, achieve, or participate in school activities. (See Figure 10.2.) Four out of five students report being harassed at school or online. Students fear attending school, withdraw from friends and activities, and suffer sleep and eating difficulties. More than half of students harassed do not share the abuse with anyone; one in four talk with family, and only 9 percent report the harassment to an adult at school.[30]

Title IX is the federal law that prohibits sex discrimination, including sexual harassment, in schools. The law recognizes two broad categories of sexual harassment: *quid pro quo* and *hostile environment*.[31] *Quid pro quo* is a Latin phrase meaning "this for that." This type of sexual harassment occurs when a person with authority, like Mr. Amando in this scenario, abuses

FIGURE 10.2

Who harasses whom?

SOURCE: Harris Interactive, *Bullying, Teasing and Sexual Harassment in School.* (Washington, DC: American Association of University Women, 2008).

REFLECTION: As a teacher, if you observed each of these four kinds of harassment, how would you respond?

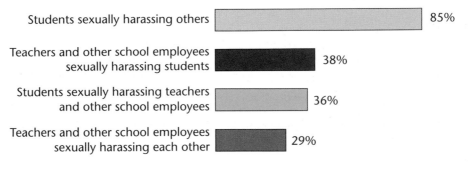

When students were asked for their perceptions of who is harassing whom in their own schools, they reported:

Students sexually harassing others — 85%

Teachers and other school employees sexually harassing students — 38%

Students sexually harassing teachers and other school employees — 36%

Teachers and other school employees sexually harassing each other — 29%

that authority to get sexual favors. *Hostile environment* consists of unwelcome sexual behavior so severe or widespread that it creates an abusive environment. This hostile behavior can be inappropriate spoken or written comments or physical conduct. Here's an example of a hostile environment:

> Albert is slender and not athletically inclined. In the locker room before gym class, his male peers tease him about his weight and clumsiness. They call him "fag," "sissy," and "girl," and snap their wet towels on his butt. Several times when Albert opened his locker, he found a bra and girls' panties with his name written on them. Albert now tries to skip gym class.

In *Franklin v. Gwinnett County Public Schools,* the Supreme Court extended the reach of Title IX, allowing students to sue a school district for monetary damages in cases of sexual harassment. The Gwinnett County case involved a Georgia high school student who was sexually harassed and abused by a teacher. The school district was instructed to pay monetary damages to the student—establishing a precedent.[32]

Two relatively recent Court decisions make collecting personal damages from school districts more difficult, although an individual accused of sexual harassment can still be sued for personal damages. In *Gebser v. Lago Independent School District* and *Davis v. Monroe County Board of Education,* a more conservative Supreme Court ruled that a school district must show "deliberate indifference" to complaints about teacher and peer sexual harassment before a district would be forced to pay damages. That means that complaining to a teacher or even a principal is now not enough; the complaint has to go higher.[33]

Sexual harassment complaints against teachers have been increasing. Teachers need to realize that sexual harassment laws prohibit not only overt actions but also offensive words and inappropriate touching. While a teacher's intention might be pure and caring, a student's perception can be quite different. The threat of the legal broadside that can result from this gap between teacher intentions and student perceptions has sent a chill through many school faculties. Teachers now openly express their fears about the dangers of reaching out to students, and some teachers are vowing never to touch a student or be alone in a room with a student, no matter how honorable the intention. Many teachers lament the current situation, recalling earlier times when a teacher's kindness and closeness fostered a caring educational climate, rather than a legal case.[34]

Scoring   What is your RQ (rights quotient)?

13 to 16 correct:	Legal eagle
11 or 12 correct:	Lawyer-in-training
9 or 10 correct:	Paralegal
7 or 8 correct:	Law student
6 or fewer correct:	Could benefit from an LSAT prep course

www.mhhe.com/sadker10e

INTERACTIVE ACTIVITY

Practice with Court Cases. Match names of court cases with their description.

This brief review of the legal realities that surround today's classroom is not meant to be definitive. These situations are intended to highlight the rapid growth and changing nature of school law and the importance of this law to teachers. It will be your responsibility to become informed, and stay current, on legal decisions that influence your actions inside and outside your classroom. Ignorance of the law, to paraphrase a popular saying, is no defense. More positively, knowledge of fundamental legal principles allows you to practice "preventive law"—that is, to avoid or resolve potential legal conflicts so that you can attend to your major responsibility: teaching.

Teaching and Ethics

FOCUS QUESTION 3

What are the ethical responsibilities of teachers and students?

Many citizens believe that the most important issues facing U.S. schools are ethical. Beyond simply following the law, students need to understand right from wrong. Cheating, for example, is not only against the rules, most consider it morally wrong. Social networking creates an ever-growing hyper-connective world that creates new ethical challenges for schools. Child abuse is yet another moral issue most teachers confront.

Cheating: The Dishonor Role

An overwhelming majority of students say: "It's not worth it to lie or cheat, because it hurts your character." The problem is, 90 percent of teens admit they cheat. (See Figure 10.3.) Why this troubling disconnect? Students blame pressure to perform, the competitive college-admissions process, and apathy toward schoolwork.[35] People always seem to find good reasons to do not-so-good things. Adults, the role models for the young, are caught in similar hypocrisies. From politicians to salespeople, from professional athletes to media stars, students are immersed in a less-than-honest culture. That does not mean cheating is okay; it means we need to look in and beyond schools to remedy the problem.

Cheating in school has become easier. Forget the traditional crib sheet tucked away under a sleeve; students today have discovered more high-tech forms of cheating. Invisible-ink pens, cell phones, and other palm-size gadgets are the new crib sheets at school, and the Internet has become a powerful temptation at home. The Internet has made it easy for students to cut-and-paste their way to a term paper, downloading a few sentences or even entire essays and then weaving them into their papers, without crediting the original sources. Such practice constitutes plagiarism, grounds for suspension from many schools. Yet many students admit to this "cut-and-paste" method to complete assignments. Some do not even cut and paste; they buy ready-made term papers from commercial websites.[36] Online companies, such as Turnitin.com, offer schools plagiarism detection programs. Students submit their completed work online, and the detection program then produces a report for teachers that

FIGURE 10.3

The dishonor role.

SOURCE: Josephson Institute for Youth Ethics: *The Ethics of American Youth* (2011).

REFLECTION: This is from a recent study of 40,000 public and private high school students. Has cheating become an acceptable norm in American schools? Why or why not? As a teacher, how will you address cheating?

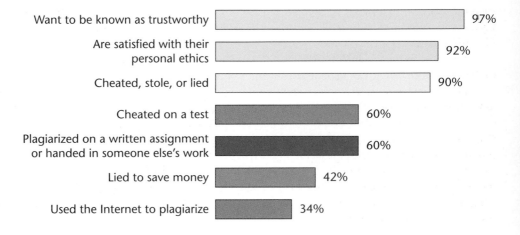

Percentage of students who:

Want to be known as trustworthy — 97%
Are satisfied with their personal ethics — 92%
Cheated, stole, or lied — 90%
Cheated on a test — 60%
Plagiarized on a written assignment or handed in someone else's work — 60%
Lied to save money — 42%
Used the Internet to plagiarize — 34%

highlights material copied from other sources. Teachers can also simply type a suspicious sentence or two from a student essay into a search engine such as Google to identify plagiarized material.

Perhaps most important, teachers can be proactive and work with students to promote honesty over deceit. Not only is plagiarism dishonest, it may also be a sign that students lack certain academic skills: Develop those skills and plagiarism will decrease. For example, some students are unable to synthesize and then summarize information. Unable to do these intellectual tasks, they resort to plagiarizing. If teachers can help students learn these skills— summarize information, use citations properly, and develop their own insights—plagiarism may well decrease. Finally, when teachers help students to explore values related to cheating, such as integrity and honesty, and when a consistent no-cheating policy is applied, students get the message and cheating is less likely.[37]

Social Networking Comes to School

Cheating is only one of a myriad of ethical issues teachers and students will confront in and beyond the classroom; the digital world is also proving to be a tricky ethical challenge. Half of all teens send at least sixty text messages a day; one in five send more than 200; and three out of four youth prefer texting to talking. Three-quarters of teenagers use social networking tools, such as Facebook and Twitter, daily. And it's not just teens using digital media. Club Penguin is the number-one social networking choice for pre-teens, and the site is visited more times every day than the *New York Times*.[38] In the face of such rocketing popularity, do students (and adults) have the skills and ethics to responsibly participate in social media? Do students understand their privacy rights? What personal information should they give online? How will they decide what to share? What are the potential consequences of their social media choices? Brainstorm other questions that will help you, as a teacher, provide lessons in *digital citizenship*. (In Chapter 11, we will explore how technology can support effective instruction.)

Some teachers have started using social media tools such as Facebook and Twitter to improve class discussions, build rapport, answer questions about class assignments, and keep students informed about school activities. Teachers report that by connecting with students on social networking sites, they often discover interests or hobbies that help them engage kids in the classroom, positively affecting academic performance. Posting class schedules and assignments online keep students and their parents up-to-date on school happenings. But potential pitfalls loom. Because most e-communication lacks facial or voice clues, even the most well-intentioned interactions can be misinterpreted. Boundaries can quickly blur when teachers "friend" their students. Some students worry about looking like the "teacher's favorite." Others say it would be "creepy" to have a teacher as a social networking friend. And sometimes "friending" has turned criminal. A small, but increasing, number of teacher–student cyber-interactions have led to sexual encounters.[39]

Finding what role, if any, social networking, texting, and other cyber-inspired communications play in schools can be challenging. Some schools prohibit any teacher–student interaction via texting and social networking sites. Others are trying to find a balance and allow cyber-communications for educational purposes only. (See the Teaching Tip: Social Networking Guidelines for specific suggestions on how to safely and ethically navigate the online world with your students).

Digital social networking is an integral part of students' lives. What might be the impact on learning? Brain development? Social skills?

Teaching Tip

SOCIAL NETWORKING GUIDELINES

Teachers are held to a high standard of professional conduct. Think before you post, text, or e-mail. Anything that is publicly available online could be seen by your students, their parents, or school administrators. Before you post any information or images, consider whether it could cause you embarrassment or potentially damage your reputation or career. Here are some tips to consider when using Facebook, Twitter, or other social networking accounts:

- Inform parents that you might text message students or communicate with them through Facebook about school-related issues. Establish an opt-out opportunity if parents are uncomfortable.
- Establish clear rules for connecting with students via cell phones, texting, Twitter, or the Internet.
- Communicate only about classroom and school matters.
- Create *separate* professional and personal sites.

- Do not accept students as friends on personal social networking sites.
- Limit personal information made available to students.
- Do not discuss students or co-workers or publicly criticize school policies or personnel.
- Do not post images that include students without parental permission.
- Check personal sites regularly if the public has access to them. Even if you don't post inappropriate material, that doesn't mean your "friends" won't.

REFLECTION: Do you think these guidelines are fair? Why or why not? What additional social networking suggestions would you offer to teachers, or to anyone?

Protecting Your Students

Sam, the new student, seems so awkward in school, and he is often late. You have asked him more than once why he can't get to class on time, but he is barely audible as he mumbles, "I dunno." What's more, his behavior is strange. He seems to have an aversion to chairs, and, whenever possible, he prefers to stand in the back of the room alone. His clothes are not the neatest or cleanest, which is unusual in your class, where most of the children come from middle-class homes and dress fairly well. You have never seen Sam laugh or even smile. Every day, even on the hot ones, he wears a long-sleeve shirt. What is that all about?

Then, one day, Sam arrives in class with some bruises on his face, and you begin to suspect that there is more to this story. You ask Sam, who shrugs it off and says that he fell and bruised his face. But you are not so sure. You arrive at a frightening thought: Could Sam be an abused child? Now, what do you do?

In this case, you are confronting both an ethical dilemma and a legal challenge. Maybe you should speak to Sam's parents. Or should you press Sam for more information? Checking with other teachers makes sense, to see how they would handle the problem. Or perhaps it is time to go to the administration and let them find out what is going on.

Wait a second. What if you are wrong? Sam says he fell down and bruised himself. Maybe that is all it is. You should not go around accusing people without real evidence. Are you responsible for Sam's family situation? Is that a private concern rather than your business? Maybe the prudent course of action would be to monitor the situation for now and keep your suspicions to yourself. What would you do?

The ethical issue is pressing. The potential for harm to Sam is simply too great to remain silent. Many would suggest that the most ethical course to follow would be to share your concerns with an appropriate person in your school, perhaps a school psychologist, counselor, or

A Closer Look   Child Abuse

Types of Abuse

Physical abuse (11%)

Psychological abuse (8%)

Sexual abuse (8%)

Medical neglect (2%)

Neglect (78%)

*A child may suffer multiple types of abuse, so numbers add to more than 100 percent

Children who suffer abuse and neglect may

- Exhibit signs of injury—burns, black eyes, welts, or bite marks
- Wear long sleeves even in very warm weather
- Not show emotion—no joy, pain, or anger
- Be apathetic toward school and friends
- Be frequently absent or tardy
- Be unusually eager to please
- Demonstrate hostility or distress
- Be dirty or unbathed
- Show signs of an eating disorder or extreme hunger
- Exhibit unusually sophisticated knowledge of sexual behavior

- Create stories or drawings of an unusually sexual nature
- Have difficulty sitting or walking
- Be frequently absent or tardy
- Show signs of depression
- Lack concentration
- Fear adults

SOURCE: Childhelp USA (2012), www.childhelpusa.org.

REFLECTION: If one of your students showed warning signs of abuse, whom in your school would you approach first? How would you phrase your concern?

administrator, or to notify Child Protective Services, a report that can be confidential. Sharing your concern is not the same as making an accusation of child abuse, which may be false. By bringing the situation to the school's attention, you start the wheels in motion to uncover facts.

Child abuse and neglect include a range of mistreatments, including physical, emotional, and sexual harm. (See A Closer Look: Child Abuse.) Child abuse occurs at every socioeconomic level, across ethnic and cultural lines, within all religions, and at all levels of education. An estimated 6 million children are reported abused each year.[40] The American Humane Institute, however, notes that very few child abuse reports come from educators. As far as reporting suspicion of child abuse is concerned, an ethical responsibility is reinforced by the law. Most states require that teachers report suspected cases of abuse, and failure to report such cases can result in the loss of a teacher's license. Most of these laws also protect teachers from any legal liability for reporting such cases.[41]

As a teacher, you will be called to follow your ethical compass to protect the physical and emotional well-being of your students and to guide students' own ethical development.

Here is an idea to help you along this ethical path. Do an Internet search of Teacher Code of Ethics. Both the National Education Association (NEA) and the American Federation of Teachers (AFT) have teacher codes of ethics. Read them to get an idea about what they believe is important. Also, it might be interesting to read the ethical codes of other careers to see how they are similar and different. Ethics is too little talked about in our culture, but it is at the heart of leading an honorable personal and professional life.

Moral Education: Programs That Develop Ethics and Values

During the American colonial experience, schools transmitted a common set of values. Back then (and in many places today), the teacher inculcated ideas of diligence, hard work, punctuality, neatness, honesty, conformity, and respect for authority, both civil and religious. It was thought that instilling these values in children would produce virtuous adults. This approach continued in college where the most important course was moral philosophy, required of all students and often taught by the college president. But not everyone agrees that preaching such values is the only or the best way to produce moral citizens. Today, schools choose from different approaches to moral education and ethics, and three of the most widely known are (1) character education, (2) values clarification, and (3) moral stages of development.

Character Education **Character education** programs assume that there are core attributes of a moral individual that children should be directly taught in school. Most states are either recipients of federal character education grants or require character education through legislation. What values are promoted? Core values include trustworthiness, respect, responsibility, fairness, caring, and good citizenship, and these values are encouraged through the school culture, conduct codes, curriculum, and community service. Younger students may be asked to find examples of these qualities in literature and history, and older students may consider these values through ethical reasoning exercises. Along with developing core values, character education programs can challenge students to act on these values. For example, students may debate how best to implement a school's honor code, organize a food drive, or plan a ceremony honoring local military veterans. Some character education programs include training in conflict resolution to develop problem-solving skills and respect.

Not everyone is enamored with character education. Opponents view this approach as superficial, artificially forcing a diverse student population into a simplistic and narrow set of unexamined values that does not really alter behaviors. (A nationwide study of more than 6,000 students at eighty-four schools that have implemented character education programs in all classes and activities did, in fact, find no improvement in student behavior or academic performance.[42]) Other critics believe that character education is little more than the old-fashioned "fix-the-kids" approach, a return to a traditional or religious agenda that simply rewards students who do what adults desire. Who selects the values or the way the values are taught are issues at the heart of these concerns.[43]

Values Clarification The controversial **values clarification** program is designed to help students develop and eventually act on their values. Students might explore questions such as: What qualities do you value in a friend? When is lying acceptable? Would you be willing to donate your body to science when you die? How do you feel about competition? Would you welcome a person of a different race into your neighborhood? Throughout such values clarification exercises, students begin to bring their private values into a public light, where they can be analyzed, evaluated, and eventually put into action. This allows students to respond to each others' beliefs, to consider different points of view, and to analyze their own values. Many believe that values, like plants, need light and thoughtful nurturing to be healthy.

You Be The Judge

MORAL ETHICS IS BEST DEVELOPED BY

Caring and Wise Adults Who . . .

INSTILL A SHARED SET OF VALUES THAT AFFIRM A NATIONAL IDENTITY

Americans believe in a common code of values to teach our children: respect, patriotism, trustworthiness, and responsibility. Our national fabric is built on such values, and our nation's future depends on them.

HELP SHAPE UNFORMED MINDS

Throughout history, educators have recognized that children have "impressionable" minds. Teaching common values develops an ethical compass. Without moral direction at a young age, as Theodore Roosevelt once noted, youth can quickly become "a menace to society."

COUNTER MEDIA CORRUPTION

Television, music, videos, and online media bombard children with commercialism, violence, and sex. Schools must be proactive in helping families instill traditional moral values, such as hard work and citizenship, in an effort to counter the disturbing and negative influences of the media.

Engaged and Independent Students Who . . .

REPRESENT OUR COUNTRY'S INCREASING DIVERSITY

In a nation of citizens with different cultural backgrounds, instilling a single fixed set of values is unrealistic and undemocratic. Our diverse population can celebrate and benefit from values nurtured in different cultures, creating a safe, caring, and fair democracy marked by tolerance and acceptance.

LEARN TO MAKE MEANINGFUL MORAL CHOICES

Rather than being "told" what values to follow, it is far better for teachers to help students become reflective and critical thinkers. When students are given the opportunity to develop their values, they are more likely to own and act upon them in meaningful ways.

CHALLENGE SOCIAL INJUSTICE

Typical traditional American values instilled in the young often ignore pressing social needs such as poverty, violence, racism, and sexism. When students investigate the world, they are more likely to see these injustices, and become active in eliminating them, creating a more just and vibrant democracy.

www.mhhe.com/sadker10e

YOU DECIDE . . .

What role should moral education play in public schools? Examine textbooks and curriculum used in a local school to determine the major values being taught to students. Are students expected to accept the values or to critically examine them? Which strategy do you support?

Critics charge that values clarification is itself valueless. In this approach, all values are treated equally, and there is no guarantee that good and constructive values will be promoted or that negative ones will be condemned. If, for example, a student decides that anti-Semitism or fascism is a preferred value, values clarification might do little to contradict that view. This "value neutral" stance is troubling to some and has led to the barring of values clarification in some school districts.

Moral Stages of Development Based on the work of Jean Piaget, the psychologist who identified stages of intellectual development (see "The Hall of Fame" online in Chapter 7), a schema proposed by **Lawrence Kohlberg** identifies **moral stages of development.** The earliest stages focus on simple rewards and punishments. Young children are taught "right" and "wrong" by learning to avoid physical punishment and to strive for rewards. Most adults function at a middle, or conventional, stage, in which they obey society's laws, even laws that may be unjust. At the highest level, individuals act on principles, such as civil rights or pacifism, that may violate conventional laws. Kohlberg believes that teachers can facilitate student growth to higher stages of morality. In Kohlberg's curriculum, students are encouraged to analyze moral dilemmas presented in brief scenarios. For example, one such scenario might tell the story of someone breaking into a store and stealing, and the question is posed: Isn't stealing always wrong, or could it ever be justified? What if the person was stealing medicine needed to save a life; would that justify the theft? The teacher's role in this curriculum is to help students move to higher stages of moral development.

Kohlberg's stages are intellectually based. Some critics believe that behavior, not intellect, is the real measure of one's morality. Detractors also express concern that traditional (what Kohlberg calls "conventional") values are attacked. Kohlberg pushes toward higher levels of moral development, principled beliefs that may run counter to current law. Other critics point out that Kohlberg's theory was developed on an all-male population and that females may go through different stages of moral reasoning. Harvard professor Carol Gilligan, for example, found that women and men react differently when responding to moral dilemmas. Whereas males seem to strongly value those who follow the rules and laws, females value relationships and caring. Kohlberg rated males as reaching a higher level of moral development than females, because the scales he developed were male-oriented.[44]

Now that we have reviewed three approaches to teaching about values and ethics, it is worth noting that some teachers "mix and match," creating a hybrid, or **comprehensive values education,** approach. For example, traditional values such as honesty, caring, and responsibility may be taught directly. Because other values are less straightforward, such as favoring or rejecting the death penalty, students might be taught the analytical skills to help them make their own decisions. There is an appropriate place in the school curriculum for character education, values clarification, and moral development, and many teachers instinctively apply multiple approaches.[45]

Classrooms That Explore Ethical Issues

For many educators and parents, concerns about values are daily events, too important to be left solely to a specific program or curriculum. How should teachers handle matters of ethics that appear on a daily basis? Consider that as a teacher, you might find

A student complains that her Vietnamese culture is being demeaned by the Christian and Western classroom activities.

A student with learning disabilities is ignored by classmates at lunchtime. Rather than sitting alone in the cafeteria, he hides in the bathroom.

A gifted student with advanced verbal skills is frequently bullied by a classmate in the locker room before gym class. Other students remain bystanders and do not stop or report the bullying.

Your best student, the one you just recommended for a special award, stored exam answers on her cell phone.

How are teachers to navigate this tricky moral minefield? Educators have offered several recommendations, summarized here:[46]

The Setting

Climate. Create an environment that respects and encourages diverse points of view and that promotes the sharing of diverse opinions, by both the teachers and the students.

School and class rules. Requiring that students unquestioningly follow rules does not lead to democratic values. School and class rules need to be explained to students, and the reasons behind them understood. Many teachers go further and ask students to participate in formulating the rules they will live by.

Parents and community. Citizens and community leaders should participate with the school in developing mission statements and ethical codes of responsibility. One way to encourage such cooperation is to plan joint efforts that tie the family and civic organizations into school-sponsored programs. The key is to reinforce ethical lessons in the school, the home, and the community.

The Teacher

Model. You need to demonstrate the ethical lessons you teach. Teacher behavior should reflect such values as tolerance, compassion, forgiveness, and open-mindedness. (Values are often "caught not taught".)

Interpersonal skills. You need effective communication skills to encourage students to share their concerns. A critical component of interpersonal skills is empathy—the ability to see problems from more than one point of view, including through the eyes of students.

Commitment. It takes determination and courage on your part to confront ethical dilemmas, rather than to take the easier path of indifference or even inattention.

Reflection skills. To unravel moral questions, you must know how to analyze a dilemma objectively and how to evaluate its essential components. Teachers with effective and deliberate reasoning skills are best suited for this challenge.

Personal opinions. You should not promote or indoctrinate students with your personal points of view, nor should you shy away from showing students that you have strong beliefs. The key is to create a classroom in which individuals can freely agree or disagree, as they see fit.

Whereas laws direct us to what we can and cannot do, moral guidelines direct us in what we feel we need and need not do. Moral issues will continue to be a major concern in the years ahead, in many ways a measure of the quality of our culture. Indeed, even as our society grows in wealth and makes great scientific strides and technological breakthroughs, the final measure of our worth may not be our materialistic accomplishments, but the way we treat one another.

GLOBAL VIEW

Seeds of Peace is a nonprofit, nonpolitical organization that helps teenagers from regions of conflict learn the skills to end the cycles of violence and make peace. www.seedsofpeace.org

ONLINE VIDEO ALBUM TO ACCOMPANY *TEACHERS, SCHOOLS, AND SOCIETY, 10E*

Visit the Online Learning Center for a range of contemporary videos with content related to this chapter.

www.mhhe.com/sadker10e

THE *TEACHERS, SCHOOLS, AND SOCIETY* READER WITH CLASSROOM OBSERVATION VIDEO CLIPS

Go to your *Teachers, Schools, and Society* Reader CD-ROM to:

READ CURRENT AND HISTORICAL ARTICLES

41. **Putting a Face to Faith,** by Charles C. Haynes, *Educational Leadership,* September 2011.

42. **Improve Relationships to Improve Student Performance,** by Richard Arum, *Phi Delta Kappan,* October 2011.

43. **Ethics: From Thought to Action,** by Robert J. Sternberg, *Educational Leadership,* March 2011.

44. **Please Help Me Learn Who I Am,** by Barry Boyce, *Shambhala Sun,* January 2007.

ANALYZE CASE STUDIES

18. **Amanda Jackson:** A teacher discovers that her principal has a drinking problem, which is well known but never discussed among the staff. She faces a dilemma when she realizes that the principal is planning to drive a student home during a snowstorm.

19. **Ellen Norton:** A teacher whose concern for a shy, underachieving student has led to the student becoming her "shadow" learns that another student may be the victim of child abuse at home. The teacher has to decide if she should become involved.

OBSERVE TEACHERS, STUDENTS, AND CLASSROOMS IN ACTION

15. Classroom Observation: Students and a Teacher Discuss Cheating

As a teacher, you will be faced with difficult decisions that will test your ethics. In this two-part observation, you will observe a scenario in which students cheat during an exam. In part one, when the teacher is called out of class during an exam, some students take to cheating. When the teacher returns, some students tell him what happened, and he must decide how to deal with the cheating. In part two, the students and teacher discuss the incident during an interview.

KEY TERMS AND PEOPLE

academic freedom, 308

Buckley Amendment, 312

character education, 326

child abuse, 325

comprehensive values
education, 328

copyright laws, 310

corporal punishment, 314

Dees, Morris, 313

due process, 314

educational malpractice, 309

establishment clause, 304

fair use, 310

First Amendment, 304

Fourth Amendment, 304, 318

Fourteenth Amendment,
304, 314

in loco parentis, 318

Kohlberg, Lawrence, 327

malfeasance, 309

misfeasance, 308

moral stages of
development, 327

nonfeasance, 308

sexual harassment, 320

Title VII of the Civil Rights Act
(1964), 305

Title IX of the Education Amendments (1972), 305, 320

values clarification, 326

zero-tolerance policy, 314

U.S. Supreme Court cases
 Engel v. *Vitale,* 317

 Franklin v. *Gwinnett County
 Public Schools,* 321

 Goss v. *Lopez,* 314

 *Hazelwood School District
 v. Kuhlmeir,* 319

 Pickering v. *Board of
 Education,* 310

 Tinker v. *Des Moines
 Independent Community
 School District,* 316

www.mhhe.com/sadker10e

CHAPTER REVIEW

Go to the Online Learning
Center to take a chapter self-
quiz, practice with key terms,
and review concepts from the
chapter.

DISCUSSION QUESTIONS AND ACTIVITIES

1. If you were to suggest a law to improve education, what would that law be? Would you make it federal, state, or local? Why?

2. The role of religion and prayer in schools has always been controversial, and teachers are advised to neither *encourage* nor *discourage* religious observances. As a teacher, what religious celebrations or practices might you encounter in your class? How would you respond to these issues while maintaining your neutrality?

3. Construct an argument to support the principle that students and their property should not be searched without the students' consent.

4. Which of the paths to moral education (values clarification, moral development, character education, or an integrated approach) appeals to you most? Why?

5. Describe some steps you might explore to promote ethical student behavior in your classroom.

REFLECTIVE ACTIVITIES AND YOUR PORTFOLIO

Part III: Foundations

3:1 Money Matters

Purpose: Most state offices of education work to equalize per-pupil expenditures (though not always successfully). Still, children live with very different financial realities at home and at school. A family's income influences a student's physical, social, emotional, moral, and cognitive growth.

Activity: To better understand and meet the needs of your learners, consider how economics has affected you and your education.

Artifact: "Finances and Me." Under each developmental area, list ways your education was helped and/or hindered by money. Although we may realize to one degree or another that money matters, we rarely take the time to consider specifically how it has shaped our own lives.

INTASC STANDARD 1
Learner Development

www.mhhe.com/sadker10e

FORM

Developmental Areas
and Socioeconomic Class

INTASC STANDARD 2
Learner Differences

Developmental Areas and Socioeconomic Class
Physical (such as size, shape, fitness, health, medical resources):
Social (such as autonomy, civility, relationships):
Emotional (such as expressiveness, empathy, motivation):
Moral (such as ethics, honesty, good will):
Cognitive (such as intellectual resources, academic services, inherent abilities):

Reflection: Consider how your childhood financial security (or lack thereof) contributed to your educational reality. How were your growth and development influenced by economic class? How might your life have been different if you had been raised with a very different financial base? What is the possible correlation between financial resources and academic success? Attach your reflection to the artifact and include it in your portfolio.

3:2 Philosophy on the Big Screen

Purpose: The philosophies of education are captured not just in this section of the book, but also in classic and contemporary films about schools. Movies reflect diverse (and sometimes overdramatized versions) of teaching philosophies, and watching these movies critically can help you analyze and explore your own philosophical preferences.

Activity: Choose a film about schools and teaching. Before you choose a movie to watch, refresh your memory of the major philosophies by scanning the philosophy discussion in Chapter 8 (essentialism, perennialism, progressivism, existentialism, social reconstructionism).

Artifact: "Philosophy in Action." Use the simple chart that follows to record evidence of the major philosophies that appeared in the film. As you watch (with or without popcorn), attend to the various techniques the teachers use to meet the different needs of learners. Can you match the theories of philosophy to the cast of characters? Take notes and try to capture the indicators of educational philosophy that appear in the film.

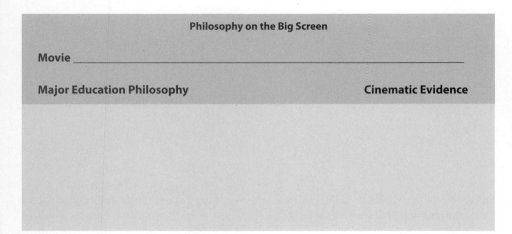

Philosophy on the Big Screen

Movie _____

Major Education Philosophy	Cinematic Evidence

www.mhhe.com/sadker10e

FORM

Philosophy on the Big Screen

Reflection: What philosophy was most prevalent? Why do you think the filmmaker chose to highlight this philosophy? What appealed or disappointed you about the film? What did you learn about teaching and educational philosophies from this film? How did the educational philosophies relate to different ways students learn? What traits of the cinematic teacher might you adapt . . . avoid?

3:3 What You See and What You Get

Purpose: The philosophy of a classroom can be seen, felt, and heard, yet future teachers sometimes have a difficult time "getting" it, even when examples of educational philosophy surround us. This activity will help you connect with specific clues that signal a teacher's philosophy.

Activity: Arrange to observe several classrooms of the age of student you would like to teach. If this is not possible, do this activity in your college classrooms. Record observations on the following chart (See page 334). Gather at least three different observations.

Artifact: Philosophy-in-the-Classroom Observations

INTASC STANDARD 3
Learner Environments

www.mhhe.com/sadker10e

FORM

Indicators of Education
Philosophy

Course: _____

Room arrangement:

Teacher-student interactions:

Student-initiated actions:

Instructional grouping and organization (full class, individuals/groups, centers/stations):

Instructional resources:

Other:

Reflection: What classroom indicators have you observed? What do these indicators suggest about the philosophy of your teachers, classes, program, or institution? How did these indicators shape the classroom learning environment? Which elements do you want to include in your teaching? Which would you prefer to omit or avoid?

3:4 Self-Fulfilling Prophecy

INTASC STANDARD 4
Content Knowledge

Purpose: Someday, at the end of your career in education, you will no doubt recall your early hopes and dreams. Will you have realized your goals? Project yourself into the future and imagine you have accomplished all that you set out to do. An orientation toward the future can help you attain your goals.

Activity: Time flies: A new generation has decided to become teachers and they open _Teachers, Schools, and Society_ (25th edition!). They turn to the history chapter and begin reading the profiles in the "Hall of Fame." And you are there. Why? Let's find out.

Artifact: "My Hall of Fame Entry." Write yourself into _The Education Hall of Fame_ by following the format in Chapter 7. Provide a graphic image, a statement of significant contribution, and about 250 words that detail your accomplishments in education. Be sure to include your unique skills and expertise to describe your achievement.

Reflection: The activity should help you define your professional values. What actions might help you reach your long-time goals? What steps should you consider now? Are there mentors and professional relationships that might help support your success? Keep this _Hall of Fame_ entry in your portfolio. You could even seal and date it in an envelope to be opened when you teach your first class of students, receive your doctorate in education, are named U.S. Secretary of Education, or attend your retirement dinner.

3:5 Putting Your Philosophy into the Classroom

INTASC STANDARD 5
Application of Content

Purpose: How does your educational philosophy influence the way you teach your content fields? Even before that, what is your educational philosophy? Is it teacher-centered or student-centered? Do you subscribe to essentialism, perennialism, progressivism, existentialism, or social reconstructionism? Or do you prefer a combination approach—picking and choosing from several philosophies? A strong sense of your educational philosophy will guide and shape your development as an educator. Refining and declaring your beliefs will allow you to sharpen your professional communication skills.

Activity: Using as a guide the background on educational philosophies presented in Chapter 8, formulate your educational philosophy. Begin by brainstorming thoughts and ideas about your own beliefs. Work to hone your beliefs into a concise one-page declaration. It may be useful to begin a number of your philosophy statements with the phrase "I believe . . ." Now choose some subjects that you will be teaching, like history or mathematics, and then offer examples of how your philosophy will influence your teaching.

Artifact: "My Philosophy of Education." Using this one-page declaration as a guide, create a poster describing your philosophy. Use pictures and words (or be more creative) to convey your philosophy. Offer examples of how your philosophy will emerge in your teaching. Challenge classmates to guess your philosophy by viewing your poster or to deduce your philosophy based on a description of how you will approach teaching. Can your poster be shared with your students when you begin teaching?

Reflection: Was it difficult to formulate a philosophy? How did your beliefs evolve during the course of this assignment? What surprised you about this activity? What did you learn about yourself from this activity? How well did you connect your philosophy with teaching particular topics or skills? Do you have—or are you moving toward—a consistent philosophy? Were classmates able to guess your philosophy? Include your one-page philosophy statement in your portfolio.

3:6 Assessing the Assessor

INTASC STANDARD 6
Assessment

Purpose: With all the attention being given to the performance of American students on national, state, and local tests, it makes sense for you to explore the promise and problems assessment.

Activity: Invite a school district administrator with assessment responsibilities to your class or study group for one hour. Ask your guest to describe the district's history and current evaluation procedures.

Artifact: "Testing Practices." Use the following questions (or your own) to expand your guest's commentary. Record the answers.

- What are the purposes behind these tests?
- Give examples of when these policies and procedures work effectively—and when there are problems.
- What is the best thing about these tests, and what is the worst?
- What is the biggest problem you face?
- What role does the public (parents, media, chamber of commerce) play?
- How do special interest groups influence testing policies?
- How do teachers, students, and parents react to these tests?
- Can you suggest other approaches to gauge achievement?

www.mhhe.com/sadker10e

FORM

Testing Practices

335

Bonus Artifact: Assume you are writing for a newspaper and turn the administrator's presentation and interview into a story for your local newspaper.

Reflection: What have you learned? What information surprised you? What do you still have on your "need to know" list? Do you support the current testing culture? What are the pros and cons?

3:7 Students' Bill of Rights and Responsibilities

Purpose: When rights and responsibilities are handed down from higher authorities, or if a teacher simply reads out loud "class rules" at the beginning of the semester, democracy and the value and meaning of individual rights may well be lost. But when students actively participate and write these rules, they are creating a living social contract and are more likely to understand, appreciate, and follow them. This RAP helps you to establish a classroom climate that promotes learning, an appreciation of individual rights, and ethical behavior among students.

Activity: Using the following outline developed by Madeline Hunter, plan a lesson that implements student rights and responsibilities.

Dr. Madeline Hunter's Seven-Step Lesson Plan

Anticipatory Set (focus)—Focus learners' attention on the instruction that is about to begin. This should motivate students and also facilitate their learning. This could be a teacher demonstration, a video, a story, a puzzle, or a handout before the actual lesson. This is also known as a "grabber" and it's a way to get your students' attention and interest. In this case, you want the students to develop the norms, rules, and responsibilities they will follow in your class. This is a real sharing of responsibility, and students should appreciate an authentic sharing of both power and responsibility.

Purpose (objective)—The purpose presents a clear explanation of what learners will understand and be able to do as a result of the lesson. This section should answer the question, "Why is this important to learn?" In this lesson, the students are creating their own community, and they are defining their rules as citizens of that community—a rather motivating reason to be involved in this lesson and an important preparation for adult responsibilities.

Instructional Strategy—What needs to be taught and how should it be taught to accomplish this task? What is an effective strategy to use for teaching the content and the skills of this lesson? In this example, you need to decide what strategies you will use to help students create the ground rules for building their community. Perhaps role-plays to demonstrate the rules will be useful. Students organizing their thoughts among themselves, and bringing their ideas and suggestions to their classmates for approval would be useful, so a student-centered learning strategy is called for. Certainly you as the teacher, a member of the class community, have a voice to include rules and responsibilities you would like to see, but the students should develop their own voice as well, their own agency in this process. Here is a wonderful and authentic opportunity for students to develop the values they want to see manifested in their classroom.

Modeling (show)—At this step, the rules need to be explored and demonstrated. Seeing the rules in action in trial runs of several days will help students to improve them.

Guided Practice—Monitor learners as they apply these rules. Work to promote consistency as students try out these classroom rules and responsibilities.

Check for Understanding—Evaluate whether learners understand the rules and why they are in place. They should be able to explain the rationale for the rules, as well implement them.

Independent Practice—Over the next few days and weeks, ensure that the students practice the rules they created. As they become more comfortable with them, the rules and values they reflect will become the norm.

Artifact: This activity is a challenging one because you may not be able fully to implement this RAP until you begin teaching, but there are several useful lessons for you nonetheless. For example, before you begin teaching, it is a good idea to understand classroom rules and responsibilities created by other teachers and students. Research those norms in preparation for your own classroom. What do you learn from how others implement rules and responsibilities? How will you approach creating your classroom rules? What role will your students play? The second benefit of this RAP is to consider the Hunter format for lesson planning. This is a seven-step approach to lesson planning. You may want to pick other topics or skills that you will be teaching and see how you can apply Hunter's seven-step lesson planning.

Reflection: How do you predict that students will respond to this rules and responsibilities activity? What are the differences between teacher-imposed rules and rules that students develop? How can you work to encourage students to follow these rules and not forget them? What are the rules and responsibilities that speak to your heart? What are the challenges in planning an instructional strategy that focuses on student decisions? As you plan a subject- or skills-oriented lesson using the Hunter format, do you find this approach helpful? Why or why not?

3:8 The Great Lecture Theory of Learning

Purpose: Most of us have attended, even been moved by, a great lecture. Yet, when we learn about strategies for classroom instruction, the lecture is often relegated to the least effective method or, simply, disparaged. Lecturing is not inherently evil. Although it can be tiresome and boring, it also be motivating, filled with information, clearly understood, and easily recalled. In some cases, the lecture format may be the best way to convey information. There are reasons that great lecturers are great, and the sooner you figure out some of those reasons, the sooner you will be able to give terrific lectures yourself.

Activity: Check around the campus with friends and acquaintances to find out which professors give great lectures. You may also want to inquire at a local elementary, middle, or high school. Choose one teacher to observe and ask permission to attend a class.

Artifact: "Effective Lecture Ideas." Take notes, but not on the specific lecture information—rather on presentation strategy and style. Ask some of the following questions about lecture technique:

www.mhhe.com/sadker10e

FORM

Effective Lecture Ideas

- What pulled you into the lecture? (a great story? a provocative question?)
- How did you know where the lecture was going? (Was the purpose or objective stated or implied?)
- How did the speaker use presentation or communication skills?

  Facial expressions?

  Gestures?

  Eye contact?

  Voice?

  Movement?

  Interaction with the audience?

  Other skills?
- What technical aids or materials (DVDs, PowerPoint presentation) enhanced your understanding and interest?
- Did the speaker use vivid examples, stories, metaphors, or role play to enhance your comprehension?

- How might you assess the speaker's expertise in the lecture's content?
  - Was the lesson too long, the right amount of time, or too brief? (Now that's rare!)

Reflection: All in all, was this lecturer worthy of his or her reputation? Why? How are you when it comes to public speaking? What's your comfort zone? Given what you know about yourself, which of the observed lecturer's strengths might be strengths of yours as well? Which might you want to add to your repertoire?

3:9 Publication of the Month

INTASC STANDARD 9
Personal Learning and
Ethical Practice

Purpose: Professional journals and magazines often include the best writing in our field. Journal articles are submitted and reviewed by educational experts, selected for their high standards of excellence. To be a reflective and responsible teacher, you will need to keep current by reading one or more professional journals.

Activity: Pick a journal or an educational magazine that is new to you. Try one at your professor's suggestion or use sources listed in the endnotes of this text. Spend at least one hour reading through the journal.

Artifact: "Journal Review." Harvest a sense of what this journal offers by analyzing its intended audience, format, content, style, policy, and readability. Write up your findings in a review format and present to the class or a small group of classmates. You may want to create a class scrapbook that describes these journals by sharing all the descriptions created by your classmates.

Refection: In describing this journal to your peers, what are its positive points? Its weaknesses? Does it appeal to you now? Might you find it more useful in the future? If you could read only one journal a month, would it be this one, or perhaps another reviewed by a classmate? Why?

3:10 Get on Board

INTASC STANDARD 10
Leadership and
Collaboration

Purpose: One seemingly distant group, the school board, influences every teaching day. As an elected agency of the community, school boards hold regular meetings, usually open to the public. Because their norms and procedures vary, you have to see one to understand one. The purpose of this activity is to better understand how school boards function and how they might influence your life in the classroom.

Activity: Attend a school board meeting or watch one on television. (Many are broadcast by local cable networks.) Imagine you are covering the meeting for your district's teacher association. Note what is going on. Try to grasp the formal curriculum (old and new business and procedures). Look also at the hidden curriculum, the cultural cues, and the nonverbal signals that tell you what else is going on.

Artifact: "A School Board Column." Write your notes into a news column for a teachers' newsletter that might be distributed in a local school system. Limit your article to a single page. Share your article in class and lead a class discussion.

Reflection: What were your personal and professional impressions of the meeting? What rituals and routines did you observe? How were your assumptions about school boards and meetings altered, if at all? Were underlying politics evident? How were attendees treated? Were any teachers present? Did any of the school board's decisions directly affect district teachers? How? On the basis of your observation of the school board meeting, would you consider teaching in this district? Would you consider running for a school board position? Why or why not?

PART IV

Your Classroom

Chapter 11

Teacher Effectiveness   340

Chapter 12

Your First Classroom   373

Chapter 13

Q and A Guide to Entering the
Teaching Profession   400

Teacher Effectiveness

FOCUS QUESTIONS

1. Are teachers born or made?
2. How is learning time organized in the classroom?
3. What classroom management skills foster academic achievement?
4. What are the roles of teachers and students in the pedagogical cycle?
5. How can teachers set a stage for learning?
6. What questioning strategies increase student achievement?
7. How can teachers best tap into different student learning styles?
8. How can teachers use technology to support effective instruction?
9. What are several salient models of instruction?

The mediocre teacher tells. The good teacher explains. The superior teacher demonstrates. The great teacher inspires.

—WILLIAM A. WARD

CHAPTER PREVIEW

Albert Einstein believed that they awakened the "joy in creative expression and knowledge." Ralph Waldo Emerson believed that they could "make hard things easy." About whom are these talented geniuses talking? You guessed it: teachers. Some individuals seem to take to teaching quite naturally. With little or no preparation, they come to school with a talent to teach and touch the lives of students. Others bring fewer natural talents to the classroom yet, with preparation and practice, become master teachers, models others try to emulate. Most of us fall in the middle, bringing some skills to teaching but also ready to benefit and grow from teacher preparation and practice teaching.

In this chapter, we present recent research findings on effective instruction and classroom management, focusing on a core set of skills that constitute good teaching. We also detail the prevailing models of instruction, such as cooperative learning, problem-based learning, and differentiated instruction—classroom approaches that have become particularly popular in recent years. You may draw on these skills and models in your own classroom, selecting those that best fit your subject, students, and purpose.

For inspirational stories about people who have had a powerful impact on the lives of others, go to the Online Learning Center and read "Class Acts."

www.mhhe.com/sadker10e

WHAT DO YOU THINK? Qualities of a good teacher. Rate the qualities of a good teacher, and see how other students rated these qualities.

Are Teachers Born, or Made?

Think about the best teacher you ever had: Try to evoke a clear mental image of what this teacher was like. How do your memories compare with what some of today's teachers say about their favorite teachers from the past:

FOCUS QUESTION 1
Are teachers born, or made?

- The teacher I remember was charismatic. Going to his class was like attending a Broadway show. But it wasn't just entertainment. He made me understand things. We went step-by-step in such a clear way that I never seemed to get confused—even when we discussed the most difficult subject matter.

- I never watched the clock in my English teacher's class. I never counted how many times she said uh-huh or okay or paused—as I did in some other classes. She made literature come alive—I was always surprised—and sorry—when the bell rang.

- When I had a problem, I felt like I could talk about it with Mrs. Garcia. She was my fifth-grade teacher, and she never made me feel dumb or stupid—even when I had so much trouble with math. After I finished talking to her, I felt as if I could do anything.

- For most of my life, I hated history—endlessly memorizing those facts, figures, dates. I forgot them as soon as the test was over. One year I even threw my history book in the river. But Mr. Cohen taught history in such a way that I could understand the big picture. He asked such interesting, provocative questions—about our past and the lessons it gave for our future.

The debate has been raging for decades: Are teachers born, or made? What do you think?

If you think it is a combination of both, you are in agreement with most people who have seriously considered this question. Some individuals—a rare few—are naturally gifted teachers. Their classrooms are dazzlingly alive. Students are motivated and excited, and their enthusiasm translates into academic achievement. For these truly talented educators, teaching seems to be pure art or magic.

But behind even the most brilliant teaching performance, there is usually well-practiced skill at work. Look again at those brief descriptions of favorite teachers: Each of them used proven skills—structure, motivation, clarity, high expectations, and effective questioning.

- "We went step-by-step in such a clear way that I never seemed to get confused—even when we discussed the most difficult subject matter." *(structure and clarity)*

- "She made literature come alive." *(motivation)*

- "After I finished talking to her, I felt as if I could do anything." *(high expectations)*

- "He asked such interesting, provocative questions—about our past and the lessons it gave for our future." *(questioning)*

Although there is ample room for natural talent, most teaching is based on "tried and true" practices. Research helps us distinguish between what we "think" will work and what really works. And we know that good teachers matter: A study that followed 2.5 million students over twenty years found that teachers who helped improve their students' achievement also had positive effects on those students' lives beyond academics, including lower teenage pregnancy rates, less obesity, greater college matriculation, and higher adult earnings.[1]

In this chapter, we describe what research tells us about teaching skills and models of instruction that raise student achievement. If you decide to teach, it will be your responsibility to keep up with the expanding and sometimes shifting teacher effectiveness research through conferences, coursework, and education journals. For now, let's explore the current findings supporting teacher effectiveness.

Learning Time

FOCUS QUESTION 2

How is learning time organized in the classroom?

One constant in schools is time. What is startling is how differently teachers use their classroom time. For example, a large study showed that one teacher in a California school system spent 68 minutes a day on reading, while another spent 137 minutes; one elementary school teacher in Florida spent only 16 minutes per day on mathematics, while another spent more than three times that amount.[2] Similarly, John Goodlad's comprehensive research study, *A Place Called School,* found that some schools devote approximately 65 percent of their time to instruction, whereas others devote almost 90 percent.[3] The variation is enormous.

Research shows that students who spend more time pursuing academic content achieve more. That's the commonsense part, and it's hardly surprising. Although allocating adequate time to academic content is obviously important, making time on the schedule is not enough. How this allocated time is used in the classroom is the real key to student achievement. To analyze the use of classroom time, researchers have developed the following terms: allocated time, engaged time, and academic learning time.

Allocated time is the time a teacher schedules for a subject—for example, thirty minutes a day for math. The more time allocated for a subject, the higher student achievement in that subject is likely to be.

Engaged time is that part of allocated time in which students are actively involved with academic subject matter (intently listening to a lecture, participating in a class discussion, writing an essay, solving math problems). When students daydream, doodle, write notes to each other, talk with their peers about nonacademic topics, or simply wait for instructions, they are not involved in engaged time. When there is more engaged time within allocated time, student achievement increases. As with allocated time, the amount of time students are engaged with the subject matter varies enormously from teacher to teacher and school to school. In some classes, engaged time is 50 percent; in others, it is more than 90 percent.[4]

Academic learning time is engaged time with a high success rate. Many researchers suggest that students should get 70 to 80 percent of the answers right when working with a teacher. When students are working independently, and without a teacher available to make corrections, the success rate should be even higher if students are to learn effectively. Some teachers are skeptical when they hear these percentages; they think that experiencing difficulty challenges students and helps them achieve. However, studies indicate that a high success rate is positively related to student achievement.[5]

In the following sections, you will learn about research-based teaching skills that you can use to increase academic learning time and student achievement. Because much time can be frittered away on organizational details and minor student disruptions (see Figure 11.1), we will look first at effective strategies for classroom management. Then we will consider the instructional skills that seem consistently to produce higher academic achievement in students.

Academic learning time is engaged learning time in which students have a high success rate. When working independently, as here, the success rate should be particularly high.

FIGURE 11.1

Estimated Time Available for Academic Learning.

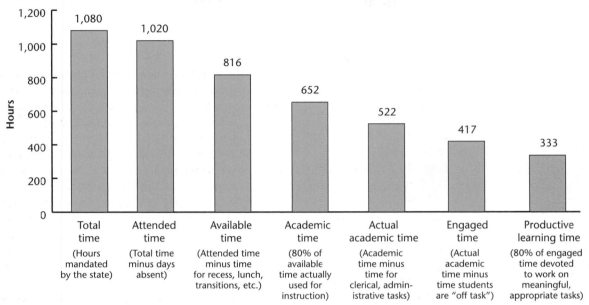

SOURCE: Carol Weinstein, Molly Romano, and Andrew Migano Jr., *Elementary Classroom Management: Lessons from Research and Practice,* 5th ed. (New York: McGraw-Hill, 2010).

REFLECTION: Identify three classroom practices that you can implement to recapture productive learning time available to your students.

Classroom Management

The observer walked to the back of the room and sat down. It seemed to him that the classroom was a beehive of activity. A reading group was in progress in the front of the room while the other children were working with partners on math examples. The classroom was filled with a hum of children working together, and in several languages—but the activity and the noise were organized and not chaotic.

The observer had been in enough schools over the past twenty years to know that this well-managed classroom did not result from magic but that carefully established and maintained procedures were at work. The observer scrutinized the classroom, searching for the procedures that allowed twenty-six students and one teacher to work together so industriously, harmoniously, and effectively.

First he examined the reading group, where the teacher was leading a discussion about the meaning of a story. "Why was Tony worried about the trip he was going to take?" the teacher asked (a few seconds' pause, all the children with eyes on the teacher, several hands raised). "Sean?"

As Sean began his response, the observer's eyes wandered around the rest of the room, where most of the children were busy at work. Two girls, however, were passing notes surreptitiously in the corner of the room.

During a quick sweep of the room, the teacher spotted the misbehavior. The two girls watched the teacher frown and put her finger over her lips. They quickly returned to their work. The exchange had been so rapid and so quiet that the reading group was not interrupted for even a second.

FOCUS QUESTION 3

What classroom management skills foster academic achievement?

Another student in the math group had his hand raised. The teacher motioned Omar to come to her side.

"Look for the paragraph in your story that tells how Tony felt after his visit to his grandmother," the teacher instructed the reading group. "When you have found it, raise your hands."

While the reading group looked for the appropriate passage, the teacher quietly assisted Omar. In less than a minute, Omar was back at his seat, and the teacher was once again discussing the story with her reading group.

At 10:15, the teacher sent the reading group back to their seats and quietly counted down from ten to one. As she approached one, the room became quiet and the students' attention was focused on her. "It is now time for social studies. Before you do anything, listen carefully to *all* my instructions. When I tap the bell on my desk, those working on math should put their papers in their cubbies for now. You may have a chance to finish them later. Then all students should take out their social studies books and turn to page 67. When you hear the sound of the bell, I want you to follow those instructions." After a second's pause, the teacher tapped the bell, and the class was once again a sea of motion, but it was motion that the teacher had organized while the students were now taking responsibility for their own learning.

The observer made some notes. There was nothing particularly flashy or dramatic about what he had seen. But he was satisfied, because he knew he had been witnessing a well-managed classroom.

Can you remember from your childhood those activity books in which you had to find the five things wrong in a picture? Let us reverse the game: Try re-reading this classroom vignette and look for all the things that are *right* with the picture. Underline four or five examples of what the teacher did well.

The teacher in this vignette used several strategies to avoid interruptions and to keep instruction proceeding smoothly and keep students on task. Did you notice that:[6]

1. The teacher used a questioning technique known as *group alerting* to keep the reading group involved. By asking questions first and then naming the student to respond, she kept all the students awake and on their toes. If she had said, "Sean, why did Tony feel concerned about his trip?" the other students in the group would have been less concerned about paying attention and answering the question. Instead, she asked her question first and then called on a student to respond.

Good classroom management requires constant monitoring of student behavior.

2. The teacher seemed to have "eyes in the back of her head." Termed *withitness* by researcher Jacob Kounin, this quality characterizes teachers who are aware of student behavior in all parts of the room at all times. While the teacher was conducting the reading group, she was aware of the students passing notes and the one who needed assistance.

3. The teacher was able to attend to interruptions or behavior problems while continuing the lesson.

A Closer Look   Times of Transition

Teachers must manage more than many major transitions every day. During these transitions, discipline problems occur twice as often as in regular classroom instruction. Classroom management expert Jacob Kounin identified five common patterns that can derail classroom management during *times of transition:*

- *Flip-flops*. In this negative pattern, the teacher terminates one activity, begins a new one, and then flops back to the original activity. For example, in making a transition from math to spelling, the teacher says, "Please open your spelling books to page 29. By the way, how many of you got all the math problems right?"

- *Overdwelling*. This bad habit includes preaching, nagging, and spending more time than necessary to correct an infraction of classroom rules. "Anna, I told you to stop talking. If I've told you once, I've told you 100 times. I told you yesterday and the day before that. The way things are going, I'll be telling it to you all year, and, believe me, I'm getting pretty tired of it. And another thing, young lady . . . "

- *Fragmentation*. In this bumpy transition, the teacher breaks directions into several choppy steps instead of accomplishing the instructions in one fluid unit—for example, "Put away your reading books. You shouldn't have any spelling books on your desk, either. All notes should be off your desk," instead of the simpler and more effective "Clear your desk of all books and papers."

- *Thrusts*. Classroom momentum is interrupted by *non sequiturs* and random thoughts that just seem to pop into the teacher's head. For example, the class is busily engaged in independent reading, when their quiet concentration is broken by the teacher, who says, "Where's Roberto? Wasn't he here earlier this morning?"

- *Dangles*. Similar to the thrust, this move involves starting something, only to leave it hanging or dangling—for example, "Richard, would you please read the first paragraph on page 94. Oh, class, did I tell you about the guest speaker we're having today? How could I have forgotten about that?"

SOURCE: Charles H. Wolfgang, *Solving Discipline and Classroom Management Problems*, 7th ed. (New York: Wiley, 2008).

REFLECTION: Because each of these patterns represents a problem, can you reword the dialogue to produce a more effective transition?

Kounin calls the ability to do several things at once *overlapping*. The teacher reprimanded the students passing notes and helped another child with a math problem without interrupting the flow of her reading lesson.

4. The teacher managed routine misbehavior using the principle of *least intervention*. Because research shows the time spent disciplining students is negatively related to achievement, teachers should use the simplest intervention that will work. In this case, the teacher did not make a mountain out of a molehill. She intervened quietly and quickly to stop students from passing notes. Her nonverbal cue was all that was necessary and did not disrupt the students working on math and reading. The teacher might also have used some other effective strategies. She could have praised the students who were attending to their math ("I'm glad to see so many partners working well on their math assignments"). If it had been necessary to say more to the girls passing notes, she should have alerted them to what they *should* be doing, rather than emphasize their misbehavior ("Deanne and U-Mei, please attend to your own work," *not* "Deanne and U-Mei, stop passing notes").

5. The teacher managed the transition from one lesson to the next smoothly and effectively, avoiding a bumpy transition, which Kounin termed *fragmentation*. When students must move from one activity to another, a gap is created in the fabric of instruction. Chaos can result when transitions are not handled competently by the instructor. Did you notice that the teacher gave a clear transition signal, either the countdown or the bell; gave thorough instructions so her students would know exactly what to do next; and made the transition all at once for the entire class? These may seem simple, commonsense behaviors, but countless classes have come apart at the seams because transitions were not handled effectively.

Management Models

When done well, classroom management goes unnoticed. When done poorly, it is about the only thing that is noticed. If you teach, you will develop your own style and techniques to manage a classroom. The style you select will reflect much about your own teaching philosophy. Why do you believe students misbehave? Should the focus of management be teacher control or the development of student self-control? Can misbehavior be avoided by exciting lessons and a class that feels a sense of community, or is there an overriding need for a firm set of rules and consequences? What kind of classroom climate can make both teacher and students comfortable?

Teachers disagree on the answers to those questions, and there is no single best strategy for classroom management. You might want to begin thinking about what approach appeals to you; and to help you on this journey, we describe briefly several of the best-known models for classroom management. (See Table 11.1.) If any of these models speak to your heart, we invite you to research and read more about it.

Preventing Problems

The approach you choose will require planning, and research underscores that good managers are good planners.[7] Effective classroom managers are waiting at the door when the children arrive, rather than entering a room late after noise and disruption have had a chance to build. Starting from the very first day of school, they teach standards or norms of appropriate student behavior, actively and directly. Often they model procedures for getting assistance, leaving the room, going to the pencil sharpener, and the like. The more important rules of classroom behavior are posted, as are the consequences of not following them.[8]

In traditional teacher-centered schools, rules usually mean obeying the teacher, being quiet, and not misbehaving. When schools move away from autocratic teaching styles, student responsibility and ownership of rules (or as one teacher calls them "Habits of Goodness") are embraced. Some teachers like to develop the list of rules together with their students; other teachers prefer to present a list of established practices and ask students to give specific examples or to provide reasons for having such rules. The bottom line: When rules are easily understood and convey a sense of moral fairness, most students will comply. We can create a productive learning community when rules are (1) few in number, (2) fair and reasonable, and (3) appropriate for student maturation.

Even the best rules need to be tied to consequences or the class can quickly deteriorate into chaos. Each consequence needs to be thoughtfully considered. A weak consequence might encourage rather than discourage a behavior, and a too-tough consequence might reflect an angry teacher's overreaction. Unfair consequences alienate a class and earn a teacher the reputation of being unfair. Never doubt the ability of students to detect injustices. Teachers rarely notice that they tend to penalize boys more harshly than girls for the same misbehavior. Students pick that up quickly. Subtle gender and race favoritism is alive and well in today's classrooms. Many teachers find it helpful to post a description of class rules and consequences and to send that list home to parents to forge a consistent home–school partnership on appropriate behavior.

Now is a good time to consider a question too few ask: Is the purpose of consequences to punish inappropriate behavior? More and more educators believe that we should move beyond punishment and use consequences to solve behavior issues.[9] For example, let's say a student, we'll call him Jimmy, is not paying attention in class. (We know, this is a highly

TABLE 11.1   Models of Classroom Management

Advocate	Main Focus	Belief System
Lee and Marlene Canter	Assertive discipline	Students deserve a safe and productive learning climate, and it is the teacher's job to provide it. Each student is taught how to behave responsibly through clear rules and consequences. When expectations are not met, students know that the teacher will mete out consequences.
Richard Curwin and Allen Mendler	Discipline with dignity	Students should always be treated with dignity, even when they misbehave. Interesting learning activities, positive reinforcement and opportunities for student success keep students on track, especially students with a history of misbehavior.
Barbara Coloroso	Developing inner control and discipline	Students need to take responsibility for their actions to develop their inner discipline. If students are messy, they need to learn to clean up after themselves. If they are too noisy, they need to develop strategies to allow others to do their work.
Rudolf Dreikurs	Collaborative decision making and belonging	The key in this approach is to identify the motivation behind misbehavior and, within a classroom community, to help students redirect their behavior in a positive way.
Haim Ginott	Communications	You speak to students as you, the teacher, would want to be spoken to. Model desirable behaviors and maintain your calm as a teacher. Focus on what needs to be done rather than on what was done wrong.
William Glasser	Student satisfaction	The teacher meets with the class to discuss not only behavior rules but also the curriculum being taught. The teacher plans meaningful work for the students and holds them to high standards. Students feel a part of the school, possessing a sense of fun, power, and independence.
Thomas Gordon	Discipline as control	Students are involved in making the rules about classroom life and procedures, and problem owners are identified—that is, those who are bothered by certain behaviors. The class as a group works to resolve those issues.
Jacob Kounin	Engagement and supervision	Student misbehavior is reduced by engaging lessons, and the teacher's watchful monitoring skills keep students on track.
Fritz Redl and William Wattenberg	Group dynamics	Group dynamics, insights, and peer influence are used to control misbehavior. The causes of any misbehavior are diagnosed and appropriate consequences are applied.
B. F. Skinner	Behavior modification	Desired behaviors are encouraged by immediately awarding positive reinforcement. Undesirable behaviors are ignored.

SOURCE: C. M. Charles, *Building Classroom Discipline* 10th ed. (Upper Saddle River, NJ: Prentice Hall, 2010).

REFLECTION: Are there elements in these brief descriptions that you find appealing? What are they, and what do they teach you about your own teaching philosophy?

improbable situation in your class, but let's just pretend for the moment.) Rather than the teacher imposing a punitive consequence (reprimand, time-out, no recess, detention, call to parents, etc.), the teacher can invite the class to brainstorm useful suggestions to help Jimmy stay on task. For example, Jimmy's desk could be moved closer to the teacher's desk, discouraging off-task behaviors. Jimmy could be paired with a student who can model on-task behavior, perhaps even work with Jimmy sharing ways to stay on task. Students might suggest something as obvious as a vision or hearing exam to make certain Jimmy is getting the instructions. If we had a real class of students brainstorming constructive interventions right now, they could offer us many other potential solutions to help Jimmy. The point to remember is that consequences can be constructive rather than negative.

Good managers also carefully arrange their classrooms to minimize disturbances, provide students with a sense of confidence and security, and make sure that instruction can proceed efficiently. They set up their rooms according to the following principles:[10]

- *Teaching eye-to-eye.* Teachers should be able to see all students at all times. Research shows that students who are seated far away from the teacher or the instructional activity are less likely to be involved in class discussions. As teachers intentionally move about the room, they can short-circuit off-task student behavior. Placing instructional materials (SMART board, demonstration activity, flip chart, lab station, and the like) in various parts of the room also gives each student "the best seat in the house" for at least part of the teaching day.

- *Teaching materials and supplies should be readily available.* Arranging a "self-help" area so that students have direct access to supplies encourages individual responsibility while freeing up the teacher to focus on instructional activities.

- *High-traffic areas should be free of congestion.* Place student desks away from supply cabinets, pencil sharpeners, and so on. Minor disturbances ripple out, distracting other students from their tasks.

- *Procedures and routines should be actively taught in the same way that academic content is taught.* Initial planning for classroom management is often rewarded with fewer discipline problems and smooth transitions to classroom routines and procedures. For students who come from chaotic home environments, these routines offer a sense of stability. Once established, they allow teachers and all students more time for academic learning.

www.mhhe.com/sadker10e
INTERACTIVE ACTIVITY
Create a Classroom Use this tool to create your ideal physical arrangement for a classroom.

A child's misbehavior—from minor classroom disruptions to emotional outbursts to violence—is often rooted in trauma, feelings of powerlessness, or even "normal" daily events beyond a teacher's control. Yet, teachers must understand and manage student anger and aggression. Several classroom strategies can help:[11]

- *Choice.* Constantly taking away privileges and threatening punishment can cause students to feel intimidated and victimized. Teachers can provide appropriate options to give a student a sense of some control and freedom. Encouraging a student to select a lunch mate or to choose a project topic offers a reasonable decision-making opportunity and can help avoid minor disruptions as well as aggressive acts.

- *Responsibility.* Rechanneling student energy and interest into constructive activities and responsibilities can reduce misbehavior. When instruction is meaningful and worthwhile, boredom and fooling around are less likely to occur. When students are empowered, they are less likely to act out.

- *Laughter.* Learning doesn't have to always be so serious, nor do we or our students. Sometimes, when tensions are high, like during testing or when difficult things are happening out in the world, we need to laugh with our students.

- *Kindness.* Take every opportunity to model kindness. Students will follow.

- *Community.* Routinely include strategies and activities in your lessons that allow students to express their thoughts and ideas, build relationships, and practice collaboration. This will help grow and maintain a feeling of emotional safety in your classroom.

- *Voice.* Listening to young people is one of the most respectful skills a teacher can model. Students who feel they are not heard feel disrespected. Hearing and honoring students' words (and feelings) reduce the likelihood of misbehavior.

Listening to students was exactly what Kathleen Cushman did when she wrote *Fires in the Bathroom.* Adolescents from around the nation were asked to tell teachers what they would like to see in their classrooms. Students advised teachers to: share your plans with me and tell me how I will be evaluated, be excited about what you teach, be firm when rules are broken, treat me fairly but remember I am an individual, give me feedback and encouragement, don't say "please" too much, and don't push yourself into my personal life.[12]

Although we can't always detect the signs of danger, we can be on the lookout and can create management plans to handle small distractions as well as major incidents. As educator David Berliner says, "In short, from the opening bell to the end of the day, the better classroom managers are thinking ahead. While maintaining a pleasant classroom atmosphere, these teachers keep planning how to organize, manage, and control activities to facilitate instruction."[13] Berliner makes an important connection between management and instruction. Effective teachers, in addition to being good classroom managers, must be good organizers of academic content and instruction.

The Pedagogical Cycle

How does one organize classroom life? Researcher Arno Bellack analyzed verbal exchanges between teachers and students and offers a fascinating insight into classroom organization, likening these interactions to a pedagogical game.[14] The game is so cyclical and occurs so frequently that many teachers and students do not even know that they are playing. There are four moves:

FOCUS QUESTION 4

What are the roles of teachers and students in the pedagogical cycle?

1. *Structure.* The teacher provides information, provides direction, and introduces the topics.
2. *Question.* The teacher asks a question.
3. *Respond.* The student answers the question, or tries to.
4. *React.* The teacher reacts to the student's answer and provides feedback.

These four steps make up a **pedagogical cycle,** diagrammed in Figure 11.2. Teachers initiate about 85 percent of the cycles, which are used over and over again in classroom interaction. When teachers learn to consciously enhance and refine each of the cycle's moves, student achievement is increased.[15]

www.mhhe.com/sadker10e

INTERACTIVE ACTIVITY

Pedagogical Cycle Identify the moves in a sample classroom dialogue.

Clarity and Academic Structure

Have you ever been to a class where the teacher is bombarded with questions? "What are we supposed to do?" "Can you explain it again?" "What do you mean?" When such questions are constant, it is a sure sign that the teacher is not setting the stage for instruction. Students need

FIGURE 11.2

Pedagogical cycle and sample classroom dialogue.

REFLECTION: Continue the classroom dialogue around the cycle again. What might the teacher and the student(s) say?

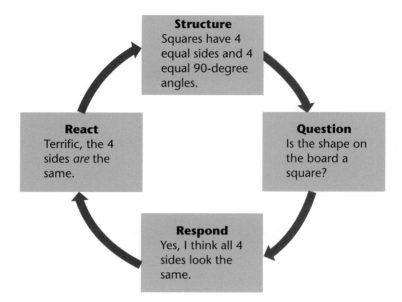

a clear understanding of what they are expected to learn, and they need motivation to learn it. Effective *academic structure* sets the stage for learning and occurs mainly at the beginning of the lesson. Although the specific structure will vary depending on the students' backgrounds and the difficulty of the subject matter, an effective academic structure usually consists of:[16]

FOCUS QUESTION 5

How can teachers set a stage for learning?

- *Objectives.* Let the students know the objectives (or purpose) of each lesson. Students, like the teacher, need a road map of where they are going and why.
- *Review.* Help students review prior learning before presenting new information. If there is confusion, reteach.
- *Motivation.* Create an "anticipatory set" that motivates students to attend to the lesson. Consider throwing out an intriguing question, an anecdote, a joke, or a challenging riddle.
- *Transition.* Provide connections to help students integrate old and new information.
- *Clarification.* Break down a large body of information. (This is sometimes called "chunking.") Do not inundate students with too much too fast. This is particularly true for young children, English language learners, and slower learners.
- *Scaffolding.* Step-by-step practice and well-crafted questions support and encourage student understanding.
- *Examples.* Give several examples and illustrations to explain main points and ideas.
- *Directions.* Give directions distinctly and slowly. If students are confused about what they are supposed to do, repeat or break information into small segments.
- *Enthusiasm.* Demonstrate personal enthusiasm for the academic content. Make it clear why the information is interesting and important.
- *Closure.* Close the lesson with a brief review or summary. If students are able to provide the summary, so much the better, for it shows that they have really understood the lesson.

Through effective and clear structure, the stage is set for the remaining steps of the pedagogical cycle.

Questioning

Good questioning is at the very core of good teaching. Using an interactive whiteboard, having students work independently or in cooperative groups, lecturing, or using technology in the classroom can all be engaging and meaningful. But designing good questions is key to success in any lesson format. As John Dewey said,

> To question well is to teach well. In the skillful use of the question more than anything else lies the fine art of teaching; for in it we have the guide to clear and vivid ideas, and the quick spur to imagination, the stimulus to thought, the incentive to action.[17]

Questioning is key in guiding learning, and all students should have equal access to classroom questions and academic interaction. Yet sitting in the same classroom taught by the same teacher, students experience significant differences in the number of questions they are asked. Research shows that male students are asked more questions than female students, and white students are asked more questions than nonwhite students. One of the reasons boys get to answer questions as well as to talk more is that they are assertive in grabbing teacher attention. Boys are more likely than girls to call out the answers to the questions. In addition, when boys call out the answers to questions, teachers are likely to accept their responses. When girls call out the answers, teachers often remind them to raise their hands. Teacher expectations also play a role and are frequently cited as one of the reasons white students (perceived as higher achievers) receive more questions and more active teacher attention than students who are members of other racial and ethnic groups.[18]

FOCUS QUESTION 6

What questioning strategies increase student achievement?

What strategies will you use to ensure that all students are heard in your classroom?

If you want all students, not just the quickest and most assertive, to answer questions, establish a protocol for participation. For example, make a rule that students must raise their hands and be called on before they may talk. Too many classes offer variations of the following scene:

TEACHER: How much is 60 + 4 + 12? *(Many students raise their hands—both girls and boys.)*

TONY: *(Shouts out)* 76!

TEACHER: Okay. How much is 50 + 9 + 8?

This scene, repeated again and again in classes across the country, is a typical example of the squeaky wheel—not necessarily the most needy or most deserving student—getting the educational oil. Once you make the rule that students should raise their hands before participating, *hold to that rule.*

Many teachers are well intentioned about having students raise their hands, but, in the rapid pace of classroom interaction, they sometimes forget their own rule. If you hold to that "wait to be recognized" rule, you can make professional decisions about who should answer which questions and why. If you give away this key to classroom participation, you are abandoning an important part of your professional decision making in the classroom.

Although the distribution and ownership of questions are important, the type of question asked is also meaningful. This section provides more information about the different levels of classroom questions, as well as strategies for using them fairly and effectively.

FIGURE 11.3
Bloom's Taxonomy.

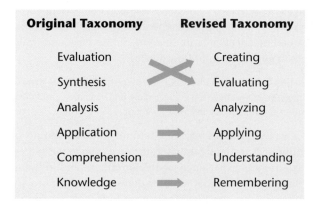

REFLECTION: Why do think the authors of the revised version decided to use verbs instead of nouns to describe each level? The revised version puts "Creating" as the highest level, indicating it is a more demanding intellectual activity than "Evaluating." What do you think?

Many educators differentiate between factual, lower-order questions and thought-provoking, higher-order questions. The oldest and most widely used system for determining the intellectual level of questions is Benjamin **Bloom's taxonomy,** which proceeds from the lowest level of questions, remembering, to the highest level, creating.[19] (By the way, *taxonomy* is another word for *classification.*)

About a decade ago, some educators revised Bloom's taxonomy, transposing and renaming some of the categories.[20] Take a look at the original and revised versions and see what similarities and differences you find. (See Figure 11.3.)

The six levels of Bloom's original and revised taxonomy represent questions that require a different kind of thought process. In a sense, Bloom is offering us a blueprint of how we think, from simple (lower-order questions) to complex (higher-order questions). Teachers should be able to formulate questions on each level so that their students can engage in a range of cognitive processes, from lower to higher order questions. (See A Closer Look: Bloom's Revised Taxonomy Applied to Questioning Levels.)

A **lower-order question** can be answered through memory and recall (levels I and II of the taxonomy). For example, "What is four plus one?" or "What is the name of the largest Native American nation?" are lower-order questions. Without consulting outside references, one could respond with the correct answer only by remembering previously learned information. (Cherokee for those who do not recall.) Either students know the answer or they don't. Research indicates that 70 to 95 percent of a teacher's questions are lower order.

A **higher-order question** demands more thought and usually more time before students reach a response (generally, levels III through VI of the taxonomy). These questions may ask for evaluations, comparisons, causal relationships, problem solving, or creative, open-ended thinking. Following are examples of higher-order questions:

1. What similarities in theme emerge in the three Coen movies: *True Grit, No Country for Old Men,* and *Fargo?*

2. What could happen if our shadows came to life?

Although higher-order questions have been shown to produce increased student achievement, most teachers ask very few of them.[21]

www.mhhe.com/sadker10e

INTERACTIVE ACTIVITY
Questioning Levels Match questions to the different questioning levels.

A Closer Look

Bloom's Revised Taxonomy Applied to Questioning Levels

LEVEL I: REMEMBERING

Requires student to recall or recognize information. Student is not asked to manipulate information, but to rely on memory or senses to provide the answer. To answer a question on this level, the student must simply remember facts, observations, and definitions.

Sample Questions What does "quixotic" mean?

List the first ten presidents of the United States.

Sample cue words define, list, review, who, what, where, when

LEVEL II: UNDERSTANDING

Requires student to go beyond simple recall and to demonstrate sufficient comprehension to organize and arrange information mentally. Student must use previously learned information by putting it in his or her own words and rephrasing it.

Sample Questions In our story, the author discusses why the family left Oklahoma. Can you summarize why in your own words?

Explain the main idea of this chart?

Sample cue words describe, explain, compare, contrast, rephrase, summarize

LEVEL III: APPLYING

Requires student to apply previously learned information to answer a problem. At this level, the student uses a rule, a definition, a classification system, or directions in solving a problem with a specific correct answer.

Sample Questions Identify the proper noun in the following sentences. *(applying a definition)*

Solve the quadratic equation. *(applying a rule)*

Sample cue words choose, classify, demonstrate, diagram, illustrate, solve

LEVEL IV: ANALYZING

Requires student to use three kinds of cognitive processes: (1) to identify causes, reasons, or motives (when these have not been provided to the student previously), (2) to analyze information to reach a generalization or conclusion, (3) to find evidence to support a specific opinion, event, or situation.

Sample Questions Why do you think King Lear misjudged his daughter? *(identify motives)*

What generalizations can you make about the climate of Egypt near the Nile River basin? *(analyze information to reach a conclusion)*

Many historians think that Abraham Lincoln was our finest president. What evidence can you find to support this statement? *(find evidence to support a specific opinion)*

Sample cue words investigate, justify, support, why

LEVEL V: EVALUATING

Requires student to judge the merits of an aesthetic work, an idea, or the solution to a problem.

Sample Questions Which U.S. senator do you think is most effective? Support your selection.

Decide why young children should or should not be allowed to read any book they want. Explain your answer.

Sample cue words argue, conclusion, decide, do you agree, explain

LEVEL VI: CREATING

Requires student to use original and creative thinking: (1) to develop original communications, (2) to make predictions, and (3) to solve problems for which there is no single right answer.

Sample Questions Write a short story about life on another planet. *(developing an original communication)*

What do you think life would be like if Germany had won World War II? *(making predictions)*

How would you measure the height of a building without being able to go into or onto it? *(solving problems for which there is no single right solution)*

Sample cue words imagine, improve, predict, synthesize, what would happen if . . .

REFLECTION: Create a question for each level of Bloom's taxonomy. Were some levels easier than others? Why or why not?

Many educators think that different questioning levels stimulate different levels of thought. If you ask a fifth-grade student to define an adjective, you are working on lower-level basic skills. If you ask a fifth-grade student to write a short story, making effective use of adjectives, you are working on a higher level of student achievement. Both lower-order and higher-order questions are important and should be matched to appropriate instructional goals:

Ask Lower-Order Questions When Students Are

- Being introduced to new information
- Working on drill and practice
- Reviewing previously learned information

www.mhhe.com/sadker10e

INTERACTIVE ACTIVITY
The Question Master
Game Test your knowledge
of Bloom's Taxonomy

Ask Higher-Order Questions When Students Are

- Working on problem-solving skills
- Involved in a creative or affective discussion
- Asked to make judgments about quality, aesthetics, or ethics
- Challenged to manipulate already established information in more sophisticated ways

Student Response

If you were to spend a few minutes in a high school English class, you might hear a classroom discussion go something like this:[22]

> TEACHER: Who wrote the poem "Stopping by Woods on a Snowy Evening"? Tomás?
>
> TOMÁS: Robert Frost.
>
> TEACHER: Good. What action takes place in the poem? Kenisha?
>
> KENISHA: A man stops his sleigh to watch the woods get filled with snow.
>
> TEACHER: Yes. Michael, what thoughts go through the man's mind?
>
> MICHAEL: He thinks how beautiful the woods are and how he would like to stay and watch. *(Pauses for a second)*
>
> TEACHER: Yes—and what else? Rita? *(Waits half a second)* Well, why does he feel he can't stay there indefinitely and watch the woods and the snow?
>
> RITA: He knows he's too busy. He's got too many things to do to stay there for so long.
>
> TEACHER: Good. In the poem's last line, the man says that he has miles to go before he sleeps. What might sleep be a symbol for? Krista?
>
> KRISTA: Well, I think it might be . . . *(Pauses for a second)*
>
> TEACHER: Think, Krista. *(Waits for half a second)* All right then—Dustin? *(Waits again for half a second)* Brian? *(Waits half a second)* What's the matter with everyone today? Didn't you do the reading?

The teacher is using several instructional skills effectively. His is a well-managed classroom. The students are on task and engaged in a discussion appropriate to the academic content. By asking a series of lower-order questions ("Who wrote the poem?" "What action takes place in the poem?"), the teacher works with the students to establish an information base. Then the teacher builds to higher-order questions about the poem's theme and meaning.

If you were to give this teacher suggestions on how to improve his questioning techniques, you might point out the difficulty students have in answering the more complex questions. You might also note the lightning pace at which this lesson proceeds. The teacher fires questions so rapidly that the students barely have time to think. This is not so troublesome when they are answering factual questions that require a brief memorized response. However, students begin to flounder when they are required to answer more complex questions with equal speed.

Although it is important to keep classroom discussion moving at a brisk pace, sometimes teachers push forward too rapidly. Slowing down at two key places during classroom discussion can usually improve the effectiveness and equity of classroom responses. In the research on classroom interaction, this slowing down is called **wait time.**[23]

Mary Budd Rowe's research on wait time shows that after asking a question, teachers typically wait only one second or less for a student response (wait time 1). If the response is not forthcoming in that time, teachers rephrase the question, ask another student to answer it, or answer it themselves. If teachers can learn to increase their wait time from one second to three to five seconds, significant improvements in the quantity and quality of student response usually will take place.

There is another point in classroom discussion when wait time can be increased. After students complete an answer, teachers often begin their reaction or their next question before a second has passed (wait time 2). Once again, it is important for teachers to increase their wait time from one second to three to five seconds. On the basis of her research, Mary Budd Rowe has determined that increasing the pause after a student gives an answer is equally important as increasing wait time 1, the pause after the teacher asks a question. When wait time 1 and wait time 2 are increased, classroom interaction is changed in several positive ways.

Changes in Student Behavior

- More students participate in discussion.
- Fewer discipline problems disrupt the class.
- The length of student response increases dramatically.
- Students are more likely to support their statements with evidence.
- Speculative thinking increases.
- There are more student questions and fewer failures to respond.
- Student achievement increases on written tests that measure more complex levels of thinking.

Changes in Teacher Behavior

- Teacher comments are less disjointed and more fluent. Classroom discussion becomes more logical, thoughtful, and coherent.
- Teachers ask more sophisticated, higher-order questions.
- Teachers begin to hold higher expectations for all students.

Research indicates that teachers give more wait time to students for whom they hold higher expectations. A high-achieving student is more likely to get time to think than is a low-achieving student. If we do not expect much from our students, we will not get much. High expectations and longer wait times are positively related to achievement. Researchers suggest that white male students, particularly high achievers, are more likely to be given adequate wait time than are females, English language learners, students with a disability, quiet students, and students of color. Students who are quiet and reserved or who think more slowly may especially benefit from increased wait time. In fact, a key benefit of extended wait time is an increase in the quality of student participation, even from students who were previously silent.[24]

Usually when teachers learn that they are giving students less than a second to think, they are surprised and have every intention of waiting longer, but that is easier said than done! In the hectic arena of the classroom, it is all too easy to slip into split-second question-and-answer patterns.

Teachers can adopt self-monitoring cues to slow themselves down at the two key wait-time points. For example, one teacher says that he puts his hand behind his back and counts on his fingers for three seconds to slow himself down. Another teacher says that she covers her mouth with her hand (in a thoughtful pose) to keep herself from talking and thereby destroying "the pause that lets them think."

As mentioned previously, wait time is more important in some cases than in others. If you are asking students to repeat previously memorized math facts and you are interested in developing speed, a three- to five-second wait time may be counterproductive. However, if you have asked a higher-order question that calls for a complicated answer, be sure that wait times 1 and 2 are ample. Simply put, students, like the rest of us, need time to think, and some students may need more wait time than others. For example, when a student speaks English as a newly acquired language, additional wait time could help that student accurately translate and respond to the question. And many of us could profit by less impulsive, more thoughtful responses, the kind that can be engendered by longer wait times.

When teachers allow more wait time, the results can be surprising. As one teacher said, "I never thought Andrea had anything to say. She just used to sit there like a bump on a log. Then I tried calling on her and giving her time to answer. What a difference! Not only does she answer, she asks questions that no one else has thought of."

Reaction or Productive Feedback

"Today," the student teacher said, "we are going to hear the story of *The Three Billy Goats Gruff.*" A murmur of anticipation rippled through the kindergarten children comfortably seated on the carpet around the flannel board. This student teacher was a favorite, and the children were particularly happy when she told them flannel-board stories.

"Before we begin the story, I want to make sure we know what all the words mean. Who can tell me what a troll is?"

A five-year-old nicknamed B.J. raised his hand. "A troll is someone who walks you home from school."

"Okay," the teacher responded, a slightly puzzled look flickering over her face. "Who else can tell me what a troll is?"

Another student chimed in, "A troll is someone with white hair sticking out of his head."

"Okay," the teacher said.

Another student volunteered, "It hides under bridges and waits for you and scares you."

"Uh-huh," said the teacher.

Warming to the topic, another student gleefully recounted, "I saw a green troll named Shrek who lives in the woods."

"Okay," the teacher said.

Wide-eyed, B.J. raised his hand again, "I'm sure glad we had this talk about trolls," he said. "I'm not going home with them from school anymore."

"Okay," the teacher said.

This is a classroom in which several good teaching strategies are in operation. The teacher uses effective academic structure, and the students are on task, interested, and involved in the learning activity. The teacher is asking lower-order questions appropriately, to make sure the students know key vocabulary words before the flannel-board story is told. The problem with this classroom lies in the fourth stage of the pedagogical cycle: This teacher does not provide specific reactions and adequate feedback. Did you notice that the teacher reacted with "uh-huh" or "okay," no matter what kind of answer the students gave? Because of this vague feedback and "okay" teaching style, B.J. was left confused about the difference between a troll and a patrol. This real-life incident may seem amusing, but there was nothing funny to B.J., who was genuinely afraid to leave school with the patrol.

Recently, attention has been directed not only at how teachers ask questions but also at how they respond to student answers. When Myra and David Sadker analyzed classroom interaction in more than one hundred classrooms in five states, they found that teachers generally use four types of reactions:[25]

1. *Praise.* Positive comments about student work, such as "Excellent, good job."
2. *Acceptance.* Comments such as "Uh-huh" and "okay," which acknowledge that student answers are acceptable. These are not as strong as praise.
3. *Remediation.* Comments that encourage a more accurate student response or encourage students to think more clearly, creatively, or logically. Sample remediation comments include "Try again," "Sharpen your answer," and "Check your addition."
4. *Criticism.* A clear statement that an answer is inaccurate or a behavior is inappropriate. This category includes harsh criticism ("This is a terrible paper"), as well as milder comments that simply indicate an answer is not correct ("Your answer to the third question is wrong").

Which of these reactions do you think teachers use most frequently? The Sadkers' study found that acceptance was the most frequent response, accounting for more than half of all teacher reactions from grade school to graduate school. The second most frequent teacher response was remediation, accounting for one-third of teacher reactions. Used infrequently, praise made up only 11 percent of reactions. The rarest response was criticism. In two-thirds of the classrooms observed, teachers never told a student that an answer was incorrect. In the classrooms where criticism did occur, it accounted for only 5 percent of interaction. (See Figure 11.4.)

In *A Place Called School,* John Goodlad writes that "learning is enhanced when students understand what is expected of them, get recognition for their work, learn about their errors, and receive guidance in improving their performances."[26] But many students claim that they are not informed or corrected when they make mistakes.[27] Perhaps this is caused by overreliance on the acceptance response, which is the vaguest kind of feedback that teachers can offer. Because there is more acceptance than praise, criticism, and remediation combined, some educators are beginning to wonder: "Is the 'okay' classroom okay?"

Because achievement is likely to increase when students get clear, specific productive feedback about their answers, it is important for teachers to reduce the "okay" reaction and to be more varied and specific in the feedback they provide. Researchers have studied the links between praise and student achievement and found that praise is most effective when:[28]

1. *Praise is contingent upon student performance.* Praise should closely follow student behavior the teacher wants to recognize.
2. *Praise is specific.* When teachers praise, they should clearly indicate what aspect of the student behavior is noteworthy (e.g., creative problem solving or good use of evidence to support an argument).

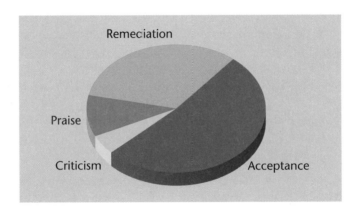

FIGURE 11.4

Teacher Reactions.

REFLECTION: Most teacher reactions fall in the acceptance category. Suggest three reasons this might occur.

3. *Praise is sincere.* Praise should reflect the experiences, growth, and development of the individual student. Otherwise, it may be dismissed as being disingenuous.

4. *Praise lets students know about their competence and the importance of their accomplishments*—for instance, "The well-documented review of studies on your website and the connection you made between the two tobacco filters may eventually have an impact on the industry."

5. *Praise attributes success to ability or effort*—for example, "Your analysis of the paintings of the Impressionists is excellent. I'll bet you spent a long time studying their work in the museum" *(attribution to effort).* Or "This story is fantastic. You've got a real flair for creative writing" *(attribution to ability).* When praise is attributed to abilities or effort, students know that successful performance is under their own control.

6. *Praise uses past performance as a context for describing present performance*—for example, "Last week you were really having trouble with your breast stroke kick. Now you've got it together—you've learned to push the water behind you and increase your speed."

When praise does not embody these characteristics, it can be detrimental. A growing body of research shows that easy, unearned praise does not help students and instead interferes with learning and emotional well being. In study after study, children rewarded for being smart become more likely to shy away from hard assignments that might tarnish their star reputations. But children praised for trying hard or taking risks tend to enjoy challenges and find greater success. Children also perform better in the long term when they believe that their intellect is not a birthright but something that grows and develops as they learn new things.[29]

Just as students need to know when they are performing well, they need to know when their efforts are inadequate or incorrect. If students do not have information about their weak areas, they will find it difficult to improve. Here are some tips for effective feedback:

1. *Constructive feedback is specific and contingent on student performance.* The teacher's comments should closely follow the student behavior the teacher wants to improve.

2. *Critical comments focus on student performance and are not of a personal nature.* All of us find it easier to accept constructive criticism when it is detached from our worth as a person, when it is not personal, hostile, or sarcastic.

3. *Feedback provides a clear blueprint for improvement.* If you merely tell a student that an answer is wrong and nothing more, the student has clear feedback on level of performance but no strategies for improvement. Effective feedback suggests an approach for attaining success, such as "Check your addition," or "Let's conjugate this verb in both French and English, to see where the error is."

4. *An environment is established that lets the student know it is acceptable to make mistakes.* "We learn from our errors. Hardly any inventions are perfected on the first try."

5. *Constructive feedback relates eventual success to effort.* "Now you have demonstrated the correct sequence in class. Give yourself a solid half-hour tonight working on this, and I bet that you will get most of it correct. I'll check with you tomorrow."

6. *Constructive feedback recognizes when students have made improvements in their performance.* "Last week you were having trouble identifying which of Newton's laws are applicable in each of these time motion studies. Now you've mastered the skill. You've done a good job."

An "okay classroom" allows student error and misunderstanding to go uncorrected; it lets B.J. think that the patrol will eat him up after school. In classrooms where there is appropriate use of remediation and constructive criticism, students know not only when they have made mistakes but also how to correct them. They also recognize that this process leads to growth and achievement.

Variety in Process and Content

Variety is the spice of life, the saying goes—the spice of lessons also, because variety can enhance both teaching effectiveness and student achievement. Have you ever listened to a lecture for an hour and found your initial interest lapsing into daydreams? Have you ever watched a class begin a seatwork assignment with active concentration and found, after thirty minutes, that involvement had turned into passing notes and doodling? Students learn more when joy and excitement are part of classroom life (but we bet you knew that).[30]

As any savvy teacher knows, student interest can be maintained by moving from one activity to another during a single lesson. For example, a sixty-minute lesson on the American Revolution might begin with a ten-minute overview providing the structure for the class, then move into a fifteen-minute question-and-answer session, then change to a twenty-five-minute video, and conclude with a ten-minute discussion and closure. Another motivation to vary content and process in teaching is to accommodate different student learning styles. Some students might miss what is said in a lecture (not being auditory learners) but easily get it when the teacher shows pictures (because the visual connection is clear). Research on different ways of learning, including Howard Gardner's inventory of intelligences, (introduced in Chapter 2) offers strong arguments for instructional variety. Following is a sample of activities teachers can use to maintain student interest by varying the pattern of the lesson:

FOCUS QUESTION 7
How can teachers best tap into different student learning styles?

www.mhhe.com/sadker10e
INTERACTIVE ACTIVITY
Create a Class Schedule
What do you think your students' week should consist of?

Discussions	Student presentations	Music activities
Lectures	Tests	Art activities
Films, DVDs	Podcast	Creating digital portfolios
PowerPoint	Silent reading	Spot quizzes
Role plays	Games	Panel discussions
Simulations	Field trips	Brainstorming sessions
Small-group activities	Creative writing	Peer tutoring
Guided practice	Theater and drama	Debates
Guest speakers	Community service	Cooperative learning activities
Independent seatwork	Learning centers	*What would you add?*

Many of these activities can be described as "hands-on" or active learning and can be captivating for students, but more is needed. Variety alone will not produce achievement: Connections with content must be made, or variety will be reduced to mere activity. Teachers must consider individual students and tailor activities according to their interests, learning styles, and abilities. This is no easy task. Consider an elementary student happily pasting animal pictures on charts, but unable to explain what (if anything) he is learning about animal families. Students in a middle school may be dressing up for an evening on the *Titanic,* and from the lower to the upper decks, their clothing and accents reflect different social classes. Yet, if students have not connected their dress with social class and deck classifications, then they may miss learning about the relationship between social class and survival rate. Challenging students with engaging activities is admirable, but the effort must clearly connect the activity to both the content and the student.[31]

Technology as a Tool for Effective Teaching

FOCUS QUESTION 8
How can teachers use technology to support effective instruction?

Today's technology transports students around the world via virtual field trips, provides individualized tutorials and drill-and-practice of certain skills, and instantly and inexpensively adds millions of books, articles, and videos to a teacher's curriculum. Technology holds the potential to profoundly reshape education, and currently about forty states and the District of Columbia require formal teacher training in technology.[32] Educators today use technology to:[33]

- *Motivate students* through multimedia materials that capture their interest.
- *Increase basic skills* in math, reading, and writing, as well as content areas, through sample quizzes, drill-and-practice, and additional course-related information. This becomes particularly attractive in this era of standardized testing.
- *Promote higher-order thinking and increased content understanding* by introducing simulations, problem-based learning, Internet research, collaborative work, and student authoring programs.
- *Increase academic resources* by bringing the unlimited written and visual assets of the Internet into local schools.
- *Increase responsiveness to different learning styles,* including children with special needs or students for whom the typical classroom culture means academic and/or social distress.
- *Improve workplace preparation* as students learn keyboarding skills, software applications, video production and other technological operations common to future employment.
- *Save work for teachers* by creating a class website, class Facebook page, or Twitter account. Homework assignments, worksheets, notes, and exam dates can be posted online. Parent communication can be accomplished through e-mail or texting. Grading software can track attendance, average grades, and chart the results while even more cutting-edge programs use artificial intelligence, such as the Intelligent Essay Assessor (IEA), to grade essays.
- *Strengthen student learning* by adding resources, such as SMART boards or online videos to create more dramatic and effective teacher presentations.
- *Modernize the school culture* by reshaping American education for the twenty-first century, moving beyond pencil and paper, chalk and chalkboards, to the world's digital resources.

Teachers can discover online an enormous amount of curriculum in a variety of formats, including audio and video pieces. Helpful sites include:

- Discovery Education's Lesson Plan Library (http://school.discoveryeducation.com/lessonplans).
- TeachersFirst.com (www.teachersfirst.com/index.cfm).
- Thinkfinity (www.thinkfinity.org/lesson-plans).

Technology also offers an array of tools for effective instruction. As examples, teachers can engage students in Twitter-like classroom discussions with

GLOBAL VIEW
YouTube for Schools is a wonderful free resource designed for teachers of all grade levels. Lessons, lectures, and interactive conversations from across the curriculum and the world are available. Check out learning possibilities from around the globe at www.youtube.com/user/teachers

Computers can be used for basic skills or for more high-order thinking and creative activities.

You Be The Judge

TECHNOLOGY—EDUCATIONAL MARVEL OR MENACE?

Technology is a *Marvel* Because It . . .

IMPROVES LEARNING

With technology we can individualize instruction, grant students autonomy, and empower them to learn at their own pace, while offering a global perspective on the curriculum. Each learner benefits from having an omnipresent tutor to individually tailor schoolwork to putting the focus on learning rather than teaching.

REACHES MORE STUDENTS

Computers, the Internet, smart phones, and the like expand the educational horizons of children in rural communities and those with limited resources, as well as homebound and disabled learners. Students fearful of going to school because of bullying or violence can learn safely at home using technology.

OFFERS STUDENTS A WEALTH OF RESOURCES

Through technology, students have so much more than a school or local library, for they can use technology to tap into resources around the world. Students can now access limitless books, articles, pictures, sound clips, and newspapers; follow links to experts or virtual field trips; and participate in real-time communications across the globe.

PREPARES STUDENTS FOR THE FUTURE

Technology encourages interdisciplinary and collaborative efforts, facilitates problem-based learning, and encourages student creativity; the skills many believe will be in high demand in the future economy. Students at ease with technology will be assets to future employers.

Technology is a *Menace* Because . . .

EFFECTIVE TEACHING IS COMPROMISED

Good teaching requires a personal connection. A teacher gazing at a student who is gazing at a computer is not a productive connection. Technology also often competes with teachers. Too many students become distracted from academic pursuits by cell phones, tablets, and iPods. When this happens, focus is lost and even the most effective teachers are compromised.

IT MAY LEAVE MORE STUDENTS OUT OF THE LOOP

Technology does not equalize many disparities, and in some cases amplifies economic inequalities. Children from families with means and resources, children with high-tech homes attending well-resourced schools have technological advantages not available to poorer students and schools. Poor students soon discover technology's unwelcome mat tripping them up at the door of most career options.

STUDENTS ARE FLOODED WITH MISINFORMATION

Many of today's youngsters can surf the Internet but are unable to sort truth from fiction. The Internet is home to countless narrow-interest groups that promote political and other causes by disseminating misinformation. While some books and periodicals might have done this in the past, technology has made all kinds of misinformation accessible to impressionable children who can be easily misguided.

WE MAY BE BUILDING A NOT-SO-WONDERFUL FUTURE

Technology is creating a world of superficial friendships, and shallow learning. Computer health risks include increased eyestrain, repetitive motion injury, and obesity that come from a more sedentary life-style. What other dangers lurk in a more technological world?

www.mhhe.com/sadker10e

YOU DECIDE . . .

Do you believe that technology is an educational marvel or menace?

Explain. In what ways has your education been enriched—or diminished—by technology?

Edmodo, bring experts into the classroom via Skype, guide students in creating digital portfolios with Mahara, and take virtual field trips around the world using Google Earth.

Doesn't all this sound exciting? We Americans love our technology, and cool computers are high on our gadget love list. Unfortunately, in all this tech-glitz, perspective can get lost. (See You Be the Judge: Technology-Educational Marvel or Menace?) Software developer and educator George Brackett reminds us, "Thoughtful, caring, capable people change schools, sometimes with the help of technology, sometimes not, and sometimes even despite it. Too often we focus on the technology rather than the reform."[34] Technology should be seen as a teacher's tool, and not the other way around. The first step is deciding how best to use that tool.

In the following section, we describe some well-known models of instruction, from direct teaching to differentiated instruction, and include examples of how each model is used in a classroom. Then we describe how technology could be used within that teaching model.

Models for Effective Instruction

FOCUS QUESTION 9
What are several salient models of instruction?

Part of the challenge for teachers is knowing which model of instruction to choose for particular educational purposes. The following models differ dramatically from one another, yet each may be helpful in your classroom.

Direct Teaching

Also called *systematic, active,* or *explicit teaching,* the **direct teaching** model emphasizes the importance of a structured lesson in which presentation of new information is followed by student practice and teacher feedback. In this model, which has emerged from extensive research, the role of the teacher is that of a strong leader, one who structures the classroom and sequences subject matter to reflect a clear academic focus.

Researchers put forward seven principles of effective direct teaching.[35]

1. *Daily review.* At the beginning of the lesson, teachers review prior learning. Frequently, teachers focus on assigned homework, clarify points of confusion, and provide extra practice for facts and skills that need more attention.

2. *Anticipatory set.* This is also known as a "grabber" and is a way to get students' attention and interest. This could be a teacher demonstration, a video, a story, a puzzle, or a handout before the actual lesson. The anticipatory set builds a bridge from previous knowledge to new information. If successful, the anticipatory set will get students mentally or physically ready for the lesson.

3. *New material.* Teachers begin by letting students know the objectives to be attained. New information is broken down into smaller bits and is covered at a brisk pace. Teachers illustrate main points with concrete examples. Teachers ask questions frequently to check for student understanding and to make sure that students are ready for independent work using new skills and knowledge.

4. *Guided practice.* Students use new skills and knowledge under direct teacher supervision. During guided practice, teachers ask many content questions ("What is the definition of a paragraph?") and many process questions ("How do you locate the topic sentence in a paragraph?"). Teachers check student responses for understanding, offering prompts and providing corrective feedback. Guided practice continues until students answer with approximately 70 to 80 percent accuracy.

5. *Specific feedback.* Correct answers to questions are acknowledged clearly, so that students will understand when their work is accurate. When student answers are hesitant, the teacher provides process feedback ("Yes, Juanita, that's correct because . . . "). Teachers correct inaccurate responses immediately, before errors become habitual. Frequent errors are a sign that students are not ready for independent work, and guided practice should continue.

With direct instruction, teachers present a carefully structured lesson, such as this chemistry lesson on molecular structures.

6. *Independent practice.* Similar to guided practice, except that students work by themselves at their seats or at home. Independent practice continues until responses are assured, quick, and at a level of approximately 95 percent accuracy. Cooperative learning (see the next section) and student tutoring of one another are effective strategies during independent practice.

7. *Weekly and monthly reviews.* Regular reviews offer students the opportunity for more practice, a strategy related to high achievement. Barak Rosenshine, a pioneering researcher in developing the principles of direct teaching, recommends a weekly review every Monday, with a monthly review every fourth Monday.

One of the best-known supporters of direct teaching was Madeline Hunter. Her ideas on direct teaching have become the foundation for writing lesson plans. Direct teaching works well when you are teaching skill subjects, such as grammar or mathematics, or helping students master factual material. The direct teaching model is particularly helpful during the first stages of learning new and complex information, but it is less helpful when imaginative responses and student creativity are called for.

Technology Presentation software, such as PowerPoint or Prezi, are some of the more ubiquitous technologies to enhance direct teaching. Such software can help organize and add energy to student or teacher presentations. Savvy teachers also use these presentation tools with more esoteric technology, such as digital microscopes, or can bring an expert speaker into the classroom through a webcam.

Direct teaching can sometimes make it difficult for teachers to engage all students in class discussions. Technology can encourage student participation. For example, students can use a handheld computer, or "clicker," to answer instructor-initiated questions. Teachers using such devices report that along with increasing participation, students are more attentive and better prepared. (See Teaching Tip: Classroom Clicks on p. 364.)

Cooperative Learning

In a classroom using **cooperative learning,** students work on activities in small, heterogeneous groups, and they often receive rewards or recognition based on the overall group performance. Although cooperative learning can be traced back to the 1920s, it seems startling or new because the typical classroom environment is frequently competitive. For example, when grading is done on a curve, one student's success is often detrimental to others. This competitive structure produces clear winners and losers, and only a limited number of A's are possible. But a cooperative learning structure differs from competitive practices, because students depend on one another and work together to reach shared goals.

In cooperative learning, students work together to gain new understandings on a topic, such as this chemistry lesson on molecular structures.

According to researchers, cooperative learning groups work best when they meet the following criteria.[36] Groups should be *heterogeneous* and, at least at the beginning, should be *small,* perhaps limited to two to six members. Because face-to-face interaction is important, the groups should be *circular* to permit easy conversation. Positive *interdependence* among group members can be fostered by a *shared group goal, shared division of labor,* and *shared materials,* all contributing to a sense that the group sinks or swims together.

Robert Slavin, a pioneer in cooperative learning techniques, developed student team learning methods in which a team's work is not completed until all students on

Teaching Tip

CLASSROOM CLICKS

How many times has a teacher wanted to ask a great question to all the students in the class? But of course, after one student provides an answer, the power of that question for others is diminished. Here comes technology to the rescue: Clickers (also known as Classroom Response Systems or Student Response Systems).

Clickers look like a simple TV remote that allows each student to respond to a question embedded in a specially designed PowerPoint-like presentation. Each student clicks the answer he or she thinks is correct, and those responses are shown to the instructor. Often teachers post, via a SMART board or computer projector, class summaries of student responses in real time, so the entire class can view the results. Interested in exploring clickers? Here are some thoughts for you to consider:

Why and when to use clickers: Clickers allow instructors to encourage active student learning and small group interactions, even during lectures. Ask clicker questions sparingly, but strategically, to highlight the concepts you most want to emphasize.

Clicker questions: Clickers work well for presenting multiple-choice questions, such as selecting the best answer, or opinion polling.

- Keep questions short to optimize legibility in a slide.
- Offer no more than five answer options.
- Avoid requiring complex calculations that may encourage students to guess rather than think through the question.

How to use clickers: Encourage active discussion among students. Post a question and ask students to discuss their answers with each other before collecting answers. Before revealing the correct answer, discuss the answer options and allow students to explain their reasons for choosing various answers. Be sure to allow time for discussion—thinking, not clicking, is the goal.

Assessing learning: Student responses enable teachers (and often students as well) to evaluate learning progress and gaps:

- Pre-assessments: before a new topic
  - What do students already know?
  - What are students' misconceptions?
- Mid-assessments: in the middle of a topic or lecture
  - Do students understand this concept?
  - Has student thinking changed?
- Post-assessments: at the end of a topic or class
  - Can students synthesize the concepts to solve problems?
  - How has students' understanding changed?

REFLECTION: Describe some advantages and disadvantages of using clickers.

---

the team understand the material being studied. Rewards are earned only when the entire team achieves the goals set by the teacher. Students tutor one another so that everyone can succeed on individual quizzes, and each member of the group is accountable for learning. Because students contribute to their teams by improving prior scores, it does not matter whether the student is a high, average, or low achiever. Increased achievement by an individual student at any level contributes to the overall performance of the group, resulting in equal opportunity for success.[37]

Research shows that cooperative learning promotes both intellectual and emotional growth:

- Students make higher achievement gains; this is especially true for math in the elementary grades.
- Students have higher levels of self-esteem and greater motivation to learn.
- Students have a stronger sense that classmates have positive regard for one another.
- Understanding and cooperation among students from different racial and ethnic backgrounds are enhanced.[38]

However, the practical realities of cooperative learning are not all commendable. Some students, accustomed to starring roles in full class instruction, continue to dominate the small groups. Accurate grading requires an analysis of both the individual and the group performance. And even the most committed practitioners acknowledge that cooperative learning may take more time than direct teaching. Still, as ability grouping becomes more controversial, educators are growing increasingly interested in cooperative learning as a strategy for working success-fully with mixed-ability groups and diverse classroom populations.

Technology Sometimes technology can isolate students, so some software products are spe-cifically designed to encourage student cooperation and collaboration. TakingIT-Global (www.tigweb.org/), for example, provides the tools for students from around the world to communicate and discuss various political, environmental, and social issues from a wide range of perspectives.

Mastery Learning

Mastery learning programs are committed to the credo that, given the right tools, all children can learn. Stemming from an individualized reward structure, these programs are used from early childhood to graduate school. For example, after years of dismal test scores and lack of student motivation, the Chugach School District in Alaska adopted a student-centered, mas-tery learning approach. Unlike the standard grade-level system where students worry about passing into the next grade, with school-wide mastery learning, each student moves at an individual pace and focuses on becoming proficient in ten specific academic areas, such as reading, mathematics, and service learning, as well as nonacademic subjects such as cultural awareness and career development. Some students achieve proficiency and graduate at age 14; some do not get there until 21. Not only are test scores and attendance greatly improved, but students also report feeling motivated to learn.[39]

Mastery learning programs require specific and carefully sequenced learning objectives. The first step is to identify a **behavioral objective,** a specific skill or academic task to be mas-tered. Students are taught the skill or material in the objective; then they are tested to determine if the objective has been reached. Students who complete the test successfully go on for accel-eration or enrichment, while the students who fail to demonstrate mastery of the objective receive corrective instruction and are retested. The success of mastery learning rests on *instruc-tional alignment,* which is a close match between what is taught and what is assessed.

In mastery learning, students typically work at their own pace, often with individualized written or digital materials. The teacher provides assistance and facilitates student efforts, but mastery still remains a student responsibility. Studies have shown that many students, par-ticularly younger ones, find it hard to take charge of their own instruction, so mastery learning programs highlight the role of the teacher as instructional leader, motivator, and guide.

Studies suggest that mastery learning can be beneficial across grade levels and subject areas. In mastery learning classrooms:[40]

- Teachers have more positive attitudes toward teaching and higher expectations for their students.

- In general, students have more positive attitudes about learning and their ability to learn.

- Students achieve more and remember what they have learned longer.

Technology In Metrotech High School in Phoenix, Arizona, students prepare for careers in areas as disparate as auto mechanics and television production, but what happens outside of class makes this school special. The school uses software that diagnoses a student's academic proficiency in areas like math and reading, and then offers individualized programs designed to improve the student's mastery of these skills. All this is done outside of class, saving valu-able class time to focus on other learning.

Problem-Based Learning

Focusing on authentic or real-life problems that often go beyond traditional subject areas is at the heart of **problem-based learning (PBL).** As you might imagine, real problems are not bound by a single subject field or even by the school building. This emphasis is apparent in the other terms used to describe PBL: *experience-based education, project-based instruction,* and *anchored instruction* (because it is "anchored" in the real world). In this instructional model, a crucial aspect of the teacher's role is to identify activities that fuel students' interest, such as

- Design a plan for protecting a specific endangered species.
- How can we stop bullying and harassment in this school?
- Develop a set of urban policies to halt the deterioration of a central city.
- Formulate solutions that might have kept the United States from engaging in the Civil War.

Finding scintillating questions and projects to excite and motivate students is critical, but it is only one aspect of PBL. Other characteristics include:[41]

- *Learner cooperation.* Similar to cooperative learning, PBL often depends on small groups or pairs of students collaborating as they explore and investigate various issues. This approach de-emphasizes competition. For teachers, the goal is to guide and challenge a dozen such small groups simultaneously.

- *Higher-order thinking.* Exploring real and complex issues requires students to analyze, synthesize, and evaluate material.

- *Cross-disciplinary work.* PBL encourages students to investigate how different academic subjects shed light on one another. In exploring ecological issues, for example, students touch not only on biology and chemistry but also on economics, history, sociology, and political science.

- *Artifacts and exhibits.* Students involved in PBL demonstrate what they learn in a very tangible way. Students may produce a traditional report or may create a video, a physical model, a digital portfolio of artifacts, or even a presentation, such as a play or a debate. Teachers might organize a class or school-wide exhibit to share the progress made by PBL students.

Problem-based learning allows students to discover answers to real life issues, such as how to improve children's nutrition by growing and harvesting healthy foods.

- *Authentic learning.* Students pursue an actual unresolved issue. They are expected to define the problem, develop a hypothesis, collect information, analyze that information, and suggest a conclusion, one that might work in the real world.

Technology At John McDonough High School in New Orleans, teachers helped students write digital stories about their lives and their neighborhood. The Neighborhood Story Project collected nonfiction stories, in-depth interviews, and digital photographs. The project produced five best-selling books, and when Hurricane Katrina devastated the city, some of the area's rich cultural history was preserved by the work these students and teachers had done. (Visit www.neighborhoodstoryproject.org.)

Profile in Education   Larry Cuban

A veteran of the classroom for nearly five decades, **Larry Cuban** has examined America's schools from varying perspectives. He has been a professor at Stanford University and a teacher in an inner-city social studies classroom. But it was when Cuban was appointed superintendent in Arlington, Virginia, that Sharon Steindam first met him, and discovered some remarkable traits. Steindam was a newly appointed school principal, and quite nervous about being evaluated by the new superintendent. But as she remembers, "He was the only superintendent that I worked for who truly used a variety of information about the school to help him determine how I was doing. He wanted to know why I felt certain students were doing well and others were not. And he was the most human superintendent I ever worked with. He would greet you in the grocery store and ask about your family. Cuban was a true leader, holding high expectations, providing meaningful feedback, and personally engaging."[a]

Cuban has witnessed many exciting efforts to reform and change America's schools. And yet, after sorting out nearly a century of change, he came to a fascinating insight: Teaching remains strikingly similar year in and year out. In *How Teachers Taught: Constancy and Change in American Classrooms, 1890–1980,* Cuban explores why.

Historically, schools have been built around teachers, not students. Not just philosophically but physically as well. Classrooms featured desks all facing front, bolted to the floor, physically reinforcing the notion that the teacher is the center of instruction. As if the nuts and bolts were not strong enough, the curriculum proved the clincher. To survive instructing very large classes in eight or ten subjects, teachers became dependent on reading and dictating assignments directly from the text. Uniformity and standardization were emphasized. Principals told teachers what to do, and teachers told students what to do. The organizational climate did not nurture new teaching techniques.

As if all these in-school barriers were not enough to defeat change, teacher training all but guaranteed that the status quo would be maintained. New teachers were brought into the profession through a modeling or an apprenticeship program, doing their student teaching under the tutelage of veteran, often conventional, older teachers. It was a system geared to the passing down of traditional approaches and conservative attitudes from one generation of teachers to the next.

Cuban also believes that the suppression of student-based instruction was no accident. Schools were designed to mold a compliant workforce; student-centered instruction was viewed as rebellious, dangerous, and threatening to educational and economic stability.

To Cuban, technology is another phony revolution. In studying effective classrooms, he notes that teachers are very concerned with choosing electronic tools that are efficient. Teachers ask: How much time and energy do I have to invest in learning to use the technology versus the return it will have for my students? When students use the technology, will there be disruption? Will it bolster or compromise my authority to maintain order and cultivate learning? Even teachers eager to make use of new technologies face a serious stumbling block, given the pressures to design curriculum around standardized tests. And comprehensive teacher training to use technology effectively is still lacking. Only a small fraction of teachers find the new technologies efficient. The result: "Computers become merely souped-up typewriters and classrooms continue to run much as they did a generation ago."[b]

Although Cuban recognizes that classrooms have undergone a few minor reforms—experimenting with online learning, greater informality between teacher and student, and even movable chairs—he concludes that instruction at the dawn of the twenty-first century looks strikingly similar to classroom instruction nearly 100 years ago.

[a] Sharon Steindam, personal communication (June 26, 2001).
[b] Larry Cuban, *Oversold and Underused: Computers in Classrooms 1980–2000* (Cambridge, MA: Harvard University Press, 2001).

To learn more about Larry Cuban, click on *Profiles in Education.*

www.mhhe.com/sadker10e

REFLECTION: Think of a few teaching reforms that are currently taking place in a school, district, or state. Which reforms do you think will stick? Why? Which do you believe are likely to fade away? Why?

367

Differentiated Instruction

It would make a teacher's life easier if all students learned the same way, but they do not. Student needs, learning styles, life experiences, and readiness to learn differ. To connect effectively with all your students, you will need to abandon the notion that all students fit comfortably into a particular teaching or testing style. **Differentiated instruction** responds to student differences by offering multiple options for instruction and assessment. Carol Ann Tomlinson, a pioneer in the field, defines differentiated instruction broadly as "doing whatever it takes to ensure that struggling and advanced learners, students with varied cultural heritages, and children with different background experiences all grow as much as they possibly can."[42]

Differentiated instruction organizes instructional activities around student needs rather than content. At first glance, this may seem to be in conflict with the current emphasis on standards-based instruction, but Tomlinson sees it as quite complementary. As she describes it, standards-based curriculum tells us *what* curriculum to teach; differentiation tells us *how* to teach any curriculum well. Notes Tomlinson,

> Typically, what we're being asked to teach kids are facts and skills, but you can wrap them in understanding. You give kids a sense of how this makes sense in the world, how it all fits together, and what they can do with it as people. . . . No one would ask teachers not to teach what they feel responsible for. But you can teach those things in ways that are more meaningful and richer.[43]

Differentiation can show us how to teach the same standards to diverse learners by using different teaching and learning approaches, so teaching becomes a blend of whole-class, group, and individual instruction. Differentiated instruction creates a classroom climate where all students—from the gifted to special needs—can learn together. To help you see how this works, compare the following differentiated instructional approaches with traditional instructional practices:[44]

Traditional/Standardized Instruction	*Differentiated Instruction*
Literature is not Ethan's favorite class. Class discussions focus on analyzing the themes, characters, symbols, and writing styles of classic novels. Ethan struggles to see how these novels relate to his life, and his interest wanes.	Ethan's teacher works hard to link literacy concepts and skills with student interests. For example, students examine how the rules of writing vary in novels, journalism, music, science, and so on. They also explore how the concept of interdependence is exhibited in athletics, the arts, science, families, governments, and literature, their primary content area.
Latisha has a learning disability. She understands ideas well but has difficulty reading quickly and writing clearly. Nearly all assessments in Latisha's class are written. Most tests and papers have strict time limits. Latisha struggles to earn a passing grade.	Latisha and her teacher work together to establish timetables for her written assignments. This flexibility enables her to write with less tension and to proofread her work. The teacher also provides more than one way to express ideas. For example, Latisha and other students can use diagrams, sketches, oral presentations, or hands-on demonstrations to show their knowledge and skill.

Technology A WebQuest is an Internet student-inquiry activity that lends itself to differentiated instruction. The teacher posts several open-ended questions on a topic, and students choose a question that interests them. To help students get started and to target different reading levels among students, the teacher may bookmark an initial list of websites. Following their online quests, students, individually or as a group, share their findings with the class through a podcast, student-produced video, graphic organizers, discussions, role plays, or other methods that reflect their preferred learning style. (To explore WebQuests across subject areas, visit www.techtrekers.com/webquests/. More information on WebQuests can be found at http://webquest.org/.)

A Few More Thoughts on Effective Teaching

Teaching is hard. Teaching well is fiercely so. Often confronted by too many students, a schedule without breaks, a pile of papers that regenerates daily, and incessant demands from every educational stakeholder, teachers can become predictable and mundane in their practices. Nevertheless, innovative, engaged, and reflective teaching is the path to effective teaching. Here are some ideas for you to consider.

"Less is more" is an aphorism attributed to education reformer Ted Sizer. According to Sizer, today's schools are misguided in their emphasis on "covering" material. The goal seems to be teaching and learning a vast body of information, in order to have a sense of accomplishment or to score well on the ever-growing number of standardized tests. But international tests in science, for example, show that although U.S. students have studied more science topics than have students in other countries, they have not studied them in depth, and their lower test scores reflect this superficiality. In Sizer's vision of effective instruction, good teachers limit the amount of content they introduce but develop it sufficiently for students to gain in-depth understanding.

This direction for teaching and schooling marks a radical departure from the current emphasis on uniform standards, test performance, and competition. In marked contrast to the superficial nature of such test-centered curriculum, Sizer advocates deep teaching. In *deep teaching*, teachers work to organize their content around a limited set of key principles and powerful ideas and then engage students in discussing those concepts. The emphasis is on problem solving and critical thinking, rather than on memorizing.[45]

This vision of deep teaching highlights the social nature of learning and of the classroom. As the builder of a classroom **learning community,** the teacher is called on to be a guide or facilitator, skillful in conducting discussions, group work, debates, and dialogues. In this way, the teacher empowers the students to talk with one another and to rehearse the terminology and concepts involved in each discipline. Learning becomes a community effort, not an individual competition.[46]

The classroom as a learning community creates an emotionally safe and intellectually engaged space for collective inquiry.

It is not surprising, therefore, that educators are reconceptualizing schools to create more nurturing learning communities. When learning communities work well, students and teachers get to know each other well and they can develop shared academic goals. Learning communities can be encouraged through several strategies, including looping and block scheduling. In **looping,** schools "promote" teachers along with their students, a process that allows the teacher an extra year or more to get to know students in depth, to diagnose and meet their learning needs, and to develop more meaningful communication with their parents and families. Looping offers students an increased sense of stability and

community. Similarly, **block scheduling** increases teacher–student contact by increasing the length of class periods. The longer periods allow teachers to get to know these students better, and the students benefit from an uninterrupted and in-depth academic study. If you were to teach in a school with block scheduling, you might have 75 students on any given day or in a particular semester, instead of 150.

This notion of a learning community, like deep teaching, contrasts sharply with many current practices that emphasize state- and school-mandated curriculum followed by standardized testing. It points to a more thoughtful classroom, one in which the teacher is a reflective practitioner. **Reflective teachers** continually and intensely analyze their own practices to improve performance. Reflective teachers ask themselves such questions as these:

- What teaching strategies did I use today? How effective were they? What might have been even more effective?

- Were my students engaged with the material? What seemed to motivate them the most? If I were to reteach today's class, how could I get even more students involved?

- What did I do to help my students think more deeply during today's lesson? How can I further develop their critical thinking skills?

- What values and attitudes did my students cultivate from today's learning?

- How did I assess my students' learning today? Would there have been a better way to measure their learning? How well did the students grasp the main points of today's lesson? Do I need to reteach some of these concepts?

- What did I learn today? What did my students teach me?

- Can I fine-tune tomorrow's or next week's lessons to capitalize on the gains made today?

Such questions are designed to raise consciousness, encourage self-scrutiny, and move you toward more effective teaching. Becoming a reflective teacher involves growing beyond your current concerns with instructional and management techniques, the "how to" questions (where many beginning teachers naturally start) and moving toward "what" and "why" questions, the questions and answers that transform teachers into insightful and gifted instructors.[47]

Reflection has many paths. A teaching journal is one way to record each day's reactions and insights. Reviewing the journal over time will hopefully provide a record of your professional growth. Asking a colleague to observe your teaching and share his or her insights can initiate a useful professional dialogue. Returning the favor and observing your colleagues can provide ideas not only for your colleagues, but for you as well. Of course, you can be your own observer through the magic of technology. Video record your teaching behaviors and do your own analysis. As you see, there are many valuable routes to reflection.

You don't have to wait until student teaching to start being a reflective teacher. You can start right now by asking yourself:

- What roles, official and unofficial, does a teacher have?

- What roles, official and unofficial, does a student have?

- What qualities do good teachers have?

- What teaching strategies do I prefer?

- What is the purpose of school?

- How will I motivate myself to be a reflective teacher in the years ahead?

So let us take a moment to reflect. After reading this chapter, we trust that you can appreciate the complexity of effective instruction. But understanding the technical aspects of teaching should never overshadow the human qualities that are the foundation of great teaching. Being a teacher has a built in arrogance. The title alone implies "I know a lot and will teach you things that you do not know." But don't let the title mislead you; we are all teachers and we are all learners. Bring humility to your work. You will interact with peers, immigrants, children, old people, and strangers, as well as friends and family; and you will learn from all of them, if you are humbled and let them be your teachers. Humility as a generosity of spirit, self-modesty, and an open heart will serve you and your students well. We are confident that mastering the strategies and techniques in this chapter will help you become a skilled teacher; we hope your humility will make you a great teacher.

ONLINE VIDEO ALBUM TO ACCOMPANY *TEACHERS, SCHOOLS, AND SOCIETY, 10E*

Visit the Online Learning Center for a range of contemporary videos with content related to this chapter.

www.mhhe.com/sadker10e

THE *TEACHERS, SCHOOLS, AND SOCIETY* READER WITH CLASSROOM OBSERVATION VIDEO CLIPS

Go to your *Teachers, Schools, and Society* Reader CD-ROM to:

READ CURRENT AND HISTORICAL ARTICLES

45. **Classroom Misbehavior Is Predictable and Preventable,** by Timothy J. Landrum, Amy S. Lingo, and Terrance M. Scott, *Phi Delta Kappan,* October 2011.

46. **The Perils and Promises of Praise,** by Carol S. Dweck, *Educational Leadership,* October 2007.

47. **Mapping a Route Toward Differentiated Instruction,** by Carol Ann Tomlinson, *Educational Leadership,* September 1999.

48. **Learning to Love Assessment,** by Carol Ann Tomlinson, *Educational Leadership,* December 2007.

ANALYZE CASE STUDIES

20. **Ken Kelly:** A teacher having trouble with questioning and with discussion teaching visits a teacher who is holding a Socratic discussion with a fourth-grade class. He questions the applicability of her methods to his situation.

21. **Judith Kent:** A teacher engages her students in whole-class discussion, and then the students work with partners on an assignment. She explains the planning process she went through to reteach the lesson after it had not worked in the previous class.

OBSERVE TEACHERS, STUDENTS, AND CLASSROOMS IN ACTION

Have High Expectations!

16. Classroom Observation: Teachers Discuss Their Methods for Effective Teaching

Part of being an effective teacher is creating a positive learning community. In this observation you will observe classroom teachers explaining how they use different strategies to create exciting learning communities.

KEY TERMS AND PEOPLE

www.mhhe.com/sadker10e

CHAPTER REVIEW

Go to the Online Learning Center to take a chapter self-quiz, practice with key terms, and review concepts from the chapter.

academic learning time, 342

allocated time, 342

behavioral objective, 365

block scheduling, 370

Bloom's taxonomy, 352

cooperative learning, 363

Cuban, Larry, 367

differentiated instruction, 368

direct teaching, 362

engaged time, 342

higher-order question, 352

learning community, 369

looping, 369

lower-order question, 352

mastery learning, 365

pedagogical cycle, 349

problem-based learning (PBL), 366

reflective teaching, 370

Rowe, Mary Budd, 354

Slavin, Robert, 363

wait time, 354

DISCUSSION QUESTIONS AND ACTIVITIES

1. Do you think teachers are born, or made? Debate a classmate who holds the opposite point of view. Interview elementary and secondary teachers and ask them what they think about this question. Do some of them say that it is a combination of both? If so, why? Which part is art, which part skill?

2. Why do you think there is so much variation in how different teachers and schools use time for learning? Observe in your own college classrooms to determine how much time is used productively and how much is wasted. For each class observed, keep a fairly detailed record of how time is lost (students six minutes late, class ends fifteen minutes early, PowerPoint presentation takes four minutes to set up, and so on).

3. Research suggests that to achieve, students should be functioning at a very high success rate. Do you agree that this is likely to lead to higher achievement? Or do you think that students need to cope with failure and be "stretched" to achieve? Defend your position.

4. Analyze teacher reactions to student answers in elementary and secondary classrooms where you are an observer and in the college classrooms where you are a student. Are most of these classrooms "okay" classrooms? Why do you think some teacher reactions are vague and diffuse? What observations can you make about the use of praise, remediation, and criticism?

5. In an interview for a teaching position, you are asked your opinion of educational technology and your plans, if any, for incorporating technology into your teaching. How would you answer? Include at least five reasons to support your position.

Your First Classroom

CHAPTER 12

FOCUS QUESTIONS

1. What are the stages of teacher development?
2. What resources do school districts provide for a teacher's first year in the classroom?
3. What are the real rewards of teaching?
4. What are the differences between the National Education Association and the American Federation of Teachers?

One cannot lead a life that is truly excellent without feeling that one belongs to something greater and more permanent than oneself.

—MIHALY CSIKSZENTMIHALYI

CHAPTER PREVIEW

It looks so small: the distance between the students' chairs and the teacher's desk. But traveling from a student's desk to a teacher's desk represents an enormous journey. This chapter is intended to prepare you for that transformation, from student to teacher.

As you enter your first classroom, chances are that you will focus on lesson planning, classroom management, and preparing for those visits by your supervisor. In short, you will be all about classroom survival. With time and experience, you will begin to refine your teaching strategies and focus less on survival skills and more on ways to enhance student learning. Although we would love to serve up some ready-to-use answers to help you meet these first-year classroom challenges, truth is, there are many questions that only you will be able to answer. Here are just a few for you to consider: Where should I teach? How can I win that ideal (at least satisfying) teaching position? What will my first year be like? Should I join a teachers' association? Should I stay in teaching long term? If so, what are the routes to advancement? How will I be evaluated? And with all the negative press I read about schools, is this something that I want to do? This chapter provides you with some insights and practical advice about making that first year of teaching a successful one, and perhaps the beginning of many rewarding years.

www.mhhe.com/sadker10e

WHAT DO YOU THINK? What teaching skills are of most value? Check off the teaching skills you believe are most important. See how your criteria compare with those of your colleagues.

Stages of Teacher Development

Will I be able to manage this class? Can I get through the curriculum? Do I know my subject well enough? Will the other teachers like me? Will the administrators rehire me? Am I going to be a good teacher? Will I like this life in the classroom?

FOCUS QUESTION 1

What are the stages of teacher development?

When you begin teaching, the questions that occupy you are mostly about your ability, about visits by supervisors, and about managing students. By the second year, teachers are more experienced (and confident), and they usually move beyond those questions, shifting the focus of their attention to improving instruction and student performance. For example, experienced teachers might spend time analyzing the needs of individual students, exploring a new curriculum strategy, and asking such questions as: How can I help this shy child? and Why is this student encountering learning problems? If a colleague is achieving success using a new teaching strategy, an experienced teacher might observe, and then adapt that strategy. As talented and experienced teachers mature, their interests and vision extend beyond their own classrooms. At this more advanced stage, they work to develop programs that could benefit large numbers of students. Figure 12.1 suggests stages that teachers pass through as they become more skilled in their craft.[1]

Attempts to reform education and improve student achievement are dependent on our ability to move teachers through these developmental stages. Although earlier studies by James Coleman and others seemed to call into question the educational impact of teachers, comprehensive studies in the 1990s found that teacher performance is critical. Investments in improving teacher skills and professional growth improve students' academic performance more than funds invested in other educational areas. Although efforts to reduce class size (particularly for the early grades) or provide schools with up-to-date computer technology can be helpful, research reveals that teacher competence is *the* most important factor in improving student achievement.[2]

What do we mean by a competent teacher? The most effective teachers not only demonstrate mastery of the subjects they teach but also are skilled in the methods of teaching and understand student development. Teaching is complex work that cannot be fully mastered in the short period of teacher education. Like doctors, lawyers, engineers, and architects, you will continue to learn on the job, especially in your early teaching years. In the past, too few teachers received quality support in their first crucial years in the classroom, making growth to a more sophisticated level of teaching difficult. Some teachers even struggle to survive that first year. One out of three teachers leaves the classroom within three years, almost half leave within five years. That is why a growing number of districts are investing resources in induction and mentoring programs to ensure that when you step into your first classroom, you will not be alone.

Your First Year: Induction into the Profession

FOCUS QUESTION 2

What resources do school districts provide for a teacher's first year in the classroom?

We wish we could relive the excitement and intensity of our first year in the classroom. Okay, it was not always wonderful, and yes, it was often tough, but truth is, it was magical. Your first year could also be a captivating time of learning and growing—or it could be quite the opposite. The quality of support you receive once you begin teaching may be the difference. Half a century ago, that support was rarely there as sociologist Dan Lortie compared new teachers to Robinson Crusoe, marooned on an island. Things are different today, and most school districts build bridges to those teacher islands, bridges called induction programs. **Induction programs** "provide some systematic and sustained assistance to beginning teachers for at least one school year," in the hope that such support will create the first of many wonderful

FIGURE 12.1

Stages of Teacher Development.

Stage 1: Survival

Teachers move from day to day, trying to get through the week and wondering if teaching is the right job for them. Concerns about classroom management, visits by supervisors, professional competence, and acceptance by colleagues dominate their thoughts. Support and professional development at this stage are particularly critical.

Stage 2: Consolidation

At stage 2, the focus moves from the teacher's survival to the children's learning. The skills acquired during the first stage are consolidated, synthesized into strategies to be thoughtfully applied in the class. Teachers also synthesize their knowledge of students and are able to analyze learning, social, or classroom management problems in the light of individual student differences and needs.

Stage 3: Renewal

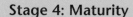

Once teaching skills and an understanding of student development have been mastered, and several years of teaching experience have been completed, predictable classroom routines can become comforting, or boring. Teachers at stage 2 face a decision: stay at stage 2, comfortable in the classroom but exploring little else, or move toward stage 3, renewal. In stage 3, new approaches are sought as teachers participate in regional or national professional development programs and visit successful colleagues to seek new ideas for teaching and learning.

Stage 4: Maturity

Teachers move beyond classroom concerns and seek greater professional perspective. At this stage, the teacher considers deeper and more abstract questions about broad educational issues: educational philosophy, ways to strengthen the teaching profession, and educational ideas that can enhance education throughout the school, region, or nation. Regrettably, many teachers never reach stage 4.

SOURCE: Based on the work of Lillian Katz.

REFLECTION: Have you been taught by teachers representing each of these four developmental stages? Describe behaviors at each of the four levels. If you were to build in strategies to take you from stage 1 to stage 4, what might they be?

years.[3] Induction programs will match you with an experienced instructor, sometimes called a consulting teacher or mentor, who observes your teaching for one to three or more years, counsels and co-plans with you, as well as provides you with a continuous source of feedback about your teaching. Nearly nine out of ten new teachers will find themselves in an induction program, and that is good news. The bad news is that too many induction programs fall short of a quality experience, a costly omission.[4] A growing number of educators believe that there is no "teacher shortage" in America; rather, there is a teacher retention problem. Teachers leaving the classroom costs the United States more than $7 billion yearly, but effective induction programs stem that exit.[5]

Effective mentoring is a crucial aspect of a beginning teacher's induction into the profession.

Mentors

A critical component of the induction program are **mentors,** experienced teachers selected to guide new teachers through the school culture and norms, shedding light on the *official* and the *hidden* school culture (which memos need a quick response, which do not; who keeps the key to the supply room; where the best DVD players are hidden), offering a shoulder to lean on during those very difficult days, and so much more. What makes a strong mentor relationship? Here are some characteristics for you to keep in mind. You are more likely to be in an effective mentor relationship if you are in close physical proximity to your mentor, if your mentor teaches in the same grade-level and/or subject area as you do, and if the school provides time for you and your mentor to meet during the school day. Then there is that intangible factor: chemistry. We don't have to explain why it will be a much better experience if you and your mentor have compatible personalities. (In fact, if you feel that you and your mentor are not compatible, you might want to discuss this problem, and possibly request a different mentor.) Thoughtful mentors are your co-thinkers and co-planners, helping you to reframe challenges, organize and modify your teaching, and analyze how best to promote student learning. Mentors strive for a balance between supporting you as a new teacher and challenging you to grow, and a good mentor program provides continuous advanced training not only to you, but to your mentor as well. If you are fortunate enough to find yourself in such a program in the first few years of your teaching career, you are more likely to stay a teacher for many years to come.[6]

If having a mentor sounds appealing, and you find yourself in a school district that does not provide an official or a quality mentoring experience, you can certainly connect with an unofficial mentor to help you through those first few years. You might want to ask colleagues or administrators about teachers known for creative lessons or effective classroom management, someone who can lend you a helping hand. Perhaps you can observe their teaching and meet with this teacher to explore lesson plans and ideas. The Internet also has sites where you can find tele-mentors, also called *e-mentors,* who answer questions and offer advice and support.

Mentors may provide more than friendly support to you; they have an official responsibility to assess new teachers and to file reports to school supervisors. A poor performance report from a mentor can result in a recommendation for extra training for an intern teacher, which could be absolutely wonderful in resolving a persistent problem.

Observation

Whether new teachers are assigned a mentor, find a mentor, or are mentorless, they are likely to have their classroom teaching observed. It is not unusual for teachers to be observed three or four times in their first year and, in some districts, much more frequently. Teachers are the most important school-level factor in student learning, so observing and evaluating how well or poorly they are doing is quite important.[7] Currently, observations come in two varieties: *diagnostic,* designed to help the teachers, and *evaluative,* intended to be used for employment decisions. Teachers benefit from the diagnostic evaluation, which helps them grow, but often fear the evaluative observation, which might be used for tenure, salary or other personnel decisions. When one observation is used for both helping and evaluating a teacher there are problems. Often these different purposes can work against each other, promoting fear rather than learning.

Although many teachers find classroom observations a bit nerve-wracking, the truth is that as currently used, they have not been very effective. A survey of teacher evaluation systems in fourteen large American school districts found that 98 percent of teachers studied were given a "satisfactory" evaluation.[8] It is true that on Garrison Keillor's NPR radio series, "A Prairie Home Companion," Lake Wobegon is a place where "the women are strong, the men good looking, and all the children are above average," but it is doubtful that virtually all of America's teachers live in Lake Wobegon. We know that students in some classes achieve a great deal, and in others not so much, and that each of us has had teachers who we found inspiring, as well as teachers who made time stand still (not in a good way).

Some districts are working to improve teacher observations. Well-done observations inform the district of the strengths and weaknesses of each faculty member, and for you the teacher, such observations help you refine your teaching skills. A number of school districts recognize the professionalism and autonomy of teachers and include them as observers of other teachers, a process called **peer review.** Sometimes a district will augment their observation teams with educators from outside the school district. You are likely to go through several reviews of your teaching during your first few years, so to get the most out of these observations, here are a few ideas for you to consider.

A good first step is to meet with your mentor, colleague, and/or supervisor to discuss the goals, what they see as effective teaching. You may not agree with everything they say, but with research as a guide, you should all agree on much of it. It is also a good idea for you to ask a mentor or a colleague precisely how your teaching skills and your students' performance will be assessed. In some school systems, administrators use a standard observation form as the accepted norm, so reviewing that form will help. In other instances, teachers and administrators work together to develop an observation system, an approach that builds consensus for what constitutes high-quality instruction, developing teachers' trust and confidence in the process.

Let's briefly offer some examples of observation strategies. The Cincinnati, Ohio, school district had administrators and teachers develop an observation framework that specifies both effective learning goals for students and the related teaching behaviors. This observation system worked: Teachers scoring high on classroom observations were teaching students also scoring high in math and reading. Let's take a closer look at two of the categories—instructional teaching strategies and content knowledge. A teacher who routinely uses a broad range of effective and appropriate teaching strategies or appropriate and accurate content scores well on the observation, but one who uses ineffective or inappropriate strategies or content would score poorly. (See Figure 12.2 for a description.) Such observations lead to productive conversations between teacher and supervisor, exploring the teaching plan.

Farmington, Connecticut Public Schools also offers a clear framework for teachers to refine their teaching skills.[9] (See a brief overview of the Farmington approach in Figure 12.3). Using critical principles associated with effective education, the school district identified both teacher and student behaviors related to each principle. One principle, for example, is intended to create a challenging educational environment for students. To attain this goal, teachers are advised to pursue several behaviors (including maintaining high expectations for each student) and to clearly communicate learning goals. Students are expected to ask questions if they need clarity and to persist even in the face of challenging learning tasks. Teaching and learning are presented as a joint responsibility. In addition, teachers are encouraged to identify individual goals for each academic year. This evaluation approach is the result of teachers and administrators working together to create a productive observation experience, one in which teachers can grow professionally.

FIGURE 12.2
How Teachers Are Evaluated in Cincinnati: A Sample.

One sample standard from the Cincinnati evaluation rubric

Standard 3.2: Teacher demonstrates knowledge . . .

	Distinguished	Proficient	Basic	Unsatisfactory
Instructional Strategies	Teacher routinely uses a broad range of multiple instructional strategies that are effective and appropriate to the content.	Teacher uses instructional strategies that are effective and appropriate to the content.	Teacher uses a limited range of instructional strategies that are effective and appropriate to the content.	Teacher uses instructional strategies that are ineffective and/or inappropriate to the content.
Content Knowledge	Teacher conveys accurate content knowledge, including standards-based content knowledge.	Teacher conveys accurate content knowledge, including standards-based content knowledge.	Teacher conveys some minor content inaccuracies that do not contribute to making the content incomprehensible to the students.	Teacher conveys content inaccuracies that contribute to making the content incomprehensible to the students.

SOURCE: Cincinnati Public Schools Teacher Evaluation System 2005

SOURCE: Thomas J. Kane, Eric S. Taylor, John H. Tyler, and Amy L. Wooten, "Evaluating Teacher Effectiveness: Can Classroom Observations Identify Practices that Raise Achievement?" *Education Next* Summer 2011 / Vol. 11, No. 3. Reprinted courtesy of Education Next.

REFLECTION: Do you see this approach for evaluating you as a teacher as helpful in developing and improving your teaching skills? Why or why not?

FIGURE 12.3

Farmington, Connecticut, Framework for Teaching and Learning.

Priniciple # 1: ACTIVE LEARNING COMMUNITY
Students learn best when they have a sense of belonging to a positive learning community in which they have regular opportunities to work collaboratively.
Teachers . . .
☐ Organize the classroom environment with clearly established routines and behavioral expectations
☐ Create effective systems to hold students accountable for individual and group responsibilities
☐ Model thinking and share learning as a member of the classroom community
☐ Provide direct instruction and guided practice in the skills and dispositions of effective collaborative work
☐ Encourage questions, nurture multiple points of view and value intellectual risk-taking
☐ Facilitate student to student discourse, developing effective communications skills
☐ Structure opportunities for students to share work publicly
☐ Promote learning through engagement with others as mentors and critics
Students . . .
☐ Establish and reflect on classroom and small group norms for respectful behavior and effective communication
☐ Participate actively in discussions and collaborative tasks
☐ Speak and write clearly to communicate with others
☐ Exchange meaningful and constructive feedback
☐ Clarify ideas by asking questions, listening to others
☐ Investigate and appreciate multiple points of view
☐ Share their work publicly and engage in dialogue about process and product
OTHER PRINCIPLES INCLUDE:
Principle # 2: CHALLENGING EXPECTATIONS
Students learn best when they understand performance expectations and are individually supported in meeting challenging standards
Principle # 3: MEANINGFUL KNOWLEDGE
Students learn best when they see content as meaningful and organized around big ideas and questions and can transfer learning to new contexts.
Principle # 4: PURPOSEFUL ENGAGEMENT
Students learn best when they are actively engaged in authentic learning tasks and given opportunities to construct meaning and develop understanding.
Principle # 5: INDIVIDUAL RESPONSIBILITY
Students learn best when they make choices about and take responsibility for their own learning goals and progress.

SOURCE: An abbreviated presentation of the Farmington Public Schools Teacher Observation form, Farmington, Connecticut, CT 06032. For a complete view of this observation approach, visit http://fpsct.org/page.cfm?p=4701.

REFLECTION: Why do you think Farmington included for each of these principles, not only what teachers should be doing, but student behavior as well? Are there any principles you would disagree with? Any you would add?

As you glance over the form, which skills do you see as your strengths? Which ones need more study and practice? What specific steps in your teacher education program will prepare you to successfully pass this evaluation?

Observations, whether official or informal, are usually followed by a conference in which the mentor or the supervisor shares the high points and the "not-as-high-as-we-would-like" points of your teaching. Take notes and carefully consider these comments. You may find the comments to be useful, even insightful, offering you wise counsel on how to improve. Your attitude and openness in these conferences indicates your willingness to analyze your teaching, refine your teaching skills, and grow professionally.

Your First Day: Creating a Productive Classroom Climate

The way you organize your classroom on that very first day sends a powerful message about who you are as a teacher. If that first day is done well, you are on your way to a smoother teaching year. On the other hand, any mistakes made early in the year enter an echo chamber—they keep returning until June arrives. Here are some suggestions for creating a productive class climate.

Physical Considerations   Before school starts, look around your classroom and ask yourself: "What do I want my room to say to the students?" Some of the physical features, such as doors, windows, and built-ins, are beyond your control. But there is still much you can do. Did you ever hear the phrase "If the walls could talk"? Guess what—they do. What do you want displayed on your classroom walls? Multicultural images of males and females, images of creative ideas, motivational statements, and fascinating facts can send powerful messages. (Blank walls convey their own messages, don't they?) When students walk into a thoughtfully prepared room, they appreciate the effort. But there are times when even a blank area of the wall can be positive—if it is designated as a student display area, postings that students will manage in the future. Walls do talk.

Do you want student desks all facing the front, or arranged for students to work in groups, or in a circle around the room for children to introduce themselves, or changing as activities change? You will also need a space for your instructional materials, a place easy to get to so there are no long delays as you move from one class activity to another. Where will you be positioned? You should select a place where you can see the entire class, a place with no blind spots so you can spot a student who needs help—or is causing a disturbance. Some teachers plan to teach from different areas of the room, placing their desk in one place, audio-visual equipment in another, the day's agenda in yet another area, and even their water, tea, or coffee in yet another place. This ensures that they will be visiting different areas, be near different students, and not be locked in the front of the room. Have you thought about any special touches that you want to bring in? Plants, carpet, pillows, posters? It is your room, and you get to create the ambience for you and your students.

This could be your first classroom, and exciting new chapter in your life.

Good Cop/Bad Cop   After decades of observing first-year teachers, we can tell you that classroom management, or as some call it, classroom discipline, is a real challenge. Beginning teachers, still learning their way, can be intimidated by the fact that they are now in charge of keeping an orderly learning environment. Some novice teachers are convinced that the key to maintaining order is a strong set of rules with tough enforcement. For them, a quiet, tightly managed class is a sign of a good teacher. A stern image can give a beginning teacher a sense of security, a feeling that the teacher is really in control. This often is an illusion. Repressing students' behavior can lead to harsh reactions later in the year. Other new teachers are just as convinced that kindness will do the trick, that a teacher who is a cross between Mr. Rogers and your sweet Aunt Bess will win the students over and avoid management confrontations. They believe caring teachers creating a friendly and open climate do not need harsh rules. But this approach is a bit naïve, and students may be confused about what this new "friend" is all about, and how they are expected to behave.

As you might imagine, or perhaps recall from your own student days, these extremes—good cop/bad cop—confuse students. Students come to your class with their own school experiences and expectations. When one teacher is a strict disciplinarian, and another is laid back and laissez-faire, the students' world gets very confusing. The school you will teach in already has norms and expectations, and if you drift too far from those norms, you will have problems. If you are a Mr. Rogers teacher in a Prussian military school, your students may get out of control quickly. On the other hand, a tough-cop teacher who wanders into Mr. Rogers's neighborhood will engender a great deal of hostility.

It is wise to check out the school climate during your job search to make certain that you feel comfortable in that school. In some schools, students are expected to control and monitor their own behaviors; in others, law and order is a priority and teachers enforce firm rules. But once you accept a position, you don't want to manage a class that is in conflict with school norms. At the beginning of the year, especially your first day, students expect a familiar and orderly climate. In most cases, that means avoiding the extremes of good cop/bad cop.

Rules and Consequences We discussed classroom management in Chapter 11, so you may want to revisit that discussion for a refresher, but because management is so crucial to your first day, we will reinforce some key points here. First a story: When David, one of the authors of this book, was flying to Asia, his plane made a refueling stop in Dubai. After forty-five minutes at the airport, there was an announcement that the passengers should line up to reboard the plane. So David went to the gate and to the end of the line to reboard. There were about one hundred people in that line, but when the plane door opened, a mob of passengers from all around the terminal bolted to the front of the line and scampered on the plane. Those of us in line watched in dismay as this group pushed their way to the front. In their cultures, the idea of waiting in a line did not make much sense; when a door opens, you go in. Several of the in-line community murmured a mix of anger and amusement. But after all, the announcement did not say line up to get on the plane; people made their own assumptions and did what they were comfortable doing. When you think of your classroom, think of the Dubai airport: Students also need to understand and follow the same rules, or chaos and discord will follow.

It is a good idea to develop a clear set of rules that first day, making certain that the students (and their parents) understand the rules. Many teachers engage their students in developing these rules, creating a sense of community and joint responsibility. Here are some sample classroom rules you may want to consider: Show respect and courtesy to everyone, avoid dangerous situations, always be honest, do not interrupt others, and no physical or verbal abuse. It is a good idea to post the rules in your classroom, along with consequences for violations. It is also a good idea to share these rules with parents. Remember, the consequences for breaking a rule need not be punitive; consequences can be instructive. For example, if a student constantly shouts out an answer instead of waiting his or her turn, the first consequence might be the other students putting their fingers to their lips as a reminder to wait. The rules are intended to create a shared sense of community, to make certain that all students feel comfortable and safe in the classroom.

Know Your Students Do you remember how it felt when the teacher called you by a wrong name, or no name at all—almost as if you did not exist? Don't forget that feeling, and dedicate yourself to learning your students' names. This is an easier assignment for teachers with one class of students than it is for a teacher with five classes a day, but the sooner all teachers learn the names of their students the smoother the class will run. Seating charts can help, as well as name signs on desks. You may hear student grunts at your suggestion for student name signs (anonymity can be a student strategy), but you can explain that the signs will disappear when everyone knows each other's name. And here is a special reminder: If a student is from another culture and has an unfamiliar-sounding name, work to learn the correct pronunciation. It will be much appreciated by the student and will help you grow as well.

Prepare for a Strong First Day This first class creates a first impression, and first impressions happen only once. Take the time to plan some exciting and meaningful activities for that first day. You may also want to share your vision and goals for the entire year with the class: what students will be learning and why that is important. An exciting and thoughtful beginning to the school year can create the tone for the weeks and months that follow.

Professional Development Programs

School systems, universities, and others offer programs that enable teachers to satisfy state requirements for renewal of teacher licensure, work toward an endorsement or a license in a second teaching field, attend a summer institute to master new skills, obtain an advanced degree, or earn a higher salary. Often, teacher pay schedules are connected to how much professional development and graduate credits they have earned, so that a teacher who takes thirty graduate credits at a college or thirty training hours offered by a school district would get a salary increase.

School districts vary greatly in their approaches to professional training. Sometimes districts identify a topic (e.g., student portfolio development or technology), invite in one or more speakers to make a presentation on that topic, and require the whole faculty to participate. These professional development efforts are scheduled before, during, and at the end of the academic year. Teachers call them *in-service* days; students are more likely to consider them vacation days. Many have criticized these one-time programs as "dog and pony" shows, charging that brief presentations given to a large group of educators lack long-term impact. Research backs this up. While teachers report engaging in about forty-four hours of professional development annually, these activities are typically brief and sporadic. Research suggests that for professional development to have significant effects on student achievement, teachers need at least forty-nine hours on a specific topic and at least a hundred hours in math and science. Some school districts and states, while supporting the idea of professional development, are not increasing time or resources devoted to professional training and, instead, are basing salaries and employment decisions on classroom performance, including student test scores.[10]

Other school districts are developing professional development strategies that require more time and offer greater focus on a specific subject or skill area. Examples of this more in-depth approach include meetings and workshops over the course of a year or more to improve the science program, monthly sessions on relevant software, and weekly conferences to create anti-bully curricula. Recent research has underscored the value of teacher-designed programs, closely tied to practical classroom skills. Educational reformers suggest that the best **professional development** programs:

- Connect directly to the teacher's work with students
- Link subject content with teaching skills
- Use a problem-solving approach
- Reflect research findings
- Are sustained and supported over time[11]

How can professional development programs incorporate these characteristics? One way is to ask teachers to prepare portfolios for a teacher's license, board certification, or merit review. Portfolio construction encourages teachers to develop insight and reflection about their instruction by creating tangible examples of their competence. The Teacher Performance Assessment, currently being developed at Stanford, would require beginning teachers to apply for a teacher's license by submitting a portfolio that includes lesson plans, reflections of their work and a video of their classroom interactions with students.[12] (See Chapter 13 for a discussion of portfolios and the Teacher Performance Assessment.) Over the years, such portfolios could provide a time-lapse portrait of a teacher's professional growth, the kind of long-term reflection that makes a difference in teacher effectiveness and student learning.

Collaborative action research (CAR) is yet another avenue for professional growth, but in this case through the use of research. In nations such as Finland, the idea of the teacher as researcher is commonplace and is viewed as simply another dimension of professionalism. Collaborative action research is based on that premise. Typically in CAR, a group of teachers identifies a genuine problem in their school or classes, designs ways to address the problem, and then evaluates their success. If the teachers are concerned about the poor performance of girls in high school science courses, for example, they might decide to experiment with new methods to improve that performance. One teacher might try cooperative learning strategies in her science class, while a second teacher develops techniques to involve parents in their daughters' science work. A third teacher might initiate a new science curriculum designed to motivate female students. Each of these approaches would be evaluated and the most effective selected for use by all teachers. CAR encourages thoughtful, objective analysis of real teacher concerns.

Professional development takes many forms: graduate degree programs, collaborative action research projects, web-based programs, teaching academies, or in-service days. A quick glance at Figure 12.4 offers a sample of the wide range of professional development options. Yet, finding the time for professional development can be a challenge. Teachers in the United States average 1,080 hours per year in classroom teaching, leaving little time for nonclassroom activities. The case is very different in industrialized European and Asian nations, where the teachers' workweek includes time for professional development and collaboration on instructional issues. (See Figure 12.5.) These countries schedule between fifteen and twenty hours per week for teachers to grade, prepare lessons, meet with students and parents, and do collaborative action research projects. U.S. teachers have, on average, only three to five hours a week for such activities.[13] It is unfortunate that collaboration is not more common in our schools.

FIGURE 12.4
These Announcements Provide a Taste of the Continuous Learning Opportunities Available to Educators.

Professional Development
Once a Teacher, Always a Learner

Institute for New Heads by the Southern Association of Independent Schools, Decatur, GA

Making Connections: The Art and Science of Teaching, Groton, MA

Assessing English Language Learners Chicago, IL

Colonial Williamsburg Teacher Institute, Williamsburg, VA

We the People Teacher Institute, by the Center for Civic Education, Denver, CO

What Works in Schools—Increasing Student Achievement Through Research-Based Practices, Alexandria, VA

The Role of the Arts in the Transformation of School Culture, Cambridge, MA

Learning & the Brain: Using Brain Research as the Pathway to Student Memory, Motivation, and Achievement, Cambridge, MA

Common Core Standards, New Orleans, LA

Making Algebra Child's Play, Buffalo, NY

Hands-on Science workshop by the American Association for the Advancement of Science, K–6, Washington, DC

Think Tank on Global Education, Cambridge, MA

Educational Theatre Association: Lighting for Musicals, Orlando, FL

Teachers' Symposium, American Montessori Society, Albuquerque, NM

Urban Education, Atlanta, GA

Learning Disabilities: Attention Deficit/Hyperactivity Disorder teachers grades 1–6, NYC

Rap, Rhythm, and Rhyme, Transforming Teaching, KIPP Academy, Bronx, NY

Reaching All Students: Assessment in a Standards-Based Environment, Worcester, MA

The Nuts and Bolts of Operating a Local Teacher Organization by the National Association of Catholic School Teachers, Philadelphia, PA

Character Education Training and Information Conference, Baltimore, MD

Success, Standards, and Struggling Secondary Students: K–12 educators who work with at-risk youth, Renton, WA

National 1 Day Conference for Substitute Teachers, Petersburg, VA

Making Sense of Looping: Non-Graded Primary and Multi-age Classrooms, Cleveland, OH

Integrating the Curriculum with Multiple Intelligences: The Balancing Act, Bloomington, IN

Council of School Attorneys' Advocacy Seminar and School Law Retreat, San Antonio, TX

Raising Standards in Rural Education, Fort Collins, CO

SOURCE: Adapted from *Education Week on the Web; Teacher Magazine,* 2009, 2012.

REFLECTION: Which of these opportunities do you find most interesting? Why? (You might need to consider numerous factors from personal interests to finances.)

Personalizing Schools

From a new teacher's perspective, what were familiar school surroundings remembered as a student now become a bit alien: teachers and students see school very differently. As a teacher, you will likely be shocked by the endless stream of paperwork that engulfs you, and

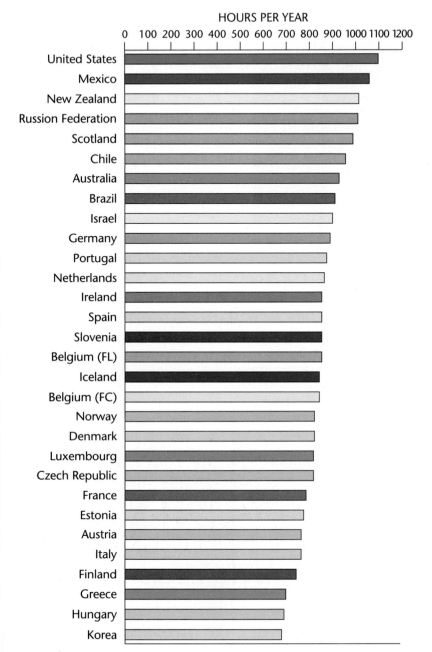

HOURS PER YEAR

United States, Mexico, New Zealand, Russion Federation, Scotland, Chile, Australia, Brazil, Israel, Germany, Portugal, Netherlands, Ireland, Spain, Slovenia, Belgium (FL), Iceland, Belgium (FC), Norway, Denmark, Luxembourg, Czech Republic, France, Estonia, Austria, Italy, Finland, Greece, Hungary, Korea

FIGURE 12.5

International Comparison of Teaching Hours Per Year.

SOURCE: Report: Teachers Lagging in Professional Learning, *Education Week* 2, no. 2 (March 16, 2009).

REFLECTION: Why do you believe the United States lags behind these other nations in providing professional time for teachers?

you will struggle to learn the names of the students in your classes, as many as 150 students or more at the secondary level. You will work even harder getting to know the people behind the names. Typically, you will have only three to five scheduled hours a week to prepare your lessons or coordinate with your colleagues. You will find little time to meet with individual students, much less their parents. Much of your professional day will be spent trying to manage

Exciting learning opportunities await beyond the classroom walls.

students in a world of adult isolation. This school organization is at least a century old, and new teachers, as well as experienced ones, often find it both dehumanizing and inadequate.

It is not surprising, therefore, that some educators would like to create schools that are more responsive to the intellectual and emotional needs of both teachers and students. As you contemplate where you want to begin your teaching career, you may want to consider the school organization: Does the school climate build or detract from a sense of community?

One effort intended to nurture a more intimate and goal-oriented school environment is the creation of learning communities. When **learning communities** are established, students and teachers get to know each other both personally and intellectually as they develop shared academic goals and values. Reducing class size and lengthening school periods are two of several organizational changes that can reduce student alienation and build learning communities.

In other nations, teachers assume a greater number of responsibilities; as a result, they work more intensively with each student. In Japan, Germany, Switzerland, and Sweden, for example, teachers serve as counselors as well as instructors and have a greater range of interactions with their students. To meet their expanded responsibilities, teachers are given additional time to confer with their colleagues and plan their lessons. There are fewer support staff and administrators in these countries, and greater emphasis is placed on the teacher–student connection. Whereas teachers constitute 60 to 80 percent of the school staff in European and Asian countries, they represent less than half of the education staff in the United States. In fact, in the United States, the number of administrators and nonteaching staff members has more than doubled over the past three decades. Reformers believe student performance will not improve unless we reverse this trend.[14]

Many of the activities in this book, including the You Be the Judge in the first chapter, the inventory of your educational philosophy in Chapter 8, and the *RAPs,* will help you answer these questions. Once you sort out your priorities and identify the schools that are right for you, the next task is to get that first job.

The Intangible (But Very Real) Rewards of Teaching

Project yourself into the future. You have worked hard in your school, and you are widely acclaimed as a terrific teacher. (Congratulations!) After some wonderful years in the classroom, you begin to think about what lies ahead. Having parents, students, and colleagues sing your praises is wonderful, but is there more than that? How are dedicated and excellent teachers recognized and rewarded? Without formal and meaningful recognition, frustration may well follow, a sentiment captured in all-too-typical teacher comments, such as the following:

> How would I describe my teaching? Well, let me put it this way—I work hard. Free time is a thing of the past. My students are really important to me, and I'm willing to go the extra mile to give them feedback, organize field trips and projects, meet with them or their parents, and give them a stimulating classroom. In fact, most Saturdays I'm working on grades or new projects. And I think it pays off—my kids are blossoming! That's a great feeling. But sometimes I wonder if it's all worth it. Is anyone ever going to notice my hard work? Brad down the hall just comes in and does his job without a second thought, and his paycheck looks just like mine. It doesn't seem fair. Teachers who deserve it should be able to earn something more—more money, more respect.

Teaching Tip

FREE ADVICE FOR YOUR FIRST YEAR

Education World asked second-year teachers to reflect on their first year in the classroom—their successes and failures—and offer advice for new teachers:

- *Take charge.* Have a clear management plan, with well-defined rewards and consequences. Explain it to the students, send it home to the parents, and ask for signatures on the plan.
- *Keep students busy and engaged.* Have a number of potential class activities available. Bored kids get into trouble; busy kids stay out of trouble.
- *Get peer support.* If you are not assigned an official mentor, find an unofficial one.
- *Get parental support.* From extra supplies to celebration plans, parents are a hidden teacher resource, but only if they are pulled into class activities.
- *Organize yourself.* Develop a system that will keep you organized. There is a lot going on in teaching, grading, and monitoring dozens of children for hours each day.

- *Organize your students.* Teach students how to organize their homework, notebooks, etc.
- *Write and reflect.* Keep a journal to help you reflect on your first year, and become a stronger teacher your second year.
- *Have fun.* Teaching is not only stressful; it is joyful. Get into it and have fun!
- *Renew:* Enjoy your life and interests outside the classroom.

SOURCE: *Education World* (www.educationworld.com).

REFLECTION: Compare this advice with the more formal areas of teacher effectiveness cited in the research and by the National Board for Professional Teacher Standards described in Chapter 1. What are the similarities and differences?

This teacher hit the nail on the head. Teachers deserve more pay and more respect, and there are some hopeful developments in this area. In the first chapter, we discussed two such trends: merit pay and the creation of the National Board for Professional Teaching Standards. With merit pay, there is the possibility that better teachers will be financially rewarded. The challenge is in the details. If merit pay is based solely on student test scores, or if it leads to destructive competition, it is not likely to be helpful. Later in an educator's career, talented teachers can be recognized as "board certified" by The National Board for Professional Teaching Standards. By passing a number of challenging tests, including observations of their teaching, experienced teachers are acknowledged for their professional expertise. How this recognition might be translated into greater influence or higher pay is yet to be determined. Another approach is career ladders.

A *career ladder* is a different way of looking at both teachers and administrators. Rather than teach one class, and perhaps eventually be "promoted" to principal, teachers are able to increase their influence, responsibility, and pay while continuing to teach. The Rochester, New York, *Career in Teaching* plan is a good example. Here, an outstanding teacher can move beyond a single class and climb the career ladder to become a master teacher and mentor other teachers, perhaps teach larger classes, write curricula and select instructional materials, and/or plan staff development programs. The significant difference here is that the teacher does not have to leave teaching for a position in administration.[15] Good teaching itself is rewarded. Some critics argue that career ladders have the same drawbacks as merit pay—a lack of clear standards or appropriate evaluation tools—but others claim that career ladders can be more effective because they are rooted in professionalism, and groups of educators are involved in observing teaching and assessing which teachers are the most skilled.

FOCUS QUESTION 3

What are the real rewards of teaching?

All teacher recognition plans share the goal of making the teaching profession more attractive and more rewarding, whether through professional recognition, financial compensation, or increased responsibility. As you enter the teaching profession, you will want to consider these incentives, as well as the invisible ones.

There is a reward that does not depend on professional boards or committees, on any external recognition, but is central to a teacher's happiness: the psychic reward of doing something meaningful, doing it well, and making a positive difference in the world. There is joy you will feel as students are moved by a new idea, stunned by an amazing fact, or emotionally moved by an exciting class. That intrinsic reward, that warm glow, becomes a regular presence in your heart. Some people go to work every day and never feel that glow, never really enjoy what they do. They are bored and call their workday a daily grind. Others may receive a huge paycheck but actually be ashamed of their job. Their work role in life is not feeding their soul; often it depletes their soul. But when we teach, when we see a room of children energized, we know that our contribution here is positive beyond words. Not many jobs do that for you, but teaching can. And one more word of advice: When that joy of teaching is gone, it is time for you to be gone, to do something new. But for us, your authors, that spark is still in our classrooms, and we still love teaching, and we hope you will too.

We are not just waxing romantic about teaching; a growing body of research supports the idea that twenty-first-century work is less about external rewards and more about satisfying your inner needs.[16] Let's demonstrate this idea by sharing a little brainteaser with you. Imagine it is 1996 and you are asked to predict twenty years into the future and decide on which of two digital encyclopedias will be more successful in 2016. Encyclopedia A is being developed by Microsoft, which is sparing no expense in hiring authors and editors to write thousands of entries for the first CD-ROM encyclopedia. (Remember, it's 1996.) Well-paid Microsoft managers will oversee every aspect of the project to ensure quality and timeliness. Microsoft has looked into the future and realized that digital encyclopedias will become a huge product. The second encyclopedia, let's call it Encyclopedia B, will compete with Microsoft, but no company is willing to invest in it, and there are no paid managers or writers to actually produce the encyclopedia, a bit of a problem. So which encyclopedia will dominate the market, and which will be defunct? You are undoubtedly leaning toward the Microsoft Encyclopedia A, but that seems too easy, and you are wondering what the trick might be in this puzzle. Could the unpaid, nonprofessional volunteers working on Encyclopedia B beat Microsoft? Did you ever hear of Encarta? Microsoft's encyclopedia was Encarta, terminated in 2009 after millions of dollars were invested. Ever hear of Wikipedia? Wikipedia is now the largest, most successful encyclopedia every produced. Unpaid volunteers wrote more than 17 million articles in 270 languages, and trumped Microsoft. And it's not just Wikipedia. The Firefox browser, the Apache web server, and the Linux operating system were all developed primarily by unsalaried volunteers. Similar stories are emerging the world over: What does this mean?

Simply put, it means that people are motivated by more than wages and bonuses. Certainly, extrinsic rewards like merit pay motivate workers in some situations, like piecework on an assembly line. But life is more than an assembly line and a salary. Intrinsic motivation, the sense of accomplishment in doing something meaningful and worthwhile, is today's driving force. That is in part why educators in Finland are happy with the work even on a modest salary. They work collaboratively: They make the decisions on teaching methods and the curriculum, and they witness their students' success. A meaningful job well done creates joyful workers. When the reward and motivation are internal, then productivity, creativity, and a sense of accomplishment are the results. And contrary to conventional wisdom, external motivations like bonuses often stifle creativity and productivity. Rewards can narrow focus away from enjoyable, productive, fulfilling work to just getting the reward, sometimes at any cost. There is much more to a human being than winning carrots and avoiding sticks. In fact, deploying rewards without knowing the negative consequences can cause more harm than good.[17]

Not convinced? Here's another example. In Sweden, women who were willing to donate blood were divided into three groups. The first group was told that if they gave blood, each woman would receive 50 Swedish kronor (about $7). A second group would also receive the 50 kroner for their blood donation, but they were given the option of donating this money immediately to a children's cancer fund. The third group was told that their blood donation was completely voluntary—that is, there would be no monetary reward. Which group donated the most blood? A majority of the women who received no money as well as a majority of the women who immediately donated the money to charity. Who gave the least blood? The women who were paid. More than two-thirds of the women who were paid for giving blood decided not to donate blood. The 50 kronor "reward" crowded out the altruistic goals, as example of a reward doing damage.[18]

People are not donkeys chasing a carrot. Teachers and students desire to be autonomous, to accomplish something meaningful, and to find inner satisfaction. A student who is rewarded for doing math homework will do the homework each day for the reward but will likely lose interest in math in the long run. Teaching offers meaningful and purposeful work, the invisible rewards that drive twenty-first century workers. It is why so many of us are drawn to teaching. Your authors doubt that merit pay plans will be the key to higher student test scores. But we do believe that if all teachers were paid a decent salary, given the freedom to collaborate and plan together, then student achievement would in fact increase.

It is indeed unfortunate that teachers are not consulted and trusted more, and that the teaching profession in the United States is not as selective as it is in other countries. But there are strong voices trying to change that, voices such as Andy Baumgartner. When Baumgartner, National Teacher of the Year in 2000, criticized the lack of significant teacher representation on a commission to reform education in his home state of Georgia, he quickly became *persona non grata*. The governor would not have his photo taken with him, and several politicians roundly criticized him for his audacity.[19] The attitude expressed by the governor is not new; nor is the courage demonstrated by Andy. This incident is an example of why teachers have established organizations dedicated to protecting their rights and promoting professional growth. So let's turn our attention to these teacher organizations, because your first year in the classroom, you may want to consider joining either the NEA or the AFT. What's the difference between the two? Glad you asked.

Educational Associations

Today, teaching is one of the most organized occupations in the nation, and teachers typically belong to one of two major teacher organizations, the **National Education Association (NEA),** created in 1857, or the **American Federation of Teachers (AFT),** created in 1916 and affiliated with the American labor movement. The NEA and the AFT work to improve the salaries and the working conditions of teachers through **collective bargaining** (i.e., all the teachers in a school system bargaining as one group through a chosen representative), organized actions (including strikes), and influencing education policy. In your first few years as a teacher, you will find yourself in a new environment and without the protection of tenure. Even as an experienced teacher in some states, you will not be protected by tenure. Teacher associations, such as the NEA and the AFT, can help alleviate that sense of vulnerability by providing you with collegial support, opportunities for professional growth, and the security that one derives from participating in a large and influential group. Nine out of ten teachers

FOCUS QUESTION 4
What are the differences between the National Education Association and the American Federation of Teachers?

belong to either the NEA or the AFT, and most are represented by one or the other in collective bargaining. It is not too early for you to start thinking about which may better represent you. So let's attend a faculty meeting here in Mediumtown and find out.

The NEA and the AFT

You have been a teacher in Mediumtown for all of two weeks, and you know about five faces and three names of other faculty members. You have just learned that there will be a teachers' meeting about the services provided by the National Education Association (NEA) and the American Federation of Teachers (AFT). Although you hear about these two organizations all the time, you know next to nothing about either. So to get to meet some of your new colleagues, and to find out about these organizations, you decide to attend.

At the meeting, you flip through the NEA brochure. You learn that the NEA is the largest professional and employee organization in the nation, with nearly 3 million members. If you join the NEA, you will benefit from publications such as *NEA Today,* free legal services, and training opportunities on issues from technology to academic freedom. The NEA is a political force as well, and it works to elect pro-education candidates and to promote legislation beneficial to teachers and students. (See www.nea.org.) You like political involvement and the NEA seems like a perfect fit. But then a speaker from the AFT takes the floor:

> "When John Dewey became our first member back in 1916, he recognized that teachers need their own organization. That is why the AFT will continue to be exclusively of teachers, by teachers, and for teachers.
>
> It was the AFT that backed school desegregation years before the 1954 Supreme Court decision that established the

The two largest teacher organizations are the National Education Association (NEA) and the American Federation of Teachers (AFT).

principle that separate is not equal. We ran freedom schools for Southern black students, and we have a strong record on academic freedom and civil rights.

It was the AFT that demanded and fought for the teacher's right to bargain collectively. It was the AFT leaders who went to jail to show the nation their determination that teachers would no longer stand for second-class status.

And, as part of the great labor movement, the AFL-CIO, the AFT continues to show the nation that through the power of the union the voice of America's teachers will be heard."

You take a look at the AFT brochure. With more than a million members, the AFT has significant influence. The AFT's image as a streetwise, scrappy union has shifted since the 1970s, and today the AFT takes a leadership role in education reform. The AFT supported national standards for teachers, charter schools, and induction programs that enable new teachers to work with master teachers and the active recruitment of people of color into the teaching profession.[20] The AFT provides services similar to the NEA, although on a smaller scale. (See www.aft.org.)

As you weigh the relative merits of the two organizations, you overhear some teachers muttering that they don't care to join either and that in their opinion the NEA and the AFT put the salaries of teachers above the needs of children. Listening more closely, you hear these teachers claim that teacher associations have pitted administrators against teachers, and teachers against the public, creating needless hostility. Even worse, these critics charge, unions too often protect incompetent teachers who should be removed from the classroom. The idea of protecting incompetent teachers is disturbing to both the public and most educators. Nearly one in five U.S. educators no longer support teachers unions, and one-third support ending tenure for teachers. The increasing willingness to do away with unions and tenure has grown in recent years. But teachers who do belong to a union believe that union membership "has never been more important."[21] They argue that as some states, like Wisconsin, have stripped away teachers' rights to collective bargaining, making teachers vulnerable to political and other pressures, and that unions have never been more needed. You are intrigued by the promise of collective action by teachers, but concerned about some of these not-so-flattering comments. You commit yourself to finding out more about the NEA and the AFT.

Professional Associations and Resources

In addition to the NEA and the AFT, you will find many resources that can help you in your professional development. Publications such as *Education Week* keep teachers abreast of educational developments. (The online version is available at www.edweek.org.) Journals, professional training, university courses, and professional associations can help you not only in those critical first few years but throughout your teaching career as you refine your teaching techniques and adapt curricular resources. The Internet is a great source of classroom ideas and practical advice. Inspiring Teachers (www.inspiringteachers.com) is typical of the online resources now available. And sometimes, just talking to others and learning about techniques for stress reduction can make all the difference in that first job, which is the idea behind Education World (www.education-world.com).

Here are a few organizations that you may find helpful:

- *The Association for Supervision and Curriculum Development* is an international, nonprofit, nonpartisan association of professional educators whose jobs cross all grade levels and subject areas. (www.ascd.org)

- *National Middle School Association* works to improve the educational experiences afforded young adolescents, ages 10 to 15 years. (www.nmsa.org)

www.mhhe.com/sadker10e

INTERACTIVE ACTIVITY

Who Said What? Match statements with the educational organizations they came from.

GLOBAL VIEW

Nearly every week, the powerful teachers union and the government officials in Finland meet to discuss education. Why are unions seen as constructive partners in Finland, but so controversial in the states?

Profile in Education   Margaret Haley

"America is on trial," declared **Margaret Haley,** standing before the National Education Association convention. Poor salaries, overcrowded classrooms, and the lack of teacher voice in school policy and curricular decisions, she argued, all undermine teachers' effectiveness.

Though Haley's charges sound disquietingly current, she was not critiquing today's curricular standards created by nonteachers, or the growing dependence on standardized tests to measure both students and teachers, or even the top-down management style of some current school administrators. In fact, Margaret Haley gave this speech a century ago. In 1904, she became the first woman and the first teacher to speak from the floor of an NEA convention. Her speech, "Why Teachers Should Organize," condemned as undemocratic the practice of treating a teacher as an "automaton, a mere factory hand whose duty it is to carry out mechanically and unquestioningly the ideas and orders of those clothed with the authority."[a]

Haley was born in 1851 in Joliet, Illinois, to Irish immigrant parents who valued education and fairness. Haley learned to read from her mother, who used the Bible and a pictorial history of Ireland to educate her daughter. Her father was an active member of local stone quarry and construction unions, who shared accounts of heated union rallies with young Margaret as bedtime stories. Her father also championed the rights and talents of women, and taught Margaret about suffragette Susan B. Anthony and America's first woman physician, Elizabeth Blackwell. Such lessons planted the seeds for Margaret Haley's later efforts to empower women teachers.

At Cook County Normal School, Haley eagerly studied the progressive ideas set forth by John Dewey, embracing the school as a democratic training ground for students and teachers. But when she entered the classroom in Chicago's poor stockyard district, she encountered a vastly different reality. The curriculum she used was uninspiring and imposed by educational bureaucrats, and she was expected to teach it to fifty or sixty sixth-graders. In the warm months, swarms of bugs visited her classroom, and in the winter, Haley shivered along with her students. Working in such deplorable conditions, she increasingly understood that teachers needed to fight the factory mentality of schools.

After twenty years of teaching in Chicago schools, Haley left the classroom to devote herself full-time to educational reform efforts through unions. As vice president and business agent for the Chicago Teachers' Federation (CTF), Haley transformed the fledgling organization into a national voice fighting for, "the right for the teacher to call her soul her own."[b]

Haley's first action for the CTF was to force the Illinois Supreme Court to wrest unpaid taxes from five public utility companies—money that was earmarked for teachers' salaries. For Haley, now known as the "Lady Labor Slugger," the victory was one for both education and democracy: Teachers were given a raise and Chicago businesses were forced to uphold their civic responsibility.

Unlike other teacher associations of the time, Haley deliberately limited the CTF to elementary school teachers. Women consequently dominated the organization, challenging the prevailing wisdom that women should remain quiet, confined to their classrooms. Through the CTF, teachers could become social activists. Under Haley's leadership, Chicago teachers won a tenure law and a pension plan and were given power over curriculum and discipline. Haley also engineered a successful campaign to affiliate her union with the Chicago Federation of Labor. The status of teachers, in Haley's mind, was little more than that of a white-collar proletariat, strikingly similar to blue-collar manual workers. Although the CTF's alliance with labor shocked many teachers, the union ultimately helped the CTF gain political power. Though women could not yet vote, they worked with male labor workers to support a range of progressive issues: child labor laws, women's suffrage, and equal wages for men and women.

A century ago, Margaret Haley called for teachers "to save the schools for democracy and to save democracy in the schools."[c] Her tireless efforts and astute political skills helped create more humane schools for both teachers and students. Haley died in 1939.

[a] Nancy Hoffman, *Woman's "True" Profession: Voices from the History of Teaching* (Old Westbury, NY: The Feminist Press, 1981), p. 291.
[b] David Neiman (Producer), *Only a Teacher,* Part 2: *Those Who Can . . . Teach* (Princeton, NJ: Films for the Humanities and Sciences, 2000).
[c] Ibid.

To learn more about Margaret Haley, click on *Profiles in Education.*

www.mhhe.com/sadker10e

REFLECTION: Had you heard of Margaret Haley before reading this profile? If not, you are not alone. Why do we know so few of education's heroes, teachers whose efforts have improved the lives of teachers?

- *National Association for the Education of Young People* pulls together preschools, child care, primary schools, cooperatives, and kindergarten educators and parents in projects to improve the quality and certification of these schools. (www.naeyc.org)

- *National Association for Gifted Children* advances the opportunities and school programs for gifted students. (www.nagc.org)

- *The Council for Exceptional Children* is the largest international professional organization dedicated to improving educational outcomes for individuals with exceptionalities, students with disabilities, and the gifted. (www.cec.sped.org)

If you are interested in subject matter specialties, many organizations, journals, and websites can meet your needs. Here is a brief sample:

- *American Alliance for Health, Physical Education, Recreation and Dance* (www.aahperd.org)

- *National Council for Teachers of English* (www.ncte.org)

- *National Council for the Social Studies* (www.ncss.org)

- *National Science Teachers Association* (www.nsta.org)

- *Teachers of Speakers of Other Languages* (www.tesol.org)

- *National Council for the Teachers of Mathematics* (www.nctm.org)

As a teacher, you will find yourself in a learning community, not only teaching students, but also continually improving your own knowledge and skills. We hope that these resources and others in this text will set you on that path of continuous learning and improvement. You may still have a question or two about teaching, which we will try to answer in the last chapter. Before we bring this chapter to a close, let's consider two questions that you confront right now. The first is: Are America's public schools working?—the topic for our final You Be the Judge feature. And the second question we will consider is to try to envision what your classroom might look like in the years ahead: can we interest you in a peak into the future?

GLOBAL VIEW

If you are interested in teaching overseas, there are both private and government opportunities. Here's a start: www.educatorsoverseas.com, www.state.gov/, and www.dodea.edu/.

Tomorrow's Classroom?

It is never too soon to begin thinking about tomorrow. So as you prepare for your first classroom, let's have a little fun and imagine what tomorrow's schools might be like. The future can happen very quickly.

Daniel Pink's book, *A Whole New Mind: Why Right-Brainers Will Rule the Future,*[22] describes major changes he believes will reshape America in the years ahead, changes that could dramatically affect schools. He may or may not be right in his views, but it is fun to explore the possibilities of change.

We know that professionals in India and China are performing many of our nation's technical and scientific operations, and Pink contends that low-cost Asian labor and the growth of technology will continue to supplant American workers in the years ahead. Why, then, do Americans continue to promote science, technology, and math careers when others do it so well for a fraction the cost? Pink argues it is time for America to forge a new path, to be more imaginative in the jobs we fashion if we are to thrive in this new world economy. To compete in the twenty-first century, Pink believes our schools should focus less on the skills we thought were so important (logic, math, science, thinking sequentially, technology) and more on the right-brain skills we typically neglect. These right-brain skills are the ones that will become important in the future, skills such as using our intuition, being creative, appreciating our

You Be The Judge

HAVE PUBLIC SCHOOLS FAILED OR SERVED SOCIETY?

American Schools Have Failed Society Because . . .

INTERNATIONAL TESTS DOCUMENT POOR STUDENT PERFORMANCE

How embarrassing for the students in the richest, most powerful nation in the world to do so miserably on tests. Our students typically trail students in Finland, Korea, Japan, and most of Western Europe.

TOO MANY STUDENTS DROP OUT OR ACT OUT

The lack of discipline, decorum, and control in America's schools is a sign that basic values are missing, poor management is commonplace, and school violence and dropouts are rampant.

WORKERS LACK BASIC SKILLS

America does not produce enough scientists, engineers, and mathematicians, and our workers lack not only key technical skills but basic reading and writing competencies as well. American companies are now forced to provide remedial instruction to our ill-prepared workers.

SCHOOLS HAVE BECOME A MONOPOLY

The power of teacher unions and the inertia of the school bureaucracies have robbed schools of initiative and creativity. Competition through vouchers and charter schools is the answer.

American Schools Have Served Society Well Because . . .

INTERNATIONAL TEST SCORES MISS THE POINT

Americans value individuality and creativity, characteristics absent from these tests. Lower scores are due to the high number of American poor taking these tests and the poor treatment of our teachers—both society's failure.

STUDENT SUCCESS IS REAL

Graduation rates are up for the poor, for non-English speakers, and for special education students. And incidences of violence have actually been reduced.

WORKERS ARE AMONG THE BEST IN THE WORLD

Many Americans are unaware of the fact that our colleges produce a very high number of engineers and scientists, and our workers are among the most educated and skilled in the world. America is an economic superpower because of our worker productivity.

THEY REPRESENT THE DEMOCRATIC IDEAL

Jefferson and Mann were right: The nation's future rests on public schools. Vouchers and privatization take money from already underfunded public schools and hurt free, democratic education.

www.mhhe.com/sadker10e

YOU DECIDE . . .

Why do Americans struggle over such a basic question? Do arguments about school effectiveness influence your decision to teach?

Do school critics serve a useful purpose by prodding the public to create more effective schools, or are they more likely to mislead the public and discourage teachers?

---

emotions, developing artistic talents, and looking beyond materialism to find meaning in our lives. Here are some of the skills Pink would have our schools teach:

Design. Today's products are quite reliable. Our cars, laptops, and toasters all work well, so the big question facing consumers is which product to buy. Pink argues that design now plays a key role in that decision: We choose products that appeal to us. Many people buy an Apple computer because they like the way it looks: an endearing glowing apple, great graphics, and user-pleasing software. Some Apple fans argue that it is a better computer than a PC (and we're not going to get into that debate), but people agree that those much-maligned PCs work quite well and are much cheaper. But because the Apple looks cooler, its design trumps its higher cost. (Have you noticed that the newer PCs are beginning to look a lot like Apples?) Appealing design also applies to that cool red toaster or that neat retro clock for sale. Don't expect the red toaster to toast bread any better than the chrome one, or the retro clock to be more accurate than the one that costs half the price. But they are pleasing to look at, and that is a good enough reason to select one product over another.

The point we are making is not that people should buy the cheaper but just-as-good product. The point is that people want to be surrounded by objects that please them, and that's okay. You may use the toaster only once a day, but you look at it much more often. Pink believes that schools should teach students fine arts skills so they can design attractive and pleasing products. Perhaps in the future, businesses will be seeking more MFAs, and fewer MBAs.

Boundary crossers. Our society has traditionally promoted specialization. Today, people earn doctorates in esoteric fields such as fifteenth-century Polish grammar or plant life in ancient Botswana. Doctors with medical specialties are more highly valued and paid than general practitioners. Everywhere you look, "experts" are recruited to solve problems. But Pink argues that this is overspecialization, that the future will belong to boundary crossers. Boundary crossers are broad rather than narrow thinkers, able to be creative as they work in different disciplines, cultures, and languages. A physician using both Western and Eastern medicine to heal patients is such a boundary crosser. He or she is a doctor who knows about Western medicine with its endless drugs and sophisticated equipment, as well as its limits. This medical boundary crosser is also a healer familiar with ancient therapeutic remedies such as acupuncture and reiki. This medical boundary crosser can offer a wider array of healing options, offering patients more choices in their own healing. With our increasingly interdependent world economy, a successful businessperson of the future might be someone who can cross cultural and linguistic boundaries. This business boundary crosser might speak several languages and work comfortably in different cultures as he or she connects the needs of an American company with the technical expertise of an Indian computer programmer. As a teacher, you can be a boundary crosser as well. Perhaps you will team-teach a social studies class over the Internet with a colleague in another country, sorting out strategies that your students can use to alleviate hunger or promote a healthy ecosystem. Or perhaps you will develop curriculum that crosses typical disciplines, such as art and science, to teach your students how to become boundary crossers.

Here are a few of the other suggestions that Pink suggests to prepare for the future. How often have you heard companies emphasize their commitment to a joyful work environment? Not often is probably what you are thinking, but it is a growing trend. "People rarely succeed at anything unless they are having fun" is a Southwest Airline motto. More and more companies are realizing that happiness, yes happiness, is an important goal and incorporate games, humor, laughing, and play into their workplaces. Such efforts increase productivity, satisfaction, and health. Wouldn't it be exciting for a teacher to bring more happiness to schools, to have students experience the joy of learning?

Americans have acquired great material wealth. But bigger houses and bigger cars seem only to lead to the desire for still bigger houses and even bigger cars. Many people have confused material wealth with happiness. Pink believes that in the future, Americans will seek more meaning in their lives and develop a sense of greater purpose. He cites the increase in meditation, yoga, public service, and spirituality as examples of our search for meaningful lives.

A Closer Look A First Year Teacher

A CLASSROOM CHALLENGE I JUST HAD TO TAKE

By Mathina Carkci

Mathina Carkci, who wrote about education as a reporter for suburban Maryland newspapers for three years, became a fourth-grade teacher at Bailey's Elementary School in Fairfax County, Virginia.

The most surprising thing about being a teacher is how often I feel like a failure. I knew that teaching fourth grade would be hard, but I expected to be able to keep up with everything and to succeed. So it's disheartening, just two months into my first job, to feel the weight of things left undone, questionable decisions made and professional duties unmet.

My teacher friends say they used to feel the same way. Some admit they still do. My student-teaching supervisor sympathetically cautions that the first two years are so unlike the "real thing" that they don't count. The teacher across the hall reminds me to take baby steps. My mom, a university professor, promises it will get better. I'm too hard on myself, a former professor tells me; it takes time to grow into the teacher I want to be.

I take some comfort from the fact that friends who were in the same one-year master's certification program at the University of Maryland last year have found it hard from the word go. I called Natalie the evening of her first day, a week before I started.

"If you told me I didn't have to go tomorrow," she said, "I wouldn't."

I called Al on his second day. "After the kids left today, I shut the door and cried," he said.

My friends and family told me I'd be a great teacher. They said they imagined a group of children gazing up at me, accompanying me on exciting journeys that would fill their minds with wonder. "You're such a good person," my husband told me. "The kids are going to love you." It gave me the chills, the way good classical music does, to think of myself and my merry band of students, gallivanting through the curriculum.

So it's difficult to admit now how hard it is to be a first-year teacher: how every single day I feel as if I am drowning; how I spend 12 hours at school each day working and four hours at home worrying; how each evening as I leave school, I have to decide which of 100 equally important things I should leave undone; how I feel so far behind that I will never catch up until Christmas, when I have 10 days "off."

When I get to school, anywhere from an hour and a half to two hours before the kids, a list of tasks swims through my head, and, as the minutes tick away until 8:40 arrives, I run through my priorities. With any luck, I'll have put up the day's schedule, written the daily message to the students and created the math warm-up exercise the night before. I might respond to kids' journals but change my mind when I realize the math lesson I had planned misses an important element. (Half my mind, all this time, is wondering what the best way is to teach kids to determine the volume of solid shapes.) I might

walk to the copier, see the line of other teachers and decide instead to swing by the library to schedule a block of time for my students. Or I might run into the guidance counselor and discuss ways to help a student who's been misbehaving.

Then I notice a student's desk that seems to be exploding papers and books, and wonder how best to help the child get organized: Does she need me to go through the pile with her, paper by paper? (And when would I do that?) Or should I write her a note and carve out a chunk of the day for her to organize things herself? Or do I need to have a talk with the whole class about keeping things straight?

It isn't as if I wasn't well prepared or don't have support. My year-long internship, including 12 weeks of student teaching, gave me a taste of the challenges I'd face. A mentor at my school, Bailey's Elementary, meets with me regularly, and Fairfax County bends over backward to provide new teachers with help. Bailey's teems with kind, helpful colleagues. Volunteers, including my mom who comes in every Friday, offer assistance of all sorts. Short of having a personal assistant 12 hours a day, I don't think there's anything more anyone could do to ease my transition.

Idealistic grad school conversations about pedagogy and democracy in the classroom made me surer than ever that I was right to go into teaching, that here was where I would make my impact on a part of the world that mattered to me. The master's program helped me build a solid educational philosophy based on wanting children to discover for themselves how rewarding learning can be.

I never thought my career switch would be easy. I had covered education when I was a newspaper reporter, so I'd seen the kinds of tightropes that many teachers walk. But I wanted to do something more active than writing about them. As a teacher, I could be with students every day and show them in tangible ways that their ideas mattered.

I try to make this happen in the classroom, but as we all know, theory and practice don't always overlap. I spend more time thinking up ways to get students to hand in homework than I do thinking about how to help them to pursue their own questions, or promoting their curiosity. Despite having vowed not to use rewards and punishments as a method of controlling the class, I have found myself giving kids extra recess for walking quietly in line or sending them back to their seats if they seem disruptive. My interactions with kids are less positive than I once hoped they would be, and I say "No," without explanation, far more often than I would like. Instead of designing creative, hands-on lessons in every subject, I sometimes teach straight from the book in science and social studies classes.

But, in the end, I don't think I'm really a failure. We have meetings, where my whole class tries to solve problems anyone puts on the agenda. I play with the kids at recess, which might make me seem more like another kid than like a teacher, but I think it also helps them to see me as someone worth following. I've managed to avoid being ruled by the lesson plan. The other day, two boys invented their own way of conducting a science project that involved analyzing rocks, and, when I realized their way was better, I encouraged the rest of the class to go with it instead of following the instructions.

I may not be on the same social studies textbook chapter as the other fourth-grade teachers, and I'll probably be late returning standardized tests to the assistant principal, but I think my kids know they're important to me. I see it in tiny, fleeting moments. I see it when a student says, "Mrs. Carkci, I wish you could come to my house for the weekend. That would be fun." I see it when a boy writes to me to ask if I will take him to the movies, or when a girl gives me a goofy smile after I've led the class down the hall taking giant, silly steps. I'm proud that a girl believes it is okay to ask "Why in America do people speak lots of languages, while in Vietnam, they only speak one language?" Or that a boy knows I will encourage him to pursue his question, "Who invented the planets?"

Once or twice, early on, I considered quitting. But no longer. I like helping my 21 students learn about the four regions of Virginia; I enjoy encouraging them to write and to use new paragraphs for new ideas; and I thrive on watching them become mathematical thinkers. Just the other day a student told me, out of the blue, that he'd noticed how the desks in our classroom were like intersecting lines. It was our geometry unit made real.

I can't imagine what it will be like in two years, when I have figured out a good response to tattling and when I have prepared a classroom set of spelling games. I don't love teaching yet, but I am beginning to catch glimpses of what it will be like when I do.

SOURCE: Copyright 1998, Mathina Carkci, published in *The Washington Post* Company, Sunday, November 8, 1998, C3.

REFLECTION: What insights and clues suggest that Mathina will succeed as a teacher? Do you share any of her attributes? Which teaching skills might you need to further refine?

Perhaps our greatest scientist, Albert Einstein, had it right when he wrote: "The intuitive mind is a sacred gift; the rational mind, its servant." Why do schools honor the servant (rational thinking) and ignore the sacred gift (intuition)? How can schools help people develop and honor their intuition, another right-brain activity that Pink believes should become center stage in the years ahead?

Although it is a challenge to imagine how some of Pink's ideas would look in your classroom, it is useful to begin visualizing a future that undoubtedly will hold many surprises. As Einstein observed: "Imagination is more important than knowledge."

www.mhhe.com/sadker10e

INTERACTIVE ACTIVITY

Edspeak Do you know what these education-related terms mean?

ONLINE VIDEO ALBUM TO ACCOMPANY *TEACHERS, SCHOOLS, AND SOCIETY, 10E*

Visit the Online Learning Center for a range of contemporary videos with content related to this chapter.

www.mhhe.com/sadker10e

THE *TEACHERS, SCHOOLS, AND SOCIETY* READER WITH CLASSROOM OBSERVATION VIDEO CLIPS

Go to your *Teachers, Schools, and Society* Reader CD-ROM to:

READ CURRENT AND HISTORICAL ARTICLES

49. **Exemplary Teacher Voices on Their Own Development,** by Rachael Gabriel, Jeni Peiria Day, and Richard Allington, *Phi Delta Kappan,* May 2011.

50. **Surviving to Thriving,** by Sonia Nieto in *Burned In: Fueling the Fire to Teach* by Audrey E. Friedman and Luke Reynolds (eds.), 2011, New York: Teachers College Press.

51. **It's Not on the Test: A Search for Existential Meaning in Three Acts,** by Christopher L. Doyle in *Burned In: Fueling the Fire to Teach* by Audrey E. Friedman and Luke Reynolds (eds.), 2011, New York: Teachers College Press.

52. **Lina's Letter: A 9-Year-Old's Perspective on What Matters Most in the Classroom,** by David Pratt, *Phi Delta Kappan,* March 2008.

ANALYZE CASE STUDIES

22. **Christie Raymond:** A mature woman in the first month of her first full-time position teaching music in an elementary school loves the work as long as the children are singing, but dislikes the school's emphasis on and her part in disciplining the students. The case describes Christie's classroom teaching in detail as well as her after-school bus duty.

23. **Melissa Read:** An enthusiastic young student teacher struggles to gain the respect and improve the behavior of her senior-level composition class and is devastated by one of her student's papers, which is full of vindictiveness and hatred toward her.

OBSERVE TEACHERS, STUDENTS, AND CLASSROOMS IN ACTION

Beverly High School Teachers
Beverly, MA

17. Classroom Observation: Respect and Salary for Teachers

The public views teachers as important but seems unwilling to pay them according y. The segment explores some reasons for this by noting a connection between the feminization of teaching and persistent negative stereotypes. In addition, the segment recognizes the "psychic" salary for teachers who love what they do.

KEY TERMS AND PEOPLE

www.mhhe.com/sadker10e

CHAPTER REVIEW

Go to the Online Learning Center to take a quiz, practice with key terms, and review concepts from the chapter.

American Federation of Teachers (AFT), 389

collaborative action research (CAR), 383

collective bargaining, 389

Haley, Margaret, 392

induction programs, 374

learning communities, 386

mentors, 376

National Education Association (NEA), 389

peer review, 377

professional development, 383

stages of teacher development, 375

DISCUSSION QUESTIONS AND ACTIVITIES

1. How might you redefine or modify any of the stages of teacher development? Can these stages be applied to other careers? Think of teachers you have observed. What are the specific behaviors and skills that place a teacher at each of these stages?

2. Survey local school districts and analyze their first-year induction programs. What resources do they provide new teachers to assist them in making a successful transition into teaching? Will this affect your decision as to where to teach? You might want to research first-year teacher induction programs in the library or on the Internet to get a sense of the range of resources offered to first-year teachers.

3. What do you look for in a mentor? What strategies can you use to recruit such a mentor in your first teaching job?

4. To get a sense of the breadth of professional opportunities available to you, add to the list started in this book. Pull together notices of professional service courses, workshops, and other opportunities available to teachers. To do this, you may want to review professional journals and also contact local school districts, professional associations, state department of education, and colleges.

5. Develop some potential topics for a collaborative action research project. Consider undertaking this project as a research activity during your teaching education program.

CHAPTER 13

Q and A Guide to Entering the Teaching Profession

FOCUS QUESTIONS

1. What does the education job market look like? (Or, put another way, will I be able to find a satisfying teaching position?)
2. How can new teachers increase their chances of working in a school of their choice?
3. What do I need to know about certification and licensing?
4. What teacher competency tests do I need to take?
5. Why do teachers seek tenure? (And should I?)
6. Are there jobs in education outside of the classroom?

Curiosity is the wick in the candle of learning.

—WILLIAM ARTHUR WARD

CHAPTER PREVIEW

Beyond questions concerning education as a field of study, students often have personal and practical questions about teaching, the kinds of questions that are more likely to be asked after class or during office hours. Students considering an education career want to know everything from where the jobs are to how to land a teaching position, from how teachers are licensed to what kinds of education careers are available beyond the classroom. We trust that this chapter will answer some of the questions you are asking, and even some you never thought to raise.

www.mhhe.com/sadker10e

WHAT DO YOU THINK? What Questions Do You Have? Click on Ask the Author to submit any questions you still have.

What are my chances of finding a teaching position?

This is a practical and quite natural question for you to be asking right now. After all, you are investing time, energy, money, and talent in preparing yourself to become a teacher.

When pondering where to apply for your first teaching position, you may want to make a list of issues that matter to you:

What subject or grade level do I prefer? What kind of community and students do I want to serve? What part of the country appeals to me? Is there a particular school organization I like? What educational philosophy and school culture am I most comfortable with? How important to me are external incentives for superior teaching? What salary and benefits am I seeking? Am I more interested in a private or public school, or perhaps a charter or magnet school? Am I flexible and open to different options or focused in my preferences?

Many of the activities in this book, including the "You Be the Judge" in the first chapter, the inventory of your educational philosophy in Chapter 8, and the *RAPs,* will help you answer these questions.

Since the great recession began in 2008, many public schools have seen deep cuts in funding, often resulting in larger classes and fewer teachers. Yet, the U.S. Department of Labor still projects nearly a 20 percent increase in the number of teachers needed over the next decade because of growing student enrollments and retiring educators.[1] Even though there are few guarantees when it comes to predicting national labor needs, the good news is there likely will be a teaching position available when you graduate. But because changes in student enrollments vary by state and economic conditions, so will your teaching opportunities. (See Figure 13.1.)

FOCUS QUESTION 1
What does the education job market look like? (Or, put another way, will I be able to find a satisfying teaching position?)

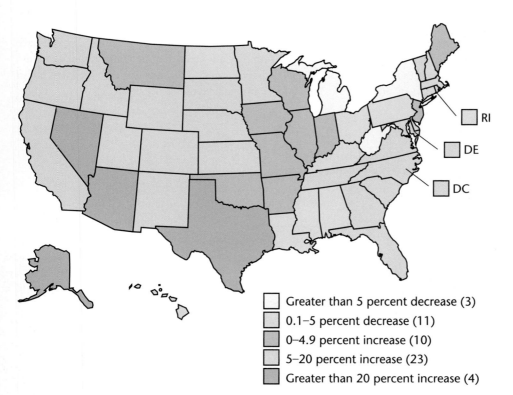

FIGURE 13.1
Where the Students Are. Projected Percentage Change in K–12 Public School Enrollment by State: 2008–2021.

SOURCE: U.S. Department of Education, "Participation in Education, Indicator 2: Public Enrollment," *The Condition of Education, 2011.*

REFLECTION: Will these state trends influence where you might choose to teach? Why or why not?

☐ Greater than 5 percent decrease (3)
☐ 0.1–5 percent decrease (11)
☐ 0–4.9 percent increase (10)
☐ 5–20 percent increase (23)
☐ Greater than 20 percent increase (4)

States and local communities also differ in their financial resources and priorities. Districts with high salary schedules and positive teacher morale, often located in popular locations with education-friendly communities, have little need to lure candidates. Because candidates flock to these districts, you will have a tougher time competing for one of these positions. Many rural and urban areas, however, struggle to find qualified teachers and adequate resources, so your application will likely be welcomed.

School reform efforts and school choice have spawned diverse teaching opportunities, from charter schools and online instruction to private and religious schools. (We discuss many of these schools in Chapter 5.) As you explore different schools, you are wise to ask about each school's philosophy and policies on merit pay, tenure, professional development, class size, and any other issues important to your teaching job.

Where you want to teach is important when applying for that first job; so is *what* you teach. If you are licensed or have an endorsement in certain fields such as special education, bilingual education, chemistry, math, and physics, may find yourself courted by many school districts. (Isn't that nice!) One way to make yourself more marketable is to consider course work and school experiences in subjects and skills that are in demand. But we encourage you not to force yourself into a subject area. Follow your interests and heart when choosing what you teach. That passion will help carry you through the joys and challenges of teaching.

Who are my teaching colleagues? What are the demographics of today's teachers?

There are more than 3 million teachers in America. Your colleagues will be overwhelming white and female. Although about 15 percent of students are African American, only 7 percent of all teachers are African American; whereas 22 percent of students are Hispanic, only 7 percent of teachers are Hispanic. More than three out of four teachers are women, and recruiting men and people of color to teaching remains a challenge.[2] (See Figure 13.2.)

You will not be alone as a new teacher: Nearly one in four of your colleagues will have begun teaching within the past five years. Your next few years may also mirror their activities, because more than half of your colleagues have earned a master's degree, and three out of four participate in annual professional development activities.[3]

FIGURE 13.2a

K–12 Public School Teachers by Race/Ethnicity.

SOURCE: "Characteristics of Full-Time School Teachers," *Condition of Education*, 2012.

REFLECTION: How can schools recruit more teachers of color?

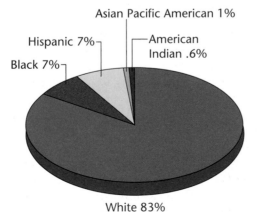

Racial/Ethnic Distribution of K–12 Teachers

Asian Pacific American 1%

Hispanic 7%

American Indian .6%

Black 7%

White 83%

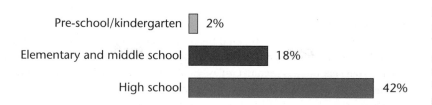

FIGURE 13.2b
Where Are the Male Teachers?

SOURCE: "Characteristics of Full-Time School Teachers," *Condition of Education*, 2012.

REFLECTION: How can schools recruit more men?

What are my chances for earning a decent salary?

The truth is that teaching offers incredible rewards, and as we discussed in Chapter 12, those intangible rewards go beyond salary. If you love teaching, as we do, it will be a joy to go to work—and a worthy way to invest your life. That joy, however, does not appear on your pay stub, and we are not alone in our belief that teachers are not paid what they deserve. Starting teachers now average more than $30,000 a year, and experienced teachers (15 or more years) average in the low to mid $50,000. But those are only averages. Some school districts pay teachers six figures, and others barely pay $25,000 a year.[4] It would be wise to contact specific school districts of interest for a copy of their salary schedule. A reality faced by many teachers is the need to supplement their salaries by working a second job at night or on the weekends.

Do private schools pay less than public schools?

Yes, most (but not all) private schools pay less than public schools. Although the salaries are lower, many private (also called independent) schools offer teachers a different set of benefits— smaller classes, motivated students, supportive parents, a sense of community, a sense of teacher autonomy, a shorter school year, a more challenging curriculum, and sometimes, housing and meals. Many extraordinary teachers work in private schools, although as a group, private school teachers have less professional preparation and less experience and partici- pate less in professional development than do public school teachers—differences that some cite to explain their lower salaries. Private schools, like their public counterparts, vary signifi- cantly in their academic standing, salaries, and employment practices. Although some pri- vate schools are incredibly strong academically and compete with local public schools in employment benefits, others do not fare as well. If you are interested in teaching in a private school, remember that each school needs to be evaluated on an individual basis.

How do I apply for a teaching job? Do I need a résumé or a portfolio?

The most crucial documents in your job search may well be your résumé and your portfolio. A résumé presents a concise description of your strengths and competencies, whereas a port- folio offers a more comprehensive profile, which might include videos of your teaching; sam- ple lesson plans; journals; supervisor's observations; letters from parents, students, and administrators; and examples of student work. The first step is to prepare a résumé to submit to prospective employers. When your résumé is strong, school districts will want a closer look, and that's when a portfolio or an interview will be requested. Résumés and portfolios open doors, so let's take a closer look at how best to construct them.

At the top of your résumé, list your contact information: name, address, telephone number, and e-mail address. But the heart of the **résumé** is your relevant education and experiences that highlight your accomplishments. Indicate your formal education background—your col- lege and university, your major and your minor (if you have one)—and describe your student

FOCUS QUESTION 2
How can new teachers increase their chances of working in a school of their choice?

teaching experience, as well as other educational accomplishments. Summarize relevant work and volunteer experiences. If you offered private instruction, worked as a camp counselor or at a religious school, or volunteered at a day care center or in a recreation program for the elderly, include those and note dates of employment, salient responsibilities, and accomplishments. Many candidates include professional objectives and a brief educational philosophy at the beginning of a résumé. If you take that approach, you might write an employment objective that details the type of teaching position you are seeking. You could also include some of the reasons that propel you to teach and perhaps a brief statement about your educational philosophy and beliefs. Your résumé should be typed in a clear and readable format; there are software templates available to help you. Check if the school districts you are interested in prefer hard copy or e-mail.

Employers rely on references and recommendations to get a clearer picture of applicants. Remember, as you list professors, supervisors, previous employers, and cooperating teachers as references, you need to ask their permission and give them a "heads up" that they may be contacted. This is not only a basic courtesy but also a way to measure their willingness to recommend you. Consider supplying them with "talking points" to aid them in preparing your recommendation.

Today, many school districts are going beyond résumés and recommendations, and are asking for a more in-depth view of you and your skills. A **portfolio** is a collection of materials that demonstrates your knowledge, competencies, and accomplishments as a teacher candidate. A portfolio does more than document your qualifications for a prospective teaching job (as a résumé does); it is a purposeful and reflective presentation of your professional development as a teacher.

Typically, portfolios include:[5]

I. Statement of Teaching Philosophy

II. Teaching Credentials
  A. Résumé
  B. Transcripts
  C. Letters of Reference
  D. Teaching Certificate/License
  E. Endorsement(s)

III. Teaching-Related Experiences
  A. Student Teaching
    1. Evaluations by University Supervisor
    2. Evaluations by Cooperating/Mentor Teacher
    3. Letters from Students and Parents
    4. Sample Lesson Plans
    5. Sample Classroom Floor Plans/Management Plans
    6. Reflective Teaching Journal
    7. Examples of Student Work
    8. Photographs of Students/Classrooms
    9. Videotape of Teaching
  B. Employment in Child-Related Fields
  C. Volunteer Work with Children

This text is designed to start you on the road to building a portfolio. The *RAP* activities guide your portfolio development. The "You Be the Judge" feature and reflection questions infused throughout the text are intended to help you consider relevant issues and form your own educational views and beliefs. In organizing the contents of your portfolio, consider using national standards (such as the INTASC standards identified in the *RAPs*) or the state or local standards of the school district to which you are applying for a job. Many teaching candidates rely on a looseleaf-type notebook to organize their portfolio work, allowing for flexibility incorporating and removing material. Recently, digital formats have become popular. With a digital or *e-portfolio,* you can simultaneously present your qualifications and demonstrate your technological proficiency. In developing your portfolio, ask for input from university supervisors and cooperating teachers; and it is a good idea to practice presenting your portfolio to them as well. (See *Reflective Activities and Your Portfolio: Introduction,* p. 87, for more on the purpose and development of portfolios.)

How do I prepare for a successful interview?

If your résumé and the portfolio do their job, you will be invited for an interview. Interviews take two forms: online and in-person. A number of districts do their initial screening through an online series of questions. Candidates who successfully respond to these questions advance to the next step and are considered for employment. The questions usually assess one's teaching philosophy, approach to a subject, and the like. The best way to prepare for such an online interview is to thoughtfully consider your educational philosophy, your approach to teaching, your long-term educational goals, your strategies for managing a class, and your plans to further develop your teaching skills. Reviewing the *RAPs* that you have prepared in this text as well as your portfolio can assist in this process.

In-person interviews may be conducted by one or more administrators, a panel of teachers, or a combination of teachers and parents, and the average interview usually lasts thirty minutes to an hour.[6] So how can these precious minutes work for you?

When you walk in for your interview, the first thing that will strike an interviewer is appearance. Your prospective interviewer (or interview team) will be looking not only for appropriate professional attire but also for such qualities as poise, enthusiasm, self-confidence, and an ability to think quickly and effectively on your feet. Appropriate grammar, a well-developed vocabulary, and clear speech and diction are important. You should be focused about your teaching philosophy and goals if you want to appear confident and purposeful in the interview. If you have developed a portfolio of teaching materials or other information that you are particularly proud of, you should take it to the interview. It cannot hurt to have it present, and it might help win the day.

It is important to be prepared for likely questions. Common interview topics include your personal philosophy of teaching, your teaching strengths and weaknesses, professional goals, employment history, teaching style, and approach to classroom management. (See the "Teaching Tip: That First Mistake" to consider how you might describe your approach to a not so comfortable topic—teaching mistakes.) Interviewers commonly look for enthusiasm, warmth, caring, leadership skills, willingness to learn new things, and confidence.[7] You may also want to note what questions cannot legally be asked—for example, questions about your religion or your marital or parental status. Such questions do not relate to your qualifications as a teacher. (In Chapter 10, we explore how to handle illegal interview questions)

Do your homework: Find out as much as possible about both the particular school and community. Talk to friends involved in the school or community, check local newspapers, explore the local library, search the Internet, and, better yet, stop by the school to talk with teachers, students and others, scour the bulletin boards, and pick up available literature. Once you obtain information about a school or a school system, you can begin matching your particular interests and skills with the school district's programs and needs.

Teaching Tip

THAT FIRST MISTAKE

It will happen, count on it: your first mistake. Perhaps you will mispronounce a student's name, incorrectly compute a student's grade, misspell a word on the board, or unintentionally embarrass a student, or yourself. Mistakes create defining moments in your class because how you respond reveals your personality, your authenticity, and your maturity. How you handle your first misstep may set the tone for the school year.

We'd like to share our insights for turning a mistake (difficult to believe, but your authors do make mistakes!) into a teachable moment.

• First of all, thank the student for pointing out your error. You can't do anything about a gaffe if you are not aware you made one.

• If you're not making any errors, you are either perfect, unaware, or teaching a class that is not being challenged.

• Slip-ups can be corrected, and in that process, they offer the teacher and the student a chance to learn and grow.

• Making mistakes is human; learning from a mistake is teaching.

REFLECTION: Have you seen a teacher make a mistake? How did the class respond? How did the teacher respond? What did you learn from those responses?

Important as such preparatory work is, the most important way of learning what an interviewer is looking for is to listen. Sometimes interviewers state their needs openly, such as "We're looking for a teacher who is fluent in both Spanish and English." In other cases, interviewers merely imply their needs—for example, "Many of the children who attend our school are Hispanic." In this case, you have first to interpret the interviewer's remark and then to check your interpretation with a statement such as "Are you looking for someone who is fluent in both Spanish and English?" Or "Are you looking for someone who has experience in working with Spanish-speaking children?"

After interviewing, it is wise to send the interviewer a brief follow-up note, reminding her or him of how your qualifications meet the school system's needs. The interviewer may have talked with dozens of candidates, and under such circumstances it is easy to be forgotten in a sea of faces—your job is to make sure you stand out.

One word of caution: When a job offer comes your way, analyze the school system to make sure that you really want to teach there before signing on the dotted line. Try to find out

• Do the teachers in the district view it as a good place to work?

• Have there been personnel problems recently and, if so, for what reasons?

• What are the benefits and potential problems in the teachers' contract?

• What is the typical class size?

• What kinds of support services are available?

• Is the school adopting organizational changes to personalize the school climate?

If the answers do not please you, you may want to look elsewhere. It is unwise to accept a position with the notion that you will leave as soon as a better offer is made. That attitude can quickly lead to a job-hopping profile that may stigmatize you as someone who is either irresponsible or unable to work well with others. In short, do not simply jump at the first available job offer if it doesn't feel right. If your credentials are good and you know how to market yourself, you will get other teaching offers.

What do I need in order to teach—a license or certification? By the way, what's the difference?

FOCUS QUESTION 3
What do I need to know about certification and licensing?

Project yourself a few years into the future. You have just completed your teacher preparation program. You stop by your local public school office and make a belated inquiry into teacher openings. The school secretary looks up from a cluttered desk, smiles kindly, and says, "We may have an opening this fall. Are you certified? Do you have a license?"

Oops! Certified? License? Now I remember. It's that paperwork thing. . . . I should have filled out that application back at school. I should have gone to that teacher licensure meeting. And I definitely should have read that Sadker and Zittleman textbook more carefully. I knew I forgot something. Now I'm in trouble. All that work and I will not be allowed to teach. What a nightmare!

And then you wake up.

Many people use the terms *teacher certification* and *teaching license* interchangeably. But it is important for you to be able to distinguish between a professional certification and a legal license, so we make the distinction in this book. **Teacher certification** confers professional standing; a **teacher's license** is a legal document.

Teacher certification indicates that a state department of education recognizes (certifies) that an individual has met certain requirements to teach. These standards include a college degree, completion of certain education courses, student teaching experience and passing a mastery exam. States vary in the specific coursework, student teaching, and exam requirements. (Appendix 2, pp. A-2, provides contact information for all State Offices of Teacher Certification and Licensure where you can find requirements for your state.) If your college or university has a *state-approved* teacher education program, then it likely meets state standards for certification and licensure. If you are reading this book, the odds are good that you are enrolled in such a program and will be well prepared to meet your state's certification requirements. But do check with your college or with your state department of education to find out for certain.

Once you meet a state's certification requirements, you can apply for your state teacher's license. Teaching licenses are awarded by each of the fifty states and the District of Columbia. A teacher's license, issued by the state government, grants the legal right to teach, not unlike a driver's license, which grants the legal right to drive. Both licenses mean that the "minimum" state requirements have been met. If you have been out on the roads recently, you know that meeting the minimum requirements to drive is not an indication that a person can, in fact, drive very well. It is the same with a teacher's license: Not all holders can teach well, especially if they are teaching a subject without adequate training in that field, a sad but not uncommon practice. Nevertheless, the intent of certification and licensure is to maintain high standards for teachers.

Many states offer a variety of teaching licenses beyond those for general elementary or high school teaching. These include licenses for early childhood education, early elementary grades, later elementary grades, middle school, special education, English as a second language, and specific licenses for high school subjects, such a biology, English, mathematics, performing arts, social studies, art, and a foreign language. Knowing the types of licenses offered in your state and the specific licenses for which your teacher education curriculum is preparing you will help avoid confusion and disappointment when you start looking for that first job.

What if you plan to teach at a charter or private school? Charter schools are independent public schools, each governed by a public board that has the authority to hire teachers according to their own established standards. In some states, charter schools can hire teachers regardless of state certification and licensing requirements. In others, charter schools must hire only certified and licensed teachers. On the other hand, private schools are not regulated

GLOBAL VIEW
There are many teaching positions available worldwide that do not require U.S. teaching certification. Most are English language teaching positions for which the only requirements are a BA degree and native English fluency. Interested? The TEFL Institute is a great place to begin your search: www.teflinstitute.com.

by state government and can set their own standards. While some private schools require teachers to be certified, many do not. You will need to contact individual schools to learn whether they require teacher certification and licensing.

When you have questions about obtaining teacher certification and a license, consult with your college adviser, teacher education placement office, or contact the appropriate state department of education. Do not depend on friends, whose well-intentioned advice may not be accurate.

If I want to teach in another state, do I need another teacher's license?

Each state issues its own teaching license. If you have a license in one state but want to teach in another, you must reapply for a license there. Although this may sound challenging, many states offer *reciprocity,* so if you have met certification requirements and have been awarded a license from one state, most other states will recognize your teacher license.

What if you are graduating from a program in one state and want to apply to teach in another state? If your teacher education program is approved by the *National Council for the Accreditation of Teacher Education* (NCATE) or the *Teacher Education Accreditation Council* (TEAC), then it has met a set of standards widely accepted by most states for certification and licensing. (It is a good idea to find out if the program you are in is NCATE or TEAC approved.) If you graduate from such an accredited teacher education program, you will find that when you apply to most other states, you will receive at least a probationary license. You may be given a year or two while you are teaching to take additional courses or exams required by that state for certification.

What is an endorsement?

In some cases, a candidate may be licensed to teach in an additional subject area through what is termed an **endorsement.** For many teachers, especially those teaching in areas that have a large supply of candidates, endorsements can give you the edge over other applicants. You may want to give some consideration to this option. Carefully planning your courses can help you get a second teaching area. So can practical experience. For instance, a teacher may have a state license in U.S. history but finds herself teaching biology courses as well. Or perhaps she has taken a number of college courses in biology and decides she wants to be recognized as a biology teacher as well as a history teacher. Because she already has certification and a professional license (in history), she need not apply for a new license. Instead, she applies to the state for an *endorsement* in biology. Although she did not take biology methods or student-teach in biology, her teaching experience and background are considered for her endorsement in biology. The endorsement means that the state has approved her teaching both history and biology.

What are "alternative" or nontraditional routes to getting a teacher's license?

Few innovations in American education have created more controversy and debate than the alternative teacher certification. What officially began in the early 1980s as a way to ward off projected shortages of teachers has become part of the teacher education landscape. The term "alternative teacher certification" refers to nontraditional avenues for acquiring teacher training and licensure. Alternative programs are designed to attract individuals who have not gone through traditional teacher preparation programs in college. Although these candidates have not earned a teaching degree, they typically hold a bachelor's degree, bring nonteaching experiences to the classroom, and are willing to learn how to teach while they teach. Alternative teacher preparation typically focuses on a structured apprenticeship, a sort of on-the-job training. For example, a candidate might learn the fundamentals of teaching in a one-semester or summer intensive program, then start teaching and continue to take university-level education courses in the evening, on weekends, or in the summer. At the end of a year, or perhaps two years, the individual can apply for certification and licensure.

One of the best known of these alternative approaches is *Teach for America (TFA)*, which recruits motivated applicants who want to make a positive contribution to society by teaching in an under-resourced inner-city or rural school. The altruism of many *TFA* Corps members is reminiscent of Peace Corps volunteers, and their academic backgrounds are typically quite strong. *Troops to Teachers* is another alternative program offering veterans a way to continue to serve their country and their communities as they pursue second careers. Many believe that these programs create a healthy competition with the more traditional approaches and welcome their emphasis on the practical. Today, nearly all states and the District of Columbia offer some form of alternative teacher training, though requirements vary among the six hundred programs. (Visit teach-now.org for details.) More than 40 percent of new teachers annually enter the field through nontraditional alternative programs, and this figure is on the rise.[8]

Although it is no surprise that older and more life-experienced people enter teaching through this nontraditional route, it is interesting to note that a higher percentage of men and nonwhites are drawn to teaching through these programs. Teachers prepared through alternative programs share the following characteristics:[9]

- 70 percent are older than 30 years of age, 38 percent are male and 30 percent are nonwhite.
- 46 percent are teaching in a large city.
- Nearly half were working in a noneducation occupation the year before entering an alternative route program.
- "Being able to teach while getting certified" and "receiving a teacher's salary and benefits" were the most important variables in their choosing an alternative route to teaching.
- "Teaching full time as a teacher of record during the program" far outranked any other variable as the most helpful component of the alternative route program in developing competence to teach.
- Nine out of ten teachers entering the field through alternative routes say they feel competent in several aspects of teaching.

Not everyone views alternative routes to teacher preparation as a terrific innovation. For one thing, the attrition rate for these programs is quite high: Many who volunteer to join also volunteer to leave. Moreover, with limited preparation, these rookies wade into challenging teaching situations in some of the nation's most troubled and impoverished communities. Some fear that the alternative preparation of teachers signals a retreat from efforts toward full teacher professionalism. Studies of the effectiveness of these programs will undoubtedly continue in the years ahead. For now, they offer an interesting comparison with traditional programs, and while growing, still prepare only relatively few teachers. (See Chapter 1 for an in-depth discussion on alternative routes to teaching.)

What are teacher competency tests?

To complete your certification process and apply for a teaching license, you will likely need to pass one or more teacher competency tests, which are now mandated by most states. These tests assess basic skills such as reading and mathematics, pedagogical skills related to

IMAGINE...

Worthy Investments

The amount spent *every minute* on weapons worldwide could feed 2,000 malnourished children for a year. The cost of one military tank could provide classrooms for 30,000 students. What would our world be like if the balance shifted, and we invested more in children and education than in military defense?

SOURCE: Nazrul Islam *Reforming the United Nations,* 2010.

FOCUS QUESTION 4

What teacher competency tests do I need to take?

teaching practices, and subject matter knowledge. Most people sail through teacher competency exams, but not all do. You should realize that such exams are high-stakes gatekeepers used to restrict entry to professional training and to a career in teaching. These teacher tests carry the force of law. Results on this single test override all other state requirements in receiving a teacher's license. Why are such tests required (and are they a good idea)?

States that use teacher exams for certification and licensing commonly require **Praxis Assessment for Beginning Teachers (PRAXIS),** a two-part teacher test. The *PRAXIS I: Academic Skills Assessment* focuses on reading, writing, and mathematics. These basic tests apply to prospective teachers in all fields and all grades and are required in most states for admission into teacher education programs or to obtain an initial teacher license. The *PRAXIS II: Principles of Learning and Teaching and Subject Assessments* focuses on subject area, pedagogy, and professional education knowledge and is taken upon completion of your teacher training.[10] Not all states, though, rely on PRAXIS. An increasing trend is for states to develop their own individual teacher competency exams. (See Appendix 1 to learn what assessments apply to you.)

You should also be aware of a new national teacher exam currently being developed by Stanford University and Pearson Publishing. The *Teacher Performance Assessment* (TPA) requires teachers applying for their teaching credentials to submit to Pearson two 10-minute videos of classroom instruction, complete a forty-page take-home exam, and pay a $300 exam fee. Supporters of this exam believe that the uniform standards and assessment offered by TPA will answer critics who contend that teacher education programs send far too many unprepared instructors into the classroom. But even before most states consider signing on to TPA, a protest is emerging. Beyond basic concerns for confidentiality protections of the schoolchildren in the teaching videos being sent to Pearson, many worry about the corporatization of public education. Some student teachers argue that their professors and supervising teachers who observe and work with them daily in real school settings can do a better job judging their skills than a corporation (such as Pearson) can by viewing twenty minutes of video.[11] Despite the controversy, several states have already signed on adopt the Teacher Performance Assessment in the next few years, so it would be wise for you to consult with your adviser or state department of education to learn about the current status of this assessment and how it may affect you.

Educators differ as to whether the Praxis series, TPA, and other competency tests are necessary. Those who support competency exams maintain that the exams lend greater credibility and professionalism to the process of becoming a teacher. They claim that such tests identify well-educated applicants who can apply their knowledge in the classroom. They cite examples of teachers who cannot spell, write, or perform basic mathematical computations, and they plead persuasively that students must be protected from such incompetent teachers.

Some critics of the teacher exams argue that they are incredibly easy and not a real measure of competence. Other critics believe that such tests are more a political gesture than a way of improving education. Still others worry that we do not really know what makes good teachers, and we know even less about how to create tests to separate the good from the bad. We don't have tests that can measure enthusiasm, dedication, caring, and sensitivity—qualities that students associate with great teachers. Yet with strong public sentiment favoring such tests, they are likely to be a part of the teacher education landscape for the foreseeable future.[12]

How do teaching contracts work?

Congratulations! You have been hired by the school system of your choice, and a contract is placed before you. Before you sign it, there are a few things you should know about teacher contracts. This contract represents a binding agreement between you and the school district. It will be signed by you as the teacher being hired and by an agent of the board of education, often the superintendent. The contract usually sets the conditions of your work, perhaps including specific language detailing your instructional duties, and, of course, your salary and benefits.

If you do not have tenure, you will receive a new contract each year. Once you earn tenure (if your district still recognizes tenure), you will be working under a continuing contract and will probably be asked to notify the school district each year as to whether you plan to teach for the district the following year.

What are some advantages of tenure?

FOCUS QUESTION 5
Why do teachers seek tenure? (And should I?)

A teacher was once asked to leave his teaching position in Kentucky because he was leading an "un-Christian" personal life. He was Jewish.

A second-grade teacher was dismissed from her teaching assignment in Utah because of her dress. She wore miniskirts.

In Massachusetts, a teacher was fired because of his physical appearance. He had grown a beard.

Fortunately, these teachers all had one thing in common: **tenure.** And tenure prevented their school districts from following through on dismissal proceedings.

How does tenure work? A newly hired teacher is considered to be in a probationary period. The probationary teaching period can be two, three, or even five years for public school teachers and about six years for college professors. After demonstrating teaching competence for the specific period, the teacher is awarded tenure, which provides a substantial degree of job security. Tenure is intended to protect teachers from arbitrary and unfair dismissal. Unlike tenure for university professors, tenure for K–12 teachers does not shield them from dismissal. Instead, it guarantees due process—that is, if a teacher is fired, it will be for cause. Generally, a tenured teacher can be fired only for gross incompetence, insubordination, or immoral acts or because of budget cuts stemming from declining enrollments. In practice, public schools rarely fire a tenured teacher.

Most of America's public school teachers believe tenure protects them from district politics, favoritism, and the threat of losing their jobs to newcomers who would earn less.[13] Without tenure, hundreds, perhaps thousands, of financially pressed school systems could respond to pressure from taxpayers by firing their experienced teachers and replacing them with lower-paid, less experienced teachers. This would significantly reduce school budgets, usually the largest cost item in the local tax structure. After two or three more years, these teachers would also face the financial ax. In short, teachers would once again become an itinerant, poorly paid profession. Would anyone really benefit?

Without tenure, the fear of dismissal would cause thousands of teachers to avoid controversial topics, large and small. Many teachers would simply become a mirror of their communities, fearing to stir intellectual debate or to teach unsettling ideas because job security had become their prime objective. Classrooms would become quiet and mundane places, devoid of the excitement that comes from open discussion of controversial ideas.

In short, tenure provides teachers with the fundamental security that allows them to develop and practice their profession without fear of undue pressure or intimidation. While many states currently have tenure laws, tenure is increasingly under scrutiny, as we shall see in the next section. You are wise to research tenure laws in the state where you wish to teach.

What are some disadvantages of tenure?

Tenure can have the unintended consequence of insulating some weak teachers from dismissal. (Did you ever have an awful teacher protected by tenure? Not much fun.) Many of these ineffective teachers view tenure as a right to job security without acknowledging a corresponding responsibility of competency in the classroom. Feeling that they are no longer subject to serious scrutiny, such teachers fail to keep up with new developments in their field, and each year they drag out old lesson plans and fading lecture notes for yet another outdated performance. In fact, a majority of teachers believe that tenure does not necessarily recognize good teaching and acknowledge that some tenured teachers "fail to do a good job and are simply going through the motions."[14]

But many others worry that without tenure, it may not be just the weak teachers who are removed. Teachers may be fired because of personality conflicts, disputes with administrators, or other reasons unrelated to teaching skills. Although tenure protections are still in place in most school districts, much consideration is being given to the best ways to identify and remove incompetent teachers, and possibly eliminating tenure entirely.

As you can see, tenure is a double-edged sword. It serves the extremely important function of preserving academic freedom and protecting teachers from arbitrary and unjust dismissal. But it also provides job security for ineffective teachers, bad news for the students of these teachers or for the new and more competent teachers trying to enter the profession.

Are untenured teachers protected?

Many believe that until tenure is granted, they are extremely vulnerable, virtually without security. This is not true. During the 1970s, in *Goldberg* v. *Kelly, Board of Regents* v. *Roth,* and *Perry* v. *Sinderman,* the U.S. Supreme Court outlined several of the rights that are enjoyed by nontenured teachers. In many circumstances, these rights include advance notice of the intention to dismiss a teacher, clearly stated reasons for termination, and a fair and open hearing.[15] In addition, teacher organizations, such as the National Education Association (NEA) and the American Federation of Teachers (AFT), provide legal assistance for teachers who might be subjected to the arbitrary and unjust action of a school system.

If, during your probationary years, you feel that you have been unfairly victimized by the school administration, you should seek legal advice. Even nontenured teachers possess rights, but these rights are effective only if they are exercised.

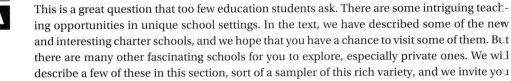

What teaching positions exist in unique school settings?

This is a great question that too few education students ask. There are some intriguing teaching opportunities in unique school settings. In the text, we have described some of the new and interesting charter schools, and we hope that you have a chance to visit some of them. But there are many other fascinating schools for you to explore, especially private ones. We will describe a few of these in this section, sort of a sampler of this rich variety, and we invite you to explore these and others on your own.

Quaker Education and Friends Schools. Quaker education differs from many other religious approaches because it does not seek to inculcate a particular set of religious beliefs or doctrines. Quakers believe in the "Inner Light," that each individual has a piece of God within. (Some people think of this as our conscience.) Emphasis on Bible instruction is not what Quakers are about. They believe each person should follow that inner voice, that we are all teachers and learners, and that each of us has unique gifts and talents to be honored and nurtured.

Quakers call their schools *Friends schools,* and they are located throughout the United States and overseas. Students attending Friends schools are quite diverse, coming from different cultural, religious, racial, and socioeconomic groups. The school tone is one of respect and caring for one another. Quaker schools foster the ideals of service and social action, and many of the students spend time overseas helping a community in a developing country. The schools also emphasize personal responsibility, experiential learning, spirituality, and environmental stewardship.

Waldorf Education. Developed by Rudolf Steiner in 1919, Waldorf education includes preschool through high school, and Waldorf teachers are trained to focus on the whole child's development. Art, music, gardening, foreign languages, and a sense of spirituality are elements of Waldorf schooling, what they call an education for the heart, hands, and head. In fact, academic focus is de-emphasized in the early years, and most children are not reading independently until the middle or the end of second grade. Rather than using textbooks, young students produce their own, recording their experiences and what they've learned. Computers and television watching by young children are strongly discouraged.

As an elementary teacher in a Waldorf school, you would get to see something few teachers witness: your students' growth and development over a seven-year period. Waldorf education is based on the notion that students go through specific developmental stages, so if you will teach in a Waldorf elementary school, you will be their teacher for one entire development cycle—seven years. That means you will teach all the grades and most of the subjects to your elementary class, what you might call seven years of student–teacher connection.

There are approximately nine hundred Waldorf schools worldwide, and most are nonprofit, independent schools, with no public financial support, although some countries do support Waldorf schools with government funding. In the United States, several schools have been established as Waldorf-methods "charter schools" within the public school system. But to teach in a Waldorf school, you will need to go through a Waldorf teacher preparation program.

Montessori Education. Beginning her work a century ago, Italian pediatrician Maria Montessori developed an educational approach based on her understanding of children's natural learning tendencies. The Montessori classroom environment contains specially designed manipulative materials that promote learning. Teachers guide children to use these materials, cultivating their concentration, motivation, and self-discipline. Although many of the Montessori schools in the United States are for younger children, the Montessori approach can be used at all levels of education. In the United States, there are more than four thousand private Montessori schools and more than two hundred public schools with Montessori-style programs. Here, too, if you are interested, you will need specialized teacher training in Montessori education. (See the History Hall of Fame in Chapter 7 to learn more about Maria Montessori.)

What kinds of educational careers are available beyond classroom teaching?

Good news! Your education degree has prepared you not only for a teaching career, but for many interesting education-related careers. If you are interested in school administration or a counseling career, starting as a classroom teacher makes a lot of sense and gives you an important perspective that will serve you well in these other school careers. But beyond administration and counseling lie many other options. The following list is intended to give you some idea of the less typical but potentially quite rewarding *nontraditional educational careers* available to you in the United States and internationally. (See also "A Closer Look: Education Want Ads.")

FOCUS QUESTION 6
Are there jobs in education outside of the classroom?

A Closer Look Education Want Ads

You may find your education niche beyond the traditional classroom. Here are some employment opportunities you might find in the "want ads".

EDUCATIONAL CONSULTANT
We are seeking an experienced Education Consultant with classroom teaching background for per diem contracted and long-term assignments, with expertise in one or more of the following: dimensions of learning, performance assessments, state learning standards, early literacy, cooperative learning, differentiated instruction.

PRIVATE GIRLS' HIGH SCHOOL
seeks Director of Technology/Computer Teacher, Classroom Experience Necessary.

ELEMENTARY ZOO INSTRUCTOR
The Education Department of the Zoo, one of the country's foremost institutions of informal science teaching, is seeking a dynamic instructor for its elementary-level programs. A highly interactive teaching approach, creativity, and a theatrical background will be helpful. This position involves program development for parents and teachers in addition to direct instruction of children ages 4–12. Excellent oral and written communication skills required.

EDITOR/WRITER
Familiar with higher edu. issues needed for Publications Dept. Will work with campus colleagues and assoc. staff to develop a natl. quarterly newsletter for faculty & administrators. Must know curriculum development, have solid editorial and publications mgmt. skills, research aptitude, & good writing skills.

Major nonprofit YOUTH SERVICE AGENCY seeks to fill the following positions (Bilingual, Spanish/English preferred): YOUTH COUNSELOR: B.A. 2 years experience in social service setting, PROGRAM COORDINATOR: B.A. 3–5 years experience, strong supervisory/communication skills necessary.

EDUCATIONAL RESEARCHER
Research and develop abstracts for www-based project about science and math education. Writing skills, attention to detail, ability to synthesize information quickly, and confident phone skills. Background in education helpful.

EDUCATIONAL COORDINATOR
The Historical Society seeks a creative, self-motivated team player to plan, implement, & promote educational programs for schools, families, & adults. Responsibilities incl.: organizing public programs & tours: coordinating National History Day, providing services for schools.

YMCA CHILD CARE DIRECTOR
Join our management team! Nonprofit corporate-sponsored child care management co., looking for a talented director to manage our state-of-the-art center. Must have ECE experience and have been through NAEYC accred. process.

LEARNING CENTERS offering individualized diagnostic and prescriptive programs are looking for dynamic PT cert. teachers to instruct students of all ages in reading, writing, math, and algebra.

SUBSTANCE ABUSE PREVENTION INTERVENTION SPECIALISTS
Seeking experienced professionals to provide services to students in substance abuse prevention and intervention. Will provide both group and individual counseling and conduct peer leadership groups for students at risk at various schools.

PROGRAM ASSISTANT
New vision in schools seeks a program assistant to provide support to a major school reform initiative. Must be meticulous with details & be able to write well, handle multiple projects, & meet deadlines. Interest in public schools is preferred.

COLLEGE GRAD
Prestigious sports program for children sks highly motivated coaches. Sports background & a love for children a must. Education majors a +.

EDUCATIONAL SALES REPS
See our ad in the SALES section under "Education."

VIOLENCE PREVENTION PROGRAM
Peace Games seeks F/T director to create curricula & resources for students, parents, & teachers.

TEACH ENGLISH ABROAD
BA/BS required. Interested in education. No exp nec.

SPECIAL EDUCATION
The Learning Center, a place for emotionally disturbed children, has the following possible positions: Resource Counselor, Cert. Teacher, Music Teacher, Level III Secretary, Therapist Assistant.

MIGRANT EDUCATOR
State Migrant Education Program needs teachers for positions working with the children and families of migrant workers. ELL is particularly helpful with his population.

CAN YOU TEACH?
If you enjoy explaining new material and engaging adult learners, transfer your teaching skills to corporate training. Develop new employee orientation sessions and montly professional development trainings. Candidates must demonstrate excellent communication skills and creativity.

COMMUNITY/NON-PROFIT ORGANIZATION
Boys and Girls Club is looking for Teen Program Director to lead activities in our Education & Career Development, Health & Life Skills, Character & Leadership and Recreation programs. Bachelors degree required. Strong communication skills, both verbal and written, and understanding of group dynamics higly desired.

AMERICAN INTERNATIONAL SCHOOL
High school teacher needed; no cert. required. AIS is a fully accredited school serving families from Hong Kong's local and international communities. AIS successfully delivers rigorous US standards-based education for students from Early Chlildhood through Grade 12. Join our richly diverse and highly talented internatial faculty!

REFLECTION: Which of these careers do you find most appealing? Which is least appealing? Have you ever explored nonteaching education careers? Why or why not?

Early Childhood Education. If you want to stay in touch with teaching and children but prefer a climate other than the typical classroom, you may want to explore such options as day care centers. Early childhood education is a vital component of the nation's educational system. Working parents seek quality options, not only for child care, but for child education and development as well.

Although day care rarely offers much pay or status, a number of talented educators find early childhood education incredibly satisfying. If you are creative and flexible, you might even endeavor to develop your own facility. For example, a growing number of businesses offer day care and early childhood education programs for employees' children. Fitness centers and shopping malls also provide childcare services for parents. You might consider creating a similar early childhood program and marketing your "children's center" in the business world. (Check out your state's laws regarding operating standards, building restrictions, number of children permitted, and so on.) If you enjoy working with young children, you will find opportunities galore in this growing field.

Adult Education. If you prefer to work with a mature population, you might be attracted to adult (continuing) education programs. These programs are offered through city and county governments, local school systems, and nearby colleges and universities. In addition, some private businesses sponsor courses that are related to their products—recreation, crafts, cooking, technical training, and so forth. As the ranks of the retired swell with baby boomers, you can expect this field to grow rapidly. Older Americans often have the time, interest, and income to pursue education in topics, skills, and hobbies that have long eluded them. Elder hostels around the world are responding to the educational demand created by retirees. With a little research, you are likely to discover a variety of adult learning programs that can provide nontraditional teaching opportunities.

Colleges and Universities. You will find many nonteaching, yet education-related, jobs in colleges and universities. As examples, academic advisers work primarily on a one-to-one basis with students, discussing courses of study; admissions officers respond to the needs of students; alumni relations personnel conduct fund-raising campaigns, organize alumni events, and maintain job placement services; and student services personnel do psychological and vocational counseling, advise international students, and administer residential programs. Most colleges offer their employees tuition benefits, so if you want to pursue graduate studies, this may be a good way to gain both experience and an advanced degree.

Community Organizations. Think of a community group. Chances are that group has an educational mission. Churches, synagogues, mosques, YMCAs, Boys and Girls Clubs, museums, parks, hospitals, clinics, and senior centers can use creative instructors and program planners. For example, a former English teacher, disturbed by the demeaning, artsy-craftsy programs in a local assisted living home, inspired the residents to write their life histories, an experience they found very stimulating. Recreation and community centers hire instructors, program planners, and directors for their numerous programs. Hospitals and health clinics need people to plan and deliver training to their professional and administrative staffs. Some of the large municipal zoos conduct programs to protect endangered animal species and to interact with school groups. Libraries and media centers require personnel to maintain and catalog resources and equipment, as well as to train others in their use. Art galleries and museums hire staff to coordinate educational programs for school and civic groups and to conduct tours of their facilities.

The Media. The publishing and broadcasting industries hire people with education backgrounds to help write and promote their educational products. For example, large print and online newspapers, such as *The New York Times* and *Huffington Post,* maintain staff writers whose job is to cover education, just as other reporters cover crime, politics, and finance. Some newspapers even publish a special edition of their paper for use in schools. Likewise, textbook publishers, educational journals, magazines, Internet media sites and blogs, and television talk shows need people familiar with educational principles to help develop their articles and programs.

Private Industry and Public Utilities. Large public and private corporations often rely on education graduates in their programs to train their staffs in areas such as organizational effectiveness, new technology training, civil rights and safety laws, and basic company policies and practices. Some companies maintain permanent learning centers and seek people with education backgrounds to plan and run them. If you like writing, you may want to work on pamphlets, brochures, curricula, online media, and other materials describing a company's services and products.

Technology. The blossoming of the Internet, social media, and even mobile phones has divided the population into those who are computer literate and those who are computer challenged (sometimes called technophobic). Those who are not yet citizens of cyberworld represent a ready population of potential students. If you enjoy computers and the digital world, you may want to become a tech-teacher/consultant, teaching computer skills from texting to social networking to digital photography in either formal or informal settings (adult education classes, computer stores, YMCAs or senior centers, to name just a few possibilities). You may also consider a position as a technology consultant for schools, helping to design websites, to create networks, or to select software. Or you may choose to work outside a school organization, as a company's Internet marketing representative.

With the dramatic increase in the use of educational software in the classroom, many software companies are also soliciting people with experience in education as consultants to help develop new programs. Creativity, familiarity with child psychology, and knowledge of the principles of learning are important resources for developing tech-related devices, programs, and software that will appeal to a diverse and competitive education market.

Educational Associations. National, state, and regional educational associations hire writers, editors, research specialists, administrators, lobbyists, and educators for a host of education-related jobs, from research and writing to public relations to web design. There are hundreds of these associations, from the NEA to the American Association of Teachers of French.

Government Agencies. A host of local, state, and federal government agencies hire education graduates for training, policy planning, management, research, and so on. Various directories can help you through the maze of the federal bureaucracy. Among these is the *United States Government Manual* (Office of the Federal Register, National Archives and Records Service), which describes the various programs within the federal government, including their purposes and top-level staffs. The Internet is another useful source for exploring career opportunities in government-related education programs.

Global Opportunities. Want an international experience? Consider Department of Defense schools, private international schools, religious and international organizations, military bases offering high school and college courses to armed forces personnel, and the Peace Corps.

A number of foreign companies now hire U.S. college graduates to teach English to their workers, positions that are sometimes very well paid. No matter the wages, high or low, the excitement of teaching in another culture (while learning about that culture) is hard to match.

As we indicated (more than once!), we love classroom teaching, but you should know there are many ways that you can serve society with an education background. You may want to explore one or more of these nonclassroom careers, perhaps as an intern or a volunteer at first, to see if these career paths appeal to you.

In this chapter—and in this text—we have tried to answer your questions about teaching. (If we missed one, we invite you to visit the OLC and submit your question via the Ask the Author button.) We hope that you have found this text chock-full of useful and interesting information, and that you have enjoyed reading this book. In fact, we hope that you enjoyed it so much that you choose to keep the book as a useful reference in the future. But more than that, we hope that you are gaining greater clarity on your decision about whether teaching is for you, and whatever that decision turns out to be, we wish you the best of luck!

GLOBAL VIEW

A premier international teacher job fair is held annually at the University of Northern Iowa. To learn more, visit, www.uni.edu.

KEY TERMS

endorsement, 408

portfolio, 404

Praxis Assessment for
Beginning Teachers, 410

résumé, 403

teacher certification, 407

teacher's license, 407

tenure, 411

www.mhhe.com/sadker10e

CHAPTER REVIEW

Go to the Online Learning Center to review concepts from the chapter.

REFLECTIVE ACTIVITIES AND YOUR PORTFOLIO

Part IV: Your Classroom

4:1 Developmental and Psychosocial Stages of Students

Purpose: Who is the average 5-year-old? 10-year-old? 15-year-old? What can they do academically? How do they behave in class? What can a teacher do to help them grow and succeed? We organize schools by age, so understanding the developmental patterns of children's growth can be quite useful. An understanding of student developmental patterns will help you to develop objectives, plan activities, and assess classroom behaviors. Do you know the typical psychosocial issues of the students you plan to teach?

Activity: Psychologist Erik H. Erikson describes life's eight developmental stages, which he calls "psychosocial stages." Understanding these stages can help you prepare to teach your students. In this activity, we ask you to observe the behavior of the students you wish to instruct.

First step, let's make sure we understand Erikson's work. If you are not already familiar with him and his ideas, do an Internet search, or find some books on the topic. Once you read about these stages, you will realize that you will likely be teaching students in Erikson's stage 3, 4, or 5:

- Stage 3: Early Childhood (approximately 4–5 years old)
- Stage 4: Elementary and Middle School Years (approximately 5–12 years old)
- Stage 5: Adolescence (approximately 13–19 years old)

Artifact: Choose the stage or stages that apply to the students you will likely teach, and consider the characteristics of their psychosocial stage. (Remember, these are broad categories and not all children arrive or leave these stages at the same time. Moreover, some of the stages are quite broad, so you will have to focus on the parts within a stage, as we do in the following example.)

Developmental and Psychosocial Stages

Stage:

Specific Age:

Characteristics of This Stage/Age:

Evidence Observed:

Here is an example of how your chart might look with some of your notations:

Example
Developmental and Psychosocial Stages

Stage: 3—Early Childhood (ages 5–12)
Specific Age: 6

www.mhhe.com/sadker10e

FORM

Developmental and
psychosocial stages

Characteristics of This Stage/Age: Children have newfound power at this stage as they develop motor skills and social interest with people around them. They now must learn to achieve a balance between eagerness for more adventure and more responsibility, and learning to control impulses and childish fantasies. Children at this age are becoming more aware of themselves, and they work at "being responsible, being good and doing it right." They are learning to share and cooperate.

Evidence Observed: I observed a first-grade class and the students would listen to the teacher's every word, but often lose their focus and begin talking to the person next to them. The students were anxious to handle scissors and other tools of the classroom. Some of the students would hold hands with friends whenever they would venture around the room, while others would quietly watch. The children were generally very polite to each other, though one child cried because of a disagreement with another student.

Reflection: What did you learn from this activity? Any surprises? Has this activity influenced your decision about teaching at a particular grade level? What more would you like to learn about the students? How can the concept of "average" or "typical" become an obstacle? What stage are you? What does that say about you? Does it ring true?

4:2 Observing Different Teaching Strategies

INTASC STANDARD 2
Learning Differences

Purpose: Teachers report that observing other teachers is one of the most useful activities for improving their own teaching. Reading about different teaching styles and strategies is informative, but seeing these styles in action brings these ideas to life.

Activity: The first (and perhaps toughest) challenge in this activity is arranging classroom observations. If you can, plan on observing teachers at the grade level or in the subject area of your choice, using various teaching strategies. If you want to teach lower elementary grades, visit some local elementary schools, meet with the principal at each school, and share with them your interest in observing some diverse teaching styles. Hopefully, the principal will have some recommendations and help you schedule some observations. Same is true at the secondary school. If you want to teach English, ask the principal if you can visit some English instructors who use different teaching styles. Perhaps your teacher education program has relationships with local schools and can assist you in this effort. If none of these approaches work for you, you can always ask friends, teachers, and other students to recommend teachers they know who will allow you to observe. One additional option is to observe different teaching styles on your own campus, although observing elementary and secondary teachers would be more appropriate.

Record your impressions on the accompanying observation form. (If you want to learn more about observation techniques, visit the Classroom Observations section on the Online Learning Center.)

Artifact: Spend the first few minutes getting a feel for the classroom. When you are ready, begin to fill out the form, which is intended to help you organize your observations and reactions. Write down the teaching style (cooperative learning, mastery learning, direct teaching—or you may want to create your own title to capture the essence of this style). Then record specific examples of this strategy. Write down what you see as the assets and the liabilities of this strategy, as well as whether this strategy appeals to you. Try to enrich your insights by speaking with the teacher or with some students about the teaching style after class. Finally, consider what assumptions this strategy makes about the learner. Record your reactions on the Teaching Strategies Observation Form.

www.mhhe.com/sadker10e

FORM

Teaching strategies
observation form

Teaching Strategies Observation Form

Teaching Style: _____

Class: _____

Examples:

Assets:

Concerns:

What appealed to you?

What are the learning assumptions inherent in this strategy?

Reflection: Visiting and observing other teachers can provide rich insights into teaching methods and whether these styles meet the needs of students' different learning styles. What insights did you take away from your observations? Did any of the observations surprise you? Which strategies did you find appealing? Will you try some of these styles and strategies in your own classroom? Which styles did not appeal to you? What do your preferences tell you about your own approach to teaching and learning?

4:3 Rules, Rituals, and Routines

INTASC STANDARD 3
Learning Environments

Purpose: Most teachers struggle to balance motivating students with managing them. Sometimes, in an attempt to keep it "all together and in control," teachers over-regulate a class. At other times, they wait too long to rein in exuberant students. As a prospective teacher, it is never too early to begin sorting out how you will manage your classroom. This activity will help you consider various behavior management techniques and how they shape the learning environment.

Activity: Arrange to visit a few classrooms at the grade level you want to teach. Use the following chart to record your observations. You may find it helpful to review the section on classroom management and the findings of classroom management discussed in the text before you record your observations. This form will focus on Jacob Kounin's work, but you can explore other management strategies as well by developing your own observation approach to capture those strategies.

Artifact:

Management/Motivation Observation
Examples
Group alerting
Withitness
Overlapping
Least intervention
Flip-flops
Overdwelling
Fragmentation
Thrusts
Dangles

www.mhhe.com/sadker10e

FORM

Management/motivation observation

Reflection: Were you able to find evidence/examples of some/none/all the categories on the Kounin chart or on another management approach that you are observing? What successful management strategies did you see? How might you employ what you learned from this teacher in your own classroom? If you observed a teacher struggling with classroom management, what lessons did you take from this experience? What, if any, evidence of the hidden or implicit curriculum did you witness? What do you believe is the most difficult aspect of management? Describe the learning environment created by the management techniques you observed—the good and the bad.

4:4 Teaching Is Learning

INTASC STANDARD 4
Content Knowledge

Purpose: Teachers know a secret: If you really want to learn a subject, teach it. Planning to teach, reviewing key points, and considering unexpected student questions all help you to learn a subject in far greater depth than simply reading about it. Providing clear and timely feedback to students as they learn a topic enhances their learning, and your understanding of the student's learning challenges as well.

Activity: This activity requires a teaching or tutoring situation. Perhaps your teacher education program might offer you the opportunity to tutor or assist in local schools. Or you can volunteer to tutor. If you can find such an opportunity, it would be very useful to audiotape or videotape your sessions for thirty minutes or so each time you tutor or teach. (You may need to get permission from the student or parent as well as the school before taping.) If this is too difficult, find a colleague who can observe your teaching or tutoring. The key is to capture your behaviors, something you cannot do by yourself while engaged in teaching.

The feedback teachers give students also provides useful insights into subject matter, a key to learning. Chapter 11 discusses four feedback reactions to student answers: praise, acceptance, remediation, and criticism. Using these four types of feedback effectively is a challenge. Teachers who use praise, criticism, and remediation typically are involved in more precise and active instruction than teachers who rely on imprecise acceptance reactions. In this tutoring session, we ask you to monitor and interpret your feedback. We want your recording or colleagues' observations to inform you of how many or each kind of feedback you give, and offer some examples of each.

Providing adequate wait-time 1 allows a student to think through an answer, and adequate wait time 2 allows you to think through your reaction so that you can give effective feedback. It may be useful to review wait-time 1 and 2 in Chapter 11 as well. Using the recording, see how long these wait times are. If a colleague is helping you, he or she may have to cease counting feedback types for a while, and using a second hand, spend a few minutes measuring the length of wait times 1 and 2.

Artifact: Use the following chart to record your teacher feedback from the audiotape or videotape, or from a colleague who can observe your class. You may find it helpful to review the criteria for each type of feedback as well as wait time beforehand.

Feedback (Sample Entries)	Number of Responses
Part I	
Praise:	
Good job!	18
Acceptance:	
Okay.	32
Remediation:	
Now read all the word parts together.	12
Criticism:	
No, that's not the way to pronounce it. Try again.	1
Part II	
Wait-time 1: (How many seconds do you wait after asking a question?)	
Seconds: 0.5, 1, 1, 1, 0, 2, 0, 0, 0.5, 1, 0	
Wait-time 2: (How many seconds do you wait after the student responds?)	
Seconds: 0, 2, 0, 0, 0.5, 1, 0, 0.5, 1, 1, 1, 0	

Reflection: What did you notice about the type and frequency of your feedback? How did your use of feedback compare with that of the typical teacher who uses acceptance more than half the time? Sometimes acceptance is quite useful, such as encouraging student responses and acknowledging student ideas, but the risk is in overusing this form of feedback. If you used acceptance, what form did your acceptance comments take (okay, aha, silence)? Did you overuse acceptance, and thus not give the kind of precise feedback that is useful in grasping a subject? Did your use of praise represent the attributes identified in Chapter 11? Was criticism clear and appropriate (and content related—that is, not personal)? Was remediation specific enough to allow the student to improve? Was wait time 1 adequate for students to thoughtfully respond? Was wait time 2 adequate enough to give you time to provide thoughtful feedback? How would you assess your use of these feedback skills? How would you assess your use of wait time? What activity can you devise to help you practice and improve your wait time and feedback?

What inferences can you make about your knowledge of the subject—and your student's knowledge of the subject—from the types and frequency of feedback? Can you see a connection between using adequate wait time, as well as praise, remediation, and criticism and subject matter mastery? Describe these connections. Include this chart and reflection in your portfolio.

4:5 Class Comedy Club

INTASC STANDARD 5
Application of Content

Purpose: For all the crises in classrooms and children at risk, humor in schools survives and even thrives. Thank goodness! Healthful humor (as opposed to targeted humor and sarcasm) can motivate students to participate and learn. Positive student humor, often unintentional, can be a major factor in keeping you happy and in the business of teaching. Although you may never aspire to be a comic, integrating humor into a lesson will help you practice setting a positive and welcoming learning climate. (We know some of you are a bit frightened at telling jokes or using comedy. If you want to skip this activity, no problem. But if you want to give it a try, remember there is humor all around us, so worry less and try to enjoy the experience!)

Activity: Do you have a funny story about yourself, friends, or family? Or did you read a story that you found funny? Can that story teach your students a useful lesson or offer a helpful insight? Practice sharing that story with friends, to give you practice and confidence. Encourage your friends to help your delivery and perhaps add colorful commentary, body language, and well-timed punch lines. Hone your presentation until you are comfortable.

Artifact: Videotape or record your "Teaching and Humor" in a comfortable environment. If you feel comfortable, present your education comedy sketch to your classmates.

Reflection: How hard was this activity for you? Can you picture yourself using humor in the classroom? What did you learn about yourself from this activity?

www.mhhe.com/sadker10e

FORM

Class comedy club

4:6 Pruning Your Portfolio: Dyads

INTASC STANDARD 6
Assessment

Purpose: The *RAP* activities, reflections, and artifacts (hopefully) helped you create a *working* portfolio. Now is the time to assess your portfolio and decide what is worth keeping or upgrading.

Activity: Evaluate your *working* portfolio. Use the following portfolio assessment rubric to chart the status of your collection. Score your portfolio according to how well it meets the criteria listed, either yes or no, or on a 1 to 5 scale. Provide some evidence to support your position. Select a partner to discuss and share your *working* portfolios and the assessment charts. Then analyze their portfolio. This dialogue should help both of you to improve your portfolios.

Artifact:

www.mhhe.com/sadker10e

FORM

Portfolio assessment

	Portfolio Assessment	
	Yes	Not yet
Item		
Does your portfolio include:		
Statement of teaching philosophy.		
Statement of your teaching methodologies.		
Description of your efforts to improve your teaching.		
Representative lesson plans.		
Summary of teaching evaluations.		
Videos of your teaching.		

	Quality Review				
	Not at All				Very
	1	2	3	4	5
Does each item reflect Quality work:					
Clear Purpose:					
Thoughtful:					
Collaboration:					
Diversity:					
Connection to an INTASC Standard:					
Other:					
Overall Appraisal:					

Reflection: What have you learned about your portfolio, including both its strengths and its weaknesses? What did your discussion with your partners teach you? How could your portfolio be improved? How do you see this portfolio helping you become an effective instructor? How do you see this portfolio helping you grow professionally?

4:7 Technology in the Classroom: Bane or Boom?

INTASC STANDARD 7
Planning for Instruction

Purpose: Technology's effectiveness relies heavily on your instructional planning. This exercise will help you incorporate the assets that technology offers and hopefully avoid the pitfalls.

Activity: Consider what you have read about and explored in educational technology. When you walk into the classroom, what are your plans, and your boundaries regarding technology? What uses do you want to promote, and what misuses do you want to avoid? You will need to do some original research for this activity, discovering what teachers have said about the specific pitfalls and assets of technology in the classroom.

Artifact: You can prepare a PowerPoint presentation, a chart, or a handout to be used with your own students to explain how technology will be used in your classroom and what aspects of technology will disallowed. Here's an example: The Internet may be used as a research tool in your classroom. But the sources of your Internet research must be cited, verified, and documented. And you must find out if these resources are sound and appropriate.

What other rules and guidelines can you develop?

Reflection: How will you invite your students into this discussion of classroom technology guidelines? How difficult is it to bring this huge innovation down to the classroom level? What did you learn about how you will plan for technology in your teaching? What types of technology are you likely to use in your teaching? Which ones will you avoid? Why?

4:8 Memories of a Teacher

INTASC STANDARD 8
Instructional Strategies

Purpose: Many of us choose education because of a special teacher. You may not have been consciously aware of all those skills and traits when you were a student, but you knew the class was interesting, challenging, productive, and maybe even arduous. Perhaps you had friends in the class and you accomplished projects in a collaborative and meaningful way. Whatever the story, we suspect you have one (and hope you have many). Connecting your memories with the research on effective teaching should help you be more mindful in your own classroom.

Activity: Consider one terrific educator from your past. First, brainstorm memories from that class. On the left side of a piece of paper, list each item. See what you can generate at this point without reading further. (It's tempting to peek but worth the effort to wait.)

After your first and open response, use the following cues to generate even more memories.

- How did the teacher treat you?
- Were there special rules or activities that you remember?
- Was the room arranged in a special way?
- Was the subject a favorite of yours, or did the teacher make it one?
- Do you remember how the class was managed (or was that not much of an issue)?
- Can you recall anything about tests (their kind, frequency, and resultant anxiety level)?
- Were term papers, major projects, or special event days part of the curriculum?
- What else made this teacher the one who made a difference for you?

Artifact: You may want to title your description "Memories of a Special Teacher," or some related title. These memories can become a touchstone, a place to return and read and reflect on what mattered to you when you sat on the other side of the desk.

Beyond an Artifact: Why not write and send a letter explaining the assignment and why you chose this teacher as your focus. Teachers don't receive enough of this sort of recognition for their time and talent. Receiving such a letter will probably be quite meaningful.

Reflection: Now, read your terrific teacher memories and meander back through Chapter 11. Consider each point you described. What connections can you make between the research on instructional quality and your memorable teacher? What insights about effective instruction did you acquire? What connections to this teacher go beyond such studies, and have more to do with the teacher's personality or caring? What does that teach you?

4:9 Website of the Month

INTASC STANDARD 9
Personal Learning and Ethical Practice

Purpose: Online resources can help your teaching and professional development. Unfortunately, quality control does not exist on the Internet. To be a reflective and responsible practitioner, you must learn to evaluate Internet sources (and help your students do the same!). Why don't we begin by compiling a bank of sound educational websites that you can draw on at any time.

www.mhhe.com/sadker10e

FORM

Assessing websites

Activity: Search the Internet for at least three educational websites that look useful. Choose one that is relevant to a subject matter area; another that is interactive, including opportunities to chat with colleagues; and a third that is monitored or sponsored by a professional organization such as the NEA or the AFT. Use (and add to) the following rubric to evaluate each of these sites.

Artifact: Assessing Websites

	Need to Improve				Did This Well
	1	2	3	4	5
Well-Researched Sources					
Objectivity					
Usefulness					
Current					
Ease of Navigation					
Valuable Links					
_____ (Your criterion)					
_____ (Your criterion)					
Overall Appraisal:					

Reflection: What criteria can you use to decide if an online resource is reliable? Are there techniques and shortcuts to finding sound and reliable educational sites? Did you discover websites that offer lesson plans and practical ideas? Others that provide emotional support for new teachers? Perhaps some with curricular insights? A forum or blog for an ongoing professional dialogue?

4:10 Showtime: Go on an Information Interview

INTASC STANDARD 10
Leadership and
Collaboration

www.mhhe.com/sadker10e

FORM

Information interview

Purpose: Interviewing for employment can be a daunting experience. As with all new and difficult endeavors, the more experience you gain the easier the task becomes. Perhaps you might want to begin this process by participating in an information interview. This type of interview is relatively low-stress and involves learning about a potential employer, job, and current situation. It is not about "landing" a job.

Activity: Check with your college about arranging for an informational interview with a local school official, or call the personnel office and arrange for one yourself. Perhaps the following questions might offer you a helpful starting point. Feel free to add other questions as well. Record both the questions and the answers for future reference.

Artifact: "Information Interview"

1. What does the school district or charter school look for in a teacher candidate?
2. Is there any special training or experience beyond the certification teaching license that is desired?
3. What subject areas and what grade levels have the greatest need?
4. What should a teacher candidate know about the students and the families in this community?
5. How are teachers evaluated?
6. How important are standardized tests?
7. What is the average class size?
8. Does the district or charter school have induction and mentor programs for new teachers, and if so how do they work?
9. What extracurricular clubs, athletics, and activities are available for new faculty members to supervise?
10. What else should I know about your school?

Reflection: How did the interview go? Were you nervous? What did you learn? What might you do differently next time? Did anything surprise you? Did you form any potentially helpful relationships? Would you want to work in this district? Do you want to pursue employment in this district? Do you now feel more comfortable about future interviews?

APPENDICES

Text Appendices

1. Teacher Competency Exams
2. State Offices for Teacher Certification and Licensure
3. INTASC Standards: Concepts and Content in *Teachers, Schools, and Society,* Tenth Edition

Online Appendices

Online Appendix A: Classroom Observation Guidelines
Online Appendix B: State Offices for Teacher Certification and Licensure

www.mhhe.com/sadker10e

A

APPENDIX 1

Teacher Competency Exams

Pearson Assessments—developer of National Evaluation Systems (NES)—and Educational Testing Service (ETS)—developers of Praxis™—are two of the largest companies to provide tests and other services for states to use as part of their teacher certification process. Some colleges and universities use these assessments to qualify individuals for entry into teacher education programs. Because more and more states are choosing to develop their own teacher competency exams, be sure to check with your specific teacher education program or state department of education for information on your particular testing requirements.

National Evaluation Systems

Although the Praxis assessments from ETS have received a great deal of attention, assessing more than half a million aspiring teachers, National Evaluation Systems assesses as many or more prospective teachers but is less well known. The reason is that NES customizes its exams for individual states. NES teacher competency assessments include those covering pedagogy and content-specific subject matter. For more information about NES visit www.nestest.com. To see if you need to take an NES competency exam as part of your certification requirements, check with your specific teacher education program or state department of education (sound familiar?). You can find contact information for all state departments of education and their certification/licensure offices in Appendix 2. Some states use both NES and Praxis exams to assess their teachers, so let's also take look at Praxis.

Praxis

Praxis is a common part of many states certification requirements. Different states and institutions require different tests in The Praxis Series™ and determine their own passing score requirements. So if your state includes Praxis as part of its certification process, be sure you know which tests you need before you register by checking with your teacher education program or state department of education (See Appendix 2).

There are currently two categories of assessments in The Praxis Series:

Praxis I:™ Academic Skills Assessment. This assessment measures reading, writing, and mathematics skills and includes multiple-choice questions and an essay. The tests are designed to evaluate whether you have the academic skills needed to prepare for a career in education. In addition to licensure, these tests are often used to qualify candidates for entry into a teacher education program.

Praxis II: Principles of Learning and Teaching and Subject Assessments. Consists of three parts:

1. The Principles of Learning and Teaching exam assesses aspiring teachers' general pedagogy-related knowledge and skills at four grade levels: Early Childhood, Grades K–6, Grades 5–9, and Grades 7–12.

2. The Teaching Foundations Tests measure pedagogy in five areas: multisubject (elementary), English, Language Arts, Mathematics, Science and Social Science. *Praxis II* tests include multiple-choice questions and essay and constructed-response questions.

3. The Subject Assessments measure candidates' knowledge of the content areas they will teach, as well as how much they know about teaching that subject.

 If you are planning to take one or more of these tests, visit the Praxis website (www.ets.org/praxis) to register, learn more about the testing process, and access study guides.

State Offices for Teacher Certification and Licensure

ALABAMA
Alabama Department of Education
Teacher Education and Certification
50 North Ripley Street
P.O. Box 302101
Montgomery, Alabama 36104
Telephone: (334) 242-9700
Email: tcert@alsde.edu
www.alsde.edu

ALASKA
Alaska Department of Education
Teacher Education and Certification
801 West 10th Street, Suite 200
P.O. Box 110500
Juneau, AK 99811-0500
Telephone: (907) 465-2831
Email: eed.webmaster@alaska.gov
www.educ.state.ak.us

ARIZONA
Arizona Department of Education
Educator Certification
Phoenix office:
1535 West Jefferson Street
Phoenix, Arizona 85007
Telephone: (602) 542-4367
Email: Certification@azed.gov
http://ade.state.az.us
Tucson office:
400 West Congress Street, #118
Tucson, Arizona 85701
Telephone: 520-628-6326
Email: TucsonCertificationInbox@azed.gov
http://ade.state.az.us

ARKANSAS
Arkansas Department of Education
Office of Professional Licensure
Four Capitol Mall
Room 107B
Little Rock, AR 72201
Telephone: (501) 682-4342
Email: ADE.Communications@arkansas.gov
http://arkansased.org/

CALIFORNIA
California Commission on Teacher
Credentialing
P.O. Box 944270

Sacramento, CA 94244-2700
1900 Capitol Avenue
Sacramento, CA 95814
Telephone: (916) 445-7254
Toll Free: (888) 921-2682
Email: credentials@ctc.ca.gov
www.ctc.ca.gov/

COLORADO
Colorado Department of Education
Educator Licensing
201 East Colfax Avenue
Denver, CO 80203
Telephone: (303) 866-6600
Email: educator.licensing@cde.state.co.us
www.cde.state.co.us

CONNECTICUT
Connecticut State Department of
Education
Bureau of Educator Preparation,
Certification, Support and Assessment
CT State Department of Education
Bureau of Educator Standards and
Certification
165 Capitol Avenue, Room 243
Hartford, CT 06106
Telephone: (860) 713-6969
Fax: (860) 713-7017
Email: teacher.cert@ct.gov
www.state.ct.us/sde/

DELAWARE
Delaware Department of Education
Licensure/Certification Office
Collette Education Resource Center
35 Commerce Way, Suite 1
Dover, DE 19904
Telephone: (302) 857-3388
www.doe.k12.de.us/

DISTRICT OF COLUMBIA
District of Columbia Board of Education
Office of the State Superintendent of
Education
810 1st Street NE
Washington, DC 20002
Phone: (202) 741-5881
Email: educator.licensurehelp@dc.gov
http://osse.dc.gov/

FLORIDA
Florida Department of Education
Bureau of Educator Certification
Suite 201, Turlington Building
325 West Gaines Street
Tallahassee, Florida 32399-0400
Telephone: (800) 245-0505
Outside U.S.: (850) 245-5049
www.fldoe.org/edcert

GEORGIA
Georgia Department of Education
Georgia Professional Standards
Commission
Two Peachtree Street
Suite 6000
Atlanta, GA 30303
Telephone: (404) 232-2500
Toll Free: (800) 869-7775
Email: mail@gapsc.com
www.gapsc.com

HAWAII
Hawaii State Department of Education
Hawaii Teacher Standards Board
650 Iwilei Road #201
Honolulu, HI 96817
Telephone: 808.586.2603
Email: licensingsection@htsb.org
www.htsb.org

IDAHO
Idaho State Department of Education
Certification/Professional Standards
Commission
P.O. Box 83720
650 West State Street, Room 251
Boise, ID 83720-0027
Telephone: (208) 332-6882
Email: certification@sde.idaho.gov
www.sde.idaho.gov/

ILLINOIS
Illinois State Board of Education
Education Certification Division
100 North First Street
Springfield, IL 62777-0001
Telephone: 217-557-6763
Toll Free: (866) 262-6663
www.isbe.net

INDIANA
Indiana Department of Education
Office of Licensing and Professional
Standards
101W. Ohio Street, Suite 300
Indianapolis, IN 46204
Telephone: (317) 232-9010
www.doe.in.gov/student-services/licensing

IOWA
Iowa Department of Education
Board of Educational Examiners
Licensure
Grimes State Office Building
400 East 14th Street
Des Moines, IA 50319-0146
Telephone: (515) 281-3245
http://educateiowa.gov/

KANSAS
Kansas State Department of Education
Teacher Education and Licensure Team
120 SE 10th Avenue
Topeka, KS 66612-1182
Telephone: (785) 291-3678
www.ksde.org/

KENTUCKY
Kentucky Department of Education
Education Professional Standards Board
100 Airport Road, 3rd Floor
Frankfort, KY 40601
Phone: (502) 564-4606
Toll Free: (888) 598-7667
www.kyepsb.net/

LOUISIANA
Louisiana State Department of Education
Teach Louisiana
P.O. Box 94064
Baton Rouge, LA 70804-9064
Toll Free: (877) 453-2721
Email: customerservice@la.gov
www.teachlouisiana.net/

MAINE
State of Maine Department of Education
Certification Office
23 State House Station
Augusta, ME 04333-0023
Telephone: (207) 624-6603
E-mail: cert.doe@maine.gov
www.maine.gov/education/cert

MARYLAND
Maryland State Department of Education
200 West Baltimore Street
Baltimore, MD 21201
Telephone: (410) 767-0412
www.marylandpublicschools.org/

MASSACHUSETTS
Massachusetts Department of Education
Elementary and Secondary
75 Pleasant Street
Malden, MA 02148-4906
Telephone: (781) 338-3000
www.doe.mass.edu/educators

MICHIGAN
Michigan Department of Education
608 West Allegan Street
P.O. Box 30008
Lansing, MI 48909
Telephone: (517) 373-3324
www.michigan.gov/mde

MINNESOTA
Minnesota Department of Education
Educator Licensing
1500 Highway 36 West
Roseville, MN 55113
E-mail: mde.commissioner@state.mn.us
http://education.state.mn.us/mde

MISSISSIPPI
Mississippi Department of Education
Office of Educator Licensure
Central High School Building, Suite 225
P.O. Box 771
Jackson, MS 39205-0771
Telephone: (601) 359-3483
Email: teachersupport@mde.k12.ms.us
www.mde.k12.ms.us/educator-licensure

MISSOURI
Missouri Department of Elementary and
Secondary Education
Educator Certification
P.O. Box 480
205 Jefferson Street
Jefferson City, MO 65102
Telephone: (573) 751-4212
http://dese.mo.gov/

MONTANA
Montana Office of Public Instruction
Montana Educator Licensure Program
P.O. Box 202501
Helena, MT 59620-2501
Telephone: (406) 444-3150
Email: cert@mt.gov
http://opi.mt.gov/cert/index.html

NEBRASKA
Nebraska Department of Education
301 Centennial Mall South
P.O. Box 94987
Lincoln, NE 68509
Telephone: (402) 471-0739
www.education.ne.gov/tcert/

NEVADA
Nevada Department of Education
Teacher Licensing Office—Southern Office
9890 South Maryland Parkway,
Suite 231, Room 234
Las Vegas, NV 89183
Telephone: (702) 486-6458
Teacher Licensing Office—Northern Office
700 East Fifth Street
Carson City, NV 89701
Telephone: (775) 687-9115
http://nvteachers.doe.nv.gov/

NEW HAMPSHIRE
New Hampshire
Department of Education
101 Pleasant Street
Concord, NH 03301-3860
Telephone: (603) 271-3494
www.education.nh.gov/certification/

NEW JERSEY
New Jersey Department of Education
Office of Licensure & Credentials
P.O. Box 500
Trenton, NJ 08625-0500
Telephone: (609) 292-2070
www.nj.gov/education/educators/
license/

NEW MEXICO
New Mexico Public
Education Department
Jerry Apodaca Education Building
Professional Licensure Bureau
300 Don Gaspar
Santa Fe, NM 87501
Telephone: (505) 827-5821
Email: LicensureUnit@state.nm.us
www.ped.state.nm.us/licensure/

NEW YORK
New York State Education Department
Teacher Certification Unit
89 Washington Avenue
Albany, New York 12234
Telephone: (518) 474-3901
www.nysed.gov/

NORTH CAROLINA
North Carolina Department of Public
Instruction
Licensure Section
6365 Mail Service Center
Raleigh NC 27699-6365
Telephone: (800) 577-7994
(within North Carolina)
Telephone: (919) 807-3310
(outside of North Carolina)
www.ncpublicschools.org/licensure/

NORTH DAKOTA
North Dakota Education Standards and
Practices Board
2718 Gateway Avenue, Suite 303
Bismarck, ND 58503-0585
Telephone: (701) 328-9641
E-mail: espbinfo@nd.gov
www.nd.gov/espb/

OHIO
Ohio Department of Education
Office of Educator Licensure
25 South Front St.
Columbus, OH 43215-4183
Telephone: (614) 466-3593
Toll Free: (877) 644-6338
www.ode.state.oh.us/

OKLAHOMA
Oklahoma State Department of Education
Teacher Certification
Hodge Education Building—Room 212
2500 North Lincoln Boulevard
Oklahoma City, OK 73105-4599
Telephone: (405) 521-3301
Email: sdeservicedesk@sde.ok.gov
www.ok.gov/sde/

OREGON
Oregon Department of Education
The Teacher Standards and Practices
Commission
250 Division St. NE
Salem, OR 97301
Telephone: (503) 378-3586
Email: contact.tspc@state.or.us
www.oregon.gov/tspc

PENNSYLVANIA
Pennsylvania Department of Education
Teacher Certification
333 Market Street
Harrisburg, PA 17126-0333
Telephone: (717) 728-3224
E-mail: ra-teachercert@state.pa.us
www.pde.state.pa.us/

RHODE ISLAND
Rhode Island Department of Elementary
and Secondary Education
Office of Educator Quality and Certification
Room 400
The Shepard Building
255 Westminster Street
Providence, RI 02903-3400
Telephone: (401) 222-4600

Email: EQAC@ride.ri.gov
www.ride.ri.gov

SOUTH CAROLINA
South Carolina Department of Education
Office of Educator Certification,
Recruitment, and Preparation
Landmark II Office Building, Suite 500
3700 Forest Drive
Columbia, SC 29204
Telephone: (803) 734-8466
Toll Free: (877) 885-5280 (in South Carolina)
http://ed.sc.gov/agency/se/
Educator-Certification/

SOUTH DAKOTA
South Dakota Department of Education
Certification
700 Governors Drive
Pierre, SD 57501
Telephone: (605) 773-3134
E-mail: certification@state.sd.us
www.doe.sd.gov/oatq/teachercert.aspx

TENNESSEE
Tennessee Department of Education
Office of Teacher Licensing
4th Floor Andrew Johnson Tower
710 James Robertson Parkway
Nashville, TN 37243-0377
Telephone: (615) 532-4885
E-mail: Education.Licensing@state.tn.us
www.tn.gov/education/lic/

TEXAS
Texas Education Agency
Educator Certification & Standards
1701 North Congress Avenue
Austin, TX 78701-1494
Telephone: (512) 463-9734
www.tea.state.tx.us/index.aspx

UTAH
State of Utah Office of Education
250 East 500 South
P.O. Box 144200
Salt Lake City, UT 84114-4200
Telephone: (801) 538-7740
www.schools.utah.gov/cert/

VERMONT
Vermont Department of Education
120 State Street
Montpelier, VT 05620
and
1311 U.S. Route 302,

Berlin, VT 05602
Phone: (802) 828-2445
E-mail: DOE-LicensingInfo@state.vt.us
http://education.vermont.
gov/new/html/maincert.html

VIRGINIA
Virginia Department of Education
Division of Teacher Education and
Licensure
P.O. Box 2120
Richmond, VA 23218
Telephone: (804) 371-2471
www.doe.virginia.gov/teaching/licensure

WASHINGTON
Office of Superintendent of Public
Instruction
Old Capitol Building
600 Washington Street, SE
P.O. Box 47200
Olympia, WA 98504-7200
Telephone: (360) 725-6400
Email: cert@k12.wa.us
www.k12.wa.us/certification/

WEST VIRGINIA
West Virginia Department of Education
1900 Kanawha Boulevard East
Charleston, WV 25305
Telephone: (800) 982-2378
Toll Free 1-932-962-2378
http://wvde.state.wv.us/certification

WISCONSIN
Wisconsin Department of Public
Instruction
Teacher Education, Professional
Development, and Licensing
125 South Webster Street
P.O. Box 7841
Madison, WI 53707-7841
Telephone: (608) 266-1027
Email: licensing@dpi.wi.gov
http://dpi.wi.gov/tepdl/licensing.html

WYOMING
Wyoming Department of Education
Professional Teaching
Standards Board
1920 Thomes Avenue
Suite 400
Cheyenne, WY 82002
Telephone: (307) 777-7291
Toll free: (800) 675-6893
http://ptsb.state.wy.us/

INTASC Standards: Concepts and Content in
Teachers, Schools, and Society, Tenth Edition

As you use the book, you will discover that each chapter typically touches upon several INTASC standards. However, for extra guidance, this chart identifies specific chapters and *RAP (Reflective Activities and Your Portfolio)* activities related to a specific INTASC standard.

INTASC Standard	*Teachers, Schools, and Society* **Chapter, Page**	*RAP**
Standard 1: Learner Development The teacher understands how children learn and develop, recognizing that patterns of learning and development vary individually within and across the cognitive, linguistic, social, emotional, and physical areas, and designs and implements developmentally appropriate and challenging learning experiences.	Multiple Intelligences, Ch. 2, p. 26 Emotional Intelligence, Ch. 2, p. 29 Learning Styles, Ch. 2, p. 31 Do Boys and Girls Learn Differently? Ch. 2, p. 33 The Gifted and Talented, Ch. 2, p. 36 Special Education, Ch. 2, p. 39 The Gendered World of Elementary and Middle Schools, Ch. 4, p. 109 High School: Lessons in Social Status, Ch. 4, p. 113 Social Challenges Come to School, Ch. 4, p. 116 Poverty, Ch. 4, p. 118 Children at Promise or at Risk?, Ch. 4, p. 121 Obesity and eating disorders, Ch. 4, p. 125	Getting to Know Whom, RAP 1.1, p. 90 Scoping School Culture, RAP 2.1, p. 201 Money Matters, RAP 3.1, p. 332 Developmental and Psychosocial Stages of Students, RAP 4.1, p. 418
Standard 2: Learning Differences The teacher uses understanding of individual differences and diverse cultures and communities to ensure inclusive learning environments that enable each learner to meet high standards.	Multiple Intelligences, Ch. 2, p. 26 Emotional Intelligence, Ch. 2, p. 29 Learning Styles, Ch. 2, p. 31 Do Boys and Girls Learn Differently? Ch. 2, p. 33 The Gifted and Talented, Ch. 2, p. 36 Special Education, Ch. 2, p. 39 Failing at Fairness, Ch. 3, p. 52 Lesbian, Gay, Bisexual, and Transgender Students (LGBT), Ch. 3, p. 54 Putting a Price on Racism, Ch. 3, p. 56 Theories of Why Some Groups Succeed and Others Do Not, Ch. 3, p. 57 From the Melting Pot to Cultural Pluralism, Ch. 3, p. 58 Bilingual Education, Ch. 3, p. 60 Multicultural Education Ch. 3, p. 66 Culturally Responsive Teaching Ch. 3, p. 69 Family Patterns, Ch. 4, p. 116 The Struggle for a Chance to Learn: Black Americans, Hispanics, Asian Americans and Pacific Islanders, Arab Americans, and Women, Ch. 7, p. 225–236	Multiple Intelligence Bingo, RAP 1.2, p. 90 Curriculum Bias Detectors, RAP 2.2, p. 202 Philosophy on the Big Screen, RAP 3.2, p. 332 Observing Different Teaching Strategies, RAP 4.2, p. 419
Standard 3: Learning Environments The teacher works with others to create environments that support individual and collaborative learning, and that encourage positive social interaction, active engagement in learning, and self-motivation.	Culturally Responsive Teaching, Ch. 3, p. 69 Rules, Rituals, and Routines, Ch. 4, p. 101 Teaching and Ethics, Ch. 10, p. 322 Classroom Management, Ch. 11, p. 343 Models for Effective Instruction, Ch. 11, p. 362 Your First Day: Creating a Productive Classroom Climate, Ch. 12, p. 380	Why Teach? RAP 1.3, p. 91 Effective Schools, RAP 2.3, p. 202 What You See and What You Get, RAP 3.3, p. 333 Rules, Rituals, and Routines, RAP 4.3, p. 420

Standard 4: Content Knowledge The teacher understands the central concepts, tools of inquiry, and structures of the discipline(s) he or she teaches and creates learning experiences that make the discipline accessible and meaningful for learners to ensure mastery of the content.	American Schools: Better Than We Think?, Ch. 1, p. 17 What Is the Purpose of School?, Ch. 5, p. 134 What Makes a School Effective?, Ch. 5, p. 141 Curriculum, Standards, and Testing, Ch. 6, p. 166 The Visible Curriculum, Ch. 6, p. 168 The Invisible Curriculum, Ch. 6, p. 168 Who and What Shape the Curriculum?, Ch. 6, p. 170 Common Core State Standards, Ch. 6, p. 177 Five Philosophies of Education, Ch. 8, p. 250	Teacher Interview in Your Subject Area, RAP 1.4, p. 92 State and National Curricular Standards RAP 2.4, p. 203 Self-Fulfilling Prophecy, RAP 3.4, p. 333 Teaching is Learning, RAP 4.4, p. 421
Standard 5: Application of Content Knowledge The teacher understands how to connect concepts and use differing perspectives to engage learners in critical thinking, creativity, and collaborative problem solving related to authentic local and global issues.	Multiple Intelligences, Ch. 2, p. 26 Emotional Intelligence, Ch. 2, p. 29 Learning Styles, Ch. 2, p. 31 Do Boys and Girls Learn Differently? Ch. 2, p. 33 The Gifted and Talented, Ch. 2, p. 36 Special Education, Ch. 2, p. 39 Culturally Responsive Teaching, Ch. 3, p. 69 Today's Classroom, Ch. 3, p. 74 Teacher-Centered Philosophies, Ch. 8, p. 250 Student-Centered Philosophies, Ch. 8, p. 254 Learning Time, Ch. 11, p. 342 Classroom Management, Ch. 11, p. 343 The Pedagogical Cycle, Ch. 11, p. 349 Technology as a Tool for Effective Teaching, Ch. 11, p. 360 Models for Effective Instruction, Ch. 11, p. 362 Your First Day: Creating a Productive Classroom Climate, Ch. 12, p. 380	Creating a Career Information Document, RAP 1.5, p. 93 A Public Service Announcement: The Purpose of School, RAP 2.5, p. 203 Putting Your Philosophy into the Classroom, RAP 3.5, p. 334 Class Comedy Club, RAP 4.5, p. 423
Standard 6: Assessment The teacher understands and uses multiple methods of assessment to engage learners in their own growth, to monitor learner progress, and to guide the teacher's and learner's decision making.	America's Schools: Better Than We Think? Ch. 1, p. 17 The Other Side of the Tracks, Ch. 4, p. 105 What Makes a School Effective?, Ch. 5, p. 141 The Testing Legacy of *No Child Left Behind*, Ch. 6, p. 176 Common Core State Standards, Ch. 6, p. 177 The Problem with Standardized Tests, Ch. 6, p. 179 Evaluating Teachers by Student Test Scores, Ch. 6, p. 186 Alternatives to High-Stakes Testing, Ch. 6, p. 187 A Few More Thoughts on Effective Teaching, Ch. 11, p. 369 The Intangible (But Very Real) Rewards of Teaching, Ch. 12, p. 386 How Do I Apply for a Teaching Job? Do I need a Résumé or a Portfolio?, Ch. 13, p. 403 What Are Teacher Competency Tests? Ch. 13, p. 409	A Novel Read, RAP 1.6, p. 93 Memoirs of a Time-Tested Student, RAP 2.6, p. 204 Assessing the Assessor, RAP 3.6, p. 335 Pruning Your Portfolio Dyads, RAP 4.6, p. 423
Standard 7: Planning for Instruction The teacher plans instruction that supports every student in meeting rigorous learning goals by drawing upon knowledge of content areas, curriculum, cross-disciplinary skills, and pedagogy, as well as knowledge of learners and the community context.	Culturally Responsive Teaching, Ch. 3, p. 69 Rules, Rituals and Routines, Ch. 4, p. 101 Watching the Clock, Ch. 4, p. 102 The Teacher as Gatekeeper, Ch. 4, p. 104 Learning Time, Ch. 11, p. 342 The Pedagogical Cycle, Ch. 11, p. 349 Direct Teaching, Cooperative, Learning, Mastery Learning, Problem-Based Learning, and Differentiated Instruction, Ch. 11, p. 362–369 Technology as a Tool for Effective Teaching, Ch. 11, p. 368 A Few More Thoughts on Effective Teaching, Ch. 11, p. 369	Planning for Diversity: A Lesson Plan, RAP 1.7, p. 94 A Real In-Service Program, RAP 2.7, p. 205 Students' Bill of Rights and Responsibilities, RAP 3.7, p. 336 Technology in the Classroom: Bane or Boom? RAP 4.7, p. 424

Standard 8: Instructional Strategies The teacher understands and uses a variety of instructional strategies to encourage learners to develop deep understanding of content areas and their connections, and to build skills to apply knowledge in meaningful ways.	Multiple Intelligences, Ch 2, p. 26 Emotional Intelligence, Ch. 2, p. 29 Learning Styles, Ch 2, p. 31 Do Boys and Girls Learn Differently? Ch 2, p. 33 The Gifted and Talented, Ch 2, p. 36 Special Education, Ch 2, p. 39 Bilingual Education, Ch. 3, p. 60 Multicultural Education, Ch. 3, p. 66 Culturally Responsive Teaching, Ch. 3, p. 69 Teacher-Centered Philosophies, Ch. 8, p. 250 Student-Centered Philosophies, Ch. 8, p. 254 Direct Teaching, Cooperative, Learning, Mastery Learning, Problem-Based Learning, and Differentiated Instruction, Ch. 11, p. 362–369	If the Walls Could Speak, RAP 1.8, p. 95 Visit a "Choice" School, RAP 2.8, p. 205 The Great Lecture Theory of Learning, RAP 3.8, p. 337 Memories of a Teacher, RAP 4.8, p. 425
Standard 9: Professional Learning and Ethical Practice The teacher engages in ongoing professional learning and uses evidence to continually evaluate his/her practice, particularly the effects of his or her choices and actions on others (learners, families, other professionals, and the community), and adapts practice to meet the needs of each learner.	The reflection questions throughout the text in the graphs, figures, and features will help guide your professional development. A Teaching Career—Is it Right For You? Ch. 1, p. 3 Professionalism at the Crossroads, Ch. 1, p. 8 From Normal Schools to Board-Certified Teachers, Ch. 1, p. 8 Social Challenges Come to School, p.4, 116 What Is the Purpose of School? Ch. 5, p. 134 What Makes a School Effective?, Ch. 5, p. 141 Teachers, Students, and Reform, Ch. 5, p. 158 Finding Your Philosophy of Education, Ch. 8, p. 246 Teaching and Ethics, Ch. 10, p. 322 A Few More Thoughts on Effective Teaching, Ch. 11, p. 369	Nontraditional Hero, RAP 1.9, p. 96 Reflections of a High School Yearbook, RAP 2.9, p. 206 Publication of the Month, RAP 3.9, p. 338 Web Site of the Month, RAP 4.9, p. 425
Standard 10: Leadership and Collaboration The teacher seeks appropriate leadership roles and opportunities to take responsibility for student learning, to collaborate with learners, families, colleagues, other school professionals, and community members to ensure learner growth, and to advance the profession.	The reflection questions throughout the text in the graphs, figures, and features will help guide your professional development. Family Patterns, Ch. 4, p. 116 What Makes a School Effective?, Ch. 5, p. 141 Teachers, Students, and Reform, Ch. 5, p. 158 Governing America's Schools, Ch. 9, p. 288 Stages of Teacher Development, Ch. 12, p. 374 Your First Year: Induction into the Profession, Ch.12, p. 374 Educational Associations, Ch. 12, p. 389 Who Are My Teaching Colleagues? What Are the Demographics of Today's Teachers? , Ch. 13, p. 402	Special Education Services, RAP 1.10, p. 44 Support Staff Interview, RAP 2.10, p. 128 Get on Board, RAP 3.10, p. 292 Go on an Information Interview, RAP 4.10, p. 405

* The first number of each RAP reflects the part of the text where it is located. The second number is the related INTASC Standard.

Glossary

A

A Nation at Risk: The Imperative for Education Reform A 1983 federal report that characterized U.S. schools as mediocre, putting the nation at risk of losing economic and technological ground to other countries. The report called for renewed emphasis on core academic subjects and ushered in the era of "back-to-basics" education.

ability grouping The assignment of pupils to homogeneous groups according to intellectual ability or level for instructional purposes.

academic freedom The opportunity for teachers and students to learn, teach, study, research, and question without censorship, coercion, or external political and other restrictive influences.

academic learning time The time a student is actively engaged with the subject matter and experiencing a high success rate.

academy A classical secondary school in colonial America that emphasized elements of Latin and English grammar schools and by the nineteenth century became more of a college preparatory school. Also the name of the ancient Greek school founded by Plato.

accelerated program The more rapid promotion of gifted students through school.

accountability The obligation of schools and teachers to be held responsible for student performance.

accreditation Certification of an education program or a school that has met professional standards of an outside agency.

acculturation The acquisition of the dominant culture's norms by a member of the nondominant culture. The nondominant culture typically loses its own culture, language, and sometimes religion in this process.

achievement tests Examinations of the knowledge and skills acquired, usually as a result of specific instruction.

adequate education A legal approach that ensures educational opportunities for poorer students based on state constitution guarantees for an efficient, thorough, or uniform education. Calls for adequate education have replaced previous calls for equal educational expenditures.

Advanced Placement (AP) A curriculum that offers college-level courses to high school students. Students who score high enough on a qualifying exam can earn college credit.

aesthetics The branch of philosophy that examines the nature of beauty and judgments about it.

affective domain The area of learning that involves attitudes, values, and emotions.

affirmative action A plan by which personnel policies and hiring practices reflect positive steps in the recruiting and hiring of women and people of color.

allocated time The amount of time a school or an individual teacher schedules for a subject.

American Federation of Teachers (AFT) A national organization of teachers that is primarily concerned with improving educational conditions and protecting teachers' rights.

American Spelling Book An early elementary textbook written by Noah Webster that focused on the alphabet, grammar, and moral lessons.

Americanization The acculturation of American norms and values.

appropriate education A part of Public Law 94-142 that protects the right of students with disabilities to an education that reflects an accurate diagnosis.

assimilation See **enculturation.**

assistive (adaptive) technology Devices that help the disabled to perform and learn more effectively, from voice-activated keyboards and mechanical wheelchairs to laptops for class note taking and personal scheduling.

authentic assessment A type of evaluation that represents actual performance, encourages students to reflect on their own work, and is integrated into the student's whole learning process. Such tests usually require that students synthesize knowledge from different areas and use that knowledge actively.

B

back to basics During the 1980s, a revival of the back-to-basics movement evolved out of concern for declining test scores in math, science, reading, and other areas. Although there is not a precise definition of back to basics, many consider it to include increased emphasis on reading, writing, and arithmetic, fewer electives, and more rigorous grading.

behavior modification A strategy to alter behavior in a desired direction through the use of rewards.

behavioral objective A specific statement of what a learner must accomplish to demonstrate mastery.

behaviorism A psychological theory that interprets human behavior in terms of stimuli-response.

bilingual education Educational programs in which students of limited or no English-speaking ability attend classes taught in English, as well as in their native language. There is great variability in these programs in goals, instructional opportunity, and balance between English and a student's native language.

block grants Federal dollars provided to the states, with limited federal restrictions, for educational aid and program funding.

block scheduling The use of longer "blocks" of time to schedule classes, resulting in fewer but longer periods given to each subject. It is designed to promote greater in-depth study.

Bloom's taxonomy A classification system in which each lower level is subsumed in the next higher level. The Bloom's taxonomy describes simple to more complex mental processes, and usually is used to classify educational objectives or classroom questions.

board of education Constituted at the state and local levels, an agency responsible for formulating educational policy. Members are sometimes appointed, but more frequently are elected at the local level.

bond A certificate of debt issued by a government guaranteeing payment of the original investment plus interest by a specified future date. Bonds are used by local communities to raise the funds they need to build or repair schools.

Brown v. Board of Education of Topeka U.S. Supreme Court ruling that reversed an earlier "separate but equal" ruling and declared that segregated schooling was inherently unequal and therefore unlawful.

Buckley Amendment The 1974 Family Educational Rights and Privacy Act granting parents of students under 18, and students 18 or over the right to examine their school records.

busing A method for remedying segregation by transporting students to create more ethnically or racially balanced schools. Before busing and desegregation were linked, busing was not a controversial issue, and, in fact, the vast majority of students riding school buses are not involved in desegregation programs.

C

Campbell's law The more any quantitative social indicator is used for social decision making, the more subject it will be to corruption pressures and the more apt it will be to distort and corrupt the social processes it was intended to monitor.

career ladder A system designed to create different status levels for teachers by developing steps one can climb to receive increased pay through increased responsibility or experience.

career technical education A program to teach elementary and secondary students about the world of work by integrating career awareness and exploration across the school curriculum.

Cartesian dualism The belief that reality is composed of both materialism and idealism, body and mind.

categorical grant Financial aid to local school districts from state or federal agencies for specific purposes.

certification State government's or a professional association's evaluation and approval of an applicant's competencies.

character education A model composed of various strategies that promote a defined set of core values to students.

charter school A school established by a charter between a local school board or a state government and a group of teachers, parents, and even businesses. A charter school is exempt from many state and local regulations. Designed to promote creative new schools, the charter represents legal permission to try new approaches to educate students. The first charter legislation was passed in Minnesota in 1991.

chief state school officer The executive head of a state department of education. The chief state school officer is responsible for carrying out the mandates of the state board of education and enforcing educational laws and regulations. This position is also referred to as *state superintendent*.

child abuse Physical, sexual, or emotional violation of a child's health and well-being.

child-centered instruction (individual instruction) Teaching that is designed to meet the interests and needs of individual students.

classroom climate The physical, emotional, and aesthetic characteristics, as well as the learning resources, of a school classroom.

Coalition of Essential Schools (CES) A reform effort founded by Theodore Sizer that creates smaller schools, learning communities, and more in-depth study of the curriculum.

cognitive domain The area of learning that involves knowledge, information, and intellectual skills.

Coleman report A study commissioned by President Johnson (1964) to analyze the factors that influence the academic achievement of students. One of the major findings of James Coleman's report was that schools in general have relatively little impact on learning. Family and peers were found to have more impact on a child's education than the school itself did.

collaborative action research (CAR) A program that connects teaching and professional growth through the use of research relevant to classroom responsibilities.

collaborative decision making An effort to empower teachers in which teachers share power with the school principal and actively participate in curricular, budgetary, and other school policy decisions.

collective bargaining A negotiating procedure between employer and employees for resolving disagreements on salaries, work schedules, and other conditions of employment. In collective bargaining, all teachers in a school system bargain as one group through chosen representatives.

Comer model A program created and disseminated by James Comer of Yale that incorporates a team of educational and mental health professionals to assist children at risk by working with their parents and attending to social, educational, and psychological needs.

Common Core State Standards Identifies the skills and content a student should master at each grade level from kindergarten through grade 12.

common school A public, tax-supported school. First established in Massachusetts, the school's purpose was to create a common basis of knowledge for children. It usually refers to a public elementary school.

community schools Schools connected with a local community to provide for the educational needs of that community.

compensatory education Educational experiences and opportunities designed to overcome or compensate for difficulties associated with a student's disadvantaged background.

competency The ability to perform a particular skill or to demonstrate a specified level of knowledge.

comprehensive high school A public secondary school that offers a variety of curricula, including vocational, academic, and general education programs.

comprehensive values education An approach to moral education that integrates traditional and progressive strategies for teaching values.

compulsory attendance A state law requiring that children and adolescents attend school until reaching a specified age.

computer-assisted instruction (CAI) Individualized instruction between a student and programmed instructional material stored in a computer.

computer-managed instruction (CMI) A recordkeeping procedure for tracking student performance using a computer.

consolidation The trend toward combining small or rural school districts into larger ones.

constructivism With roots in cognitive psychology, an educational approach built on the idea that people construct their understanding of the world. Constructivist teachers gauge a student's prior knowledge, then carefully orchestrate cues, classroom activities, and penetrating questions to push students to higher levels of understanding.

content standards The knowledge, skills, and dispositions that students should master in each subject. These standards are often linked to broader themes and sometimes to testing programs.

cooperative learning An instructional model in which students work on activities in small groups and receive rewards based on the overall group performance.

copyright laws (Copyright Act) A federal law that protects intellectual property, including copyrighted material. Teachers can use such material in classrooms only with permission, or under specific guidelines.

core curriculum A central body of knowledge that schools require all students to study.

core knowledge Awareness of the central ideas, beliefs, personalities, writings, events, etc. of a culture. Also termed *cultural literacy*.

corporal punishment The physical disciplining of a student by a school employee.

covert power This is the unofficial power wielded in schools by parents, vocal individuals, a school secretary, businesses, community and other groups not a part of official school governance.

creationism The position that God created the universe, the earth, and living things on the earth in precisely the manner described in the Old Testament, in six, 24-hour periods.

critical pedagogy An education philosophy that unites the theory of critical thinking with actual practice in real-world settings. The purpose is to eliminate the cultural and educational hegemony and encourage students to apply critical thinking skills to the real world, becoming agents for social change.

critical thinking skills Higher-order intellectual skills such as comparing, interpreting, observing, summarizing, classifying, creating, and criticizing.

cultural difference theory A theory that asserts that academic problems can be overcome if educators study and mediate the cultural gap separating school and home.

cultural literacy Knowledge of the people, places, events, idioms and informal content of the dominant culture.

cultural pluralism Acceptance and encouragement of cultural diversity.

culturally responsive teaching An approach to multicultural education that recognizes that students learn in different ways, and that effective teachers recognize and respond to those differences. This approach also mediates the frequent mismatch between home and school cultures and honors cultural heritages.

culture A set of learned beliefs, values, and behaviors; a way of life shared by members of a society.

curriculum (formal, explicit) Planned content of instruction that enables the school to meet its aims.

curriculum development The processes of assessing needs, formulating objectives, and developing instructional opportunities and evaluation.

D

dame schools Primary schools in colonial and other early periods in which students were taught by untrained women in the women's own homes.

de facto segregation The segregation of racial or other groups resulting from circumstances, such as housing patterns, rather than from official policy or law.

de jure segregation The segregation of racial or other groups on the basis of law, policy, or a practice designed to accomplish such separation.

decentralization The trend of dividing large school districts into smaller and, it is hoped, more responsive units.

deductive reasoning Working from a general rule to identify particular examples and applications to that rule.

deficit theory A theory that asserts that the values, language patterns, and behaviors that children from certain racial and ethnic groups bring to school put them at an educational disadvantage.

delegate representative Form of representative government in which the interests of a particular geographic region are represented through an individual or "delegate." Some school boards are organized so that members act as delegates of a neighborhood or region.

demographic forecasting The study and predictions of people and their vital statistics.

descriptive data Information that provides an objective depiction of various aspects of school or classroom life.

desegregation The process of correcting past practices of racial or other illegal segregation.

differentiated instruction An approach to teaching in which instructional activities are organized in response to individual learning differences. Teachers are asked to carefully consider each student's needs, learning style, life experience, and readiness to learn.

digital divide A term used to describe the technological gap between the "haves" and the "have-nots." Race, gender, class, and geography are some of the demographic factors influencing technological access and achievement.

direct teaching A model of instruction in which the teacher is a strong leader who structures the classroom and sequences subject matter to reflect a clear academic focus. This model emphasizes the importance of a structured lesson in which presentation of new information is followed by student practice and teacher feedback.

disability A learning or physical condition, a behavior, or an emotional problem that impedes education. Educators now prefer to speak of "students with disabilities," not "handicapped students," emphasizing the person, not the disability.

distance learning Courses, programs, and training provided to students over long distances through television, the Internet, and other technologies.

dual-language instruction A language maintenance approach in which students develop cognitively in two languages, learning about the culture and history of their ethnic group as well as that of the dominant culture.

due process The procedural requirements that must be followed in such areas as student and teacher discipline and placement in special education programs. Due process exists to safeguard individuals from arbitrary, capricious, or unreasonable policies, practices, or actions. The essential elements of due process are (1) a notice of the charge or actions to be taken, (2) the opportunity to be heard, (3) and the right to a defense that reflects the particular circumstances and nature of the case.

E

early childhood education Learning undertaken by young children in the home, in nursery schools, in preschools, and in kindergartens.

eclecticism In this text, the drawing on of elements from several educational philosophies or methods.

educable child A developmentally disabled child who is capable of achieving only a limited basic learning and usually must be instructed in a special class.

educational malpractice A new experimental line of litigation similar to the concept of medical malpractice. Educational malpractice is concerned with assessing liability for students who graduate from school without fundamental skills. However, many courts have rejected the notion that schools or educators be held liable for this problem.

educational partnership A business relationship between schools and corporations through which companies offer schools services and products and often have their corporate names used in the schools.

Eight-Year Study Educator Ralph Tyler's study in the 1930s that indicated the effectiveness of progressive education.

elementary school An educational institution for children in grades 1 through 5, 6, or 8, often including kindergarten.

emergency license A substandard license that recognizes teachers who have not met all the requirements for licensure. It is issued on a temporary basis to meet the needs of communities that do not have licensed teachers available.

emotional intelligence (EQ) A new human dimension that measures personality characteristics, such as persistence. Some believe that EQ scores may be better predictors of future success than IQ scores.

empiricism The philosophy that maintains that sensory experiences, such as seeing, hearing, and touching, are the ultimate sources of all human knowledge. Empiricists believe that we experience the external world by sensory perception; then, through reflection, we conceptualize ideas that help us interpret the world.

enculturation The process of acquiring a culture; a child's acquisition of the cultural heritage through both formal and informal educational means.

endorsement The extension of a license through additional work to include a second teaching field.

engaged time The part of time that a teacher schedules for a subject in which the students are actively involved with academic subject matter. Listening to a lecture, participating in a class discussion, and working on math problems all constitute engaged time.

English as a Second Language (ESL) An immersion approach to bilingual education that removes students from the regular classroom to provide instruction in English.

English Classical School The first free public high school, established in Boston in 1821. The school initially enrolled only boys.

English grammar schools Private schools that taught commerce, navigation, engineering, and other vocational skills. The demand for a more practical education in eighteenth-century America led to the creation of these schools.

English language learners (ELL) Students whose native language is not English and are learning to speak and write English. Also referred to as *limited English proficiency* or LEP.

English-only movement (also known as Official English movement) Refers to the political effort to establish English as the only official language in the United States of America, and the only language to be used for official government activities, such as voting.

environmental education The study and analysis of the conditions and causes of pollution, overpopulation, and waste of natural resources, and of the ways to preserve Earth's intricate ecology.

epistemology The branch of philosophy that examines the nature of knowledge and learning.

equal educational opportunity A term that refers to giving every student the educational opportunity to develop fully whatever talents, interests, and abilities he or she may have, without regard to race, color, national origin, sex, disability, or economic status.

equity Educational policy and practice that are just, fair, and free from bias and discrimination.

essentialism An educational philosophy that emphasizes basic skills of reading, writing, mathematics, science, history, geography, and language.

establishment clause A section of the First Amendment of the U.S. Constitution that says that Congress shall make no law respecting the establishment of religion. This clause prohibits nonparochial schools from teaching religion.

ethics The branch of philosophy that examines questions of right and wrong, good and bad.

ethnic group A group of people with a distinctive culture and history.

ethnicity A term that refers to shared common cultural traits such as language, religion, and dress. A Latino or Hispanic, for example, belongs to an ethnic group, but might belong to the Black, Caucasian, or Asian race.

ethnocentrism The tendency to view one's own culture as superior to others, or to fail to consider other cultures in a fair manner.

evaluation Assessment of learning and instruction.

evolution As put forth by Charles Darwin, a keystone of modern biological theory and postulates that animals and plants have their origin in other preexisting types and that there are modifications in successive generations.

exceptional learners Students who require special education and related services to realize their full potential. Categories of exceptionality include retarded, gifted, learning disabled, emotionally disturbed, and physically disabled.

existentialism A philosophy that emphasizes the ability of an individual to determine the course and nature of his or her life and the importance of personal decision making.

expectation theory First made popular by Rosenthal and Jacobson, a theory that holds that a student's academic performance can be improved if a teacher's attitudes and beliefs about that student's academic potential are modified.

expulsion Dismissal of a student from school for a lengthy period, ranging from one semester to permanently.

extracurriculum The part of school life that comprises activities, such as sports, academic and social clubs, band, chorus, orchestra, and theater. Many educators think that the extracurriculum develops important skills and values, including leadership, teamwork, creativity, and diligence.

F

failing school The term given to a school when a large proportion of its students do not do well on standardized tests or other academic measures. Critics charge that students attending such schools are not receiving their constitutionally guaranteed adequate education.

fair use A legal principle allowing limited use of copyrighted materials. Teachers must observe three criteria: brevity, spontaneity, and cumulative effect.

First Amendment The constitutional Amendment that protects freedom of religion and speech. An important part of this Amendment is the establishment clause, which prohibits schools and the government from promoting or inhibiting religion in schools.

five-factor theory of effective schools A theory, developed through school effectiveness research, that emphasizes five factors: effective leadership, monitoring student progress, safety, a clear vision, and high expectations.

Flanders Interaction Analysis An instrument developed by Ned Flanders for categorizing student and teacher verbal behavior. It is used to interpret the nature of classroom verbal interaction.

formal or explicit curriculum A school's official curriculum that is reflected in academic courses and requirements.

Fourteenth Amendment: The constitutional provision that ensures due process and equal protection under the law. This amendment also grants state and federal citizenship to all persons born or naturalized in the United States regardless of race.

Fourth Amendment: The constitutional provision that protects and individual's basic privacy and security from unreasonable searches and seizures of property.

Franklin Academy A colonial high school founded by Benjamin Franklin that accepted females as students and promoted a less classical, more practical curriculum.

full-service school Schools that provide a network of social services from nutrition and health care to parental education and transportation, all designed to support the comprehensive educational needs of children.

G

gatekeeping Philip Jackson's term describing how teachers control classroom interactions.

gender bias The degree to which an individual's beliefs and behavior are unduly influenced on the basis of gender. See also **sex discrimination.**

gender similarities hypothesis A theory suggesting that males and females are more alike than different on most psychological and intellectual variables and therefore do not demonstrate gender-specific learning styles that require unique teaching approaches.

gendered career A term applied to the gender stereotyping of career and occupational fields. Teaching, for example, was initially gendered male but today is gendered female, particularly at the elementary school level.

generalizations Broad statements about a group that offer information, clues, and insights that can help a teacher plan more effectively. Generalizations are a good starting point, but as the teacher learns more about the students, individual differences become more educationally significant.

giftedness A term describing individuals with exceptional ability. The National Association for Gifted Children defines five elements of giftedness: artistic and creative talents, intellectual and academic abilities, and leadership skills. There, however, continues to be great variance in definitions of the "gifted."

global education Because economics, politics, scientific innovation, and societal developments in different countries have an enormous impact on children in the United States, the goals of global education include increased knowledge about the peoples of the world, resolution of global problems, increased fluency in foreign languages, and the development of more tolerant attitudes toward other cultures and peoples.

Golden Mean The doctrine put forth by Aristotle asserting that virtue lies in the middle ground between two extremes.

Great Books The heart of the perennialists' curriculum that includes great works of the past in literature, philosophy, science, and other areas.

green ribbon school Schools recognized by the U.S. Department of Education as offering healthier learning environments with clean air and water, nourishing and natural foods, nontoxic cleaners, and more outdoor activities. Academic performance often improves in green schools, and absenteeism decreases.

Gun-free Schools Act Legislation enacted by Congress in 1994 that requires states receiving federal funds to establish laws regarding firearms. Schools can lose federal funds if they do not have a zero-tolerance policy mandating one-year expulsions for students bringing firearms to schools. The vast majority of schools report zero-tolerance policies for firearms.

H

Head Start Federally funded pre-elementary school program to provide learning opportunities for disadvantaged students.

hidden government The unofficial power structure within a school. It cannot be identified by the official title, position, or functions of individuals. For example, it reflects the potential influence of a school secretary or custodian.

higher-order questions Questions that require students to go beyond memory in formulating a response. These questions require students to analyze, synthesize, evaluate, and so on.

homeschooling A growing trend (but a longtime practice) of parents educating their children at home, for religious or philosophical reasons.

homogeneous grouping The classification of pupils for the purpose of forming instructional groups having a relatively high degree of intellectual similarity.

hornbook A single sheet of parchment containing the Lord's Prayer and letters of the alphabet. It was protected by a thin sheath from the flattened horn of a cow and fastened to a wooden board—hence the name. It was used during the colonial era in primary schools.

humanistic education A curriculum that stresses personal student growth; self-actualizing, moral, and aesthetic issues are explored.

I

idealism A doctrine holding that knowledge is derived from ideas and emphasizing moral and spiritual reality as a preeminent source of explanation.

ideologues Homeschool advocates focused on avoiding public schools in order to impart their own set of values.

immersion A bilingual education model that teaches students with limited English by using a "sheltered" or simplified English vocabulary, but teaching in English and not in the other language.

implicit or hidden curriculum What students learn, other than academic content, from what they do or are expected to do in school; incidental learnings.

in loco parentis Latin term meaning "in place of the parents"; that is, a teacher or school administrator assumes the duties and responsibilities of the parents during the hours the child attends school.

inclusion The practice of educating and integrating children with disabilities into regular classroom settings.

independent school A nonpublic school unaffiliated with any church or other agency.

individualized education program (IEP) The mechanism through which a disabled child's special needs are identified, objectives and services are described, and evaluation is designed.

individualized instruction Curriculum content and instructional materials, media, and activities designed for individual learning. The pace, interests, and abilities of the learner determine the curriculum.

Individuals with Disabilities Education Act (IDEA) Federal law passed in 1990 that extends full education services and provisions to people identified with disabilities.

induction program A formal program assisting new teachers to successfully adjust to their role in the classroom.

inductive reasoning Drawing generalizations based on the observation of specific examples.

informal education A practice that, in many cultures, augments or takes the place of formal schooling as children learn adult roles through observation, conversation, assisting, and imitating.

infrastructure The basic installations and facilities on which the continuance and growth of a community depend.

instruction The process of implementing a curriculum.

INTASC The Interstate New Teachers Assessment and Support Consortium, an organization that has identified competency standards for new teachers.

integrated curriculum (interdisciplinary curriculum) Subject matter from two or more areas combined into thematic units (e.g., literature and history resources to study civil rights laws).

integration The process of educating different racial and ethnic groups together, and developing positive interracial contacts.

Intelligent Design The argument that instances in nature cannot be explained by Darwinian evolution, but instead are consistent with the notion of an intelligent involvement in the design of life.

interest centers Centers that provide independent student activities related to a specific subject. Usually associated with an open classroom.

International Baccalaureate (IB) An internationally recognized curriculum for students ages 3 through 19 that includes rigorous science, math, and foreign language requirements along with diverse cultural studies. The IB program is designed to develop the intellectual, emotional, and social skills students need to learn, live, and work in our increasingly connected globalizing world.

J

junior high school A two- or three-year school between elementary and high school for students in their early adolescent years, commonly grades 7 and 8 or 7 through 9.

K

Kalamazoo, Michigan, case An 1874 U.S. Supreme Court decision that upheld the right of states to tax citizens to provide public secondary education.

kindergarten A preschool, early childhood educational environment first designed by Froebel in the mid-nineteenth century.

L

labeling Categorizing or classifying students for the purposes of educational placement. One unfortunate consequence may be that of stigmatizing students and inhibiting them from reaching their full potential.

Laboratory Schools Schools often associated with a teacher preparation institution for practice teaching, demonstration, research, or innovation.

land grant colleges State colleges or universities offering agricultural and mechanical curricula, funded originally by the Morrill Act of 1862.

Land Ordinance Act A nineteenth-century federal law that required newly settled territories to reserve a section of land for schools.

language submersion A bilingual education model that teaches students in classes where only English is spoken, the teacher does not know the language of the student, and the student either learns English as the academic work progresses or pays the consequences. This has been called a "sink or swim" approach.

last mile problem A digital divide in which geography is a factor, in part because running fiber-optic cables to rural schools is often an expense that telecommunications companies avoid. See also **digital divide.**

latchkey (self-care) kids A term used to describe children who go home after school to an empty house; their parents or guardians are usually working and not home.

Latin grammar school A classical secondary school with a Latin and Greek curriculum preparing students for college.

learning communities The creation of more personal collaboration between teachers and students to promote similar academic goals and values.

learning disability An educationally significant language and/or learning deficit.

learning styles The belief that students have diverse ways of learning, comprehending, and using information and have different preferences, ranging from preferred light and noise levels to independent or group learning formats.

least-restrictive environment The program best suited to meeting a disabled student's special needs without segregating the student from the regular educational program.

limited English proficiency (LEP) A student who has a limited ability to understand, speak, or read English and who has a native language other than English.

locus of control A concept wherein learners attribute success or failure to external or internal factors. "The teacher didn't review the material well" is an example of attribution to an external factor and represents an external locus of control. In this case, the learner avoids responsibility for behavior. When students have an internal locus of control, they believe that they control their fate and take responsibility for events.

logic The branch of philosophy that deals with reasoning. Logic defines the rules of reasoning, focuses on how to move from one set of assumptions to valid conclusions, and examines the rules of inference that enable us to frame our propositions and arguments.

looping The practice of teaching the same class for several years, over two or even more grades. The purpose is to build stronger teacher–student connections.

lower-order questions Questions that require the retrieval of memorized information and do not require more complex intellectual processes.

M

magnet school A specialized school open to all students in a district on a competitive or lottery basis. It provides a method of drawing children away from segregated neighborhood schools while affording unique educational specialties, such as science, math, and the performing arts.

mainstreaming The inclusion of special education students in the regular education program. The nature and extent of this inclusion should be based on meeting the special needs of the child.

maintenance (developmental) approach A bilingual model that emphasizes the importance of acquiring English while maintaining competence in the native language.

malfeasance Deliberately acting improperly and causing harm to someone.

mastery learning An educational practice in which an individual demonstrates mastery of one task before moving on to the next.

materialism A philosophy focused on scientific observation and the belief that existence is experienced only in the physical realm.

McGuffey Reader A reading series that, for almost 100 years, promoted moral and patriotic messages and set the practice of reading levels leading toward graded elementary schools.

McKinney Vento Homeless Assistance Act The primary piece of federal legislation dealing with the education of homeless children in public schools.

mentor A guide or an adviser, and a component of some first-year school induction programs designed to assist new teachers.

merit pay A salary system that bases a teacher's pay on performance.

metacognition Self-awareness of our thinking process as we perform various tasks and operations. For example, when students articulate how they think about academic tasks, it enhances their thinking and enables teachers to target assistance and remediation.

metaphysics The area of philosophy that examines the nature of reality.

microteaching A clinical approach to teacher training in which the teacher candidate teaches a small group of students for a brief time while concentrating on a specific teaching skill.

middle schools Two- to four-year schools of the middle grades, often grades 6 through 8, between elementary school and high school.

misfeasance Failure to act in a proper manner to prevent harm.

moral stages of development A model of moral development promoted by Lawrence Kohlberg in which individuals progress from simple moral concerns, such as avoiding punishment, to more sophisticated ethical beliefs and actions.

Morrill Act Federal legislation (1862) granting federal lands to states to establish colleges to promote more effective and efficient agriculture and industry. A second Morrill Act, passed in 1890, provided federal support for "separate but equal" colleges for African Americans.

multicultural education Educational policies and practices that not only recognize but also affirm human differences and similarities associated with gender, race, ethnicity, nationality, disability, and class.

multiple intelligences A theory developed by Howard Gardner to expand the concept of human intelligence to include such areas as logical-mathematical, linguistic, bodily-kinesthetic, musical, spatial, interpersonal, intrapersonal, and naturalist.

multiracial A term that pertains to people whose ancestry consists of more than one race. This is the fastest-growing student demographic in the United States.

N

National Assessment of Educational Progress (NAEP) Program to ascertain the effectiveness of U.S. schools and student achievement.

National Board for Professional Teacing Standards (NBPTS) An organization designed to award *board certification* to extraordinary teachers whose skills and knowledge indicate their high level of achievement.

national curricular standards Nationally prescribed or recommended standards, content skills, and testing.

National Defense Education Act (NDEA) Federally sponsored programs (1958) to improve science, math, and foreign language instruction in schools.

National Education Association (NEA) The largest organization of educators. The NEA is concerned with the overall improvement of education and the conditions of educators. It is organized at the national, state, and local levels.

networking The term used to describe the intentional effort to develop personal connections with individuals who could be helpful in finding positions or gaining professional advancement.

neuroplasticity The ability of our brain to change itself and create new neural pathways.

New England Primer One of the first textbooks in colonial America, teaching reading and moral messages.

No Child Left Behind (NCLB) A federal law passed in 2001 that emphasized high-stakes standardized testing. By 2012, the federal government allowed many states to opt out as an emphasis on national core standards took hold.

nondiscriminatory education A principle, based on the Fifth and Fourteenth Amendments of the U.S. Constitution, that mandates that children with disabilities be fairly assessed so that they can be protected from inappropriate classification and tracking.

nonfeasance Failure to exercise appropriate responsibility that results in someone's being harmed.

nongraded school A school organization in which grade levels are eliminated for two or more years.

nonverbal communication The act of transmitting and/or receiving messages through means not having to do with oral or written language, such as eye contact, facial expressions, and body language.

norm-referenced tests Tests that compare individual students with others in a designated group.

normal school A two-year teacher education institution popular in the nineteenth century. Many normal schools were expanded to become today's state colleges and universities.

Northwest Ordinance (1785, 1787) Federal legislation that provided for the sale of federal lands in the Northwest territory to support public schools.

null curriculum The curriculum that is not taught in schools.

O

objective The purpose of a lesson expressed in a statement.

objective-referenced tests Tests that measure whether students have mastered a designated body of knowledge rather than how they compare with other students in a norm group.

Old Deluder Satan Law (1647) Massachusetts colony law requiring teachers in towns of fifty families or more and that schools be built in towns of one hundred families or more. Communities must teach children to read so that they can read the Bible and thwart Satan.

open classroom A system of education, that involves not only an informal classroom environment but also a philosophy of education. Students pursue individual interests with the guidance and support of the teacher; interest centers are created to promote this individualized instruction. Students may also have a significant influence in determining the nature and sequence of the curriculum. It is sometimes referred to as *open education*.

open enrollment The practice of permitting students to attend the school of their choice within their school system. It is sometimes associated with magnet schools and desegregation efforts.

open-space school A school building without interior walls. Although it may be designed to promote the concept of the open classroom, the open-space school is an architectural concept rather than an educational one.

oral tradition Spoken language is the primary method for instruction in several cultures around the world. Word problems are used to teach reasoning, proverbs to instill wisdom, and stories to teach lessons about nature, history, religion, and social customs.

outcome based education (OBE) An educational approach that emphasizes setting learning outcomes and assessing student progress toward attaining those goals, rather than focusing on curricular topics.

P

paraprofessional A layperson who serves as an aide, assisting the teacher in the classroom.

parochial school An institution operated and controlled by a religious denomination.

pay-for-performance A salary method that attempts to make teaching more accountable by linking teacher and student performance to teacher salary (see also **merit pay**).

peace studies The study and analysis of the conditions of and need for peace, the causes of war, and the mechanisms for the nonviolent resolution of conflict. Also referred to as *peace education*.

pedagogical cycle A system of teacher–student interaction that includes four steps: structure—teacher introduces the topic; question—teacher asks questions; respond—student answers or tries to answer questions; and react—teacher reacts to student's answers and provides feedback.

pedagogy The science of teaching.

peer review The practice of having colleagues observe and assess teaching, as opposed to administrators.

perennialism The philosophy that emphasizes rationality as the major purpose of education. It asserts that the essential truths are recurring and universally true; it stresses Great Books.

performance standards Statements that describe what teachers or students should be able to do, and how well they should do it.

permanent license Although some variation exists from state to state, a permanent license is issued after a candidate has completed all the requirements for full recognition as a teacher. Requirements may include a specified number of courses beyond the bachelor's degree or a specified number of years of teaching.

philosophy The love of or search for wisdom; the quest to understand the meaning of life.

phonics An approach to reading instruction that emphasizes decoding words by sounding out letters and combinations of letters (as contrasted with the whole language approach).

Plessey* v. *Ferguson An 1896 Supreme Court decision that upheld that "separate but equal" was legal and that the races could be segregated. It was overturned in 1954 by *Brown* v. *The Board of Education of Topeka*.

political philosophy An approach to analyzing how past and present societies are arranged and governed and how better societies may be created in the future.

portfolio Compilations of work (such as papers, projects, videos, online activities) assembled to demonstrate growth, creativity and competence. Often advocated as a more comprehensive assessment than test scores.

pragmatism A philosophical belief that asserts truth is what works and rejects other views of reality.

praxis The doctrine that actions should be based on sound theory and values. (It is no accident that the term *praxis* is also the name given to the teacher competency tests required by many states.)

primary school A separately organized and administered elementary school for students in the lower elementary grades, usually grades 1 through 3, and sometimes including preprimary years.

private school A school controlled by an individual or agency other than the government, usually supported by other than public funds. Most private schools are parochial.

privatization The movement toward increased private sector, for-profit involvement in the management of public agencies, including schools.

probationary teaching period A specified period of time in which a newly hired teacher must demonstrate teaching competence. This period is usually three years for public school teachers and six years for college professors. Generally, on satisfactory completion of the probationary period, a teacher is granted tenure.

problem-based learning(PBL) An approach that builds a curriculum around intriguing real-life problems and asks students to work cooperatively to develop and demonstrate their solutions.

procedural due process The right of children with disabilities and their parents to be notified of school actions and decisions; to challenge those decisions before an impartial tribunal, using counsel and expert witnesses; to examine the school records on which a decision is based; and to appeal whatever decision is reached.

professional development School district efforts to improve knowledge, skills, and performance of its professional staff.

progressive education (progressivism) Educational practices emphasizing democracy, student needs, practical activities, and school–community relationships.

progressivism An educational philosophy that organizes schools around the concerns, curiosity, and real-world experiences of students.

property tax Local real estate taxes (also cars and personal property) historically used to fund local schools.

provisional license Also referred to as a *probationary license,* a provisional license is frequently issued to beginning teachers. It may mean that a person has completed most, but not all, of the state requirements for permanent licensure. Or it may mean that the state requires several years of teaching experience before it will qualify the teacher for permanent licensure.

Public Law 94-142 Passed in 1975, this was the first law to require schools to provide free and appropriate public education to every child with special needs. This law evolved into today's Individuals with Disabilities Education Act (IDEA).

Pygmalion in the Classroom Both a concept and a book by Robert Rosenthal and Lenore Jacobson explaining the power of teacher expectations in shaping student achievement.

R

race Refers to a group of individuals sharing common genetic attributes, physical appearance, and ancestry.

racial discrimination Actions that limit or deny a person or group any privileges, roles, or rewards on the basis of race.

racism Attitudes, beliefs, and behavior based on the notion that one race is superior to other races.

rationalism The philosophy that emphasizes the power of reason and the principles of logic to derive statements about the world. Rationalists encourage schools to emphasize teaching mathematics, because mathematics involves reason and logic.

readability formulas Formulas that use objective, quantitative measures to determine the reading level of textbooks.

reciprocity A mutual exchange of rights or benefits. For example, a teacher's license in one state is recognized as valid in another.

reconstructionism (reconstructionist) A view of education as a way to improve the quality of life, to reduce the chances of conflict, and to create a more humane world. Also called *social reconstructionism.*

reflective teaching Thoughtfully analyzing one's own teaching practices and classroom.

regular education initiative The attempt to reduce the complications and expense of segregated special education efforts by teaching special needs students in the standard educational program through collaborative consultation, curricular modifications, and environment adaptations.

résumé A summary of a person's education and experiences, often used for application to school or employment.

revenue sharing The distribution of federal money to state and local governments to use as they decide.

Robin Hood reformers State legislators favoring the redistribution of revenue from wealthier to poorer communities to equalize educational funding.

romantic critics Critics such as Paul Goodman, Herbert Kohl, and John Holt who believed that schools were stifling the cognitive and affective development of children. Individual critics stressed different problems or solutions, but they all agreed that schools were producing alienated, uncreative, and unfulfilled students.

rubric A scoring guide that describes what must be done, and often describes performance levels ranging from novice to expert, or from a failing grade to excellence.

S

scaffolding Taking from the construction field, scaffolding provides support to help a student build understanding. The teacher might use cues or encouragement or well-formulated questions to assist a student in solving a problem or mastering a concept.

school boards Elected or appointed officials who determine educational policies for school systems.

school choice The name given to several programs in which parents choose what school their child will attend.

school financing A term that refers to the ways in which monies are raised and allocated to schools. The methods differ widely from state to state, and many challenges are being made in courts today because of the unequal distribution of funds within a state or among states.

school infrastructure The basic facilities and structures that underpin a school plant, such as plumbing, sewage, heat, electricity, roof, masonry, and carpentry.

school superintendent The chief administrator of a school system, responsible for implementing and enforcing the school board's policies, rules, and regulations, as well as state and federal requirements. The superintendent is directly responsible to the school board and is the formal representative of the school community to outside individuals and agencies.

School to Work Opportunities Act Federal legislation that authorizes the funding of programs that link school learning to job settings, often developed in partnerships between school and industry.

school-based management The recent trend in education reform that stresses decision making on the school level. In the past, school policies were set by the state and the districts. Now the trend is for individual schools to make their own decisions and policies.

schools without walls An alternative education program that involves the total community as a learning resource.

second-generation segregation The separation of a school's multiracial populations through tracking, extracurricular activities, and informal social events.

secondary school A program of study that follows elementary school and includes junior, middle, and high school.

secular humanism The belief that people can live ethically without faith in a supernatural or supreme being. Some critics have alleged that secular humanism is a form of religion and that publishers are promoting secular humanism in their books.

separate but equal A legal doctrine that holds that equality of treatment is accorded when the races are provided substantially equal facilities, even though those facilities are separate. This doctrine was ruled unconstitutional in regard to race.

service credit By volunteering in a variety of community settings, from nursing homes to child care facilities, students are encouraged to develop a sense of community and meet what is now a high school graduation requirement in some states.

sex discrimination Any action that limits or denies a person or group of persons opportunities, privileges, roles, or rewards on the basis of sex.

sex-role stereotyping Attributing behavior, abilities, interests, values, and roles to a person or group of persons on the basis of sex. This process ignores individual differences.

sexism The collection of attitudes, beliefs, and behavior that results from the assumption that one sex is superior to the other.

sexual harassment Unwanted, repeated, and unreturned sexual words, behaviors, or gestures prohibited by federal and some state laws.

simulation A role-playing technique in which students take part in re-created, lifelike situations.

site-based (school-based) management A school governance method that shifts decision making from the central district office to individual schools.

social Darwinism A belief similar to Darwin's notion of "survival of the fittest," that contends that society is a natural sorting system which rewards the talented and places the less deserving at the bottom of the social and economic pecking order.

social reconstructionism See **reconstructionism.**

sociogram A diagram that is constructed to record social interactions, such as which children interact frequently and which are isolates.

Socratic method An educational strategy attributed to Socrates in which a teacher encourages a student's discovery of truth by questions.

special education Programs and instruction for children with physical, mental, emotional, or learning disabilities or gifted students who need special educational services to achieve at their ability level.

stages of teacher development A presentation of four stages that teachers pass through as they become more skilled in their craft.

standards-based education Education that specifies precisely what students should learn, focuses the curriculum and instruction (and perhaps much more) on meeting those standards, and provides continual testing to see if the standards are achieved.

state adoption The process by which members of a textbook adoption committee review and select the books used throughout a state. Advocates of this process say that it results in a common statewide curriculum that unites educators on similar issues and makes school life easier for students who move within the state. Critics charge that it gives too much influence to large states and results in a "dumbed down" curriculum.

state board of education The state education agency that regulates policies necessary to implement legislative acts related to education.

state department of education An agency that operates under the direction of the state board of education, accrediting schools, certifying teachers, appropriating state school funds, and so on.

stealth censorship (self-censorship) The quiet removal of a book from a library shelf or a course of study to avoid possible problems and parental complaints. Teachers practice the same sort of self-censorship when they choose not to teach a topic or not to discuss a difficult issue.

stereotype threat A measure of how social context, such as self-image, trust in others, and a sense of belonging, can influence academic performance.

stereotypes Absolute statements applied to all members of a group, suggesting that members of a group have a fixed, often inherited set of characteristics.

street academies Alternative schools designed to bring dropouts and potential dropouts, often inner-city youths, back into the educational mainstream.

student-initiated questions Content-related questions originating from the student yet consisting of only a small percentage of the questions asked in a typical class.

superintendent of schools The executive officer of the local school district.

T

taxonomy A classification system of organizing information and translating aims into instructional objectives.

Teach for America A program that places unlicensed college graduates in districts with critical teacher shortages as they work toward attaining a teacher license.

teacher certification State government's or a professional association's evaluation and approval of an applicant's competencies.

teacher flexibility The capability to adapt a variety of skills, abilities, characteristics, and approaches, according to the demands of each situation and the needs of each student.

teacher's license A teaching credential issued by a state government that grants the legal right to teach, not unlike a driver's license, which grants the legal right to drive.

Tenth Amendment The constitutional Amendment that establishes that areas not specifically mentioned in the Constitution as federal responsibilities are left to state authority. Since education is not mentioned, each state is free to create its own school system.

tenure A system of employment in which teachers, having served a probationary period, acquire an expectancy of continued employment. The majority of states have tenure laws.

textbook adoption states States, most often those in the South and West, that have a formal process for assessing, choosing, and approving textbooks for school use.

Title I Section of the Elementary and Secondary Education Act that provides federal funds to supplement local education resources for students from low-income families.

Title IX of the Education Amendments (1972) A provision of the 1972 Educational Amendments that prohibits sex discrimination in any educational program receiving federal financial assistance.

Title VII of the Civil Rights Act (1964) Section that prohibits employment discrimination based on race, color, religion, sex, or national origin.

tracking The method of placing students according to their ability level in homogeneous classes or learning experiences. Once a student is placed, it may be very difficult to move up from one track to another. The placements may reflect racism, classism, or sexism.

transitional bilingual education A bilingual education program in which students are taught for a limited time in their own language as well as English. The goal is to move students into English-only speaking classrooms.

trustee representatives School board members viewed as representatives of the entire community, rather than of the narrower interests of a particular group or neighborhood. This conception of a school board member's role differs from the delegate approach.

tuition tax credits Tax reductions for parents or guardians of children attending public or private schools.

U

U.S. Department of Education Federal cabinet-level agency responsible for establishing national education policies, prohibiting discrimination in education, and collecting data on student achievement and other educational issues.

unobtrusive measurement A method of measuring without affecting what is measured; indirect elicitation of data.

V

value-added A statistical measure showing the contribution of teachers and schools toward growth in student achievement. Value-added measures are increasingly used to determine which teachers are rewarded and which teachers are replaced.

values clarification A model, comprising various strategies, that encourages students to express and clarify their values on different topics.

virtual school A type of distance education offered through the Internet. Virtual schools provide asynchronous learning and may offer specialized courses not typically found in traditional schools.

voucher A coupon, issued by the government, representing money targeted for schools. In a voucher system, parents use educational vouchers to "shop" for a school. Schools receive part or all of their per-pupil funding from these vouchers. In theory, good schools would thrive and poor ones would close for lack of students.

W

wait time The amount of time a teacher waits for a student's response after a question is asked and the amount of time following a student's response before the teacher reacts.

whole language approach An approach to reading instruction that emphasizes the integration of language arts skills and knowledge, with a heavy emphasis on literature (as contrasted with a phonics approach).

women's studies Originally created during the 1970s to study the history, literature, psychology, and experiences of women, topics typically missing from the traditional curriculum.

Z

zero reject The principle that no child with disabilities may be denied a free and appropriate public education.

zero-tolerance policies Rigorous rules that offer schools little or no flexibility in responding to student infractions related to alcohol, drugs, tobacco, violence, and weapons. These policies have been developed by both local school districts and a number of state legislatures, and in most cases, students who violate such policies must be expelled.

zone of proximal development The area where students can move from what they know to new learning, a zone where real learning is possible.

Notes

CHAPTER 1   BECOMING A TEACHER

1. Frederick Buechner, *Wishful Thinking: A Seeker's ABC* (San Francisco: HarperSanFrancisco, 1993) p. 119.
2. National Education Association, *Status of the American Public School Teacher, 2000–2001* (Washington, DC: NEA, 2003); see also *The Metlife Survey of the American Teacher: Past, Present and Future* (New York: Metropolitan Life Insurance Company, October, 2008), www.metlife.com/assets/cao/contributions/citizenship/teacher-survey-25th-anniv-2008.pdf; Mathew DiCarlo, Nate Johnson, and Pat Cochran, *Survey and Analysis of Teacher Salary Trends 2007* (Washington, DC: American Federation of Teachers, 2008).
3. Andrew L. Yarrow, "State of Mind," *Education Week* 29, no. 8 (October 21, 2009), pp. 21–23.
4. Kim Marshall, "Is Merit Pay the Answer?" *Education Week* 29, no. 15 (December 15, 2009), pp. 22, 28; Justin Snider, "Tying Teacher Tenure to Student Scores Doesn't Fly," *Education Week*, www.edweek.org (retrieved February 9, 2010), in print February 10, 2010, as *The Cult of Statistical Pyrotechnics*; Stephen Sawchuk, "New Teacher-Evaluation Systems Face Obstacles: Stimulus Funds Require Districts to Revamp Teacher Yardsticks," *Education Week* 29, no. 14 (December 11, 2009), www.edweek.org; Michele Kerr, "The Right Way to Assess Teachers' Performance," *Washington Post*, June 18, 2010, p. A27; Bryan Toporek, "Poll: Americans in Favor of Teacher Merit Pay," www.teachermagazine.org (retrieved September 16, 2010).
5. Trip Gabriel and Sam Dillon, "G.O.P. Governors Take Aim at Teacher Tenure," *New York Times,* February 1, 2011, pp. A1, A3; Jeremy P. Meyer, "Colorado Renews Teacher-Tenure Debate," *Denver Post,* April 13, 2010; Jason Felch, Jessica Garrison, and Jason Song, "Bar Set Low for Lifetime Job in L.A. Schools," *Los Angeles Times,* December 20, 2009, http://latimes.com/news/local/education/la-me-teacher-tenure20-2009dec20,0,2529590.story (retrieved January 3, 2010); Julie Bykowicz, "O'Malley to Push Teacher Changes Proposal that Would Add Year to Tenure Track Might Better Position Md. for Federal Funds," *Baltimore Sun,* February 14, 2010, www.baltimoresun.com/news/education/bal-md.race-14feb14,0,1490150.story (retrieved April 7, 2010).
6. Thomas Newkirk, "Stress, Control, and the Deprofessionalizing of Teaching," *Education Week*, October 21, 2009; Jillian N. Lederhouse, "Show Me the Power," *Education Week,* June 13, 2001; National Education Association, *Status of the American Public School Teacher, 2000–2001.*
7. Ron Brandt, "On Teacher Empowerment: A Conversation with Ann Lieberman," *Educational Leadership* 46, no. 8 (May 1989), pp. 23–24; *The MetLife Survey of the American Teacher: Expectations and Experience: A Survey of Teachers, Principals, and Leaders of College Education Programs* (September 26, 2006), www.metlife.com/WPSAssets/818 21402701160505871V1F2006MetLifeTeacherSurvey.pdf (retrieved January 31, 2008).
8. Adopted from Robert Howsam et al., *Educating a Profession, Report on the Bicentennial Commission of Education for Profession of Teaching* (Washington, DC: American Association of Colleges for Teacher Education, 1976), pp. 6–7.
9. Daniel Pink, *Drive: The Surprising Truth About What Motivates Us* (New York: Riverhead, 2009) p .142.
10. *Tomorrow's Teachers: A Report of the Holmes Group* (East Lansing, MI: Holmes Group, 1986).
11. Carnegie Forum on Education and the Economy, Task Force on Teaching as a Profession, *A Nation Prepared: Teachers for the Twenty-First Century* (New York: Forum, 1986).
12. Scott Stephens and Edith Starzyk, "Colleges Use Programs as Cash Cows, with Few Standards, Critics Say," *Cleveland Plain Dealer,* May 25, 2008, http://groups.google.com/group/oregon-arts-education/msg/a764bcd3a00d2bb7?pli=1 (retrieved February 20, 2009); Jay Mathews, "Breaking Down the Ivy Tower: Study Finds Schools of Ed in Poor Shape," *Washington Post,* October 31, 2006, p. A8; Doug Selwyn, "Teacher Quality: Teacher Education Left Behind," *Rethinking Schools* 20, no. 2 (Winter 2005/2006), www.rethinking-schools.org/archive/20_02/left202.shtml (retrieved May 10, 2008); George K. Cunningham, *Can Education Schools Be Saved?* Speech at the American Enterprise Institute (AEI) in Washington, DC, June 9, 2003, www.aei.org/publications/publD.17804,filter.all/pub_detail.asp (retrieved May 10, 2008); Ellen Condliffe Lagemann, "Whither Schools of Education? Whither Education Research?" *Journal of Teacher Education* 50, no. 5 (November/December 1999), pp. 373–76.
13. National Board for Professional Teaching Standards website, www.nbpts.org; "National Certification Picks Up Steam," *American Teacher* 76, no. 6 (May/June 1992), p. 3.
14. Retrieved on November 21, 2011, from www.nbpts.org/.
15. Debra Viadero and Vaishali Honawar, "National Board Teachers Found to Be Effective," *Education Week* 27, no. 42 (June 11, 2008), www.tasb.org/services/hr_services/hrexchange/2008/sept08/research_confirms_nb.asp (retrieved February 20, 2009).
16. Michael Winerip, "Chosen Few Are Teaching for America," *New York Times,* July 11, 2010; Lisa W. Foderaro, "Alternate Path for Teachers Gains Ground," *New York Times*, April 18, 2010; Paul F. Peterson and Daniel Nadler, "What Happens When States Have Genuine Alternative Certification?" *Education Next* 9, no. 1, Winter 2009, www.hoover.org/publications/ednext/34564684.html (retrieved February 12, 2009); National Center for Education Information, "Alternative Routes Are Attracting Talented Individuals from Other Careers Who Otherwise Would Not Become Teachers," www.ncei.com/part.html (retrieved February 12, 2009). See also Wendy Kopp, "Ten Years of Teach for America" in *Education Week on the Web,* June 21, 2000; Wendy Kopp, *One Day All Children Will Triumph: The Unlikely Story of Teach for America and What I Learned along the Way* (New York: Public Affairs, 2003).

17. Will Dobbie, "Teacher Characteristics and Student Achievement: Evidence from Teach For America," July 2011, www.people.fas.harvard.edu/~dobbie/research.html; Michael Birnbaum, "With Limited Training, Teach for America Recruits Play Expanding Role in Schools," *Washington Post,* August 23, 2010; Megan Greenwell, "Applicants Flock to Teacher Corps for Needy Areas," *Washington Post,* December 6, 2008, p. A1.

18. Morgaen L. Donaldson and Susan Moore Johnson, "Teach For America Teachers: How Long Do They Teach? Why Do They Leave?" *Phi Delta Kappan*, vol. 93 no. 2 (October 2011), pp. 47-51; Andrew Vanacore, "Teach for America Has Become Embedded in New Orleans Education," *The Times-Picayune*, November 27, 2011, http://blog.nola.com/education_impact/print.html?entry=/2011/11/teach_for_america_has_become_e.html (retrieved November 28, 2011).

19. Linda Darling-Hammond, "Teacher Preparation Is Essential to TFA's Future," *Education Week* 30, no.24 (March 14, 2011), pp. 25–26, 36; Megan Hopkins, "Training the Next Generation for America: A Proposal for Reconceptualizing Teach for America," *Phi Delta Kappan* 89, no. 10 (June 2008), pp. 721–725; Stephen Sawchuk, "Teach For America Elaborates Its Response to NEA Criticism," Education Week/Teacher Beat blog, July 22, 2011, http://blogs.edweek.org/edweek/teacherbeat/2011/07/teach_for_america_elaborates_o.html.

20. Stephen Sawchuk, "Teacher Residents Seen Outpacing Peers in Later Years," Education Week 31, no. 15 (published online: December 15, 2011); Stephen Sawchuk, "Teacher Residencies Make Strides, Encounter Obstacles," *Education Week* 30, no. 36 (published online: July 8, 2011).

21. Stephen Sawchuk, "Biggest Teacher-Prep School Revamped," *Education Week* 31, no. 12, (November 16, 2011), pp. 1,18–19; Stephen Sawchuk, "NEA Stakes a Claim in Teacher Effectiveness Debate," Liana Heitin, Teacher magazine's Teaching Now blog, December 8, 2011.

22. Debra Viadero, "Panel Finds No Favorite in Teacher-Prep Pathways," *Education Week* 29, no. 31 (April 29, 2010); Jill Constantine, Daniel Player, Tim Silva, Kristin Hallgren, Mary Grider, and John Deke, *An Evaluation of Teachers Trained through Different Routes to Certification* (Washington, DC: U.S. Department of Education, February 2009).

23. Charlotte Danielson, "A Framework for Learning to Teach," *Education Leadership* 66, June 2009, www.ascd.org/publications/educational-leadership.aspx (retrieved May 2010); Susan Moore Johnson and Sarah Birkeland, "Fast-Track Certification: Can We Prepare Teachers Both Quickly and Well?" *Education Week* 25, no. 23 (February 15, 2006), pp. 37, 48; "Research-Based Characteristics of High-Quality Teacher Preparation," *ASCD SmartBrief* 1, no. 4 (February 19, 2003); Linda Darling-Hammond, Deborah J. Holtzman, Su Jin Gatlin, and Julian Vasquez Heilig, *Does Teacher Preparation Matter? Evidence about Teacher Certification, Teach for America, and Teacher Effectiveness,* paper presented at the American Educational Association Annual Meeting, Montreal, April 2005, www.schoolredesign.net/srn/binaries/teachercert.pdf (retrieved July 19, 2005); Marilyn Cochran-Smith and Kenneth Zeichner, eds., *Studying Teacher Education: The Report of the AERA Panel on Research and Teacher Education* (Mahwah, NJ: Lawrence Erlbaum, 2005).

24. *Different Drummers: How Teachers of Teachers View Public Education* (New York: Public Agenda, 1997).

25. C. Emily Feistritzer, *Profile of Teachers in the U.S. 2011* (Washington, DC, National Center for Education Information, 2011), p. 30.

26. Linda Darling-Hammond, "Keeping Good Teachers: Why It Matters What Leaders Can Do," *Educational Leadership* 60, no. 8 (May 2003), pp. 7–13.

27. Darrel Drury and Justin Baer, The American Public School Teacher: *Past, Present, and Future* (Cambridge, MA: Harvard University Press, 2011); C. Emily Feistritzer, The Context of Teaching in the U.S. (Washington, DC: National Center for Education Information, National Center for Alternative Certification, 2011).

28. David C. Berliner, "A Personal Response to Those Who Bash Teacher Education," *Journal of Teacher Education* 51, no. 5 (November/December 2000), pp. 358–71; Suzanne M. Wilson, Robert E. Floden, and Joan Ferrini-Mundy, "Teacher Preparation Research: An Insider's View from the Outside," *Journal of Teacher Education* 53, no. 3 (May/June 2002), pp. 190–204.

29. Berliner, "A Personal Response," p. 363. See also College Board, "2005 College-Bound Seniors," www.collegeboard.com/prod_downloads/about/news_info/cbsenior/yr2005/2005-college-bound-seniors.pdf (retrieved February 11, 2006).

30. Andy Baumgartner, "A Teacher Speaks Out: Insights from the National Teacher of the Year," *The Washington Post,* March 26, 2000, p. B4.

31. Lapointe quoted in Gerald W. Bracey, "The Second Bracey Report on the Condition of Public Education," *Phi Delta Kappan* (October 1992), pp. 104–17, cited in David C. Berliner and Bruce J. Biddle, *The Manufactured Crisis* (Reading, MA: Addison Wesley, 1995), p. 54.

32. A chart of 2009 College-Bound Seniors Average SAT Scores, FairTest website, www.fairtest.org/ (retrieved February 2, 2009); Nation's Report Card, *Reading Scores* http://nces.ed.gov/nationsreportcard/reading/ (retrieved February 2, 2009); College Board, *The 5th Annual AP Report to the Nation,* www.collegeboard.com/html/aprtn/pdf/ap_report_to_the_nation.pdf (retrieved February 2, 2009); Dianne Reed, Lynn Fox, Mary Lou Andrews, Nancy Betz, Jan Perry Evenstad, Anthony Harris, Carol Hightower-Parker, Judy Johnson, Shirley Johnson, Barbara Polnick, and Phyllis Rosser, "Gender Equity in Testing and Assessment," in Susan S. Klein (ed.), *Handbook for Achieving Gender Equity through Education,* 2nd ed. (New York: Lawrence Erlbaum Associates, Taylor & Francis Group, 2007), pp. 155–69; Gerald W. Bracey, "U.S. Students: Better Than Ever," *The Washington Post,* December 22, 1995, p. A-9; Robert J. Samuelson, "Three Cheers for Schools," *Newsweek,* December 4, 1995, p. 61. See also Berliner and Biddle, *The Manufactured Crisis,* pp. 13–64.

33. "Survey Gauges Teens' View of Tech Future," *Lemelsin-MIT Invention Index,* Massachusetts Institute of Technology, January 12, 2006, web.mit.edu.

34. Berliner and Biddle, *The Manufactured Crisis*, p. 146. See also Richard Rothstein, *The Way We Were? The Myths and Realities of America's Student Achievement* (Washington, DC: Century Fund, 1998); Sara Mead, *The Evidence Suggests Otherwise; The Truth about Boys and Girls* (Washington, DC: Education Sector, 2006), pp.14–16.

YOU BE THE JUDGE NOTES

1. Amy DePaul, *What to Expect Your First Year of Teaching* (Washington, DC: U.S. Department of Education, September 1998), p. 28. There are also some worthwhile contemporary teaching experiences and insights described on the Internet. See, for example, "10 Things to Expect & Not Expect Your First Year of Teaching," at http://specialedandme.wordpress.com/2009/08/31/10-things-to-expect-not-expect-your-first-year-of-teaching-easier/.
2. Quoted in Ann Lieberman and Lynn Miller, *Teachers, Their World and Their Work* (Alexandria, VA: Association for Supervision and Curriculum Development, 1984), p. 22.
3. Lieberman and Miller, *Teachers, Their World and Their Work,* p. 47.
4. William Lyon Phelps, quoted in Oliver Ikenberry, *American Education Foundations* (Columbus, OH: Merrill, 1974), p. 389.
5. Quoted in Myron Brenton, *What's Happened to Teacher?* (New York: Coward, McCann & Geoghegan, 1970), p. 164.
6. Stephen Gordon quoted in "What Keeps Teachers Going?" *Educational Leadership* 60, no. 8 (May 2003), p. 18.
7. Shane Lopez and Sangeeta Agrawal, "Teachers Score Higher than Other Professionals in Well-Being," Gallup Poll, December 23, 2009, www.gallup.com/poll/124778/teachers-score-higher-professionals.aspx.
8. Quoted in Brenton, *What's Happened to Teacher?* p. 97.

CHAPTER 2   DIFFERENT WAYS OF LEARNING

1. Daniel Pink, *Drive: The Surprising Truth about What Motivates Us* (New York: Riverhead Books, 2011); Carol Dweck, *Mindset: The New Psychology of Success* (New York: Random House, 2006).
2. Howard Gardner and Thomas Hatch, "Multiple Intelligences Go to School: Educational Implications of the Theory of Multiple Intelligences," *Educational Researcher* 18, no. 8 (November 1989), p. 5; Seana Moran, Mindy Kornhaber, and Howard Gardner, "Orchestrating Multiple Intelligences," *Educational Leadership* 64, no. 1 (September 2006); Howard Gardner, *Frames of Mind: The Theory of Multiple Intelligences,* 3rd ed. (New York: Basic Books, 2011).
3. Gardner, *Frames of Mind: The Theory of Multiple Intelligences*; Kathy Checkley, "The First Seven . . . and the Eighth: A Conversation with Howard Gardner," *Educational Leadership* 55, no. 1 (September 1997), pp. 8–13.
4. Richard Louv, *Last Child in the Woods: Saving Our Children from Nature-Deficit Disorder* (New York: Algonquin Books, 2005).
5. Gardner, *Frames of Mind: The Theory of Multiple Intelligences*; Thomas Armstrong, *Multiple Intelligences in the Classroom,* 3rd ed. (Alexandria, VA: Association for Supervision and Curriculum Development, 2009).
6. Howard Gardner, "Can Technology Exploit the Many Ways of Knowing?" in David T. Gordon, ed., *The Digital Classroom* (Cambridge, MA: Harvard College, 2000), pp. 32–35.
7. Gardner, *Frames of Mind: The Theory of Multiple Intelligences.*
8. Thomas Armstrong, *Multiple Intelligences in the Classroom;* Evangeline Harris Stefanakis, *Multiple Intelligences and Portfolios: A Window into the Learner's Mind* (Portsmouth, NH: Heinemann, 2002).
9. Howard Gardner, *Five Minds for the Future* (Cambridge, MA: Harvard Business School Press, 2006).
10. Nancy Gibbs, "The E.Q. Factor," *Time,* October 2, 1995, pp. 60–68.
11. Daniel Goleman, *Working with Emotional Intelligence* (New York: Bantam Books, 2000); Daniel Goleman, "Emotional Intelligence: Why It Can Matter More Than IQ," *Learning* (May/June 1996), pp. 49–50.
12. Daniel Goleman, "The Socially Intelligent Leader," *Educational Leadership* 64, no. 1 (September 2006), pp. 76–81; Daniel Goleman, *Working with Emotional Intelligence.*
13. Harold Pashler, Mark McDaniel, Doug Rohrer, and Robert Bjork, "Learning Styles: Concepts and Evidence," *Psychological Science in the Public Interest* 9, no. 3 (December 2008), pp. 105–19; Heather Wolpert-Gawron, "The Bunk of Debunking Learning Styles," *Teacher Magazine,* February 17, 2010, www.teachermagazine.com; Marge Scher, "Celebrate Strengths, Nurture Affinities: A Conversation with Mel Levine," *Educational Leadership* 64, no. 1 (September 2006), pp. 8–15.
14. Wolpert-Gawron, "The Bunk of Debunking Learning Styles"; Donna Walker Tileston, *Ten Best Teaching Practices: How Brain Research and Learning Styles Define Teaching Competencies.* (Thousand Oaks, CA: Corwin Press, 2010.)
15. Norman Doidge, *The Brain That Changes Itself* (New York: Viking Press, 2007).
16. Tileston, *Ten Best Teaching Practices: How Brain Research and Learning Styles Define Teaching Competencies;* Pashler, McDaniel, Rohrer, and Bjork, "Learning Styles: Concepts and Evidence."
17. Janet Hyde, "New Directions in the Study of Gender Similarities and Differences," *Current Directions in Psychological Science* 16, (2007), pp. 259–63; Janet Hyde, "The Gender Similarities Hypothesis," *American Psychologist* 60, (2005), pp. 581–92.
18. Diane Halpern, "The Pseudoscience of Single-Sex Schooling," *Education Forum* (September 22, 2011) pp. 1706–07; Caryl Rivers and Rosalind Barnett, *The Truth About Girls and Boys: Challenging Toxic Stereotypes About Our Children* (New York: Columbia Press University, 2011); Lise Eliot, *Pink Brain, Blue Brain: How Small Differences Grow Into Troublesome Gaps—And What We Can Do About It* (Boston: Houghton Mifflin, 2010.)
19. Halpern, "The Pseudoscience of Single-Sex Schooling"; Hyde, "New Directions in the Study of Gender Similarities and Differences."
20. Pamela Davis-Keen, *Dads Influence Daughters' Interest in Mathematics.* Paper presented at Education a STEM Workforce: New Strategies for U-M and the State of Michigan, Ann Arbor, MI, 2007.

21. Eliot, *Pink Brain, Blue Brain: How Small Differences Grow Into Troublesome Gaps—And What We Can Do About It.*
22. Doidge, *The Brain That Changes Itself.*
23. These categories build on the ones described by William Heward, Sara Ernsbarger Bicard, and Rodney A. Cavanaugh, "Educational Equality for Students with Disabilities," in James Banks and Cherry Banks (eds.), *Multicultural Education,* 7th ed. (San Francisco: Jossey Bass, 2010), pp. 329–67.
24. Michael Janofsky, "Some New Help for the Extremely Gifted," *New York Times* online, October 26, 2005.
25. Walt Gardner, "Gifted Children Are Stepchildren in School Reform," *Education Week,* May 7, 2010, www.edweek.org; Christina A. Samuels, " 'Gifted' Label Said to Miss Dynamic Nature of Talent," *Education Week* 28, no. 8 (October 15, 2008), pp. 1, 18.
26. Valerie Strauss, "Looking for a Few Wise Children, *The Washington Post,* September 17, 2002, p. A11.
27. National Association for Gifted Children, "Frequently Asked Questions," www.nagc.org/ (retrieved December 12, 2011).
28. Carolyn Callahan and Jonathan Plucker, *Critical Issues and Practices in Gifted Education: What the Research Says* (Austin, TX: Prufrock Press, 2007).
29. Tamara Fisher, "I Don't Want to Be a Smarty Anymore," *Education Week* online (June 30, 2010); Callahan and Plucker, *Critical Issues and Practices in Gifted Education: What the Research Says.*
30. Fisher, "I Don't Want to Be a Smarty Anymore."
31. Callahan and Plucker, *Critical Issues and Practices in Gifted Education: What the Research Says.*
32. Ibid.
33. Ibid; Dona J. Matthews and Joanne F. Foster, "Mystery to Mastery: Shifting Paradigms in Gifted Education," *Roeper Review* 28, no. 2 (Winter 2006), pp. 64–69.
34. National Association for Gifted Children, "Frequently Asked Questions"; Callahan and Plucker, *Critical Issues and Practices in Gifted Education: What the Research Says.*
35. Tamara Fisher, "On the Up-Side," *Education Week* online (July 7, 2010).
36. Ibid.
37. Marie Killilea, *Karen* (New York: Dell, 1952), p. 171.
38. Heward, Bicard, and Cavanaugh, "Educational Equality for Students with Disabilities."
39. Ibid.
40. U.S. Department of Education, National Center for Education Statistics, "Children and Youth with Disabilities, Indicator 7-2011," *Condition of Education 2011,* http://nces.ed.gov/programs/coe/.
41. Ibid; Heward, Bicard, and Cavanaugh, "Educational Equality for Students with Disabilities."
42. U.S. Department of Education, National Center for Education Statistics, "Children and Youth with Disabilities"; Heward, Bicard, and Cavanaugh, "Educational Equality for Students with Disabilities."
43. Ibid.
44. Heward, Bicard, and Cavanaugh, "Educational Equality for Students with Disabilities."
45. U.S. Department of Education, National Center for Education Statistics, "Children and Youth with Disabilities."
46. Quoted in David Milofsky, "Schooling the Kid No One Wants," *The New York Times Magazine,* January 2, 1977, pp. 24–29.
47. For more information about special education services and adaptive technology, visit the U.S. Department of Education Office of Special Education website at www.ed.gov/about/offices/list/osers/osep/index.html.
48. Solomon Moore, "Special Ed Joins the Mainstream," *Los Angeles Times,* October 2002, online.

CHAPTER 3　TEACHING YOUR DIVERSE STUDENTS

1. National Center for Educational Statistics, U.S. Department of Education, *Status and Trends in the Education of Racial and Ethnic Groups* (Susan Aud, National Center for Education Statistics, and Mary Ann Fox and Angelina Kewal Ramani, Education Statistics Services Institute–American Institutes for Research,) July 2010, http://nces.ed.gov/pubs2010/2010015.pdf; the Center for Public Education, *At a Glance: Changing Demographics* (Washington, DC: The Center for Public Education, 2007), www.centerforpubliceducation.org/Main-Menu/Staffingstudents/Changing-Demographics-At-a-glance (retrieved August 22, 2011).
2. James A. Banks, "Multicultural Education: Characteristics and Goals," in James Banks and Cherry Banks, eds., *Multicultural Education,* 6th ed. (San Francisco: Jossey Bass, 2007), pp. 3–30.
3. The demographic information is based on the following: Debra Viadero, "Multiracial Children Attracting Interest as Visibility Increases," *Education Week* 28, no. 18 (January 21, 2009), pp. 1, 14–15; Carol Morello and Ted Mellnik, "Minorities Become a Majority in Washington Region," *The Washington Post,* August 31, 2011, retrieved online at www.washingtonpost.com; National Center for Educational Statistics, U.S. Department of Education, *Status and Trends in the Education of Racial and Ethnic Groups;* "Overview of Race and Hispanic Origin," *Census 2000 Brief* (Washington, DC: U.S. Census Bureau, March 2001); "Projections of the Resident Population by Race, Hispanic Origin, and Nativity: 2025 to 2045," *Census 2000 Brief.*
4. National Center for Educational Statistics, U.S. Department of Education, *Status and Trends in the Education of Racial and Ethnic Groups;* College Board, *2010 College Bound Seniors,* 2008, www.collegeboard.com/press/releases/213182.html (retrieved September 13, 2010); National Assessment of Educational Progress, 2011, retrieved at http://nationsreportcard.gov/; Nirvi Shah, "Study Finds Minority Students Get Harsher Punishments," *Education Week* 31, no. 07 (October 5, 2011), retrieved online at www.Edweek.org; Sara Mead, *The Evidence Suggests Otherwise; The Truth About Boys and Girls* (Washington, DC: Education Sector, 2006), pp. 14–16; "Child Poverty In America Is Absolutely EXPLODING—16 Shocking Statistics That Will Break Your Heart," http://theeconomiccollapseblog.com/, retrieved online December 18, 2011; Christopher B. Swanson, *The Real Truth about*

Low Graduation Rates, An Evidence Based Commentary (Washington, DC: The Urban Institute, 2004); U.S. Department of Education, National Center for Educational Statistics, *The Nation's Report Card,* http://nationsreportcard.gov (retrieved February 24, 2009).

5. Lowell C. Rose and Alec M. Gallup, "The 38th Annual Phi Delta Kappa/Gallup Poll of the Public's Attitude Toward the Public Schools," *Phi Delta Kappan* 88, no. 1 (September 2006), Table 20, pp. 42–53.

6. Robert Evans, "Reframing the Achievement Gap," *Phi Delta Kappan* 86, no. 8 (April 2005), pp. 582–89.

7. Gay, Lesbian, and Straight Education Network, www.glsen .com; Ian K. Macgillivray, *Gay-Straight Alliances: A Handbook for Students, Educators, and Parents* (Binghampton, NY: Haworth Press, 2007).

8. Benoit Denzet-Lewis, "Coming Out in Junior High School," *New York Times Magazine,* September 27, 2009, pp. 36–41, 52, 54–55; Jason Cianciotto and Sean Cahill, *Education Policy: Issues Affecting Lesbian, Gay, Bisexual and Transgender Youth* (New York: The National Gay and Lesbian Task Force Policy Institute, 2003).

9. Gay, Lesbian, and Straight Education Network, *Number of Gay-Straight Alliance Registrations Passes 3,500,* www.glsen. org (retrieved February 13, 2008).

10. Dan Lovett, "California to Require Gay History in Schools," *The New York Times,* July 14, 2011, retrieved online at NYTimes.com.

11. Andrew Hacker, *Two Nations: Black, White, Separate, Hostile, Unequal* (New York: Charles Scribner's, 1992), pp. 31–32.

12. Jennifer Holliday, "The ABC's of Whiteness and Anti-Racism," *Teaching Tolerance,* www.tolerance.org/teach/activities/ activity.jsp?ar=713 (retrieved March 2, 2009).

13. Michael Winerip, "Closing the Achievement Gap Without Widening a Racial One," *The New York Times,* February 13, 2011, retrieved online at NYTimes.com.

14. Ana Maria Villegas, *Culturally Responsive Pedagogy for the 1990s and Beyond* (Washington, DC: ERIC Clearinghouse on Teacher Education, American Association of Colleges for Teacher Education, 1991).

15. Israel Zangwill, *The Melting Pot* (play), 1909, cited in Pamela Tiedt and Iris Tiedt, *Multicultural Education* (Needham Heights, MA: Allyn & Bacon, 1999), p. 2.

16. James Crawford, ed., *Language Loyalties: A Source Book on the Official English Controversy* (Chicago: University of Chicago Press, 1992); see also Jonathon Zimmerman, "A Babel of Tongues," *U.S. News & World Report,* November 24, 1997, p. 39.

17. Richard Rothstein, "Bilingual Education: The Controversy," in James W. Noll ed., *Taking Sides* (Dubuque, IA: McGraw-Hill/ Dushkin, 2005), pp. 290–301.

18. James Lyon, *Legal Responsibilities of Education Agencies Serving National Origin Language Minority Students* (Chevy Chase, MD: Mid-Atlantic Equity Center, 1992), www.maec. org/lyons/contents.html (retrieved May 9, 2008).

19. The National Clearinghouse for English Language Acquisition, *The Growing Number of Limited English Proficient Students* (Washington, DC: NCELA, November 2007), www .ncela.gwu.edu/policy/states/reports/statedata/2005LEP/ GrowingLEP_0506.pdf; U.S. Department of Education, *The Condition of Education, 2007,* Indicator 6.

20. Tom Stritikis and Manka M. Varghese, "Language Diversity and Schooling," in Banks and Banks, eds., *Multicultural Education,* pp. 297–325.

21. Christine Bennett, *Comprehensive Multicultural Education: Theory and Practice,* 6th ed. (Boston: Allyn & Bacon, 2006).

22. Jens Manuel Krogstad, "Branstad: Bilingual Education Gives Students Leg Up in Global Economy," *The Des Moines Register,* November 15, 2011, retrieved online at http://blogs. desmoinesregister.com.

23. Yilu Zhao, "Wave of Pupils Lacking English Strains Schools," *New York Times,* August 5, 2002, http://query.nytimes.com/ gst/fullpage.html?res=9A01EFD9133BF936A3575BC0A9649 C8B63 (retrieved May 10, 2008).

24. James Crawford, *Hold Your Tongue: Bilingualism and the Politics of "English Only"* (New York: Addison-Wesley, 1992), pp. 111–12.

25. Gary A. Cziko, "The Evaluation of Bilingual Education: From Necessity and Probability to Possibility," *Educational Researcher* 21, no. 2 (March 1992), p. 24; J. David Ramirez, "Executive Summary," *Bilingual Research Journal* 16 (Winter/ Spring, 1992), pp. 1–245; Lisa Kocian, "Some Educators Say Pushing Immersion Before Bilingual Classes May Do More Harm than Good, *Boston Globe,* September 25, 2008, www .boston.com/news/local/articles/2008/09/25/english_ period/ (retrieved February 27, 2009); Stritikis and Varghese, "Language Diversity and Schooling."

26. Bennett, *Comprehensive Multicultural Education: Theory and Practice;* Stritikis and Varghese, "Language Diversity and Schooling."

27. Peter Schmidt, "Three Types of Bilingual Education Effective, E.D. Study Concludes," *Education Week,* February 20, 1991, pp. 1, 23.

28. Wayne Thomas and Virginia Collier, "Two Languages Are Better than One," *Educational Leadership* 55, no. 4 (December 1997/January 1998), pp. 23–26; Kenneth J. Cooper, "Riley Endorses Two-Way Bilingual Education," *Washington Post,* March 26, 2000, p. A2; Cara Simmon, "School Puts New Accent on Learning Two Languages," *Seattle Times,* April 1, 2003; Wayne Thomas and Virginia Collier, *A National Study of School Effectiveness for Language Minority Students' Long-Term Academic Achievement, Final Report 1.1,* Center for Research on Education, Diversity, and Excellence, U.S. Department of Education, Office of Educational Research and Improvement, 2008; Brian Cobb, Diego Vega, and Cindy Kronauge, "Effects of an Elementary Dual Language Immersion School Program on Junior High School Achievement, *Middle Grades Research Journal* 1 no. 1 (2006), pp. 27–47.

29. Frederick M. Hess, "Schools of Reeducation," *Washington Post,* February 5, 2006, p. B7.

30. Education Research Center, *Cities in Crisis Education Week,* April 2008; Christopher B. Swanson, *The Real Truth about Low Graduation Rates, An Evidenced-Based Commentary*

(Washington, DC: The Urban Institute, 2004); U.S. Department of Education, *The Condition of Education 2007* (Washington, DC: National Center for Education Statistics, 2007), (NCES 2007-064), Indicator 23, 2007; Gary Orfield and Chungmei Lee, *Racial Transformation and the Changing Nature of Segregation* (Cambridge, MA: The Civil Rights Project, Harvard University, 2006); Erica Frankenberg and Gary Orfield, *Lessons in Integration: Realizing the Promise of Racial Diversity in America* (Charlottesville, VA: University of Virginia Press, 2007).

31. Christine Sleeter, "Curriculum Controversies in Multicultural Education," in Margaret Early and Kenneth Rehage, eds., *Issues in the Curriculum: A Selection of Chapters from Past NSSE Yearbooks, Ninety-Eighth Yearbook of the National Society for the Study of Education* (Chicago: University of Chicago Press, 1999), p. 261; Banks, "Multicultural Education: Characteristics and Goals."

32. Banks, "Multicultural Education: Characteristics and Goals."

33. James Banks, "Approaches to Multicultural Curriculum Reform," in Banks and Banks, *Multicultural Education: Issues and Perspectives,* pp. 247–269.

34. Justin Britt-Gibson, "What's Wrong with this Picture?" *Washington Post,* March 18, 2007, p. B01; Peter Schmidt, "New Survey Discerns Deep Divisions Among U.S. Youths on Race Relations," *Education Week,* March 25, 1992, p. 5.

35. Cristina Fernandez-Pereda, "Media Falls Flat in Covering Race Relations, New Survey Says," *New America Media,* February 19, 2009, http://news.newamericamedia.org/news/view_article.html?article_id=fa22894b6bee1753da1e89c189126106.

36. Mathew Bigg, "U.S. School Segregation on the Rise: Report," *Reuters,* January 14, 2009.

37. Bennett, *Comprehensive Multicultural Education: Theory and Practice;* Gloria Ladson-Billings, *Crossing Over to Canaan: The Journey of New Teachers in Diverse Classrooms* (San Francisco: Jossey Bass, 2001); Gloria Ladson-Billings, "But That's Just Good Teaching," *Theory into Practice* 34, no. 3 (Summer 1995), pp. 159–165.

38. Geneva Gay, "Achieving Educational Equality Through Curriculum Desegregation," *Phi Delta Kappan* 72, no. 1 (September 1990), pp. 56–62.

39. Carol Gilligan, *In a Different Voice: Psychological Theory and Women's Development* (Cambridge, MA: Harvard University Press, 1982); David Sadker, Myra Sadker, and Karen Zittleman, *Still Failing at Fairness: How Gender Bias Cheats Girls and Boys in School and What We Can Do about It* (New York: Charles Scribner's, 2009). See also Mary Field Belenky, Blythe McVicker Clinchy, Nancy Rule Goldberger, and Jill Mattuck Tarule, *Women's Ways of Knowing: The Development of Self, Voice, and Mind* (New York: Basic Books, 1986).

40. Julie Chlebo, "There Is No Rose Garden: A Second Generation Rural Head Start Program," unpublished doctoral dissertation, 1999, quoted in Christine I. Bennett, *Comprehensive Multicultural Education: Theory and Practice,* 4th ed. (Needham Heights, MA: Allyn & Bacon, 1999), p. 259.

41. Joshua Aronson, "The Threat of Stereotype," *Educational Leadership* 62, no. 3 (November 2004), pp. 14–19.

42. Joshua Aronson, "The Effects of Conceiving Ability as Fixed or Improvable on Responses to Stereotype Threat," unpublished manuscript, New York University, 2004.

43. Aronson, "The Threat of Stereotype"; Carol Dweck, *Self Theories: Their Role in Motivation, Personality and Development* (Philadelphia: Taylor & Francis, 1999).

44. Bennett, *Comprehensive Multicultural Education: Theory and Practice;* Carlos Cortes, *The Children Are Watching: How the Media Teach About Diversity* (New York: Teachers College Press, 2000), pp. 149–150; Barbara J. Shade, Cynthia Kelly, and Mary Oberg, *Creating Culturally Responsive Classrooms* (Washington, DC: American Psychological Association, 1997).

45. *Common Core Data, 2005–06* (Washington, DC: U.S. Department of Education, NCES), http://nces.ed.gov/ccd/ (retrieved February 27, 2008); Children's Defense Fund, www.childrens-defense.org (retrieved February 27, 2008).

46. The information about generalizations and different group learning styles is drawn from a variety of sources, including Bobby Ann Starnes, "What We Don't Know Can Hurt Them White Teachers, Indian Children," *Phi Delta Kappan* 87, no. 5 (January 2006), pp. 384–392; Banks and Banks, *Multicultural Education: Issues and Perspectives;* Bennett, *Comprehensive Multicultural Education: Theory and Practice;* Kenneth Cushner, *Human Diversity in Action: Developing Multicultural Competencies for the Classroom* (New York: McGraw-Hill, 2006); Gary A. Davis and Sylvia Rimm, *Cultural Diversity and Children from Low Socioeconomic Backgrounds* (Boston: Allyn & Bacon, 1997); K. M. Evenson Worthley, "Learning Style Factor of Field Dependence/Independence and Problem Solving Strategies of Hmong Refugee Students," master's thesis, University of Wisconsin–Stout, July 1987 (cited in Bennett, *Comprehensive Multicultural Education: Theory and Practice*); Norene Dresser, *Multicultural Manners: New Rules of Etiquette for a Changing Society* (New York: John Wiley & Sons, 1996); Education Alliance at Brown University, *The Diversity Kit: An Introductory Resource for Social Change in Education* (Providence, RI: Northeast and Islands Regional Educational Laboratory–LAB at Brown University, 2002); Rowena Fong and Sharlene B. Furuto, *Culturally Competent Practice: Skills, Interventions, and Evaluations* (Needham Heights, MA: Allyn & Bacon, 2001); Eleanor W. Lynch and Marci J. Hanson, eds., *Developing Cross-Cultural Competence: A Guide for Working with Children and Their Families* (Baltimore, MD: Paul H. Brookes, 2004); Ian K. Macgillivray, *Sexual Orientation and School Policy: A Practical Guide for Teachers, Administrators, and Community Activists* (Lanham, MD: Rowman & Littlefield, 2004).

47. We thank Louise Wilkinson for this poignant quote. We couldn't have said it better.

48. Kent L. Koppelman with R. Lee Goodhart, *Understanding Human Differences: Multicultural Education for Diverse America* (Boston: Pearson Education, 2005), p. 344.

49. Nancy P. Gallavan, "I, Too, Am an American: Preservice Teachers Reflect upon National Identity," *Multicultural Teaching,* Spring 2002, pp. 8–12.

CHAPTER 4   STUDENT LIFE IN SCHOOL AND AT HOME

1. Philip W. Jackson, *Life in Classrooms* (New York: Holt, Rinehart & Winston, 1968); Elena Silva, *On the Clock: Rethinking the Way Schools Use Time* (Washington, DC: Education Sector, January 2007), retrieved February January 3, 2012, from www.educationsector.org/.

2. Ibid.

3. Carol Ann Tomlinson, "Notes from an Accidental Teacher," *Educational Leadership* (December 2010/January 2011), pp. 22–26; Leila Christenbury, "Flexible Teacher," *Educational Leadership* (December 2010/January 2011), pp. 46–50; Silva, *On the Clock: Rethinking How Schools Use Time.*

4. Quoted in Ernest L. Boyer, *High School* (New York: Harper & Row, 1983).

5. Warren Kubitschek, Maureen Hallinan, Stephanie Arnett, and Kim Galipeau, "High School Schedule Changes and the Effect of Lost Instructional Time on Achievement," *High School Journal* 89, no.1 (October–November, 2005), pp. 63–71; Erik Gleibermann, "Teaching Even 100 Hours a Week Leaves Children Behind," *Phi Delta Kappan* 88, no. 6 (February 2007), pp. 455–459; Bill Metzker, *Time and Learning: ERIC Digest* (2003), retrieved January 4, 2012, from www.ericdigests.org/2003-5/time.htm.

6. Jackson, *Life in Classrooms;* Silva, *On the Clock: Rethinking How Schools Use Time*

7. Ned Flanders, "Intent, Action, and Feedback: A Preparation for Teaching," *Journal of Teacher Education* 14, no. 3 (September 1963), pp. 251–60; Jill Bourne and Caery Jewiit, "Orchestrating Debate: A Multimodal Analysis of Classroom Interaction," *Reading* 37, no. 2 (July 2003), pp. 64–72; Kristiina Kumpulainen, *Investigating Classroom Research* (Rotterdam, the Netherlands: Sense Publishers, 2009); Arno Bellack, *The Language of the Classroom* (New York: Teachers College Press, 1965); Romiett Stevens, "The Question as a Measure of Classroom Practice," in *Teachers College Contributions to Education* (New York: Teachers College Press, 1912); David Sadker, Myra Sadker, and Karen Zittleman, "Questioning Skills," in James M. Cooper, ed., *Classroom Teaching Skills,* 9th ed. (Belmont, CA: Cengage, 2010), pp. 107–152.

8. Shane J. Lopez, "The Highs and Lows of Student Engagement," *Phi Delta Kappan* (October 2011), pp. 72–73; John Goodlad, *A Place Called School* (New York: McGraw-Hill, 1984/2004); K. Kumpulainen, *Investigating Classroom Research.*

9. Talcott Parsons, "The School as a Social System: Some of Its Functions in Society," in Robert Havinghurst and Bernice Neugarten (eds.), *Society and Education* (Boston: Allyn & Bacon, 1967), pp. 191–214; Jeannie Oakes, "The Tracking Wars," in *Keeping Track: How Schools Structure Inequality,* 2nd ed. (New Haven, CT: Yale University Press, 2005), pp. 214–221; Mike Rose, *Why School: Reclaiming Education for All of Us* (New York: New Press, 2009).

10. Robert Lynd and Helen Lynd, *Middletown: A Study in American Culture* (New York: Harcourt Brace Jovanovich, 1929).

11. W. Lloyd Warner, Robert Havinghurst, and Martin Loeb, *Who Shall Be Educated?* (New York: Harper & Row, 1944).

12. Jeannie Oakes, "Keeping Track: Structuring Equality and Inequality in an Era of Accountability," *Teachers College Record* 110, no. 3 (2008), pp. 12–13 (ID Number: 14610), www.tcrecord.org; Jeannie Oakes, *Keeping Track.*

13. Ray Rist, "Student Social Class and Teacher Expectations. The Self-Fulfilling Prophecy of Ghetto Education," *Harvard Education Review* 40, no. 3 (1970), pp. 411–451.

14. Jeannie Oakes, "Keeping Track: Structuring Equality and Inequality in an Era of Accountability"; Mike Rose, *Why School: Reclaiming Education for All of Us;* Eric Quiñones, "Tracking Political Impact of Racial Disparity in Schools," *Princeton Weekly Bulletin* 98, no. 24 (April 20, 2009), www.princeton.edu/pr/pwb/volume98/issue24/school/.

15. Jeannie Oakes, "Foreword," in Anne Wheelock, *Crossing the Tracks: How Untracking Can Save America's Schools* (New York: New Press, 1993), p. xiii.

16. James Rosenbaum, "If Tracking Is Bad, Is Detracking Better?" *American Educator* (Winter 1999–2000), pp. 24–29, 47; Oakes, "Keeping Track: Structuring Equality and Inequality in an Era of Accountability;" Quiñones, "Tracking Political Impact of Racial Disparity in Schools.

17. George Theoharis, *The School Leaders Our Children Deserve: Seven Keys to Equity, Social Justice, and School Reform* (New York: Teachers College Press, 2009); Carol Ann Tomlinson, "Differentiating Instruction for Academic Diversity," in James M. Cooper, ed., *Classroom Teaching Skills,* 9th ed. (Belmont, CA: Cengage, 2010), pp. 154–187.

18. Kelsey Felton and Patrick Akos, "The Transition Years," *Educational Leadership,* (April 2011), pp. 28–31; Raphaela Best, *We've All Got Scars* (Bloomington: Indiana University Press, 1983).

19. Best, *We've All Got Scars,* p. 162.

20. Felton and Akos, "The Transition Years"; Lisa Wolcott, "Relationships: The Fourth 'R,'" *Teacher,* April 1991, pp. 26–27.

21. Quoted from a student letter in the *Arlingtonian,* May 13, 1993.

22. Sarah Sparks, "Study Links Academic Setbacks to Middle School Transition," *Education Week* online (November 28, 2011); Tara Malone, "Study: College Success Starts Early," *Chicago Tribune,* December 11, 2008, retrieved January 10, 2012, from http://chicagotribune.com; Jaana Juvonen et al., *Focus on the Wonder Years: Challenges Facing the American Middle School* (Santa Monica, CA: RAND Corporation, 2004), retrieved January 10, 2012, from www.rand.org/pubs/monographs/2004/RAND_MG139.pdf.

23. Sparks, "Study Links Academic Setbacks to Middle School Transition."

24. Jay Matthews, "Traditional Social Focus Yielding to Academics," *The Washington Post,* October 4, 2005, p. A04.

25. Lopez, "The Highs and Lows of Student Engagement."

26. Karen R. Zittleman, "Gender Perceptions of Middle Schoolers: The Good and the Bad," *Middle Grades Research Journal* 2, no. 2 (Fall 2007), pp. 65–97.

27. Ibid.

28. Benoit Denzet-Lewis, "Coming Out in Junior High School," *New York Times Magazine,* September 27, 2009, pp. 36–41, 52, 54–55.

29. Girls Inc., *The SuperGirl Dilemma: Girls Feel the Pressure to Be Perfect, Accomplished, Thin, and Accommodating* (New York, 2006).

30. U.S. Department of Education, National Center for Education Statistics, "Elementary and Secondary Enrollments," *Digest of Education Statistics,* 2010, p. 59, available at http://nces.ed.gov/pubs2011/2011015.pdf.

31. K. M Pierce, "Posing, Pretending, Waiting for the Bell: Life in High School Classrooms," *High School Journal* 89, no. 2 (December 2005/January 2006), pp. 1–15.

32. Quoted in Jeremy Iverson *High School Confidential: Secrets of an Undercover Student* (New York: Atria Books, 2007), p. 202.

33. David Owen, *High School* (New York: Viking Press, 1981).

34. Iverson, *High School Confidential: Secrets of an Undercover Student.*

35. Patricia Hersch, *A Tribe Apart: A Journey into the Heart of American Adolescence* (New York: Random House, 1999).

36. Candy Schulman, "Burnt Out on the High School Treadmill," *Washington Post online* (May 29, 2011); Iverson, *High School Confidential: Secrets of an Undercover Student.*

37. Schulman, "Burnt Out on the High School Treadmill."

38. Sean Slade, "Relationships Matter," *Huffington Post* (November 23, 2011), www.huffingtonpost.com

39. *America's Children: Key National Indicators of Well-Being, 2011,* www.childstats.gov/americaschildren/.

40. William Jeynes, *Parental Involvement and Academic Success* (New York: Routledge, 2010); William Jeynes, *Divorce, Family Structure, and the Academic Success of Children* (New York: Routledge, 2002).

41. Carol Morello, "Married Couples at Record Low," *Washington Post online* (December 13, 2011); "Study: Older, More Educated Moms on the Rise," *Arizona Daily Star,* May 6, 2010, p. A13.

42. *Statistics on Stepfamilies in the United States* (New York: The Stepfamily Foundation, 2012), www.stepfamily.org/statistics.html.

43. U.S. Census Bureau, *Statistical Abstract of the United States: 2012,* 131st ed. (Washington, DC, 2011), www.census.gov/compendia/statab, Current Population Survey 2011; Morello, "Married Couples at Record Low"; "Winding Road to Adulthood Taking Longer: Research Shows Marked Age Shifted for Marriage, Careers, Parenthood," *Arizona Daily Star,* June 13, 2010, p. A3.

44. U.S. Census Bureau, *Statistical Abstracts of the United States,* Current Population Survey 2011; Maria Shriver and the Center for American Progress, *The Shriver Report: A Woman's Nation Changes Everything* (2009), www.shriverreport.com.

45. "Study Cites Dramatic Rise in Family Togetherness," *Arizona Daily Star,* April 6, 2010, p. A14.

46. Frances Kemper Alston, *Latch Key Children* (New York: NYU Child Study Center, 2007), retrieved January 18, 2011, from www.aboutourkids.org/articles/latch_key_children.

47. Federal Interagency Forum on Child and Family Statistics, *America's Children: Key National Indicators of Well-Being, 2011,* available at www.childstats.gov/americaschildren/.

48. Quoted in John O'Neil, "A Generation Adrift?" *Educational Leadership* 49, no. 2 (September 1991), pp. 4–10.

49. Federal Interagency Forum on Child and Family Statistics, *America's Children: Key National Indicators of Well-Being, 2011.*

50. Willis D. Hawley and Sonia Nieto, "Another Incontinent Truth: Race and Ethnicity Matter," *Educational Leadership* (November 2010), pp. 66–71; Janice L. Cooper, Patti Banghart, and Yumiko Aratani, *Addressing the Mental Health Needs of Children in the Child Welfare System* (September 2010), available at www.nccp.org/publications/pub_968.html; Richard Rothstein, "Whose Problem Is Poverty?" *Educational Research* 65, no. 7 (2008), pp. 8–13; Royal Van Horn, *Bridging the Chasm between Research and Practice: A Guide to Major Educational Research* (Lanham, MD: Rowman and Littlefield Education, 2008); Rob Stein, "Research Links Poor Kids' Stress, Brain Development," *The Washington Post,* April 6, 2009, p. A6; "Early Education for Poor Kids Yields Long-term Benefits in Study," *Arizona Daily Star* January 21, 2012, p. 14.

51. Oscar Lewis, *La vida; A Puerto Rican Family in the Culture of Poverty—San Juan and New York* (New York: Random House, 1966).

52. Shirley Brice Heath, *Ways with Words: Language, Life, and Work in Communities and Classrooms* (New York: Cambridge University Press, 1983); Hawley and Nieto, "Another Incontinent Truth: Race and Ethnicity Matter."

53. Hawley and Nieto, "Another Incontinent Truth: Race and Ethnicity Matter"; Rothstein, "Whose Problem Is Poverty?"; Stein, "Research Links Poor Kids' Stress, Brain Development."

54. This material is gathered from the Big Picture Longitudinal Study. The information was compiled and sent by the research team, including Karen D. Arnold, Katherine Lynk Wartman, Shezwae Fleming, Mario A. DeAnda, Benjamin L. Castleman, and Carmen Perez. *The Summer Flood: The Gap between College Admission and Matriculation among Low-income Students* (Draft of Findings, May 2009). Funding from the Lumina Foundation and the Irvine Foundation.

55. The National Center for Family Homelessness, *America's Youngest Outcasts* (2010), www.homelesschildrenamerica.org/.

56. National Association for the Education of Homeless Children and Youth, *Fact Sheet,* (September 2011), www.naehcy.org.

57. John Holloway, "Research Link: Addressing the Needs of Homeless Students," *Educational Leadership* 60, no. 4 (December 2002/January 2003), pp. 89–90; National Center for Homeless Education, *McKinney-Vento Act,* retrieved January 20, 2012, from http://center.serve.org/nche/m-v.php.

58. "Study: Fatalistic View Possibly Tied to Kids' Risky Behavior," *The Arizona Daily Star,* June 29, 2009, p. A5.

59. Adria Steinberg and Lili Allen, "Putting Off-Track Youths Back on Track to College," *Phi Delta Kappan* 92, no.5 (February 2011), pp. 21–26; Chris Swanson, "Diplomas Count: Graduation by the Numbers," *Education Week* 29, no. 34 (June 10, 2010), pp. 4–5.

60. Steinberg and Allen, "Putting Off-Track Youths Back on Track to College," p. 23.

61. Editorial Projects in Education, "Diploma Counts 2011," *Education Week online* (June 9, 2011).

62. Editorial Projects in Education, "Diploma Counts 2011"; Steinberg and Allen, "Putting Off-Track Youths Back on Track to College," pp. 21–26.

63. National Campaign to Prevent Teen and Unplanned Pregnancy, *National Data,* 2009, www.thenationalcampaign.org/national-data/default.aspx.

64. Sexuality Information and Education Council of the United States, *Fact Sheet, 2007 & Policy Updates, January 2008,* www.siecus.org.

65. Federal Interagency Forum on Child and Family Statistics, *America's Children: Key National Indicators of Well-Being, 2011,* from www.childstats.gov/americaschildren.

66. The National Center on Addiction and Substance Abuse at Columbia University, *CASA National Survey of American Attitudes on Substance Abuse XVI: Teens and Parents* (August 2011), available at www.casacolumbia.org/.

67. Ibid.

68. Lloyd Johnston, Patrick O'Malley, Jerald Bachman, and John Schulenberg, *Monitoring the Future: National Results on Adolescent Drug Use: Overview of Key Findings, 2010* (Bethesda, MD: National Institute on Drug Abuse, 2010), available at www.monitoringthefuture.org/.

69. The National Center on Addiction and Substance Abuse at Columbia University, *CASA National Survey of American Attitudes on Substance Abuse XVI: Teens and Parents.*

70. Ibid.

71. Ibid.

72. S. Schlozman, "The Shrink in the Classroom: Why 'Just Say No' Isn't Enough," *Educational Leadership* 59, no. 7 (2002), pp. 87–89.

73. Centers for Disease Control and Prevention, *Overweight and Obesity Data and Statistics,* (2012), www.cdc.gov/obesity/.

74. Rob Hotakainen, "Bipartisan Plan Aims to Boost PE in Schools," *Arizona Daily Star,* January 8, 2012, p. A4.

75. "Schools to Serve More Nutritious Meals Under New Guidelines," *The Washington Post online,* January 25, 2012; Claudia Kalb, "Culture of Corpulence," *Newsweek,* March 22, 2010, pp. 42–44.

76. National Eating Disorders Coalition, *Stats About Eating Disorders: What the Research Shows,* January 25, 2012, www.eating.disorderscoalition.org/; Lauren Greenfield and Joan Jacobs Brumberg, *Thin* (San Francisco: Chronicle Books, 2006).

77. National Institute on Drug Abuse, *Anabolic Steroid Abuse,* NIH Publication (July 2009), www.drugabuse.gov/drugs-abuse/steroids-anabolic.

78. Centers for Disease Control and Prevention, National Center for Injury Prevention and Control, *Suicide: Facts at a Glance* (Summer 2011), www.cdc.gov/.

79. Sarah Shulkind, "Reframing Bullying in Middle Schools," *Education Spotlight on Bullying,* 2010, p. 7.

80. Jaclyn Zubrzycki, "Lawmakers Take Aim at Bullying," *Educational Leadership,* October 19, 2011) pp. 1, 16; Lesli A. Maxwell, "Principals' Views on Bullying," *Education Spotlight on Bullying,* 2010, p. 4; Josephson Institute Center for Youth Ethics, *The Ethics of American Youth: 2010* (October 2010); http://charactercounts.org/programs/reportcard.

81. Sameer Hinduja and Justin W. Patchin, "High-Tech Cruelty," *Educational Leadership,* February 2011, pp. 48–52; Jennifer Hollday, "Cyberbullying," *Teaching Tolerance,* Fall 2010, pp. 43–46.

82. Ibid, pp. 43–44.

83. Ibid., pp. 43–46; Hinduja and Patchin, "High-Tech Cruelty."

84. Hollday, "Cyberbullying," pp. 43–46.

85. Dakarai I. Aarons, "Efforts to End Bullying, A Challenge to Leaders, Gains Momentum," *Education Spotlight on Bullying,* 2010, pp. 1–3.

86. Dirk Johnson, "Dalai Lama Donates to Center in Wisconsin," *New York Times,* September 27, 2010, p. A10; Aarons, "Efforts to End Bullying, A Challenge to Leaders, Gains Momentum."

87. Lyn Mikel Brown, "Ten Ways to Move Beyond Bullying Prevention (and Why We Should Do It), *Education Spotlight on Bullying,* 2010, pp. 10–11.

CHAPTER 5 PURPOSES OF AMERICA'S SCHOOLS AND THE CURRENT REFORM MOVEMENT

1. James Shaver and William Strong, *Facing Value Decisions: Rationale Building for Teachers* (Belmont, CA: Wadsworth, 1976); Barbara Slater Stern and Karen Lea Riley, "Reflecting on the Common Good: Harold Rugg and the Social Reconstructionists," *Social Studies* 92 (2001); Michael E. James, *Social Reconstructionism through Education* (Stamford, CT: Ablex Publishing, 1995).

2. Sara Neufeld, "Photos Reveal Decrepit State of City Schools," *Baltimore Sun,* February 24, 2006, http://healthyschoolscampaign.org/news/media/environ/2006-0224_photos.php (retrieved April 17, 2009).

3. Ernest L. Boyer, *High School: A Report on Secondary Education in America* (New York: Harper & Row, 1983), pp. 209–210.

4. Linda Perlstein, " 'Serving' the Community Without Leaving School," *Washington Post,* June 28, 1999, pp. A1, A6.

5. *The Condition of Education 2001,* U.S. Department of Education, NCES, Indicator 16: Social and Cultural Outcomes, Community Service Participation in Grades 6–12, p. 142, http://nces.ed.gov/pubs2001/2001072_2.pdf; Helen M. Marks and Susan Robb Jones, "Community Service in Transition: Shifts and Continuities in Participation from High School to College," *Journal of Higher Education* 75 (2004), pp. 307–339.

6. Bill Bigelow, "The Human Lives Behind the Labels: The Global Sweatshop, Nike, and the Race to the Bottom," *Phi Delta Kappan* 79, no. 2 (October 1997), pp. 112–119.

7. Paulo Freire, *Pedagogy of the Oppressed* (New York: Herder & Herder, 1970).

8. John Goodlad, *A Place Called School* (New York: McGraw-Hill, 1984), pp. 35–39.

9. Arthur Eugene Bestor, *Educational Wastelands: The Retreat from Learning in Our Public Schools* (Urbana: University of Illinois Press, 1953), p. 75.

10. Boyer, *High School,* p. 5.

11. Lowell C. Rose and Alec M. Gallup, "The 39th Annual Phi Delta Kappa/Gallup Poll of the Public's Attitude toward the Public Schools," *Phi Delta Kappan* 89, no. 1 (September 2007), Table 33, pp. 33–48.

12. George Weber, *Inner-City Children Can Be Taught to Read: Four Successful Schools* (Washington, DC: D.C. Council for Basic Books, 1971); Ronald Edmonds, "Some Schools Work and More Can," *Social Policy* 9 (1979), pp. 28–32; Barbara Taylor and Daniel Levine, "Effective Schools Projects and School-Based Management," *Phi Delta Kappan* 72, no. 5 (January 1991), pp. 394–397. See also Herman Meyers, "Roots, Trees, and the Forest: An Effective Schools Development Sequence," paper delivered at the American Educational Research Association, San Francisco, April 1992.

13. Sara Lawrence Lightfoot, *The Good High School* (New York: Basic Books, 1983).

14. Ibid., p. 67.

15. David Clark, Linda Lotto, and Mary McCarthy, "Factors Associated with Success in Urban Elementary Schools," *Phi Delta Kappan* 61, no. 7 (March 1980), pp. 467–470; *The MetLife Survey of the American Teacher: Expectations and Experiences*, Figure 3.7, p. 50 (issued September 26, 2006), www.metlife.com/ (retrieved April 23, 2009). See also David Gordon, "The Symbolic Dimension of Administration for Effective Schools," paper delivered at the annual meeting of the American Educational Research Association, San Francisco, April 1992.

16. William Rutherford, "School Principals as Effective Leaders," *Phi Delta Kappan* 67, no. 1 (September 1985), pp. 31–34; Carl Glickman, "The Courage to Lead," *Educational Leadership* 59, no. 8 (2002), pp. 41–44. See also R. McClure, "Stages and Phases of School-Based Renewal Efforts," paper presented at the annual meeting of the American Educational Research Association, New Orleans, 1988.

17. Steven C. Schlozman, "The Shrink in the Classroom: Fighting School Violence," *Educational Leadership* 60, no. 2 (October 2002), pp. 89–90; Gay, Lesbian, and Straight Education Network, *2007 Climate Survey* (New York: GLSEN, 2008), www.glsen.org; National Center for Education Statistics, *Indicators of School Crime and Safety, 2008* (issued April 21, 2009), http://nces.ed.gov/pubs2008/2008021.pdf (retrieved April 30, 2009).

18. *The Metropolitan Life Survey of the American Teacher 1999* (New York: Harris Interactive Inc., 2001), pp. 39, 42.

19. Lowell C. Rose and Alec M. Gallup, "The 39th Annual Gallup Poll of the Public's Attitudes toward the Public Schools," *Phi Delta Kappan* 89, no. 1 (September 2007), Table 43, pp. 33–48; *The MetLife Survey of the American Teacher: Expectations and Experiences*, Figure 3.7, p. 50.

20. Lightfoot, *The Good High School*; Kevin Dwyer and D. Osher, *Safeguarding Our Children: An Action Guide* (Washington, DC: U.S. Department of Education, August 2000).

21. Wilbur Brookover, Laurence Beamer, Helen Efthim, Douglas Hathaway, Lawrence Lezotte, Stephen Miller, Joseph Passalacqua, and Louis Tornatzky, *Creating Effective Schools* (Holmes Beach, FL: Learning Publications, 1982); Harris Cooper, Jorgianne Robinson, and Erika Patall, "Does Homework Improve Academic Achievement? A Synthesis of Research," *Review of Educational Research* 76 (2006), pp. 1–62.

22. Herbert Walberg, Rosanne Paschal, and Thomas Weinstein, "Homework's Powerful Effects on Learning," *Educational Leadership* 42 (1985), pp. 76–79.

23. Robert Rosenthal and Lenore Jacobson, *Pygmalion in the Classroom* (New York: Holt, Rinehart & Winston, 1968).

24. Patrick Proctor, "Teacher Expectations: A Model for School Improvement," *Elementary School Journal,* March 1984, pp. 469–481; Karin Spader, "The Effects of Teacher Expectations on Student Achievement," paper presented at the annual meeting of the American Sociological Association, Montreal, Canada, August 11, 2006; Robert Marzano, *What Works in Schools* (Alexandria, VA: Association for Supervision and Curriculum Development, 2003).

25. *The Metropolitan Life Survey of the American Teacher 2001* (New York: Harris Interactive, Inc., 2001), p. 61.

26. Alan M. Blankstein and Pedro Noguera, "What Works in School Turnarounds?" *Ed Week* 31, no. 17 (January 18, 2012), pp. 26, 32; Debra Viadero, "Study Finds Success in NYC's 'Small Schools,'" *Education Week* 29, no. 36 (June 23, 2010); Sam Dillon, "4,100 Students Prove 'Small Is Better' Rule Wrong," *New York Times,* September 27, 2010, p. A1; Lorna Jimerson, *The Hobbit Effect: Why Small Works in Public Schools* (2006), www.smallschoolsproject.org/PDFS/RSCT_hobbit-effect.pdf (retrieved April 23, 2009); Christina A. Samuels, "Study: Effective Principals Embrace Collective Leadership" *Education Week* 29, no. 37 (July 23, 2010); Jay Feldman, Lisette Lopez, and Katherine Simon, *Choosing Small: The Essential Guide to Successful High School Conversion* (San Francisco: Jossey Bass, 2006); Douglas Ready, Valerie Lee, and Kevin Welner, "Educational Equity and School Structure: School Size, Overcrowding, and Schools-within-Schools," *Teachers College Record* 106 (2004), pp. 1989–2014; Barbara Taylor, Michael Pressley, and David Pearson, "Research-Supported Characteristics of Teachers and Schools That Promote Reading Achievement," in B. Taylor and D. Pearson, eds., *Teaching Reading: Effective Schools, Accomplished Teachers* (Mahwah, NJ: Erlbaum, 2002), pp. 361–374; Marzano, *What Works in Schools;* Anne T. Henderson, *A New Wave of Evidence: The Impact of School, Family, and Community Connections on Student Achievement* (Austin, Texas: Southwest Educational Development Laboratory, 2002), www.sedl.org/pubs/catalog/items/fam33.html (retrieved April 23, 2009); Kevin Mixon, "Making Parent Involvement a Two-Way Street," *Teacher Magazine,* December 7, 2011, www.Teacher-Magazine.org (retrieved February 8, 2012); James P. Comer, "The Rewards of Parent Participation," *Educational Leadership* 62, no. 6 (March 21, 2005), pp. 38–42; Sabrina Tavernise, "Education Gap Grows Between Rich and Poor, Studies Say," *New York Times,* February 9, 2012, www.nytimes.com (retrieved February 9, 2012).

27. Debra Viadero, "Students Learn More in Magnets than Other Schools, Study Finds," *Education Week,* March 6, 1996, p. 6; Caroline Hendrie, "Magnets' Value in Desegregating Schools Is Found to Be Limited," *Education Week on the Web,* November 13, 1996; "Research Notes," *Education Week on the Web,* September 16, 1998.

28. Alicia Mundy, "Gates 'Appalled' by High Schools," *Seattle Times,* February 7, 2005, http://seattletimes.nwsource.com/html/localnews/2002191433_gates27m.html (retrieved April 20, 2009).

29. *The Economic Impact of Achievement Gaps in America's Schools,* McKinsey Group, Social Sector Office, 2009, www.mckinsey.com/clientservice/socialsector/achievementgap.asp (retrieved April 24, 2009).

30. Alex Molnar, "Charter Schools: The Smiling Face of Disinvestment," *Educational Leadership* 54, no. 2 (October 1996), pp. 9–15; Chuck Sudetic, "Reading, Writing, and Revenue," *Mother Jones,* May/June 2001, pp. 84–95.

31. Mary Ann Zehr, "Study Finds High Dropout Rates for Black Males in KIPP Schools," *Education Week* 30, no. 27 (March 31, 2011), www.educationweek.com (retrieved February 3, 2012); John Thompson, "KIPP and Its Critics Are Both Right," *Huffington Post,* April 17, 2011, www.huffingtonpost.com/ (retrieved February 2, 2012); Mary Ann Zehr, "KIPP Middle Schools Found to Spur Learning Gains," *Education Week* 36, no. 29 (June 22, 2010); Jay Mathews, "Inside the Bay Area KIPP Schools," *Washington Post,* September 19, 2008, www.washingtonpost.com/wp-dyn/content/article/2008/09/19/AR2008091900978.html (retrieved March 27, 2009); Mary Ann Zehr, "Regular Public Schools Start to Mimic Charters," *Education Week* 30, no. 11 (November 8, 2010), pp. 1, 12, www.edweek.org/ew/articles/2010/11/10/11charter.h30.html.

32. David Brooks, "The Relationship School," *New York Times,* March 22, 2012, p. A25.

33. Winnie Hu, "In a New Role, Teachers Are Given the Chance to Run Poorer Schools," *New York Times,* September 7, 2010, pp. A1, A20.

34. Lesli A. Maxwell, "Study Finds No Clear Edge for Charter Schools," *Education Week,* June 29, 2010, www.edweek.org/ew/articles/2010/06/29/36ies.h29.html; Lesli A. Maxwell, "Study Casts Doubt on Charter School Results," *Education Week,* June 15, 2009, www.edweek.org/ew/articles/2009/06/15/36charters.h28.html; Trip Gabriel, "Despite Push, Success at Charter Schools Is Mixed," *New York Times,* May 2, 2010, pp. 1, 22, 23.

35. Leah Fabel, "Charter School Teachers More Likely to Leave Teaching," *Washington Examiner,* July 6, 2010; Jack Buckley and Mark Schneider, *Charter Schools: Hope or Hype?* (Princeton, NJ: Princeton University Press, 2007); Robin J. Lake, ed., *Hopes, Fears, and Reality: A Balanced Look at Charter Schools in 2007* (Seattle, WA: The National Charter School Research Project, December 2007), www.ncsrp.org/cs/csr/view/csr_pubs/17 (retrieved April 9, 2008); Andrew Rotherham and Sara Mead, *A Sum Greater than the Parts: What States Can Teach Each Other about Charter Schooling* (Washington, DC: Education Sector, 2007), www.educationsector.org/usr_doc/CharterSchoolSummary.pdf (retrieved April 17, 2009); Patrik Jonsson, "As New Orleans Restarts Its Schools, Most Are Now Charter Schools," *Christian Science Monitor,* September 4, 2007, www.csmonitor.com/2007/0904/p01s08-ussc.html (retrieved April 17, 2009).

36. Winnie Hu, "Charter School Battle Shifts to Affluent Suburbs," *New York Times,* July 17, 2011, www.nytimes.com/2011/07/17/education/17charters.html?_r=1&pagewanted=print (retrieved January 26, 2012).

37. *Choice Without Equity: Charter School Segregation and the Need for Civil Rights Standards,* The Civil Rights Project, UCLA, February 4, 2010; Dave Weber, "Florida Charters Less Diverse Than Other Public Schools," *Orlando Sentinel,* April 30, 2011, www.sun-sentinel.com/news/local/breakingnews/os-charter-schools-segregation-20110430,0,4650625,full.story.

38. Alyson Klein, "Needs of 'Whole Child' May Factor in ESEA Renewal; Wide Range of Supports, Services, and Enrichment Seen as Vital but Costly," *Education Week* 29, no. 30, pp. 16, 21 (April 28, 2010); Sharon Otterman, "Despite Money and Attention, It's Not All A's at 2 Harlem Schools," *New York Times,* October 13, 2010, pp. A18–19; Javier C. Hernandez, "Harlem Educator Is Said to Have Rejected Schools Chancellor Job," *New York Times,* December 10, 2010, p. 10.

39. For more on the legal dispute, see *Jackson* v. *Benson* (1998), which held that vouchers used for religious school tuition did not violate the Wisconsin state constitution; Sam Dillon, "For Parents Seeking a Choice, Charter Schools Prove More Popular than Vouchers," *New York Times,* July 23, 2005, www.nytimes.com/2005/07/13/education/13voucher.html (retrieved April 7, 2008).

40. David Stout, "Public Money Can Pay Religious-School Tuition, Court Rules," *New York Times,* June 27, 2002.

41. Erin Richards, "New Data Shows Similar Academic Results Between Voucher and MPS Students," *Milwaukee Journal Sentinel,* April 7, 2010, www.jsonline.com/news/education/90169302.html; Kavan Peterson, "School Vouchers Slow to Spread," www.Stateline.org, May 5, 2005; National Education Association, "Florida High Court Rules Against Vouchers," www.nea.org/vouchers/flvouchers1-06.html (retrieved January 5, 2006); Maria Glod and Bill Turque, "Report Finds Little Gain from Vouchers," *Washington Post,* June 17, 2008, p. B6.

42. Jeremy P. Meyer, "Douglas County School District Considers Starting Voucher Program," *Denver Post,* November 5, 2010, www.denverpost.com/news/ci_16528490; Dillon, "For Parents Seeking a Choice, Charter Schools Prove More Popular than Vouchers"; U.S. Charter Schools, "Frequently Asked Questions," March 22, 2006, www.uscharterschools.org/pub/uscs_docs/o/faq.html; Center for Education Reform, "Charter Schools," March 22, 2006, www.edreform.com; "New CER Report Gives Evidence of Charters' Impact," *Charter Schools Today,* Washington, DC, May 5, 2004; National Education Association, *Vouchers* (2008), www.nea.org/vouchers/index.html (retrieved April 7, 2008).

43. Erin Richards and Amy Hetzner, "Choice Schools Not Outperforming MPS, Latest Tests Show Voucher Scores About Same or Worse in Math and Reading," *Milwaukee Journal Sentinel,* March 29, 2011,.jsonline.com/news/education/118820339.html (retrieved February 1, 2012); Dan Hardy, "Finding that Vouchers Have Little Impact on Student Achievement Do Not Deter Advocates," *Philadelphia Inquirer,* August 08, 2011, http://articles.philly.com/2011-08-08/news/29864661_1_voucher-programs-voucher-students-voucher-proposals (retrieved February 3, 2012); Timothy McDonald, "The False Promise of Voucher," *Educational Leadership* 59, no. 7 (April 2002), pp. 33–37; Kaleem M. S. Caire, "The Truth about Vouchers," *Educational Leadership* 59, no. 7 (April 2002), pp. 38–42; National Education Association, "Vouchers," March 22, 2006,

www.nea.org/vouchers/index.html; Pat Kossan and Emily Gersema, "Arizona's High Court Bans School Vouchers," *Arizona Republic,* March 26, 2009, www.azcentral.com/arizonarepublic/news/articles/2009/03/26/20090326vouchers0326.html (retrieved March 29, 2009); National Education Association, "Florida High Court Rules Against Vouchers."

44. A. S. Byrk, Valerie Lee, and P. B. Holland, *Catholic Schools and the Common Good* (London: Harvard University Press, 1993); Public School Review, "What Is a Magnet School?" www.publicschoolreview.com/magnet-schools.php (retrieved March 22, 2006); Howard Blume, "Support for Magnet Schools Waning Despite Their Success," *Los Angeles Times,* November 26, 2008, http://articles.latimes.com/2008/nov/26/local/memagnets26 (retrieved April 1, 2009).

45. National Center of Education Statistics, *State Education Reforms. Table 4.1: Number and Types of Open Enrollment Policies, by State, 2005,* http://nces.ed.gov/programs/statereform/sssco_tab1.asp (retrieved April 7, 2008).

46. Amanda Paulson, "Virtual Schools, Real Concerns," *Christian Science Monitor,* May 4, 2004; U.S. Department of Education, National Center for Education Statistics, Fast Response Survey System (FRSS), "Distance Education Courses for Public School Elementary and Secondary School Students: 2002–03," Washington, DC; Kate Moser, "Online Courses Aren't Just for Home-Schoolers Anymore," *Christian Science Monitor,* March 30, 2006, www.csmonitor.com/2006/0330/p14s02-legn.html; Sean Cavanagh, "Survey Finds Interest in Blend of Tradition and Online Courses," *Education Week,* March 5, 2007.

47. Bill Tucker, *Laboratories of Reform: Virtual High Schools and Innovation in Public Education* (Washington, DC: Education Sector, June 2007), www.educationsector.org/research/research_show.htm?doc_id5502307 (retrieved April 10, 2008); Cavanagh, "Survey Finds Interest in Blend of Tradition and Online Courses," Moser, "Online Courses Aren't Just for Home-Schoolers Anymore"; Michelle Galley, "Despite Concerns, Online Elementary Schools Grow," *Education Week* 22, no. 16 (January 8, 2003), pp. 1, 12.

48. Diana B. Henriques, "Edison Schools' Founder to Take It Private," *New York Times,* July 15, 2003; Gerald Bracey, "The 12th Bracey Report on the Condition of Public Education," *Phi Delta Kappan* 84, no. 2 (October 2002), pp. 135–150; Chris Brennan, "Ex-Edison Official: Company Lacks Integrity," Philly.com, July 24, 2002; Michael Fletcher, "Private Enterprise, Public Woes in Phila. School," *Washington Post,* September 17, 2002, p. A1; Brian Gill, Laura S. Hamilton, J. R. Lockwood, Julie A. Marsh, Ron Zimmer, Deanna Hill, and Shana Pribesh, *Inspiration, Perspiration, and Time: Operations and Achievements in Edison Schools,* October 2005, RAND Corporation, www.rand.org/pubs/monographs/MG351.html (retrieved May 1, 2009).

49. Joel Spring, *American Education* (New York: McGraw-Hill, 1996), pp. 184–185.

50. Lyndsey Layton and Emma Brown, "Virtual Schools Are Multiplying, But Some Question Their Educational Value," *Washington Post,* November 26, 2011, www.washingtonpost.com (retrieved February 2, 2012); Dale Singer, "Missouri's

Top Educator Says Imagine Schools Should Shut Down," *St. Louis Beacon,* November 8, 2011, www.stlbeacon.org/issues-politics/95-Education/114070-missouris-top-educator-says-imagine-schools-should-shut-down (retrieved February 3, 2012); Stephanie Strom, "For School Company, Issues of Money and Control," *New York Times,* April 23, 2010, p. A1; Katrina E. Bulkley, *Recentralizing Decentralization? Educational Management Organizations and Charter Schools' Educational Programs* (National Center for the Study of the Privatization of Education, Columbia Teachers College, 2003). For additional studies on the privatization of schools and school choice, see the National Center for the Study of the Privatization of Education, www.ncspe.org/; Bill Brubaker, "Sylvan Learning Systems Renamed Laureate to Focus on Universities," *Washington Post,* May 18, 2004, p. E04; Jamie Smith Hopkins, "Sylvan, LeapFrog Plan to Tutor Kids in Big Stores: Parents Might Soon Be Able to Shop While Their Children Are Being Tutored a Few Aisles Away," *Baltimore Sun,* December 22, 2004.

51. "Live and Learn," *Harper's Bazaar,* September 1994, pp. 268–270.

52. National Center for Education Statistics, "Homeschooling in the United States: 2003," February 2006, http://nces.ed.gov/pubs2006/2006042.pdf (retrieved May 1, 2009).

53. J. A. Van Galen, "Schooling in Private: A Study of Home Education," doctoral dissertation, University of North Carolina, Chapel Hill, 1986; National Center for Education Statistics, "Homeschooled Students," *The Condition of Education* (May 2009), Indicator 6, http://nces.ed.gov/pubs2009/2009081.pdf.

54. Brian D. Ray, "Homeschooling Across America: Academic Achievement and Demographic Characteristics," August 10, 2009, www.nheri.org/Latest/Homeschooling-Across-America-Academic-Achievement-and-Demographic-Characteristics.html; Gregory J. Millman, "Home Is Where the School Is," *Washington Post,* March 23, 2008, p. B1; National Center for Education Statistics, "Homeschooling in the United States: 2003"; Moser, "Online Courses Aren't Just for Home-Schoolers Anymore." For examples of online homeschooling curricula, see HomeSchool.com at www.homeschool.com/onlinecourses/ and Online Learning Haven at www.learninghaven.com/. See also, Nancy Trejos, "Home Schooling's Net Effect," *The Washington Post,* July 16, 2000, pp. C1, C9.

55. Brian Ray, "Customization through Homeschooling," *Educational Leadership* 59, no. 7 (April 2002), p. 50.

56. "Top-Selling Home-School Texts Disparage Evolution," *Arizona Daily Star,* March 7, 2010, p. A14.

57. Rob Reich, "The Civic Perils of Home Schooling," *Educational Leadership* 59, no. 7 (April 2002), pp. 56–59.

58. Erik W. Robelen, "Environmental Literacy Making a Splash," *Ed Week,* October 10, 2011, www.edweek.com (retrieved January 2012); Lucy Hood, "The Greening of Environmental Ed: Teachers Focus on Complexity, Evidence, and Letting Students Draw their Own Conclusions," *Harvard Graduate School of Education Newsletter* 27, no. 1 (January/February 2011); Katie Ash, " 'Green Schools' Benefit Budgets and Students, Report Says Environmentally friendly Schools Seen as Good for Bottom Line," *Ed Week,* May 24, 2011, www.edweek

.org/ew/articles/2011/05/25/32greenschools_ep.h30.html (retrieved February 3, 2012); Gregory Kats, "Greening America's Schools: Costs and Benefits" (October 2006), a Capital E Report, www.cape.com/ewebeditpro/items/O59F9819. pdf; "Daylighting in Schools: An Investigation into the Relationship between Daylighting and Human Performance," Heschong Mahone Group (August 1999), www.coe.uga.edu/ sdpl/research/daylightingstudy.pdf; *Healthier, Wealthier, Wiser: A Report on National Green Schools,* a Report by Global Green USA, www.globalgreen.org/news/155 (retrieved April 2, 2009).

59. Rhonda Bodfield, "Schoolchildren Aware of Environmental Woes," *Arizona Daily Star,* January 3, 2009, www.azstarnet. com/metro/274326 (retrieved April 3, 2009); Sean Cavanagh, " 'Green' Classes Flourish in Schools," *Education Week,* 28, no. 20 (February 3, 2009), p. 1, 13; Chelsy Killebrew, "Schoolchildren Go Green: Gardens Offer Science, Art and Enviro Lessons," *Arizona Daily Star,* September 26, 2008, pp. B1, B2; No Child Left Inside, www.cbf.org/site/ PageServer?pagename5act_sub_actioncenter_federal_ NCLB (retrieved April 3, 2009); James Daly, "School Retrofits Go Green" *Edutopia,* October 28, 2009, www.edutopia.org/ green-schools-retrofitting-health-budget.

60. U.S. Environmental Protection Agency, Office of Radiation and Indoor Air, *The Inside Story: A Guide to Indoor Air Quality,* U.S. (6609J), Washington, DC, cosponsored with the Consumer Product Safety Commission, EPA 402-K-93-007, www .epa.gov/iaq/pubs/insidest.html.

61. Anna Phillips, "In State of the City, Mayor Calls for an End to Seniority Layoffs," *GothamSchools.org,* January 19, 2011; "Study Questions Seniority-Based Teacher Layoffs," *Daily Caller,* December 23, 2010, Center for Education Data and Research, www.cedr.us; Steven Greenhouse and Sam Dillon, "A Wholesale School Shake-Up Is Embraced by the President, and Divisions Follow," *New York Times,* March 7, 2010, p. 18; Jason Felch, Jason Song, and Sandra Poindexter "In Reforming Schools, Quality of Teaching Often Overlooked," *Los Angeles Times,* December 21, 2010.

62. Mitchell Landsberg, "Influence of Teachers Unions in Question," *Los Angeles Times,* November 7, 2010, http://articles.latimes.com/2010/nov/07/local/ la-me-teachers-unions-20101107.

63. Dakarai I. Aarons, "Tennessee Targets Teaching with Race to Top Winnings: State Officials See Unique Chance for Big Change in Expectations for Schools," *Education Week* 29, no. 28 (April 2, 2010), p. 28; Catherine Gewertz, "Race to Top Rules Aim to Spur Shifts in Testing," *Education Week* 29, no. 29 (April 8, 2010), www.edweek.org/ew/articles/2010/04/07 /29assessment_ep.h29.html.

64. Sam Dillon, "Teacher Ratings Get New Look, Pushed by a Very Rich Watcher," *New York Times,* December 4, 2010, pp. A1, A14; Nick Anderson, "Education Secretary Duncan and Teachers Unions Announce Summit," *Washington Post,* October 14, 2010, www.washingtonpost.com/wp-dyn/ content/article/2010/10/14/AR2010101404094.html.

65. "Is America Listening to Its Teachers? Annual MetLife Teacher Survey Reveals Two-Thirds of Teachers Say Voices Unheard," *MetLife,* B2E News Alert, February 17, 2010; Steven Brill, "The Teachers' Union Last Stand," *New York Times Magazine,* May 23, 2010, pp. 32–39, 44, 46–47.

66. Ann Duffett, Steve Farkas, Andrew J. Rotherham, and Elena Silva, *Waiting to Be Won Over: Teachers Speak on the Profession, Unions, and Reform* (Washington, DC: Education Sector, May 2008).

67. Sharon Otterman, "Once Nearly 100%, Teacher Tenure Rate Drops to 58% as Rules Tighten," *New York Times,* July 27, 2011, www.nytimes.com/2011/07/28/nyregion/tenure-granted- to-58-of-eligible-teachers-in-city.html; Doug Ireland, "N.H. Tenure Change Makes Some Happy, Some Not," *Eagle Tribune,* July 19, 2011, www.eagletribune.com/newhampshire/ x1241067726/N-H-tenure-change-makes-some-happy- some-not (retrieved January 15, 2012); Scott Martindale, "Survey: 1 in 5 Teachers Support Ending Unions," *Orange County Register,* August 3, 2011, www.ocregister.com/arti- cles/teachers-310712-percent-tenure.html.

68. Barbara Martinez, "School 'Bonus' Plan Comes Up Short," *Wall Street Journal,* April 4, 2011, http://online.wsj.com/article/ SB10001424052748703806304576236711724799444.html; Scott Travis, "Merit Pay Law Raises Questions for Florida's Specialty Teachers," *Sun Sentinel,* August 20, 2011, http:// articles.sun-sentinel.com/2011-08-20/news/fl-electives- fcat-accountability-20110820_1_new-teacher-merit-music- teacher-drama-teacher (retrieved February 4, 2012); Jocelyn Wiener, "Teachers Wary on Risk, Rewards of Merit Pay" *Sacramento Bee,* January 18, 2005.

69. Circe Stumbo and Peter McWalters, "The Effective Educator Measuring Effectiveness: What Will It Take?" *Educational Leadership* 68, no. 4 (December 2010), pp. 10–15; Juan A. Lozano, "Houston to Link Teachers' Pay, Test Scores," *The Guardian,* January 11, 2006, www.guardian.co.uk; Holly K. Hatcher and Terrence Stutz, "Incentive Pay Enters Classroom; Other States Watching as Texas Ties Teacher Bonuses to Test Scores," *Dallas Morning News,* June 12, 2006, www.dallasnews. com.

70. Stumbo and McWalters, "The Effective Educator Measuring Effectiveness"; "Teachers Willing to Talk about Merit Pay," *Chicago Daily Herald,* June 7, 2006.

71. John Norton, "These Things We Believe," *Teacher Magazine* online, February 10, 2010; Vivian Truen and Katherine C. Boles, "How 'Merit Pay' Squelches Teaching," *Boston Globe,* September 28, 2005.

72. Kenneth J. Cooper, "Performance Pay for Teachers Catches On," *Washington Post,* February 26, 2000, p. A4; Alfie Kohn, "The Folly of Merit Pay," *Education Week* 23, no. 3 (September 17, 2003), pp. 44, 31.

73. Anthony S. Byrk and Barbara Schneider, "Trust in Schools: A Core Resource for School Reform," *Educational Leadership* 60, no. 6 (March 2003), pp. 40–44.

74. Penny A. Bishop and Susanna W. Pflaum, "Student Perceptions of Action, Relevance, and Pace," *Middle School Journal* 36, no. 4 (March 2005), pp. 1–12.

75. National Center for Educational Statistics, *The Condition of Education 2007* (Washington, DC: U.S. Department of Education, 2007), Indicator 22: Student Preparedness.

76. Marge Scherer, "Perspectives/Learning: Whose Job Is It?" *Educational Leadership* 66, no. 3 (November 2008), p. 7.

77. "What Students Want from Teachers," *Educational Leadership* 66, no. 3 (November 2008), pp. 48–51.

78. Adam Fletcher, "Giving Students Ownership of Learning: The Architecture of Ownership," *Educational Leadership* 66, no. 3 (November 2008), www.ascd.org/publications/educational_leadership/nov08/vol66/num03/The_Architecture_of_Ownership.aspx (retrieved April 15, 2009).

79. *The Metropolitan Life Survey of the American Teacher 2000: Are We Preparing Students for the 21st Century?* (New York: Harris Interactive, Inc., 2000); *The MetLife Survey of the American Teacher: Expectations and Experiences,* Figure 3.9, p. 52 (issued September 26, 2006), www.metlife.com/Applications/Corporate/WPS/CDA/PageGenerator/0,4132,P2315,00.html (retrieved April 13, 2008).

80. Lightfoot, *The Good High School.* See also Anthony Jackson and Gayle Davis, *Turning Points: Educating Adolescents in the 21st Century* (New York: Teachers College Press, 2000).

81. Carrie R. Leana, "The Missing Link in School Reform," *Stanford Social Innovation Review,* Fall 2011, www.ssireview.org (retrieved February 3, 2012); Jeff Gregg and Diana Underwood-Gregg, "The Paradox of Education Reform," *Teachers College Record,* July 22, 2011, www.tcrecord.org/ (retrieved February 9, 2012); Paul Farhi, "Five Myths about America's schools," *Washington Post,* May 20, 2011, www.washingtonpost.org (retrieved February 7, 2012).

CHAPTER 6   CURRICULUM, STANDARDS, AND TESTING

1. Abner Peddiwell (Harold Benjamin), *The Saber-Tooth Curriculum* (New York: McGraw-Hill, 1939).

2. Hilda Taba, *Curriculum Development: Theory and Practice* (New York: Harcourt Brace Jovanovich, 1962).

3. Stephen Hamilton, "Synthesis of Research on the Social Side of Schooling," *Educational Leadership* 40, no. 5 (February 1983), pp. 65–72.

4. Women's Sports Foundation, *2008 Statistics—Gender Equity in High School and College Athletics: Most Recent Participation & Budget Statistics,* www.womenssportsfoundation.org/ (retrieved April 17, 2009).

5. Ibid.; National Federation High School Athletic Association, *The Case for High School Activities,* www.nfhs.org (retrieved April 17, 2009).

6. National Federation High School Athletic Association, *LaCrosse, Bowling among Nation's Emerging High Sports,* www.nfhs.org (retrieved April 17, 2009); Staci Hupp, "As Fastest Growing High School Sport, Bowling a Hit," *Dallas Morning News,* October 23, 2007.

7. June Kronholz, "Academic Value of Non-Academics: The Case for Keeping Extracurriculars," *Education Next* 12, no. 1 (Winter 2012), http://educationnext.org/.

8. National Federation High School Athletic Association, *The Case for High School Activities;* Jennifer A. Fredericks and Jacquelynne S. Eccles, "Developmental Benefits of Extracurricular Involvement: Do Peer Characteristics Mediate the Link between Activities and Youth Outcomes?" *Journal of Youth and Adolescence* 34, no. 6 (December 2005), pp. 507–520; John Holloway, "Extracurricular Activities and Student Participation," *Educational Leadership* 60, no. 1 (September 2002), pp. 80–81.

9. National Center for Education Statistics, *Trends among High School Seniors, 1972–2004* (Washington, DC: U.S Department of Education, 2008); Women's Sports Foundation, *Go Out and Play: Youth Sports in America* (October 2008), www.womenssportsfoundation.org.

10. John Hoffman, "Extracurricular Activities, Athletic Participation, and Adolescent Alcohol Use: Gender-Differentiated and School-Contextual Effects," *Journal of Health and Social Behavior* 47 (September 2006), pp. 275–290; Fredericks and Eccles, "Developmental Benefits of Extracurricular Involvement."

11. Sean Cavanaugh, "Electives Getting the Boot? It Depends on Where and What," *Education Week* 35, no. 2 (April 19, 2006), p. 7.

12. Paul Barry, "Interview: A Talk with A. Bartlett Giamatti," *College Review Board* (Spring 1982), p. 48.

13. Tamar Lewis, "Children's Publisher Backing Off Its Corporate Ties," *New York Times,* July 31, 2011, www.nytimes.com/2011/08/01/education/01scholastic.html?_r=1&pagewanted=print (retrieved April 4, 2012).

14. Bobbi Ann Starnes, "Textbooks, School Reform, and the Silver Lining," *Phi Delta Kappan* 86, no. 2 (2004), pp. 170–171; L. Fan and G. Kaeley, "The Influence of Textbooks on Teaching Strategies," *Mid-Western Educational Researcher* 13, no 4 (2000), pp. 2–9; A. Woodward and D. L. Elliot, "Textbook Use and Teacher Professionalism," in D. L. Elliot and A. Woodward, eds., *Textbooks and Schooling in the United States,* 89th Yearbook of the National Society for the Study of Education (Chicago: University of Chicago Press, 1990), pp. 178–193.

15. Harriet Tyson Bernstein, *A Conspiracy of Good Intentions: America's Textbook Fiasco* (Washington, DC: The Council for Basic Education, 1988), p. 2.

16. Russell Shorto, "How Christian Were the Founders?" *New York Times Magazine,* February 14, 2010; James McKinley Jr., "Texas Conservatives Seek Deeper Stamp on Texts," *New York Times,* March 10, 2010; Katherine Mangan, "Ignoring Experts' Pleas, Texas Board Approves Controversial Curriculum Standards," *Chronicle of Higher Ed,* May 23, 2010; "Educators Seek Delay of School Curriculum Vote," *Houston Chronicle,* April 15, 2010; Larry Dossey, "Stolen History: The Great Texas Textbook War," *Explore: The Journal of Science and Healing* 7, no. 4 (July 2011), pp. 203–211; Nick Anderson, "Teaching the Civil War, 150 Years Later," *Washington Post,* April 10, 2011, www.washington post.com (retrieved April 4, 2012).

17. Paul Weber, "Experts: Texas Textbooks are Unlikely to Spread," *ABC News (AP) San Antonio,* May 31, 2010, http://abcnews.go.com/US/Media/wireStory?id510790382 (retrieved June 21, 2010); "City Revokes Testing Word Ban," *The New York Times,* SchoolBook blog, April 2, 2012, www.nytimes.com (retrieved April 4, 2012).

18. Gilbert Sewall, "Textbook Publishing," *Phi Delta Kappan* 48, no. 1 (March 2005), pp. 498–502; Diana Jean Schemo, "Schoolbooks Are Given F's in Originality," *New York Times,* July 13, 2006, www.nytimes.com/2006/07/13/books/13textbook.html (retrieved April 17, 2009).

19. Sewall, "Textbook Publishing."

20. Kate Walsh, "Basal Readers: The Lost Opportunity to Build the Knowledge that Propels Comprehension, *The American Educator,* Spring 2003, pp. 24–27, www.aft.org/pubs-reports/american_educator/spring2003/Basal_readers.pdf (retrieved April 18, 2009); Andrew Haslett, *Political Propaganda in Elementary Reading Texts* (Chicago: The Heartland Institute, 1999). See also Michael Apple, "Regulating the Text: The Social Historical Roots of State Control," paper delivered at the annual meeting of the American Educational Research Association, San Francisco, April 1992.

21. M. Pittman and Jeff Frykholm, "Turning Points: Curriculum Materials as a Catalyst for Change," paper presented at the annual meeting of the American Educational Research Association, Seattle, April 2002; Starnes, "Textbooks, School Reform, and the Silver Lining"; Fan and Kaeley, "The Influence of Textbooks on Teaching Strategies."

22. L. Hardy, "A New Federal Role," *American School Board Journal* 189, no. 9 (September 2002), pp. 20–24.

23. Nick Anderson, "Most Schools Could Face 'Failing' Label Under No Child Left Behind, Duncan Says," *Washington Post,* March 10, 2011, www.washingtonpost.com (retrieved March 12, 2012).

24. David J. Hoff, "More Schools Facing Sanctions Under NCLB," *Education Week* 28, no. 16 (January 7, 2009), pp. 1, 14–15; Susan Saulny, "Meaning of 'Proficient' Varies for Schools Across Country," *New York Times,* January 19, 2005, www.nytimes.com/2005/01/19/education/19scores.html (retrieved September 1, 2009); Lynn Olson and Linda Jacobson, "Analysis Finds Minority NCLB Scores Widely Excluded," *Education Week,* April 26, 2006; Tamar Lewin, "States Found to Vary Widely on Education," *New York Times,* June 8, 2007, www.nytimes.com/2007/06/08/education/08scores.html (retrieved April 19, 2009); Ledyard King, "Data Suggest States Satisfy No Child Law by Expecting Less of Students," *USA Today,* June 6, 2007, www.usatoday.com/news/education/2007-06-06-schools-main_N.htm (retrieved April 19, 2009); Pauline Vu, "Do State Tests Make the Grade," *Stateline.org* (January 17, 2008), www.stateline.org/live/details/story?contentld5272382 (retrieved April 25, 2008); Daniel De Vise, " 'Safe Harbor' Offers Shelter from Strict 'No Child' Targets," *Washington Post,* April 7, 2008, pp. B01, B02.

25. Diane Ravitch, *The Death and Life of the Great American School System: How Testing and Choice Are Undermining Education* (New York: Basic Books, 2010); Alexis Hulcochea, "Education Expert Knocks Reform in Schools, Standardized Testing," *Arizona Star,* February 19, 2011, p. A5.

26. Helen Cooper, "Obama Urges Education Law Overhaul," *New York Times,* March 15, 2011, p. A22; Gail Russell Chaddock, "No Child Left Behind: Why Congress will Struggle to Hit Obama Deadline," *Christian Science Monitor,* March 14, 2011; Michele McNeil, "Majority of States Say They'll Seek Waivers Under NCLB," *Education Week,* October 13, 2011, www.educationweek.com (retrieved March 12, 2012); "The Wrong Fix for No Child Left Behind," *New York Times,* October 26, 2011, wwwnytimes.com (retrieved March 12, 2012).

27. Common Core State Standards Initiative, www.corestandards.org/ (retrieved February 17, 2011). These standards were developed by the Council of Chief State School Officers and the National Governors Association; Catherine Gewertz, "Gates Awards 15 Grants for Common-Standards Work," *Education Week* 29, no. 22 (February 18, 2010), www.edweek.org/ew/articles/2010/02/18/22gates.h29.html (retrieved January 19, 2011); David Keyes, "Classroom Caste System," *Washington Post,* April 9, 2007, p. A13.

28. Robert Rothman, "Five Myths About the Common Core State Standards," *Harvard Education Letter* 27, no. 5 (September/October 2011); Nancy Badertscher, "Teachers See Change Coming in Common Core State Standards," *The Atlanta Journal-Constitution,* September 27, 2011, www.ajc.com (retrieved March 15, 2012); University of Virginia, "Students Benefit from Depth, Rather than Breadth, in High School Science Courses," *ScienceDaily,* March 10, 2009, www.sciencedaily.com/releases/2009/03/090305131814.htm (retrieved April 19, 2009); see also Kelly Gallagher, "Why I Will Not Teach to the Test: It's Time to Focus on In-Depth Learning, Not Shallow Answers," *Education Week* 30, no. 12 (November 17, 2010), pp. 29, 36.

29. Catherine Gewertz, "Districts Gear Up for Shift to Informational Texts," *Education Week,* March 13, 2012, www.edweek.org (retrieved March 15, 2012); Tennille Tracy, "School Standards Wade into Climate Debate," *Wall Street Journal,* March 11, 2012, www.wallstreetjournal.com (retrieved March 15, 2012); Sarah D. Sparks, "Experts Say Social Sciences Are 'Left Behind'" *Education Week,* November 30, 2011, www.edweek.org/ew/articles/2011/11/30/13social.h31.html (retrieved March 21, 2012).

30. Catherine Gewertz, "Few States Cite Full Plans for Carrying Out Standards," *Education Week* 31, no. 17 (January 12, 2012), www.edweek.org (retrieved March 17, 2012); Catherine Gewertz, "Preparedness For Common Standards: A Work in Progress," *Education Week,* March 19, 2012, www.edweek.org (retrieved March 20, 2012); Stephanie Hirsh, "Common-Core Work Must Include Teacher Development; Standards Movement Must Embrace Teacher Professional Learning," *Education Week,* January 31, 2012, www.educationweek.com (retrieved March 26, 2012); Erik W. Robelen, "Literacy Wins, History Loses in Federal Budget; Foreign-Language, Civics, Economics Aid also Scrapped," *Education Week,* January 6, 2012, www.edweek.org (retrieved April 5, 2012).

31. Michael Alison Chandler, "Montgomery County Is Paving the Way for New School Standards," *Washington Post,* September 3, 2011, www.washingtonpost.com (retrieved March 12, 2012); Fernando Santos, "A Trial Run for School Standards That Encourage Deeper Thought," *New York Times,* April 24, 2011, www.nytimes.com (retrieved March 13, 2012); Catherine Gewertz, "Academics Find Common Standards Fit for College, But Academics Maintain Some Skills Are Missing," *Education Week* 31, no. 2 (August 25, 2011), pp. 1, 12–13.

32. Alfie Kohn, "Debunking the Case for National Standards," commentary in *Education Week* 29, no. 17 (January 14, 2010), pp. 28, 30; Ze'ev Wurman and W. Stephen Wilson, "The Common Core Math Standards: Are They a Step Forward or

Backward?" *Education Next* 12, no. 3 (Summer 2012); Catherine Gewertz, "Critics Post 'Manifesto' Opposing Shared Curriculum; More Than 100 Critics Sign Opposing Document," *Education Week,* May 9, 2011, updated May 17, 2011, www.educationweek.com (retrieved March 21, 2012).

33. Linda Darling-Hammond, *The Flat World and Education: How America's Commitment to Equity Will Determine Our Future* (New York: Teachers' College Press, 2010).

34. Catherine Gewertz, "New Details Surface About Common Assessments," *Education Week* 31, no. 15 (January 11, 2012), p. 10.

35. Sharon Nichols and David Berliner, *Collateral Damage: How High-Stakes Testing Corrupts America's Schools* (Cambridge, MA: Harvard Education Press, 2007).

36. John Merrow, "Undermining Standards," *Phi Delta Kappan* 82, no. 9 (May 2009), p. 655.

37. Kate Zernike, "Scarsdale Mothers Succeed in First Boycott of 8th-Grade Test," *New York Times on the Web,* May 4, 2001, http://tv.nytimes.com/learning/general/specials/testing/04SCAR.html (retrieved January 16, 2005).

38. Michael A. Fletcher, "High Stakes Rise, School Group Put Exam to Test," *Washington Post,* July 9, 2001, p. A1; Michele Kurtz, "Berkshire District to Flout MCAS Rule," *Boston Globe,* February 21, 2003, p. B5; David Hoff, "Teacher Probed for Role in Anti-Testing Activity," *Education Week* 21, no. 36 (May 15, 2002), p. 3.

39. David Keyes, "Classroom Caste System," *Washington Post,* April 9, 2007, p. A13.

40. Monty Neill, "The Dangers of Testing," *Educational Leadership* 60, no. 5 (February 2003), pp. 43–46; Nichols and Berliner, *Collateral Damage: How High-Stakes Testing Corrupts America's Schools.*

41. Alfie Kohn, *The Case Against Standardized Testing: Raising Scores and Ruining Schools* (Portsmouth, NH: Heinemann, 2000); Dalia Zabala, *State High School Exit Exams: Patterns in Gaps in Pass Rates* (Center on Education Policy, February 2008), www.cep-dc.org/ (retrieved April 27, 2008); "Only '50-50' Chance of High School Graduation for U.S. Minority Students, Weak Accountability Rules Found" (Washington, DC: The Civil Rights Project at Harvard and the Urban Institute, February 25, 2004).

42. Jennifer Booher-Jennings, "Rationing Education," *Washington Post,* October 5, 2006, p. A33.

43. "Primary Sources: 2012: America's Teachers on the Teaching Profession," *A Project of Scholastic and the Bill & Melinda Gates Foundation,* March 2012, www.scholastic.com/primarysources/download.asp (retrieved April 6, 2012); Anthony Rebora, "Teachers Place Little Value on Standardized Testing" *Education Week* 31, no. 26 (March 28, 2012) p. 14; the report is entitled and is available at www.scholastic.com/primarysources/pdfs/Gates2012_full.pdf.

44. Diane Rado, "New ISAT Lets Kids Pass with More Wrong Answers," *Chicago Tribune,* October 18, 2010, www.chicagotribune.com/news/education/ct-met-isat-answers-20101018,0,308277.story; Ben Feller, "Gaps Appear in State, Federal Test Scores," *Boston Globe,* March 3, 2006; Susan Saulny, "Meaning of 'Proficient' Varies for Schools

Across Country," *New York Times,* January 19, 2005; Nichols and Berliner, *Collateral Damage: How High-Stakes Testing Corrupts America's Schools;* David Sadker and Karen Zittleman, "Test Anxiety: Are Students Failing Tests—or Are Tests Failing Students?" *Phi Delta Kappan,* 85, no. 10 (June 2004), pp. 740–751.

45. Nichols and Berliner, *Collateral Damage;* Sadker and Zittleman, "Test Anxiety."

46. Connie Langland, "Tests No Help to Learning," *Philadelphia Inquirer,* May 29, 2003.

47. James Hoffman, Assaf Czop, Lori Paris, and Scott Paris, "High-Stakes Testing in Reading: Today in Texas, Tomorrow?" *The Reading Teacher* 54, no. 5 (February 2001), pp. 482–492.

48. Alex Kingsbury, "Schools Cut Other Subjects to Teach Reading and Math," *U.S. News and World Report,* July 25, 2007, www.usnews.com/usnews/edu/articles/070725/25nclb.htm (retrieved April 19, 2009).

49. Fran Smith, "Why Arts Education Is Crucial and Who Is Doing It Best," *Edutopia,* February 18, 2009, www.edutopia.org/arts-music-curriculum-child-development; Stephanie Perrin, "Why Arts Education Matters," *Education Week* 27, no. 21 (January 30, 2008), pp. 26–27; Shirley Dang, "Schools Pile on English, Math Classes," *Contra Costa Times,* May 19, 2007.

50. Nancy Kober, "Teaching to the Test: The Good, the Bad, and Who's Responsible," *TestTalk for Leaders,* June 2002; Michele Kurtz and Anand Vaishnav, "Student's MCAS Answer Means 449 Others Pass," *Boston Globe,* December 5, 2002, p. A1.

51. Sam Dillon, "Before the Answer, the Question Must Be Correct," *New York Times,* July 16, 2003; Karen W. Arenson and Diana B. Henriques, "SAT Errors Raise New Questions about Testing," *New York Times,* March 10, 2006.

52. Diana B. Henriques and Jacques Steinberg, "Right Answer, Wrong Score: Test Flaws Take Toll," *New York Times on the Web,* May 20, 2001; Thomas M. Haladyna, "Perils of Standardized Achievement Testing," *Educational Horizons* 85, no. 1 (Fall 2006), pp. 30–43. See also the National Center for Fair and Open Testing, www.fairtest.org; Catherine Gewertz, "More Testing Seen for High School Students," *Education Week* 30, no. 15 (December 21, 2010).

53. Michele Kurtz, "Teachers' Views Mixed on Testing," *Boston Globe,* March 5, 2003, p. B5;, "Why Arts Education Matters"; Sarah M. Fine, "Consumed by Failure," *Education Week* 28, no. 25 (March 18, 2009), pp. 22–23.

54. Kathleen Kennedy Manzo, "Protests over State Testing Widespread," *Education Week on the Web,* May 16, 2001; Howard Blume, "L.A. Teachers' Union Calls for Boycott of Testing," *Parajo Valley Federation of Teachers,* January 18, 2009, www.pvft.net.

55. Abby Goodnough, "Strains of Fourth-Grade Tests Drive Off Veteran Teachers," *New York Times on the Web,* June 14, 2001; Liz Seymour, "SOL Tests Create New Dropouts," *Washington Post,* July 17, 2001, pp. A1, A8.

56. David Clouston, "1895 Saline County Exam Continues to Raise Interest," *Saline Journal,* February 2, 2008, www.saljournal.com/news/story/1895-Eighth-grade-test-SE1-0123082008-02-22T16-03-32 (retrieved January

10, 2009). The test can be retrieved at www.salina.com/www/1895test/test_1895.pdf.

57. Michael Winerip, "Hard-Working Teachers, Sabotaged When Student Test Scores Slip," *New York Times,* March 4, 2012, www.nytimes.com (retrieved March 5, 2012).

58. "Primary Sources: 2012: America's Teachers on the Teaching Profession."

59. Linda Darling-Hammond, "Value-Added Evaluation Hurts Teaching," *Ed Week* 31, no. 24 (March 5, 2012), www.edweek.com (retrieved March 6, 2012).

60. Jack Gillum and Marisol Bello, "When Standardized Test Scores Soared in D.C., Were the Gains Real?" *USA Today,* March 28, 2011, www.usatoday.com (retrieved March 30, 2012).

61. "Schools Cheating Investigation: Atlanta Journal Constitution Flags Improbable Test Scores In Analysis," *AP/The Huffington Post,* March 25, 2012, www.huffingtonpost.com/2012/03/24/schools-cheating-investig_n_1377767.html (retrieved April 4, 2012).

62. Christina A. Samuels, "Cheating Scandals Intensify Focus on Test Pressures," *Ed Week,* August 4, 2011, www.edweek.com (retrieved April 4, 2012).

63. Ibid.

64. Richard Elmore, "Testing Trap," adapted from *Education Next* 105 (September/October 2002), p. 35; Barbara Gleason, "ASCD Adopts Positions in High-Stakes Testing and the Achievement Gap," *ASCD Conference News,* March 20–22, 2004.

65. Grant Wiggins, "Healthier Testing Made Easier," EDUTOPIQ George Lucas Educational Foundation, April 6, 2006, www.edutopia.org/magazine/.

66. "Primary Sources: 2012: America's Teachers on the Teaching Profession"; Sonja Steptoe, "How Nebraska Leaves No Child Behind," *Time,* May 30, 2007; Winnie Hu, "Schools Move toward Following Students' Yearly Progress on Tests," *New York Times,* July 6, 2007, www.nytimes.com/2007/07/06/education/06test.html (retrieved May 21, 2008).

67. Theodore Sizer, *Horace's School: Redesigning the American High School* (New York: Houghton Mifflin, 1992).

68. Craig Timberg, "Bible's Second Coming," *Washington Post,* June 4, 2000, p. A1.

69. "Public School Drops Christian Textbooks," *Washington Post,* September 17, 1999, p. 2.

70. Mark Sappenfield and Mary Beth McCauley, "God or Science?" *Christian Science Monitor,* November 23, 2004; Lisa Anderson, "Darwin's Theory Evolves into Culture War Kansas Curriculum Is Focal Point of Wider Struggle Across Nation," *Chicago Tribune,* May 22, 2005, www.religionnewsblog.com/11267/darwins-theory-evolves-into-culture-war (retrieved March 5, 2008); Scott Stephens, "Panel OKs Disputed 10th-grade Biology Plan," *Cleveland Plain Dealer,* March 10, 2004, www.cleveland.com/debate/index.ssf?/debate/more/1078914742102330.html (retrieved July 18, 2007).

71. "Tennessee Monkey Bill Becomes (Unsigned) Law," *Wall Street Journal,* April 11, 2012, www.wsj.com (retrieved April 12, 2012).

72. "Frank Newport "Four in 10 Americans Believe in Strict Creationism," December 17, 2010, www.gallup.com/poll/145286/Four-Americans-Believe-Strict-Creationism.aspx (retrieved January 12, 2011); "Why Evolution Is True," http://whyevolutionistrue.wordpress.com/2010/12/20/new-gallup-poll-america-still-creationist-surprise/ (retrieved January 16, 2007).

73. Steve Olson, "An Argument's Mutating Terms," *Washington Post,* March 20, 2005, p. B01.

74. David Van Biema, "The Case for Teaching the Bible," *Time,* March 22, 2007, www.time.com/time/magazine/article/0,9171,1601845,00.html; G. Jeffrey MacDonald, "Now Evolving in Biology Classes: A Testier Climate," *Christian Science Monitor,* May 3, 2005, www.csmonitor.com/2005/0503/p01s04-legn.html.

75. Liz Leyden, "Story Hour Didn't Have a Happy Ending," *Washington Post,* December 3, 1998, p. A3.

76. Michael Alison Chandler, "Two Guys and a Chick Set Off Tiff over School Library Policy," *Washington Post,* February 17, 2008, p. C06. For an extensive discussion on censorship and intellectual freedom, see the American Library Association www.ala.org/offices/oif/ifissues/censorshipschools.

77. American Library Association, "Frequently Challenged Books," www.ala.org/.

78. Ibid.

79. Ibid.

80. Chandler, "Two Guys and a Chick Set Off Tiff over School Library Policy."

81. Winnie Hu, "A Call for Opening Up Web Access at Schools," *New York Times,* September 28, 2011, www.nytimes.com (retrieved April 4, 2012).

82. Quoted in Lynne Cheney, *Humanities in America: A Report to the President, Congress and the American People* (Washington, DC: National Endowment for the Humanities, 1988), p. 17.

83. Allan Bloom, *The Closing of the American Mind* (New York: Simon & Schuster, 1987), p. 63.

84. E. D. Hirsch Jr., *What Your First Grader Needs to Know and What Your Second Grader Needs to Know* (New York: Doubleday, 1991).

85. James Banks, "Multicultural Education: For Freedom's Sake," *Educational Leadership* 49, no. 4 (December 1991/January 1992), pp. 32–36.

86. Todd Oppenheimer, "The Computer Delusion," *Atlantic Monthly,* July 1997, pp. 45–48, 50–56, 61–62.

87. Andrew Trotter, "Major Study on Software Stirs Debate," *Education Week,* April 4, 2007; Greg Toppo, "Computers May Not Boost Student Achievement," *USA Today,* April 11, 2006; North Central Regional Educational Laboratory, *Critical Issue: Using Technology to Improve Student Achievement* (2005), www.ncrel.org/sdrs/areas/issues/methods/technlgy/te800.htm (retrieved April 17, 2008).

88. Trotter, "Major Study on Software Stirs Debate."

89. "The Effects of Computers on Student Writing: What the Research Tells Us," *ASCD SmartBrief* 1, no. 7 (April 1, 2003), www.ascd.org; Jennifer Lee, "Nu Shortcuts in School R 2 Much 4 Teachers," *New York Times,* September 19, 2002;

Victoria Irwin, "Hop, Skip . . . and Software?" *Christian Science Monitor,* March 11, 2003.

90. Regan McMahon, "Everybody Does It," *SFGate.com,* September 9, 2007 (retrieved April 17, 2009); Don McCabe, "Levels of Cheating
    and Plagiarism Remain High," *Center for Academic Integrity* (June 2005), www.academicintegrity.org.

91. *Computer Technology in the Public School Classroom: Teacher Perspectives,* U.S. Department of Education, Institute of Educational Science, March 2005.

92. *Staying the Course: Online Education in the United States,* the Sloan Consortium, 2008; Public Act 123 and 124 of 2006, www.michigan.gov/documents/PA_123_ and124_159920_7.pdf (retrieved July 8, 2009); John Watson, Butch Gemin, Jennifer Ryan, and Mathew Wicks, *Keeping Pace with K-12 Online Learning 2009,* www.inacol.org/research/docs/KeepingPace07color.pdf.

93. *Synthesis of New Research on K-12 Online Learning,* 2005, North Central Regional Education Laboratory/Learning Point Associates, www.ncrel.org/tech/synthesis/.

94. National Educational Technology Plan 2010, executive summary, www.ed.gov/sites/default/files/NETP-2010-exec-summary.pdf (retrieved September 2, 2010).

95. Larry Cuban, *Oversold and Underused: Computers in the Classroom* (Cambridge, MA: Harvard University Press, 2003).

96. Andrew Trotter, "Closing the Digital Divide," *Education Week* 20, no. 35 (2001), pp. 37–38, 40; Maisie McAdoo, "The Real Digital Divide: Quality Not Quantity," in David T. Gordon, ed., *The Digital Classroom* (Cambridge, MA: Harvard College, 2000), pp. 143–151; U.S. Department of Education, National Center for Education Statistics, "Computers and Technology," *Digest of Educational Statistics, 2008,* Tables 427–432 (issued March 2009), http://nces.ed.gov.

97. Ellen McCarthy, "Where Girls and Tech Make a Match," *Washington Post,* March 20, 2003, p. E1; Trotter, "Closing the Digital Divide," pp. 37–38, 40; Andrew Trotter, "Minorities Still Face Digital Divide," *Education Week* 26, no. 3, (2006), p. 14.

98. U.S. Department of Education, National Center for Education Statistics, "Computers and Technology"; Chris Rother, "Teachers Talk Tech," *Technological Horizons in Education* 33, no. 3, (2005), pp. 34–36; Trotter, "Minorities Still Face Digital Divide," p. 14.

99. Glen Bull and Joe Garofalo, "Internet Access: The Last Mile," *Learning and Leading with Technology* 32, no. 1 (September 2004), pp. 16–18, 21.

100. Larry Cuban, *Growing Instructional Technology in U.S. Classrooms* (J. George Jones and Velma Rife Jones Lecture: University of Utah, Salt Lake City, 2005).

101. Tamar Lewin, "Children's Computer Use Grows, but Gaps Persist, Study Says," *New York Times,* January 22, 2001, p. A11.

102. Selma Wasserman, "Teaching for Thinking: Louis E. Raths Revisited," *Phi Delta Kappan* 68, no. 6 (February 1987), pp. 460–666; Valerie Strauss, "Relentless Questioning Paves a Deeper Path," *Washington Post,* February 18, 2008, p. B2.

103. Amy *Green,* "Push for Financial Literacy Spreads to Schools," *Christian Science Monitor,* March 9, 2009, www.csmonitor.com/2009/0309/p13s01-wmgn.html.

104. Scott Melville, "Implications of the Physical Educators' Wellness Role," *Journal of Physical Education, Recreation, and Dance* 80, no. 2 (February 2009), p. 58.

105. Erik Robelen, "U.S. Must Bolster Civic Learning in Schools Report Says," *Education Week,* September 19, 2011, www.educationweek.com (retrieved April 5, 2012); Erik W. Robelen, "Most Students Lack Civics Proficiency on NAEP," *Education Week,* May 4, 2011, www.edweek.org (retrieved April 5, 2012).

CHAPTER 7   THE HISTORY OF AMERICAN EDUCATION

1. Joel Spring, *American Education,* 15th ed. (New York: McGraw-Hill, 2011).

2. Ibid.; James Hendricks, "Be Still and Know! Quaker Silence and Dissenting Educational Ideals, 1740–1812," *Journal of the Midwest History of Education Society,* Annual Proceedings, 1975.

3. Lawrence A. Cremin, *American Education: The Colonial Experience, 1607–1783* (New York: Harper & Row, 1970). See also Spring, *American Education.*

4. L. Dean Webb, *The History of American Education: A Great American Experiment.* (Upper Saddle River, NJ: Prentice Hall, 2005); James C. Klotter, "The Black South and White Appalachia," *Journal of American History* (March 1980), pp. 832–49.

5. John H. Best, *Benjamin Franklin on Education* (New York: Teachers College Press, 1962); Spring, *American Education.*

6. Jonathon Messerli, *Horace Mann: A Biography* (New York: Alfred A. Knopf, 1972); Webb, *The History of American Education: A Great American Experiment.*

7. Lawrence Cremin, *The Transformation of the School: Progressivism in American Education, 1876–1957* (New York: Alfred A. Knopf, 1961).

8. Wilbur R. Jacobs, "The Tip of an Iceberg: Pre-Columbian Indian Demography and Some Implications for Revisionism," *William and Mary Quarterly,* 3rd Ser., 31, no. 1 (January 1974), pp. 123–32; Webb, *The History of American Education: A Great American Experiment;* K. Tsianina Lomawaima and Teresa McCarthy, *To Remain an Indian* (New York: Teachers College Press, 2006).

9. Lomawaima and McCarthy, *To Remain an Indian;* Webb, *The History of American Education: A Great American Experiment.*

10. Terry Huffman, *Theoretical Perspectives on American Indian Education: Taking a New Look at Academic Success and the Achievement Gap* (Lanham, MD: AltaMira Press, 2010); Bobby Ann Starnes, "What We Don't Know Can Hurt Them: White Teachers, Indian Children," *Phi Delta Kappan* 87, no. 5 (January 2006), pp. 384–92; Lomawaima and McCarthy, *To Remain an Indian;* Editorial Projects in Education, "Diploma Counts 2011," *Education Week online,* June 9, 2011.

11. Jackie M. Blount, "Spinsters, Bachelors and Other Gender Transgressors in School Employment, 1850–1990," *Review of Educational Research* 70, no. 1 (Spring 2000), pp. 83–101; Spring, *American Education.*

12. E. Marcus, *Making History: The Struggle for Gay and Lesbian Equal Rights, 1945–1990, An Oral History* (New York: Harper Collins Publishers, 1992); Mark Kelly, *Learning to Stand*

and Speak: Women, Educators and Public Life America's Republic (Chapel Hill: The University of North Carolina Pres, 2008).

13. Blount, "Spinsters, Bachelors and Other Gender Transgressors in School Employment, 1850–1990," p. 94.

14. Edward A. Krug, *The Shaping of the American High School, 1880–1920,* I (New York: Harper & Row, 1964). See also Joel Spring, *The American School,* 8th ed. (New York: McGraw-Hill, 2010).

15. National Commission on Excellence in Education, *A Nation at Risk: The Imperative for Educational Reform* (Washington, DC: U.S. Government Printing Office, 1983), p.1.

16. Susie King Taylor, *Reminiscences of My Life in Camp with the 33rd U.S. Colored Troop Late First S.C. Volunteers* (1902; reprinted, New York: Amo Press, 1968).

17. W. E. B. Du Bois, "The United States and the Negro," *Freedom ways* (1971), quoted in Meyer Weinberg, *A Chance to Learn* (Cambridge, UK: Cambridge University Press, 1977).

18. Spring, *American Education.*

19. National Advisory Commission on Civil Disorders, *Report of the National Advisory Commission on Civil Disorders* (Washington, DC: U.S. Government Printing Office, 1968), p. 369. See also Andrew Hacker, *Two Nations Black and White, Separate, Hostile, Unequal* (New York: Charles Scribner's, 1992).

20. Louis Fischer, Cynthia A. Kelly, and David Schimmel, *Teachers and the Law,* 8th ed. (Boston: Allyn & Bacon, 2010); "ACLU Expresses Mixed Feelings about Supreme Court Decision in School Desegregation Cases," June 29, 2007, www.commondreams.org/news2007/0629-02.htm; Gary Orfield, *Reviving the Goal of an Integrated Society: A 21 Century Challenge* (Los Angeles: The Civil Rights Project/Proyecto Derechos Civiles at UCLA, January 2009).

21. Orfield, *Reviving the Goal of an Integrated Society.*

22. Ibid; Stephanie McCrummen and Michael Birnbaum, "Study of Montgomery County Schools Shows Benefits of Economic Integration," *Washington Post online,* October 15, 2010.

23. Richard M. Merleman, "Dis-integrating American Public Schools," *Education Week,* May 19, 2002, p. 37.

24. U.S. Census Bureau, *Hispanic Americans by the Numbers,* 2011, www.census.gov.

25. Ibid.

26. Quoted in Weinberg, *A Chance to Learn.*

27. U.S. Census Bureau, *Hispanic Americans by the Numbers.*

28. Edna Costa-Belen and Carlos Santiago, *Puerto Ricans in the United States: A Contemporary Portrait* (Boulder, CO: Lynne Rienner Publishers, 2006).

29. U.S. Census Bureau, *Hispanic Americans by the Numbers.*

30. Much of the information on the history of Asian Americans is adapted from James Banks and Cherry Banks, eds., *Multicultural Education,* 8th ed. (San Francisco: Jossey Bass, 2012).

31. U.S. Department of Education, National Center for Educational Statistics, *National Assessment of Educational Progress (NAEP): Reading and Math Scores, 2011,* http://nces.ed.gov/nationsreportcard.

32. U.S. Census Bureau, *Facts for Features: Asian/Pacific American Heritage Month 2011,* www.census.gov/newsroom/releases/archives/facts_for_features_special_editions/cb11-ff06.html.

33. Ibid.

34. Ibid; Zhenchao Qian and Priyank Shah, "Educational Attainment and Intermarriage: Asian Indian and Filipino Americans Compared," paper presented at the annual meeting of The American Sociological Association, Philadelphia, Pennsylvania, August 12, 2005.

35. Laurie Olsen, "Crossing the Schoolhouse Border: Immigrant Children in California," *Phi Delta Kappan* 70, no. 3 (November 1988), p. 213.

36. James Zogby, *Arab Voices* (New York: Macmillan, 2010). For more information about Arab Americans, visit the website of the American-Arab Anti-Discrimination Committee at www.adc.org.

37. Much of the information on Arab Americans is adapted from James Banks and Cherry Banks, eds., *Multicultural Education,* 8th ed. (San Francisco: Jossey Bass, 2012).

38. For more information about Arab Americans, visit the website of the American-Arab Anti-Discrimination Committee at www.adc.org and the Arab American Institute at www.aaiusa.org.

39. David Sadker, Myra Sadker, and Karen R. Zittleman, *Still Failing at Fairness: How Gender Bias Cheats Girls and Boys in School and What We Can Do about It* (New York: Charles Scribner, 2009).

40. M. Carey Thomas, "Present Tendencies in Women's Education," *Education Review* 25 (1908), pp. 64–85; quoted in David Tyack and Elisabeth Hansot, *Learning Together: A History of Coeducation in American Schools* (New Haven, CT: Yale University Press, 1990), p. 68.

41. Adapted from "Opening the Schoolhouse Door" and "Higher Education: Peeking behind the Campus Curtain," in Sadker, Sadker, and Zittleman, *Still Failing at Fairness.*

42. Ibid.

CHAPTER 8   PHILOSOPHY OF EDUCATION

1. William Bagley, "The Case for Essentialism in Education," *National Education Association Journal 30,* no. 7 (1941), pp. 202–20.

2. Andrew J. Rotherham, "Core Convictions: An Interview with E. D. Hirsch," *Education Sector,* September 26, 2006; www.educationsector.org/publications/core-convictions.

3. Mortimer Adler, *Reforming Education* (Boulder, CO: Westview Press, 1977), pp. 84–85.

4. Robert M. Hutchins, *The Higher Learning in America* (New Haven, CT: Yale University Press, 1962), p. 78.

5. John Dewey, *Experience and Education* (New York: Macmillan, 1963).

6. Brenda Engel and Anne Martin, *Holding Values: What We Mean by Progressive Education* (New York: Heinemann, 2005).

7. Paulo Freire, *Pedagogy of the Oppressed* (New York: Continuum Press, 1989).

8. Maxine Greene, *Landscapes of Learning* (New York: Teachers College Press, 1978). See also Maxine Greene, "Reflections on Teacher as Stranger" in C. Kridel (ed.), *Books of the Century Catalog* (Columbia, SC: University of South Carolina,

Museum of Education, 2000); and *Releasing the Imagination: Essays on Education, The Acts, and Social Change* (Hoboken, NJ: Wiley, 2000).

9. Georgia East, "No Teachers, No Homework," *Sun-Sentinel* (December 5, 2010), www.sun-sentinel.com; Danna Harman, "This Is School?" *Christian Science Monitor*, May 18, 2004, p. 11.

10. Jay Mathews, "Educators Blend Divergent Schools of Thought," *The Washington Post,* May 9, 2006, p. A12.

11. Timothy Reagan, *Non-Western Educational Traditions: Alternative Approaches to Educational Thought and Practice* (Mahwah, NJ: Lawrence Erlbaum Associates, 2000).

12. *Aristotle, Politics,* trans. and intro. by T. A. Sinclair (Middlesex, U.K.: Penguin, 1978).

CHAPTER 9   FINANCING AND GOVERNING AMERICA'S SCHOOLS

1. Heller Reports Virtual Round Table, *Teacher Buying Behavior,* 2007, www.qeddata.com/MarketKno/ResearchReports/TBB%20Roundtable%20Summary.pdf (retrieved March 18, 2008).

2. Mark G. Yudof, David L. Kip, and Betsy Levin, *Educational Policy and the Law,* 3rd ed. (St. Paul, MN: West, 1992), p. 658; Betsy Levin, Thomas Muller, and Corazon Sandoval, *The High Cost of Education in Cities* (Washington, DC: The Urban Institute, 1973).

3. Barry Siegel, "Parents Get a Lesson in Equality," *Los Angeles Times* (Washington edition), April 13, 1992, pp. A-1, A-18, A-19.

4. *Robinson* v. *Cahill,* 69 N.J. 133 (1973); *Abbott* v. *Burke,* 119 N.J. 287 (1990) (known as *Abbott I); Abbott* v. *Burke,* 153 N.J. 480 (1998) (known as *Abbott V*).

5. Catherine Gerwitz, "Though N. J. Funding Formula Upheld, Abbott Intact," *Education Week* 8, no. 33 (June 10, 2009), p. 10; Peter Enrich, "Leaving Equality Behind: New Directions in School Finance Reform," *Vanderbilt Law Review* 48 (1995), pp. 101–194. For a description of this movement to adequacy arguments, visit http://nces.ed.gov/edfin/litigation/Contents.asp. For a discussion of the impact in Wisconsin, see Daniel W. Hildebrand, "2000 Significant Court Decisions," *Wisconsin Lawyer* 74, no. 6 (June 2001). Similar analyses are available in other such law updates.

6. "Financing Better Schools: Too Often, Traditional Methods of Paying for Schools Come Up Short," *Education Week* 24, no. 17 (January 6, 2005), p. 7.

7. Richard Rothstein, "Equalizing Education Resources on Behalf of Disadvantaged Children," in Richard D. Kahlenberg, ed., *A Nation at Risk: Preserving Public Education as an Engine for Social Mobility* (New York: Century Foundation Press, 2000), p. 74; Alan Odden and Lawrence O. Picus, *School Finance: A Policy Perspective,* 4th ed. (New York: McGraw-Hill, 2007).

8. Sharon Noguchi, "Some California Schools Get Twice the Funding—and More—of Others," *Mercury News,* February 26, 2012, www.mercurynews.com (retrieved April 4, 2012).

9. W. E. Thro, "The Third Wave: The Impact of the Montana, Kentucky and Texas Decisions on the Future of Public School Finance Reform Litigation," *Journal of Law and Education* 199, no. 2 (Spring 1990), pp. 219–250; Robert F. McNergney and Joanne M. Herbert, *Foundations of Education: The Challenge of Professional Practice* (Boston: Allyn & Bacon, 1995), pp. 475–478; Chris Pipho, "Stateline: The Scent of the Future," *Phi Delta Kappan* 76 (September 1994), pp. 10–11; Greg Kocher, "Group Says Education Not Getting Enough Money Due It by Law," *Lexington Herald-Leader,* June 25, 2003, www.kentucky.com.

10. Cited in *Campaign for Fiscal Equality* v. *New York,* 86 N.Y. 2d 307 (1995). See also Bess Keller, "School Finance Case Draws to Close in N.Y.," *Education Week,* August 2, 2000.

11. Lori Montgomery, "Maryland Seeks 'Adequacy,' Recasting School Debate," *Washington Post,* April 22, 2002, p. A1.

12. Liz Bowie, "As State Increased Aid, Grades Went Up," *Baltimore Sun,* January 8, 2009, www.goodschoolspa.org/pdf/news_articles/Baltimore%20Sun%201-8-09.pdf (retrieved May 15, 2009); The high rankings continued for years: visit www.edweek.org/ew/qc/2012/16src.h31.html for an update.

13. Christina A. Samuels, "Study Tallies a District's Return on Investment," *Education Week,* December 5, 2011, www.education.com (retrieved March 5, 2012).

14. Robert L. Borosage, "Sending Kids the Bill for the Mess Left By Wall Street," *Huffington Post,* October 13, 2011, www.huffingtonpost.com/ (retrieved October 30, 2011).

15. Michael A. Rebell, "The Recession—and Students' Rights," in Michael A. Rebell, Allan Odden, Anthony Rolle, and James W. Guthrie, "Four Takes on Tough Times," *The Resourceful School* 69, no. 4 (December 2011/January 2012), pp. 11–18.

16. Sean Cavanagh, "States Dogged by Lawsuits on K-12 Funding," *Ed Week* 31, no. 17 (January 18, 2012), pp. 1, 2; April Castro and Paul J. Weber, "Texas Schools Sue State, Saying Funding is Unfair," October 11, 2011, *Huffington Post,* October 13, 2011, www.huffingtonpost.com/ (retrieved October 30, 2011).

17. James W. Guthrie, "Fine-Tuning the Cuts," in Michael A. Rebell, Allan Odden, Anthony Rolle, and James W. Guthrie, "Four Takes on Tough Times," *The Resourceful School,* 69, no. 4 (December 2011/January 2012), pp. 11–18; Morgan Smith, "Rural District Is Struggling to Make Improvements," *New York Times,* April 7, 2012, www.nytimes.com (retrieved April 26, 2012).

18. Ben Wolfgang, "No Cuts Left Behind as Schools Squeeze Most Out of Budgets," *The Washington Times,* November 14, 2011, www.washingtontimes.com; (retrieved April 21, 2012); Kimberely Hefling, "Schools Brace for More Budget Cuts," *TIME.com,* October 24, 2011, www.time.com (retrieved January 4, 2012).

19. Joshua Benton, "One District Reaps the Benefit of Another's Belt-Tightening," *Dallas Morning News,* December 12, 2002, www.dallasnews.com; David Mace, "Act 60 Reform Likely," *Rutland Herald,* January 6, 2003; "Tennessee's School Funding Declared Unconstitutional Again," *Associated Press,* October 9, 2002.

20. Alfred A. Lindseth, "A Reversal of Fortunes: Why Courts Have Cooled to Adequacy Lawsuits," *Education Week* 27, no. 3 (September 10, 2007).

21. Robert Slavin, "How Can Funding Equity Ensure Enhanced Achievement?" *Journal of Educational Finance* 24, no. 4 (Spring 1999), pp. 519–528.

22. Bruce J. Biddle and David C. Berliner, "Unequal School Funding in the United States," *Education Leadership* 59, no. 8 (May 2002), pp. 48–59; Diana Jean Schemo, "Neediest Schools Receive Less Money, Report Finds," *New York Times,* August 9, 2002; Odden and Picus, *School Finance: A Policy Perspective;* Carmen G. Arroyo, *The Funding Gap* (Washington, DC: Education Trust, January 17, 2008), www2.edtrust.org/NR/rdonlyres/5AF8F288-949D-4677-82CF-5A867A8E9153/0/FundingGap2007.pdf (retrieved March 19, 2008).

23. Stephen Sawchuk, "Out-of-Field Teaching Called Worse in Poor Schools," *Education Week* 28, no. 15 (November 25, 2008).

24. "SFFF Files Public School Lawsuit," *Topeka Capital-Journal,* November 2, 2010, http://cjonline.com/news/state/2010-11-02/sfff_files_public_school_lawsuit; Lesli A. Maxwell, "Funding Formula Aims at Equity," *Education Week* 29, no. 37 (July 19, 2010); *Is School Funding Fair? A National Report Card,* National Law Center, October 12, 2010, www.schoolfundingfairness.org/.

25. Amanda Paulson, "Does Money Transform Schools?" *Christian Science Monitor,* August 9, 2005, www.csmonitor.com/2005/0809/p01s03-ussc.html (retrieved March 19, 2008).

26. Arroyo, *The Funding Gap.*

27. Debra Viadero, "Rags to Riches in U.S. Largely a Myth, Scholars Write," *Education Week* 26, no. 9 (October 25, 2006), p. 8.

28. Thomas Toch, "Separate but Not Equal," *Agenda* 1 (Spring 1991), pp. 15–17; Odden and Picus, *School Finance: A Policy Perspective.*

29. Peter Keating, "How to Keep Your State and Local Taxes Down," *Money* 24, no. 1 (January 1995), pp. 86–92; Odden and Picus, *School Finance: A Policy Perspective.*

30. Bill Norris, "Losing Ticket in Lotteries," *Times Educational Supplement,* March 19, 1993, p. 17.

31. U.S. Department of Education, *The Federal Role in Education,* 2008, www.ed.gov/about/overview/fed/role.html (retrieved March 20, 2008).

32. Stephen Sawchuk and Erik Robelen, "Stimulus Guidance Spotlights Teacher Evaluations," *Education Week* 28, no. 28 (April 1, 2009); Valerie Strauss, "Schools Chief Returns Race to the Top Money—for His Teachers," *Washington Post,* November 24, 2010, http://voices.washingtonpost.com/answer-sheet/schools-chief-returns-race-to.html; Gerald Seib, "In Education, a Chance for Change," *Wall Street Journal,* March 27, 2009; "Obama Wants Stimulus to Transform Schools," *USA Today,* February 17, 2009, www.usatoday.com/news/education/2009-02-17-stimulus-schools_N.htm (retrieved May 18, 2009); Maria Glod, "Budget Outlines Funding for Teacher Merit Pay Programs," *Washington Post,* May 7, 2009, www.washingtonpost.com/wp-dyn/content/article/2009/05/07/AR2009050703786.html (retrieved May 21, 2009); "Obama Wants 5K Closed Schools to Rebound," *USA Today,* May 11, 2009, www.usatoday.com/news/education/2009-05-11-duncan-schools_N.htm (retrieved on May 18, 2009); Libby Quaid, "Plan to Fix Schools Could Help Students," *Arizona Daily Star,* January 1, 2009, p. A3; Sam Dillon, "U.S. Stimulus Plan Would Provide Flood of Aid to Education," *New York Times,* January 28, 2009, www.nytimes.com/2009/01/28/education/28educ.html (retrieved May 23, 2009).

33. Frederick M. Hess and Linda Darling-Hammond, "How to Rescue Education Reform," *New York Times,* December 5, 2011, www.nytimes.com (retrieved January 5, 2012).

34. Juliet Schor, *Born to Buy: The Commercialized Child and the New Consumer Culture* (New York: Charles Scribner's, 2004).

35. *FTC Report Sheds New Light on Food Marketing to Children and Adolescents* (Washington, DC: Federal Trade Commission, July 29, 2008), www.ftc.gov/opa/2008/07/foodmkting.shtm (retrieved May 30, 2009).

36. Many of the examples in this section are adapted from "Commercializing Childhood: The Corporate Takeover of Kids' Lives: An Interview with Susan Linn," *Multinational Monitor* 30, no. 1 (July/August 2008), www.multinationalmonitor.org/mm2008/072008/interviewlinn.html (retrieved May 22, 2009).

37. Ibid. See also Linda Matchan, "A Sober Look at Ads and Children," *Boston Globe,* May 17, 2009, www.boston.com/ae/movies/articles/2009/05/17/a_sober_look_at_ads_and_children (retrieved May 22, 2009).

38. *FTC Issues Report on Marketing Violent Entertainment to Children* (Washington, DC: Federal Trade Commission, April 12, 2007), www.ftc.gov/opa/2007/04/marketingviolence.shtm (retrieved May 22, 2009).

39. Miriam H. Zoll, "Psychologists Challenge Ethics of Marketing to Children," American News Service, April 5, 2000, www.mediachannel.org/originals/kidsell.shtml (retrieved May 22, 2009).

40. Tamar Lewin, "In Public Schools, the Name Game as a Donor Lure," *New York Times,* January 26, 2006; Pam Belluck, "And for Perfect Attendance, Johnny Gets . . . a Car," *New York Times,* February 5, 2006; Alex Molnar and David Garia, "The Battle over Commercialized Schools," *Educational Leadership* 63, no. 7 (April 2006), pp. 78–82.

41. Neil Buckley, "Obesity Campaign Eyes School Drinks," *Financial Times,* June 23, 2003; Alex Molnar, "The Corporate Branding of Our Schools," *Educational Leadership* 60, no. 2 (October 2002), pp. 74–78.

42. "School Soda Ban Has Limited Effect," *Washington Post,* November 27, 2008, www.washingtonpost.com/wp-dyn/content/article/2008/11/27/AR2008112701843.html (retrieved July 12, 2009).

43. Alfie Kohn, "The 500-Pound Gorilla," *Phi Delta Kappan* 84, no. 2 (October 2002), p. 117; Molnar and Garia, "The Battle over Commercialized Schools."

44. Linda Lou, "Money Helps Pay for Printing Costs after Budget Cuts," *San Diego Union Tribune,* November 22, 2008, www.signonsandiego.com/news/metro/20081122-9999-1mc22rbteach.html (retrieved July 12, 2009).

45. Molnar, "The Corporate Branding of Our Schools," p. 76.

46. Bill Turque, "District Considers Longer School Day," *Washington Post,* November 8, 2010, p. B01.

47. Michael A. Rebell, Allan Odden, Anthony Rolle, and James W. Guthrie "Four Takes on Tough Times," *The Resourceful School* 69, no. 4 (December 2011/January 2012) pp. 11–18; Kris Axtman, "Schools Bend under Tight Budgets," *Christian Science Monitor,* November 20, 2002; "Schools Cut Costs with 4–Day Weeks," September 11, 2002, http://cnn.com; Richard Rothstein, "Raising School Standards and Cutting Budget: Huh?" *New York Times,* July 10, 2002; Ann E. Marimow and Rosalind S. Helderman, "Taxing Times for County Budgets," *Washington Post,* March 18, 2008, p. A01; Maria Glod, "Strapped Schools May Boost Class Sizes," *Washington Post,* December 5, 2008, p. A1.

48. Michael Alison Chandler and Emma Brown, "D.C. Area Schools Turn to Parents for More Funding as Budgets are Squeezed," *Washington Post,* April 4, 2012, www.washingtonpost.com (retrieved April 5, 2012); Sam Dillon, "Districts Pay Less in Poor Schools, Report Says," *New York Times,* November 30, 2011, www.nytimes.com (retrieved January 30, 2012); Peter Schworm, "Is It Good for Education Foundations to Fund What Taxes Don't Cover?" *Boston Globe,* February 25, 2007, www.boston.com/news/local/articles/2007/02/25/what_taxes_dont_cover/ (retrieved March 20, 2008); Jennifer Gonzalez, "Public School Endowments on the Rise," *Cleveland Plain Dealer,* June 2007, www.publiceducation.org/newsblast/June07/June15_text.htm (retrieved March 20, 2008).

49. Mary Filardo, Jared Bernstein, and Ross Eisenbrey, "Creating Jobs Through FAST!, a Proposed New Infrastructure Program to Repair America's Public Schools," *The 21st Century School Fund,* Economic Policy Institute, August 11, 2011, http://web.epi-data.org/temp727/Fix%20America%27s%20Schools_Today_FINAL.pdf (retrieved April 12, 2012).

50. Bradford Chaney and Laurie Lewis, *Public School Principals Report on Their School Facilities: Fall 2005* (NCES 2007–007) (Washington, DC: U.S. Department of Education, National Center for Education Statistics; issued January 2007), http://nces.ed.gov/pubs2007/2007007.pdf (retrieved May 5, 2009).

51. Frederick M. Hess, *School Boards at the Dawn of the 21st Century* (Arlington, VA: National School Boards Association, 2002).

52. For an insightful discussion of school boards, see Joel Spring, *American Education* (New York: McGraw-Hill, 2002), pp. 178–182.

53. Christina A. Samuels, "School Board Members' Focus Shifting, Survey Says," *Education Week* 30, no. 20 (February 3, 2011), www.edweek.com (retrieved January 7, 2012); Chester Finn, "Reinventing Local Control," in Patricia First and Herbert Walberg, eds., *School Boards: Changing Local Control* (Berkeley, CA: McCutchan, 1992); Emily Feistritzer, "A Profile of School Board Presidents," in *School Boards: Changing Local Control;* Neal Pierce, "School Boards Get Failing Grades, in Both the Cities and the Suburbs," *Philadelphia Inquirer,* April 27, 1992, p. 11; Mary Jordan, "School Boards Need Overhaul, Educators Say," *Washington Post,* April 5, 1992, p. A-51.

54. Jay Mathews, "Playing Politics in Urban City Schools," *Washington Post,* September 11, 2002; American Association of School Administrators, *The State of the American School Superintendency: A Mid-Decade Study* (September 2007), www.aasa.org/newsroom/pressdetail.cfm?ItemNumber59401 (retrieved May 5, 2009); Catherine Gewertz, "Race, Gender, and the Superintendency," *Education Week* 26, no. 24 (February 17, 2006), pp. 1, 22, 24.

55. American Association of School Administrators, *The State of the American School Superintendency: A Mid-Decade Study;* Gewertz, "Race, Gender, and the Superintendency."

56. Cited in Spring, *American Education.*

57. Jay Mathews, "Nontraditional Thinking in Central Office," *The School Administrator* Web Edition, *Washington Post,* June 2001; Tamar Lewin, "Leaders from Other Professions Reshape America's Schools, from Top to Bottom," *New York Times,* June 8, 2000; Nancy Mitchell, "Nontraditional School Bosses," *Denver Rocky Mountain News,* April 16, 2001; Abby Goodnough, "Retired General Takes on New Mission: Schools," *New York Times,* November 6, 2002; Jennifer Steinhauer, "Bloomberg Picks a Lawyer to Run New York Schools," *New York Times,* July 30, 2002; Timothy Waters and Robert J. Marzano, "The Primacy of Superintendent Leadership," *The School Administrator,* March 2007, www.aasa.org/publications/saarticledetailtest.cfm?ItemNumber58435 (retrieved May 28, 2009).

58. Valerie Strauss, "Rhee in D.C.: The Myth of the Heroic Leader," *Washington Post,* September 9, 2010, http://voices.washingtonpost.com/answer-sheet/guest-bloggers/rhee-in-dc-the-myth-of-the-her.html (retrieved November 3, 2010).

59. Joanna Richardson, "Contracts Put Superintendents to Performance Test," *Education Week,* September 14, 1994, pp. 1, 12.

60. Debra Viadero, "Turnover in Principalship Focus of Research," *Education Week* 29, no. 9 (October 28, 2009), pp. 1, 14; Emily Wax, "A Tough Time at the Head of the Classes," *Washington Post,* June 18, 2002, p. A9.

61. Cheri Carlson, "Competing Pressures Put Strain on School Principals, Study Finds," *Ventura County Star,* January 2, 2012, http://vcstar.com (retrieved April 8, 2012); Vincent L. Ferrandino, "Challenges for 21st-Century Elementary School Principals," *Phi Delta Kappan* 82, no. 6 (February 2001), pp. 440–442; Linda Borg, "The Principal Dilemma Facing Schools in R.I.," *Providence Journal,* www.projo.com/education (August 26, 2001); Jacques Steinberg, "One Principal's World (The Unscripted Version)," *New York Times,* January 1, 2003.

62. "Seeing the Big Picture" in Education Vital Signs, *American School Board Journal,* December 1999.

63. Ferrandino, "Challenges for 21st-Century Elementary School Principals."

64. *Perspectives, The School Principal as Leader: Guiding Schools to Better Teaching and Learning,* The Wallace Foundation, January 2012, www.wallacefoundation.com (retrieved March 6, 2012).

65. Elissa Gootman and Robert Gebeloff, "Principals Younger and Freer, but Raise Doubts in the Schools," *New York Times,* May 26, 2009, pp. A1, A15.

66. Jenny Upchurch, "Custodians Keep Schools Running without a Hitch," *Tennessean.com,* December 30, 2007; Edmund Janko, "The Untouchables: There Are Some People You Don't Mess With, and Many of Them Work in Schools," *Teacher Magazine* 16, no. 6 (May 1, 2005), pp. 50–51.

67. James G. Cibula, "Two Eras of Urban Schooling: The Decline of Law and Order and the Emergence of New Organizational Forms," *Education and Urban Society,* 29, no. 3 (May 1997), pp. 317–341.

68. Quoted in "Building Better Business Alliances," *Instructor* (Winter 1986, special issue), p. 21. See also Brian Dumaine, "Making Education Work," *Fortune* (Spring 1990, special issue), pp. 12–22.

69. For a good overview of school consolidation, see Karen Irmsher, "School Size," *ERIC Digest,* no. 113 (Eugene, OR: ERIC Clearinghouse on Educational Management, July 1997) (ED414615).

70. U.S. Department of Education, "Number of Public School Districts and Public and Private Elementary and Secondary Schools: Selected Years, 1869–70 through 2006–07," *Digest of Education Statistics, 2008* Table 87 (issued March 2009), http://nces.ed.gov/pubs2009/2009020_2a.pdf (retrieved May 5, 2009).

71. Catherine Gewertz, "The Breakup: Suburbs Try Smaller High Schools," *Education Week on the Web,* May 2, 2001; Craig Howley and Marty Strange and Robert Bickel, "Research about School Size and School Performance in Impoverished Communities" (Charleston, WV: ERIC Clearinghouse on Rural Education and Small Schools, December 2000); William Ayers, Gerald Bracey, and Greg Smith, "The Ultimate Education Reform? Make Schools Smaller" (Milwaukee: Center for Education Research, Analysis, and Innovation, University of Wisconsin–Milwaukee, December 14, 2000).

72. Elissa Gootman, "New York City Plans to Open Small Secondary Schools," *New York Times,* March 12, 2004.

73. See Marianne Perle and David Baker, *Job Satisfaction among America's Teachers: Effects of Workplace Conditions, Background Characteristics, and Teacher Compensation* (Washington, DC: National Center for Education Statistics, U.S. Department of Health, Education and Welfare, August 1997), pp. 41–42. See also John Lane and Edgar Epps, eds., *Restructuring the Schools: Problems and Prospects* (Berkeley: McCutchan, 1992); Jeff Archer, "New Roles Tap Expertise of Teachers," *Education Week,* May 30, 2001.

74. Fern Shen, "New Strategy for School Management," *Washington Post,* February 17, 1998, pp. B-1, B-7; Patrick McCloskey, "Vocal Arrangement," *Teacher Magazine* 17, no. 1 (September 1, 2005), pp. 30–35; Jeff Archer, "S.F. School Councils Help Chart Improvement Course," *Education Week* 25, no. 31 (April 12, 2006), p. 10.

75. Information about Finland drawn from Diane Ravitch, "What Can We Learn From Finland?" *Education Week's blogs,* October 11, 2011, www.edweek.org (retrieved January 7, 2012); David Sirota, "How Finland Became an Education Leader," *Salon.com,* July 18, 2011; Andreas Schleicher, "Is the Sky the Limit to Education Improvement?" *Phi Delta Kappan* 93, no. 2 (October 2011), pp. 58–63; Jeevan Vasagar, "Finland's Schools Flourish in Freedom and Flexibility," *The Guardian,* December 5, 2010, guardian.co.uk (retrieved April 3, 2012).

CHAPTER 10   SCHOOL LAW AND ETHICS

1. David Schimmel and Matthew Militello, "Legal Literacy of Teachers: A Neglected Responsibility," *Harvard Educational Review* 77, no. 3 (February 2007), pp. 257–284.

2. Ibid; David Schimmel, Leslie Stellman, and Louis Fischer, *Teachers and the Law,* 8th ed. (Upper Saddle, NJ: Prentice Hall, 2010).

3. Louis Fischer and David Schimmel, *The Civil Rights of Teachers* (New York: Harper & Row, 1973).

4. The legal situations and interpretations included in this text are adapted from a variety of sources, including Myra Sadker and David Sadker, *Sex Equity Handbook for Schools* (New York: Longman, 1982); Schimmel, Stellman, and Fischer, *Teachers and the Law;* Michael LaMorte, *School Law: Cases and Concepts,* 10th ed. (Boston: Allyn & Bacon, 2011); Karen R. Zittleman, "Teachers, Students and Title IX: A Promise for Fairness," in David Sadker and Ellen Silber (eds.), *Gender in the Classroom: Foundations, Skills, Methods and Strategies across the Curriculum* (Mahwah, NJ: Lawrence Erlbaum, 2007), pp. 73–107.

5. Schimmel, Stellman, and Fischer, *Teachers and the Law;* Zittleman, "Teachers, Students and Title IX."

6. *Gebser* v. *Lago Vista Independent School District* (96 U.S. 1866 (1998); Greg Henderson, "Court Says Compensatory Damages Available Under Title IX," UPI, February 26, 1992; *Franklin* v. *Gwinnett County Schools,* 503 U.S. 60 (1992).

7. *Thompson* v. *Southwest School District,* 483 F. Supp. 1170 (W.D.M.W. 1980); Schimmel, Stellman, and Fischer, *Teachers and the Law.*

8. *Kingsville Independent School District* v. *Cooper,* 611 F. 2d 1109 (5th Cir. 1980); See also Schimmel, Stellman, and Fischer, *Teachers and the Law.*

9. Schimmel, Stellman, and Fischer, *Teachers and the Law.*

10. *Pickering* v. *Board of Education of Township High School District 205, Will County,* 391 U.S. 563 (1968); Nathan L. Essex, *School Law and the Public Schools: A Practical Guide for School Leaders,* 5th ed. (Boston: Allyn & Bacon, 2011).

11. "California: Ruling Against Anti-Creationism Teacher," *The New York Times,* May 5, 2009, p. A18.

12. Javier Hernandez, "Judge Says No to Teachers' Campaign Buttons, but Yes to Certain Politicking," *The New York Times,* October 18, 2008, p. A20.

13. *Basic Books* v. *Kinko's Graphics Corp.,* 758 F. Supp. 1522 (S.D.N.Y.1991); Hall Davidson, "The Educators' Guide to Copyright and Fair Use," *Technology & Learning* 23, no. 3 (October 2002), pp. 26–32; Essex, *School Law and the Public Schools.*

14. Elizabeth Weaver, *Pennsylvania Teachers: Number One in Strikes* (Allegheny Institute for Public Policy, August 2007), www.alleghenyinstitute.org/reports/07_06.pdf; Essex, *School Law and the Public Schools.*

15. Essex, *School Law and the Public Schools.*

16. LaMorte, *School Law: Cases and Concepts.*

17. Schimmel, Stellman, and Fischer, *Teachers and the Law; Owasso Independent School District* v. *Falvo* 534 U.S. 426 (2002).

18. *Goss* v. *Lopez,* 419 U.S. 565 (1975); *Wood* v. *Strickland,* 420 U.S. 308 (1975); Essex, *School Law and the Public Schools;* "Report: Minority Students Face Harsher Punishments," *Arizona Daily Star"* (March 7, 2012), p. A22; Tara Parker-Pope, "Schools and Legal System Mistreat Gays, Study Says," *The New York Times,* December 7, 2010, p. A22.

19. The Center for Effective Discipline, "States Banning Corporal Punishment" (March 2012), www.stophitting.com; *Ingraham* v. *Wright,* 430 U.S. 651 (1977).

20. *Tinker* v. *Des Moines Independent Community School District,* 393 U.S. 503 (1969).

21. Howard Fischer, "Court: Schools Can Ban Hurtful T-Shirt Slogans," *Arizona Daily Star* (April 21, 2006), www.azstarnet.com/.

22. *Morse* v. *Frederick,* 127 S. Ct. 2618 (2007).

23. *Beussink* v. *Woodland R-IV School District,* 30 F. Supp. 2d 1175 (1998); Jamin Raskin, *We the Students: Supreme Court Cases for and about Students* (Washington, DC: CQ Press, 2000).

24. Patrik Jonsson, "Teachers Strike Back at Students' Online Pranks," *Christian Science Monitor,* February 25, 2008, www.csmonitor.com.

25. *Bethel School District No. 403* v. *Fraser,* 478 U.S. 675 (1986); *J. S.* v. *Bethlehem Area School District,* 757A. 2d 412 (2000).

26. "Religion in America: Facts and Figures," *Phi Delta Kappan* 93, no. 4 (December 2011/January 2012), pp. 44–45; *Engel* v. *Vitale,* 370 U.S. 421 (1962); *Lee* v. *Weisman,* 112 U.S. 2649, (1992); *Good News Club* v. *Milford Central Schools,* 99 U.S. 2036 (2001); *Santa Fe Independent School District* v. *Doe,* 99 U.S. 62 (2000).

27. *Bellnier* v. *Lund,* 438 F. Supp. 47 (N.Y. 1977); *New Jersey* v. *T.L.O.,* 105 U.S. 733 (1985); Jesse Holland, "Court Says Strip Search of Arizona Teenager Illegal," *Arizona Daily Star,* June 25, 2009, p. A1.

28. *Hazelwood School District* v. *Kuhlmeier,* 108 S. Ct. 562 (1988).

29. Schimmel, Stellman, and Fischer, *Teachers and the Law.*

30. Jenny Anderson, "National Study Finds Widespread Sexual Harassment of Students in Grades 7–12," *New York Times online,* November 7, 2011.

31. Ibid; Zittleman, "Teachers, Students, and Title IX: A Promise for Fairness."

32. Schimmel, Stellman, and Fischer, *Teachers and the Law.*

33. Ibid.

34. Ibid; Karen Zittleman, "Title IX and Gender: A Study of the Knowledge, Perceptions, and Experiences of Middle and Junior High School Teachers and Students," *Dissertation Abstracts International* 66, no. 11 (2005) (UMI No. 3194815).

35. Josephson Institute, Center for Youth Ethics: *The Ethics of American Youth.* (Los Angeles: The Josephson Institute, 2011), http://charactercounts.org/programs/reportcard/.

36. Ibid.

37. Rebecca Moore Howard and Laura J. Davies, "Plagiarism in the Internet Age," *Educational Leadership* 66, no. 6 (March 2009), pp. 64–67; Josephson Institute, *The Ethics of American Youth.*

38. Amanda Lenhart, *Social Media and Young Adults,* Pew Research Center Publications (April 20, 2010), http://pewinternet.org.

39. Jennifer Preston, "Rules to Stop Pupil and Teacher from Getting Too Social Online," *New York Times* online, December 17, 2011; Michelle Davis, "Social Networking Goes to School," *Education Week* 3, no. 3 (June 14, 2010), pp. 16, 18, 20, 22–23; Rhonda Bodfield, "Should Teachers, Kids Be 'Friends'?" *Arizona Daily Star,* May 24, 2009, p. A1.

40. ChildHelp, *National Child Abuse Statistics* (2012), www.childhelp.org/pages/statistics.

41. Administration on Children, Youth, and Families, U.S. Department of Health and Human Services, *Mandatory Reporter of Child Abusers and Neglect: Summary of State Laws* (April 2010), www.childwelfare.gov/systemwide/laws_policies/statutes/manda.pdf.

42. Sarah Spark, "Character Education Found to Fall Short in Federal Study," *Education Week online* 30, no. 9 (October 21, 2010).

43. Alfie Kohn, "How Not to Teach Values," *Phi Delta Kappan* 78, no. 8 (April 1997), pp. 428–437 [cited in James Noll, *Taking Sides,* 13th ed. (New York: McGraw-Hill, 2005), pp. 102–117].

44. Nel Noddings, *Caring: A Feminine Approach to Ethics and Moral Development,* 2nd ed. (Berkeley, CA: University of California Press, 2003).

45. Howard Kirschenbaum, "A Comprehensive Model for Values Education and Moral Education," *Phi Delta Kappan* 73, no. 10 (June 1992), pp. 771–776; Nel Noddings, "Handle with Care," *Greater Good,* Spring/Summer 2006, pp. 18–21.

46. Charles Haynes, "Teaching Social Responsibility," *Education Leadership* 66, no. 8 (May 2009), pp. 6–13; Katherine Simon, "Making Room for Moral Questions in the Classroom," *Education Week* 21, no. 10 (November 7, 2001), pp. 51, 68.

CHAPTER 11 TEACHER EFFECTIVNESS

1. Annie Lowrey, "Big Study Links Good Teachers to Lasting Gain," *New York Times online* (January 6, 2012).

2. Carol Weinstein, Molly Romano, and Andrew Mignano, *Elementary Classroom Management: Lessons from Research and Practice,* 5th ed. (New York: McGraw Hill, 2011).

3. John Goodlad, *A Place Called School,* 2nd ed. (New York: McGraw-Hill, 2004).

4. Deborah Loewenberg Ball and Francesca M. Forzani, "Teaching Skillful Teaching," *Educational Leadership,* December 2010/January 2011, pp. 40–45; Robert Shostak, "Involving Students in Learning," in James M. Cooper, ed., *Classroom Teaching Skills,* 9th ed. (Belmont, CA: Cengage, 2011), pp. 82–106; Sam Intrator, "The Engaged Classroom," *Educational Leadership,* September 2004, pp. 20–25; Weinstein, Romano, and Mignano, *Elementary Classroom Management.*

5. Ibid.

6. Jacob Kounin, *Discipline and Group Management in Classrooms* (New York: Holt, Rinehart & Winston, 1970); Weinstein, Romano, and Mignano, *Elementary Classroom Management.*

7. Carol Weinstein and Wilford Weber, "Classroom Management," in James Cooper, ed., *Classroom Teaching Skills*, 9th

ed. (Belmont, CA: Cengage); pp. 215–251; C. M. Charles, *Building Classroom Discipline* 10th ed (Upper Saddle River: Prentice Hall, 2010).

8. Ibid.

9. Weinstein and Weber, "Classroom Management"; Jane Nelson, Lynn Lott, and H. Stephen Glenn, *Positive Discipline in the Classroom: Developing Mutual Respect, Cooperation, and Responsibility in Your Classroom* (Roseville, CA: Prima, 2000).

10. Ibid.

11. Weinstein and Weber, "Classroom Management"; Thomas L. Good and Jere E. Brophy, *Looking in Classrooms,* 10th ed. (Boston: Allyn & Bacon, 2008); Carol Cummings, *Winning Strategies for Classroom Management* (Alexandria, VA: Association for Supervision and Curriculum Development, 2000).

12. Kathleen Cushman, *Fires in the Bathroom: Advice for Teachers from High School Students* (New York: The New Press, 2005).

13. David Berliner, "What Do We Know About Well-Managed Classrooms? Putting Research to Work," *Instructor* 94, no. 6 (February 1985), p. 15.

14. Arno Bellack, *The Language of the Classroom* (New York: Teachers College Press, 1966).

15. Several of the sections on the pedagogical cycle are adopted from David Sadker, Myra Sadker, and Karen R. Zittleman, "Questioning Skills" in in James Cooper, ed., *Classroom Teaching Skills*, 9th ed. (Belmont, CA: Cengage, 2011), pp. 107–152.

16. Ibid.; P. Smagoinsky, "The Social Construction of Data: Methodological Problems of Investigation Learning in the Zone of Proximal Development," *Review of Educational Research* 65, no. 3 (1995), pp. 191–212.

17. John Dewey, *How We Think,* rev. ed. (Boston: D. C. Heath, 1933), p. 266.

18. Sadker, Sadker, and Zittleman, "Questioning Skills."

19. Benjamin Bloom (ed.), *Taxonomy of Educational Objectives, Handbook I: Cognitive Domain* (New York: David McKay, 1956); Lorin Anderson and David Krathwohl, *A Taxonomy for Learning, Teaching, and Assessing: A Revision of Bloom's Taxonomy of Educational Objectives* (New York: Longman, 2001).

20. Sadker, Sadker, and Zittleman, "Questioning Skills; Anderson and Krathwohl, *A Taxonomy for Learning, Teaching, and Assessing.*

21. Ibid.

22. Adapted from Sadker, Sadker, and Zittleman, "Questioning Skills."

23. Mary Budd Rowe, "Wait Time: Slowing Down May Be a Way of Speeding Up!" *Journal of Teacher Education* 37 (January/February 1986), pp. 43–50; Mary Budd Rowe, "Science, Silence, and Sanctions," *Science and Children* 34 (September 1996), pp. 35–37; Jim B. Mansfield, "The Effects of Wait-time on Issues of Gender Equity, Academic Achievement, and Attitude toward a Course," *Teacher Education and Practice* 12, no. 1 (Spring/Summer 1996), pp. 86–93; Sadker, Sadker, and Zittleman, "Questioning Skills."

24. Ibid.

25. Myra Sadker, David Sadker, and Susan Klein, "The Issue of Gender in Elementary and Secondary Education," *Review of Research in Education* 17 (1991), pp. 269–334.

26. Goodlad, *A Place Called School.*

27. Intrator, "The Engaged Classroom"; Martha McCarthy, *High School Survey of Student Engagement* (Bloomington: University of Indiana Press, 2005).

28. Thomas L. Good and Jere E. Brophy, *Looking in Classrooms,* 10th ed. (Boston: Allyn & Bacon, 2008); Heidi Halvorson, *Succeed* (New York: Plume, 2011); Dan Laitsch, "Student Behaviors and Teacher Use of Approval versus Disapproval," *ASCD Research Brief* 4, no. 3 (March 27, 2006).

29. Halvorson, *Succeed;* Carol Dweck, *Mindset: The New Psychology of Success* (New York: Ballentine, 2007).

30. Judy Willis, "The Neuroscience of Joyful Education," *Educational Leadership* 4, no. 9 (Summer 2007); Intrator, "The Engaged Classroom."

31. Ibid.

32. Margaret Roblyer and Aaron Doering, *Integrating Educational Technology into Teaching,* 6th ed. (Boston, MA: Allyn & Bacon, 2012).

33. Ibid.

34. George Brackett, "Technologies Don't Change Schools—Caring, Capable People Do," in David T. Gordon, ed., *The Digital Classroom* (Cambridge, MA: Harvard College, 2000), pp. 29–30.

35. Barak Rosenshine, "Principles of Instruction: Research-Based Strategies That All Teachers Should Know" *American Educator,* Spring 2012, pp. 12–19, 39; Gary R. Morrions, *Designing Effective Instruction,* 6th ed. (Hobokon, NJ: Wiley, 2010).

36. Mary Leighton, "Cooperative Learning," in James M. Cooper, ed., *Classroom Teaching Skills,* 9th ed. (Belmont, CA: Cengage, 2011), pp. 252–295; R. Bruce Williams, *Cooperative Learning: A Standard for High Achievement* (Thousand Oaks, CA: Corwin Press, 2007); Robyn M. Gilles, *Cooperative Learning: Integrating Theory into Practice* (Thousand Oaks, CA: Sage Publications, 2007); David Johnson and Roger Johnson, *Learning Together and Alone: Cooperative, Competitive, and Individualistic Learning,* 5th ed. (Boston: Allyn & Bacon, 1999).

37. Leighton, "Cooperative Learning"; Robert E. Slavin, "Cooperative Learning in Middle and Secondary Schools," *Clearinghouse* 69, no. 4 (March/April 1996), pp. 200–204.

38. Leighton, "Cooperative Learning"; Williams, *Cooperative Learning: A Standard for High Achievement*; Gilles, *Cooperative Learning: Integrating Theory into Practice*; Robert E. Slavin, *Cooperative Learning: Theory, Research, and Practice* (Boston: Allyn & Bacon, 1995).

39. Jay Matthews, "Students Move at Own Pace toward Proficiency," *The Washington Post,* June 13, 2006, p. A8.

40. Thomas Guskey, "Mastery Learning: How It Works," *Educational Leadership,* October 2010, pp. 52–57; J. Ronald Gentile, "Assessing Fundamentals in Every Course through Mastery Learning," *New Directions in Teaching and Learning* 100 (December 2004), pp. 15–20; Jenifer M. Fox, *Your Child's Strengths: Discover Them, Develop Them, Use Them* (Toronto: Penguin Group, 2008).

41. John Barell, *Problem-Based Learning: An Inquiry Approach,* 2nd ed. (Thousand Oaks, CA: Sage Publications, 2006); Diane Ronis, *Problem-Based Learning for Math and Science,* 2nd ed. (Thousand Oaks, CA: Sage Publications, 2008); Vicki Shuster, "Camelot Teachers, Staff, Implement New Learning Techniques," *Brookings Register Online,* February 23, 2010; Diane Curtis, "The Power of Projects," *Educational Leadership* 60, no. 1 (September 2002), pp. 50–53.

42. Anthony Rebora, "Making a Difference: Carol Ann Tomlinson Explains How Differentiated Instruction Works and Why We Need It Now," *Teacher Magazine* 2, no. 1 (September 10, 2008), pp. 26, 28–31.

43. Ibid., p. 28.

44. Carol Ann Tomlinson, "Differentiated Instruction for Academic Diversity," in James M. Cooper, ed., *Classroom Teaching Skills,* 9th ed. (Belmont, CA: Cengage, 2011), pp. 153–187.

45. Kenneth Leithwood, *Teaching for Deep Understanding: What Every Educator Should Know,* (Thousand Oaks, CA: Corwin Press, 2006); Jay McTighe, Elliott Seif, and Grant Wiggins, "You Can Teach for Meaning," *Educational Leadership* 62, no. 1 (September 2004), pp. 26–30.

46. William Spady and Charles Schwahn, *Learning Communities 2.0: Educating in the Age of Empowerment* (Lanham, MD: Rowman and Littlefield Education, 2010); Jonathan Supovitz and Jolley Bruce Christman, "Small Learning Communities That Actually Learn: Lessons for School Leaders," *Phi Delta Kappan* 86, no. 9 (May 2005), pp. 649–651; Robert Blum, "A Case for Connectedness," *Educational Leadership* 62, no. 7 (April 2005), pp. 16–20.

47. James Cooper, "The Effective Teacher," in James M. Cooper, ed., *Classroom Teaching Skills,* 9th ed. (Belmont, CA: Cengage, 2011), pp. 1–20; Melody J. Shank, "Common Space, Common Time, Common Work," *Educational Leadership* 62, no. 8 (May 2005), pp. 16–19; John Ward and Suzanne McCotter, "Reflection as a Visible Outcome for Preservice Teachers," *Teaching & Teacher Education* 20, no. 3 (April 2004), pp. 243–258.

CHAPTER 12 YOUR FIRST CLASSROOM

1. Lilian Katz, "The Development of Preschool Teachers," *The Elementary School Journal* 73, no. 1 (October 1972), pp. 50–54; John L. Watzke, "Longitudinal Study of Stages of Beginning Teacher Development in a Field-Based Teacher Education Program," *Teacher Educator* 38, no. 3 (Winter 2003), pp. 209–229.

2. Linda Darling-Hammond, "Keeping Good Teachers: Why It Matters, What Leaders Can Do," *Educational Leadership,* May 2003, pp. 6–13.

3. Pam Grossman and Emily Davis, "Mentoring That Fits," *Ed Leadership* 69, no. 8 (May 2012), pp. 54–57; Deborah Bieler, "What New Teachers Want from Colleagues," *Ed Leadership* 69, no. 8 (May 2012), pp. 46–49; Andrew J. Wayne, Peter Youngs, and Steve Fleischman, "Improving Teacher Induction," *Educational Leadership* 62, no. 8 (May 2005), pp. 76–77; Mary C. Clement, "My Mother's Teaching Career—What It Can Tell Us about Teachers Who Are Not Certified," *Phi Delta Kappan* 87, no. 10 (June 2006), pp. 772–776.

4. Sharon Feiman-Nemser, "Beyond Solo Teaching," *Ed Leadership* 69, no. 8 (May 2012), pp. 10–16.

5. David Eggers and Ninive Clements Calegari, "The High Cost of Low Teacher Salaries," *New York Times,* April 30, 2011, www.nytimes.com (retrieved March 5, 2012); Linda Darling-Hammond, "Keeping Good Teachers: Why It Matters, What Leaders Can Do," *Educational Leadership* 60, no. 8 (2003), pp. 6–13; Belinda Eggen, "New Teacher Attrition and Retention," paper presented at the annual meeting of the American Association of Colleges for Teacher Education, Chicago, May 25, 2009.

6. Melody J. Shank, "Common Space, Common Time, Common Work," *Educational Leadership* 62, no. 8 (May 2005), pp. 16–19; Donna Niday, Jean Boreen, Joe Potts, and Mary K. Johnson, *Mentoring Beginning Teachers: Guiding, Reflecting, Coaching,* 2nd ed. (Portland, ME: Stenhouse Publishers, 2009); Hal Portner, *Mentoring New Teachers,* 3rd ed. (Thousand Oaks, CA: Corwin Press, 2008); Sarah Henchey, "Student Teaching: More Than a Custody Arrangement?" *Education Week,* July 26, 2011, www.edweek.com (retrieved April 2, 2012); Thomas M. McCann, Larry R. Johannessen, and Bernard Ricca, "Responding to New Teachers' Concerns," *Educational Leadership* 62, no. 8 (May 2005), pp. 30–34.

7. John Papay, "Refocusing the Debate: Assessing the Purposes and Tools of Teacher Evaluation," *Harvard Educational Review,* 82, no. 1, (Spring 2012) pp. 123–141.

8. Thomas J. Kane, Eric S. Taylor, John H. Tyler, and Amy L. Wooten, "Evaluating Teacher Effectiveness: Can Classroom Observations Identify Practices that Raise Achievement?" *Education Next* 11, no 3 (Summer 2011), www.education-Next.org (retrieved April 2, 2012).

9. Ibid.; Morgaen L. Donaldson and Gordon A. Donaldson Jr., "Strengthening Teacher Evaluation: What District Leaders Can Do," *Ed Leadership* 69, no. 8 (May 2012), pp. 78–82.

10. "Research Alert: Fewer Hours, Fewer Results," *Ed Leadership* 68, no. 4 (December 2010/January 2011), pp. 8–9.

11. Judith W. Little, "Teachers' Professional Development in a Climate of Educational Reform," *Educational Evaluation and Policy Analysis* 15 (1993), pp. 129–151; Deborah Loewenberg Ball and Francesca M. Forzani, "Teaching Skillful Teaching," *Ed Leadership* 68, no.4 (December 2010/January 2011), pp. 40–45; Linda Darling-Hammond and Milbrey W. McLaughlin, "Policies That Support Professional Development in an Era of Reform," in Milbrey W. McLaughlin and Ida Oberman, eds., *Teaching and Learning: New Policies, New Practices* (New York: Teachers College Press, 1996), pp. 208–218.

12. Erin Richards, "New Teachers Getting Ready to be Graded on Classroom Work; Wisconsin Moving Toward Portfolio-Based Assessment," *Milwaukee Journal Sentinel,* March 11, 2012, www.jsonline.com/ (retrieved May 10, 2012).

13. Anthony Rebora, "Report: Teachers Lagging in Professional Learning," *Education Week* 2, no. 2 (March 16, 2009), p. 11.

14. Organization for Economic Cooperation and Development (OECD), *Education at a Glance, OECD Indicators* (Paris: OECD, 2007).

15. Justin Baeder, "Career Ladders for Educators," *Ed Week,* December 7, 2010, www.edweek.com (retrieved May 11, 2012); Adam Urbanski, "The Rochester Contract: A Status Report," *Educational Leadership* 46, no. 3 (November 1988), pp. 48–52.
16. Bruno S. Frey, *Not Just for the Money: An Economic Theory of Personal Motivation* (Brookfield, VT: Edward Elgar, 1997).
17. Daniel H Pink, *Drive: The Surprising Truth about What Motivates Us* (New York: Riverhead, 2009); Teresa Amabie, *Creativity in Context* (Boulder, CO: Westview Press, 1996).
18. Carl Mellstrom and Magnus Johannesson, "Crowding Out in Blood Donations: Was Titmuss Right?" *Journal of European Economic Association* 6, no. 4 (June 2008), pp. 845–863.
19. Andy Baumgartner, "A Teacher Speaks Out: Insights from the National Teacher of the Year," *The Washington Post,* March 26, 2000, p. B4.
20. Albert Shanker, "Where We Stand: Is It Time for National Standards and Exams?" *American Teacher* 76, no. 6 (May/ June 1992), p. 5.
21. Scott Martindale, "Survey: 1 in 5 Teachers Support Ending Unions," *Orange County Register,* August 3, 2011, www .ocregister.com (retrieved May 13, 2012).
22. Daniel Pink, *A Whole New Mind: Why Right-Brainers Will Rule the Future* (New York: Riverhead, 2006).

CHAPTER 13   Q AND A GUIDE TO ENTERING THE TEACHING PROFESSION

1. Bureau of Labor Statistics, U.S. Department of Labor, *Occupational Outlook Handbook, 2012–13 Edition,* Kindergarten and Elementary School Teachers, www.bls. gov/ooh/education-training-and-library/kindergarten-and-elementary-school-teachers.htm
2. U.S. Department of Education, "Context of Elementary and Secondary Education: Characteristics of Full-Time Teachers," *The Condition of Education,* 2012; U.S. Department of Education, "Participation in Education, Indicator 5: Race/Ethnic Enrollment in Public Schools," *The Condition of Education, 2011;* Sarah Sparks, "Despite Downturn, Few Men Attracted to Teaching Field," *Education Week* (May 9, 2012).
3. U.S. Department of Education, "Context of Elementary and Secondary Education: Characteristics of Full-Time Teachers," *The Condition of Education,* 2012.
4. National Education Association (NEA), *Professional Pay* (Washington, DC: NEA, 2011), www.nea.org/; "David Eggers and Ninive Clements Calegari, "The High Cost of Low Teacher Salaries," *New York Times online,* April 30, 2011.
5. Patricia M. Costantino, Marie N. De Lorenzo, and Christy Tirrell-Corbin, *Developing a Teaching Portfolio: A Guide to Success,* 3rd ed. (Boston: Allyn & Bacon, 2008).
6. Charles Stewart and William Cash, *Interviewing: Principles and Practices,* 13th ed. (New York: McGraw-Hill, 2010).
7. Ibid.
8. Richard Ingersoll, Lisa Merrill, and Henry May, "Retaining Teachers: How Preparation Matters," *Educational Leadership,* May 2012, pp. 30–34.
9. National Center for Education Information, "Alternative Routes Are Attracting Talented Individuals from Other Careers Who Otherwise Would Not Become Teachers," 2009, www.ncei.com; Jill Constantine, Daniel Player, Tim Silva, Kristin Hallgren, Mary Grider, and John Deke, *An Evaluation of Teachers Trained through Different Routes to Certification* (Washington, DC: U.S. Department of Education, February 2009).
10. *The Praxis Series: Teacher Licensure and Certification,* 2012. Available at www.ets.org.
11. Michael Winetrip, "New Procedure for Teacher Licensing Draws Protests," *New York Times* online, May 6, 2012.
12. Ibid.
13. Daniel Weisberg, Susan Sexton, Jennifer Mulhern, and David Keeling, *The Widget Effect: Our National Failure to Recognize and Act on Differences in Teacher Effectiveness* (New York: New Teacher Project, 2009).
14. Steve Farkas, Jean Johnson, and Ann Duffett with Leslie Moye and Jackie Vine, *Stand by Me: What Teachers Really Think about Unions, Merit Pay and Other Professional Matter,* Public Agenda, 2003, www.publicagenda.org.
15. David Schimmel, Leslie Stellman, and Louis Fischer, *Teachers and the Law,* 8th ed. (Upper Saddle River, NJ: Prentice Hall, 2010).

CREDITS

TEXT AND LINE ART CREDITS

CHAPTER 1

Figure 1.2: "Where Teachers Teach" from C. Emily Feistritzer, *Profile of Teachers in the U.S.,* National Center for Education Information, 2011. http://www.ncei.com/Profile_Teachers_ US_2011.pdf chart 6, page 18. Reprinted by permission of the author; P. 10: Martha Groves, "Love of Writing and Students Fires Her Up," *The Los Angeles Times,* May 13, 2007. Reprinted by permission of TMS Reprints on behalf of the Los Angeles Times; Figure 1.5: "Percentage of Teens Who Feel they Have Learned Critical Skills While in High School." Adapted from *The Lemelson-MIT Invention Index 2006,* Courtesy of the Lemelson-MIT Program, 2006 Invention Index, http://web.mit.edu/invent; p. 15:

CHAPTER 2

P. 28: From *All I Really Need to Know I Learned in Kindergarten* by Robert L. Fulghum, copyright © 1986, 1988 by Robert L. Fulghum. Used by permission of Villard Books, a division of Random House, Inc, and the author, Robert Fulghum; Figure 2.3: "Appropriate education in the least restrictive environment for students with disabilities." HEWARD, WILLIAM L., EXCEPTIONAL CHILDREN: AN INTRODUCTION TO SPECIAL EDUCATION, 9th,©2009. Printed and Electronically reproduced by permission of Pearson Education, Inc., Upper Saddle River, New Jersey.

CHAPTER 3

P. 55: Adapted from "Ally Yourself with LGBT Students," *Teaching Tolerance,* Fall 2010, p. 35. Reprinted by permission of Southern Poverty Law Center; Figure 3.3: "States with Official English Language" from U.S. English, Inc. (2012). Reprinted with permission; P. 77: Text adapted from Jacqueline Irvine and Beverly Jean Armento, *Culturally Responsive Teaching: Lesson Planning for Elementary and Middle Grades.* Copyright © 2001. Adapted with permission of The McGraw-Hill Companies, Inc.; P. 84: Courtesy of Lacey Rosenbaum; P. 84: Courtesy of Mandie Rainwater.

CHAPTER 4

P. 104: From Joseph Goodlad, *A Place Called School.* Copyright © 1984. Reprinted with permission by The McGraw-Hill Companies; P. 127: "Girl acted tough, but Mom is tougher," by David Kelly. *The Los Angeles Times,* May 18, 2007. Copyright © 2007 The Los Angeles Times. Reprinted by permission.

CHAPTER 5

P. 154: Jonathan Kozol, excerpts from *Educational Leadership* 50.3 (November 1992). Copyright © 1992 by the Association for Supervision & Curriculum Development. Reprinted by permission. The Association for Supervision and Curriculum Development is a worldwide community of educators advocating sound policies and sharing best practices to achieve the success of each learner. To learn more, visit ASCD at www.ascd.org.

CHAPTER 6

P. 167: J. Abner Peddiwell, summary of and excerpt from *The Saber-Tooth Curriculum.* Copyright © 1930. Reprinted with permission by The McGraw-Hill Companies; Figure 6.3: Copyright © 2010. National Governors Association Center for Best Practices and Council of Chief State School Officers. All rights reserved; Figure 6.4: Tirupalavanam Ganesh, "Held Hostage by High-Stakes Testing: Drawing as Symbolic Resistance," *Teacher Education Quarterly* (2002). Reprinted by permission of the artist; Figure 6.5: Chart "Public Acceptance of Evolution." From *Science,* August 11, 2006, Vol. 313. no. 5788, pp. 765–766. Copyright © 2006, The American Association for the Advancement of Science. Reprinted with permission from AAAS.

CHAPTER 9

Figure 9.3: Adapted with permission from Center on International Education Benchmarking, *Finland: System and School Organization.* Figure: "Annual Expenditure by Educational Institutions per Student for All Services." CIEB: Finland. http://www.ncee.org/programs-affiliates/center-on-international-education-benchmarking/top-performing-countries/finland-overview/finland-system-and-school-organization/

CHAPTER 10

Figure 10.2: "Who Harasses Whom." Adapted from Table 6, Harris Interactive. *Hostile Hallways: Bullying, Teasing and Sexual Harassment in Schools.* Commissioned by the AAUW Educational Foundation. Research by Harris Interactive. Copyright © 2001 American Association of University Women Educational Foundation. All rights reserved.

CHAPTER 12

Figure 12.2: "How Teachers Are Evaluated in Cincinnati: A Sample." From Thomas J. Kane, Eric S. Taylor, John H. Tyler and Amy L. Wooten, "Evaluating Teacher Effectiveness: Can Classroom Observations Identify Practices that Raise Achievement?" *Education Next,* Summer 2011 / Vol. 11, No. 3. Reprinted by permission; Figure 12.3: Farmington CT, FRAMEWORK FOR TEACHING AND LEARNING. © Farmington Public Schools. http://www.fpsct.org/page .cfm?p=4701. Reprinted by permission; Figure 12.5: "Number of Teaching Hours per Year." From "Report: Teachers Lagging in Professional Learning." Reprinted with permission from *Education Week,* Vol. 2, Issue 2 (March 16, 2009). http://www.teachersourcebook.org/tsb/articles/2009/03/16/02nsdc.h02.html?qs=professional+learning. This table first appeared in the Teacher Professional Development Sourcebook, March 16, 2009. Data is from the Organisation for Economic Co-Operation and Development. Reprinted with permission from Editorial Projects in Education; P. 397: Marthina Carkci, from "A LOOK AT . . . The Desire to Teach; A Classroom Challenge I Just Had to Take." *The Washington Post,* November 8, 1998, p. C3. Used by permission.

PHOT O CREDITS

CHAPTER 1

Opener: © Image Source/PunchStock RF; p. 2: © Ryan McVay/Getty Images RF; p.4: © Comstock/PictureQuest; p. 9: Blend Images/John Lund/Marc Romanelli/Getty Images RF; p. 11: © Library of Congress Prints and Photographs Division, LC-USZ62-49011; p. 14: Ingram Publishing RF; p. 20: Courtesy of Rafe Esquith, photo by Heather Harris.

CHAPTER 2

Page 26: © Purestock/PunchStock RF; p. 34: © Blend Images/Alamy RF; p. 41: Courtesy of Randall Smith; p.42: © Stockbyte/Punchstock RF;p.46: © Bob Daemmrich/PhotoEdit.

CHAPTER 3

Page 54: © Thinkstock Images/JupiterImages RF; p. 55: Courtesy of Boulder County Public Health Department; p.56: Comstock/PictureQuest RF; p. 61: © Purestock/Getty Images RF; p.62: Courtesy of Carlos Julio Ovando; p. 73: © Image Source, all rights reserved; p. 75: Erin Patrice O'Brien/Taxi/Getty Images; p. 76(top): Comstock/PictureQuest RF; p. 76 (bottom): © Dynamic Graphics Group/Creatas/Alamy RF; p. 77: © Michael Newman/PhotoEdit; p.78(top): Digital Vision/PunchStock; p. 78(bottom): Glow Images RF; p.79(top): Image Source/Getty Images RF; p. 79(bottom): © Digital Vision/PunchStock; p.82: © Digital Vision.

CHAPTER 4

Opener: Brand X Pictures/PunchStock RF; p. 103 © Sarah/Flickr; p. 106: © BananaStock/PunchStock RF; p. 107: Courtesy of Dr. Jeannie Oakes; p. 111: © BananaStock RF; p. 114: © Digital Vision/Getty Images RF; p. 117: Buccina Studios/Getty Images RF; p. 128: © Exactostock/SuperStock RF.

CHAPTER 5

Page 137: © Tony Freeman/PhotoEdit; p. 142: Thomas Barwick/Digital Vision RF; p. 150: © James Estrin/The New York Times/Redux Pictures; p. 153(top): © Blend Images/Hill Street Studios/Getty Images; p. 153(bottom): Tetra Images/Getty Images RF; p. 154: James Wilson/Woodfin Camp & Associates; p. 157: Courtesy of Adam Mörk/3XN; p. 161: Michael Wesch, Kansas State University, From " A Vision of Students Today."

CHAPTER 6

Page 169: Image Source/PunchStock RF; p.183: Courtesy of Alfie Kohn; p.184: © David Jennings/The Image Works; p.187: Tracy A Woodward/The Washington Post via Getty Images; p.193: © Creatas/PunchStock RF.

CHAPTER 7

Opener: Comstock/PictureQuest RF; p.211: © Culver Pictures; p.214: Hisham F. Ibrahim/Getty Images RF; p.226: Library of Congress Prints and Photographs Division [LC-DIG-ppmsca-03128]; p.228: Arthur Schatz//Time Life Pictures/Getty Images; p.229: Library of Congress Prints and Photographs Division [LC-USZ62-42810]; p.230: © Bonnie Kamin/PhotoEdit; p.235: © Brown Brothers; p.238(top): New York Public Library Picture Collection; p. 238 (bottom): North Wind Pictures Archives/AP Images; p. 239 (top):

CHAPTER 8

CHAPTER 9

CHAPTER 10

CHAPTER 11

CHAPTER 12

INDEX

A

Abbott v. Burke, 277
Abbott districts, 277
Abercrombie and Fitch, 285
Ability grouping, 109
Abstinence only sex education
    curriculum, 123
Academic advisers, 415
Academic freedom, 307–308
Academic learning time, 342
Academic structure, 350
Academy, 214, 220
Academy (Plato), 266
Accelerated programs, 38–39
Acceptance, 357
Accountability, 287
Acculturation, 140
Achievement gaps, 147
"Acting white," 54
Active learning, 359
Active teaching, 362
Activities. *See also* Observation video clips
    EQ, 30
    inventory of philosophies
      of education, 247–249
    profession, 9
    purposes of schools, 139–140
    school governance quiz, 288–300
    student diversity, 74–82
Adams, Elaine, 199
Adaptive technology, 46
Additive approach (multicultural
    education), 68, 69
Adequate education, 277–278
Adler, Mortimer, 252, 263
Admissions officers, 415
Adoption states, 173, 174
Adult education, 415
Adult literacy surveys, 17
Advanced placement (AP), 18, 38, 39
Advantage Schools, 155
Aesthetics, 269
Affective domain, 31
Affective needs, 161
Afghan school curriculum, 175
African Americans. *See also* Race
    and ethnicity
    "acting white," 54
    aural and participatory learning, 71
    Black law, 238–239
    compulsory-ignorance law, 225
    discipline, 314
    generalization, 80
    giftedness, 38
    NAEP reading scores, 18

segregation. *See* School segregation
special needs students, 44
student letter to newspaper, 110
two-parent families, 116
typical student, 76
AFT. *See* American Federation of
    Teachers (AFT)
"Against the Current" (Williamson), 23
AIDS, 319
Ain't I a Woman: Black Women and Feminism
    (hooks), 263
Alexander the Great, 267
All I Really Need to Know I Learned in
    Kindergarten (Fulghum), 28
"All Our Students Thinking" (Noddings), 198
"Allegory of the Cave" (Plato), 266
Allocated time, 342
Alternative assessment, 187
Alternative teacher certification, 408–409
Alternative teacher training, 14
Alumni relations personnel, 415
American Alliance for Health, Physical
    Education, Recreation and Dance
    (AAHPERD), 394
American Education: A History (Urban/
    Wagoner), 223
American family, 116–117
American Federation of Teachers (AFT),
    172, 325, 389–391, 412
American Public School Teacher: Past, Present,
    and Future, The (Drury/Baer), 14
American Recovery and Revitalization Act
    (ARRA), 284
American School, The (Spring), 225
American Spelling Book (Webster), 215
Americanization, 140
Amy Biehl High School, 149
Anchored instruction, 366
Ancient Greek philosophers, 265–267
And Still We Rise: The Trials and Triumphs
    of Twelve Gifted Inner-city High School
    Students (Coewin), 38
Anorexia nervosa, 126
Anticipatory set, 362
Antimiscegenation laws, 117
AP. *See* Advanced placement (AP)
Appearance, 112–113
Apprenticeship, 14, 15, 212
Appropriate education, 40
Arab Americans, 79, 81, 82, 232–233
Aristotle, 267, 270
Arizona State University (ASU), 14–15
Arnold, Karen, 120
ARRA. *See* American Recovery and
    Revitalization Act (ARRA)

Artifacts and exhibits, 366
Ashton-Warner, Sylvia, 240
Asian Americans/Pacific Islanders, 229–232
    Asian Indian Americans, 230–231
    Chinese Americans, 229–230
    Filipino Americans, 230
    generalization, 80
    Japanese Americans, 231
    Southeast Asian Americans, 231–232
    typical student, 77
Asian Indian Americans, 230–231
Aspirational marketing, 285
Assertive discipline, 347
Assessment, 28
    authentic, 187–188
    tests. *See* Tests/testing
Assimilation, 60
Assistive technology, 46
Association for Supervision and Curriculum
    Development (ASCD), 391
Asylums, 39
Attention-getting devices, 16
Attribution to ability, 358
Attribution to effort, 358
Auditory learners, 32, 33
Authentic assessment, 187–188
Authentic learning, 366
Autism, 43
Awake Youth Project, 348

B

Back-to-basics, 250
Bagley, William, 250, 263
Baldwin, James, 245
Banks, James, 68, 192
Banks's approach to multicultural eduction,
    68, 69
Barefoot Heart: Stories of a Migrant Child
    (Hart), 228
Barnard, Henry, 216
Baumgartner, Andy, 17, 389
Baylin, Eric, 16
Becker, Henry Jay, 195
Beecher, Catherine, 218, 235
Behavior modification, 264, 347
Behavioral objective, 365
Behaviorism, 264
Bell Curve, The (Hernstein/Murray), 280
Bellack, Arno, 349
Berliner, David, 18, 349
Bermuda Triangle of American
    education, 111
Best Friends, Worst Enemies: Understanding
    the Social Lives of Children (Thompson/
    O'Neill), 386

Bestor, Arthur, 138, 222
Bethel School District v. Fraser, 316
Bethune, Mary McLeod, 239–240
Beyond Discipline: From Compliance to Community (Kohn), 343
Beyond Survival (Rubinstein), 381
Beyond Tracking: Multiple Pathways to College, Career, and Civic Participation (Oakes/Sanders), 109
Bial, Deborah, 182
Bias, 176
Bias busters, 202
Bible, 188
Biddle, Bruce, 18
Bilingual education, 60–66
　defined, 61
　distribution of ELL learners (map), 63
　dual-language instruction, 64
　ESL, 64
　historical overview, 61
　immersion, 64
　Lau remedies, 61
　maintenance approach, 63
　official English language laws, 65
　political controversy, 64
　research studies, 65–66
　submersion, 64
　teaching tip, 66
　transitional approach, 63
Bilingual Education Act, 61, 64, 224
Bilingual Education in the 21st Century: A Global Perspective (Garcia), 66
Bilingual education models, 63–64
Bill and Melinda Gates Foundation, 147
Black law, 238–239
Black studies, 68
Blended courses, 195
Block grants, 283
Block scheduling, 370
Bloom, Allan, 192, 251
Bloom, Benjamin, 352
Bloomberg, Michael, 150
Bloom's taxonomy, 352, 353
Board certification, 12–13, 287, 407–408
Board of Education v. Mergens, 318
Board of Regents v. Roth, 412
Boat people, 232
Bodett, Tom, 166
Bodily-kinesthetic intelligence, 26
Body rhythms, 31
Body smart, 26
Bonaparte, Napoleon, 234
Bond, 288
Bonuses, 388
Boston Latin Grammar School, 212
Boundary crossers, 395
Boyer, Ernest, 138, 158
Brackett, George, 361
Bragdon v. Abbott, 319
Brain, 32, 35

Branches of philosophy, 268
Brand name education, 285–287
Bratz, 286
Breaking Ranks in the Middle, 111
Bridging the Chasm between Research and Practice: A Guide to Major Educational Research (Van Horn), 119
Bronx High School of Science, 38
Brookline High School, 141, 144
Brougham, Lord, 8
Brown, Carol, 48
Brown, Lyn Mikel, 129
Brown, Moses, 238
Brown v. Board of Education, 40, 226, 241
Brownlee, Megan, 23
Bubble kids, 182
Buckley Amendment, 312
Budget cuts, 278, 287
Buechner, Frederick, 3
Building Classroom Discipline (Charles), 347
Bully, the Bullied, and the Bystander, The (Coloroso), 128
Bully Society, The (Klein), 128
Bullying, 127–129
"Bullying and the Culture of Peers" (Rodkin), 130
Bureau of Indian Affairs (BIA), 217
Burned In: Fueling the Fire to Teach (Friedman/Reynolds), 370, 398, 406
Business and schools, 284–287, 297
California Achievement Test, 18
Campaign for a Commercial Free Childhood, 287
Campbell, Donald T., 186
Campbell's law, 186
Canada, Geoffrey, 151
Canter, Lee and Marlene, 347
Capsule biographies. *See* Profile in education
CAR. *See* Collaborative action research (CAR)
Cardinal Principles of Secondary Education, 221
Career development. *See also* Job hunting, etc.
　coursework, 21
　extracurricular activities, 21
　first impression, 22
　information gathering, 19–21
　networking, 21
　portfolio, 22
　recommendations, 21–22
　résumé, 22
Career in Teaching plan, 387
"Career Information" document, 93
Career ladder, 387
Caring school relationship, 116
Carkci, Mathina, 396–397
Carnegie Forum, 12
Carnegie Foundation for the Advancement of Teaching, 135

Carnegie units, 221
Cartesian dualism, 268
Casa dei Bambini, 239
Categorical grants, 283
Censorship, 190–191
Center for Talented Youth (CTY), 38
Central-office personnel, 171
"Certain Degenerate Tendencies among Teachers" (Hall), 219
Certification/licensure, 12–13, 407–408, A–2 to A–4
"Challenging Assumptions: Helping Struggling Students Succeed" (Easton/Soguero), 130
Character education, 326
Charter schools, 147–150, 162, 407
Chávez, César, 228
Cheating, 322–323
Cherokee Phoenix, 217
Cherokee syllabary, 217
Chesapeake Bay Foundation, 158
Chicago Teachers' Federation (CTF), 392
Chicken Soup for the Soul: Teens Talk High School: 101 Stories of Life, Love, Learning for Older Teens (Canfield), 114
Chief state school officer, 290–291
Child abuse, 325
Children's Defense Fund (CDF), 276
Children's television, 284, 285
Chinatown, 60
Chinese Americans, 229–230
Choice, 348
Choice programs, 147–158. *See also* Education reform and school choice
Choice school instruction diary, 205–206
Christian fundamentalists, 189
Chugach School District (Alaska), 365
Churchill, Winston, 166
Cicero, 8
Cigarette smoking, 124
Cincinnati, Ohio, school district, 377, 378
Cincinnati Public Schools teacher evaluation system (2005), 378
Civics education, 197
Civil Rights Act of 1964, 226
Civil War, 234
Clarification, 350
Clark, Kenneth, 240–241
Clark, Mamie Phipps, 240
Clarke, Edward, 235
Class comedy club, 423
Class rules, 346, 381–382
Class size, 145
Classroom clicks, 364
Classroom management, 342–349, 381
"Classroom Misbehavior Is Predictable and Preventable" (Landrum et al.), 371
Classroom observation guidelines, A
Classroom observations, 376–380
Classroom response system, 364

Classroom Teaching Skills (Cooper), 352
Clearinghouse, 19
Clickers, 364
Clinton, Bill, 305
Closer look boxes
  ancient Greek philosophers, 267
  bias, 176
  Bloom's taxonomy, 353
  charter school, 149
  child abuse, 325
  common core standards, 178
  culturally responsive teaching, 77
  early textbooks, 215
  education milestones, 237
  education want ads, 414
  essentialism *vs.* perennialism, 253
  federal legislation, 224
  first-year teacher (teacher's point of
    view), 396–397
  history of American schools, 220
  levels of educational power, 292
  mermaids - people who do not fit the
    norm, 28
  names of schools, 136
  patterns of the classroom, 104
  religion and public schools, 318
  single-sex education, 35
  Socratic method, 266
  teacher, private life, 307
  teachers, core competencies, 13
  times of transition, 345
  voices of five philosophies, 263
  world without schools, 163
Closing of the American Mind, The (Bloom),
  192, 251
Closure, 350
Club Penguin, 323
Co-curriculum, 169
Coalition of Essential Schools, 187, 252
Coca-Cola, 286
Coe, Marilyn, 48
Cognitive domain, 32
Coleman, James, 146, 374
Coleman study, 280
Collaborative action research (CAR), 383
Collaborative decision making, 298
*Collateral Damage: How High-Stakes Testing
  Corrupts America's Schools* (Nichols/
  Berliner), 182
Collective bargaining, 312, 389, 390
Collier, Virginia, 65
Colonial New England education, 211–214
*Color of Water: A Black Man's Tribute to His
  White Mother, The* (McBride), 68
Coloroso, Barbara, 347
Comenius, 241
Commercializing schools, 284–287, 297
Commissioner, 290
Committee of Ten, 221
Common core state standards, 177–179, 180

Common schools, 215–216, 220
Community-building, 129
Complete Gentleman, The, 213
Comprehensive values education, 328
Compulsory-ignorance law, 225
Computers. *See* Technology/computers
Consolidation, 298
Consolidation stage of teacher
  development, 375
Constitution of the United States, 304
Constructionism, 261, 264
Constructive feedback, 358
Consuming Kids (Lynn), 286
Contraceptives, 123
Contributions approach (multicultural
  education), 68, 69
Cooney, Caroline, 232
Cooperative learning, 363–365
Copyright law, 310–311
Core curriculum, 168, 251
Core knowledge, 192
Corporal punishment, 314–315
Corporate influence in schools,
  284–287, 297
Cosby, Bill, 57
Cosmetic bias, 176
Council for Exceptional Children, 394
Council of Chief State School Officers, 172
Counts, George, 256, 263
*Courage to Teach: Exploring the Inner
  Landscape of a Teacher's Life, The*
  (Palmer), 261, 370
Covert power, 296–297
Crandall, Prudence, 238–239
Crawford, James, 64
Creating mind, 29
Creationism, 189
Cremin, Lawrence, 216
Critical consciousness, 70
*Critical Issues in Education: Dialogue and
  Dialectics* (Nelson et al.), 45
Critical pedagogy, 241
Critical-thinking skills, 196
Criticism, 19, 357
Cross-disciplinary work, 366
*Crossing Over to Canaan: The Journey of
  New Teachers in Diverse Classrooms*
  (Ladson-Billings), 386
Csikzentmihalyi, Mihaly, 373
CTF. *See* Chicago Teachers'
  Federation (CTF)
Cuban, Larry, 160, 195, 367
Cuban Americans, 229
Cultural assimilation, 63
Cultural competence, 70
Cultural difference theory, 58
Cultural differences. *See* International
  comparisons
Cultural influences on education,
  264–265

Cultural literacy, 192
*Cultural Literacy: What Every American
  Needs to Know* (Hirsch), 192, 251
Cultural pluralism, 60, 192
Cultural stereotype, 72
Cultural transmission, 134–135
Culturally responsive teaching,
  69–72, 77
Culturally Responsive Teaching (Jordan/
  Armento), 77
Culture, 52
Culture of poverty, 119, 280
Curricular canon, 192
Curricular inertia, 184
Curriculum
  censorship, 190–191
  character education, 326
  core, 168
  creationism *vs.* evolution, 190
  cultural literacy *vs.* cultural
    imperialism, 192
  curricular canon, 192
  defined, 168
  extracurriculum, 169–170
  factors to consider, 170–173
  invisible, 168–169
  multicultural education, and, 192
  null, 169
  Pink's suggested subjects, 394–395
  saber-tooth, 167
  social action, 135
  standardized testing, and, 182, 184
  technology, and, 194, 195
  tension points, 188–192
  textbook, 173–175
value clarification, 326–327
Curriculum bias detectors, 202
"Curriculum Theory and Practice: What's
  Your Style?" (Miller), 198
Curwin, Richard, 347
Cushman, Kathleen, 349
Cyber-bullying, 128
Czechoslovakia, 67

D

Daily review, 362
Dame schools, 211, 220
Damon, Matt, 187
Dangles, 345
D.A.R.E., 124
Dare the Schools Build a New Social Order
  (Counts), 256
Darling-Hammond, Linda, 145, 178, 286
Darrow, Clarence, 313
Darwin, Charles, 189
Data sensors, 194
*Davis v. Monroe County Board
  of Education,* 321
De facto segregation, 226
De jure segregation, 226

Death and Life of the Great American School System: How Testing and Choice Are Undermining Education, The (Ravitch), 176
Death at an Early Age (Kozol), 154
Decaying infrastructure, 288
Decentralization, 298
Deductive reasoning, 269
Deep teaching, 369
Dees, Morris, 313
Defensive teaching, 303
Deficit theory, 57–58
Delegate representative, 292
Demographics (teachers), 402, 403
"Demystifying the Adolescent Brain" (Steinberg), 48
Descartes, René, 268
Deschooling Society (Illich), 163
Design, 394–395
Developing a Teaching Portfolio: A Guide to Success (Constantino et al.), 404
Developmental and psychosocial stages, 418–419
Developmental approach (ELL students), 63
Dewey, John, 242, 254, 255, 263, 351
Diagnostic observation, 376
Differentiated instruction, 368–369
Digital divide, 195–196
Direct teaching, 362–363
Directions, 350
Director of instruction, 290
Disabilities. *See* Special needs students
Discipline, 314–315
Discipline as control, 347
Discipline with dignity, 347
Disciplined mind, 29
Discovery Education's Lesson Plan Library, 360
Disengaged students, 105
Dishonor role, 322
Distance learning, 153–155, 194–195
DIVERSE, 82–83
Diversity. *See* Student diversity
Divorce, 118
Dreams from My Father: A Story of Race and Inheritance (Obama), 52, 69
Dreikurs, Rudolf, 347
Drive: The Surprising Truth About What Motivates Us (Pink), 10, 388
Dropping out, 122–123, 161, 181
Drug abuse, 123–124
Drug Abuse Resistance Education (D.A.R.E.), 124
Dual-language instruction, 64
DuBois, W. E. B., 226, 242
Due process, 314
Dumbing down, 175
Dweck, Carol, 26

E
E-mentor, 376
E-portfolio, 88, 405
Early childhood education, 415
Early colonial education, 211–214
Early start, 145
Early textbooks, 215
Earth Day Network, 157
Eating disorders, 126
Ecological Intelligence (Goleman), 31
Economic downturns, 278–280
Economic Impact of the Achievement Gap in America's Schools, The, 147
Economic reconstructionists, 136–137
Edelman, Marian Wright, 276
Edgewood v. Kirby, 275
Edison, Thomas, 193
Edison Schools Inc. (Edison Learning), 155
Edmodo, 361
Educating a Profession, 8
Educating Esmé: Diary of a Teacher's First Year (Codell), 381
Education commissions and committees, 172
Education for All Handicapped Children Act, 40
Education in Popular Culture: Telling Tales on Teachers and Learners (Fisher et al.), 110
Education majors, 17
Education milestones, 237
Education of Free Men, The (Mann), 243
Education professors, 15
Education reform and school choice, 146–163, 221
  assumptions, 162–163
  charter schools, 147–150, 162
  full-service schools, 150–151
  green schools, 157–158
  home schools, 155–157
  magnet schools, 152–153
  open enrollment, 153
  rethinking reform, 162–163
  schools for profit, 155, 156
  students, 160–162
  teachers, 158–160
  trust, 160
  virtual schools, 153–155
  voucher program, 151–152
Education Sector survey, 158, 160
Education Testing Service (ETS), A–1
Education want ads, 414
Education Week, 391
Education World, 391
Educational associations, 389–391
Educational finance. *See* Financing America's schools
Educational malpractice, 309
Educational partnership, 297

Educational philosophies. *See* Philosophy of education
Edwards v. Aguillard, 318
Effective schools, 141–146
  class size, 145
  early start, 145
  expectations, 144
  how effective are they?, 394
  leadership, 141
  learning time, 145
  monitoring student progress, 143
  parental involvement/education, 145–146
  reading and math, 145
  safe and orderly climate, 142–143
  school mission, 141–142
  school size, 145
  teacher training, 145
  trust, 145
Effective schools observation, 202–203
Eight-Year Study, 223
8th grade examination graduation questions (1895), 185
Einstein, Albert, 25, 340, 397
Electronic portfolio, 88
Elementary and Secondary Education At, 224
Elementary school, 109–111, 215
Eliot, Lise, 35
ELL students, 63, 66. *See also* Bilingual education
Elstob, Elizabeth, 8
Emerson, Ralph Waldo, 230, 340
Emotional intelligence (EQ), 29–31
Emotional intelligence (Goleman), 29
Emotions, 30
Empathy, 30, 128
Empiricism, 268
Employment interview, 405–406
Emporia State University, 236
Empowering teachers, 158
Encarta, 388
Enculturation, 60
Endorsement, 408
"Engaged Classroom, The" (Intrator), 130
Engaged time, 342
Engaging activities, 359
Engaging the Disengaged (Easton), 102
Engel v. Vitale, 317, 318
English as a second language (ESL), 64
English Classical School, 219
English grammar schools, 220
English language learners (ELLs), 63, 66. *See also* Bilingual education
English-only movement, 64, 65
English standards, 178
Enthusiasm, 350
Entity theory, 26
Entrepreneurs, 148

Environment smart, 27
Environmental pollutants, 44
Environmentally friendly schools, 157
Epistemology, 267
EQ. *See* Emotional intelligence (EQ)
Equal Access Act, 55
ERICA, 46
Erikson's psychosocial stages, 418
Escape from Childhood (Holt), 271
ESL. *See* English as a second
     language (ESL)
Esquith, Rafe, 20
Essentialism, 250–252, 253, 262, 271
Establishment clause, 304
Ethical mind, 29
Ethics, 322–329
     cheating, 322–323
     defined, 269
     moral education, 326–328
     protecting your students, 324–325
     recommendations for teachers, 329
     social networking, 323, 324
"Ethics: From Thought to Action"
     (Sternberg), 330
Ethics of Teaching (Strike/Soltis), 322
Ethnicity, 52. *See also* Race and ethnicity
Ethnocentrism, 264
ETS. *See* Education Testing Service (ETS)
Evaluative observation, 376
*Everyday Antiracism: Getting Real about
     Race in School* (Pollock), 71
Evolution, 189
Examples, 350
Exceptional learners, 36. *See also* Gifted
     and talented students; Special needs
     students
Executive Order No. 9006, 231
"Exemplary Teacher Voices on Their Own
     Development" (Gabriel et al.), 397
Exhibitions, 188
Existential intelligence, 27
Existentialism, 257–259, 262
Expectation theory, 58
Experience and Education (Dewey), 271
Experience-based education, 366
Explicit curriculum, 168
Explicit teaching, 362
External motivation, 388–389
Extracurricular activities, 169–170
Extrinsic profit goals, 10
Extrinsic rewards, 388

F
Facebook, 323
Fair use, 310–311
Family patterns, 116–117
Family Rights and Privacy Act, 312
Family-to-school connection, 142, 165
Farber, Tom, 286

Farmington, Connecticut, framework for
     teaching and learning, 377, 379
Federal legislation, 224
Feedback, 356–359, 362, 421–422
Female seminaries, 234–235
Ferguson, Ronald, 57
Fernald, Grace, 40
Filipino Americans, 230
Financial literacy, 196
Financing America's schools, 274–288
     adequate education, 277–278
     block grants, 283
     budget cuts, 278, 287
     categorical grants, 283
     commercializing schools, 284–287, 297
     distribution of funds, 277
     does money matter?, 280–281
     economic downturns, 278–280
     federal government involvement, 283–284
     future directions, 287–288
     property tax, 274–275
     reforming education finance, 275–277
     Robin Hood reformers, 275
     sources of money, 277, 282
     state per-pupil expenditures, 282
"Finding Fairness for Rural Students"
     (Strange), 300
Finland, 281, 298–299, 383, 388
"Fire and Water, Reflections on Teaching in
     the City" (Miche), 164
Fires in the Bathroom (Cushman), 349
Fires in the Mind (Cushman), 349
First Amendment, 304, 310, 318
First impression, 22
First People's Project, 194
First-year teachers
     good cop/bad cop, 380–381
     induction programs, 374–375
     know your students, 382
     mentors, 376
     observation, 376–380
     one teacher's personal account, 396–397
     physical considerations, 348, 380
     rules and consequences, 381–382
     tips/advice, 387
Five-factor theory of effective schools,
     141–143
Five minds, 28–29
Five Minds for the Future (Gardner), 28, 29
*Flat World and Education: How America's
     Commitment to Equity Will Determine
     Our Future, The* (Darling-Hammond),
     178
Flawed tests, 182–184
Flip-flops, 345
For-profit schools, 155, 156
Ford, Henry, 234
Forester, Brenda, 271
Formal curriculum, 168

Forster, E. M., 230
Fourteenth Amendment, 304, 314
Fourth Amendment, 304, 318
Fragmentation, 345
*Framing Equal Opportunity: Law and
     the Politics of School Finance Reform*
     (Paris), 275
Franklin, Benjamin, 61, 66, 214
Franklin, Helen, 85
*Franklin v. Gwinnett County Public
     Schools,* 321
Franklin Academy, 214
Freedmen's Bureau, 225
Freedom of speech, 309–310, 315–317
Freedom of the press, 319
Freeman, Morgan, 226
Freire, Paulo, 137, 241, 256–257
*Friday Night Lights: A Town, A Team and
     a Dream* (Bissinger), 169
Friedman, Milton, 146, 151
Friendless children, 110
Friends schools, 413
Froebel, Friedrich, 238
Frostig, Marianne, 40
Fulghum, Robert, 28
Full inclusion, 42. *See also* Inclusion
Full-service schools, 150–151

G
Galen, Van, 155
Gandhi, Mahatma, 37
Garcia, Ana, 76, 80, 81
Gardner, Howard
     five minds, 28–29
     instructional technologies, 27
     multiple intelligences, 26–27
Gardner's multiple intelligences, 26–27
Garrison, William Lloyd, 238
Gatekeeping, 104
Gates, Bill, 146
Gay and lesbians. *See* LGBT students
Gay-Straight Alliance (GSA), 55
*Gebser v. Lago Independent School
     District,* 321
*Geeks: How Two Lost Boys Rode the Internet
     Out of Idaho* (Katz), 195
Gender. *See also* Women
     eating disorders, 126
     elementary/middle school, 109–113
     Hyde's gender similarities hypothesis, 34
     ideal body type, 126–127
     learning styles, 33–35
     male entitlements, 112
     parental conduct/expectations, 34
     questioning, 351
     second-class, 113
     service credits, 135
     special needs students, 44
     suicide, 127

Gender socialization, 35
Gender stereotypes, 34
Gender wall, 109
Gendered career, 218
General Mills, 286
Generalizations, 73–74
Genetics, 280
Geography (school enrollment by state),
    401
George Washington Carver High School
    (Atlanta), 141
Germantown, 60
G.I. Bill of Rights, 1944, 224
Giamatti, A. Bartlett, 171
Gifted and talented students, 36–39
    accelerated programs, 38–39
    challenging courses of study, 38
    definition, 36
    dropping out, 38
    elements of giftedness, 36, 37
    how many, 37
    professional association, 393
    special schools, 38
    gifted inclusion, 38
Gilbert, Rose, 10
Gilligan, Carol, 328
Ginott, Haim, 347
*Girlfighting: Betrayal and Rejection among
    Girls* (Brown), 113
Giving Kids the Business (Molnar), 286
Glass wall, 236
Glasser, William, 347
"Go Where You Belong: Male Teachers
    as Cultural Workers in the Lives of
    Children, Families, and Communities"
    (Watson/Woods), 402
Goldberg v. Kelly, 412
Golden Mean, 267
Goleman, Daniel, 29, 30
Good cop/bad cop, 380–381
Good High School, The (Lightfoot),
    141, 144
Goodbye, Mr. Chips (film), 9
Goode, Mary, 78, 80–81, 82
Goodlad, John, 104, 137, 138, 158,
    342, 357
Google Earth, 361
Gordon, Jennifer, 23
Gordon, Thomas, 347
Goss v. Lopez, 314
Governing America's schools, 288–298
    chief state school officer, 290–291
    consolidation, 298
    covert power, 296–297
    decentralization, 298
    hidden government, 296–297
    overview (figure), 291
    principal, 294–295
    quiz, 288–290

school board, 290, 292, 293
school districts, 291, 292
state board of education, 290
state department of education, 291
superintendent, 293–294
teachers, 297–298
Grabber, 336, 362
Grandparent, 117
Grant, Melinda, 199
Great Books, 252, 253
Green schools, 157–158
Greene, Maxine, 259, 263
Griffin, Marcus, 76, 80, 81
Group alerting, 344
Group dynamics, 347
Groves, Warren, 48
GSA. *See* Gay-Straight Alliance (GSA)
Guided practice, 362

H

Hacker, Andrew, 56
Haley, Margaret, 392
Hall, G. Stanley, 219
Hall, Samuel, 11
Hall of fame (profiles in education),
    236–242. *See also* Profile in education
Hands-on learning, 33
Haptic learning, 33
Harlem Children's Zone, 151
Harris, Sarah, 238, 239
Hazelwood School District v. Kuhlmeir, 319
Healthy, Hungerfree Kids Act, 125
Heath, Shirley Brice, 119
Helicopter parents, 115
Henry, Jules, 168
Herbart, Johann, 242
Herron, Carolivia, 190
Hersch, Patricia, 114
Hidden curriculum, 168
Hidden government, 296–297
*High School Confidential: Secrets of an
    Undercover Student* (Iverson), 113
High-school experience, 206–207
High school graduation rates, 67, 122
High School of Music & Art, 152
High School of Performing Arts (New York
    City), 134
High school yearbook, 206
High-stakes testing, 179–187, 199. *See also*
    Standardized testing
High-tech cheating, 193
High-traffic areas, 348
Higher-order question, 352, 354
Higher-order thinking, 366
Highland Park High School, 141
Hill, Anita, 305
Hindu beliefs, 67
Hirsch, E. D., Jr., 192, 251, 263
Hispanic studies, 68

Hispanic subgroups, 228
Hispanics. *See also* Race and ethnicity
    Cuban Americans, 229
    discipline, 314
    generalization, 80
    giftedness, 38
    Mexican Americans, 227–228
    Puerto Ricans, 228–229
    special needs students, 44
    subgroups, 228
    two-parent families, 116
    typical student, 76
Historical overview, 210–244
    academy, 214, 220
    African Americans, 225–227
    Arab Americans, 232–233
    Asian Americans and Pacific
        Islanders, 229–232
    bilingual education, 61
    Committee of Ten reports, 221
    common schools, 215–216, 220
    dame schools, 211, 220
    early colonial period, 211–214
    early textbooks, 215
    English grammar schools, 220
    federal government involvement,
        223–225
    female seminaries, 234–235
    Hispanics, 227–229
    influential educators, 238–242
    key people, 238–242
    Latin grammar schools, 212, 220
    milestones, 237
    Native Americans, 216–218
    normal schools, 216
    progressive education, 222–223
    school reform, 221
    schools, 220
    secondary school movement,
        219–221
    segregation, 225–227
    special needs students, 39–40
    teaching, 10–12
    timeline, 237
    women, 218–219, 234–236
*History of American Education:
    A Great American Experiment,
    The* (Webb), 213
HIV-infected students, 319
Holmes, Henry H., 12
Holmes Group, 12
Holocaust/Genocide Project, 194
Holt, Anne, 130
Holt, John, 163
Home schools, 155–157
Homeless families, 121
Homework, 105, 142, 143
Homogeneous classes, 106
hooks, bell, 263

Hope in the Unseen: An American Odyssey from the Inner City to the Ivy League, A (Susskind), 76

Hopwood decision, 227

Horatio Alger rags-to-riches stories, 140, 280

Hornbook, 215

Hostile environment sexual harassment, 321

"How Good Are the Asians: Refuting Four Myths About Asian-American Academic Achievement" (Zhao/Qiu), 85

How Teachers Taught: Constancy and Change in American Classrooms, 1890-1980 (Cuban), 367

Huffington Post, 416

Human potential, 73

Human relations, 197

"Humanities: Why Such a Hard Sell?, The" (Ferrero), 271

Humility, 371

Hunter, Madeline, 94, 95, 363

Hunter's seven-step lesson plan, 95

Hutchins, Robert, 253, 263

Huxley, Aldous, 192

Hybrid course, 195

Hyde, Janet, 34

Hyde's gender similarities hypothesis, 34

I

"I, too, am an American" (Rosenbaum), 84

"I, Too, Am an American: Preservice Teachers Reflect upon National Identity" (Gallavan), 85

"I, too, am an original American" (Rainwater), 84

"I, Too, Sing America" (Hughes), 83

IAEP. *See* International Assessment of Education Progress (IAEP)

IDEA. *See* Individuals with Disabilities Education Act (IDEA)

Ideal body type, 126–127

Idealism, 268

Ideologues, 155

IEA. *See* Intelligent essay assessor (IEA)

IEP. *See* Individualized education program (IEP)

If You Don't Feed the Teachers They Eat the Students (Connors), 295

Illich, Ivan, 163

Images of Schoolteachers in America (Bodin), 218

Imagine... boxes
Afghan school curriculum, 175
bathroom habits, 344
best teachers for most needy students, 82
bullying, 127
financial impact of a good teacher, 284
humorous student answers to teacher questions, 390

Matt Damon speaking at teacher rally, 187

meditation, 348

92-year-old teacher, 10

one-student school, 136

posse, 182

reflection, 250

religious freedom, 317

school superintendent gives back $800,000, 279

segregated school proms, 226

shaved heads/chemotherapy, 29

skipping school, paying for, 281

tardiness, 328

test of goodwill, 188

weapons *vs.* education, 410

yearbook signing, 326

Iman, Amanullah, 175

Immersion, 64

Immigration Act of 1882, 230

Implicit curriculum, 168

"Improve Relationships to Improve Student Performance" (Arum), 330

In a Different Voice: Psychological Theory and Women's Development (Gilligan), 328

In action, video clips. *See* Observation video clips

In-depth profiles. *See* Profile in education

In loco parentis, 212, 318

In-service days, 382

Inclusion
gifted students, 38
moral issue, 47
pros/cons, 45
special needs students, 42, 45, 46

"Inclusion in Two Languages: Special Education in Portugal and the United States" (Linn), 48

Income tax, 282

Incremental theory, 26

Independent practice, 363

Individualized education program (IEP), 42

Individuals with Disabilities Education Act (IDEA), 40–42, 224

Induction programs, 374–375

Inductive reasoning, 269

Informal education, 265

Information gathering, 19–21

Information interview, 427

Infrastructure, 288

Ingraham v. Wright, 314

Inside Charter Schools: The Paradox of Radical Decentralization (Fuller), 148

Inspiring Teachers, 391

Instructional alignment, 365

Instructional variety, 359

INTASC Reflective Activities and Your Portfolio. *See* Reflective activities and your portfolio (RAPs)

INTASC standard 1 (learner development)
developmental and psychosocial stages, 418–419
interview with person of different background, 90
money matters, 332
school observation diary, 201
text of the standard, 89
textbook page references, A–5

INTASC standard 2 (learning differences)
curriculum bias detectors, 202
multiple intelligence bingo, 90–91
observing different teaching strategies, 419–420
philosophy on the big screen, 333
text of the standard, 89
textbook page references, A–5

INTASC standard 3 (learning environments)
effective schools observation, 202–203
philosophy-in-the-classroom observations, 333–334
rules, rituals, and routines, 420–421
text of the standard, 89
textbook page references, A–5
"Why I Am Teaching" letter, 91–92

INTASC standard 4 (content knowledge)
curricular standards, 203
my hall of fame entry, 334–335
teacher: interview: subject specialty, 92–93
teaching is learning (teacher feedback), 421–422
text of the standard, 89
textbook page references, A–6

INTASC standard 5 (application of content knowledge)
"Career Information" document, 93
class comedy club, 423
"my philosophy of education" document, 335
PSA: purpose of education, 203–204
text of the standard, 89
textbook page references, A–6

INTASC standard 6 (assessment)
assessing the assessor, 335
portfolio assessment, 423–424
reading a novel, 93–94
test-taking experience, 204–205
text of the standard, 89
textbook page references, A–6

INTASC standard 7 (planning for instruction)
community service, 205
diversity lesson plan, 94–95
students' bill of rights and responsibilities, 336–337
technology in classroom (bane or boom?), 424–425
textbook page references, A–6

INTASC standard 8 (instructional strategies)
  bulletin board, 95–96
  choice school instruction diary, 205–206
  great lecture theory of learning, 337–338
  memories of a special teacher, 425
  text of the standard, 89
  textbook page references, A–7
INTASC standard 9 (professional learning and ethical practice)
  high-school experience, 206–207
  nontraditional hero, 96–97
  publication of the month, 338
  text of the standard, 89
  textbook page references, A–7
  website of the month, 425–426
INTASC standard 10 (leadership and collaboration)
  information interview, 427
  school board column, 338
  special education services, 97
  support staff interview, 207
  text of the standard, 89
  textbook page references, A–7
INTASC teaching standards. See also individual standards
  overview, A–5 to A–7
  RAPs (foundations), 332–338
  RAPs (schools and curriculum), 201–207
  RAPs (teachers and students), 90–97
  RAPs (your classroom), 418–427
  text of standards, 89
Intellect, 73
Intellectual property, 311
Intelligence
  cultural differences, 27
  defined, 26
  entity theory, 26
  Gardner's multiple intelligences, 26–27
  incremental theory, 26
  Intelligence quotient (IQ), 26
  Intelligent design, 189
  Intelligent essay assessor (IEA), 360
  Interdependence, 363
  International Assessment of Education Progress (IAEP), 17
  International Baccalaureate (IB), 38
  International comparisons. See also Finland
  administrators/nonteaching staff, 386
  intelligence, 27
  teacher responsibilities, 386
  teaching hours per year, 383, 385
International conversation, 66
"International Education: What's In a Name?" (Parker), 198
International PISA test, 299
International tests, 17–18, 299
International Walk to School Month, 126
Internet resources, 194

Interpersonal intelligence, 26
Interracial marriage, 117
Interviewing Principles and Practices (Stewart/Cash), 405
Intrapersonal intelligence, 27
Intrinsic motivation, 388
Intrinsic purpose goals, 10
Intuition, 397
Invisible curriculum, 168–169
Invisible race knapsack, 57
Iowa Test for Basic Skills, 18
IQ, 26
Is There Life After High School? (Keyes), 113
Islam, 232
Itinerant schools, 220
"It's Not on the Test: A Search for Existential Meaning in Three Acts" (Doyle), 398

J
Jackson, Amanda, 330
Jackson, Andrew, 215
Jackson, Philip W., 102, 104
Jacobson, Lenore, 144
Japanese Americans, 231
Japanese internment camps, 231
Jefferson, Thomas, 214
Jewish American students, 78, 80, 81–82
Job-hopping profile, 406
Job hunting, etc. See also Career development
  alternative teacher certification, 408–409
  analyzing the job offer, 406
  certification/licensure, 12–13, 407–408, A–2 to A–4
  chances of finding teaching position, 401–402
  employment interview, 405–406
  endorsement, 408
  nontraditional educational careers, 413–417. See also Nontraditional educational careers
  portfolio, 404–405. See also Reflective activities and your portfolio (RAP)
  résumé, 403–404
  salary, 403
  teacher competency exams, 409–410, A–1
  teaching contract, 411
  teaching in another state, 408
  tenure, 411–412
  unique school settings, 412–413
Job interview, 405–406
John F. Kennedy High School (Bronx), 141, 143
John McDonough High School, 366
Johnson, Lyndon, 226
Jones Act, 228
"Journey North: A Global Study of Wildlife Migration," 194

Juku schools, 17
Just Like Us: The True Story of Four Mexican Girls Coming of Age in America (Thorpe), 64

K
Kalamazoo, Michigan, case, 219–220
Kanner, Allen, 285
Karen (Killilea), 39
Katz, Lillian, 375
Keeping Track (Oakes), 106, 107
"Keeping Youth in School: An International Perspective" (Hoffman), 130
Kelly, Ken, 371
Kemberling, Amie, 115
Kennedy, John F., 83
Kent, Judith, 371
Kerner Commission, 226
Kettering, Chris, 164
Keyes, Ralph, 113
Kindergarten, 238
Kindness, 349
Kinesthetic/tactile learners, 32, 33
King, Lawrence, 55
King, Martin Luther, Jr., 37
KIPP schools, 148–150
Kirst, Michael, 118
Klein, Ariel, 78, 80, 81–82
Klein, Joel, 295
Knowledge Deficit, The (Hirsch), 251
Kohlberg, Lawrence, 327–328
Kohn, Alfie, 178, 182, 183
Kopp, Wendy, 14
Kounin, Jacob, 344, 345, 347
Kozol, Jonathan, 154
Krispy Kreme, 286

L
Labeling, 129
Labor rights, 311–312
Laboratory School, 255
Ladson-Billings, Gloria, 69, 70
LaGuardia, Fiorello H., 152
LaGuardia School of Arts, 152
Lamb, Christopher, 211
Land-Grant College Acts, 224
Land Ordinance Act, 224
Language submersion, 61, 64
Last mile problem, 195
Latchkey kids, 118
Latin grammar schools, 212, 220
Latino culture. See also Hispanics
Lau v. Nichols, 61
Lau remedies, 61
Laughter, 349
Leadership Academy (New York City), 295
Learner cooperation, 366
Learning community, 369, 386

Learning disabilities. *See* Special needs students
"Learning from Latino Families" (Auerbach), 84
Learning styles
  affective factors, 31–32
  brain development, 32, 35
  cognitive factors, 32
  gender, 33–35
  physiological factors, 31
  teaching tip, 33
Learning time, 145, 341, 342
"Learning to Love Assessment" (Tomlinson), 371
Learning to Stand and Speak: Women, Education, and Public Life in America's Republic (Kelly), 219
Least intervention, 345
Least restrictive environment, 42, 43
Lee v. Weisman, 318
Leetch, Amber, 136
Legal issues. *See* School law and ethics
Legal liability, 308–309
Lemelson-MIT Invention Index (2006), 18
Lemon v. Kurtzman, 151
Lemon test, 151
Lesbians. *See* LGBT students
Lesson plan, 94–95
Let Your Life Speak: Listening for the Voice of Vocation (Palmer), 3
Let's Move campaign, 126
Letters of recommendation, 21–22
"Letters to My Younger Self" (Shafto), 48
Levenson, William, 193
Levin, Joe, 313
Lewis, Oscar, 119
LGBT students, 54–55
  discipline, 314
  generalization, 81
  GSAs, 55
  safety, 142
  teaching tip, 55
  typical student, 79
Licensure, 407–408, A–2 to A–4
Life in Classrooms (Jackson), 102
Lightfoot, Sara Lawrence, 141, 143, 144, 162
"Lina's Letter: A 9-Year-Old's Perspective on What Matters Most in the Classroom" (Pratt), 398
Linguistic bias, 176
Linguistic intelligence, 26
Listserv, 142
Literature, 134
Living with Intensity: understanding the Sensitivity, Excitability, and the Emotional Development of Gifted Children, Adolescents, and Adults (Daniels/Piechowski), 38
Local school board, 171

Local school district, 291, 292
Locker search, 317–318
Locus of control, 32
Logic, 269
Logical-mathematical intelligence, 26
Looking in Classrooms (Good/Brophy), 358
Looping, 369
Lortie, Dan, 374
Lost Child in the Woods: Saving Our Children from Nature Deficit Disorder (Louv), 27
Lower-order question, 352, 353
Lower-tracked students, 106
Lyceum, 267
Lynd, Robert and Helen, 106
Lyon, Mary, 234

M
Magnet schools, 152–153
Mahara, 361
Mainstreaming, 42. *See also* Inclusion
Maintenance approach (ELL students), 63
Male entitlements, 112
Malfeasance, 309
Mama G, 10
Mama's Boy, Preacher's Son: A Memoir of Becoming a Man (Jennings), 57
Management models, 346, 347
Management/motivation observation, 421
Mann, Horace, 11, 197, 210, 215–216, 242
Manufactured Crisis, The (Berliner/Biddle), 18
"Mapping a Route Toward Differentiated Instruction" (Tomlinson), 371
Marijuana, 124
Marshmallow story, 30
Martin, Jane Roland, 258
Martin, Joan, 48
Martinez, Carlos, 79, 81, 82
Maryland, 278
Maslow, Abraham, 100
Mason, Casey, 149
Massachusetts Law of 1647, 212
Mastery learning, 365
Mastruzzi, Robert, 141
Materialism, 268
Mathematics standards, 178
Mature judgment and selection, 191
Maturity stage of teacher development, 375
McAuliffe, Christa, 8
McCarthy, Colman, 188
McCarthy, Joseph, 222
McCarty, Donald, 294
McDonald's, 286
McGuffey, William Holmes, 215
McGuffey Readers, 215
McIntosh, Peggy, 57
McKinney-Vento Homeless Assistance Act, 121
McKinsey & Company, 147
Meditation, 129, 348

Melting pot, 60, 140
Mendler, Allen, 347
Mentioning phenomenon, 175
Mentors, 376
Merit pay, 5, 159, 162, 387
"Metaphors of Hope" (Chenfield), 23
Metaphysics, 267
MetLife surveys, 4–5
Metropolitan Achievement Test, 18
Metrotech High School (Phoenix), 365
Mexican Americans, 227–228. *See also* Hispanics
Meyer v. State of Nebraska, 61
Middle school, 111–113
Middletown, 106
Mill v. D.C. Board of Education, 40
Milton Academy, 141
Mindset: The New Psychology of Success (Dweck), 26
Miner, Myrtilla, 235
Miner Normal School for Colored Girls, 235
Misfeasance, 308
Models of classroom management, 346, 347
Montessori, Maria, 239, 413
Montessori: The Science Behind the Genius (Lillard), 413
Montessori schools, 239, 413
Moral education, 326–328
Moral Education (Durkheim), 328
Moral stages of development, 327–328
Morrill Land Grant College Acts, 224
Morse v. Frederick, 316
Motivating oneself, 30
Mouawad, Ibrahim, 79, 81, 82
Mount Holyoke, 234, 235
Multicultural, 68
Multicultural education, 66–72
  approaches to, 68–69
  Banks's approach, 68, 69
  culturally responsive teaching, 69–72, 77
  curriculum, 192
  dimensions, 67–68
  factoids, 67
  Ladson-Billings research, 69–71
Multicultural reconstructionism, 68
Multiculturalism debate, 67
Multiple intelligence bingo, 90–91
Multiple intelligences, 26–27
Multiple Intelligences in the Classroom (Armstrong), 27
Multiracial, 52
Municipal overburden, 275
Music smart, 26
Musical intelligence, 26
Muslims, 232, 233
"My Pedagogic Creed" (Dewey), 243
"Myth of Pink and Blue Brains, The" (Eliot), 48
"Myth of the Culture of Poverty, The" (Gorski), 130

N

Nappy Hair (Herron), 190
Narrative of the Life of Frederick Douglass: An American Slave (Douglass), 243
Nation at Risk: The Imperative for Educational Reform, A, 146, 221
Nation Prepared, A, 12
National Association for Gifted Children (NAGC), 394
National Association for the Education of Young Children (NAEYC), 172, 394
National Board for Professional Teaching Standards (NBPTS), 12, 387
National Council for Teachers of English (NCTE), 394
National Council for the Accreditation of Teacher Education (NCATE), 408
National Council for the Social Studies (NCSS), 394
National Council for the Teachers of Mathematics (NCTM), 394
National Defense Education Act (NDEA), 223, 224
National Education Association (NEA), 4, 15, 172, 221, 325, 389–391, 412
National Educational Technology Plan, 195
National Evaluation System (NES), A–1
National Forensics Study, 169
National Governors Association, 172
National Middle School Association (NMSA), 391
National School Lunch Program, 125
National Science Teachers Association (NSTA), 394
National Teacher Recruitment Clearinghouse, 19
Native American students. *See also* Race and ethnicity
  generalization, 75
  historical overview, 216–218
  typical student, 75
Naturalist intelligence, 27
Nature deficit disorder, 27, 158
NBPTS. *See* National Board for Professional Teaching Standards (NBPTS)
NCLB. *See* No Child Left Behind Act (NCLB)
NDEA. *See* National Defense Education Act (NDEA)
NEA. *See* National Education Association (NEA)
Negligence, 308
Neighborhood Story Project, 366
Neill, A. S., 259, 263
NES. *See* National Evaluation System (NES)
Networking, 21
Neuroplasticity, 32, 35
New American Academy, 150
New England Primer, 215
New material, 362

"New Professional: The Aims of Education Revisited, A" (Palmer), 23
New York City, 295
New York Times, 416
No Child Left Behind Act (NCLB), 176–177, 224
No Child Left Inside program, 158
"No pass, no play" rules, 170
Noddings, Nel, 263
Non sequitur, 345
Nondiscriminatory education, 40–42
Nonfeasance, 308
Nontraditional educational careers, 413–417
  adult education, 415
  colleges and universities, 415
  community organizations, 415
  early childhood education, 415
  education associations, 416
  education want ads, 414
  global opportunities, 416–417
  government agencies, 416
  media, 416
  private industry and public utilities, 416
  technology, 416
Nontraditional families, 117
Nontraditional hero, 96–97
Norm-referenced tests, 143
Normal school, 11
North Carolina School for Mathematics and Science, 38
Northwest Ordinance, 224
Norton, Ellen, 330
"Notes from an Accidental Teacher" (Tomlinson), 23
Noyes Elementary, 186
Null curriculum, 169
Number/reasoning smart, 26
Nyquist case, 151

O

Oakes, Jeannie, 106–108
Obama, Barack, 52
Obama, Michelle, 126
Obesity, 125–127
Objective-referenced tests, 143
Observation video clips
  adolescent self-concept, 130
  bullying, 131
  charter school, 164, 300
  cheating, 330
  classroom bias (role play), 49
  drug abuse, 130
  essentialism, 271
  family-to-school connection, 165
  high-stakes testing, 199
  immigrant students, 85
  including students with special needs, 49
  methods of effective teaching, 372

  multiple intelligences lesson, 48
  progressivism, 243
  pros/cons of teaching, 23
  respect and salary for teachers, 398
Odd Girl Out (Simmons), 113
Odyssey of the Mind, 169
Official English language laws, 65
Old Deluder Satan Law, 212
One Day All Children....:The Unlikely Triumph of Teach for America and What I Learned along the Way (Kopp), 14
120 Banned Books: Censorship Histories of World Literature (Karolides), 191
One-student school, 136
Online Learning Center, 19
Open enrollment, 153
Opinion polls. *See* Public opinion
Opportunity-to-learn standards, 181
Oral tradition, 265
Orfield, Gary, 227
Orwell, George, 192
Out of Our Minds: Learning to Be Creative (Robinson), 38
Ovando, Carlos Julio, 62
Overdwelling, 345
Overlapping, 345
Overprotective/over-involved parents, 115
Overspecialization, 395
Owasso Independent School District v. Falvo, 312–314
Owen, David, 113

P

Pacific Islanders. *See* Asian Americans/Pacific Islanders
Page, Clarence, 69
Paideia Proposal (Adler), 252
Parent
  curriculum, and, 171
  effective schools, and, 145–146
  overprotective/over-involved, 115
  school governance, and, 297
Parent-teacher home visit project, 142
Parenting responsibilities, 117
Parker, Francis, 222
Parsons, Talcott, 106
"Pass to play" regulations, 170
Path to Purpose: How Young People Find Their Calling In Life, The (Damon), 115
Patterns of the classroom, 104
Pauper's Oath, 212
Pay-for-performance, 5
"Pay to play" rules, 170
PBL. *See* Problem-based learning (PBL)
Peabody, Elizabeth, 238
Peanuts (cartoon), 3
Pedagogical cycle, 349–359
  questioning, 351–354
  reaction/productive feedback, 356–359

structure, 349–350
student response, 354–356
Pedagogues, 155
Pedagogues of Resistance: Women Educator Activists, 1880-1960 (Crocco et al.), 235
Pedagogy, 16
Pedagogy of the Oppressed, The (Friere), 137, 241
Peer mediation program, 129
Peer review, 377
Pennsylvania Association for Retarded Children v. Commonwealth, 40
People smart, 26
People's History of the Civil War, A (Williams), 234
People's History of the United States: 1492-Present, A (Zinn), 234
Perennialism, 252–253, 262
Perestroika, 171
Performance-based work, 187
"Perils and Promised of Praise, The" (Dweck), 371
Perry v. Sinderman, 412
Personal income tax, 282
Pestalozzi, Johann Heinrich, 241
Petteway, Diane, 198
Philosophy of education, 245–272
  aesthetics, 269
  ancient Greek philosophers, 265–267
  behaviorism, 264
  Cartesian dualism, 268
  constructionism, 261, 264
  empiricism, 268
  epistemology, 267
  essentialism, 250–252, 253, 262
  existentialism, 257–259, 262
  idealism, 268
  inductive *vs.* deductive reasoning, 269
  key people, 263
  logic, 269
  materialism, 268
  metaphysics, 267
  overview (table), 262
  perennialism, 252–253, 262
  political philosophy, 269
  progressivism, 254–255, 262
  rationalism, 269
  social reconstructionism, 255–257, 262
  student-centered philosophies, 254–259, 260
  teacher-centered philosophies, 250–253, 260
Philosophy statement, 270
Physical fitness, 197
Physical setup of classroom, 348
Piaget, Jean, 242, 327
Pickering v. Board of Education, 310
Picture smart, 26
Pierce v. Society of Sisters, 318

Pink, Daniel, 393–395
Pink Brain, Blue Brain: How Small Differences Grow Into Troublesome Gaps--And What We Can Do About It (Eliot), 34
Place Called School, A (Goodlad), 104, 137, 342, 357
Plato, 266–267
Play: How it Shapes the Brain, Opens the Imagination, and Invigorates the Soul (Brown), 182
"Please Help Me Learn Who I Am" (Boyce), 330
Pledge of Allegiance, 317
Plessy v. Ferguson, 225
Podcasting lectures and discussions, 194
Political philosophy, 269
Portfolio, 22, 28, 87–88, 383, 404–405. *See also* Reflective activities and your portfolio (RAP)
Portfolio assessment, 423–424
Positive teacher-student relationship, 116
Posse Scholars, 182
Postman, Neil, 192
Poverty, 118–121
  college, 120–121
  disadvantages, 119
  early colonial period, 212
  financial fears, 120
  giftedness, 37
  rich-poor divide, 287
  rising out of poverty, 281
  soft bias, 120
  special needs students, 44
  standardized tests, 181
  verbal interactions, 119
Powell, Larry, 279
"Power of Personal Relationships, The" (Mawhinney/Sagan), 164
Power of the Arts: Creative Strategies for Teaching Exceptional Learners, The (Smith), 40
Powerful Reforms with Shallow Roots (Cuban/Usdan), 149
PowerPoint, 363
"Prairie Home Companion, A," 377
Praise, 357–358
Pravat, Kasem, 77, 80, 81
Praxis, 257
Praxis Assessment for Beginning Teachers (PRAXIS), 172, 410, A–1
PRAXIS I: Academic Skills Assessment, 410, A–1
PRAXIS II: Principles of Learning and Teaching and Subject Assessments, 410, A–1
Pregnancy, 123
Presentation software, 363
Presidential election (2008), 69
"Pretend attend," 161

Prezi, 363
Price of Privilege: How Parental Pressure and Material Advantage Are Creating a Generation of Disconnected and Unhappy Kids (Levine), 322
Principal, 141, 171, 294–295
Principle of least intervention, 345
Private school, 146, 155, 156, 403, 407–408
Privatization, 155
Problem-based learning (PBL), 366
Procedural due process, 42
Productive feedback, 356–359
Profession, 9
Professional associations, 391–393
Professional development programs, 382–384
Professional education journals, 21
Professional organizations, 172, 312
Professionalism, 8–10
Profile in education
  Cuban, Larry, 367
  Dees, Morris, 313
  Edelman, Marian Wright, 276
  Esquith, Rafe, 20
  Haley, Margaret, 392
  influential educators, 238–242
  Kohn, Alfie, 183
  Kozol, Jonathan, 154
  Martin, Jane Roland, 258
  Oakes, Jeannie, 107
  Ovando, Carlos Julio, 62
  Smith, Sally L., 41
Profit goals, 10
Progressive education, 222–223
Progressivism, 222, 254–255, 262
Project-based instruction, 366
Project Head Start, 224
Property tax, 274–275
Proposals Relating to the Youth Pennsylvania (Franklin), 214
Proposition 13, 277
Pros/cons. *See* You Be The Judge
"Pseudoscience of Single-Sex Schooling, The" (Halpern), 35
Psychological influences on education, 261–264
Public Agenda survey, 5
Public Law 94-142, 40
Public opinion
  charter schools, 147
  effectiveness of schools, 18
  evolution, 189
  factors affecting school performance, 54
  race relations, 68
  trust in various professions, 5
  voucher programs, 152
  who should become a teacher, 15
Publication of the month, 338
Publicly funded vouchers, 151–152

Publishers, 172, 173–175
Puerto Ricans, 228–229
Pullout programs, 44, 45
Punished by Rewards (Kohn), 389
Puritans, 212–214
Purpose goals, 10
"Putting a Face to Faith" (Haynes), 330
Pygmalion in the Classroom (Rosenthal/
    Jacobson), 144

Q

Quaker education, 412–413
Quaker Education in Theory and Practice
    (Briton), 413
Quakers, 213
"Questionable Assumptions about
    Schooling" (Eisner), 164
Questioning, 351–354
Quid pro quo sexual harassment, 320–321

R

Race and ethnicity
    African Americans. *See* African Americans
    Arab Americans, 79, 81, 82, 232–233
    Asian Americans. *See* Asian Americans/
        Pacific Islanders
    computer use, 196
    definitions, 52
    factoids, 52–54, 108
    high school graduation rates, 122
    Hispanics. *See* Hispanics
    invisibility, 176
    media, 69
    Native American students. *See* Native
        American students
    obesity, 125
    population (1980-2025), 53
    public opinion, 68
    service credits, 135
    teachers, 402
Race to the Top, 158
Rainwater, Mandie, 84
"Raising Teacher Quality Around
    the World" (Stewart), 23
Ramadan, 233
Ramsey, Charles, 294
Rancho Elementary School, 251
Random thoughts, 345
RAP. *See* Reflective activities and your
    portfolio (RAP)
Rationalism, 269
Ravitch, Diane, 177
Raymond, Christie, 398
Read, Melissa, 398
Reciprocity, 408
Reconstructionists, 135
Redl, Fritz, 347
Reflective activities and your portfolio (RAP)
    contents/elements, 87
    Part I (teachers and students), 90–97

Part II (schools and curriculum), 201–207
    Part III (foundations), 332–338
    Part IV (your classroom), 418–427
Reflective teachers, 370
Reform movement. *See* Education reform
    and school choice
Reformers, 148
Regular education initiative, 44–45
Relational aggression, 113
Religion, 190, 317, 318
Religious fundamentalists, 189
Religious right, 189
Remediation, 357
Renewal stage of teacher
    development, 375
"Respect--Where Do We Start?" (Beaudoin),
    300
Respectful mind, 29
Résumé, 22, 403–404
Rethinking reform, 162–163
"Reviving the Goal of An Integrated
    Society: A 21st Century Challenge"
    (Orfield), 243
Rewards of teaching, 386–389
Rich-poor divide, 287
Rickover, Hyman, 222
Right-brain skills, 393–394
Rights quotient (RQ), 303, 321
Riley, Lindsey Maria, 75, 81
Rist, Ray, 106
Robin Hood reformers, 275
Roosevelt, Franklin, 231, 273
Roosevelt, Theodore, 218
Rosenbaum, Lacey, 84
Rosenthal, Robert, 144
Rothman, Amy, 164
Rousseau, Jean-Jacques, 241
Rowe, Mary Budd, 354, 355
Rules and consequences, 346, 381–382
Rural white students, 78, 80–81, 82

S

Saber-tooth curriculum, 167
Saber-Tooth Curriculum, The (Peddiwell),
    167
Sadker, Myra and David, 356
Safe and Drug-Free Schools program, 124
Safe school learning environments,
    142–143
Salary, 5, 7, 403
Sales tax, 282
Salovey, Peter, 30
San Antonio v. Rodriguez, 275
*Santa Fe Independent School District v. Jane
    Doe*, 318
SAT reading and mathematics tests, 18
Savage Inequalities (Kozol), 154
Scaffolding, 264, 350
Schaffer, Robert, 8
Scholars Bowl, 169

School
    administrative structure, 290–295
    curriculum. *See* Curriculum
    effectiveness, 141–146, 394
    gendered world, 109–113
    goals, 137–140
    infrastructure, 288
    middle, 111–113
    name of, 136
    passing the cultural baton, 134–135
    patterns of the classroom, 104
    purpose of, 134–140
    reform. *See* Education reform and school
        choice
    social status, 113–115
    time, 103
    tool for change, as, 135–137
    unique school settings, 412–413
School administrators, 290–295
School-based management, 298
School board, 171, 290, 292, 293, 338
School choice, 147–158. *See also* Education
    reform and school choice
*School Choice Policies and Outcomes:
    Empirical and Philosophical Perspectives*
    (Feinberg/Lubienski), 147
School curriculum. *See* Curriculum
School custodian, 297
School districts, 291, 292
School effectiveness, 141–146, 394. *See
    also* Effective schools
School funding. *See* Financing America's
    schools
"School Funding's Tragic Flaw" (Carey/
    Roza), 300
School goals, 137–140
School governance. *See* Governing
    America's schools
School governance quiz, 288–300
*School in the United States: A Documentary
    History, The* (Fraser), 213
School Law: Cases and Concepts (LaMorte),
    304
School law and ethics, 302–331
    copyright law, 310–311
    corporal punishment, 314–315
    ethics. *See* Ethics
    freedom of speech, 309–310, 315–317
    freedom of the press, 319
    HIV-infected students, 319
    labor rights, 311–312
    legal liability, 308–309
    overview, 304
    school prayer, 317
    search and seizure, 317–318
    sexual harassment, 305, 320–321
    student records, 312–314
    student's rights and responsibilities,
        312–321
    suspension and discipline, 314–315

teacher's academic freedom, 307–308
teacher's application for a job, 304–305
teacher's personal lifestyle, 306, 307
teacher's rights and responsibilities, 304–312
untenured teachers, protection of, 412
School Law and the Public Schools: A Practical Guide for School Leaders (Essex), 303, 307
School Managers: Power and Conflict in American Public Education, The (McCarty/Ramsey), 294
School mascots, 217
School meals, 125, 126
School mission, 141–142
School name, 136
School observation diary, 201
School prayer, 317
School secretary, 296
School segregation
    Civil Rights Act of 1964, 226
    court decisions, 225–226, 227
    de jure/de facto segregation, 226
    high-poverty schools, 67
    magnet schools, 152
    resegregation, 67, 69, 227
    second-generation segregation, 226
    separate but equal, 225
    single-sex education, 35, 236
School size, 145
School superintendent, 293–294
Schools for profit, 155, 156
Schools That Learn: A Fifth Discipline Fieldbook for Educators, Parents, and Everyone Who Cares About Education (Senge), 296
Schools.com, 153–155
Schurz, Margaretta, 238
Scientific theories, 189
Scott, Leigh, 85
Search and seizure, 317–318
Second-generation segregation, 226
Secondary school movement, 219–221
Secretary of education, 290
See Me After Class: Advice for Teachers from Teachers (Elden), 402
Seeds of Peace, 329
Segregated school proms, 226
Segregation. *See* School segregation
Self-censorship, 191
Self-esteem, 34, 70
Self-help area, 348
Self smart, 27
Separate but equal, 225
Separation of church and state, 318
Serrano v. Priest, 275
Service credit, 135
Servicemen's Readjustment Act, 224
SES. *See* Socioeconomic status (SES)
Sex in Education (Clarke), 235

Sex-role stereotyping, 285
Sexist artifacts, 112
Sexual harassment, 305, 320–321
Sexually transmitted diseases (STDs), 123
Shades of White: White Kids and Racial Identities in High School (Perry), 57
Shame of the Nation: The Restoration of Apartheid in America, The (Kozol), 226
Shared division of labor, 363
Shared group goal, 363
Shared materials, 363
Sherman, Ruth, 190
Simulations, 194
Sin tax, 282
Single-group studies, 68
Single-parent families, 116–117
Single-sex education, 35, 236
Site-based management, 298
Sizer, Theodore, 158, 187, 369
Skinner, B. F., 242, 264, 347
Skype, 361
Slavin, Robert, 363
Smith, Sally L., 41
Smith v. YMCA, 313
Smith-Hughes Act, 224
Snyder, Greg, 348
Social action approach (multicultural education), 68, 69
Social action curriculum, 135
Social Darwinism, 257
Social democratic reconstructionists, 135
Social injustice, 70
Social Intelligence (Goleman), 31
Social issues
    bullying, 127–129
    divorce, 118
    dropping out, 122–123
    eating disorders, 126
    family patterns, 116–117
    homeless families, 121
    latchkey kids, 118
    obesity, 125–127
    poverty, 118–121. *See also* Poverty
    substance abuse, 123–124
    teen pregnancy, 123
    wage earners and parenting, 117
    youth suicide, 127
Social networking, 124, 323, 324
Social reconstructionism, 255–257, 262
Social status, 113–115
Socioeconomic status (SES). *See also* Poverty
    books, 119
    factoids, 108
    giftedness, 38
    special needs students, 44
    verbal interactions, 119
Sociogram, 110
Socrates, 265–266, 267
Socratic method, 265, 266

Soft bias, 120
Solving Discipline and Classroom Management Problems (Wolfgang), 345
Southeast Asian Americans, 231–232
Southern Poverty Law Center (SPLC), 313
Southwest Airlines, 395
Spatial intelligence, 26
Special interest groups, 172
Special needs students, 39–47
    appropriate education, 40
    continuum of choices, 43
    gender, 44
    historical overview, 39–40
    IEP, 42
    inclusion, 42, 45, 46
    least restrictive environment, 42, 43
    legislation, 40
    nondiscriminatory education, 40–42
    procedural due process, 42
    professional association, 390
    pullout programs, 44, 45
    regular education initiative, 44–45
    teaching tip, 47
    technological advances, 46
    types of impairments, 36, 44
    zero reject, 40
Spirituality, 189–190
Split verse, 118
St. John's College, 253
St. Paul's High School (Concord), 141
Stages of teacher development, 374, 375
Standardized testing, 179–187
    Campbell's law, 186
    curriculum, 182, 184
    dropouts, 181–182
    evaluating teachers, and, 186–187
    flawed tests, 182–184
    poverty, 181
    pros/cons, 180
    student performance, 182
    teacher education programs, 172
    teacher stress, 184
Standards-based education, 177–179, 180. *See also* Standardized testing
State board of education, 290
State department of education, 291
State offices for teacher certification and licensure, A–2 to A–4
State per-pupil expenditures, 282
State superintendent, 290–291
STDs. *See* Sexually transmitted diseases (STDs)
Stealth censorship, 191
Steiner, Rudolf, 413
Stepfamily, 117
Stereotype, 72, 176
Stereotype threat, 72–73
Sternberg, Robert, 36–37
Stewart, Potter, 274, 302

Still Failing at Fairness: How Gender Bias Cheats Girls and Boys in School and What We Can Do About It (Sadker et al.), 34, 235
Stone v. Graham, 318
Stowe, Harriet Beecher, 235
Structure of school system, 290–295
Student
  access to records, 312–314
  curriculum, and, 171
  dropping out, 122–123, 161
  eating disorders, 126
  HIV, and, 319
  humorous incorrect answers to teacher questions, 390
  obesity, 125–127
  pedagogical cycle, and, 354–356
  pregnancy, 123
  purposeful activities, 115
  rights and responsibilities, 312–321
  school reform, and, 160–162
  seventh grade English class, 102
  sexual harassment, 320–321
  social temptation, 103
  substance abuse, 123–124
  suicide, 127
  suspension and discipline, 314–315
Student-centered philosophies, 254–259, 260
Student diversity, 51–86. *See also* Race and ethnicity
  bilingual education. *See* Bilingual education
  cultural difference theory, 58
  deficit theory, 57–58
  DIVERSE, 82–83
  diversity assets, 81–82
  example (seventh-grade class), 74–82
  expectation theory, 58
  generalizations, 73–74
  LGBT students, 54–55. *See also* LGBT students
  melting pot, 60
  multicultural education. *See* Multicultural education
  separating students, pros/cons, 59
  stereotypes, 72–73
Student newspaper, 319
Student records, 312–314
Student response, 354–356
Student response system, 364
Student services personnel, 415
Student-teacher relationship, 116
Stuyvesant High School, 152
Submersion, 64
Substance abuse, 123–124
Succeed: How We Can Reach Our Goals (Halvorson), 358
Sudbury Valley School, 259

Suicide, 127
Sullivan, Kate, 300
Summerhill, 259
Sumner, William G., 265
Superintendent, 290, 293–294
Support staff interview, 207
Survival stage of teacher development, 375
"Surviving to Thriving" (Nieto), 398
Suspension and discipline, 314–315
Sylvan Learning Systems, 155
Synthesizing mind, 29
Systematic teaching, 362

T

Taba, Hilda, 168
"Tackling the Toughest Turnaround--Low-Performing High Schools" (Duke/Jacobson), 164
TakingIT-Global, 365
Tales out of School: Contemporary Writers on Their Student Years (Shreve/Shreve), 114
Tantalus, 103
Taylor, Suzie King, 225
Teach for America (TFA), 14, 409
teach-now.org, 409
Teacher retention problem, 374, 375
Teacher. *See also* Teacher effectiveness; Teaching tips
  academic freedom, 307–308
  artist, as, 6–7
  attention-getting devices, 16
  board certification, 12–13, 287, 407–408
  career development. *See* Career development
  core competencies, 13
  curriculum, and, 170
  expectations regarding own performance, 144
  feedback, 356–359, 362, 421–422
  first year of teaching. *See* First-year teachers
  freedom of speech, 309–310
  gatekeeper, as, 104
  humility, 371
  in-depth profiles. *See* Profile in education
  job hunting. *See* Job hunting, etc.
  knowledge of subject and instructional skills, 16
  labor rights, 311–312
  legal liability, 308–309
  merit pay, 159, 162
  MetLife surveys, 4–5
  moral education, 329
  nature *vs.* nurture, 341
  pedagogical cycle, and, 356–359
  personal life, 306, 307
  preparation programs, 14–15
  professional development programs, 382–384

professional/semiprofessional status, 9
  pros/cons, 6–7
  protecting your students, 324–325
  Public Agenda survey, 5
  race/ethnicity, 402
  reasons for teaching, 4
  reflective, 370
  rewards of teaching, 386–389
  rights and responsibilities, 304–312
  salary, 5, 7, 403
  school governance, and, 297–298
  school reform, and, 158–160
  self-monitoring cues (wait time), 355
  seventh grade English class, 101
  sexual harassment, 305
  stages of development, 374, 375
  standardized tests, and, 184, 186–187
  tenure, 8, 158–159
  termination, 307
  that first mistake, 406
  unions, 162–163
  urban legends, 15–17
  value added, 158
Teacher (Ashton-Warner), 240
Teacher-ages, 218
Teacher associations, 389–391, 412
Teacher-centered philosophies, 250–253, 260
Teacher certification, 407
Teacher codes of ethics, 325
Teacher competency exams, 409–410, A–1
Teacher Education Accreditation Council (TEAC), 408
Teacher effectiveness
  block scheduling, 370
  classroom management, 342–349
  cooperative learning, 363–365
  deep teaching, 369
  differentiated instruction, 368–369
  direct teaching, 362–363
  instructional variety, 359
  learning time, 341, 342
  looping, 369
  mastery learning, 365
  pedagogical cycle, 349–359
  physical setup of classroom, 348
  problem-based learning, 366
  reflective teachers, 370
  rules, 346
  technology, 360–362
Teacher expectations, 58, 106, 144
Teacher feedback, 356–359, 362, 421–422
Teacher liability, 308
Teacher observations, 376–380
Teacher of Speakers of Other Languages (TESOL), 394
Teacher performance assessment (TPA), 383, 410
Teacher preparation programs, 14–15

Teacher reactions, 356–359
Teacher recognition plans, 388
Teacher seniority, 158
Teacher-student relationship, 116
Teacher training, 145
Teacher unions, 158, 162–163
Teachers and the Law (Schimmel et al.), 412
TeachersFirst.com, 360
"Teaching against Idiocy" (Parker), 164
Teaching and Its Predicaments (Cohen), 17, 380
Teaching as a Moral Practice: Defining, Developing, and Assessing Professional Dispositions in Teacher Education (Murrell et al.), 10
Teaching contract, 411
Teaching contract (1920), 11
Teaching eye-to-eye, 348
Teaching journal, 370
Teaching license, 407
Teaching residency program, 14
Teaching standards. *See* INTASC teaching standards
Teaching strategies observation form, 420
Teaching the culturally different, 68
Teaching tips
   clickers, 364
   connecting teachers and families, 142
   ELL students, 66
   first-year teaching, 387
   getting student's attention, 16
   helicopter parents, 115
   history classes, 234
   learning styles, 33
   LGBT students, 55
   philosophy statement, 270
   social networking guidelines, 324
   special needs students, 47
   teaching the student, 198
   that first mistake, 406
Teaching to Transgress: Education as the Practice of Freedom (hooks), 263
Teaching with Fire: Poetry That Sustains the Courage to Teach (Intrator/Scribner), 369
Technology/computers, 193–196
   cooperative learning, 365
   curriculum, and, 194, 195
   differentiated instruction, 368–369
   digital divide, 195–196
   direct teaching, 363
   downside of, 193
   ethical dilemmas, 193
   helpful sites, 360
   hybrid course, 195
   mastery learning, 365
   multiple intelligences, 27
   problem-based learning, 366
   pros/cons, 361, 424–425

   uses, 360
   virtual education, 194–195
Teen pregnancy, 123
Teenage Liberation Handbook: How to Quit School & Get a Real Life & Education (Llewellyn), 155
Tele-mentor, 376
Television marketing to children, 284, 285
Ten Best Teaching Practices: How Brain Research and Learning Styles Define Teaching Competencies (Tileston), 32
Tenth Amendment, 223, 290
Tenure, 8, 158–159, 389, 411–412
Terrorist, The (Cooney), 232
Test-tampering, 186
TESTED: One American School Struggles to Make the Grade (Perlstein), 181
Tests/testing
   Campbell's law, 186
   international tests, 17–18, 299
   norm-referenced tests, 143
   objective-referenced tests, 143
   standardized testing. *See* Standardized testing
   Texas State Board of Education, 174
Textbook, 173–175
Textbook adoption states, 173, 174
Textbook publishers, 172, 173–175
TFA. *See* Teach for America (TFA)
"The Bridge to Excellence," 278
They Led by Teaching (Field/Berson), 377
Thinkfinity, 360
Thomas, Clarence, 305
Thomas, M. Carey, 235
Thomas, Wayne, 65
Thompson v. Southwest School District, 306
Thoreau, Henry David, 230
"Threat of Stereotype, The" (Aronson), 84
Thrusts, 345
Thurman, Howard, 2
Times of transition, 345
Tinker v. Des Moines Independent Community School District, 316, 318
Tinkering toward Utopia: A Century of Public School Reform (Tyack/Cuban), 146
Title IX, 224, 236, 305, 320
Title VII, 305
To Remain an Indian: Lessons in Democracy from a Century of Native American Education (Lomawaima/McCarthy), 218
Toledo Plan, 380
Tolstoy, Leo, 133
Tomlinson, Carol Ann, 368
Tomorrow's Teachers, 12
Tong, Barbara, 20
TPA. *See* Teacher performance assessment (TPA)
Tracking, 106–109, 226

Traditional/standardized instruction, 368
Traditional teacher education path, 14
Transformation approach (multicultural education), 68, 69
Transformation of the School, The (Cremin), 216
Transformation Teaching: Waldorf-Inspired Methods in the Public School (Gorel), 413
Transition times, 345
Transitional approach (ELL students), 63
Traveling teachers, 220
Tribe Apart: A Journey into the Heart of American Adolescence, A (Hersch), 114
Troops to Teachers, 409
Troy Female Seminary, 234, 235
Truman, Harry, 125
Trust, 145
Trustee representative, 292
Truth About Girls and Boys: Challenging Toxic Stereotypes About Our Children (Rivers/Barnett), 34
Tuesdays with Morrie: An Old Man, a Young Man (Albom), 246
Turning Points: Preparing American Youth for the 21st Century, 161
Turnitin.com, 322
Tutors, 220
Twain, Mark, 6, 234
Twitter, 323
Two Americas, Two Educations: Funding Quality Schools for All Students (Cummins), 275
Two Nations: Black, White, Separate, Hostile, Unequal (Hacker), 56
Tyack, David, 160
Tydings-McDuffie Act, 230

U
Un-schooling, 163
"Understanding Unconscious Bias and Unintentional Racism" (Moule), 84
Understanding Waldorf Education: Teaching from the Inside Out (Petrash), 413
Unions, 312, 389–391
Unique school settings, 412–413
United States
   administrators/nonteaching staff members, 386
   educational values, 17
   leaders, 19
   material wealth, 395
   school enrollment by state, 401
   search for meaningful lives, 395
   teaching hours per year, 383, 385
United States Government Manual, 416
University of Michigan decision, 227
University placement office, 21
Urban legends, 15–17
U.S. Constitution, 304

V

Value added, 158, 186
Value clarification, 326–327
Venn diagram
    choice/nonchoice school, 206
    curricular standards, 203
Video clips. See Observation video clips
Vincent, Jane, 300
Virtual education, 194–195
Virtual field trip, 194
Virtual schools, 153–155
Visible curriculum, 168
"Vision of Students Today, A" (YouTube), 161
Visual learners, 32, 33
Vocation, 3
Voucher program, 151–152

W

Wage earners and parenting, 117
Wait time, 354–356
Waiting for a Miracle: Why Schools Can't Solve Our Problems--and How We Can (Comer), 146
Wakefield High School, 261
Walberg, Herbert, 143
Waldorf school, 413
Walker, Alice, 51
Wallace v. Jaffree, 318
Ward, William A., 340, 400
Warner, W. Lloyd, 106
Waronker, Shimon, 150
Warren, Marsha, 130
Washington, Booker T., 242
Watkins, Tom, 148
Watson, Michael, 271
Wattenberg, William, 347
WebQuest, 368–369
Website of the month, 425–426
Websites, 21
Webster, Noah, 215
Weekly and monthly reviews, 363
Werner, Heinz, 40
West Virginia State Board of Education v. Barnette, 318

What Color Is Your Parachute? (Bolles), 24
What Your First Grader Needs to Know (Hirsch), 192
"Where Have All the Strong Poets Gone?" (Jones), 300
Where teachers teach, 4
White Teacher Talks about Race, A (Landsman), 227
WhitePrivilege.pdf, 57
Whitmore Lake High School, 158
Withitness, 344
Who Said School Administration Would Be Fun: Coping with a New Emotional and Social Reality (Sigford), 294
Whole New Mind: Why Right-Brainers Will Rule the Future, A (Pink), 196, 393–395
"Why Are All the Black Kids Sitting Together in the Cafeteria?" And Other Conversations about Race (Tatum), 108
"Why Has High-Stakes Testing So Easily Slipped into Contemporary American Life?" (Nichols/Berliner), 198
"Why I Am Teaching" letter, 91–92
Why We Teach (Nieto), 393
Why We Teach: Learning, Laughter, Love and the Power to Transform Lives (Alston), 403
Wikipedia, 388
Willard, Emma Hart, 234, 235, 242
Williams, David, 234
Wisdom, 37
Women. *See also* Gender
    female seminaries, 234–235
    historical overview, 218–219, 234–236
    labor force, 117
    personal experience (first-hand observation), 71
    wages, 117
Women's studies, 68
Wood v. Strickland, 314
Woods, Tiger, 52
Word smart, 26
Work Hard, Be Nice: How Two Inspired Teachers Created the Most Promising Schools in America (Mathews), 150

World Data on Education (WDE), 290
World Wise Schools, 194
"Worthy Texts: Who Decides?" (Gilmore), 198
www.corestandards.org, 177
www.pthvp.org, 142
www.recruitingteachers.org, 19
www.teach-now.org, 14

X

Xenophobia, 61

Y

Yearbook signing, 326
YES College Preparatory School, 261
Yoga, 129
You Be The Judge
    educational equity *vs.* educational adequacy, 279
    for-profit schools, 156
    homework, 105
    moral ethics, 327
    school effectiveness, 394
    school mascots, 217
    separating students by shared characteristics, 59
    special needs students, 45
    standards-based education, 180
    teacher- *vs.* student-centered approaches to education, 260
    teaching career, 6–7
    technology, 361
Youth suicide, 127
Yugoslavia, 67

Z

Zangwill, Israel, 60
Zealots, 148
Zelman v. Simmons-Harris, 152, 318
Zen and the Art of Public School Teaching (Perricone), 246
"Zen for High Schoolers," 348
Zero reject, 40
Zero-tolerance policy, 314